data structures and pl/I programming

data structures and pl/I programming

Moshe Augenstein

Aaron Tenenbaum

Department of Computer and Information Science
Brooklyn College
City University of New York

Prentice-Hall, Inc.
Englewood Cliffs, New Jersey 07632

Library of Congress Cataloging in Publication Data

Augenstein, Moshe (date)
Data structures and PL/I programming.

Bibliography: p.
Includes index
1. Data structures (Computer science) 2. PL/I
(Computer program language) I. Tenenbaum, Aaron M.,
joint author. II. Title.
QA76.9.D35A93 001.6'424 78-21002
ISBN 0-13-197731-8

To my wife, Gail, and my parents, Melech and Ruth.
M. A.

To my wife, Miriam, and my mother, Genia.
A. T.

Editorial/production supervision and interior design by Nancy Milnamow
Cover design by Edsal Enterprises
Manufacturing buyer: Gordon Osbourne

Printed in the United States of America

10 9 8 7 6 5 4

Prentice-Hall International, Inc., *London*
Prentice-Hall of Australia Pty. Limited, *Sydney*
Prentice-Hall of Canada, Ltd., *Toronto*
Prentice-Hall of India Private Limited, *New Delhi*
Prentice-Hall of Japan, Inc., *Tokyo*
Prentice-Hall of Southeast Asia Pte. Ltd., *Singapore*
Whitehall Books Limited, *Wellington, New Zealand*

contents

5

queues and lists 263

6

pl/I list processing 314

7

trees and graphs 357

8

sorting 455

preface

This text is designed for a two-semester course in data structures and programming. For several years, we have taught a course in data structures to students who have had a semester course in PL/I programming and a semester course in assembly language programming. We found that a considerable amount of time was spent in teaching programming techniques because the students had not had sufficient exposure to programming and were unable to implement abstract structures on their own. The brighter students eventually caught on to what was being done. The weaker students never did. Based on this experience, we have reached the firm conviction that a first course in data structures must go hand in hand with a second course in programming. This text is a product of that conviction.

The text introduces abstract concepts, shows how those concepts are useful in problem solving, and then shows how the abstractions can be made concrete by using a programming language. Equal emphasis is placed on both the abstract and the concrete versions of a concept, so that the student learns about the concept itself, its implementation, and its application.

The language used in this text is PL/I. PL/I is ideally suited to such a course since it contains the control structures necessary to make programs readable and allows basic data structures such as stacks, linked lists, and trees to be implemented in a variety of ways. This allows the student to appreciate the choices and tradeoffs which face a programmer in a real situation. The only prerequisite for students using this text is a one-semester course in programming. Students who have had a course in programming using such languages as FORTRAN or PASCAL can use this text together with one of the elementary PL/I texts listed in the bibliography. Chapters 1 and 2 also provide information necessary for such students to acquaint themselves with PL/I.

Chapter 1 is an introduction to data structures. Section 1.1 introduces the concept of an abstract data structure and the concept of an implementation. Sections 1.2 and 1.3 introduce arrays and structures in PL/I. The implementations of these two data structures as well as their applications are covered.

Chapter 2 forms the foundation of a second course in programming and discusses such issues as control structures, structured programming, top-down program development, modularity, testing, debugging, program correctness, and program efficiency.

Chapter 3 discusses stacks and their PL/I implementation. Since this is the first new data structure introduced, considerable discussion of the pitfalls of implementing such a structure is included. Section 3.4 introduces postfix, prefix, and infix notations. Section 3.5 discusses BEGIN blocks and CONTROLLED storage in PL/I.

Chapter 4 covers recursion, its applications, and its implementation. Chapter 5 introduces queues and linked lists and their implementations using an array of available nodes.

Chapter 6 discusses PL/I BASED storage and the implementation of stacks, queues, and linked lists using BASED storage.

Chapter 7 discusses trees and graphs.

Chapter 8 covers sorting and Chapter 9 covers searching.

Chapter 10 discusses memory management algorithms, including garbage collection, best-fit and first-fit, and the buddy system. The first section of the chapter discusses general lists and list processing systems.

At the end of each chapter, we list several references and suggestions for further reading. At the end of the text, we have included a more comprehensive bibliography.

A second course in programming consists of Section 1.2 and 1.3, Chapters 2 through 4, Chapter 8 except for Section 8.3, and Section 9.1. A one-semester course in data structures consists of Chapter 1 and Chapters 3 through 9. Sections 7.5 and 7.6 (graphs) and parts of Chapters 8 and 9 can be omitted if time is pressing, and Chapter 1 can be assigned to students independently.

The text is suitable for course I1 of Curriculum 68 (*Communications of the ACM*, March 1968), courses UC1 and UC8 of the Undergraduate Programs in Information Systems (*Communications of the ACM*, Dec. 1973) and course CS2 of the Curriculum Recommendations for the Undergraduate Program in Computer Science (*SIGCSE Bulletin*, June 1977). In particular, the text covers parts or all of topics P1, P2, P3, P4, S2, S4, D1, D2, and D3 of the last-mentioned report.

Algorithms are presented as intermediaries between English language descriptions and PL/I programs. They are written in PL/I style interspersed with English. These algorithms allow the reader to focus on the method used to solve a problem without concern about declaration of variables and the peculiarities of a real language. In transforming an algorithm into a program, we introduce these issues and point out the pitfalls which accompany them.

Most of the concepts in the text are illustrated by several examples. Some of these examples are important topics in their own right (e.g. postfix notation, multi-word arithmetic, etc.) and may be treated as such. Other examples illustrate different implementation techniques (such as sequential storage of trees). The instructor is free to cover as many or as few of these examples as he wishes. Examples may also be assigned to students as independent reading. It is anticipated that an instructor will be unable to cover all the examples in sufficient detail within the confines of a one or two semester course. We feel that at the stage of a student's development for which the text is designed, it is more important to cover several examples in great detail rather than to cover a broad range of topics cursorily.

There are a large number of exercises geared to each section of the text in a separate Exercise Manual. While considerations of cost and length prohibited the inclusion of these exercises within the text itself, they are an integral part of the entire work. We consider it essential that any instructor who uses this book as a text should also have a copy of the Exercise Manual. We also consider it advisable for students to obtain the manual. Copies of the manual are available from the publisher.

The exercises vary widely in type and difficulty. Some are drill exercises to ensure comprehension of topics in the text. Others involve modifications of programs or algorithms presented in the text. Still others introduce new concepts and are quite challenging. Often, a group of successive exercises includes the complete development of a new topic which can be used as the basis for a term project or an additional lecture. The instructor should use caution in assigning exercises so that an assignment is suitable to the student's level. We consider it imperative for students to be assigned several (from five to twelve, depending on difficulty) programming projects per semester. The exercises abound with projects of this type.

All the programs and algorithms in this text have been tested and debugged using PL/C (wherever possible), IBM PL/I-F, and the IBM Optimizing Compiler. We wish to thank Irving and Tobe Goldfinger for their invaluable assistance in this task. Their zeal for the task was above and beyond the call of duty and their suggestions were always valuable. Of course, any errors that remain are the sole responsibility of the authors.

Because of the disparity in the rules governing the ENTRY attribute among the various compilers, we have not included this attribute in any of the routines presented in the text. Restrictions which apply to PL/C are noted in the text, as are certain other incompatibilities between PL/I-F and the PL/I Optimizing Compiler (such as the need to declare the NULL built-in function explicitly in the Optimizer and the illegality of declaring a VARYING character string with the BASED attribute in PL/I-F). The instructor should describe the requirements of the particular compiler being used. In the interest of simplicity, we have declared almost all integer variables FIXED rather than FIXED BINARY, although the latter attributes often lead to more efficient code.

We would like to acknowledge the encouragement and advice of the following members of the Department of Computer and Information Science at Brooklyn College: Frank Beckman, Jack Wolfe, Pat Sterbenz, Michael Barnett, Steven Brodt, Raymond Kanner, Jack Meth, Marvin Stein, Ronnie Templeman, Joseph Thurm, and Gershon Weintraub.

We would also like to thank the following for their invaluable assistance: A. Beatty, Y. Brodt, C. Chow, B. Davidowics, D. Elefant, E. Hylton, J. Jones, W. Kelly, J. Lopez, M. Lowenthal, V. Melamud, M. Mishkovsky, E. Rich, J. Rothschild, I. Setton, D. Shapiro, A. Stok, R. Teich, S. Templeman, T. Wagner, G. Weiss, M. Yoselovsky, and N. Zeldes. Gail Augenstein did an excellent job of typing the initial manuscript. Because of the devotion she displayed in typing into the late hours of the night it was possible to submit the manuscript on time. Miriam Tenenbaum was most helpful in proofreading portions of the manuscript. Her advice was always appropriate.

The staff of the City University Computer Center deserves special mention. They were extremely helpful in assisting us in using the excellent facilities of the Center. The same can be said of the staff of the Brooklyn College Computer Center.

We would like to thank the editors and staff at Prentice-Hall and the reviewers for their helpful comments and suggestions.

Finally, we thank our families for their patience and encouragement during the long and arduous task of producing such a book.

Moshe Augenstein

Aaron Tenenbaum

chapter **1**

introduction to data structures

A computer is a machine which manipulates information. The study of computer science includes the study of how information is organized in a computer, how it can be manipulated, and how it can be utilized. Thus it is exceedingly important for a student of computer science to understand the concepts of information organization and manipulation in order to continue study of the field.

1.1. Information and Meaning

If computer science is fundamentally the study of information, the first question which arises is: What is information? Unfortunately, although the concept of information is the bedrock of the entire field, this question cannot be answered precisely. In this sense, the concept of information in computer science is similar to the concepts of point, line, and plane in geometry: they are all undefined terms about which statements can be made but which cannot be explained in terms of more elementary concepts.

In geometry, it is possible to talk about the length of a line despite the fact that the concept of a line itself is undefined. The length of a line is a measure of quantity. Similarly, in computer science, we can measure quantities of information. The basic unit of information is the ***bit***, whose value asserts one of two mutually exclusive possibilities. For example, if a light switch can be in one of two positions but not in both simultaneously, the fact that it is either in the "on" position or the "off" position is one bit of information. If a device can be in more than two possible states, then the fact that it is in a particular state is more than one bit of information. For example, if a dial has eight possible positions, then the fact that it is in position 4 rules out seven other possibilities; whereas the fact that a light switch is on rules out only one other possibility.

Another way of thinking of this phenomenon is as follows. Suppose we had only two-way switches, but could use as many of them as we needed. How many such switches would be necessary to represent a dial with eight positions? Clearly, one switch can represent only two positions (see Fig. 1.1.1(a)). Two switches can represent four different positions (Fig. 1.1.1(b)), and three switches are required to represent eight different positions (Fig. 1.1.1(c)). In general, n switches can represent 2^n different possibilities.

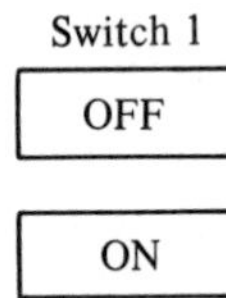

(a) One switch (two possibilities).

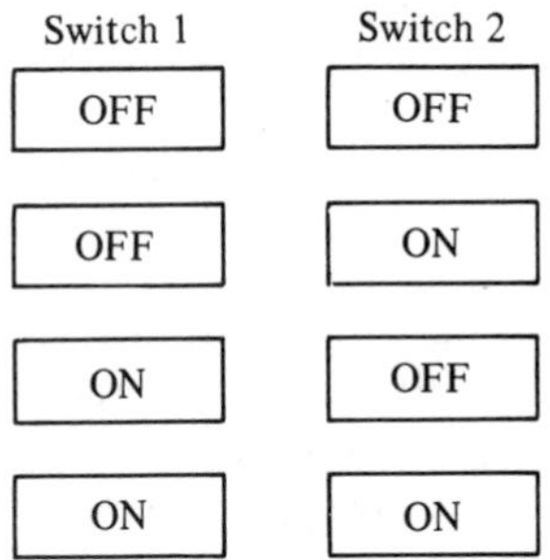

(b) Two switches (four possibilities).

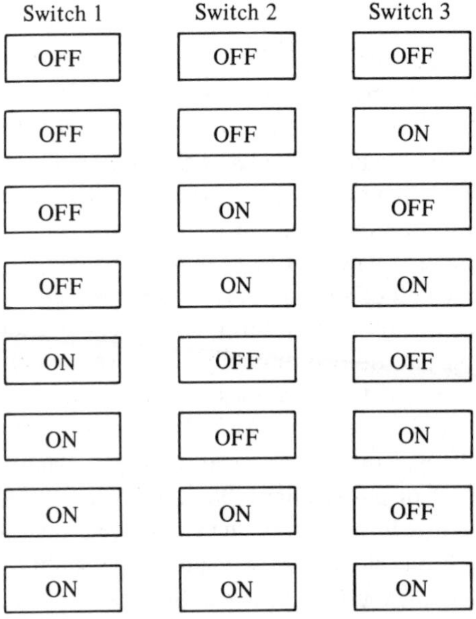

(c) Three switches (eight possibilities). **Figure 1.1.1.**

The binary digits 0 and 1 are used to represent the two possible states of a particular bit (in fact, the word "bit" is a contraction of the words "binary digit"). Given n bits, a string of n 1s and 0s is used to represent their settings. For example, the string 101011 represents six switches, the first of which is "on" (1), the second of which is "off" (0), the third on, the fourth off, and the fifth and sixth on.

We have seen that three bits are sufficient to represent eight possibilities. The eight possible configurations of these three bits (000, 001, 010, 011, 100, 101, 110, and 111) can be used to represent the integers 0 through 7. However, there is nothing intrinsic about these bit settings which implies that a particular setting represents a particular integer. Any assignment of integer values to bit settings is equally valid as long as no two integers are assigned to the same bit setting. Once such an assignment has been made, a particular bit setting can be unambiguously interpreted as a specific integer. Let us examine several widely used methods for interpreting bit settings as integers.

Binary and Decimal Integers

The most widely used method for interpreting bit settings as nonnegative integers is the ***binary number system***. In this system each bit position represents a power of 2. The rightmost bit position represents 2^0, which equals 1; the next position to the left represents 2^1, which is 2; the next bit position represents 2^2, which is 4; and so on. An integer is represented as a sum of powers of 2. A string of all 0s represents the number 0. If a 1 appears in a particular bit position, then the power of 2 represented by that bit position is included in the sum; but if a 0 appears, then that power of 2 is not included in the sum. For example, the group of bits 00100110 has 1s in positions 1, 2, and 5 (counting from right to left with the rightmost position counted as position 0). Thus 00100110 represents the integer $2^1 + 2^2 + 2^5 = 2 + 4 + 32 = 38$. Any string of bits represents a unique nonnegative integer, and any nonnegative integer can be represented by a unique string of bits of minimum length.

However, the binary number system is by no means the only method by which bits can be used to represent nonnegative integers. For example, a string of bits may be used to represent integers in the decimal number system, as follows. Four bits can be used to represent a decimal digit between 0 and 9 in the binary notation described above. A string of bits of arbitrary length may be divided into consecutive sets of four digits, where each set represents a decimal integer. The string then represents the number which is formed by those decimal digits in conventional decimal notation. For example, in this system, the bit string 00100110 is separated into two strings of four bits each: 0010 and 0110. The first of these represents the decimal digit 2 and the second represents the decimal digit 6, so that the entire string represents the integer 26. This representation is called ***binary coded decimal***.

One important feature of the binary coded decimal representation of nonnegative integers is that not all bit strings are valid representations of a decimal integer. Four bits can be used to represent 1 of 16 different possibilities since there are 16 possible states for a set of 4 bits. However, in the binary coded decimal integer representation, only 10 of those 16 possibilities are used. That is, codes such as 1010 and 1100 whose binary values are 10 or larger are invalid in a binary coded decimal number.

Character Strings

As we all know, information is not always interpreted numerically. Such things as names, job titles, and addresses must also be represented in some fashion within a computer. To enable the representation of such nonnumeric objects, still another method of interpreting bit strings is necessary. Such information is usually represented in character string form. For example, in some computers, the eight bits 00100110 are used to represent the character '&'. A different eight-bit pattern is used to represent the character 'A', another to represent 'B', another to represent 'C', and still another for each character which has a representation in a particular machine. A Russian machine uses bit patterns to represent Russian characters, while an Israeli machine uses bit patterns to represent Hebrew characters. (In fact, the characters being used are irrelevant to the machine; the character set can be changed by using a different print chain on the printer.) If eight bits are used to represent a character, up to 256 different characters can be represented since there are 256 different eight-bit patterns. If the string 11000000 is used to represent the character 'A' and 11000001 is used to represent the character 'B', then the character string 'AB' would be represented by the bit string 1100000011000001. In general, a character string STR is represented by the concatenation of the bit strings which represent the individual characters of STR.

As in the case of integers, there is nothing intrinsic about a particular bit string which makes it suitable for representing a particular character. The assignment of bit strings to characters may be entirely arbitrary, but it must be adhered to consistently. It may be that some convenient rule is used in assigning bit strings to characters. For example, two bit strings may be assigned to two letters so that the one with a smaller binary value is assigned to the letter which comes earlier in the alphabet. However, such a rule is merely a convenience; it is not mandated by any intrinsic relation between characters and bit strings. In fact, computers even differ over the number of bits used to represent a character. Some computers use seven bits (and therefore allow only up to 128 possible characters), some use eight (up to 256 characters), and some use ten (up to 1024 possible characters). The number of bits necessary to represent a character in a particular computer is called the ***byte size***, and a group of bits of that number is called a ***byte***.

Note that using eight bits to represent a character means that 256 possible characters can be represented. It is not very often that one finds a computer which uses so many different characters (although it is conceivable for a computer to include upper and lower case letters, special characters, italics, boldface, and other type characters), so that many of the eight-bit codes are not used to represent characters. Again, there is a possible "waste" of information.

Thus we see that information itself has no meaning. Any meaning can be assigned to a particular bit pattern, as long as it is done consistently. It is the interpretation of a bit pattern which gives it meaning. For example, the bit string 00100110 can be interpreted as the number 38 (binary), the number 26 (binary coded decimal), or the character string '&'. A method of interpreting a bit pattern is often called a ***data type***. We have presented three data types: binary nonnegative integers, binary coded decimal nonnegative integers, and character strings. The key questions are how to determine what data types are available to interpret bit patterns and which data type to use in interpreting a particular bit pattern.

The ***memory*** (also called ***storage*** or ***core***) of a computer is simply a set of bits (switches). At any instant of the computer's operation any particular bit in memory is either 0 or 1 (off or on). The setting of a bit is called its ***value*** or its ***contents***.

The bits in a computer memory are grouped together into larger units such as bytes. (In some computers, several bytes are grouped together into units called ***words***.) Each such unit (byte or word, depending on the machine) is assigned an ***address***, which is a name identifying a particular unit among all the units in memory. This address is usually numeric, so that we may speak of byte 746 or word 937. An address is often called a ***location***, and the contents of a location are the contents of the bits which make up the unit at that location.

Every computer has a set of "native" data types. This means that it is constructed with a mechanism for manipulating bit patterns in a way that is consistent with the objects they represent. For example, suppose a computer contains an instruction to add two binary numbers and place that sum at a given location in memory for subsequent use. Then there is a mechanism built into the computer to:

1. extract bit patterns from two given locations
2. produce a third bit pattern representing the binary number which is the sum of the two binary numbers represented by the two operands, and
3. store the resultant bit pattern at a given location

The computer "knows" to interpret the bit patterns at the given locations as binary integers because the hardware which executes that particular instruction is designed to do so. This is akin to a light "knowing" to be on when the switch is in a particular position.

If the same machine also has an instruction to add two binary coded decimal numbers, then there is a separate built-in mechanism to interpret operands as decimal numbers. Two distinct instructions are necessary for the two operations, and each instruction carries within itself an implicit identification of the types of its operands as well as their explicit locations.

Therefore, it is the programmer's responsibility to know which data type is contained in each location that is used. It is the programmer's responsibility to choose between using a binary or decimal addition instruction to obtain the sum of two numbers.

A high-level programming language aids in this task considerably. For example, if a PL/I programmer declares

```
DCL (X,Y) FIXED BINARY,
    (A,B) FIXED DECIMAL;
```

then space is reserved at four locations for four different numbers. These four locations may be referenced by the ***identifiers*** X, Y, A, and B. Such an identifier is used instead of a numerical address to refer to a particular memory location because of its convenience for the programmer. The contents of the locations reserved for X and Y will be interpreted as binary numbers, while the contents of A and B will be interpreted as decimal numbers. The PL/I compiler which is responsible for translating PL/I programs into machine language will translate the "+" in the statement

```
X = X+Y;
```

into binary addition, and will translate the "+" in the statement

```
A = A+B;
```

into decimal addition. An operator such as "+" is really a ***generic*** operator because it has several different meanings depending on its context. The compiler relieves the programmer of specifying the type of addition that must be performed by examining the context and using the appropriate version.

A statement such as

```
Y = X;
```

involves only moving a bit pattern from location X into location Y, but a statement such as

```
Y = B;
```

involves converting the bit pattern of the decimal number at B into the bit pattern for the same number in binary representation at Y. Fortunately, the compiler takes care of all these details automatically. However, a blind reliance on the compiler's "good judgment" in making decisions as to conversions and types of operations can sometimes lead to surprising and unwanted results.

It is important to recognize the key role played by the DECLARE statement in the PL/I language. It is by means of declarations that the programmer specifies how the contents of the computer memory are to be interpreted by the program. In doing this, a declaration specifies how much memory is needed for a particular entity (for example, the precision of a numerical variable or the length of a string), how the contents of that memory are to be interpreted (as a binary or decimal number or as a string), and other vital details. The DECLARE statement also specifies to the compiler exactly what is meant by the operation symbols which are subsequently used.

The Concept of Implementation

Thus far, we have been viewing data types as a method of interpreting the memory contents of a computer. The set of native data types which a particular computer can support is determined by what functions have been wired into its hardware. However, we can view the concept of "data type" from a completely different perspective: not in terms of what a computer can do, but in terms of what the user wants done. For example, if a human wishes to obtain the sum of two integers, he does not care very much about the detailed mechanism by which that sum will be obtained. The human is interested in manipulating the mathematical concept of an "integer," not in manipulating hardware bits. The hardware of the computer may be used to represent an integer and is useful only insofar as the representation is successful.

Once the concept of "data type" is divorced from the hardware capabilities of the computer, there are a limitless number of data types which can be considered. A data type is an abstract concept defined by a set of logical properties. Once such an abstract data type is defined and the legal operations involving that type are specified, we may ***implement*** that data type (or a close approximation to it). An implementation may be a ***hardware implementation*** in which the circuitry necessary to perform the required operations is designed and constructed as part of a computer. Or it may be a ***software implementation*** in which a program consisting of already existing hardware instructions is written to interpret bit strings in the desired fashion and to perform the required operations. Thus, a software implementation includes a specification of how an object of the new data type is represented by objects of previously existing data types, as well as a specification of how such an object is manipulated in conformance with the operations which have been defined for it. Throughout the remainder of this text, the term "implementation" is used to mean "software implementation."

An Example

Let us illustrate these concepts with an example. Suppose the hardware of a computer contains an instruction

MOVE (FROM,TO,*length*)

which copies a character string of *length* bytes from an address specified by FROM to an address specified by TO. The length must be specified by an integer, and for that reason we indicate it with lower case letters. FROM and TO can be specified by identifiers which represent storage locations. An example of this instruction is MOVE(A,B,3), which copies the three bytes starting at location A to the three bytes starting at location B.

Note the different roles played by the identifiers A and B in this operation. The first operand of the MOVE instruction is the contents of the location specified by the identifier A. The second operand, however, is not the contents of location B, since these contents are irrelevant to the execution of the instruction. Rather, the location itself is the operand, since the location specifies the destination of the character string. Although an identifier always stands for a location, it is common for an identifier to be used to refer to the contents of that location. It is always apparent from the context whether an identifier is referencing a location or its contents. The identifier appearing as the first operand of a MOVE instruction refers to the contents of memory, while the identifier appearing as the second operand refers to a location.

We also assume the computer hardware to contain the usual arithmetic and branching instructions, which we indicate by using PL/I-like notation. For example, the instruction

```
Z=X+Y;
```

interprets the contents of the bytes at locations X and Y as binary integers, adds them, and inserts the binary representation of their sum into the byte at location Z. (We do not operate on integers greater than one byte in length and we ignore the possibility of overflow.) Here again, X and Y are used to reference memory contents while Z is used to reference a memory location, but the proper interpretation is clear from the context.

Sometimes, it is desirable to add a quantity to an address to obtain another address. For example, if A is a location in memory, we might want to reference the location four bytes beyond A. We cannot refer to this location as A+4 since that notation is reserved for the integer contents of location A plus four. We therefore introduce the notation A(4) to refer to this location. We also introduce the notation A(X) to refer to the address given by adding the binary integer contents of the byte at X to the address A.

The MOVE instruction requires the programmer to specify the length of the string to be copied. Thus, it deals with an operand which is a fixed-length character string (i.e., the length of the string must be known). A fixed-length string and a byte-sized binary integer may be considered native data types of that particular machine.

Suppose we wished to implement varying-length character strings on this machine. That is, we want to enable programmers to use an instruction

```
MOVEVAR(FROM,TO)
```

to move a character string from location FROM to location TO without being required to specify any length.

In order to implement this new data type, we must first decide on how it is to be represented in the memory of the machine and then indicate how that representation is to be manipulated. Clearly, it is necessary to know how many bytes must be moved in order to execute this instruction. Since the MOVEVAR operation does not specify this number, the number must be contained within the representation of the character string itself. Thus, a varying-length character string of length l is represented by a contiguous set of l+1 bytes ($l < 256$). The first byte contains the binary representation of the length l, and the remaining bytes contain the representations of the characters in the string. Representations of three such strings are illustrated in Fig. 1.1.2. (Note that the digits 5 and 9 in these figures do not stand for the bit patterns representing the characters '5' and '9' but rather for the patterns 00000101 and 00001001 (assuming eight bits to a byte), which represent the integers 5 and 9. Similarly, 14 in Fig. 1.1.2(c) stands for the bit pattern 00001110.)

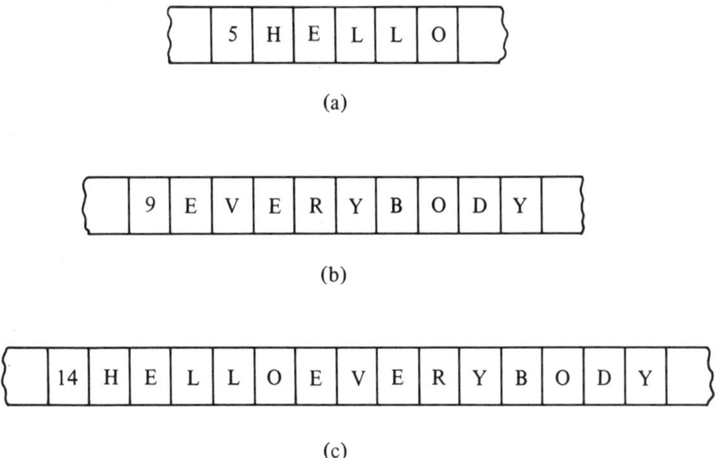

Figure 1.1.2. Varying-length character strings.

The program to implement the MOVEVAR operation can be written as follows (I is an auxiliary memory location):

```
MOVE(FROM,TO,1);
do I=1 to TO by 1;
   MOVE(FROM(I),TO(I),1);
end;
```

Similarly, we can implement an operation CONCATVAR(C1,C2,C3) to concatenate two varying-length character strings at locations C1 and C2 and place the result at C3. Figure 1.1.2(c) illustrates the concatenation of the two strings in Figs. 1.1.2(a) and (b):

```
/*       move the length        */
Z=C1+C2;
MOVE(Z,C3,1);

/*     move the first string    */
do I=1 to C1 by 1;
   MOVE(C1(I),C3(I),1);
end;

/*   move the second string     */
do I=1 to C2 by 1;
   X=C1+I;
   MOVE(C2(I),C3(X),1);
end;
```

However, once the operation MOVEVAR has been defined, CONCATVAR can be implemented using MOVEVAR as follows:

```
   /*       move the second string        */
MOVEVAR(C2,C3(C1));

   /*       move the first string         */
MOVEVAR(C1,C3);

   /*  update the length of the result    */
Z = C1+C2;
MOVE(Z,C3,1);
```

Figure 1.1.3 illustrates phases of this operation on the strings of Fig. 1.1.2. Although this latter version is shorter, it is not really more efficient, since all the instructions used in implementing MOVEVAR are performed each time that MOVEVAR is used.

The statement Z=C1+C2; in both of the above algorithms is of particular interest. The addition instruction operates independently of the use of its operands (in this case, parts of varying-length character strings). The instruction is designed to treat its operands as single-byte integers regardless of any other use which the programmer has for them. Similarly, the reference to C3(C1) is to the location whose address is given by adding the contents of the byte at location C1 to the address C3. Thus the byte at C1 is treated as holding a binary integer, although it is also the start of a varying-length character string. This illustrates the fact that a data type is a method of treating the contents of memory and that those contents have no intrinsic meaning.

If we use the representation of varying-length character strings, then the concatenation operation is invalid if the resulting string is more than 255 characters long. Since the result of such an operation is undefined, the implementor has a wide variety of actions which he can take if that operation is attempted. One possibility is to use only the first 255 characters of the result. Another possibility is to ignore the operation entirely and not move anything to the result field. There is also a choice of printing a warning message or of assuming that the user wants to achieve whatever result the implementor decides on.

Note that this representation of varying-length character strings allows only strings whose length is less than or equal to the largest binary integer which fits into a single byte. If a byte is eight bits, this means that the largest such string is 255 (which is 2^8-1) characters long. To allow for longer strings, a different representation must be chosen and a new set of programs must be written.

Once a representation has been chosen for objects of a particular data type and routines have been written to operate on those representations, the programmer is free to use that data type to solve his problems. The original hardware of the machine plus the programs for implementing more complex data types than those provided by hardware can be thought of as a "better" machine than the one consisting of the hardware alone.

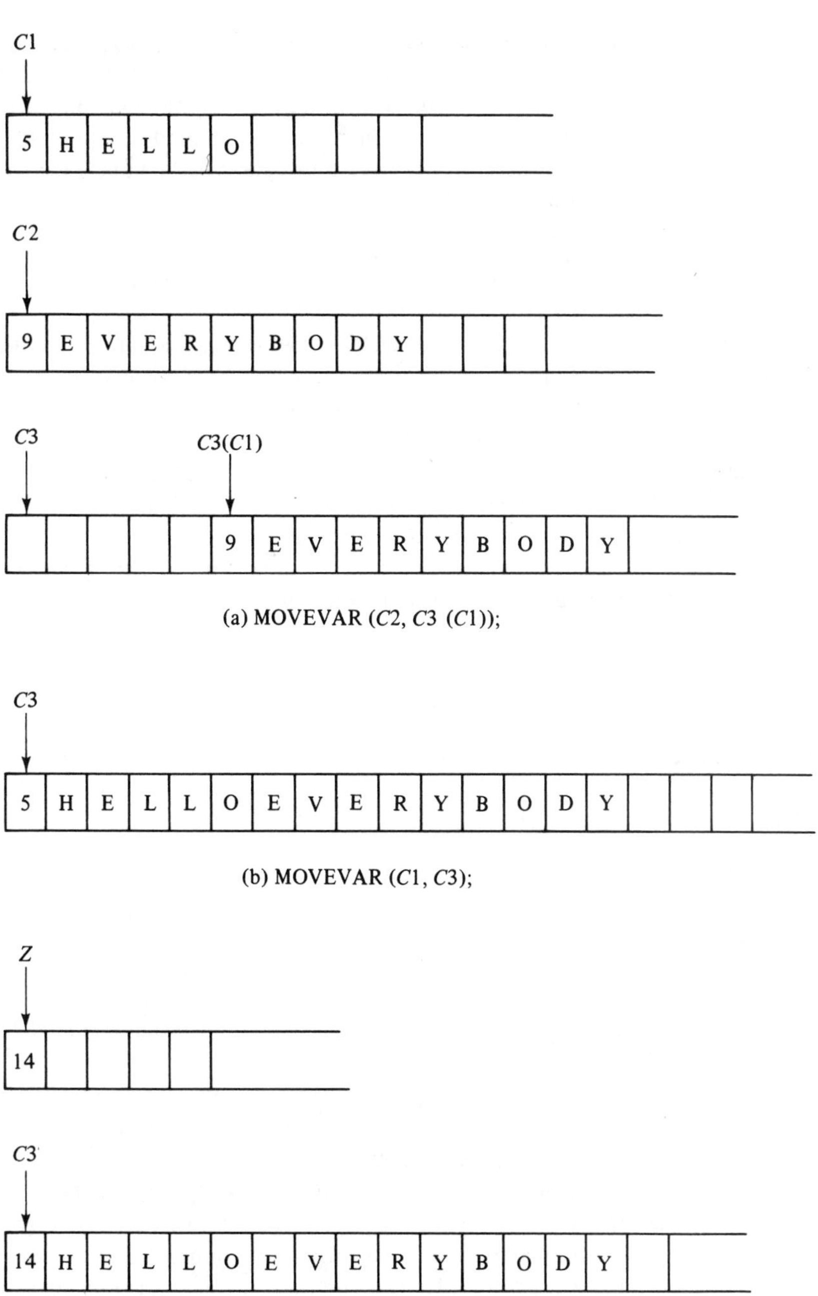

(a) MOVEVAR (C2, C3 (C1));

(b) MOVEVAR (C1, C3);

(c) $Z = C1 + C2$; MOVE (Z, C3, 1);

Figure 1.1.3. The CONCATVAR operation.

The programmer of the original machine need not worry about how the computer is designed and what circuitry is being used to execute each instruction. He need only know what instructions are available and how those instructions can be used. Similarly, the programmer who uses the "new" machine (which consists of hardware and software) need not be concerned with the details of how various data types are implemented. All the programmer needs to know is how they can be manipulated and what operations are available for those manipulations.

Data Types in PL/I

The PL/I language contains many data types such as fixed-point, float, binary and decimal numbers, fixed and varying character and bit strings, etc. A good many of these are not native data types in the hardware of the computers for which the language is implemented. Therefore, a set of routines must exist to implement these data types and the PL/I operations which are defined on them. These routines are present in the software of the PL/I system. Thus the PL/I programmer need understand only the PL/I definitions of the data types and need not worry about implementation details.

For example, the varying-length character string data type described above exists within PL/I (although it is implemented somewhat differently). To declare variables A, B, C with such strings as values, the programmer may code

```
DCL (A,B,C) CHAR(255) VAR;
```

To move such a string from B to A, he simply codes

```
A=B;
```

and to concatenate A and B and place the result in C, he can code

```
C=A||B;
```

The PL/I system supplies routines such as MOVEVAR and CONCATVAR which are necessary for interpreting memory contents as varying-length character strings and operating on those contents accordingly.

A PL/I declaration performs several functions. First, it causes an amount of storage in the computer to be reserved for a specific use. Second, it associates an identifier with that storage space so that the space can be referenced by name. Third, it causes the contents of that storage space to be interpreted according to the PL/I implementation of the attributes appearing in the declaration, when the storage space is referenced by name.

A PL/I programmer can think of the PL/I language as defining a larger machine with its own capabilities, data types, and operations. The user can state his problem solution in terms of the higher-level PL/I constructs rather than in terms of lower-level machine language constructs. Thus, he is able to solve a larger class of problems more easily because he has a larger set of tools available.

In the same way that PL/I data types allow easy solutions to a larger class of problems, even higher-level data types than are found in PL/I allow easier solutions to even more complex problems. If such data types were made available to programmers, they could be used directly in problem solving in much the same way that varying-length character strings are used by PL/I programmers.

The study of data structures therefore involves two complementary goals. The first goal is to identify and develop useful mathematical entities and operations and to determine what classes of problems can be solved by using those entities and operations. The second goal is to determine representations for those abstract entities and to implement the abstract operations on those concrete representations. The first of these goals views a high-level data type as a tool which can be used to solve other problems, while the second views the implementation of such a data type as a problem to be solved using already existing data types. In determining representations for abstract entities, we must be careful to specify what facilities are available for constructing such representations. For example, it must be stated whether all of PL/I is available or if we are restricted to the hardware facilities of a particular machine.

In the next two sections of this chapter, we examine two data structures which already exist in PL/I: the array and the structure. We focus on the abstract definitions of these data structures and how they can be useful in problem solving. We also examine how they could be implemented if PL/I were not available (although a PL/I programmer can simply use the data structures as defined in the language without concerning himself with most of these implementation details). Additionally, we describe facilities which are available in PL/I for utilizing these structures.

In the remainder of the book (except for Chapter 2, which deals with PL/I programming techniques), we develop more complex data types and show their usefulness in problem solving. We also show how to implement these data types using the data types which are already available in PL/I. Since the problems which arise in the course of attempting to implement high-level data structures are quite complex, this will also allow us to investigate the PL/I language more thoroughly and to gain valuable experience in the use of that language.

Often, no implementation, hardware or software, can model a mathematical concept completely. For example, it is impossible to represent arbitrarily large integers on a computer since the size of such a machine's memory is finite. Thus it is not the data type "integer" which is represented by the hardware but rather the data type "integer between x and y," where x and y are the smallest and largest integers representable by that machine.

It is important to recognize the limitations of a particular implementation. Often it will be possible to present several implementations of the same data type, each with its own strengths and weaknesses. One particular implementation may be better than another for a specific application, and the programmer must be aware of the possible tradeoffs that might be involved.

One important consideration in any implementation is its efficiency. In fact, the reason that the high-level data types which we discuss are not built into PL/I is because of the significant overhead that they would entail. There are languages of significantly higher level than PL/I which have many of these data types already built into them, but all of them are highly inefficient and are therefore not in widespread use.

Efficiency is usually measured by two factors: time and space. If a particular application is heavily dependent on manipulating high-level data structures, then the speed at which those manipulations can be performed will be the major determinant of the speed of the entire application. Similarly, if a program uses a large number of such structures, then an implementation which uses an inordinate amount of space to represent the data structure will be impractical. Unfortunately, there is usually a tradeoff between these two efficiencies, so that an implementation which is fast uses more storage than one which is slow. The choice of implementation in such a case involves a careful evaluation of the tradeoffs among the various possibilities.

1.2. Arrays in PL/I

In this section and the next we examine two data structures which are an invaluable part of the PL/I language. We will see how to use these structures and how they can be implemented. Both of these structures are ***composite structures***; that is, they are made up of simpler data types which exist in the language. The study of these structures involves an analysis of how the simpler structures combine to form the composite and how to extract a specific component from the composite. We expect that you have already seen these data structures in an introductory PL/I programming course and that you are aware of how they are declared and used in PL/I. In these sections, therefore, we will not dwell on the many details associated with these structures, but instead will highlight those features which are interesting from a data structure point of view.

The first of these data structures is the ***array***. The simplest form of an array is a ***one-dimensional array***, which may be defined abstractly as a finite, ordered set of homogeneous elements. By "finite" we mean that at any given moment there is a specific number of elements in the array. This number may be large or small, but it must exist. By "ordered" we mean that the elements of the array are arranged so that there is a first, second, third, etc. By "homogeneous" we mean that all the elements in the array must be of the same data type. For example, an array may contain all integers or all character strings, but may not contain both.

There are two basic operations which can be performed on a one-dimensional array. The first is the extraction of a particular element from an array. The inputs to this operation are the array and an indication of which element of the array is to be referenced. This indication is given as an integer, called an ***index***. Thus the function

extract (A,5)

returns element number 5 of the array A. The second operation stores an element into an array. For example, the operation

store (A,5,X)

stores the value of the variable X into element number 5 of the array.

Thus far, we have introduced an abstract data structure and two abstract operations. PL/I includes an implementation of this data structure and these operations. To declare a one-dimensional array named A with 100 elements, all of which are decimal integers, the programmer may write

```
DECLARE A(100) FIXED;
```

The function *extract* (A, 5) is written in PL/I as A(5), which refers to element number 5 of array A. The operation *store*(A,5,X) is written as

```
A(5) = X;
```

A(1) need not be the first element of an array A. For example, the declaration

```
DCL A(10:100) FIXED ;
```

declares A to be an array of 91 integers. The first element in the array is A(10), the second is A(11), and the ninety-first is A(100). The smallest index in the array is called the ***lower bound*** and the largest is the ***upper bound.*** If a lower bound is not specified in the declaration (as in the first example above), the lower bound is 1 by default. Thus, in the first example above, the lower bound of A is 1 and the upper bound is 100; in the second example, the lower bound is 10 and the upper bound is 100. The number of elements in a one-dimensional array, called the ***range*** of the array, is equal to 1 more than the difference between the upper and lower bounds. If l is the lower bound, u the upper bound, and r the range of a one-dimensional array, then $r = u - l + 1$.

One important feature of a PL/I array is that once such an array is created, it is static; that is, its lower bound and its upper bound (and therefore its range) cannot be changed. Thus, a PL/I array must have a fixed number of elements throughout its existence. Before any values can be stored in the array, its size must be established.

Using One-dimensional Arrays

A one-dimensional array is used when it is necessary to keep a large number of items in memory and reference all the items in a uniform manner. Let us see how these two requirements apply to practical situations.

Suppose we wish to read 100 integers, find their average, and determine by how much each integer deviates from that average. The following program accomplishes this (without the use of the PL/I built-in SUM function):

```
AVER: PROC OPTIONS (MAIN);
      DCL NUM(100) FIXED,             /*   set up array for the    */
                                      /*   one hundred numbers     */
          TOTAL    FIXED(7) INIT(0),  /*   sum of the numbers      */
          AVG      FIXED(7,2),        /*       the average         */
          DIFF     FIXED(7,2),        /*  difference between the   */
                                      /*  number and the average   */
          I        FIXED;             /*      loop variable        */
```

```
INPUT:      /*             read the numbers into the array            */
        DO I = 1 TO 100;
            GET LIST (NUM(I));
            TOTAL = TOTAL + NUM(I);
        END INPUT;

            /*       at this point, TOTAL contains the sum of the     */
            /*                        numbers                         */
        AVG = TOTAL/100;
            /*                     print headings                     */
        PUT SKIP LIST ('NUMBER', 'DIFFERENCE');

            /*         print each number and the difference           */
PRINT:  DO I = 1 TO 100;
            DIFF = NUM(I) - AVG;
            PUT SKIP LIST (NUM(I), DIFF);
        END PRINT;

        PUT SKIP(2) EDIT('AVERAGE IS:',AVG) (A,X(2),F(8,2));
      END AVER;
```

This program uses two groups of 100 numbers. The first group is the set of input integers and is represented by the array NUM, and the second group is the set of differences which are the successive values assigned to the variable DIFF in the loop PRINT. The question arises as to why an array is used to hold all the values of the first group simultaneously but only a single variable is used to hold one value of the second group at a time.

The answer is quite simple. Each difference is computed and printed and is never needed again. Thus the variable DIFF can be reused for the difference of the next integer and the average. However, the original integers which are the values of the array NUM must all be kept in memory. Although each can be added into TOTAL as it is input, it must be retained until after the average is computed in order for the program to compute the difference between it and the average. Therefore, an array is used.

Of course, 100 separate variables could have been used to hold the integers. The advantage of an array, however, is that it allows the programmer to declare only a single identifier and yet obtain a large amount of space. Furthermore, in conjunction with the DO loop, it also allows the programmer to reference each element of the group in a uniform manner instead of forcing him to code a statement such as

```
GET LIST (NUM1,NUM2,NUM3, . . . ,NUM99,NUM100);
```

A particular element of an array may be retrieved through its index. For example, suppose a company is using a program in which an array is declared by

```
DCL SALES (1950:1969)   FIXED (10,2);
```

The array will hold sales figures for a 20-year period. Suppose that each input card to the program contains a year and a sales figure for that year and it is desired to read the sales figure into the appropriate element of the array. This can be accomplished by executing the statement

```
GET LIST(YR,SALES(YR));
```

within a loop. In this statement, a particular element of the array is accessed directly by using its index. Consider the situation if 20 variables SALES1950, SALES1951, . . . , SALES1969 had been declared. Then even after executing GET LIST(YR); to set YR to the integer representing the year, the sales figure could not be read into the proper variable without coding something like:

```
IF YR=1950 THEN GET LIST (SALES1950);
IF YR=1951 THEN GET LIST (SALES1951);
                   .
                   .
                   .
IF YR=1969 THEN GET LIST (SALES1969);
```

This is bad enough with 20 elements–imagine the inconvenience if there were 100 or 1000.

Implementing One-dimensional Arrays

A one-dimensional array can be easily implemented. The PL/I declaration

```
DCL B (100) FIXED;
```

reserves 100 successive memory locations, each large enough to contain a single FIXED number. The address of the first of these locations is called the ***base address*** of the array B and is denoted by *base*(B). Suppose that the size of each individual element of the array is *esize*. Then a reference to the element B(1) is to the element at location *base*(B), a reference to B(2) is to the element at *base*(B) + *esize*, a reference to B(3) is to the element *base*(B) + 2∗*esize*. In general, a reference to B(I) is to the element at location *base*(B) + (I–1)∗*esize*. Thus it is possible to reference any element in the array, given its index.

To implement an array declared with a lower bound other than 1, there is one minor change in the formula for computing the address of an element. For example, if the array C is declared by

```
DCL C (10:100) FIXED;
```

then *base* (C) refers to the location of C (10) which is the first element of the array C, C(11) is at location *base*(C) + *esize*, C(12) at *base*(C) + 2∗*esize*, and C(I) is at location *base*(C) + (I–10)∗*esize*. In general, if *l* is the lower bound of an array D, then D(I) is located at *base*(D) + (I–*l*)∗*esize*.

If the elements of an array do not have a fixed size, however, this method cannot be used to implement the array. (An example of this is an array of varying-length character strings.) This is because this method of calculating the address of a specific element of the array depends upon knowing the fixed size *esize* of each preceding element. If not all the elements have the same size, a different implementation must be used.

One method of implementing an array of varying-sized elements is to reserve a contiguous set of memory locations, each of which holds an address. The contents of each such memory location is the address of the varying-length array element in some other portion of memory. For example, Fig. 1.2.1(a) illustrates an array of five varying-length character strings under this implementation. The arrows in that diagram indicate addresses of other portions of memory. The character 'ƀ' indicates a blank.

Since the length of each address is fixed, the location of the address of a particular element can be computed in the same way that the location of a fixed-length element was computed in the previous examples. Once this location is known, its contents can be used to determine the location of the actual array element. This, of course, adds an extra level of indirection to referencing an array element by involving an extra memory reference, which in turn decreases efficiency. However, this is a small price to pay for the convenience of being able to maintain such an array.

A similar method for implementing an array of varying-sized elements is to keep all fixed-length portions of the elements in the contiguous array area, in addition to keeping the address of the varying-length portion in the contiguous area. For example, in the implementation of varying-length character strings presented in the last section, each such string contains a fixed-length portion (a one-byte length field) and a variable-length portion (the character string itself). One implementation of an array of varying-length character strings keeps the length of the string together with the address, as shown in Fig. 1.2.1(b). The advantage of this method is that those parts of an element which are of fixed length can be examined without an extra memory reference. For example, the LENGTH function for varying-length character strings can be implemented with a single memory lookup. The fixed-length information for an array element of varying length which is stored in the contiguous memory area of the array is often called a ***header***.

Two-dimensional Arrays

An array need not be a linear set of homogeneous elements; it can also be multidimensional. A ***two-dimensional array*** is one in which each element is accessed by two indices: a row number and a column number. Figure 1.2.2(a) illustrates such a two-dimensional array declared by the PL/I statement

```
DCL A (3,5) FIXED;
```

The element which is darkened in Fig. 1.2.2(a) is referred to as A(2,4) since it is in row 2

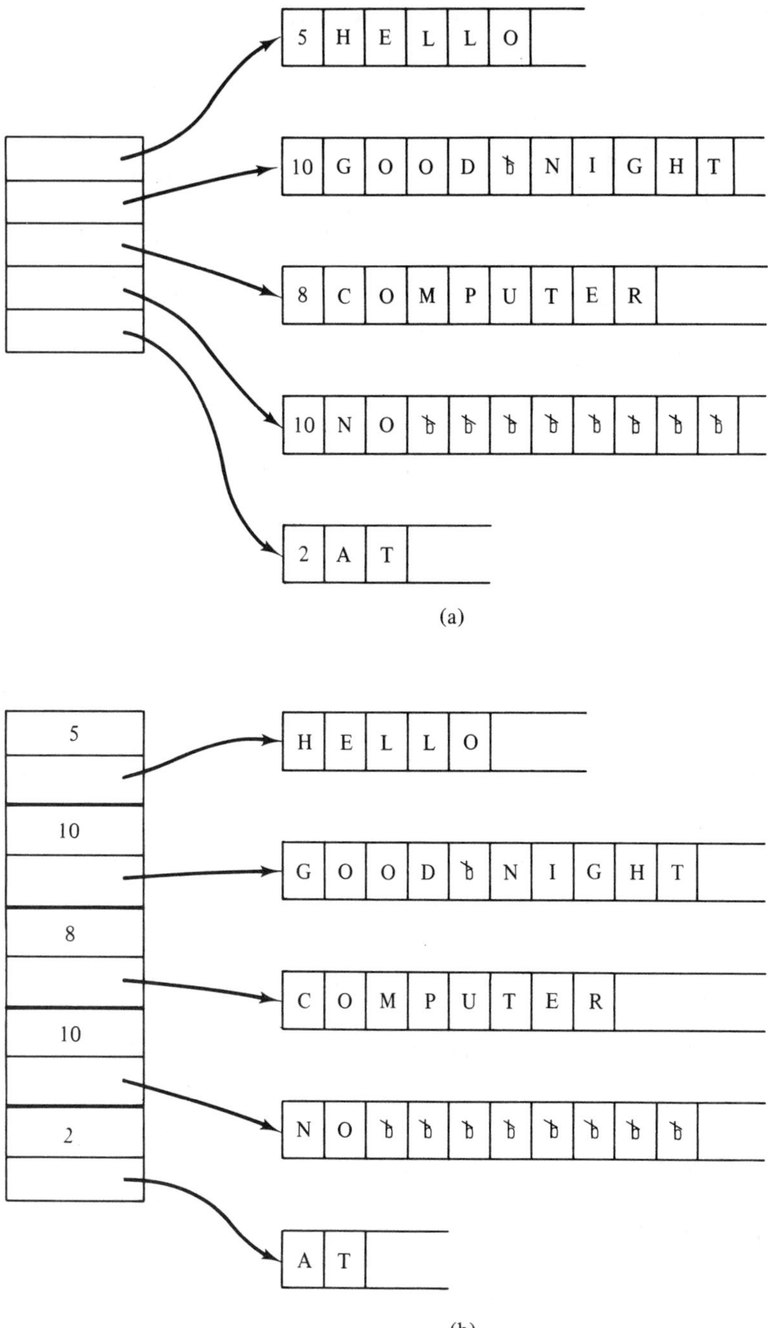

Figure 1.2.1. Two implementations of an array of varying length strings.

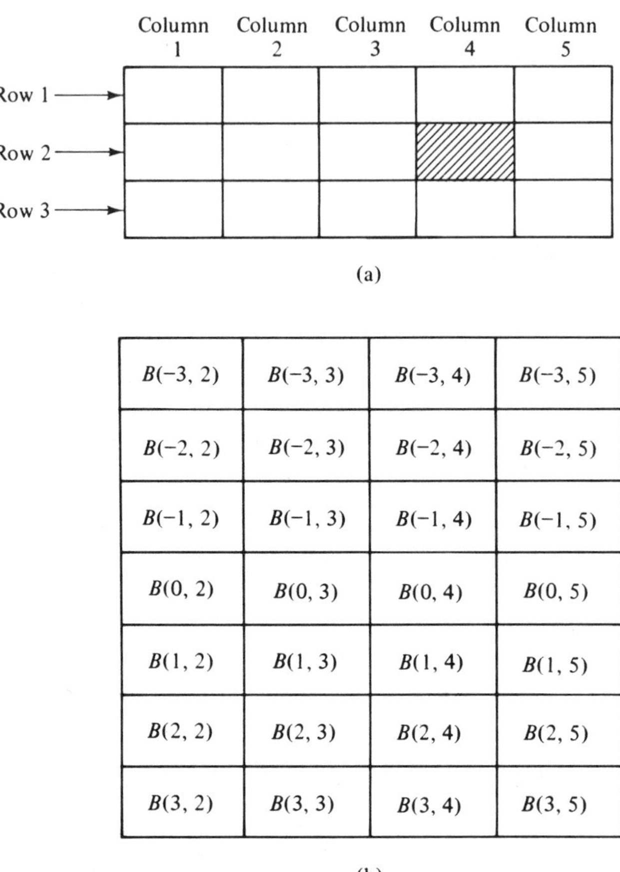

Figure 1.2.2. Two-dimensional arrays.

and column 4. As in the case of a one-dimensional array, if a lower bound is not specified, it is 1 by default. A different lower bound than the default may be specified for either or both of the dimensions. For example, Fig. 1.2.2(b) illustrates an array declared by

```
DCL B (-3:3,2:5) FIXED;
```

and names each element of the array. The number of rows or columns is equal to the upper bound minus the lower bound plus 1. This number is called the ***range*** of the dimension. In the array A above, the range of the first dimension is 3–1+1, which is 3, and the range of the second dimension is 5–1+1, which is 5. Thus the array A has three rows and five columns. In the array B, the number of rows is 3–(–3)+1=7 and the number of columns is 5–2+1=4. The number of elements in a two-dimensional array is equal to the product of the number of rows and the number of columns. Thus, the array A contains 3*5=15 elements, and the array B contains 7*4=28 elements.

A two-dimensional array clearly illustrates the differences between a ***logical*** and a ***physical*** view of data. A two-dimensional array is a logical data structure which is useful in programming and problem solving. For example, such an array is useful in describing an object which is physically two-dimensional, such as a map or a checkerboard. It is also useful in organizing a set of values which are dependent upon two inputs. For example, a program for a department store which has 20 branches, each of which sells 30 items, might include a two-dimensional array declared by

```
DCL SALES (20,30) FIXED (7,2);
```

Each element SALES (I,J) represents the amount of item J sold in branch I.

However, although it is convenient for the programmer to think of the elements of such an array as being organized in a two-dimensional table and programming languages do indeed include facilities for treating them as a two-dimensional array, the hardware of most computers have no such facilities. An array must be stored in the memory of a computer, and that memory is usually linear. By this we mean that the memory of a computer is essentially a one-dimensional array. A single address (which may be viewed as a subscript for a one-dimensional array) is used to retrieve a particular item from memory. In order to implement a two-dimensional array, it is necessary to develop a method of ordering its elements in a linear array and of transforming a two-dimensional reference to the linear representation.

One method of representing a two-dimensional array in memory is the ***row-major*** representation. Under this representation, the first row of the array occupies the first set of memory locations reserved for the array, the second row occupies the next set, etc. There may also be several locations at the start of the physical array which serve as a header and which contain the upper and lower bounds of the two dimensions. (This header should not be confused with the headers discussed above. This header is for the entire array, whereas the headers mentioned earlier are headers for the individual array elements.) Figure 1.2.3 illustrates the row-major representation of the two-dimensional array B declared above and illustrated in Fig. 1.2.2(b). Alternatively, the header need not be contiguous to the array elements, but could instead contain the address of the first element of the array. Additionally, if the elements of the two-dimensional array are variable-length objects, the elements of the contiguous area could themselves contain the addresses of those objects in a form similar to those of Fig. 1.2.1 for linear arrays.

Let us suppose that a two-dimensional array is stored in row-major sequence, as in Fig. 1.2.3, and let us suppose that, for an array AR, *base*(AR) is the address of the first element of the array. That is, if AR is declared by

```
DCL AR(L1:U1,L2:U2) FIXED;
```

where L1, U1, L2, and U2 are the integer upper and lower bounds, then *base*(AR) is the address of AR(L1,L2). For example, for the array A of Fig. 1.2.2(a), *base*(A) is the address of A(1,1), and for the array B of Fig. 1.2.2(b), *base*(B) is the address of B(–3,2). Let us define R2 (the range of the second dimension) as U2–L2+1. We also assume that

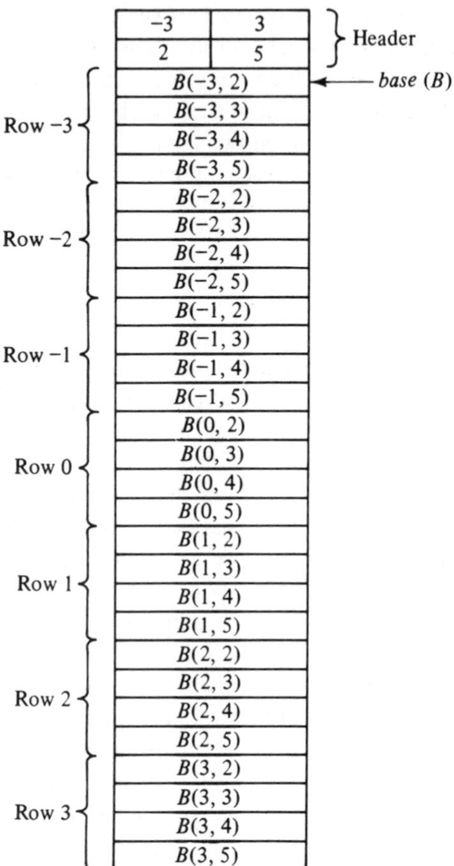

Figure 1.2.3. Representing a two-dimensional array.

esize is the size of each element in the array. Let us calculate the address of an arbitrary element, AR(I1,I2). Since the element is in row I1, its address can be calculated by computing the address of the first element of row I1 and adding the quantity (I2–L2)**esize* (this quantity represents how far into row I1 the element at column I2 is). But in order to reach the first element of row I1 (which is the element AR(I1,L2)), it is necessary to pass through (I1–L1) complete rows, each of which contains R2 elements (since there is one element from each column in each row), so that the address of the first element of row I1 is at *base*(AR) + (I1–L1)*R2**esize*. Therefore, the address of AR(I1,I2) is at

base(AR) + [(I1–L1)*R2 + (I2–L2)] **esize*.

As an example, consider the array B of Fig. 1.2.2(b) whose representation is illustrated in Fig. 1.2.3. In this array, L1=–3, U1=3, L2=2, and U2=5, so that *base*(B) is the address of B(–3,2) and R2 equals 4. Let us also suppose that each element of the array requires a single unit of storage so that *esize* equals 1. (This is not necessarily true since B was declared as an array of FIXED items and a FIXED item may need more than one unit of memory on a particular machine. For simplicity, however, we accept this assumption.) Then the location of B(0,4) may be computed as follows: In order to reach row 0, we must skip over rows –3, –2, and –1. Each of those rows contains four elements consisting of one memory location each. Thus, the first element of row 0 (which is B(0,2)) is 12 elements past the address of B(–3,2), which is *base*(B). The element B(0,4) is two elements past B(0,2). The above formula yields the address of B(0,4) as:

```
base(B) + [ (0–(–3))*4 + (4–2) ] *1
```

which is

```
base(B) + 12+2 = base(B)+14.
```

You may confirm the fact that B(0,4) is 14 units past *base*(B) in Fig. 1.2.3.

Multi-dimensional Arrays

PL/I allows arrays which have more than two dimensions. For example, a three-dimensional array may be declared by

```
DCL C(3:5, 2, 4) FIXED;
```

and is illustrated in Fig. 1.2.4(a). An element of this array is specified by three subscripts, such as C(4,1,3). The first subscript specifies a plane number, the second subscript a row number, and the third a column number. Such an array is useful when a value is determined by three inputs. For example, an array of temperatures might be indexed by latitutde, longitude, and altitude.

For obvious reasons, the geometric analogy breaks down when we go beyond three dimensions. However, PL/I does allow an arbitrary number of dimensions. For example, a six-dimensional array may be declared by

```
DCL D(7, 15, 3, –2:2, 8, 5:6) FIXED;
```

Referencing an element of this array would require six subscripts, such as D(3,14,1,–1, 7,6). The number of different subscripts which are allowed in a particular position (the range of a particular dimension) equals the upper bound of that dimension minus its lower bound plus 1. The number of elements in an array is the product of the ranges of all its dimensions. For example, the array C above contains (5–3+1) * (2–1+1) * (4–1+1) = 3*2*4 = 24 elements, while the array D contains 7*15*3*5*8*2 = 25,200 elements.

The row-major representation of arrays can be extended to arrays of more than two dimensions. Figure 1.2.4(b) illustrates the representation of the array C of Fig. 1.2.4(a).

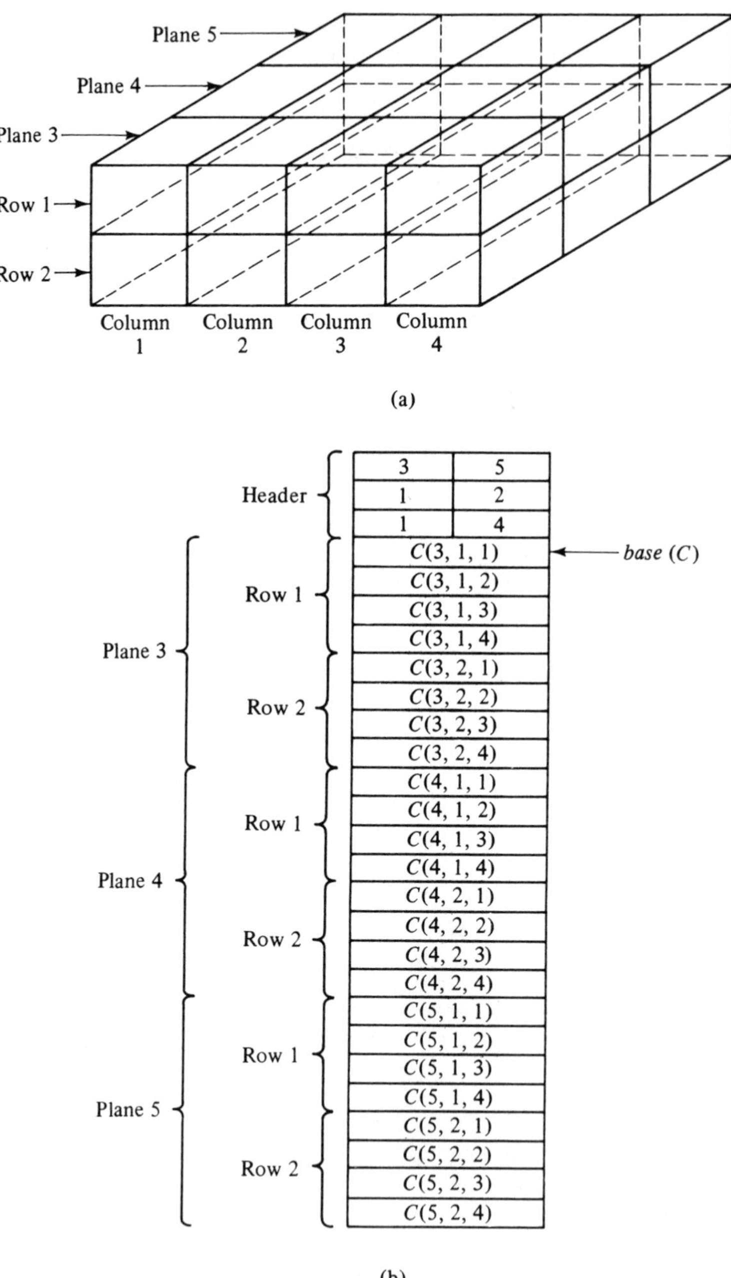

Figure 1.2.4. A three-dimensional array.

The elements of the six-dimensional array D described above are ordered as follows:

```
D(1,1,1,–2,1,5)
D(1,1,1,–2,1,6)
D(1,1,1,–2,2,5)
D(1,1,1,–2,2,6)
D(1,1,1,–2,3,5)
      . . .
      . . .
D(7,15,3,2,6,5)
D(7,15,3,2,6,6)
D(7,15,3,2,7,5)
D(7,15,3,2,7,6)
D(7,15,3,2,8,5)
D(7,15,3,2,8,6)
```

That is, the last subscript varies most rapidly, and a subscript is not increased until all possible combinations of the subscripts to its right have been exhausted. This is similar to an odometer (mileage indicator) of a car, where the rightmost digit changes most rapidly.

What mechanism is needed to access an element of an arbitrary multidimensional array? Suppose that AR is an n-dimensional array declared by

DCL AR(L_1:U_1, L_2:U_2, . . . ,L_n:U_n) FIXED;

which is stored in row-major order. Each element of AR is assumed to occupy *esize* storage locations, and *base*(AR) is defined as the address of the first element of the array (which is AR(L_1,L_2, . . . , L_n)). R_i is defined as U_i–L_i+1 for all i between 1 and n. Then in order to access the element

AR(I_1, I_2, . . . , I_n)

it is first necessary to pass through (I_1–L_1) complete "hyperplanes," each consisting of R_2∗R_3∗ . . . ∗R_n elements to reach the first element of AR whose first subscript is I_1. Then it is necessary to pass through an additional (I_2–L_2) groups of R_3∗R_4∗ . . . ∗R_n elements in order to reach the first element of AR whose first two subscripts are I_1 and I_2 respectively. A similar process must be carried out through the other dimensions until the first element whose first n–1 subscripts match those of the desired element is reached. Finally, it is necessary to pass through (I_n–L_n) additional elements to reach the element desired.

Thus the address of $AR(I_1, I_2, \ldots, I_n)$ may be written as *base*(AR) + *esize* * $[(I_1-L_1)*R_2* \ldots *R_n + (I_2-L_2)*R_3* \ldots *R_n + \ldots + (I_{n-1}-L_{n-1})*R_n + (I_n-L_n)]$, which can be evaluated more efficiently by using the equivalent formula:

$$base(AR) + esize * [I_n - L_n + R_n*(I_{n-1}-L_{n-1} + R_{n-1}*(\ldots \ldots + R_3*(I_2-L_2+R_2*(I_1-L_1)) \ldots))]$$

This formula may be evaluated by the following algorithm (assuming arrays *i*, *l*, and *r* of size *n* to hold the indices, lower bounds, and the ranges respectively):

```
offset=0;
do j = 1 to n;
   offset = r(j)*offset + (i(j)-l(j));
end;
addr=base(AR) + esize* offset;
return(addr);
```

Handling Subscript Errors

Suppose, as is often the case, a programmer uses a subscript which is not within the range of the array bounds. For example, the programmer references A(I), where A is an array with subscripts 1 to 100 and where the current value of I is 101. Such mistakes are quite common when expressions are used as subscripts, or inside a DO loop which is repeated once too often. Because the reference is illegal, the results of such a reference are unspecified by the PL/I language. Since the programmer is not programming in legal PL/I, he cannot expect PL/I to define what his results will be. Therefore, each PL/I implementation may produce a different result for this eventuality.

Let us examine some of the alternative actions which might be taken when a subscript is out of bounds. The simplest alternative is to do nothing. That is, whenever a reference to an array element A(I) is made, the machine proceeds to compute the address of that element using the formula given above as though the subscript were legitimate. For example, if the size of each array element (*esize*) is one storage unit and the array were declared with bounds 1 and 100, a reference to the element with subscript 101 will result in the address which is 100 storage units past the first element of the array. That address is no longer within the array and may even be outside of the area in memory set aside for the entire program. The system may take whatever action is appropriate. If the address is outside the program's memory area, this usually involves printing an error message and stopping the program. However, the error message will not indicate an illegal array reference; it will only state that an attempt is being made to access a location which is nonexistent or is not allocated to the program.

It may be that the computed address is within the program area but the information at that address is not of the proper format for an array element. For example, the array may consist of decimal numbers, but the information at the computed location may contain bit patterns which are not legitimate decimal numbers. When an attempt is made to interpret that information as a decimal number, the system will produce an error message stating that the information is in incorrect format. Again, there is no indication that the cause of the error was a subscript which was out of bounds.

Even if the programmer receives one of these imprecise messages, he should consider himself lucky. A far more distressing possibility is that the computed location is within the program area and that the information contained therein is in proper format. In that case, the system will simply use that information and will give no indication that anything is wrong. Instead, it will proceed to produce incorrect results based on that information. Often the programmer will have no indication that the results are incorrect. Or he may see that they are obviously incorrect but will have no indication of where his large program went wrong.

In all of the above cases, the PL/I implementation relies on the backup error detection system of the hardware or of the operating system. It does not itself check for whether the subscript is within bounds of the specific PL/I array. The reason for this "do-nothing" attitude is twofold: Since a subscript may be a variable or an expression, there is no way to determine at compilation (when the program is translated into machine code) whether or not its value will be within bounds. Therefore, such a check would have to be made at execution time if it is to be made at all. A check that can be made at compilation is usually made only once for each statement. A check that is made during execution must be made each time that the statement is executed. Thus if a particular statement appears within a loop which is repeated 1000 times, a compilation check would involve only a single check, while an execution check would involve 1000 checks. In addition, a production program (one that is in constant use and is not changed) need be compiled only once but may be executed many times. An execution check means that every array reference involves not only an address computation but also a check for validity. This sharply decreases efficiency. Furthermore, in order to be able to check a subscript for validity, it is necessary to keep the upper and lower bounds of the array in memory during execution time. This means that extra information is necessary within each array and that the format of an array is more complex.

The alternative to doing nothing is to forgo efficiency for clarity and ease of debugging. An array is not represented solely by the elements of which it is composed. Rather, each array has a header which contains its upper and lower bounds. This header could be located at the beginning of the contiguous area which holds the array elements, or it could be a separate entity and contain the base address of the array as well as the upper and lower bounds. Whenever a reference to an array element is made during execution, a test is made to ensure that the subscript lies between the bounds before computing the element's address. If the subscript is out of bounds, a detailed error message giving the name of the array and the value of the illegal subscript can be printed.

The PL/I language allows the user the option of having the system check for subscript errors. Ordinarily, there is no checking performed unless the programmer enables the SUBSCRIPTRANGE condition. (However, in PL/C the SUBSCRIPTRANGE condition is initially enabled so that such errors are detected.) We will describe this condition and its use more fully in Section 2.3.

Array Operations

Thus far, arrays have been treated as collections of elements. However, PL/I allows an array to be treated as an entity in itself. For example, if A is declared by

```
DCL A(5) FIXED;
```

then the statement

```
GET LIST (A);
```

is equivalent to the statement

```
GET LIST(A(1), A(2), A(3), A(4), A(5));
```

A reference in a program to an identifier without subscripts implies a reference to each of the array elements in turn. Thus if arrays B and C had also been declared by

```
DCL (B,C)(5) FIXED;
```

then the statement

```
A = B+C;
```

is equivalent to the five statements

```
A(1) = B(1) + C(1);
A(2) = B(2) + C(2);
A(3) = B(3) + C(3);
A(4) = B(4) + C(4);
A(5) = B(5) + C(5);
```

Similarly, the statement

```
A = B+7;
```

is equivalent to

```
A(1) = B(1) + 7;
A(2) = B(2) + 7;
A(3) = B(3) + 7;
A(4) = B(4) + 7;
A(5) = B(5) + 7;
```

In general, if an array identifier appears on the left side of an assignment statement, then the right side may be any arithmetic expression involving array identifiers and scalars (single-element objects). However, all the array identifiers in such an assignment statement must have the same number of dimensions and the same upper and lower bounds for each dimension.

The PL/I array manipulation facilities for multidimensional arrays are built around their row-major representation. For example, if the array A is declared by

```
DCL A(3,5) FIXED;
```

as illustrated in Fig. 1.2.2(a), then the statement

```
GET LIST (A);
```

is equivalent to the statement

```
GET LIST (A(1,1), A(1,2), A(1,3), A(1,4), A(1,5), A(2,1),. . .
. . . , A(2,5), A(3,1), A(3,2), A(3,3), A(3,4), A(3,5));
```

This means that the data must appear in row-major order on the input medium.

If an arithmetic or string built-in function is applied to an array, it is applied to the elements of the array in row-major order. For example, if arrays S and T are declared by

```
DCL (S,T) (2,2) CHAR(30)VAR;
```

then the statement

```
S=SUBSTR(T,4,3);
```

is equivalent to

```
S(1,1)=SUBSTR(T(1,1),4,3);
S(1,2)=SUBSTR(T(1,2),4,3);
S(2,1)=SUBSTR(T(2,1),4,3);
S(2,2)=SUBSTR(T(2,2),4,3);
```

Similarly if A, B, and C are declared by

```
DCL (A,B,C) (2,2) FIXED;
```

then the statement

```
A=MAX(B,C);
```

is equivalent to

```
A(1,1)=MAX(B(1,1),C(1,1));
A(1,2)=MAX(B(1,2),C(1,2));
A(2,1)=MAX(B(2,1),C(2,1));
A(2,2)=MAX(B(2,2),C(2,2));
```

Note that the MAX and MIN functions cannot be used to compute the maximum and minimum elements of a single array since they are applied elementwise and not to the array as a whole.

However, PL/I does contain some built-in functions which manipulate entire arrays. For example, if A is an array of numbers, then SUM(A) returns the sum of all the elements of A, and PROD(A) returns the product of all the elements of A. These functions can accept either one-dimensional or multidimensional arrays.

There is also a facility in PL/I for obtaining a cross section of a multidimensional array. For example, suppose an array A was declared by

```
DCL A(10,5) FIXED;
```

and it was desired to print the elements in the fourth row of A. A statement which accomplishes this is

```
PUT LIST (A(4,*));
```

The asterisk as the second subscript indicates a reference to all elements of a particular row—in this case the fourth, since the first subscript is 4. Similarly, A(*,2) refers to all the elements in the second column of the array A.

A cross section of a two-dimensional array may be used as a one-dimensional array. For example, if A, B, and C are declared by

```
DCL (A(5), B(5,7), C(10,5)) FIXED;
```

then the PL/I statement

```
A=B(*,3)+C(8,*);
```

is equivalent to the five statements

```
A(1)=B(1,3)+C(8,1);
A(2)=B(2,3)+C(8,2);
A(3)=B(3,3)+C(8,3);
A(4)=B(4,3)+C(8,4);
A(5)=B(5,3)+C(8,5);
```

Similarly, if A is declared as a three-dimensional array such as

```
DCL A(9,5,6) FIXED;
```

then a reference to A(6,*,3) is to the five-element, one-dimensional array formed by A(6,1,3), A(6,2,3), A(6,3,3), A(6,4,3), and A(6,5,3). A reference to A(*,*,6) is to the two-dimensional array of nine rows and five columns formed by the elements of the array whose last subscript is 6.

Arrays as Parameters

When an array is passed as an argument to a PL/I procedure, the corresponding formal parameter must be declared as an array. For example, the following function computes the average of 100 numbers stored in a one-dimensional array.

```
AVG100:  PROC(A) RETURNS(FLOAT);
           DCL A(100)            FLOAT,
               H                 FLOAT INIT (100);
           RETURN(SUM(A)/H);
         END AVG100;
```

(This function does not work correctly in PL/C, for reasons which will be explained shortly.) If in a main routine, an array X is declared by

```
DCL X(100) FLOAT;
```

then the average of the 100 elements of X can be printed by the statement

```
PUT LIST (AVG100(X));
```

When the function AVG100 is invoked, the identifier A which is the parameter of the function refers to the original array X.

However, suppose it is desired to have a function which computes the average of the numbers in an array whose size is larger or smaller than 100. PL/I contains a facility which makes it unnecessary to specify the size of an array parameter in a subprocedure. This can be done by using an asterisk in the declaration for the array parameter, as illustrated in the following function. The function computes the average of all the elements in an array A of size N.

```
AVG:     PROC(A,N) RETURNS (FLOAT);
           DCL A(*)        FLOAT,
               N           FIXED;
           RETURN (SUM(A)/N);
         END AVG;
```

The asterisk means that the array A is declared to be of the same size as the array which is passed as an argument to the function. N still appears as a parameter, however, since it is still necessary to know the number of elements being averaged in order to compute the average.

It is possible to eliminate N as a parameter entirely by using a PL/I built-in function. The function HBOUND (A,I), where A is an array and I an integer, returns the upper bound of the Ith dimension of the array A. For example, if we declared

```
DCL (X(5,7), Y(13), Z(3:8, -4:-2, 0:5)) FIXED;
```

then HBOUND(X,2) is 7, HBOUND(Y,1) is 13, and HBOUND(Z,2) is −2. Using this function, it is possible to rewrite the function AVG to compute the average of all the elements in a one-dimensional array as follows:

```
AVG2:    PROC(A) RETURNS (FLOAT);
           DCL A(*)              FLOAT;
           RETURN (SUM(A)/HBOUND(A,1));
         END AVG2;
```

Of course, if it is desired to find the average of only the first N elements of an array of arbitrary size, then N must be passed as a parameter and an explicit loop must be used as follows:

```
AVGN:    PROC(A,N) RETURNS (FLOAT);
           DCL (A(*),S)          FLOAT,
               (N,I)             FIXED;
           S=0;
LOOP:      DO  I=1 TO N;
               S=S+A(I);
           END LOOP;
           RETURN (S/N);
         END AVGN;
```

To use this function, the programmer codes the expression AVGN(X,N), after the first N elements of an array X have been initialized.

There are two other built-in functions similar to HBOUND. LBOUND(A,I) returns the lower bound of the Ith dimension of array A, and DIM(A,I) returns the range of the Ith dimension of array A. In the above example, where we declared

```
DCL (X(5,7), Y(13), Z(3:8, -4:-2, 0:5))  FIXED;
```

LBOUND(X,2) is 1, LBOUND(Y,1) is 1, LBOUND(Z,2) is −4, and LBOUND (Z,3) is 0. Also in the above example DIM(X,1) is 5, DIM(Y,1) is 13, DIM(Z,1) is 6, and DIM(Z,2) is 3. These functions are most useful in a subprocedure where an array parameter is declared with the asterisk notation, leaving the bounds and range of the array unknown at the time that the subroutine is written.

The asterisk notation may be used for multidimensional arrays as well. For example, a ***magic square*** is one in which the elements of each row, column, and diagonal add up to the same value, as in the following:

```
8  1  6
3  5  7
4  9  2
```

The following function returns '1'B (true) if a square two-dimensional array forms a magic square and '0'B otherwise.

```
SQUARE:  PROC(A) RETURNS(BIT(1));
           DCL A(*,*)                    FIXED,
               (SIZE,I,S1,S2,VALUE)      FIXED;

           SIZE=HBOUND(A,1);
           IF SIZE¬=HBOUND (A,2) THEN
               /*   the array is not square    */
                                         RETURN ('0'B);
           VALUE=SUM (A(1,*));

               /*   The identifier VALUE now contains the sum     */
               /*        of the first row. If the sum of any of   */
               /*   the rows or columns is not the same, then A   */
               /*              is not a magic square.             */
           IF VALUE¬=SUM(A(*,1)) THEN RETURN ('0'B);
LOOP:      DO  I=2 TO SIZE;
               IF VALUE¬=SUM(A(I,*)) | VALUE¬=SUM(A(*,I))
                                             THEN RETURN ('0'B);
           END LOOP;

               /*              check the two diagonals            */
           S1,S2=0;
DIAG:      DO  I=1 TO SIZE;
               S1=S1+A(I,I);
               S2=S2+A(I,SIZE+1-I);
           END DIAG;
           IF S1¬ =VALUE | S2¬ =VALUE THEN RETURN ('0'B);
                                       ELSE RETURN ('1'B);
         END SQUARE;
```

The asterisk notation may also be used for parameters which are character strings to indicate that the length of a formal parameter should be taken from its corresponding argument. For example, the following function returns the number of times that letter LETT occurs in a character string STR:

```
COUNT:   PROC(STR,LETT)  RETURNS (FIXED);
           DCL STR                 CHAR(*),
               LETT                CHAR(*),
               NUM                 FIXED INIT (0),
               I                   FIXED;
LOOP:      DO I=1 TO LENGTH(STR);
              IF SUBSTR (STR,I,1) =  LETT THEN NUM=NUM+1;
           END LOOP;
           RETURN (NUM);
         END COUNT;
```

Users of PL/C should be aware of the fact that, in PL/C, parameter array bounds and character string lengths must be specified with asterisks.

Another important feature of PL/I is that in order to change a value in an array passed to a procedure as a parameter (or in any parameter), the attributes of the argument and the attributes of the formal parameter must match exactly. If the attributes do not match, different compilers may take different actions. Some compilers (e.g., IBM PL/I Optimizer) perform conversions automatically, while others (e.g., IBM PL/I–F) do not. It may be necessary to use the ENTRY attribute to force such conversions.

It is always a good idea to make sure that the attributes of an argument and its corresponding formal parameter match exactly. One attribute for which this correspondence is often overlooked is the VARYING attribute for character string parameters. Despite the fact that the length of a character string parameter is specified by an asterisk, if the argument is declared with the VARYING attribute, then the formal parameter should also be declared with that attribute if it is to refer to the same storage area. We will have more to say about these issues in Sections 2.2 and 4.3.

1.3 Structures in PL/I

In this section we examine the PL/I data structure that is actually called a ***structure***. We assume that you are already familiar with PL/I structures from an introductory course. In this section we review some of the highlights of this PL/I data structure and point out some interesting and useful features which we will need for a more general study of data structures.

A structure is a set of items in which each item is given its own identifier and in which the items are arranged in hierarchical order. The items in a structure need not be homogeneous. Let us consider an example. The PL/I declaration at the top of page 35 may be used to describe an employee record in a personnel file.

This structure may be viewed as a tree-like hierarchy, as shown in Fig. 1.3.1(a). The entire structure EMP_REC is called a ***major structure***, while those structures such as NAME_ADDR, NAME, ADDRESS, and POSITION which are included within EMP_REC are called ***minor structures***. Objects such as FIRST, MIDINIT, LAST, STRADDR, CITY, STATE, ZIP, DEPTNO, JOBTITLE, SALARY, NUMDEP, HEALTH_PLAN, and DATE_HIRED which have no subparts are called ***elementary items***. Only elementary items contain actual information. The identifiers associated with major and minor structures are used only to establish the hierarchy and to group various items together. Since only the elementary items contain data, only they are declared with attributes such as FIXED and CHAR which describe the interpretation of information.

Figure 1.3.1(b) illustrates how memory is allocated to a structure. A structure occupies a contiguous area of storage which includes enough space for all its elementary items. These elementary items are assigned storage in the order in which they are declared. An identifier representing an elementary item refers to the storage space allocated to that item. An identifier representing a structure, whether major or minor, refers to the entire space which is allocated to all the elementary items included within that structure.

Level numbers are positive, unsigned integers used to define the hierarchy of a PL/I structure. They appear immediately to the left of the identifiers in the declaration of a

```
DCL 1 EMP_REC,
      2 NAME_ADDR,

        3 NAME,
          4 FIRST       CHAR(10),
          4 MIDINIT     CHAR(1),
          4 LAST        CHAR(20),

        3 ADDRESS,
          4 STRADDR     CHAR(40),
          4 CITY        CHAR(10),
          4 STATE       CHAR(2),
          4 ZIP         CHAR(5),

      2 POSITION,
        3 DEPTNO        CHAR(3),
        3 JOBTITLE      CHAR(20),

      2 SALARY          FIXED(8,2),
      2 NUM_DEP         FIXED,        /*    number of dependents         */
      2 HEALTH_PLAN     BIT(1),       /* whether or not employee is    */
                                      /*   enrolled in health plan      */
      2 DATE_HIRED      CHAR(8);      /*    in form MM/DD/YR             */
```

structure, separated from the identifiers by one or more blanks. A major structure must be declared with a level number of 1. If an identifier A is declared with a level number *la* and an identifier B is declared immediately after A with a level number *lb* greater than *la*, then B is a part of A. If identifier C is declared immediately after B with a level number *lc* which is less than or equal to *lb* but greater than *la*, then C is also a subpart of A and is on the same level of the hierarchy as B. If, however, *lc* is less than or equal to *la* (but greater than the level number of the structure containing A), then C is on the same level of the structure hierarchy as A. Indentation is irrelevant to establishing a structure's hierarchy and is used only for readability. For example, the following declaration establishes a hierarchy as shown in Fig. 1.3.2.

```
DCL 1 A, 5 B, (12 C, 7 D) FIXED, 4 E, 5 F, (7 G, 6 H) FIXED,
      2 I FIXED;
```

It is highly recommended that sequential level numbers be used to declare increasingly lower levels in the hierarchy and that a reasonable indentation pattern is followed in structure declarations, as was done in the declaration of EMP_REC. Note that in the above structure, all the variables have the FIXED attribute. Although this could have been done using an array, it is sometimes helpful to place homogeneous variables in a structure. One advantage of this is that each variable has its own identifier.

The declaration of EMP_REC illustrates that not all elementary items need be de-

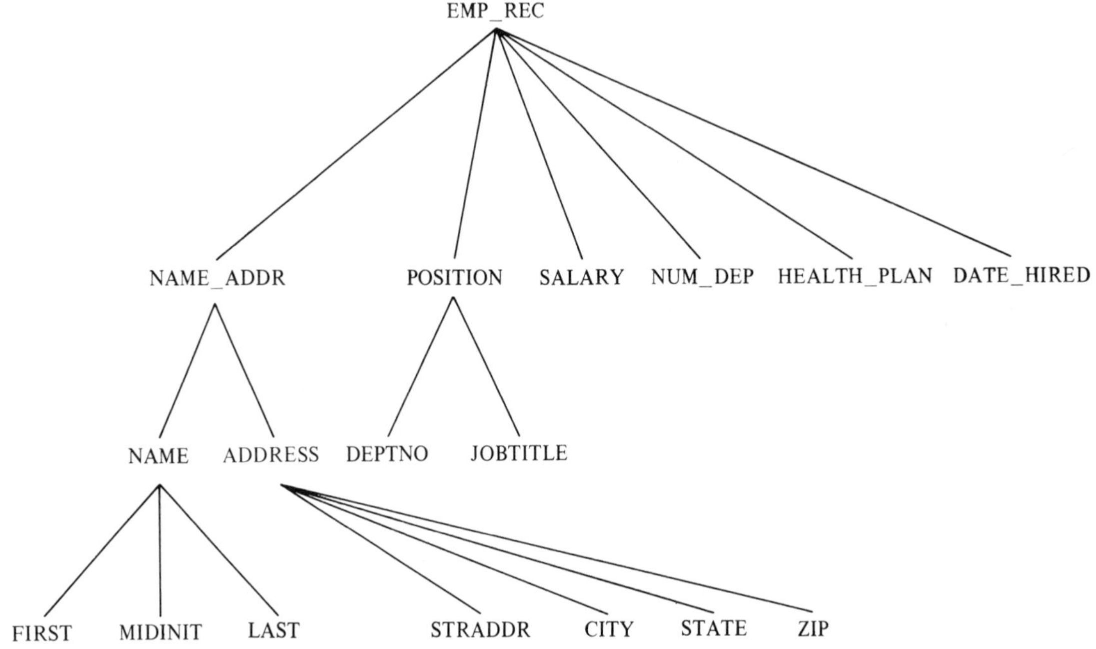

(a) A structure as a hierarchy.

EMP_REC												
NAME_ADDR												
NAME			ADDRESS				POSITION					
FIRST	MIDINIT	LAST	STRADDR	CITY	STATE	ZIP	DEPTNO	JOBTITLE	SALARY	NUM_DEP	HEALTH_PLAN	DATE_HIRED

(b) Storage allocation for a structure.

Figure 1.3.1.

clared at the same level. In that structure, elementary items appear on levels 4 (e.g., FIRST), 3 (e.g., DEPTNO) and 2 (e.g., SALARY). The decision as to which items are to be grouped together is a practical one, as we shall soon see.

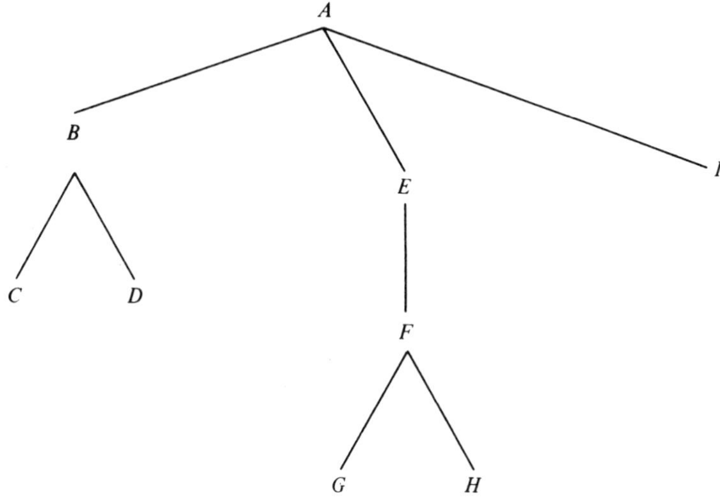

Figure 1.3.2. A structure hierarchy.

The main reason for declaring a structure is so that an entire group of items can be referenced by a single name. For example, the full name of an employee can be printed by the single statement

```
PUT SKIP EDIT(NAME) (A,X(1));
```

and the entire name and address can be printed by the statement

```
PUT SKIP EDIT (NAME_ADDR) (3(A,X(1)),SKIP,A,SKIP,3(A,X(1)));
```

(Note that one data-format item (in this case, the A format) is needed for each elementary item to be printed. In the first example, the A format is repeated three times in printing NAME. However, in printing NAME_ADDR, different format items are needed in order to print the name and address on three separate lines. The format could have been shortened to (3(A,X(1)),SKIP,A,SKIP).)

In declaring the structure EMP_REC, we assumed that it would not be necessary to process the entire payroll information (SALARY, NUM_DEP, HEALTH_PLAN, DATE_HIRED) as a unit. In order to print the employee's name and payroll information it would be necessary to code

```
PUT SKIP EDIT (NAME,SALARY,
          NUM_DEP,HEALTH_PLAN,DATE_HIRED) (/*   format list   */);
```

If the latter part of the structure EMP_REC had been declared by

```
2 PAYROLL,
  3 SALARY        FIXED(8,2),
  3 NUM_DEP       FIXED,
  3 HEALTH_PLAN   BIT(1),
  3 DATE_HIRED    CHAR(8);
```

then it would suffice to code

```
PUT SKIP EDIT (NAME,PAYROLL) (/*  format list  */);
```

In the same way that an entire structure can be printed, values can be input or assigned to an entire structure. Thus the statement

```
GET LIST(EMP_REC);
```

would read 13 items from a data card and assign those items to the 13 elementary items in the structure in the order that the items appear in the structure declaration.

Suppose another structure had been declared as follows:

```
DCL 1 ADDR,
        2 STR   CHAR(40),
        2 CTY   CHAR(10),
        2 ST    CHAR(2),
        2 ZP    CHAR(5);
```

Then the assignment statement

```
ADDRESS=ADDR;
```

is equivalent to the four assignment statements

```
STRADDR=STR;
CITY=CTY;
STATE=ST;
ZIP=ZP;
```

Qualification and Ambiguity

As we have seen, an individual element of a PL/I structure may be referenced through its own identifier. For example, if an employee is represented by the structure EMP_REC, his department number can be referenced using the identifier DEPTNO. The full name of this variable is EMP_REC.POSITION.DEPTNO, but since there is no other variable in the program with the identifier DEPTNO, it is permissible to reference the department number using only its identifier. The variable can also be referenced as EMP_REC.DEPTNO or as POSITION.DEPTNO. Such a reference, in which the name of a containing structure is explicitly used, is called a ***qualified reference***. A reference which uses the names of all containing structures (such as EMP_REC.POSITION.DEPTNO) is called a ***fully qualified reference***.

A PL/I identifier can refer to more than one variable as long as the variables have different fully qualified names. For example, suppose that a structure is declared as follows:

```
DCL 1 LIFE_REC,
        2 NAME          CHAR(30),
        2 BIRTH,
          3 PLACE,
            4 CITY      CHAR(10),
            4 STATE     CHAR(2),
          3 DATE        CHAR(8),
        2 DEATH,
          3 PLACE,
            4 CITY      CHAR(10),
            4 STATE     CHAR(2),
          3 DATE        CHAR(8);
```

Each of the identifiers PLACE, CITY, STATE, and DATE is declared twice. However, within each pair of declarations, the identifier refers to two different variables. For example, one variable with identifier CITY is the variable with full name LIFE_REC. BIRTH.PLACE.CITY, while the other has full name LIFE_REC.DEATH.PLACE.CITY.

Each time that a reference is made to an identifier, it must be clear which variable is being referenced. For example, given the previous declaration, a reference to CITY without any qualification is ***ambiguous*** and therefore illegal since there is no way of determining which of the two variables named CITY is meant. A reference to PLACE.CITY is still ambiguous since there are two variables with that name. In order to achieve a nonambiguous reference, one of the identifiers BIRTH or DEATH must be used to qualify CITY. Thus BIRTH.PLACE.CITY or even BIRTH.CITY would legally reference one of the variables, while DEATH.PLACE.CITY or DEATH.CITY would legally reference the other.

There is one exception to the above. Suppose that, in addition to the structure LIFE.REC, a structure PLACE had also been declared as follows:

```
DCL 1 PLACE,
        2 CITY      CHAR(10),
        2 STATE     CHAR(2);
```

Then a reference to PLACE.CITY would be valid and would refer to an element of this last structure despite the fact that there are three variables with that name. This is because there is only a single variable for which PLACE.CITY is a fully qualified name, and therefore that is the variable which is referenced by that name. However, a reference to CITY would still be ambiguous, since it is not a fully qualified name.

Implementing Structures

A structure may be thought of as a map of a segment of the machine's storage. For example, a structure declared by

```
DCL 1 ORDER,
        2 QUANTITY  FIXED,
        2 PRICE     FIXED(4,2),
        2 DATE      CHAR(8);
```

reserves a section of storage as illustrated in Fig. 1.3.3(a). Enough storage is reserved to include all the elementary items of the structure. Thus, the variable QUANTITY occupies the space required for a FIXED variable, PRICE occupies the space required for a variable which is FIXED(4,2), and DATE occupies the space specified by CHAR(8). Since the length of each part of the structure is known, the offset of any particular elementary item within the structure can be calculated by adding the lengths of all preceding elementary items. (This is not strictly true since data must often be aligned to conform with some property of the computer's hardware, but we ignore this exception in our discussion.)

(a)

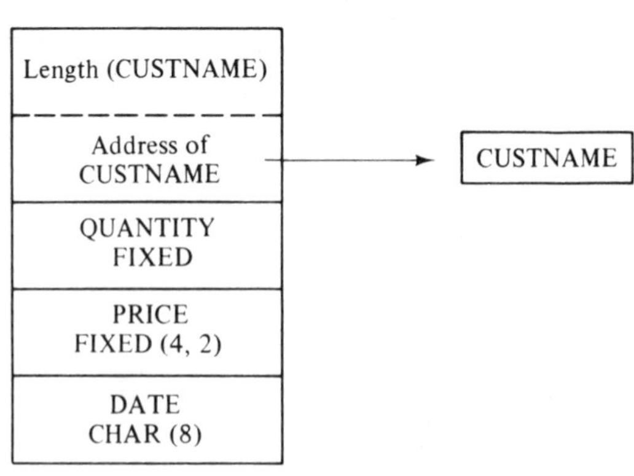

(b)

Figure 1.3.3. Storage assigned to two structures.

Thus far, all the items in our structures have been of fixed length. However, it is possible to have varying-length objects contained in a structure. For example, consider the structure ORDER2 declared by

```
DCL 1 ORDER2,
        2 CUSTNAME    CHAR(30) VAR,
        2 QUANTITY    FIXED,
        2 PRICE       FIXED(4,2),
        2 DATE        CHAR(8);
```

When reference is made to QUANTITY, PRICE, or DATE within this structure, it must be possible to calculate the address of that particular elementary item. However, since CUSTNAME is of varying length, if its value were kept within the storage area reserved for ORDER2, it would be impossible to calculate those addresses. Of course, one solution is to reserve enough space to allow for the longest possible length, in this case 30 characters. However this would probably waste space since most of the time the value of a varying-length string does not take up the maximum length.

A similar problem arose in implementing arrays of varying-length character strings in the previous section, and the solutions to the two problems are similar as well. Only the fixed-length portion of a varying-length elementary item is kept within the structure's storage area together with the address of a varying-length portion. This is illustrated in Fig. 1.3.3(b).

Arrays and Structures

Just as PL/I allows the declaration of an array of FIXED numbers or of character strings, it allows the declaration of an array of structures. For example, suppose we wanted to keep a record of the high, low, and average temperature and precipitation for each of the 12 months of the year. Then we might declare an array of structures as follows:

```
DCL 1 WEATHER(12),
        2 TEMP,
           3 HI     FIXED(4,1),
           3 LO     FIXED(4,1),
           3 AV     FIXED(4,1),
        2 PRECIP,
           3 HI     FIXED(5,2),
           3 LO     FIXED(5,2),
           3 AV     FIXED(5,2);
```

The beginning of this array of structures as it would exist in the computer's memory is illustrated in Fig. 1.3.4. The statement

```
PUT LIST(WEATHER);
```

would print out 72 items, in the order

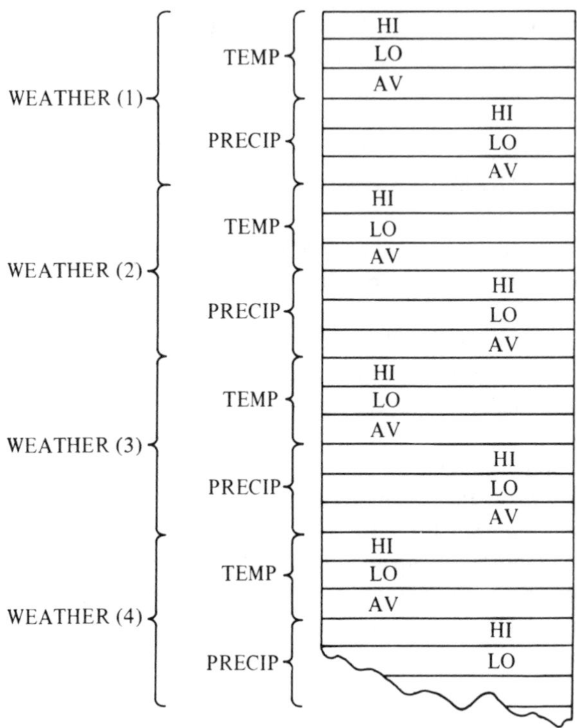

Figure 1.3.4. Storage representation of WEATHER.

```
WEATHER(1).TEMP.HI
WEATHER(1).TEMP.LO
WEATHER(1).TEMP.AV
WEATHER(1).PRECIP.HI
WEATHER(1).PRECIP.LO
WEATHER(1).PRECIP.AV
WEATHER(2).TEMP.HI
        .
        .
        .
WEATHER(12).PRECIP.AV
```

The high temperature for June would be referred to as WEATHER(6).TEMP.HI. It can also be referred to as WEATHER.TEMP(6).HI or as WEATHER.TEMP.HI(6) or as TEMP(6).HI or as TEMP.HI(6). The subscript can be placed after any identifier in a qualified reference. Of course, the variable cannot be referenced as HI(6) since HI is ambiguous. However, if such a reference were unambiguous, then it would be legal. For example, suppose a company employed 500 people. A program for keeping track of those employees might include an array of 500 employee records declared by

```
DCL 1 EMP_REC(500),
        2 NAME_ADDR,
          3 NAME,
            4 FIRST      CHAR(10),
            4 MIDINIT    CHAR(1),
            4 LAST       CHAR(20),
          3 ADDRESS,
            4 STRADDR    CHAR(40),
            4 CITY       CHAR(10),
            4 STATE      CHAR(2),
            4 ZIP        CHAR(5),
        2 POSITION,
          3 DEPTNO       CHAR(3),
          3 JOBTITLE     CHAR(20);
```

In this case, a reference to MIDINIT(376) would be the middle initial of the 376th employee.

Similarly, a multidimensional array of structures could be declared. For example, to keep track of the high, low, and average temperature and precipitation for each day of the year, accessible by the month and day within the month, we might declare:

```
DCL 1 WEATHER(12,31),
        2 TEMP,
          (3 HI,
           3 LO,
           3 AV)    FIXED(4,1),
        2 PRECIP,
          (3 HI,
           3 LO,
           3 AV)    FIXED(5,2);
```

The array WEATHER contains 2232 (= 12*31*6) elementary items. The high temperature for June 17 could be referred to as WEATHER(6,17).TEMP.HI, WEATHER.TEMP(6,17).HI, WEATHER.TEMP.HI(6,17), TEMP.HI(6,17), or TEMP(6,17).HI. We could also split the two subscripts between two different variables. The preceding references are all equivalent to TEMP(6).HI(17), WEATHER(6).TEMP.HI(17), or WEATHER(6).TEMP(17).HI. The first subscript always refers to the first dimension, and the second subscript refers to the second dimension.

A structure may also contain an array as a component. This component may be a minor structure or an elementary item. For example, suppose we wanted to keep a record of the high, low, and average temperature and precipitation level for each month as well as for each day of the year. Then we might declare WEATHER as follows:

```
DCL 1 WEATHER(12),
        2 MTEMP,
          (3 HI,
           3 LO,
           3 AV)   FIXED(4,1),
        2 MPRECIP,
          (3 HI,
           3 LO,
           3 AV)   FIXED(5,2),
        2 DTEMP(31),
          (3 HI,
           3 LO,
           3 AV)   FIXED(4,1),
        2 DPRECIP(31),
          (3 HI,
           3 LO,
           3 AV)   FIXED(5,2);
```

In this structure, the minor structures MTEMP and MPRECIP contain the monthly highs, lows, and averages, while DTEMP and DPRECIP contain the daily highs, lows, and averages. The high temperatures for June 17 may be referred to in a number of ways, including WEATHER(6).DTEMP(17).HI, WEATHER(6,17).DTEMP.HI, and DTEMP.HI(6,17). The variables DTEMP and DEPRECIP may be thought of as two-dimensional arrays of structures, while MTEMP and MPRECIP can be thought of as one-dimensional arrays of structures. The entire structure WEATHER contains 2304 (=12*(3 + 3 + 31*3 + 31*3)) items.

Representing Other Data Structures

Throughout the remainder of this text, PL/I arrays and structures will be used to represent the more complex data structures which are studied. PL/I structures are useful for this purpose because they enable us to group objects of different types within a single entity and to name each of these objects appropriately according to its function.

As an example of how structures can be used in this fashion, let us consider the problem of implementing multidimensional arrays in a system that allows only simple variables, one-dimensional arrays, and structures. We will illustrate the implementation of three-dimensional arrays; the reader will see that the analogue for any other number of dimensions is straightforward.

There are essentially two operations which must be implemented for a three-dimensional array: storing a value into the array at a specified position and extracting a value from a specified position within the array. These two operations will be denoted by

```
STORE(A,S1,S2,S3,V)
```

and

```
EXTRACT(A,S1,S2,S3)
```

respectively. In each of these, A is the structure representing the array, and S1, S2, and S3 are the three subscripts. In the STORE operation, V is the value stored at the specified position. The EXTRACT operation is a function which returns the value extracted from the specified position.

Suppose that we wish to implement an array declared by

```
DCL ARRAY(5:10,7,2:4)      FIXED;
```

This can be done by declaring a structure such as

```
DCL 1 ARRAY,
        2  LOBOUND(3)      FIXED INIT(5,1,2),
        2  HIBOUND(3)      FIXED INIT(10,7,4),
        2  ELEMENT(126)    FIXED;
```

The values in the array LOBOUND are the lower bounds of the three dimensions, and the values in HIBOUND are their upper bounds. The array ELEMENT contains the actual elements of the array. The size of ELEMENT is equal to 126, which is the number of elements in the three-dimensional array ((10-5+1) * (7-1+1) * (4-2+1)). The elements are stored in row-major order so that ELEMENT(1) represents ARRAY(5,1,2), ELEMENT(2) represents ARRAY(5,1,3), etc.

The routines STORE and EXTRACT involve computing the offset for an array reference and using that offset as a subscript in the one-dimensional array ELEMENT. The routine STORE may be written as follows:

```
STORE:    PROC(A,S1,S2,S3,V);
            DCL 1  A,
                     2 LB(*)              FIXED,
                     2 HB(*)              FIXED,
                     2 EL(*)              FIXED,
                  (S1,S2,S3,OFFSET,V)     FIXED;

            /*    error checking     */
            IF S1<LB(1) | S1>HB(1) |
               S2<LB(2) | S2>HB(2) |
               S3<LB(3) | S3>HB(3) THEN DO;
                               PUT SKIP LIST('ILLEGAL SUBSCRIPT');
                               STOP;
                                        END;

            OFFSET= (S1—LB(1))*(HB(2)—LB(2)+1);
            OFFSET= (OFFSET+ (S2—LB(2))) * (HB(3)—LB(3)+1);
            OFFSET= OFFSET+ (S3—LB(3)+1);
            EL(OFFSET)=V;
            RETURN;
          END STORE;
```

The routine EXTRACT may be written as follows:

```
EXTRACT: PROC(A,S1,S2,S3) RETURNS(FIXED);
         DCL 1  A,
                  2 LB(*)              FIXED,
                  2 HB(*)              FIXED,
                  2 EL(*)              FIXED,
                (S1,S2,S3,OFFSET)      FIXED;

         /*    error checking     */
         IF S1<LB(1) |S1>HB(1) |
            S2<LB(2) |S2>HB(2) |
            S3<LB(3) |S3>HB(3) THEN DO;
                              PUT SKIP LIST ('ILLEGAL SUBSCRIPT');
                              STOP;
                                     END;

         OFFSET= (S1-LB(1))*(HB(2)-LB(2)+1);
         OFFSET= (OFFSET+ (S2-LB(2))) * (HB(3)-LB(3)+1);
         OFFSET= OFFSET+(S3-LB(3)+1);
         RETURN(EL(OFFSET));
       END EXTRACT;
```

These routines use the formulas developed in Section 1.2 for computing the offset of a specific element in a multidimensional array. As exercises, you are asked to generalize the above routines so that the number of dimensions of the array can also be passed as a parameter.

Bibliography and References

Any text on the machine language for a particular machine contains information on the hardware data types of that machine. The software data structures implemented in a particular language processor are usually described in the manuals for that processor. For a description of arrays and structures in PL/I, see the PL/I texts and manuals in the Bibliography at the end of the text. For a discussion of how arrays and structures are implemented, see (Gries, 1971) and (Pratt, 1975) as well as the data structure texts in the Bibliography.

chapter 2

programming

A program is a device by which a problem can be solved using a computer. In this chapter, we discuss some of the major steps in producing a correct program. We also consider several programming techniques that help improve the efficiency of the programmer and his product.

2.1. Program Structure

There are many different styles in programming, probably one for every programmer. As computing evolves and programming projects grow in scope and sophistication, more attention is being paid to the form of a program and to the style in which it is written. By no means does attention to these issues excuse a programmer for writing incorrect programs. Yet, given the primary importance of writing a correct program, structure and style can play important roles.

One of the major objectives of using good style in writing a program is to make the program readable. The reason that readability is so important is that it is often necessary to modify the program. If the programmer who is to make the modifications is not the author of the original program, and if the program is almost impossible to understand, then the programmer faces a difficult task. The task is even more difficult if the documentation is as bad as the program. Even when the program's author is responsible for subsequent modifications, he often forgets the function of various detailed portions of code as time passes. This results in a situation where either significant time must be spent to modify a small portion of a program, or the entire program must be rewritten because no one can figure out which parts of the program are doing what. In either case, much time and effort is wasted.

As pointed out, each programmer develops his own style as he learns and practices his craft. Although no two programmers program exactly alike, there are some programming habits which are considered desirable and others which are generally considered poor. In this section and the next, we illustrate some of these practices and indicate why they are desirable or undesirable. We consider those aspects of style which are related to how the final program "looks" and how it reads. We also consider methods of deciding which PL/I constructs to use in specific situations so that the resultant program is easier to read and to modify.

Flow of Control

We begin by considering several types of programming constructs and how they appear in PL/I. PL/I executable statements fall into one of two major categories: simple statements that accomplish a single operation or a set of operations, and compound statements which group statements together to form an overall control structure.

The following statements are examples of the simple constructions:

```
GET LIST(X);

PUT DATA(Y,Z);

FINAL = ORIG + NEW*DISC;
```

Each of the above statements is "simple" in that it performs a single task. A task may consist of two operations (such as PUT DATA(Y,Z); which prints two values), but each such task basically represents a single operation. One such statement is executed sequentially after another in the order in which they appear in the code.

On the other hand, the following constructs are examples of the compound type:

```
IF A=B THEN PUT LIST (X);

IF A=B THEN Y=7;
        ELSE Y=8;

DO WHILE (X>0);
    PUT LIST (X);
    X=X-1;
END;
```

These constructions determine the sequence in which the simple operations which they include are to be performed. In such constructions, the simple statements are not necessarily executed in the order in which they appear. The sequence of their execution cannot be determined by simply looking at the code; it depends on conditions (A=B or X>0) which are tested during program execution. The sequence in which instructions are executed is called the ***flow of control*** of a program. We shall discuss several types of flow of control and illustrate how they may be implemented in PL/I.

Sequential Flow

Sequential flow means that statements are executed sequentially in the order in which they appear. Sequential flow is achieved by simply writing simple statements in the order in which they are to be executed. As discussed later in this section, the code is easier to read if each statement appears on a separate line and all the statements are indented to the same column. If the computation that is being performed is not clear from the code, then a comment at key points in the code should be used to explain the purpose and the intended effects of each group of statements.

Conditional Flow

Conditional flow is "almost" sequential in that the statements, if executed, are executed in their order of appearance. However, a statement or group of statements may or may not be executed in certain cases. This type of flow is achieved by an IF statement such as

```
IF condition THEN statement;
```

or

```
IF condition THEN statement1;
                  ELSE statement2;
```

In the first version, if *condition* is satisfied, then *statement* is executed; if the *condition* fails, then *statement* is not executed. In either case the next statement to be executed is the one that follows the IF THEN construction.

In the second version, if the *condition* is satisfied, then *statement*1 is executed but *statement*2 is not. If *condition* fails, then *statement*1 is not executed but *statement*2 is. In either case, one of the two statements (but not both) is executed. After executing either *statement*1 or *statement*2, the computer next executes the statement immediately following the complete IF THEN ELSE construction. Actually, the first version is merely a shortcut for writing the special case of the second in which *statement*2 is the null statement.

The IF THEN ELSE construction is easy to use in cases that require alternative action depending upon the outcome of a test. Frequently, it is necessary to implement code where *statement*1 and/or *statement*2 are sequences of statements rather than single statements. In such cases, the sequence of statements is included between the statements DO; and END; to form a ***DO group*** as in the following:

```
IF A>B | C<D THEN DO;
                       X=2;
                       Y=3;
                  END;
              ELSE Z=7;
```

By writing code in this way and grouping those actions that are to be performed together, the code is easy to read and understand. It is possible to follow the flow of control easily and to insert additional statements in the DO group, if necessary.

Conditions are represented in PL/I by bit strings of length 1. The *true* condition is represented by '1'B and the *false* condition by '0'B. Thus in writing

```
IF A=B THEN . . .
```

we are not really asking whether A is equal to B; rather we are making the claim that A is equal to B and testing whether that claim is true or false. In this fashion, the most complicated test is reduced to a single logical value which is either true or false and therefore has the value '1'B or '0'B.

Since a logical value is represented by a bit, a bit variable can be used as a condition. For example, suppose we wish to replace all occurrences of X in a FIXED array with 0 and to print a message indicating whether any such occurrences were found. The following code could be used to accomplish this:

```
        DCL   FOUND           BIT(1)  INIT('0'B);
FIND:   DO I=1 TO N;
           IF A(I)=X THEN DO;
                              FOUND='1'B;
                              A(I)=0;
                           END;
        END FIND;

        IF FOUND THEN PUT SKIP EDIT(X,'WAS FOUND')
                                  (F(2),X(1),A);
                 ELSE PUT SKIP EDIT(X,'WAS NOT FOUND')
                                  (F(2),X(1),A);
```

Note that it is not necessary to code IF FOUND='1'B. IF FOUND is sufficient. Any expression which evaluates to a bit string may also be used as a condition as in

```
IF ¬FOUND THEN . . .
```

Very often, however, the underlying logic of a problem's solution does not fit into two alternatives. The outcome of a test may have many alternatives, each of which requires a different set of actions to be performed. For example, suppose it is necessary to assign a value to the variable X based on the value of a nonnegative integer A as follows:

If A is between	Then X is
0 and 10	A–7
11 and 20	2*A
21 and 30	3*A+5
31 and 40	4
41 and 50	A–5
51 and 60	6*A–3
61 and 70	7*A
71 and 80	87–3*A
A greater than 80	0

In some PL/I compilers (e.g., the IBM PL/I Optimizing Compiler), such a multiway test is handled by the SELECT statement. There are two forms of the SELECT statement. The more general form is as follows:

```
SELECT;
   WHEN (condition1)  statement1;
   WHEN (condition2)  statement2;
          .
          .
          .
   WHEN (conditionn)  statementn;
   OTHERWISE          statementn+1;
END;
```

When the SELECT is executed, the *condition*s 1 through n are tested in sequence. If *condition*i is the first to be satisfied, then *statement*i is executed and execution of the SELECT statement terminates. Execution resumes with the statement following END;. If none of the conditions are satisfied, then the object of the OTHERWISE clause (*statement*n+1) is executed. If the OTHERWISE clause is omitted, then none of the *statement*s 1 through n is executed when all the conditions are false. Each of the *statement*s 1 through n+1 may be any other valid PL/I construction (e.g., a DO loop, a BEGIN block, etc.).

Thus to process the multiway test of the above example, we could code the following:

```
SELECT;
   WHEN (A<=10)  X = A–7;
   WHEN (A<=20)  X = 2*A;
   WHEN (A<=30)  X = 3*A+5;
   WHEN (A<=40)  X = 4;
   WHEN (A<=50)  X = A–5;
   WHEN (A<=60)  X = 6*A–3;
   WHEN (A<=70)  X = 7*A;
   WHEN (A<=80)  X = 87–3*A;
   OTHERWISE     X = 0;
END;
```

There is a more restricted form of the SELECT statement which is more concise. It is used only when testing the value of a single expression for equality with other expressions. For example, if we wish to assign X the value of 1, 2, or 3 depending on whether the third character of the character string A is 'X', 'L', or 'P' respectively, we can code the following:

```
SELECT  (SUBSTR(A,3,1));
   WHEN ('X')      X = 1;
   WHEN ('L')      X = 2;
   WHEN ('P')      X = 3;
END;
```

By specifying the expression to be tested in parentheses immediately after the keyword SELECT, it becomes unnecessary to code the complete condition in the WHEN portion of the statement; it is necessary to code only the expression to which equality is being tested.

An expanded version of this form of the SELECT statement allows several possibilities to be coded in each WHEN clause. For example, to set DAYS to the number of days in a month of a non-leap year, one can code:

```
SELECT(MONTH);
   WHEN('APR', 'JUN', 'SEP', 'NOV') DAYS=30;
   WHEN('FEB') DAYS=28;
   OTHERWISE DAYS=31;
END;
```

Although the SELECT statement does provide a logical solution to problems that depend upon multiway tests, it is not implemented on most PL/I compilers. Because of this, it is necessary to translate such tests into a succession of two-way tests by using nested IF THEN ELSE constructions. It is instructive to see how this is done.

One possible coding of the first example above is as follows:

```
IF A<=40 THEN IF A<=20 THEN IF A<=10THEN X=A–7;
                                   ELSE X=2*A;
                         ELSE IF A<=30 THEN X=3*A+5;
                                   ELSE X=4;
           ELSE IF A<=60 THEN IF A<=50 THEN X=A–5;
                                   ELSE X=6*A+3;
                         ELSE IF A<=70 THEN X=7*A;
                                   ELSE IF A<=80 THEN X=87–3*A;
                                             ELSE X=0;
```

The above code, although correct, is difficult to read and even more difficult to modify. For example, in order to determine when the statement X=6*A+3; is executed, one must start from the top and struggle through the tests to discover that ¬(A<=40), (A<=60), and ¬(A<=50), which reduces to the interval 51 to 60. Also consider the problem of splitting an interval into two or of joining part of one interval with another. Such modifications require reworking the entire block of code.

Consider the following alternate solution:

```
IF A<=10 THEN X=A–7;
   ELSE IF A<=20 THEN X=2*A;
      ELSE IF A<=30 THEN X=3*A+5;
         ELSE IF A<=40 THEN X=4;
            ELSE IF A<=50 THEN X=A–5;
               ELSE IF A<=60 THEN X=6*A–3;
                  ELSE IF A<=70 THEN X=7*A;
                     ELSE IF A<=80 THEN X=87–3*A;
                                 ELSE X=0;
```

While this code appears formidable, a little practice makes it easy to understand. In order to determine under what circumstances a particular assignment is executed, one need merely travel sequentially through the successive tests until the first one that is satisfied is reached.

In general, the first form of the SELECT statement can be translated into nested IF statements as follows:

```
IF condition1 THEN statement1;
   ELSE IF condition2 THEN statement2;
                 . . .
                 . . .
            ELSE IF conditionn THEN statementn;
                  ELSE statementn+1;
```

One can argue that the latter coding is inefficient because it may sometimes require up to seven tests, whereas the former version requires at most three. We shall have more to say on the subject of efficiency in Section 3. However, it is usually not worthwhile to sacrifice readability and modifiability in order to save a few instructions.

Finally, we should point out that nested IFs are often unnecessary in solving a particular problem. For example, suppose it is necessary to set X to 10 if A is between 100 and 200. One version is

```
IF A>=100 THEN IF A<=200 THEN X=10;
```

Such code is overly complicated. There is no need to use a nested IF when a single (compound) test will do, as in

```
IF (A>=100) & (A<=200) THEN X=10;
```

The second version mirrors the statement of the problem more closely than the first. In general, it is easier to read single statements involving compound tests (when those tests are connected with the same logical operators) than nested control structures.

Since most PL/I compilers do not support the SELECT statement, the programs that appear subsequently in the text will use only IF THEN ELSE constructions. Users who do have the SELECT statement available will find it easier to use.

There is a common pitfall in using compound tests. For example, suppose A is an array declared by

```
DCL A(10) FIXED;
```

and it is desired to determine whether a subscript I is within the bounds of the array and whether A(I) is negative. A novice might use the following scheme:

```
IF (I>=1) & (I<=10) & (A(I)<0) THEN . . .
```

However, this code is incorrect because in the case that the subscript I is out of bounds, the reference to A(I) is undefined. For example, suppose I equals 12. Then the expression (I>=1) is evaluated as '1'B (true) and the expression (I<=10) is evaluated as '0'B (false). But when the expression (A(I)<0) is evaluated, an error results since A(I) does not exist. The code can be rewritten correctly as

```
IF (I>=1) & (I<=10) THEN IF A(I)<0 THEN...
```

It should be noted that in some optimizing compilers the first statement executes correctly. In a sequence of tests connected by the "&" operation, as soon as one operand is found to be false, no further testing of the other conditions is necessary. Similarly, when one component of a sequence of tests connected by the "|" operation is found to be true, the entire expression is assumed to be true and no further testing is performed. When writing programs for such compilers, a judicious ordering of the tests will make statements such as the former usable. In other compilers, however, such tests will result in an error.

The choice of whether to use logical operators or nested IFs should be made on the merits of each particular case. However, within the limits of a correct program, one should select the version that is clearest and most readable.

Repetitive Flow

The next control structure is ***repetitive flow***, in which a statement or group of statements is executed repeatedly until some halting condition is reached. This type of structure is called a ***loop***. The computing done by most programs (whether to calculate π correct to 500 decimal places, or to calculate and print payroll checks for several thousand employees) is basically a repetitive process involving some sort of looping. Most high-level programming languages provide for some form of automatic looping. Let us examine the basic types of looping structures that arise in programming and show how they are implemented in PL/I.

The most basic looping construct is one which loops as long as a condition is met, as in

```
DO WHILE(condition);
   /*   body of the loop   */
END;
```

Whenever the DO statement is encountered, *condition* is tested. If it is found to be true, then the body of the loop is executed. When the END statement is encountered, control is sent back to the DO statement, where the process is repeated. At some time (hopefully) *condition* becomes false. When this occurs, control passes to the statement immediately following the END statement.

The number of iterations through a loop may be 0, 1, 2, or 5000. The body of the loop is repeated as long as the condition in the WHILE clause is true. Of course, it is the programmer's responsibility to make sure that the loop does not execute forever.

For example, the following loop prints all powers of two less than TOP:

```
          POWER=1;
LOOP:     DO WHILE (POWER<TOP);
               PUT LIST (POWER);
               POWER=POWER*2;
          END LOOP;
```

Note that the value of POWER is changed within the loop so that eventually POWER is greater than or equal to TOP and the loop terminates. One of the requirements for the normal termination of a DO WHILE loop is that the value of some variable appearing within the WHILE condition is altered within the loop body so that the condition eventually becomes false. The condition within the WHILE clause is tested before each execution of the loop body.

There is another type of loop which is useful. This is the DO UNTIL loop. The form of the loop is as follows:

```
DO UNTIL (condition);
          /*   body of the loop    */
END;
```

When such a loop is encountered, the loop body is executed once. Then, *condition* is tested. If *condition* is satisfied, then the loop is terminated; otherwise, the body is repeated until *condition* is satisfied. The basic differences between the DO WHILE and the DO UNTIL is that in the former a condition is tested before the loop body is executed, while in the latter the condition is tested after the loop body is executed. Thus a DO UNTIL loop body is executed at least once, whereas a DO WHILE loop body need not be executed at all. A second difference between the two is that a DO WHILE loop is exited when the condition fails, while a DO UNTIL loop is exited when the condition is satisfied.

As an example of the use of the DO UNTIL, consider the problem of computing the root of a continuous function $f(x)$. Suppose we are given two values $v1$ and $v2$ such that $f(v1)<0$ and $f(v2)>0$. The graph of such a function is shown in Fig. 2.1.1(a). It can be shown that, because the function is continuous and changes sign between $v1$ and $v2$, there is a number x between $v1$ and $v2$ such that $f(x)=0$. Since x is a real number which may have an infinite number of decimal positions, it is desired to approximate x to within some range *err* of its true value.

The problem may be approached as follows. Let x be the midpoint between $v1$ and $v2$. Then $x=(v1+v2)/2$. If $f(x)=0$, then x is the desired answer. If not, then either $f(x)>0$ or $f(x)<0$. If $f(x)>0$, then the function changes sign between $v1$ and x; and if $f(x)<0$, then the function changes sign between x and $v2$. Figure 2.1.1(b) illustrates the latter situation. In either case, repeat the process (of finding the midpoint and determining in which half the sign change occurs) with the new, smaller interval (either $v1$ to x or x to $v2$) in which the function changes sign. The process halts when the length of the

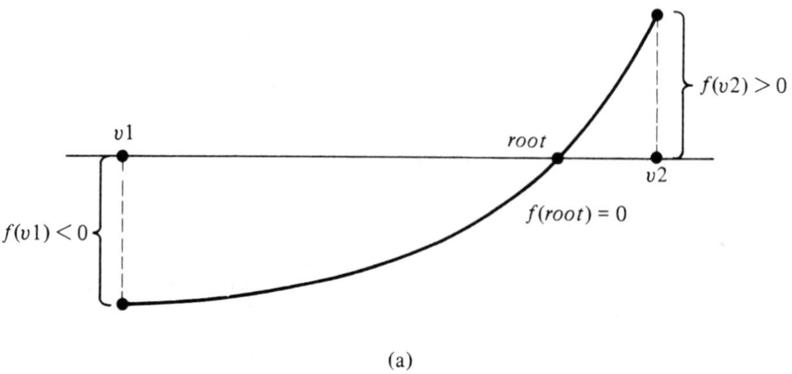

(a)

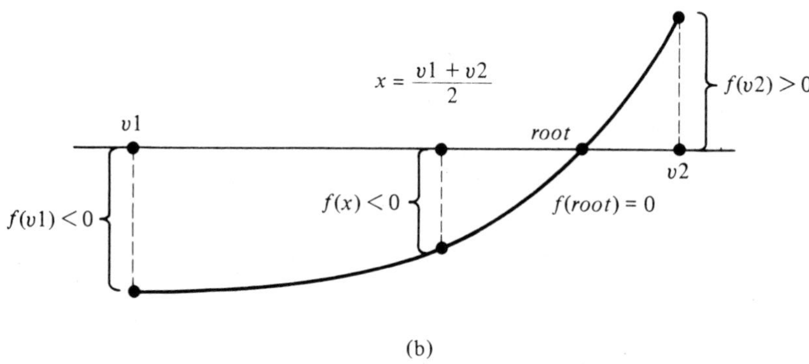

(b)

Figure 2.1.1. A continuous function changing signs in the internal (*v1*, *v2*).

interval being considered is less than *err*, at which time any value within the interval may be selected as the answer.

A program segment to compute and print the answer may be written as follows:

```
LB = V1;    /*  initialize interval   */
UB = V2;    /*       bounds           */
DO UNTIL (UB-LB<ERR  |  F(X)=0);
   X=(LB+UB)/2;
   IF F(X)<0 THEN LB=X;
             ELSE UB=X;
END;
PUT LIST(X);
```

Why is the DO UNTIL preferable to the DO WHILE in this case? Consider the following code, which makes use of a DO WHILE loop to compute and print an acceptable value of X.

```
LB=V1;
UB=V2;
X=(LB+UB)/2;
DO WHILE (UB-LB>=ERR & F(X) ¬ =0);
   IF F(X)<0 THEN LB=X;
             ELSE UB=X;
   X=(LB+UB)/2;
END;
PUT LIST(X);
```

The body of a DO UNTIL loop must be executed at least once. Therefore, since X is given a value within the body of the loop, we are sure in the first version that the value of X can be printed after the loop has been completed. In the second version, control may exit the loop even though the loop body has never been executed (for example, if V2–V1 < ERR). Thus, the variable X must be given a value outside of the loop in order to assure than an error will not result when its value is printed. The effect of this is that the statement

```
X=(LB+UB)/2;
```

must be coded twice if a DO WHILE is used. Additionally, the condition in the DO WHILE statement uses the value of X. Since the condition is evaluated before the loop body is executed, X must be given a value before the loop. In the DO UNTIL, the condition is not evaluated until after the loop body is executed, so X need not be initialized outside the loop.

As is the case for the SELECT statement, the DO UNTIL is not implemented on most PL/I compilers. Thus, unless the programmer is certain that his programs will be run only under compilers that do support this feature, it is important that he know how to translate the DO UNTIL construction into other PL/I constructs. The simplest and most direct translation of the DO UNTIL involves repeating the code in the body of the loop before the DO statement, replacing the DO UNTIL with a DO WHILE, and replacing the condition with its negation. Thus

```
DO UNTIL(condition);
  /*   body of the loop   */
END;
```

is logically equivalent to

```
/*   body of the loop   */
DO WHILE (¬condition);
  /*   body of the loop   */
END;
```

An alternative is to use a bit as a flag, as in the following;

```
FIRST = '1'B;
DO WHILE(FIRST |¬ condition);
    FIRST = '0'B;
    /*   body of the loop    */
END;
```

While the second version probably involves less coding than the first, it is inferior from a logical point of view. Use of special flags and switches in programs to perform such tricks is to be avoided since it significantly reduces the readability of the code. Also, flags which are not supposed to change value during a loop sometimes have a way of doing so (usually through programmer oversight). Debugging such code is more difficult. If the body of a loop is large so that the first version requires a significant amount of extra coding, the code can be placed in a subroutine so that the total amount of coding for the body is reduced to two subroutine calls.

PL/I contains another very popular and useful loop structure in which a counter is automatically incremented (or decremented) after each execution of the loop body. When the counter becomes greater than (or less than) some test value, the loop is terminated. For example, consider the following loop:

```
DO IND = start TO finish BY step;
   /*   body of loop    */
END;
```

The variable IND (known as the ***index*** or the ***control variable*** of the loop) is initialized to *start* and is tested against *finish*. If the result of the test is true, the loop body is repeated. If the result is false, the loop is skipped. The type of test depends on the sign of *step*. If *step* is positive, then the test is whether IND≤*finish*. If *step* is negative, then the test is whether IND≥*finish*. When the END statement is encountered, the variable IND is incremented by *step* and is again tested against the original value of *finish*. When the test fails (even if the loop body has never been executed), execution resumes with the statement immediately following the END statement.

It should be noted that the value of IND may be changed within the body of the loop (not recommended), a practice which may have an effect on the number of iterations. However, changes to the values of *step* or *finish* have no effect on the loop iteration. If the BY *step* portion is omitted, then the increment is set to 1. If the TO *finish* portion is omitted, then no test is made and the loop executes indefinitely. If both of these clauses are omitted, then the construct is no longer a DO loop but a DO group which is executed once with the value of IND equal to *start*.

This type of loop can be used to control a simple count of the number of times a particular process is executed. It may be combined with other types of looping mechanisms to perform a significant amount of work.

For example, here is another method for printing all powers of 2 less than TOP:

```
LOOP:  DO I=0 BY 1 WHILE (2**I<TOP);
          PUT LIST (2**I);
       END LOOP;
```

The value of I starts at 0. It is increased by 1 and its power of 2 printed, as long as that power is less than TOP. Note that the loop has no TO clause. The value of I is increased by 1 indefinitely with no upper limit. The loop is terminated only if 2^I becomes greater than TOP.

There are advantages and disadvantages between this method and the previous method, which used only a DO WHILE loop. In this method, each power of 2 is computed separately, while in the previous method, each power of two is computed by doubling the previous power of 2. Thus, the above version is somewhat easier to understand. It clearly states that powers of 2 are being computed. An appropriate comment would help clarify the previous version. On the other hand, the previous version uses a multiplication operation to compute each power of 2, while the above version uses exponentiation. It happens that multiplication can be performed much more efficiently than exponentiation on most computers. Further, the above version involves two exponentiations each time through the loop, while the previous version requires only one multiplication. The question of efficiency versus clarity is a common one, which we discuss in a later section.

In one sense, however, the previous version is somewhat clearer than this version. This is because of the use of a variable named POWER which documents the fact that successive powers of 2 are being computed. In fact, it is the use of the variable POWER which allows the previous version to avoid repeating the multiplication, since once a product is computed, it is stored in that variable for later retrieval. A similar savings can be made in the above version as follows:

```
       POWER=1;
LOOP:  DO I=1 BY 1 WHILE (POWER<TOP);
          PUT LIST (POWER);
          POWER=2**I;
       END LOOP;
```

Note that it is necessary to initialize POWER outside the loop so that the test in the WHILE clause can be made the first time through the loop. It is also necessary to change the starting value of I from 0 to 1, since the "zero"th power of 2 (which is 1) is computed outside the loop. Also note that in this version as well as the first version, the old value of POWER is printed before the new value is computed. This is somewhat awkward.

It would be instructive for you to attempt to improve the above version by using an UNTIL clause instead of a WHILE clause. Is it possible to compute the power of 2 before printing it within the loop body? What happens if the value of TOP is negative?

Suppose it is also desired to print the largest value of I for which 2^I is printed (that is, the largest value of I for which 2**I<TOP). One version which does this is

```
LOOP: DO I=0 BY 1 WHILE (2**I<TOP);
          PUT LIST(2**I);
      END LOOP;
      PUT LIST(I–1);
```

After the loop is completed, the value of I is that value which caused termination of the loop. In this case, it is the smallest value of I for which 2**I<TOP is false. Thus I–1 is the largest value for which 2**I<TOP is true, and this value is printed. Note that the value of I is increased by the BY clause before the test in the WHILE clause is made.

If the variable POWER is used in computing the powers of 2, then I–2 is the value which must be printed at the end of the loop:

```
      POWER=1;
LOOP: DO I=1 BY 1 WHILE(POWER<TOP);
          PUT LIST(POWER);
          POWER=2**I;
      END LOOP;
      PUT LIST(I–2);
```

Make sure that you can explain why.

The control variable of a loop is frequently used to index an array. For example, suppose the first N elements of an array A are in increasing numerical order. It is desired to insert the element X in its proper numerical sequence within the array. The following code accomplishes this:

```
FIND:   DO I=1 TO N WHILE (X>A(I));
        END FIND;

             /*  At this point X<=A(I). Thus X should    */
             /*   be inserted immediately before A(I)    */
        N=N+1;
PLACE:  DO J=N TO I+1 BY –1; /*  move each element in   */
            A(J)=A(J–1);     /*  the array larger than X  */
        END PLACE;
        A(J)=X;
```

Make sure that you understand how the indices are manipulated in each of the above loops. Such techniques should be standard tools of programming since they are used in many applications.

Occasionally it is necessary to repeat the loop body for a known set of values that do not follow an arithmetic incrementing rule and cannot be easily computed from one another within the body of the loop. In such cases the values may be listed explicitly as in:

```
DO J=1,3,5,-18,12;
    /*  body of the loop   */
END;
```

The loop body is performed for the values of J specified in the DO statement.

Finally, all the forms can be combined within a single DO statement, as in

```
DO J = -5,76,8 TO K BY C WHILE (A(J)>0),12;
    /*  body of the loop   */
END;
```

As the index of the loop is assigned each successive value, the body of the loop is executed. If one test should fail (e.g., A(J)<0), then the process continues with the next value (e.g., 12). Such loops are extremely powerful, but should be used with caution.

Some loops are not terminated by a condition in a WHILE or UNTIL clause. Instead, the logical tests that cause loop termination are made within the body of the loop body. In such cases, we desire a loop which is inherently infinite unless it can somehow be terminated from within. One example of such a loop is the following:

```
DO I=1 BY 1;
    /*  body of the loop   */
END;
```

where the value of I is increased by 1 ad infinitum (or until the value is too large for the variable I). Another method uses a WHILE clause with a condition which is always true, as in

```
DO WHILE(1=1);
    /*  body of the loop   */
END;
```

Because all conditions evaluate to either '0'B (false) or '1'B (true), the simplest and most direct method is to use '1'B as the condition. Such a loop is coded as

```
DO WHILE ('1'B);
    /*  body of the loop   */
END;
```

Of course the programmer must provide a mechanism for exiting from within the body of such a loop. Let us see how such a loop can be terminated prematurely and why such premature termination may be desirable.

Premature Exiting from Loops

Suppose there is an array A into which values are to be inserted. We wish to read a set of data cards, each of which contains two integers. The first integer is an array index, and the second is a value which is to be inserted into that array position. The last card in the set contains a 0 as its first integer and indicates the end of this portion of data. There may be other data after this set which is needed for another portion of the program.

The simplest way of coding this is as follows:

```
LOOP:   DO WHILE('1'B);
            GET LIST(POSITION, VALUE);
            IF POSITION=0 THEN GO TO OUT;
            A(POSITION)=VALUE;
        END LOOP;
OUT:    /*  remainder of the program    */
```

The body of the loop accomplishes two purposes: reading a data card and inserting a value into the array. However, after reading a data card, we may discover that the entire loop is to be terminated. A GO TO statement is used to exit the loop prematurely.

Historically, the GO TO statement was the most powerful and most commonly used tool for altering the sequence of execution control. However, we have not made use of this statement in our discussion thus far. The reason for this is that programs containing many GO TOs are difficult to read and debug, and almost impossible to modify properly. Because of this, structured programming favors the use of loops and subroutines and tries to stay away from using GO TO statements.

The above example, however, represents a legitimate use of the GO TO statement. Other methods of implementing the desired logic are clumsier and less readable. For example, one alternative is the following:

```
        GET LIST(POSITION,VALUE);
LOOP:   DO WHILE(POSITION¬=0);
            A(POSITION)=VALUE;
            GET LIST(POSITION,VALUE);
        END LOOP;
            /*  remainder of the program    */
```

Here, the order of the operations of input and array insertion are reversed within the loop so that each execution of the loop inserts the value input by the previous loop execution and then reads the next value. Aside from the fact that this necessitates an additional initializing input statement before the loop is entered, there is another reason to prefer the earlier version. The logical specification of the operation to be performed by the loop body is to read information and process it. The first version more directly implements this specification and is therefore more understandable.

Another alternative is more general and involves the use of a bit flag. For example, the above logic can be implemented as follows:

```
       FLAG='1'B;
LOOP:  DO WHILE(FLAG);
          GET LIST(POSITION,VALUE);
          IF POSITION=0 THEN FLAG='0'B;
                        ELSE A(POSITION)=VALUE;
       END LOOP;
         /*  remainder of the program  */
```

The variable FLAG indicates whether the loop is to be continued or terminated. FLAG is initialized to '1'B to indicate that the loop is to be executed at least once. If the condition for loop termination (POSITION=0) is not met, then the value read from the data card is inserted into the array and the value of FLAG is unchanged so that the loop is executed once more. If however, the condition is met, then the value is not inserted. Instead, the value of FLAG is reset to '0'B to indicate that the loop is to be terminated.

The introduction of a logical variable can transform any loop which includes premature termination into one which does not. To see this, note that the code

```
LOOP:  DO WHILE(condition1);
          /*  group1 of statements  */
          IF condition2 THEN GO TO OUT;
          /*  group2 of statements  */
       END LOOP;
OUT:   /*  remainder of the program  */
```

can be transormed into:

```
       FLAG='1'B;
LOOP:  DO WHILE(condition1 & FLAG);
         /*  group1 of statements  */
         IF condition2 THEN FLAG='0'B;
                       ELSE DO;
                                /*  group2 of statements  */
                            END;
       END LOOP;
       /*  remainder of the program  */
```

The version which includes a GO TO statement is preferable to a version in which a variable that has no counterpart in the program specification is introduced just for the sake of structure. Such "structure," rather than elucidating the purpose of the code, obfuscates it so that a good deal of head scratching is necessary before the code can be understood.

We should note that some newer PL/I compilers (e.g., the IBM PL/I Optimizer) allow the use of a LEAVE statement to terminate a loop prematurely. We illustrate the use of this statement to code the previous example.

```
LOOP: DO WHILE('1'B);
          GET LIST(POSITION, VALUE);
          IF POSITION=0 THEN LEAVE LOOP;
          A(POSITION)=VALUE;
      END LOOP;
      /*  remainder of the program     */
```

The effect of the statement LEAVE LOOP; is a branch to the statement immediately following the loop LOOP. Thus, it is essentially a controlled version of the GO TO. If such a statement is available, then its use leads to the clearest coding of the above example. However, most PL/I compilers do not allow such a statement.

Another way of handling the problem is to use a subroutine. Such a subroutine may be written as follows:

```
SUB:  PROC(A);
        DCL A(*)                  FIXED,
            (POSITION, VALUE)FIXED;
LOOP:   DO WHILE ('1'B);
          GET LIST(POSITION, VALUE);
          IF POSITION=0 THEN RETURN;
          A(POSITION)=VALUE;
        END LOOP;
      END SUB;
```

Then, whenever it is necessary to perform this operation, the programmer simply codes

```
CALL SUB(A);
```

This solution is perfectly acceptable and is well structured. However, the programmer may not wish to introduce a separate subroutine for such a simple task, especially if it is only performed once in the entire program.

In the above example, a GO TO statement is used to exit a loop in order to avoid an illegal array reference. There is another case in which it might be convenient to use a GO TO to exit a loop. For example, suppose it is desired to print the number of years required for doubling an initial principal, PRINC, invested at an annual interest rate, RATE, compounded annually. One way to do this is as follows:

```
AMT=PRINC;
DO YEAR = 1 BY 1 WHILE (AMT<2*PRINC);
   AMT = AMT + RATE*AMT;
END;
PUT LIST (YEAR-1);
```

As already noted, it is necessary to print the value YEAR–1 since YEAR is incremented before the test in the WHILE clause is made. This is somewhat confusing.

An alternative is to eliminate the WHILE clause and use an IF statement with a GO TO instead:

```
        AMT = PRINC;
        DO YEAR = 1 BY 1;
           AMT = AMT + RATE*AMT;
           IF AMT>=2*PRINC THEN GO TO OUT;
        END;
OUT:    PUT LIST(YEAR);
```

A related situation occurs when it is necessary to skip over a loop body for certain values but it is necessary to continue the loop for several remaining values. For example, if three numbers a, b, and c are the coefficients of a quadratic equation

$$a*x^2 + b*x + c = 0$$

then the values of x which satisfy the equation are computed by the statements

```
X1 = (-B+SQRT(B**2-4*A*C))/(2*A);
```

and

```
X2 = (-B-SQRT(B**2-4*A*C))/(2*A);
```

However, if the value of B**2–4*A*C is negative, then the quadratic equation has no real roots since we cannot take the square root of a negative number. (We ignore complex numbers in this discussion.)

Suppose we wanted to read a deck of cards where each card contains three numbers a, b, and c which are coefficients of a quadratic equation. If the equation has real roots, then a, b, c, and the two roots are to be printed; otherwise, the next set of input coefficients are to be processed. Let us also assume that at the start of the deck is a card containing the number of data cards which follow.

There are two methods of coding the solution to this problem: one using a GO TO, the other using a DO group. The following code uses a GO TO:

```
         GET LIST(N);
LOOP:    DO I = 1 TO N;
            GET LIST (A,B,C);
            DISC = B**2-4*A*C;
            IF DISC<0 THEN GO TO OVER;
            X1 = (-B+SQRT(DISC))/(2*A);
            X2 = (-B-SQRT(DISC))/(2*A);
            PUT SKIP LIST(A,B,C,X1,X2);
OVER:    END LOOP
```

The alternate method uses a DO group:

```
         GET LIST(N);
LOOP:    DO I=1 TO N;
            GET LIST(A,B,C);
            DISC=B**2-4*A*C;
            IF DISC>=0 THEN DO;
                      X1 = (-B+SQRT(DISC))/(2*A);
                      X2 = (-B-SQRT(DISC))/(2*A);
                      PUT SKIP LIST(A,B,C,X1,X2);
                           END;
         END LOOP;
```

Generally, the second method using a DO group is preferable. However, there are cases where the entire DO loop is nested within several other constructs, and adding another level of nesting causes additional confusion. In other cases, it is necessary to terminate an inner loop and continue an outer loop simultaneously. In these situations the use of the GO TO statement is preferable.

The ENDFILE Condition

Let us reconsider the program which reads a set of array indices and values from data cards and inserts the values into the array. Let us however remove the card containing 0, which signals the end of the data. Rather, let us assume that the end of data is indicated by the absence of any further input cards.

Consider the loop:

```
LOOP:    DO WHILE ('1'B);
            GET LIST(POSITION,VALUE);
            A(POSITION)=VALUE;
         END LOOP;
```

Note that the IF statement which tests for the 0 index has been removed since there is no longer a 0 in the data. The loop executes properly, repeatedly reading a position and a value and inserting the value into the array at the specified position, until it has read the last card. It then attempts to read yet another card and finds that no more cards exist. This condition of no more data existing is called the ENDFILE condition. Unlike other conditions which are part of the program logic and can be tested for (such as POSITION=0), the ENDFILE condition is an event which occurs outside the program's logic but rather as a result of a real-world circumstance–there are no cards left. Ordinarily the occurrence of such a condition causes an error, and the program's execution halts.

However, PL/I allows a programmer to specify the action which is to be taken when such a condition occurs. An ON statement of the form

```
        ON ENDFILE(SYSIN) on-unit;
```

specifies that when the condition occurs, the on-unit is to be executed. Execution then resumes with the statement following the statement which raised the ENDFILE condition. However, if the on-unit is a GO TO statement, then execution resumes with the statement which is the target of the GO TO.

Thus, one way of programming the example is as follows:

```
        ON ENDFILE(SYSIN) GO TO OUT;
LOOP:   DO WHILE ('1'B);
            GET LIST(POSITION, VALUE);
            A(POSITION)=VALUE;
        END LOOP;
OUT:    /*  remainder of the program    */
```

Another way of programming the example is to use a bit flag and rearrange the code of the DO loop:

```
        ON ENDFILE(SYSIN) FLAG='0'B;
        FLAG='1'B;
        GET LIST(POSITION,VALUE);
LOOP:   DO WHILE (FLAG);
            A(POSITION)=VALUE;
            GET LIST (POSITION,VALUE);
        END LOOP;
        /*  remainder of the program    */
```

When the ON statement is encountered, it establishes the fact that the on-unit for the ENDFILE condition is the statement FLAG='0'B;. However, the on-unit is not executed at this point since the ENDFILE condition has not been raised. The flag is then initialized to '1'B, which indicates that the loop is to be repeated. As long as there are additional data cards, the flag maintains its value of '1'B and the loop continues. When a GET statement finds no data remaining, the ENDFILE condition is raised for the SYSIN file (which is the default input file in PL/I) so that the flag's value is set to '0'B. Execution resumes with the END statement following the GET LIST. This causes the test at the head of the loop to be made. Since FLAG is '0'B, the loop is terminated and the remainder of the program is executed.

The first program is clearly preferable to the second. The second program introduces an extra flag which is not part of the program logic—its use is a trick to "fool" the program into executing properly. Furthermore, it requires the programmer to keep in mind that once the ENDFILE condition has occurred and the on-unit has been executed, execution resumes at a statement which is not in proximity to the ON statement and is not explicitly referenced by that statement. In addition, the second program involves a rearrangement of the statements within the loop into an unnatural order (although this can be avoided by adding an additional IF statement within the loop).

An on-unit may not consist of a DO group or a DO loop. However, it may consist of a BEGIN block. We will discuss BEGIN blocks in detail in Section 3.5, but for now we note that a group of PL/I statements may be enclosed between the statements BEGIN; and END; and used as an on-unit. For example, consider the following code to solve the problem:

```
       ON ENDFILE(SYSIN) BEGIN;
                            /*   remainder of the program   */
                            STOP;
                         END;
LOOP:  DO WHILE('1'B);
          GET LIST(POSITION,VALUE);
          A(POSITION)=VALUE;
       END LOOP;
```

Here, the remainder of the program is placed into a BEGIN block to form the on-unit which is executed when the data is exhausted. Thus, when no data remains and the ENDFILE condition is raised, the remainder of the program will be executed within the on-unit. Note that a STOP; statement must be placed at the end of the on-unit in order to terminate the program's execution. Otherwise, execution will resume with the statement A(POSITION)=VALUE;.

The first version using a GO TO is preferable to this version as well. The first program is executed in the order that it is written; after the loop is complete, the remainder of the program is executed. In the last version, a substantial body of code which appears earlier in the program is actually executed later. This can be very confusing.

ON Conditions

The ENDFILE condition is only one example of a large number of conditions which may be detected. When such a condition is detected, it is said to be ***raised***. An ON statement is used to specify the action which is taken when such a condition is raised. The ON statement is an executable statement, so that one action may be taken if an ON condition is raised at one point in a program, while another action may be taken if the same condition is raised in another section of the program. For example, consider the following code:

```
          DCL X FIXED INIT(1);
          ON ENDFILE (SYSIN) GO TO NEXT;
LOOP1:    DO WHILE (X¬=0);
              GET LIST(X);
              . . .
          END LOOP1;

          ON ENDFILE (SYSIN) GO TO OUT;
LOOP2:    DO WHILE ('1'B);
              GET LIST(A,B);
              . . .
          END LOOP2;

NEXT:     PUT SKIP LIST ('END OF FILE FOR X');
          RETURN;
OUT:      PUT SKIP LIST ('END OF FILE FOR A,B');
          RETURN;
```

If the data does not include a 0, then the statement labeled NEXT is executed: otherwise, the statement at OUT is executed. The RETURN statement is not permitted within an on-unit, so that the above code cannot be rewritten using BEGIN blocks as on-units.

Examples of ON conditions are the following:

ENDPAGE (*filename*) occurs when the end of a page is reached in a print file. Usually *filename* is the system output file SYSPRINT.

FIXEDOVERFLOW occurs when a FIXED arithmetic expression results in a value too large for the particular machine.

ZERODIVIDE occurs when division by 0 is attempted.

OVERFLOW or UNDERFLOW occurs when the result of a floating-point expression is either too large or too small for a particular machine.

SIZE occurs when digits are lost in assigning a value to a variable which is too small to contain the value.

SUBSCRIPTRANGE occurs when an array index is out of bounds. (This condition is discussed in more detail in Section 3.)

STRINGRANGE occurs when a nonexistent position is referenced in a bit or character string.

There are many other ON conditions which are not mentioned here. The interested reader is referred to a PL/I manual.

An ON condition may be ***enabled*** or ***disabled***. Some conditions such as ENDFILE and ENDPAGE are always enabled and cannot be disabled. Others, such as FIXEDOVERFLOW, ZERODIVIDE, OVERFLOW, and UNDERFLOW are initially enabled but can be disabled and reenabled by the programmer through the use of *condition prefixes*. Such a prefix consists of a condition name enclosed in parentheses. The prefix is placed at the beginning of a PL/I statement, separated from the statement by a colon. If the prefix is meant to disable a condition, then the condition name is preceded by the two letters "NO". A condition prefix placed before any statement other than a PROCEDURE or BEGIN statement affects only that single statement. A prefix placed before a PROCEDURE or a BEGIN statement affects all statements within the procedure or block.

For example, to disable the OVERFLOW condition for the statement

```
X=X*Y;
```

the programmer codes

```
(NOOVERFLOW):  X=X*Y;
```

To disable the ZERODIVIDE condition for an entire procedure EXPROC, the programmer codes

```
(NOZERODIVIDE):  EXPROC:  PROC(X,Y);
```

To reenable the ZERODIVIDE condition for a single statement within EXPROC, the programmer codes

```
(ZERODIVIDE):  X = X/Y;
```

Other conditions, such as SIZE and SUBSCRIPTRANGE are initially disabled but may be enabled or redisabled through the use of condition prefixes. (However, in PL/C these two conditions are initially enabled.)

If a condition is enabled, there is a standard system action which is taken when the condition is raised. For example, when the SIZE condition is raised, and no on-unit has been specified for it, the standard system action is to print an error message and halt execution. However, if an on-unit has been established by an ON statement, then whatever action is specified within that on-unit is taken.

If an on-unit contains a GO TO statement to a statement outside the on-unit and that GO TO statement is executed, then the on-unit is said to be ***abnormally terminated***. In such a case, execution resumes at the target of the GO TO after the on-unit has been executed. If, however, a GO TO statement is not executed within an on-unit, then the on-unit is ***normally terminated***. In such a case, there is a standard action which is taken. For example, in the case of the ENDFILE condition, that standard action is to resume execution with the statement following the statement which raised the condition. In the case of the ZERODIVIDE condition, that standard action is to return to the point immediately following the point at which the condition was raised (even if that point is in the middle of a statement).

Each ON condition has its own standard system action in case an on-unit has not been established for that condition, and its own normal termination action in case its on-unit is normally terminated. The reader is referred to the PL/I manual for his particular compiler and installation. The details of which conditions are initially enabled and disabled and the actions which take place when conditions are disabled also vary from compiler to compiler. Again, a PL/I manual should be consulted.

One very useful ON condition is the ENDPAGE condition. It is particularly useful in printing reports or forms by computer. The condition is permanently enabled and is raised when the line number on the current output page is increased beyond the number of lines which belong on a page (specified by the PAGESIZE option of the OPEN statement or 60 by default. We assume 60 lines per page in the ensuing discussion.) If an on-unit for this condition is not specified, the standard system action is to advance the output to the next page and then resume processing at the point where the condition was raised. Thus, for example, in a statement such as

```
PUT LIST (A,B,C,D,E,F);
```

where A through E are printed on line 60 of a page, an attempt to print F on the next line increases the line counter to 61. This raises the ENDPAGE condition. In the absence of an ON ENDPAGE(SYSPRINT) statement, the line counter is reset to 1 and the forms in the printer are advanced to the start of the new page. Since no on-unit exists, execution resumes at the point of interruption, so that F is printed on the first line of the new page.

Suppose it is desired to print a heading on each new page of a program's output. Then the following ON statement may be executed:

```
ON ENDPAGE(SYSPRINT) BEGIN;
                           PUT PAGE;
                           PUT EDIT   (/* heading */) (/* format */);
                           PUT SKIP;
                         END;
```

As a final example, suppose that it is desired to print a page number at the head of each new output page and at the bottom of each page. Usually, the number of lines printed per page leaves several empty lines at the bottom of a page in which information may be printed by an ENDPAGE on-unit. Consider the following code:

```
DCL PGCNT                  FIXED INIT(1);
PUT EDIT ('PAGE',PGCNT) (X(100),A,F(3));
PUT SKIP;
ON ENDPAGE(SYSPRINT) BEGIN;
      PUT SKIP EDIT('PAGE',PGCNT) (X(100),A,F(3));
      PUT PAGE;
      PGCNT=PGCNT+1;
      PUT SKIP EDIT('PAGE',PGCNT) (X(100),A,F(3));
      PUT SKIP;
                           END;
      /*   remainder of program    */
```

After the last regular line is printed on the page, the ENDPAGE condition is raised, a line is skipped, and the page number is printed in the second line of the bottom margin. Then, the page is advanced and the page count is increased and printed on the first line of the new page. After skipping a line, the program resumes printing its output.

In Section 3, we examine the use of ON conditions in debugging PL/I programs.

Program Layout

Now that we have examined some of the programming constructs of PL/I and have shown how they should be used to produce logical, readable, and correct programs, let us turn our attention to the physical text of the program. Consider the following program segment:

```
GET LIST(A,B,C);   IF A<B THEN GO TO P;
IF B<C THEN GO TO Q;   /*   branch to Q   */
D=C;   /*   assign C to D   */   GO TO S;
P:   IF A  <  /*   less than   */   C THEN
GO TO R;   D=C;   GO TO S;   /*   unconditional branch   */  Q:
D=B;   GO TO S;   R:   D=A;
S:   PUT SKIP LIST(D);
```

Before reading further, see if you can figure out what the program segment does. The above code reads three numbers A, B, and C, assigns the smallest to D, and prints D. The above code, although it accomplishes its task, is a far cry from the type of program one would like to read and modify. Let us examine what is wrong with it. First, the layout of the code is very disorganized. While the PL/I language imposes few restrictions on the format of source code, good programmers use formats that are consistent with easy reading and understanding. In particular, rarely should more than one statement appear on a line. In addition, the individual lines should be placed so that labels of statements stand out at the left. This allows the reader to scan the left margin and quickly determine the objects of branches.

The following version incorporates these improvements:

```
      GET LIST(A,B,C);
      IF A<B THEN GO TO P;
      IF B<C THEN GO TO Q;   /*   branch to Q   */
      D=C;   /*   assign C to D   */
      GO TO S;
P:    IF A  <  /*   less than   */   C THEN GO TO R;
      D=C;
      GO TO S;   /*   unconditional branch   */
Q:    D=B;
      GO TO S;
R:    D=A;
S:    PUT SKIP LIST(D);
```

Certainly the second version is better than the first, although it is far from a "good" program. One of the difficulties in reading the above code is that little is done to help the reader decipher which portions of code do what. There are two methods of remedying this: use of meaningful identifiers and good comments.

Meaningful Identifiers

Let us consider the identifiers first. Even if the programmer has no control over the names A, B, and C (they might have been passed on from some previous portion of the program), he can still select a more meaningful name than D for the smallest number. By using a variable name such as SMALL, the programmer gives a good indication of what his program does. As another illustration, suppose that the variables of a program to compute interest on a principal are named A, B, C, and D rather than PRINC, AMT, YEAR, and RATE. Such an assignment of variable names adds significantly to the time required to understand a program.

In some cases the programmer may feel that it is more expedient to use "simple" variable names such as X and Y. However, the added time spent in trying to determine, at some later date, just what these variables represent probably costs more than any time initially spent in selecting meaningful names. It is, however, usually considered acceptable to use simple variable names such as I, J, K as indices of a loop.

Another good programming practice is to declare all identifiers explicitly. In fact, the DECLARE statement is an excellent place to explain the purpose of a variable with a short comment.

But variable names are not the only identifiers in a program. Any program in which there is a considerable amount of transfer of control (such as subroutine calls or GO TOs) will have a large number of labels. These labels usually represent the start of portions of code that accomplish specific subtasks. It is usually a good idea to use labels that describe the purpose of the next portion of code. In the above example, the labels P, Q, R, and S yield no information about what the following sections of code are expected to accomplish. More meaningful labels could be chosen. For example, the label P (at which point it is known that either A or C is smallest) could be replaced by the label NOTB. Similarly, Q, R, and S could have been replaced by the labels BLOW, ALOW, and OUTP respectively. Careful choice of label identifiers to reflect what is actually occurring at those labels helps the reader (and the original programmer) to determine just what the following statements are doing. These selections are best made when the code is first written rather than as a subsequent patch-up to an originally poor job.

Documentation

A second way in which the programmer can aid the reader in understanding his program is by using good documentation. Documentation, in its most general interpretation, refers to anything that the programmer provides (in addition to the code) to help explain the program to the user and to anyone who wants to make changes at some future point. Included are flow charts, instructions on the format of the inputs, and explanations of the outputs. More narrowly, documentation has been used to refer to comments in the actual code.

There are several points to be made concerning comments. If a program is well written, then it is not necessary to insert comments at each elementary stage. A good program is self-explanatory so that the reader does not have to plow his way through a long series of comments in order to determine what some small portion of code is doing.

Let us analyze the comments in the above example. One thing that is worse than no comment is a useless comment. Each of the comments in the above program fits remarkably well into this category. The comment

```
/*    branch to Q    */
```

says nothing more than the statement

```
GO TO Q;
```

immediately preceding it. The comment serves only to clutter up the layout of the code and perhaps mislead the reader into thinking that something more substantial than actually indicated by the code is really going on. Likewise, the last comment

```
/*    unconditional branch    */
```

is of use only to the novice programmer who is totally unfamiliar with the terminology of programming. Cluttering up code with such meaningless comments serves only to confuse the reader.

Worst of all, however, is the comment in the middle of a statement. It is impossible to read the statement without being interrupted by such a diversionary comment. Rarely should a comment appear in the middle of a statement, and then only to clarify an obscure structure or operation that might otherwise confuse the reader. In other cases, comments should either precede or follow a statement. Because this example does not use any significant new concepts or techniques, there is no excuse for a comment in the middle of a statement.

How then should comments be used to help rather than hinder the reader of a program? First, as mentioned earlier, the code should be written in such a way that many comments are not necessary. Among the techniques that promote this goal are the use of meaningful identifiers and the use of basic constructs such as DO loops and IF statements.

Yet, even if all the right techniques are used, comments are sometimes necessary. In general, an explanation should be provided at the beginning of a procedure or self-contained block of code. These comments should be concise but complete so that the reader knows the function of the code. In addition, there should usually be a comment at the beginning of a loop explaining the purpose of the loop, and unless it is completely obvious, the comment should also specify the conditions for exiting the loop. Finally, those portions of code whose actions are not clear should be fully commented. These ideas should be used as guidelines and not as rules; the programmer must make the ultimate decision in deciding which statements or groups of statements should be commented.

Another useful technique is to include explanatory output messages. A program which produces a page of numbers is often useless. Make sure that all output include messages which identify the final result.

To improve readability, code should be interspersed with blank lines so that individual groups of statements stand out as being related to each other. Incorporating the above suggestions, the above example can be rewritten as follows:

```
        /*   compute the smallest of three numbers   */
        GET LIST (A,B,C);
        IF A<B THEN GO TO NOTB;
        IF B<C THEN GO TO BLOW;
        SMALL=C;
        GO TO OUTP;

          /*   check whether A or C is smallest   */
NOTB:   IF A<C THEN GO TO ALOW;
        SMALL=C;
        GO TO OUTP;

          /*   B is smallest   */
BLOW:   SMALL=B;
        GO TO OUTP;

          /*   A is smallest   */
ALOW:   SMALL=A;
OUTP:   PUT SKIP EDIT('SMALLEST IS ',SMALL) (A,F(6));
```

Avoiding Needless Branches

Unfortunately, although we have improved the layout of the code and the documentation, there is very little that can be done to make an inherently poor program understandable. The problem with the above code is its structure and organization. The major fault of the code is that upon finding a condition to be true or false, it transfers control to a different portion of code. This problem is compounded when, upon completing that second portion of code, control is again transferred around some third portion of code. As the complexity of the program increases, this problem is compounded until the final product becomes totally unreadable. The final product of such programming practice is known as "spaghetti." The problem is not one that can be easily remedied by patching up poorly structured code; it requires careful planning and attention from the start. We shall say more about this planning in the next section; for the moment, let us rewrite the existing code.

The smallest of a set of numbers must be less than or equal to each of the other numbers in the set. However, it is not necessary to compare each number with every other number in order to locate this smallest number. Suppose that as the set of numbers is scanned, the program keeps track of the smallest number encountered thus far in a variable SMALL. Then each time a new number is considered, it need be compared only with SMALL. If the new number is less than SMALL, then it is also less than each of the numbers previously encountered; if the new number is not less than SMALL, then SMALL retains the property of being the smallest. Using this analysis, the solution can be coded in either of the following ways:

```
GET LIST(A,B,C);
      /*   SMALL is set to the smallest of A, B, and C    */
IF A<=B THEN SMALL=A;
         ELSE SMALL=B;
IF C<SMALL THAN SMALL=C;
PUT SKIP EDIT('SMALLEST IS', SMALL) (A,F(6));
```

or

```
GET LIST(A,B,C);
      /*   SMALL is set to the smallest of A, B, and C    */
SMALL=A;
IF B<SMALL THEN SMALL=B;
IF C<SMALL THEN SMALL=C;
PUT SKIP EDIT('SMALLEST IS',·SMALL) (A,F(6));
```

Contrast either of these versions with any of the three earlier versions. These new versions solve the problem directly by making use of the simple relationship described above. As soon as a condition which requires an action is detected, the appropriate action is performed by a statement which is in close proximity to the condition. No branching is used. Even the casual reader should have little difficulty in following the actions since the program reads sequentially. It is unnecessary to intersperse comments to explain the more intricate parts of the code since there are no intricate parts to explain. The earlier versions, on the other hand, contain an additional comparison, four labels, and six branches. Of course, not all of these branches are taken on any single run of the program. Yet, in order for a reader to determine just what is actually going on, he would have to understand every possible sequence of statements. Without doing this, he could never be certain that the code actually accomplishes its task.

Visual Spacing

There are several other things the programmer can do in order to make his program more readable. One of these is the use of visual spacing for portions of code. Such spacing includes the use of blank lines to group different portions of code together physically. This enables the reader to detect logical sections of the program by their physical separation. In addition to using blank lines, separate routines should be placed on separate pages. Certainly, major subroutines should not begin on the same page as a main program and then continue on succeeding pages. Even within a single routine, skipping to a new page can be a very effective way of helping the reader focus on a single concept at a time. By separating logical portions of code through the use of blank lines and separate pages, the programmer can provide simple visual aids to the reader.

Most PL/I compilers allow the use of a set of carriage control characters to control the printing of the source program. In particular, for most compilers a "1" in column 1 of a card causes a page to be skipped before the card is printed. Many PL/I compilers and printers provide the ability to overprint the previous line by inserting a plus sign in column 1. This allows the user to type two identical comment cards, with a plus sign in column 1 of the second card so that the comment is printed twice on the same line and thus appears darker than the rest of the program. Such techniques can provide effective visual aids to the reader when used properly.

Still another visual feature which enhances program readability is the use of indentation. PL/I is a free-form language in that there are almost no restrictions as to the position of parts of a statement on a card. For example, a statement may span two or more lines of code, and conversely, two or more statements may be placed on a single card. Some programmers use this freedom to code programs haphazardly, paying little attention to the position and the layout of the statements. This carelessness yields a program that is difficult to read. For example, consider the following code:

```
IF A>100 THEN IF B>100 THEN C=8;
ELSE IF B=100 THEN C=9;
ELSE C=10;
ELSE C=11;
```

The above code is not an especially obnoxious example of this practice, yet it is quite unreadable. The purpose of the code is to assign a value to C based on the current values of A and B in accordance with the following table:

A	B	C
>100	>100	8
>100	=100	9
>100	<100	10
≤100	anything	11

The problem is that it is difficult to determine at a glance which ELSEs are to be matched to which IF THENs. Let us rewrite the code by indenting each ELSE clause so that it begins immediately under its matching THEN clause as follows:

```
IF A>100 THEN IF B>100 THEN C=8;
                        ELSE IF B=100 THEN C=9;
                                       ELSE  C=10;
         ELSE C=11;
```

By presenting the program in this way, the programmer helps the reader comprehend which statements or groups of statements are executed for a specific set of conditions. Needless to say, this readability is well worth the effort required to format and indent the statements. (Some users prefer to nest the ELSE statement under the word IF rather than under the word THEN, but in most of the examples of the text we adhere to the form illustrated above.)

The code could be rewritten to test each of the above four mutually exclusive conditions. Such a revision would eliminate the need for any of the ELSE clauses.

```
IF A>100 & B>100 THEN C=8;
IF A>100 & B=100 THEN C=9;
IF A>100 & B<100 THEN C=10;
IF A<=100 THEN C=11;
```

However, such a rewriting often obscures the logic in which B must be tested only if A is greater than 100. Thus, it may be difficult for a reader to understand how the above code corresponds to the problem specification. Additionally, the above version is less efficient since it requires 10 operations (7 comparison and 3 logical) in the case where A is less than 100, whereas the previous version requires only one.

There are some PL/I compilers which accept an "unformatted" program and format it according to guidelines similar to the ones presented here. While the use of such compilers is not to be discouraged, the programmer should be encouraged to format his own code as he writes it so that he can more easily understand what he is doing. It is a disturbingly frequent occurrence for a programmer to forget what he meant to do 10 statements earlier.

Another set of constructs whose readability is improved by indentation includes PROCEDURE and BEGIN blocks and DO groups and loops. It is a good idea to keep the PROCEDURE and END or DO and END statements even with the surrounding statements and indent the statements contained within the block or group several columns. This improves readability and the structure of the entire code. For example, consider the following:

```
LOOP:  DO I=1 TO N-1;
       DO J=1 TO N-I;
       IF A(J)>A(J+1) THEN DO;
       HOLD=A(J);
       A(J)=A(J+1);
       A(J+1)=HOLD;
       END LOOP;
```

You may recognize the above sequence of statements as being part of a sort program; but to someone unfamiliar with the particular technique involved, the code is difficult to understand. Contrast the above with the following version:

```
OUTER:  DO I=1 TO N-1;
INNER:     DO J=1 TO N-1;
              IF A(J)>A(J+1) THEN DO;
                                   HOLD=A(J);
                                   A(J)=A(J+1);
                                   A(J+1)=HOLD;
                                      END;
           END INNER;
        END OUTER;
```

There are several features that make this version easier to read than its predecessor. First the DO loops are labeled, and each DO and its END are indented to the same depth. The body of statements within each DO loop is indented several columns so that it may be easily distinguished from the control structure (the DO and END statements). If the level of nesting is sufficiently deep so that it is impossible to indent the loop body any further, then exceptions and accommodations can be made. In the code above, for example, the body of the DO group which interchanges the two array elements is not indented past the DO and END. Nevertheless, the statements in the loop body are all indented to the same column, and it is rather easy to detect that they belong together as the body of the DO. Note that the two loops are labeled, while the DO group is not. There are no established rules; the programmer should use his judgment by labeling those DOs whose control structure might otherwise be obscure.

There is one additional difference between the two versions. The first version contains only a single END statement, whereas the latter contains three. You might be aware that when an END statement includes a label, then the labeled loop (or group or block) is closed only after all other loops, groups, and blocks which appear after the labeled loop header are closed. Thus the control structure of the first version is equivalent to that of the second version. The compiler automatically inserts two additional END statements preceding END LOOP; even if they are omitted by the programmer. However, people are not compilers, and because of this, the reader should not be burdened with the responsibility of trying to determine precisely where those imaginary END statements belong. By adhering to the rule that every DO, PROC, or BEGIN should be closed with its own END statement even if it is not syntactically necessary, a program and its overall control structure becomes more understandable.

"Clever" Code

Finally, the programmer should stay away from "clever" code. For example, the following statement prints all numbers less than N that are perfect squares. For example, if N=50, then the statement prints 1, 4, 9, 16, 25, 36, and 49. (The statement does not work in PL/C.)

```
PUT SKIP EDIT('PERFECT SQUARES LESS THAN',N) (A,X(1),F(5))
                 ('') (SKIP,A)
                 ((I DO I=1 TO N-1))
                   (SKIP(FLOOR(SQRT(I))**2=I),
                   F(5*(FLOOR(SQRT(I))**2=I)));
```

This is a prime example of the type of coding that should never be used (except perhaps to show off a repertoire of clever tricks). This statement is based on automatic conversion from bit strings to binary numbers. Let us see how it works.

The FLOOR function returns the largest integer less than or equal to its argument. Thus FLOOR(8)=8, FLOOR(8.5)=8, and FLOOR(–8.5)=–9. If an integer I is a perfect square, then SQRT(I) is an integer, say J, and FLOOR(J)=J. Squaring J yields I. On the other hand, if I is not a perfect square, then SQRT(I) is a noninteger, say X, so that FLOOR(X) < X. When FLOOR(X) is squared, it does not yield I. Thus, a number I is a perfect square only if it equals

```
FLOOR(SQRT(I))**2.
```

In the program, the logical expression

```
FLOOR(SQRT(I))**2=I
```

is used as the argument of format specifications where a number is expected, so its value ('0'B if false and '1'B if true) is converted to a binary integer. Thus the arguments of SKIP and F in the last format portion of the PUT EDIT will both be 0 if the condition fails. Thus when I is not a perfect square, nothing is printed. When the condition is true, the value of the expression is '1'B, which is converted to the integer 1. In this case the arguments of SKIP and F are 1 and 5 respectively so that I is printed on a new line.

A program that is loaded with such "clever" code is doomed to failure should it ever be modified. Unless the original author remembers precisely how the program works, it is almost impossible to decipher such code. The above example is an extreme. Unfortunately, many programs in use today are permeated with tricks that only the original author understands. While such tactics do make the author indispensable to the maintenance of the program (and may for this reason be a guarantee of a lifetime job), they have no place in an environment where well-styled and modifiable programs are run. A simpler version of the above code would be

```
PUT SKIP EDIT('PERFECT SQUARES LESS THAN',N) (A,X(1),F(5));
PUT SKIP;
DO I=1 TO N;
    IF FLOOR(SQRT(I))**2 = I THEN PUT SKIP LIST(I);
END;
```

This second version is clearer than its predecessor and does not require any extra code (although it does use five PL/I statements).

An even simpler version is

```
PUT SKIP EDIT('PERFECT SQUARES LESS THAN',N) (A,X(1),F(5));
PUT SKIP;
SQ=1;
DO I=2 BY 1 WHILE(SQ<N);
    PUT SKIP LIST(SQ);
    SQ=I**2;
END;
```

Conclusion

In this section we have mentioned many points which form a list of dos and don'ts in writing code. We summarize this list.

Code only one statement per line.

Use meaningful identifiers.

Use proper documentation including proper comments and explanatory output for the user.

Use blank lines and separate pages.

Use indentation (for DO, IF THEN ELSE, etc.).

Avoid needless transfers.

Match DO and END statements.

Label DO statements.

Avoid clever code.

The above rules should be used as a guide, but they are not inflexible. The programmer must make the decision as to when rules may be broken and when exceptions should be made. Programming does require initiative and originality. However, a programmer who adheres to the above guidelines will develop his own style. A style built on these suggestions contributes to making the final program easy to read and therefore easier to debug and modify when necessary.

2.2. Problems, Solutions, Algorithms, and Programs

We all have an intuitive idea of the relationship between a problem and a solution. We think of a problem as the formulation of a question that is presented to us and the solution as the response to that question.

For large problems, we are not the sole problem solvers. Most problem solutions that involve large amounts of data or that require a process to be performed many times are processed by a computer (so that humans can devote their time to more worthwhile endeavors). The programmer's job is essentially to formulate the solution so that a machine can be used to carry out the mechanics of that solution. Computer design has not yet reached the level where one can walk up to a computer and ask it "What is 2+2?" or "What is the value of π correct to 5000 decimal places?" It is therefore necessary to write programs to enable a machine to answer these questions. The program is a vehicle with which we may arrive at answers to these and other questions.

In the process of producing a solution from a problem, the work of the programmer must pass through several stages:

1. problem formulation
2. choice of algorithm and data structures
3. coding a solution

Let us examine each of these three stages in turn.

Formulating the Problem

The problem formulation phase is an extremely important one. It has been said that specifying a problem well is half the solution. As a problem is specified in more and more detail, it becomes clearer what resources are necessary for the problem's solution and how those resources are to be utilized in achieving that solution.

For example, suppose that you are hired by a firm to produce a computerized payroll system for its employees. While this may be enough of a description for specifying the requirements of a programming position, it is by no means sufficient information from which to write a program. The problem must be defined precisely so that the programmer knows exactly what inputs the program may expect and what outputs are expected from it. The inputs and outputs may be specified by company management, in which case the programmer has no choice other than to accept the specifications handed to him and write the program (or else possibly quit his job). On the other hand, the programmer may have some input into the specification of the program. In that case, he can exercise some degree of control over the specification so that the programming may be simplified and the value of the final product to its users enhanced. For example, it may be determined that certain informaion which is difficult to compute is not really necessary until a later phase of the project, when it is easier to obtain. Or it may be determined that such information is not needed at all. Similarly, it may turn out that some procedure or process is really a very inefficient method of obtaining a result, whereas a simpler method produces the same or similar results at a much lower cost.

In any case, a final, precise, definition of the problem is arrived at—usually with input from both the programmer and the user. It should be pointed out that no programming should be attempted or even outlined before the problem is completely specified. Projects that enter the coding stage prematurely usually end up requiring large amounts of time in constant revision of code as the needs of the final product evolve. Worse yet, such code is frequently patched up to get around sticky points based on invalid initial assumptions which stem from an incomplete understanding of the original problem. The time that a programmer spends in writing and refining the specification of the problem and its solution will be retrieved by eliminating much debugging, reorganizing, and rewriting portions of code too hastilv written.

Let us return to the payroll problem. Suppose that the company involved pays its employees once every four weeks. Employees are paid on an hourly basis, earning a base amount for every hour up to 40 hours per week and a higher amount for every hour over 40 in a given week. This description contains sufficient information for computing the gross pay for an employee. From the gross pay of each employee, the company must withhold federal and state tax. The employees at this particular company work in five states, so that a federal tax schedule and five separate state tax schedules are needed to compute the taxes withheld from all employees.

We would like to print each employee's name, social security number, gross income, federal tax, state tax, and net income. Also, we would like to print totals for each of the numerical fields. The inputs and outputs are therefore as follows:

```
INPUTS:    federal tax table
           state tax tables (one for each state)
           for each employee:
              social security number
              name
              hours worked (in each of four weeks)
              hourly rate (regular)
              hourly rate (overtime)

OUTPUTS:   for each employee:
              social security number
              name
              gross income
              federal tax
              state tax
              net income
           total gross income
           total federal income tax
           for each state:
              total income tax for that state
           total state income tax
           total net income
```

The practice of explicitly specifying the inputs and outputs of a program is extremely valuable. Aside from serving as a summary of problem specification, such a list helps focus on the question of whether each output can be computed from the given set of inputs. It is often the case that one or two inputs have been unintentionally omitted from the problem specification. This omission can be detected at this point before any programming has been done, at a time when the machinery necessary to obtain missing inputs can be put into effect. For example, if the state tax table for a particular state is not available, a letter can be sent to the state's tax agency requesting such a table. Actually, one of the inputs necessary to the payroll program has been omitted from the above list. See if you are able to spot this omission.

Developing an Algorithm

A list of inputs and outputs naturally leads to the next phase of program development: choosing algorithms and data structures. An ***algorithm*** is a process by which the outputs are computed from the inputs. A good programmer realizes that no solution is completely specified unless an algorithm for the solution has been described. In developing such an algorithm, the programmer must ask how each of the outputs can be derived from the inputs, i.e., which of the outputs can be derived directly from the inputs and which need intermediate quantities or other output quantities for their derivation. For example, the name and social security number of an employee is given by the input. The gross pay must be derived from the hours worked and the hourly rates. The federal tax for an employee must be derived from the federal tax table (which is an input) and the gross pay (which is itself an output). Note that this implies that the gross pay must be computed before the federal tax.

During the process of writing and modifying an algorithm, the good programmer uncovers remaining gaps in the problem specification. In general, programming is not a straight-line activity in which one can proceed from one step to another. Rather, at every stage, decisions which were made in previous stages must be reexamined and sometimes modified. Other decisions which were consciously postponed in previous stages must be made in later stages. For example, specifications might be modified during the actual coding in the interests of increasing the program's efficiency. Of course, any such change of specification must be agreed to by the user as well as the programmer. A first attempt at an algorithm for the payroll program might be the following:

```
read (federal tax table);
do (for each state);
    read (state tax table);
end;

initialize  total gross, total federal tax,
            total state tax for each state,
            total net to 0;

do (for each employee);
    read  (social security number, name,
          regular rate, overtime rate,
          hours worked each week);
    gross=0;
    do    week=1 to 4;
          compute salary earned that week;
          add weekly salary to gross;
    end;
    compute federal tax from federal tax table;
    compute state tax;
    compute net income;
    update total gross, total federal tax,
          total state tax for employee's state,
          total net;
    print (employee output information);
end;
print  (total gross, total federal tax,
       total state tax for each state,
       total state tax for all states, total net);
stop;
```

The above algorithm can be regarded as a logical description of the solution, but it cannot be used directly to construct a program. In order to write a PL/I program from such an algorithm it is necessary to be able to translate every statement in the algorithm into equivalent PL/I code. This requires two things: descriptions of how the data is maintained (i.e., the data structures to be used) and the actual computations involved. It is also necessary to describe the mechanism for controlling the loops.

We will shortly return to the problem of how to transform the algorithm into PL/I code. For now, let us examine the data structures which are necessary for the problem's solution.

Choosing Data Structures

There are two types of inputs to the payroll problem: tax tables and employee data. Tax tables are not organized in a uniform manner among the states and the federal government. Thus it is necessary either to handle each case separately or to first convert all the tables to some uniform format. To simplify the program, we assume a uniform table organization in which the tables are organized in intervals, where each interval contains a base amount and a percentage. For example, if one interval is \$200 to \$399 and the base and percentage are \$15 and 10% respectively, then an employee making \$300 pays the base tax of \$15 and 10% of the amount over \$200, giving a total tax bill of \$25. Since the tax tables are constantly referenced during the tax computation, they are stored in an array. For each tax table, there may be any number of intervals (we assume a maximum of 20). For each interval, the table specifies the lower limit of the interval, the base tax amount, and the additional tax rate. Finally, each table includes a state name code so that the appropriate table may be referenced for each state. The federal tax table has the same structure as the state tables, except that only one such table is needed. The tables are declared as follows:

```
DECLARE 1  FED_TABLE,
             2 NAME          CHAR(5),
             2#INTERVALS     FIXED,        /*  number of intervals   */
                                           /*     in the table       */
             2 INTERVALS(20),
               3 LOWER       FIXED(8,2),   /* lower bound of interval */
               3 BASE_TAX    FIXED(8,2),   /*      minimum tax        */
               3 ADDNL_RATE  FIXED(8,2);   /* additional percentage   */
                                           /*         rate            */
DECLARE STATE_TABLE(5)       LIKE FED_TABLE;
```

The second of the above statements creates an array of five structures, each with substructures identical to those of the structure FED_TABLE. (Note that the LIKE attribute may not be used in PL/C.)

Several hard decisions are made when data structures are chosen. For example, implicit in the decision to have a uniform format for all tax tables is a decision to provide conversion routines to convert from each state's tax table format into the uniform format. The decision to allow for only five state tax tables is justified by the problem specification which stipulates that the company's employees are located in only five states. There are good reasons for allowing for all 50 state tax tables. The company might decide to expand to other states, or a new employee might live in a sixth state. If this happens, the program would have to be modified. It is possible that the program could run correctly for years, and then suddenly an employee in a different state is hired. The program suddenly produces errors or aborts, giving no indication of the reason. In the meantime, the original programmer has left long ago, and no one else understands the program.

However, keeping all 50 tables in the memory of the machine is a drain on a valuable resource. In a real-world situation, such tables might be stored off-line on a direct access device. In the remainder of this text, we assume that all necessary information (except input data) is kept in memory and do not deal with issues concerning external storage.

Note that each tax table contains a NAME field which contains the name of the state for which the table applies. For the sake of uniformity, the federal table also contains such a field, although it is really unnecessary. In this way, any operation which is to be performed using a tax table can expect that table to be in a single, specific format.

Note also that it is unnecessary to keep both a lower and upper bound for each interval since the upper bound of one interval is the same as the lower bound of the next. However, by eliminating upper bounds from the data structure, we are requiring the intervals of the table to be kept in increasing order. Otherwise, it is difficult (but not impossible) to determine the interval for a particular gross pay. Therefore the code which initializes the tables must ensure that this restriction is enforced. The simplest way of doing this is to require that the intervals in the input must already be in increasing order. This is an example of programming efficiency considerations impacting the specification of the problem.

Next, it must be decided what information to keep for each employee. For identification purposes, the employee's social security number and name are needed. In order to compute the gross pay, the regular and overtime rates and the actual number of hours worked by the employee during each week of the period are required. For purposes of computing the state tax, the state name of the employee is required.

Note that in the process of choosing data structures, an input (the employee's state name) which had not previously been considered has been identified. The state name is needed in order to select the appropriate state tax table for that employee. Again, we are forced to revise the specification during the course of programming.

The programmer may note at this point that it would be more efficient to keep an integer from 1 to 5 as the code identifying an employee's state. Then, for example, if an employee's state code is 3, the program would use STATE_TABLE(3). This would eliminate the need for a NAME field in the tax tables. In the current situation, where a character string is used to identify a state's name, it becomes necessary to search the array STATE_TABLE for the table whose NAME field matches the employee's state name. Since such a search must be performed for every employee, keeping the state code as an integer would yield significant savings.

If the programmer is able to convince the user to supply a state code rather than a state name with each employee, then so much the better. However, he may find that the input employee data has already been prepared with state names. Therefore, he has no choice but to write the program as specified.

Finally, for output purposes, the gross pay, the federal tax, the state tax, and the net pay are needed. At this point, the programmer must make a choice between combining the input and output information about an employee into a single structure EMPLOYEE or separating them into two distinct structures EMPIN and EMPOUT. An argument can be made for either of the two choices. Placing all the information into one structure has the advantage of segregating all information about a logical entity in one place. Separating the input and output information has the advantage of focusing the program development process on obtaining all the outputs from the input. Additionally, it may be convenient for the programmer to code

```
GET EDIT (EMPIN)    (/*    format list    */);
```

and

```
PUT EDIT (EMPOUT)   (/*    format list    */);
```

rather than to specify exactly which items of EMPLOYEE must be input or output. On the other hand, since there are items which appear in both the input and the output (such as the employee's name and social security number), it is wasteful to declare two separate memory areas (one in EMPIN, the other in EMPOUT) to hold the same information and to move that information from one structure to the other.

We choose to declare a single EMPLOYEE structure as follows:

```
DCL 1 EMPLOYEE,
      2 SOC_SEC          CHAR(9),
      2 ENAME            CHAR(20),    /*       employee name          */
      2 STATE_NAME       CHAR(5),     /*       employee's state       */
      2 RATE,
        3 REG            FIXED(7,2),  /*       regular rate           */
        3 OVER           FIXED(7,2),  /*       overtime rate          */
      2 HOURS_WORKED(4)  FIXED,       /*  hours worked during each    */
                                      /*   week of salary period      */
      2 INCOME,
        3 GROSS          FIXED(9,2),  /*       gross income           */
        3 FED_TAX        FIXED(9,2),  /*       federal tax            */
        3 STATE_TAX      FIXED(9,2),  /*       state tax              */
        3 NET            FIXED(9,2);  /*       net income             */
```

It is unnecessary to declare an array of structures, one for each employee in the company. To see why this is so, let us reexamine the algorithm. The algorithm may be rewritten in less detail as follows:

```
read (tax tables);
initialize variables;
do (for each employee);
   read (employee input information);
   compute employee output information;
   update totals;
   print (employee output information);
end;
print (totals);
stop;
```

This global view of the algorithm leads to the realization that once an employee's output information has been printed, neither his input nor output information is ever used again. Rather, the program loops to obtain the next employee's input information. Thus only one employee's information is ever used at any one time. Although the totals (such as total federal taxes) are accumulations of many employees' information, they are updated within the loop so that running totals are kept.

If an array of employees were used, the totals would not have to be updated within the loop. Rather, an algorithm such as the following could be used (the numbers on the left are for future reference):

```
1 read (tax tables);
2 read (all employees' input information into an array);
3 compute all employee's output information;
4 print (all employees' output information);
5 compute totals from information in the array;
6 print (totals);
7 stop;
```

However, if there are several thousand employees in the company, several thousand units of memory would be required for the elements of the array. This is too much space if an alternative is available.

Another reason for preferring the first algorithm to the second is that each of lines 2 through 5 in the latter algorithm must be expanded into a loop of the form

```
do (for each employee);
   /*   take some action based on that employee's information   */
end;
```

For example, line 4 would expand into

```
do (for each employee);
   print (that employee's output information);
end;
```

while line 5 would expand into

```
initialize totals to zero;
do (for each employee);
   add that employee's information to the totals;
end;
```

Thus the looping mechanism involved in cycling through all the employees would have to be performed four times in the latter algorithm, whereas it would have to be repeated only once in the former. (It should be noted that although the latter algorithm requires an array, the former algorithm does not imply its absence. The input information for a particular employee could be stored within an array element. However, the former algorithm does not require an array. It is also preferable to the latter because the looping mechanism is not repeated. Thus there is no valid reason for using the large amount of space that an array would require.)

Note the interaction between choice of algorithm and choice of data structure. Each phase of the programming activity interacts with every other phase, so that the programmer must "look ahead" to anticipate decisions that will have to be made later and must be constantly ready to revise decisions that have already been made.

At this time, the variables which hold the totals may be selected, given meaningful names, and declared:

```
DCL TOTAL_GROSS     FIXED(9,2),  /*   total gross pay     */
    TOTAL_FED       FIXED(9,2),  /*   total federal tax   */
    TOTAL_NET       FIXED(9,2),  /*   total net pay       */
    TOTAL_STATE(5)  FIXED(9,2);  /*   total state taxes   */
```

As an algorithm is developed into a program, additional variables are identified as necessary. Throughout the program development process, the programmer should keep and update a list of the variables which must be declared in the program. This list can be translated directly into DECLARE statements when the program is written. Of course, variables may be deleted from the list as well as added to it as decisions which have already been made are revised.

Algorithm Refinement

Once an algorithm has been chosen and outlined and the major data structures have been decided upon, the programmer proceeds to convert the algorithm into a program. Again, there are no hard and fast rules which will guarantee a "good" program. If such rules existed, an algorithm outline would be the final goal of the programmer since a machine could follow the rules as well as (or better than) a person. However, a group of guidelines has been developed and has been found to be enormously helpful in the design of successful programs. We present these guidelines with the warning that programming is an art as well as a science and that the mark of the true artist is the knowledge of when to adhere to established guidelines, when to bend those guidelines, and even when to break them.

We have presented two versions of the payroll program's algorithm. (A third version which required an EMPLOYEE array was dismissed as being wasteful of time and space.) One version eliminates most detail and presents only the global scheme. We repeat that version here with line numbers to the left so that we may refer to it more easily. (The line numbers begin with the letter G for "global.")

```
G1     read (tax tables);
G2     initialize variables;
G3     do (for each employee);
G4        read (employee input information);
G5        compute employee output information;
G6        update totals;
G7        print (employee output information);
G8     end;
G9     print (totals);
G10    stop;
```

The algorithm basks in glorious generality. As much detail as possible has been squeezed out of the algorithm. Rather than specifying the actual variables that are necessary for a program, it refers to "tax tables," "variables," "employee input information," "employee ouput information," and "totals." Still, this outline yields useful information about the final program. The outline is a skeleton which can be fleshed out component by component. The programmer can focus on line G1 without worrying about the remaining parts of the outline. The outline exhibits how the pieces of the final program fit together into a useful whole and allows the programmer to concentrate on the individual pieces separately.

This process of beginning with global specification of the entire program and proceeding to greater and greater levels of detail until the final program is written is called ***top-down programming***. The process of specifying an algorithm in greater and greater detail until it can be translated directly into a program is called ***step-wise algorithm refinement***. The two processes are intimately related and imply each other.

For example, let us repeat the more detailed version of the payroll program algorithm and see how it is a refinement of the global version. (The line numbers begin with the letter I for "intermediate.") We also include the state name of each employee as an input.

```
I1     read (federal tax table);
I2     do (for each state);
I3        read (state tax table);
I4     end;
I5     initialize  total gross, total federal tax,
                   total state tax for each state,
                   total net to 0;
```

```
I6     do (for each employee);
I7        read   (social security number, name, state,
                 regular rate, overtime rate,
                 hours worked each week);
I8        gross=0;
I9        do week=1 to 4;
I10          compute salary earned that week;
I11          add weekly salary to gross;
I12       end;
I13       compute federal tax;
I14       compute state tax;
I15       compute net income;
I16       update total gross, total federal tax,
                 total state tax for employee's state,
                 total net;
I17       print (employee output information);
I18    end;
I19    print (total gross, total federal tax,
             total state tax for each state,
             total state tax for all states,
             total net);
I20    stop;
```

Let us compare the two outlines. Outline G says "**read** (tax tables);" in line G1. Outline I expands this single line into lines I1 through I4. Thus lines I1 through I4 are a refinement of line G1. The programmer who initially writes algorithm G can focus on line G1 and expand it into lines I1 through I4 without paying attention to the remainder of the program. In this expansion, the programmer makes several decisions: there are to be separate tables for the federal taxes and each of the state taxes; the federal tables precede the state tables in the input; variables must be declared to hold these tables.

Each one of these decisions is small and almost insignificant. But any program represents a collection of small decisions. Making many small decisions at once almost always leads to either overlooking one "tiny" detail or making a "wrong" decision. Often, decisions are made by default without the programmer realizing the fact that they have been made until it is too late. In the divide-and-conquer strategy which we are presenting, the programmer has a chance to recognize that a decision is being made and to consider the consequences of each individual decision.

Similarly, line I5 is a refinement of line G2. In line I5, the programmer identifies those variables which need initialization and what their initial values should be. Line I7 is a refinement of G4; lines I8 through I15 are a refinement of G5; I16 is a refinement of G6; and I19 is a refinement of G9. It would be instructive for you to examine what decisions are implicit in each of these refinements.

Note that some lines such as I6, I17, I18, and I20 are taken directly from outline G. This illustrates that the process of algorithm refinement is heavily dependent on programmer style and is not an exact procedure. The programmer may choose to expand certain segments of an algorithm and choose to leave the expansion of other segments to a later time.

There is another path which may be taken from a global outline such as G to a final program. Each line of that outline may be translated directly into a PL/I statement. We present such a PL/I version of outline G. (The letter P in the line numbering stands for "program.")

```
P1    CALL READTABLES;
P2    CALL INITVARS;
P3    DO EMPNUM=1 BY 1;
P4        CALL READINPUT;
P5        CALL COMPOUTPUT;
P6        CALL UPDTOTALS;
P7        CALL PRINTEMPL;
P8    END;
P9    CALL PRINTTOT;
```

Almost every line of the outline has been transformed into a statement calling a subroutine to perform the operation specified by that line. Thus the algorithm is immediately transformed into a PL/I program, and the top-down development proceeds with the program itself. We will see shortly how this is done. For the moment, let us make an observation.

Statement P3 introduces a new variable EMPNUM to serve as a counter of employees. If EMPNUM equals 100, then the program is processing the hundredth employee; if EMPNUM equals 1000, then the program is processing the thousandth employee. Thus we have identified another variable which must be declared. The value of EMPNUM is a count of which employee is currently being processed. Since there is no TO clause in the DO statement, EMPNUM will be increased by 1 indefinitely, and the only way to leave the loop is by an occurrence of the ENDFILE condition.

Statement P3 could be replaced by a statement such as DO WHILE('1'B);, which accomplishes the same thing without using the variable EMPNUM. Such a statement is more efficient than P3 since it does not involve incrementing a variable each time through the loop. Why then should statement P3 appear?

The answer to this question illustrates one of the most important rules of the program development process. If there is a conflict between clarity and efficiency, the programmer should choose clarity. P3 is the preferred statement in this situation because it more clearly describes what is being done. Statement P3 acts as a comment and says: "The following process is repeated starting with employee number 1 and for each subsequent employee." The primary consideration at this early stage is that the resulting program be correct. A program which is confusing is rarely correct. Even when it is correct, it is rarely efficient. By aiming for clarity, the programmer often surprises himself with the overall efficiency of the result. This occurs despite the fact that local decisions have been made which tend to decrease rather than increase efficiency. We will have more to say about efficiency considerations later in this chapter.

Coding the Program

We have indicated two paths from a global algorithm outline (such as outline G) to a final program. The first path begins by expanding the outline into an intermediate version (such as outline I) and then continues from that intermediate version. The second path immediately translates the global outline into a series of CALL statements (such as program segment P) and continues from that program segment.

There are advantages and disadvantages to both methods. The advantage of immediately translating into a program is that the programmer must translate only a few lines of an algorithm into actual code. Thus, he can ensure that those lines are translated correctly. The process continues by developing a global algorithm outline for each of the individual subroutines, coding them as a series of subroutine calls, and then repeating the process with those subroutines. This continues until each subroutine consists of a simple task which can be coded directly into a series of PL/I statements.

In the other method, the intermediate algorithm is expanded further and further into more and more detailed versions until each line corresponds to one or two single statements. By keeping the entire program together, the programmer can focus on the interrelationships between various parts of the program. This is more difficult to do in the subroutine method, where each subroutine is developed in isolation. However, the power to examine interrelationships is a curse as well as a blessing. The interrelationships among various parts of a large program are so complex that the programmer often gets lost in their complexity. The reason for introducing the top-down development method in the first place is to reduce the number of factors which a programmer must consider at any one time.

As usual, the best approach is a compromise between two extremes. In this case, the preferred way of proceeding is to first expand algorithm outline G into outline I. But then, instead of continuing algorithm refinement, outline I is translated into a program segment.

During the translation of algorithm I into a program, additional factors become apparent. These factors can be divided into three groups. The first group consists of the need for additional variables. For example, in translating line I2, it becomes apparent that a variable STATE is necessary to control the loop consisting of lines I2 through I4. The values of this variable proceed from 1 to 5. Another example is in line I5, where it becomes apparent than an array TOTSTATE(5) is necessary to hold the total state taxes for all of the five states.

The second group consists of the realization that processes or statements were inadvertently omitted from the algorithm. An example of this is that headings should be printed at the top of the columns of employee output information. We were so concerned with the processing and printing of numbers that we ignored specifying the printout's format in developing an algorithm. This oversight may not be detected until a test run of the program actually produces output without headings. The patch-up job to correct the program at that point is a simple one. In general, however, it is a good idea to detect such oversights as early as possible since they may be far more significant and not so easily correctable at a later stage.

The discovery of such an omission and its correction implies a revision of the original global algorithm. This illustrates that the algorithm and even the specification of the problem (in deciding exactly what the headings should say) may have to be altered during the coding phase.

The third group consists of coding that is made necessary by the nature of the programming language. For example, the loop consisting of lines I6 through I20 cannot be repeated forever. Eventually, the input runs out and the ENDFILE condition is raised. To continue processing after the input has run out, an ON statement is required.

Each line of outline I is translated into one or more PL/I statements. Many of these are calls on subroutines which must be further expanded. The PL/I statements corresponding to the algorithm can be preceded by appropriate declarations and enclosed between PROCEDURE and END statements to produce the main routine of the final program. The statements of global algorithm G can serve as comments to the major portions of the program. We do this for the main routine of the payroll program as follows:

```
PAYROLL: PROC OPTIONS(MAIN);

   /*              declare tax tables              */
  DCL 1 FED_TABLE,
          2 NAME                 CHAR(5),
          2 #INTERVALS           FIXED,
          2 INTERVALS(20),
             3 LOWER             FIXED(8,2),
             3 BASE_TAX          FIXED(8,2),
             3 ADDNL_RATE        FIXED(8,2),
        STATE_TABLE(5)           LIKE FED_TABLE;

   /*          declare employee variables          */
  DCL 1 EMPLOYEE,
          2 SOC_SEC              CHAR(9),
          2 ENAME                CHAR(20),
          2 STATE_NAME           CHAR(5),
          2 RATE,
             3 REG               FIXED(7,2),
             3 OVER              FIXED(7,2),
          2 HOURS_WORKED(4)      FIXED,
          2 INCOME,
             3 GROSS             FIXED(9,2),
             3 FED_TAX           FIXED(9,2),
             3 STATE_TAX         FIXED(9,2),
             3 NET               FIXED(9,2);

          /*     declare summary statistics       */
  DCL     EMPNUM                 FIXED,        /*   number of employee    */
          TOTAL_GROSS            FIXED(9,2),   /*   total gross paid      */
          TOTAL_FED              FIXED(9,2),   /*   total federal tax     */
                                               /*          paid           */
```

```
        TOTAL_NET            FIXED(9,2),  /*     total net paid         */
        TOTAL_STATE(5)       FIXED(9,2);  /*   total state tax paid     */
                                          /*      to each state         */
   DCL  (WEEK, STATE)        FIXED;

      /*   read tax tables    */
      CALL READTAX (FED_TABLE);

READ: DO STATE=1 TO 5;
         CALL READTAX (STATE_TABLE(STATE));
      END READ;
      CALL PRINTHEADING;

       /*    initialize summary statistics     */
      TOTAL_GROSS,TOTAL_FED,TOTAL_NET=0;
      TOTAL_STATE=0;
      ON ENDFILE(SYSIN) GO TO PRINT_SUMMARY;

       /*    process individual employees     */
LOOP: DO EMPNUM=1 BY 1;

            /*   read employee input information    */
            CALL READEMP (EMPLOYEE);

            /*   compute employee output information    */
            GROSS=0;
NEXT_WEEK:  DO WEEK=1 TO 4;
               IF HOURS_WORKED (WEEK) <=40 THEN
                  GROSS= GROSS + HOURS_WORKED (WEEK)*REG;
                                              ELSE
                  GROSS= GROSS + 40*REG +
                                 (HOURS_WORKED(WEEK)-40)*OVER;
            END NEXT_WEEK;

            /*           compute taxes             */
            FED_TAX=TAX(GROSS,FED_TABLE);
            STATE=FIND(STATE_NAME);
            IF STATE=0 THEN DO;
               PUT SKIP EDIT(SOC_SEC,ENAME,'HAS INVALID STATE CODE')
                              (A,X(2));
               STATE_TAX=0;
                              END;
                      ELSE STATE_TAX=TAX(GROSS,STATE_TABLE(STATE));
            NET=GROSS - FED_TAX - STATE_TAX;
```

```
                /*     update summary statistics     */
               TOTAL_GROSS=TOTAL_GROSS + GROSS;
               TOTAL_FED=TOTAL_FED + FED_TAX;
               TOTAL_STATE(STATE)=TOTAL_STATE(STATE)
                                                      + STATE_TAX;
               TOTAL_NET=TOTAL_NET + NET;

               /*     print employee record     */
               CALL PRINTEMP (EMPLOYEE);
          END LOOP;

PRINT_SUMMARY:     /*     print the totals     */
        CALL PRINTTOT;
      END PAYROLL;
```

Note the use of subroutines to implement most of the operations of algorithm I. At this point in the coding process, the programmer must specify explicitly what the inputs and outputs to each subroutine are and exactly what processing each subroutine is to perform. This is exactly the same process that was performed for the entire program as a whole. Recall that the first step in programming is the specification of the problem. Each subroutine is now viewed as a program in itself. Each individual subroutine must itself be specified, an algorithm and data structures for its implementation must be chosen, and finally, the subroutine must be coded.

Let us specify the purpose of each of the subroutines mentioned in the above program:

READTAX is a subroutine which reads a tax table from the program's input and places it into a data structure representing that table in interval format. Note that READTAX is used to initialize the federal as well as all state tax tables.

PRINTHEADING prints headings for the information which is to be printed for each employee.

READEMP reads a single employee's input information into the structure EMPLOYEE.

TAX accepts an income and a tax table and returns the amount of tax which must be paid on that income according to the table. TAX is used to find both the federal and the state tax.

FIND is a function which accepts a state name and searches through the array STATE_TABLE to find the index of that state within the array. FIND returns an integer between 0 and 5. If it returns 0, then there is no tax table for that state in the array of structures and an error message is printed. The employee's state tax is set to 0. If the value returned by FIND is I, then STATE_TABLE(I).NAME is equal to STATE_NAME.

PRINTEMP accepts an employee structure and prints all the information concerning that employee which is to be printed.

Finally, PRINTTOT prints summary statistics in a neatly labeled format.

Before illustrating how the program development proceeds in coding these subroutines, let us recapitulate what we are trying to do and discuss the use of subroutines in general.

Subroutines

The subroutine is a most helpful programming tool when used effectively. We assume that the reader is already familiar with the basic concepts of the subroutine and function as used in PL/I.

Although a main routine controls a program, it should only act in a supervisory fashion. In other words, the main routine should act as a manager which organizes the work that is to be done and assigns specific tasks to specific subroutines. Each routine, in turn, organizes the job which it must do and breaks up the work into components to be assigned to still other, lower-level routines. This process continues until the lowest level routines are written. These routines can perform their job easily enough without calling other routines.

The main program is written first. The first version of the main program may leave gaps in the code because it has not yet been decided how to handle certain features. These features are left to a subroutine by inserting a statement such as

```
CALL  PHASE1;
```

It is helpful to include a comment describing the action that the subroutine is expected to accomplish. The programmer may then proceed to complete the main routine as though the desired actions have been performed. In this way, a complete main routine is constructed. The program cannot yet be executed because of the gaps that must be filled. However, the programmer can consider the major problem to be solved. All that is required is the solution of several simple subproblems.

The programmer then proceeds to solve the subproblems. At this time it is necessary to specify those subproblems more precisely. In particular, it is necessary to determine exactly what information the subroutine can access when it is called and what actions it is expected to take. Once the purpose of the subroutine is completely specified, the subroutine may be coded using the same techniques that were used in coding the calling program. This process continues until there are no more algorithms to refine and no more subgoals to accomplish.

The question that must be faced for each problem is how to divide the chores among a main routine and its subroutines. This question does not have a clear answer, and must be answered by the programmer for each individual program. Yet, there are two general guidelines that are helpful in selecting those tasks which are to be performed in a calling program and those which are relegated to a subprogram.

The first criterion is that segments of a program that include a large amount of detail which is secondary to the solution of the problem should be placed in a subroutine. When writing and reading a routine, a programmer does not want to concern himself with the details of how certain subtasks are accomplished; he merely wants to be able to be sure that they are done. Included in this category is any task whose actual actions may be modified at a later date. A program that is permeated with code that is "to be improved" may prove to be very difficult to improve. On the other hand, if that code is placed into compact subroutines, then each subroutine can be modified and tested independently of the calling routine so that the calling routine need not be changed at all. When the modification is complete, the new subroutine replaces the old and the total program works correctly. This concept of being able to replace one version of a routine by another is called ***modularity*** and the individual routines are called ***modules***. Programming in a modular style, in which each routine is a self-contained unit which is easily replaceable, enables subsequent modifications to be performed efficiently, correctly, and without worrying about possible side effects of one piece of code on all the others.

For example, in the payroll program all input and output has been relegated to subroutines such as READTAX, READEMP, PRINTHEADING, PRINTEMP, and PRINTTOT. The reason for this is that we do not wish to focus on the format of the input and the output at this stage of program development. By the use of subroutines, we acknowledge that information must be input or output at this point of the program's execution, but that we will determine exactly what information is necessary and what form it takes at a later stage.

After the entire program has been written and debugged, company management might decide that it wishes the output in a different format. Instead of searching through a large complex program for the appropriate statements to modify, the programmer can simply replace one version of PRINTTOT (for example) with another.

A second criterion for placing a specific operation or set of operations in a subroutine is its usefulness to other portions of the program. For example, if a particular process (such as sorting) is required at several points in a program, then it is helpful to code this process as a subroutine and access the routine through a CALL statement. Thus, the code need not be repeated at several points in the program, and hence it need not be debugged several times.

Accessing Information in a Subroutine

A subroutine can access storage which has been declared in another routine in two ways. The first method is by referencing a ***global variable***. The second method is by referencing a ***parameter***.

There are two types of procedures in PL/I: ***external*** procedures and ***internal*** procedures. An external procedure is one which is written separately from any other routine and does not access any variable which is not declared (possibly by default) within its own body. An internal procedure is one which is contained within some other procedure. If procedure B is internal to procedure A, it usually appears immediately before the statement END A;. (However, by the rules of PL/I, it can appear between any two statements of A.) Procedure B can access any variable declared within procedure A simply by referencing it by name. For example, if PRINTTOT is written as an internal procedure of PAYROLL, then PRINTTOT can reference the variables EMPNUM, TOTAL_GROSS, TOTAL_FED, TOTAL_NET, and TOTAL_STATE, all of which it must access in order to print their values. Such variables are called ***global***. These variables may not be redeclared within PRINTTOT since we wish to access the same storage which PAYROLL accesses in referencing those variables. Global variables are discussed in more detail in Section 3.5.

A global variable may be used by a subroutine in three ways. An ***input variable*** is one which has been given a value before the internal procedure is called and whose value is used by that procedure. An ***output variable*** is one whose value is changed by the internal procedure. A variable may also be used as both an input and an output variable. For example, consider the following program:

```
MAIN:   PROC OPTIONS (MAIN);
          DCL X              FIXED INIT(1),
              Y              FIXED,
              Z              FIXED INIT(3),
              W              FIXED;
          W=7;
          CALL SUB;
          PUT SKIP LIST(X,Y,Z,W);
SUB:      PROC;
            PUT SKIP LIST(X);
            Y=X+Z;
            Z=Z**2;
            W=12;
            RETURN;
          END SUB;
        END MAIN;
```

X, Y, Z, and W are all global variables to the procedure SUB since they are all used without being redeclared within SUB. X is an input variable since its previous value (1) is used within SUB (in the PUT statement as well as to give Y a value). X is not an output variable since its value is not changed within SUB. Y is an ouput variable since it is given a value within SUB, but it is not an input variable since it has not even been initialized when SUB is called. Z is both an input and ouput variable since its previous value is used within SUB and its value is changed by SUB. Although W has a value when SUB is called, W is not an input variable for SUB since that value is never used within SUB. Rather, W is given a new value and is therefore an ouput variable. The terms input and output variable refer to how a global variable is used within a subroutine.

Global variables are very useful since they allow an internal procedure to access all the information accessible to its containing procedure. However, their use involves certain elements of danger as well. The first danger is that it is difficult to determine from the text of a program the global variables that are being used by an internal procedure. The variables are not declared within the procedure nor are they explicitly segregated and labeled as global variables. Thus a subroutine may use a certain variable as a global input variable, but that variable has not been given a value by the calling routine. Such errors are extremely difficult to trace.

An even greater danger stems from the use of a global output variable. Such a variable is modified by the subroutine, so that after the subroutine returns, the variable has a new value. However, no mention of the fact that the variable might have its value changed appears in the calling routine. Thus if such a variable is found to have an incorrect value at some later stage of the calling procedure (or in some other procedure which is called by the calling procedure), it is extremely difficult to trace the source of the incorrect value.

Thus, the elimination of global variables is strongly recommended wherever possible. The objection to the use of global variables arises from the fact that such use is not explicitly noted in the calling routine so that a program which uses such variables becomes difficult to debug. This objection can be removed by passing information to and from a subroutine by the use of parameters.

Parameters

We assume that you are familiar with the basic concept of a parameter and how it is used in PL/I. If you are not, then you should read an introductory PL/I text for the basic information before proceeding.

The major point which we wish to make is that statements such as

```
CALL SUB(A,B,C);
```

or

```
X = FUNC(R,S,T);
```

explicitly refer to the variables A, B, C, R, S, T. These variables may be used or altered by the subroutine or function. However, because of their explicit mention in a CALL statement, it is easier to trace an error in their values to the actions of the subroutine.

Before discussing the details of how parameters are transmitted, we present some terminology. If a subroutine is invoked by the statement

```
CALL SUB (A,B);
```

and SUB is a routine whose first statement is

```
SUB:    PROC(X,Y);
```

then A and B are called ***actual parameters*** or ***arguments***, and X and Y are called ***formal parameters*** or ***parameters***. We use the terms ***argument*** and ***parameter***.

There are two basic methods of transmitting parameters in PL/I: ***call by reference*** and ***call by dummy argument***. In call by reference, the address of the argument within the calling program is transmitted to the subroutine. For example, consider the following program:

```
INCR:  PROC (X);
          DCL X           FIXED;
          X=X+1;
          RETURN;
       END INCR;
```

Suppose a calling program contained the statements

```
DCL A     FIXED;
A=5;
PUT LIST(A);
CALL INCR(A);
PUT LIST(A);
```

Suppose that the variable A in the calling program is assigned to location 100 in memory. Then all references to A in the calling program are to location 100. This is depicted in Fig. 2.2.1(a). When the first statement PUT LIST(A); is encountered, the content of location 100 (the value 5) is printed out. When SUB is called, the parameter is transmitted by reference, i.e., the address of A (which is 100) is transmitted. Since parameter X corresponds to argument A, the address of X is also 100, and the statement X=X+1; increases the content of location 100 by 1.

Thus after returning from the subroutine, the content of location 100 (which is the value of A) is 6. Therefore the second PUT statement prints 6. In effect, then, any operation performed on a parameter by a subroutine is actually an operation performed on the original argument.

In some cases, call by reference is not practical. These cases occur when:

- The argument is a constant.
- The argument is an expression consisting of more than a single variable.
- The attributes of the argument and the parameter do not match.

In these cases, PL/I uses a call by *dummy argument*. In this type of call a copy of the value of the argument is made in a dummy location within the area of the calling program. The attributes of this dummy location are those specified by the subroutine for its parameter. It is the address of this dummy location that is transmitted to the subroutine. For example, assume the routine INCR above and further assume that the sequence of statements in the calling program is

```
DCL A     FLOAT;
A=5;
PUT LIST(A);
CALL INCR(A);
PUT LIST(A);
```

As before, A is at location 100, so the first PUT LIST prints the value 5 (as a floating-point number). When INCR is called, the mode of transmission is by dummy argument (why?). Thus a dummy area is created, say at location 200, and is initialized to the current content of location 100. The address of this dummy area is passed to the subroutine. Thus when the statement X=X+1; in the subroutine is executed, location 200 is the object of the operation, as shown in Fig. 2.2.1(b). When the program returns, location 100 remains unchanged and the second PUT statement again prints 5. Thus, in a call by dummy argument the value of the original argument cannot be changed.

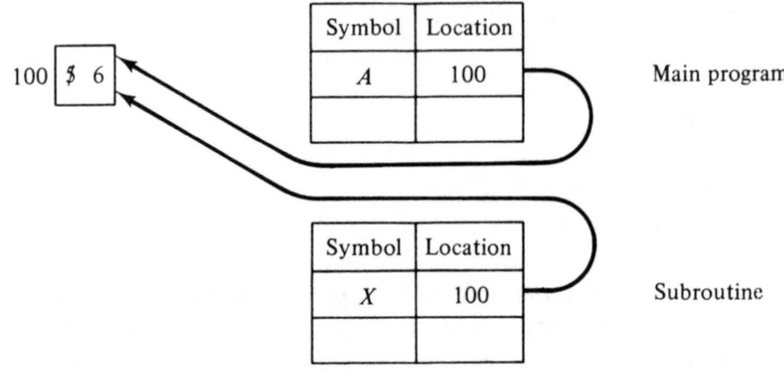

(a) Call by reference.

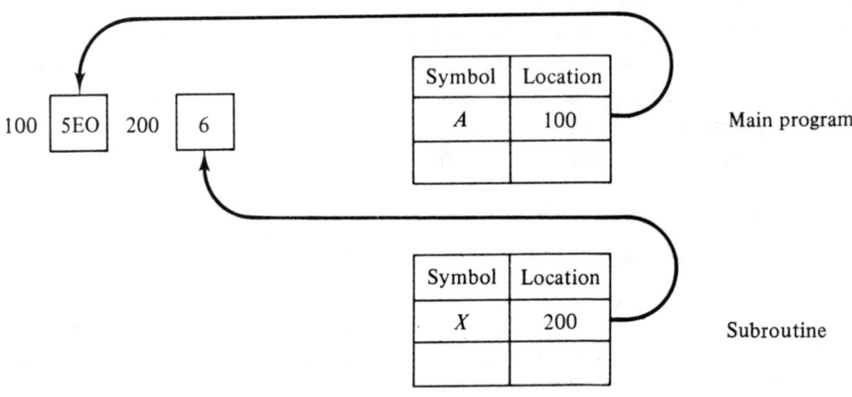

(b) Call by dummy argument.

Figure 2.2.1. Subroutine calls in PL/I.

Just as in the case of a global variable, we may make a distinction between an input parameter and an output parameter. An input parameter is one whose corresponding argument has been assigned a value before the subroutine is called and whose value is used by the subroutine. An output parameter is one which is assigned a value within the subroutine so that its corresponding argument is changed by the subroutine.

For example, consider the following program:

```
MAIN:   PROC OPTIONS(MAIN);
          DCL  X          FIXED INIT(1),
               Y          FIXED,
               Z          FIXED INIT(3),
               W          FIXED;
          W=7;
          CALL SUB (X,Y,Z,W);
```

```
SUB:        PROC(R,S,T,U);
               DCL(R,S,T,U)FIXED;
               PUT SKIP LIST(R);
               S=R+T;
               T=T**2;
               U=12;
               RETURN;
            END SUB;
         END MAIN;
```

All four arguments are passed by reference. R is an input parameter, S is an output parameter, T is both an input and an output parameter, and U is an output parameter.

Note that the passing mechanism (reference or dummy argument) is a property of the argument, while the mode in which a parameter is used (input, output, or both) is a property of the parameter.

An argument which corresponds to an output parameter should not be passed by dummy argument. One of the purposes of a subroutine which has an output parameter is to give a value to the corresponding argument. But if that argument is not passed by reference, then its value is not changed when the output parameter is assigned a value.

It is therefore important for a programmer to understand the function of each of his parameters and to be sure that the corresponding arguments are passed correctly.

Coding the Subroutines

Let us now proceed to examine each of the subroutines of the payroll program and identify its global variables and parameters.

READTAX has a single parameter consisting of a tax table in interval format. This parameter is an output parameter since READTAX initializes this table. READTAX is used to initialize both the federal and state tax tables. Since the same routine is used for all the tables, they must all appear in the same format in the input to the program. Note that this uniform format need not be interval format. READTAX could call on a routine CONVERT which would be responsible for converting the table from the form it appears in the input to the format of the tax tables in the program. The decision as to the exact format of the tables in the input may be postponed until READTAX is actually coded. We leave the coding of the actual routine as an exercise for the reader.

The routine PRINTHEADING does not involve any parameters or global variables at all. It is responsible only for printing a set of character strings as appropriate headings in appropriate columns. This implies that a decision must be made as to the exact format of the employee output table before PRINTHEADING can be coded. We leave this decision and the coding of PRINTHEADING as an exercise for the reader.

READEMP has a single output parameter which represents an employee structure. The routine is responsible for reading an employee's name, social security number, state name, regular and overtime rates, and the hours worked by the employee in each of four weeks from the input, and initializing the corresponding fields in the EMPLOYEE structure. Notice that not all items in EMPLOYEE are changed by this routine. The remaining items retain their old values (these values are changed by other statements in the program). Before coding READEMP, a decision must be made as to the format of the employee input information in the input file. The coding of this routine is also left as an exercise for the reader.

TAX is a function which accepts two input parameters. The first is a gross income and the second is a tax table in interval format. The function TAX returns the amount of tax due on the gross income according to the table. An algorithm to do this is straightforward. Let *#intervals* be the number of intervals to the table, *gross* be the gross income, *lower*(*int*) be the lower limit of the interval *int*, and let *base_tax*(*int*) and *addl_rate*(*int*) be the base tax and the additional rate for interval *int*.

```
/*        search for the correct interval          */
do int = 1 to# intervals while (lower(int) < gross);
end;
int = int-1;

/*     if gross is smaller than the lower limit     */
/*      of the first interval, then pay no tax      */
if int = 0 then return (0);

/*    compute the tax    */
taxamt = base_tax(int) + (gross-lower(int))*addnl_rate(int);
return (taxamt);
```

Note that this algorithm assumes that the intervals are stored in ascending order of lower limit. At this point, the programmer should check the routine READTAX to make sure that the tables are initialized properly. Note also that the programmer must consider all cases, including such remote possibilities as the gross income being smaller than the lowest limit of the table. If READTAX ensured that the lowest limit in each tax table is zero, then it would not be necessary to check for this possibility. However, it would still be a good idea to insert such a test to guard against such unlikely events as *gross* being negative.

The algorithm can be translated directly into a program:

```
TAX:   PROC(GROSS,TABLE) RETURNS(FIXED(9,2));
         DCL GROSS                FIXED(9,2),
               1 TABLE,
                 2 NAME           CHAR(*),       /*       state name        */
                 2 #INTERVALS     FIXED,         /*  number of intervals    */
                 2 INTERVALS(*) ,
                   3 LOWER        FIXED(8,2),    /*      lower bound        */
                   3 BASE_TAX     FIXED(8,2),    /*        base tax         */
                   3 ADDNL_RATE   FIXED(8,2),    /*       additional        */
                                                 /*       percentage        */
               TAXAMT             FIXED(9,2),
               INT                FIXED;
```

```
FINDINT: DO INT=1 TO #INTERVALS WHILE (LOWER(INT)<GROSS);
         END FINDINT;
         INT=INT-1;

         IF INT=0 THEN RETURN(0);
         TAXAMT= BASE_TAX(INT)
                          + (GROSS-LOWER(INT))* ADDNL_RATE (INT);
         RETURN(TAXAMT);
      END TAX;
```

Note that the routine TAX assumes that the largest tax bracket is the one to be used if the GROSS income is greater than the lower limits of all the intervals.

The function FIND accepts a state name as an input parameter and uses the set of state tax tables as an input global variable. It returns the integer between 1 and 5 corresponding to the state name, or 0 if the state name does not exist in the table.

It can be coded as follows:

```
FIND:     PROC(NM)   RETURNS(FIXED);
            DCL NM               CHAR(*),   /*   name of state    */
                ST               FIXED;
SEARCH:     DO ST=1 TO 5;
               IF STATE_TABLE(ST).NAME=NM THEN RETURN(ST);
            END SEARCH;
            RETURN (0);
          END FIND;
```

The routine allows for the possiblity that the state name, as specified in the employee record, is incorrect. It is a good idea to make a program "bugproof" against incorrect data as in the above routine.

Note that FIND uses STATE_TABLE as a global variable rather than as a parameter. There is no reason why this must be so, and there are arguments to be made for either decision. The programmer might wish to use a global variable in order to avoid redeclaring the entire STATE_TABLE array. However, he might wish to use a parameter for documentation purposes so that it is clear that FIND uses the state tax tables.

The result of FIND is used in two different places: in determining which state tax table to use and in determining which element of the array TOTAL_STATE to update.

The routine PRINTTOT is responsible for printing the totals, including TOTAL_GROSS, TOTAL_FED, TOTAL_NET, the total number of employees (EMPNUM), and the total state taxes for each of the five states (the array TOTAL_STATE). All of these are input global variables. The main task of programming PRINTTOT is in deciding how these totals should appear in the final printout. Other global input variables might be used as well. For example, it might be decided to print a message such as:

```
TOTAL STATE TAX FOR CALIF. IS:   XXXXXXX.XX
```

In that case, the array of state names STATE_TABLE. NAME must be an input variable as well. One reason for not specifying the totals as parameters to PRINTTOT is that it is not yet clear what quantities are need by PRINTTOT.

The Final Program

After all the routines have been designed and written, they must be combined into a single program. In doing this, the programmer must decide whether he wishes to place each procedure as an ***internal*** or ***external*** routine.

An internal procedure is one which is inserted within another procedure. Usually, if procedure SUBA is internal to procedure SUBB, SUBA is placed immediately before the statement END SUBB; or immediately after the declarations of SUBB, as shown in Fig. 2.2.2. However, SUBA may be placed between any two statements of SUBB. All the variables declared in SUBB may be used as global variables by SUBA. Additionally, all variables which may be used as global variables in SUBB (for example, if they were declared in SUBC which contains SUBB as an internal routine) may also be used as global variables by SUBA. SUBA may be called from within SUBB or from any other routine which is internal to SUBB, but may not be called from any other routine. For example, the situation of Fig. 2.2.3(a) is illegal because MAIN calls SUBA, but the situation of Fig. 2.2.3(b) is legal.

```
SUBB:   PROC . . . ;
            DCL /* variables of SUBB */ . . . ;
                    . . .
            /* body of SUBB */
                    . . .
SUBA:       PROC . . . ;
                DCL /* local variables and parameters of SUBA */ . . . ;
                    . . .
                /* body of SUBA */
                    . . .
            END SUBA ;
        END SUBB ;
```

(a)

```
SUBB:   PROC . . . ;
            DCL /* variables of SUBB */ . . . ;
SUBA:       PROC . . . ;
                DCL /* local variables and parameters of SUBA */ . . . ;
                    . . .
                /* body of SUBA */
                    . . .
            END SUBA ;
                    . . .
            /* body of SUBB */
                    . . .
        END SUBB ;
```

(b)

Figure 2.2.2. Placement of an internal routine.

```
MAIN:   PROC  OPTIONS (MAIN) ;
              . . .
              CALL SUBB ;
              . . .
              CALL SUBA ;
              . . .
SUBB:         PROC . . . ;
              . . .
                CALL SUBA ;
                . . .
SUBA:           PROC . . . ;
                . . .
                END SUBA ;
              END SUBB ;
        END MAIN;
```

(a)

```
MAIN:   PROC  OPTIONS (MAIN) ;
              . . .
              CALL SUBB ;
              CALL SUBA ;
              . . .
SUBB:         PROC . . . ;
              . . .
                CALL SUBA ;
                . . .
              END SUBB ;
SUBA:         PROC . . . ;
              . . .
              END SUBA ;
        END   MAIN ;
```

(b)

Figure 2.2.3. Illegal and legal calling patterns.

An external routine is one which is not contained within any other routine. Each installation has a different method of linking a set of external procedures into a single program. An external procedure may safely be used in one program and later in another. Figure 2.2.4 illustrates a set of external procedures formed into a program. Note that any external procedure may call any other as long as they have been linked together into a single program. The ENTRY attribute should be declared for any external procedure name which is referenced within a procedure. Because the requirements for ENTRY attributes are compiler-dependent, we do not discuss them here. For further details, see a PL/I text or manual.

An external procedure may not use any global variables since it is not contained within any other procedure. Although it is possible for two external procedures to access the same variable if it is declared in both procedures with the EXTERNAL attribute, the usual method of communication between two external procedures is through parameters (or by having one procedure write something onto a file which is to be read by the other procedure). This means that an external procedure is truly an independent module. A disadvantage of using an external procedure is that it must be linked to the other external procedures of the program. The main procedure of a program is always external.

In the case of the payroll program, the procedures FIND and PRINTTOT use global

```
MAIN:   PROC OPTIONS (MAIN) ;
                 ...
              CALL SUBB ;
                 ...
              CALL SUBC ;
        END MAIN ;
```
A card which is dependent on the installation goes here.
```
SUBB:   PROC . . . ;
          ...
          CALL SUBA ;
        END SUBB ;
```
A card which is dependent on the installation goes here.
```
SUBA:   PROC . . . ;
          ...
        END SUBA ;
```
A card which is dependent on the installation goes here.
```
SUBC:   PROC . . . ;
            ...
            CALL SUBB ;
        END SUBC ;
```

Figure 2.2.4. External procedures.

variables and therefore must be internal to PAYROLL. The other procedures may be either internal or external.

The purpose of going through the payroll program was not to solve that problem itself; we assume that students who have had an introductory course in programming are capable of handling such a problem. Rather, it is to present a general method of proceeding from a problem to its solution. The first step in producing a solution is a complete understanding of the problem. Once the problem is specified, it is a good idea to outline the solution in the form of an algorithm. This allows the programmer to see what parts of the problem are still vague. To the extent that the programmer is involved in program specification, he can make the final version more efficient and easier to write.

The above example has illustrated how a common data processing problem goes through several stages between the initial problem statement and the final solution. Most of these stages are related to the refinement of the problem statement. The process of refining the payroll algorithm uncovers no earthshaking computational techniques; rather it points out what data is to be kept in memory and how data may be processed and destroyed. Also, it points out the need for clarifying how data is to be input to and output from the program, something which is usually relegated to subroutines.

Finally, this method points to the deficiencies of the solution, i.e., limitations on what the final program can and cannot do. For example, the tax tables are assumed to be all of the same format; in reality, each state may use a different method to compute its withholding tax. In addition, the company may need to keep records on total taxes paid to date for each employee to aid in end-of-year reports. This is one aspect which our program ignores completely.

Choosing an Algorithm

Although the payroll program is typical of a great many real-world data processing problems, there are a great many other problems which present quite different challenges to the programmer. One important feature of the payroll problem is that the algorithm for its solution is straightforward and fairly "obvious." The main work in developing the payroll program is in refining the algorithm, choosing the data structures, and organizing the entire program. Very little work was necessary to decide the basic method by which the problem was to be solved. To be sure, we did present two different methods of solution, but both were immediately apparent and one was seen to be clearly superior to the other.

A different class of problems exists for which the choice of algorithm is a difficult chore. For such problems, it is often difficult to be sure that a solution exists at all. Even if a solution does exist, that solution might not be unique. If a unique solution is known to exist, there may still not be any known method to find that solution. Finally, even if a method is known, that method may be so inefficient in terms of time and space that it is impractical even for modern computers.

To illustrate this, let us consider the well-known problem of finding a needle in a haystack. One method for its solution is to toss the haystack with a pitchfork until the needle is found. Unfortunately, there is no guarantee that this method will ever find the needle.

A solution which is more certain of termination is to sift through the haystack straw by straw, carting away each straw as it is examined until the needle is found. Since the number of straws in the haystack is finite, eventually all the straws will have been removed and either the needle will have been found in the process or the needle remains alone on the barn floor. (We presume the floor has no cracks.) Certainly the solution works, but the cost in time is prohibitive.

Another solution is to place an extremely powerful electromagnet above the haystack while vibrating the entire stack. The needle will be attracted to the magnet, and the vibrations will loosen the straws sufficiently to allow the needle to rise to the top. We might be sure that the solution will work in short enough time, but the cost of such a powerful electromagnet and vibrating equipment is prohibitive.

A great deal of problem solving by computer involves the search for efficient algorithms. Many such efficient algorithms depend on clever insights into the true nature of the original problem. There are no general guidelines for the development of clever algorithms as there are for the development of an algorithm into a program. Usually, a great deal of study and hard work precedes the discovery of such algorithms.

However, in the short history of computer science, many such problems have been attacked and many clever algorithms have been discovered. The more frequently a problem must be solved, the more likely it is that someone has already come up with a solution. Further, when an efficient algorithm is discovered, it is usually found to be applicable to a wide group of similar problems. Therefore it is important for a good programmer to have a large "bag of tricks;" that is, to know a large class of techniques so that he can reach into his bag of tricks to come up with the right solution. Of course, another element in the art of programming is knowing which solution to apply to which problem. Still another element is knowing how to tailor a particular solution to the peculiar needs of a specific problem.

Let us analyze a problem which is specified quite simply and examine several algorithms for its solution. These algorithms are not obvious (although they are neither overly complicated nor farfetched) and illustrate the kinds of decisions which must be made.

Consider the problems of generating prime numbers. A ***prime number*** is an integer greater than 1 whose only proper divisors are itself and 1. Thus 2, 3, 5, and 71 are primes but 8 (=2*4), 15 (=3*5), and 93 (=31*3) are not. There is not much to be gained from a long discussion of inputs/outputs and problem specification. We desire a program to read a number *n* and to enumerate the first *n* prime numbers in an array *p*. Thus the inputs and outputs are simply defined; we need supply only the algorithm, its data structures, and a program.

We can approach the problem directly and use the following global method:

```
do i=1 to n;
   p(i) = ith prime number;
end;
```

Clearly this algorithm solves the problem, providing we can produce some method to implement the "*i*th prime number" routine. However, we note that it is unnecessary to be able to determine the *i*th prime number given an arbitrary integer *i*. Rather, it is sufficient to be able to find the next prime after a given number. The first two prime numbers are 2 and 3, and each succeeding prime number *p*(*i*) can be found from *p*(*i*–1) by the following method:

```
cand = p(i–1)+2;
do while ( ¬ prime (cand));
   cand=cand+2;
end;
p(i)=cand;
```

The variable *cand* takes on the value of the next candidate for a prime number. All primes greater than 2 are odd (since an even number is divisible by 2), so that only odd numbers need be considered as candidates. The above algorithm sequences through all odd numbers greater than *p*(*i*–1) until it finds one which is a prime. The function *prime*(*cand*) returns the logical value *true* if *cand* is a prime and *false* otherwise.

The next task, then, is to develop an algorithm for the function *prime*. To determine if *cand* is a prime, it is necessary to test all possible divisors of *cand* other than 1 and *cand* itself. If such a divisor is found, then *cand* is not a prime; otherwise, it is. It suffices to test only for divisors that are less than or equal to the square root of *cand* (why?). Also it is only necessary to test for prime divisors (why?). Thus the function *prime* can be coded as follows:

```
temp=sqrt(cand);
do j=1 to i–1 while (p (j) ≤ temp);
   if mod(cand,p(j))=0 then return (false);
end;
return (true);
```

The algorithm uses the *mod* function which returns the remainder of its first argument divided by its second. Incorporating these modules into a single program produces a working solution to the problem. A sample program using this algorithm follows:

```
GEN_PRIMES: PROC OPTIONS (MAIN);
              DCL N                              FIXED;
              GET LIST(N);
              BEGIN;
                DCL P(N)                         FIXED,
                    (I,CAND)                     FIXED;

                P(1)=2;
                P(2)=3;
LOOP:           DO I=3 TO N;
                  CAND=P(I-1)+2;
TEST:             DO WHILE ( ¬PRIME(CAND));
                    CAND=CAND+2;
                  END TEST;
                  P(I)=CAND;
                END LOOP;

                /*    print primes    */
                PUT SKIP EDIT ('THE FIRST',N,'PRIME NUMBERS ARE')
                              (A,F(8),X(1),A);
PRNT:           DO I=1 TO N;
                   PUT SKIP EDIT(I,P(I)) (F(10));
                END PRNT;

PRIME:          PROC(CAND) RETURNS(BIT(1));
                  DCL (CAND,J,TEMP)               FIXED;

                  TEMP=SQRT(CAND);
TRY:              DO J=1 TO I-1 WHILE (P(J)<=TEMP);
                     IF MOD (CAND,P(J))=0 THEN RETURN ('0'B);
                  END TRY;
                  RETURN('1'B);
                END PRIME;

              END;
            END GEN_PRIMES;
```

Have we satisfactorily written a program to generate prime numbers? The answer is that "it depends." Given unlimited machine time, and enough time to wait for the answer, then we have a working solution. Clearly, storage space presents no problem because our storage needs consist only of an array P and several simple variables. Suppose that this program is used to generate 10, 100, or even 1000 primes. While the execution times for these cases grow rapidly, they are within reason for most machines. However, suppose a program is asked to generate 10,000, 100,000, or 1 million primes. Would the program work as well (or would it even work at all)? The answer depends, of course, on the resources available to the user and on the speed of the machine. You are asked to run the program for various values of N as an exercise and measure its speed (or lack of it). It will become evident that as N becomes very large the time requirements of the program increase even more, to the point where the program becomes unusable. Thus for large values of N it will be necessary to use some other method, if one can be found.

It frequently turns out that where one algorithm is not satisfactory because of the overhead it places on execution time or space, a second algorithm might be found to be more suitable in these respects. For example, in our problem there is another well known method to generate prime numbers known as the ***sieve of Eratosthenes***. While this method also ultimately succumbs to limitations of time and space, it turns out to be faster than the previous method and is therefore usable in some cases where the previous method is not.

The logic behind the sieve of Eratosthenes is that instead of examining each candidate to determine if it is prime, each of the primes generated thus far may be used to eliminate all its multiples. To see how this works, consider the list of numbers in Fig. 2.2.5. This list represents the set of all candidates less than or equal to 23. Begin by asserting that 2 is a prime so that all multiples of 2 may be eliminated (line 2). The next number is 3, and since it has not been eliminated, it is not a multiple of any smaller prime and is therefore a prime. All multiples of 3 are then eliminated (line 3). The next number not eliminated is 5, which is the next prime. All multiples of 5 that were not already removed should now be removed, but there are no such numbers in the list. This same process is repeated for all numbers remaining in the list. When all the numbers have been processed, the numbers remaining in the list are the set of primes less than or equal to 23.

Line 1:	2	3	4	5	6	7	8	9	10	11	12	13	14	15	16	17	18	19	20	21	22	23
Line 2:	2	3	~~4~~	5	~~6~~	7	~~8~~	9	~~10~~	11	~~12~~	13	~~14~~	15	~~16~~	17	~~18~~	19	~~20~~	21	~~22~~	23
Line 3:	2	3	~~4~~	5	~~6~~	7	~~8~~	~~9~~	~~10~~	11	~~12~~	13	~~14~~	~~15~~	~~16~~	17	~~18~~	19	~~20~~	~~21~~	~~22~~	23

Figure 2.2.5. The Sieve of Eratosthenes.

Let us write an algorithm using this method. One problem immediately encountered is that the process begins with an initial set of numbers and it is not clear how large this set must be since the size of the nth prime is not known. For simplicity we rephrase the problem to compute all prime numbers less than or equal to m, rather than to compute the first n prime numbers.

Suppose an array of bits $a(2{:}m)$ is declared, where $a(j)$ equals '1'B if j is a candidate for a prime and $a(j)$ equals '0'B if j has been removed from the list of candidates. All the elements of the array are initialized to '1'B, and individual bits are changed to '0'B when their array indexes are found to be multiples of already known primes. The algorithm may be outlined as follows:

```
read(m);
/*   initialize    */
do i=2 to m;
   a(i)='1'B;
end;

cand=2;
do while (cand<=m);
   /*   find next prime    */
   do cand=cand to m while ( ¬a(cand));
   end;

   /*         cand is the next prime          */
   /*     remove all multiples of cand        */
   do j=cand**2 by cand to m;
      a(j)='0'B;
   end;
   cand=cand+1;
end;
```

The set of numbers j for which $a(j)$ equals '1'B is the set of all primes less than or equal to m.

The actual coding of this algorithm is left as an exercise. However, it should be clear that the algorithm requires that a significant amount of space be set aside for the elimination process. Moreover, in the case where the problem actually requires the computation of the first n primes rather than all primes less than m, it is not clear how large to declare the initial array a. (It can be shown that there is an upper bound on the nth prime, but this is usually a gross overestimate and would require a tremendous amount of wasted space.)

Let us see if the algorithm can be modified so that it makes more efficient use of memory. In the first algorithm, a nonprime is recognized as such only after it becomes a candidate for the next prime. In the second algorithm, a nonprime is recognized as soon as one of its factors is discovered to be prime. The third algorithm which we now present is similar to both of these methods.

For each already discovered prime $p(i)$, let $e(i)$ be the next multiple of $p(i)$ which might be recognized as a nonprime because it is a multiple of $p(i)$. Initially, $e(i)$ equals the square of $p(i)$ since any nonprime number smaller than $(p(i))^2$ can be recognized as a multiple of a prime smaller than $p(i)$ (why?). When the current value of $e(i)$ is recognized as a nonprime, $e(i)$ is increased by $p(i)$. Similarly, when a value larger than $e(i)$ becomes a candidate for a prime, $e(i)$ can also be increased by $p(i)$ since all smaller candidates have already been recognized as nonprimes.

The method used to determine whether a candidate *cand* is a prime or not is the following. Suppose the first k primes have been found and *cand* is being considered as a candidate for the (k+1)th prime. Search the array e starting at $e(1)$. For each position i in the array e, perform the following operation. If $e(i)$ is equal to *cand*, then *cand* is not a prime. Increment $e(i)$ by $p(i)$ and proceed to the next candidate. If $e(i)$ is greater than *cand*, then proceed to compare *cand* against $e(i+1)$ (unless i equals k, in which case *cand* is the (k+1)th prime so that $p(k+1)$ is set to *cand* and $e(k+1)$ is set to $cand^2$). If $e(i)$ is smaller than *cand*, increment $e(i)$ by $p(i)$ repeatedly until it is greater than or equal to *cand* and then take the action appropriate for that case.

To illustrate the process, consider Fig. 2.2.6, which illustrates the contents of the arrays p and e in processing candidates 27 through 35. After candidate 26 has been processed, the arrays p and e are as in Fig. 2.2.6(a). To process *cand*=27, *cand* is first compared to $e(1)$=28. Since 27<28, $e(1)$ is unchanged and *cand* is compared to $e(2)$. Since they are equal (27 is a multiple of $p(2)$), 27 is recognized as a nonprime. Thus, the value of $e(2)$ is increased by $p(2)$ to become 30, and the next candidate (28) is processed (Fig. 2.2.6(b)). Since 28 equals $e(1)$, it is a nonprime; $e(1)$ is increased by $p(1)$, and 29 is processed (Fig. 2.2.6(c)). 29 is smaller than every entry in the e array, so it is a prime. It is therefore added as $p(10)$, and $e(10)$ is set to its square (Fig. 2.2.6(d)). Then 30 is processed. It is equal to $e(1)$, so it is nonprime and $e(1)$ is increased (Fig. 2.2.6(e)).

The processing of 31 is more interesting. 31 is less than $e(1)$, so $e(1)$ is left un-

	After *cand* = 26		After *cand* = 27		After *cand* = 28		After *cand* = 29	
i	$p(i)$	$e(i)$	$p(i)$	$e(i)$	$p(i)$	$e(i)$	$p(i)$	$e(i)$
1	2	28	2	28	2	30	2	30
2	3	27	3	30	3	30	3	30
3	5	30	5	30	5	30	5	30
4	7	49	7	49	7	49	7	49
5	11	121	11	121	11	121	11	121
6	13	169	13	169	13	169	13	169
7	17	289	17	289	17	289	17	289
8	19	361	19	361	19	361	19	361
9	23	529	23	529	23	529	23	529
10							29	841
11								
	(a)		(b)		(c)		(d)	

After *cand* = 30		After *cand* = 31		After *cand* = 32		After *cand* = 33		After *cand* = 34		After *cand* = 35	
2	32	2	32	2	34	2	34	2	36	2	36
3	30	3	33	3	33	3	36	3	36	3	36
5	30	5	35	5	35	5	35	5	35	5	40
7	49	7	49	7	49	7	49	7	49	7	49
11	121	11	121	11	121	11	121	11	121	11	121
13	169	13	169	13	169	13	169	13	169	13	169
17	289	17	289	17	289	17	289	17	289	17	289
19	361	19	361	19	361	19	361	19	361	19	361
23	529	23	529	23	529	23	529	23	529	23	529
29	841	29	841	29	841	29	841	29	841	29	841
		31	961	31	961	31	961	31	961	31	961
(e)		(f)		(g)		(h)		(i)		(j)	

Figure 2.2.6. The arrays p and e.

changed. 31 is greater than $e(2)$, so $e(2)$ is increased by 3. Now 31 is less than $e(2)$, so it is compared to $e(3)$. 31 is greater than $e(3)$, so $e(3)$ is increased by 5. Now 31 is less than $e(3)$, so it is compared to $e(4)$. 31 is less than $e(4)$ through $e(10)$, so it is established as a prime. $p(11)$ is set to 31 and $e(11)$ is set to its square (Fig. 2.2.6(f)). The reader is invited to trace the process through *cand*=35 and compare the results with Fig. 2.2.6(g) through (j).

Several modifications are obvious from this illustration as well as from the discussion of the first algorithm. First of all, even numbers greater than 2 need not be considered as candidates. They will always equal the current value of $e(1)$. Second, odd numbers need not be compared against $e(1)$ since they are always less than $e(1)$. Third, since only odd numbers are candidates and since they never need be compared against $e(1)$, the value of $e(1)$ is irrelevant to the algorithm. Thus, it need not be updated. Fourth, the value of $e(i)$ may be incremented by $2*p(i)$ since $e(i)$ is initially odd (all primes greater than 2 are odd, and the square of an odd number is odd). Adding $p(i)$ which is also odd produces an even number, but even numbers are not considered as candidates. By incrementing $e(i)$ by $2*p(i)$, $e(i)$ always equals an odd multiple of $p(i)$. Fifth, it is only necessary to compare *cand* against $e(i)$ for those i for which $p(i) \leqslant sqrt(cand)$. This is because if $p(i) > sqrt(cand)$ and *cand* is a multiple of $p(i)$, then there is a $j<i$ such that *cand* is a multiple of $p(j)$.

Figure 2.2.7 illustrates the revised method for *cand* between 27 and 35. The algorithm to find the first n primes by this method is as follows:

```
/*    last is the number of the last prime found      */
last=1;
/*                initialize the p table              */
p(1)=2;
/*   test all candidates   */
do cand=3 by 2 while(last<n);
   if prime(cand) then do;
                           last=last+1;
                           p(last)=cand;
                           e(last)=cand**2;
                        end;
end;
```

The function *prime(cand)* returns *true* or *false* and uses the following algorithm:

```
x=sqrt(cand);
do i=2 to last while (p(i)<x);
   do while (e(i)<cand);
      e(i)=e(i)+2*p(i);
   end;
   if e(i)=cand then do;   /*   cand is not prime     */
                           e(i)=e(i)+2*p(i);
                           return (false);
                     end;
end;
/*   cand is a prime   */
return (true);
```

	After *cand* = 25		After *cand* = 27		After *cand* = 29		After *cand* = 31		After *cand* = 33		After *cand* = 35	
i	$p(i)$	$e(i)$	$p(i)$	$e(i)$	$p(i)$	$e(i)$	$p(i)$	$e(i)$	$p(i)$	$e(i)$	$p(i)$	$e(i)$
1	2		2		2		2		2		2	
2	3	27	3	33	3	33	3	33	3	39	3	39
3	5	35	5	35	5	35	5	35	5	35	5	40
4	7	49	7	49	7	49	7	49	7	49	7	49
5	11	121	11	121	11	121	11	121	11	121	11	121
6	13	169	13	169	13	169	13	169	13	169	13	169
7	17	289	17	289	17	289	17	289	17	289	17	289
8	19	361	19	361	19	361	19	361	19	361	19	361
9	23	529	23	529	23	529	23	529	23	529	23	529
10					29	841	29	841	29	941	29	841
11							31	961	31	961	31	961
	(a)		(b)		(c)		(d)		(e)		(f)	

Figure 2.2.7. The revised method.

We have not discussed the question of the relative efficiency of the routines. That is, for what values of n is one algorithm more efficient than the others and at what point do they all become impractical? We leave these questions as exercises.

2.3. Program Reliability

Let us summarize the stages of the program development process. We start with a possibly imprecise problem statement. The problem statement is refined so that it is clear exactly what the inputs to the program are and exactly what outputs are expected of it. An algorithm for solution is chosen; this algorithm might be well known or it might be one which the programmer has to derive on his own. The algorithm contains several statements which can be translated directly into a programming language. Others are vague in that they specify only that some task be done without specifying how. Such statements require further clarification and are usually specified by a subalgorithm. This subalgorithm may, in turn, require other subalgorithms. This process continues until the lowest-level algorithms can be readily translated into program statements. In the course of developing each algorithm, the data structures that must be used in its implementation are specified.

Once the algorithms have been written, they can be translated into actual code. If the programmer follows the coding suggestions of the previous sections, the resulting program will be easy to read, understand, and modify. The programmer might congratulate himself on a job well done.

Or are such congratulations a bit premature? It would seem that the programmer should be able to answer some questions about the program. The first question is: "Does it work?" If a program does not work, then it is worthless regardless of how well it was planned or how nicely the code is documented or how neat the output looks. A "yes" answer to the question of whether a program works requires that the program always works, and not just sometimes. The program that fails to work only for certain inputs in exceptional cases will invariably be presented with just those inputs in just those cases and will, of course, fail to work.

Even if a program does work, the question arises "How well does it work?" If a payroll program that is to be run on a machine with two hours of available time requires eight hours to run, then that program is of no help to the user. Efficiency may seem at times to be an academic question, but when one is programming on a real machine with real constraints, the question may become crucial.

Questions of whether a program works, and if so, how well, form the subject of ***program reliability***. Throughout the remainder of this section we consider some areas of program reliability. It is not possible to cover all aspects of reliability because there is no general way of determining whether an arbitrary program does what it is supposed to for all inputs within specific time and space constraints. However, if a programmer avoids some obvious blunders and makes a strong effort to program properly, he strongly improves the chances that his program is correct and does not require an exorbitant amount of resources.

In this section, we consider three major questions in program reliability: "Is the algorithm correct?" "Does the program produce the results intended by the algorithm?" "Is the program reasonably efficient?"

Program Correctness

A logic error reflects a serious flaw in the programmed solution which cannot be attributed to its implementation. As a trivial example consider the following problem and proposed solution, both in algorithmic and program form. Suppose it is necessary to read two numbers from data cards and to compute and print out their sum. The following is a proposed algorithm solution.

```
read(n1,n2);
ans=n1*n2;
print(ans);
```

To implement the above algorithm as a program, we can code:

```
SOL:  PROC OPTIONS(MAIN);
        DCL   (N1,N2)    FIXED,         /*  input numbers   */
              ANS        FIXED;         /*     answer       */
        GET LIST(N1, N2);
        ANS=N1*N2;
        PUT SKIP EDIT('ANSWER IS',ANS) (A,X(1),F(5));
      END SOL;
```

The above solution is obviously incorrect, but it is important to understand where its fault lies. A casual reader of the problem statement and the program SOL might say that the error is a keypunch error (an '∗' was typed instead of a '+'). However, the reader who has followed the solution from start to finish should note that the program is a correct implementation of the algorithm given above. In fact the program is correct; it only solves the "wrong problem." The real mistake in this case is in the algorithm; instead of adding two numbers, it multiplies them. Such an error is called a logic error and is one of the most difficult errors to find. (In fact, if the programmer tests the program using the inputs 2 and 2, he will not even know that there is anything wrong with it.)

How does one ascertain that a program is logically correct? There is no easy answer to this question. In some cases, as in the above example, it is possible to verify by inspection whether a program is correct or not. In fact, most programs that require only that a set of computations be done can be verified for correctness in this way. However, most programs that do any substantial computation normally involve conditional executions and loops. Such control structures are not as easy to follow, especially if the number of iterations through a loop is variable.

There are methods that can be used to determine whether a program is correct. One of these is ***symbolic execution***. In this method, the program is executed for symbolic values of its inputs rather than on a sample set of values (which may not identify errors which occur for a different sample). At the end of the program, it is necessary to show that the symbolic values of the computed expressions do indeed satisfy the requirements specified in the problem statement. For example, consider the problem of computing the smallest of three numbers. A sample program might be the following:

```
        SMALL = A;
        IF B<SMALL  THEN SMALL=B;
        IF C<SMALL  THEN SMALL=C;
                /* at this point SMALL is the smallest of A, B, and C  */
```

A symbolic execution of the above program can proceed in one of several ways. One method is to assign symbolic values to each of the input variables (A, B, and C) and to trace through the execution for each possible set of values. For example, suppose we assign the values a, b, and c to the variables A, B, and C respectively. Assuming that A, B, and C are all distinct (this is by no means guaranteed), there are six possible relations among a, b, and c:

1. $a < b < c$
2. $a < c < b$
3. $b < a < c$
4. $b < c < a$
5. $c < a < b$
6. $c < b < a$

In order to show that the program is correct, it is necessary to simulate the execution of the program for each of the possible relations 1 through 6 above. If the program is correct for each of those cases (plus those cases where two or three of the inputs are equal), then it can be considered correct.

Let us illustrate how to trace the execution for one such relation, say (4). We trace through the actions of the program line by line. Initially, A=a, B=b, and C=c. To the right of each line we show the values of each of the program variables (A, B, C, and SMALL) after execution of that line.

Code	A	B	C	SMALL
Start of program	*a*	*b*	*c*	—
SMALL=A;	*a*	*b*	*c*	*a*
IF B<SMALL THEN SMALL=B;	*a*	*b*	*c*	*b*
IF C<SMALL THEN SMALL=C;	*a*	*b*	*c*	*b*
end of program	*a*	*b*	*c*	*b*

This shows that in case 4 the above program segment does indeed compute the smallest of A, B, and C (namely B). To prove that the program works in all cases, it would be necessary to simulate the execution of the code for the other five cases.

A similar approach to ascertaining program validity which also involves symbolic execution involves the construction of an ***execution tree*** to simulate the execution of the program. A sample execution tree for the above program is shown in Fig. 2.3.1. In that figure, each of the circled numbers (called a ***node*** of the tree) represents a line number in the program (2.5 and 3.5 represent the THEN clauses of the respective IF statements). As execution proceeds through each node in the tree, the respective values of A, B, C, and SMALL are noted adjacent to it. Based on an initial assumption at step 0, we can proceed down the tree until a STOP node is reached. Such a node signals the end of the program. At this point it can be easily verified whether or not the program does, in fact, produce the required results.

For example, let us use this tree to trace the execution of the program for case 4 in which $b<c<a$. At node 0, SMALL has no value, but at nodes 1 and 2 its value is a. At node 2, the left branch is taken (since $b<a$), and at nodes 2.5 and 3, the value of SMALL is b. At node 3, the right branch is taken (since $c>b$), so execution proceeds to node 4 (where SMALL is b) and halts. The value of SMALL is b, which is indeed the smallest of the three inputs in this case. Thus, the program is correct for this case. If the remaining five cases can also be validated, the correctness of the program can be established.

Unfortunately, methods such as symbolic execution or the use of an execution tree are not helpful in most cases. There are two primary reasons for this. First, the number of different initial possibilities is usually significantly larger than six. (Even in this case, for example, we ignored the possibility that two or more of the variables are equal.) Thus even in a relatively simple program, tracing through all the different possibilities might prove too tedious. Furthermore, the actions taken by complicated statements may not lend themselves to easy subdivision. For example, if one of the statements in a program computes the root of a quadratic equation using the quadratic formula

```
X = (–B + SQRT(B**2 – 4*A*C))/(2*A);
```

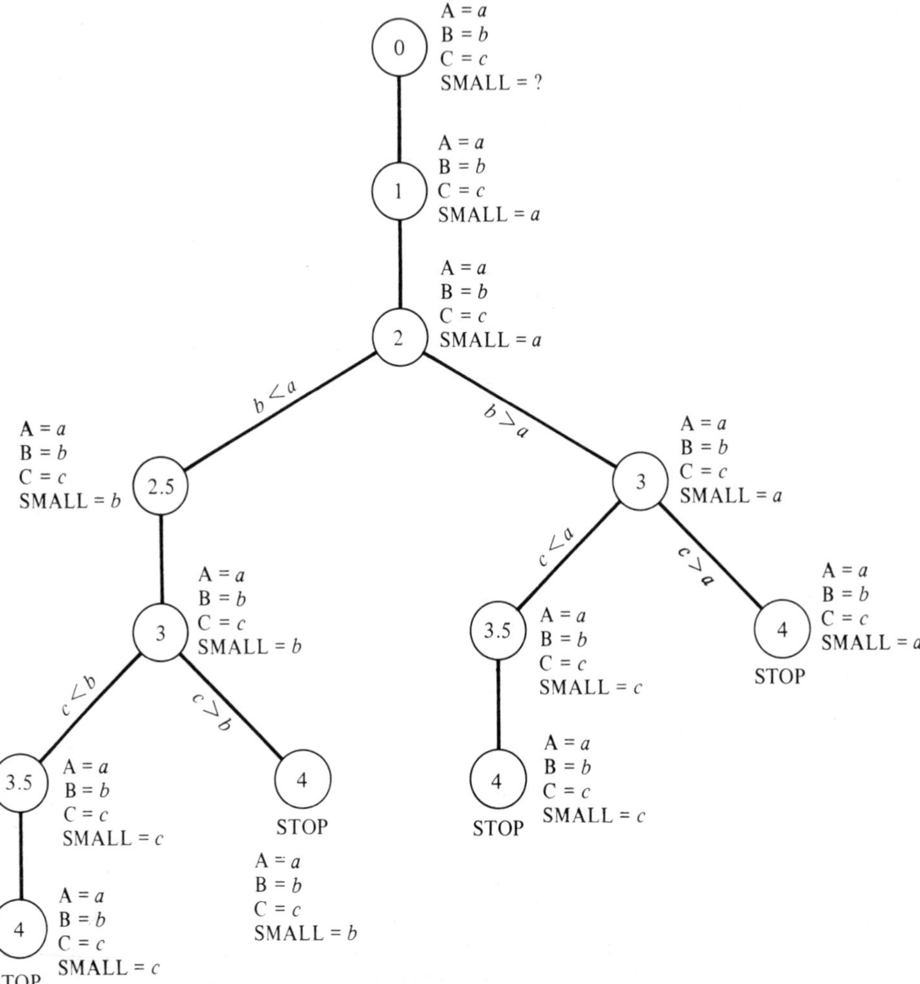

Figure 2.3.1. A sample execution tree.

and then the value of X is tested for being positive or negative, it is difficult to determine whether X is positive or negative without knowing more about A, B, and C. This would necessitate a further subdivision of the number of cases, thus generating even more possibilities to consider.

Even more important, however, are the problems that arise in the treatment of loops. In most cases the number of iterations through a loop is represented by a variable or by the satisfaction of a set of conditions. In this case, symbolic execution or use of an execution tree could involve an infinite number of cases or nodes. Of course, it is impossible to test all possibilities in an infinite set. The only real way to prove that a set of conditions is satisfied by such a program is to use mathematical induction. Some of you may already know about this technique; others may not. In practice, even programmers who are well versed in mathematics find such techniques too difficult or troublesome to perform on every single program written.

Thus it is necessary to rely on techniques that are less than perfect for verifying program correctness. Such techniques are not always perfect, but can help eliminate logic errors when combined with good programming practice and common sense. The programmer should code all logical portions of the program as separate entities. Each of these entities should be preceded by a comment describing the state of affairs before that portion of the program is executed. This is particularly important in the case of loops. Each portion of the code should be written clearly so that the reader who understands the situation before the code is executed should be able to understand the situation after that portion of code is executed. If any portion of the code is unclear, it should be documented more fully, with an explanation of precisely what actions are to be taken.

If this process is followed consistently from the beginning of the program to its end, then the program includes, as comments, a series of assertions about the values of the program variables. The code of the program should read as proof that a particular assertion is valid, based on the previous assertion and the code between the two assertions. Thus the reader should be able to follow the transformations of the program variables from start to finish. If the transformations imply that the desired output is not correct, then there is something wrong with the logic of the program.

A related approach to proving a program correct is to use ***invariant relationships*** in describing the execution of a loop. An invariant relationship is one that holds true throughout the loop, regardless of any transformations that take place on the program variables within the loop. By using such relationships (when they can be found), one can sometimes prove conclusively that the program does do what it was intended to.

Let us consider an example. Suppose it is desired to reverse the elements of an array (e.g., if an array of seven elements contains 3, 8, 2, 7, 6, 4, 9, after the transformation it should contain 9, 4, 6, 7, 2, 8, 3). There are several approaches to solving this problem. One of these is to declare an auxiliary array of the same size as the original array and to fill the second array with the elements of the first in the reverse order. A second approach is to start with the first element of the array and interchange it with the last element. Then advance to the second element and interchange it with the next to the last. This process continues until the middle two elements have been interchanged (if there are an even number of elements in the array) or the middle element has been reached (if there are an odd number of elements). Clearly, the second approach is more efficient in terms of space than the first.

A simple program to implement this approach is seen on page 122.

The following invariant relationship describes the state of affairs each time the body of the loop is about to be executed: All values of A between position 1 and START–1 (if any) and their counterparts between FIN+1 and N (if any) have been interchanged. Those elements of the array between positions START and FIN inclusive must yet be interchanged. To verify this contention, note that it is true initially (initially there are no elements between 1 and START–1) and after each interchange START and FIN are adjusted so that it remains true. Figure 2.3.2 illustrates this state of affairs.

```
REV:    PROC(A,N);

              /*  program to reverse the N elements of A  */
            DCL (A(*),N,START,FIN)   FIXED;
            START=1;
            FIN=N;
LOOP:       DO WHILE(START<FIN);
                /*  interchange  */
                HOLD=A(START);
                A(START)=A(FIN);
                A(FIN)=HOLD;
                /*  adjust pointers  */
                START=START+1;
                FIN=FIN-1;
            END LOOP;
            RETURN;
          END REV;
```

To use the invariant relationship to show that the program is correct, note that initially START and FIN are at 1 and N respectively, implying that the entire array must be reversed. At the conclusion of the algorithm START and FIN are at the same position (if there are an odd number of elements in the array) or FIN is 1 less than START (if there are an even number of elements in the array). In either case the area in the middle of "elements not yet interchanged" has shrunk to 0. Thus as the program proceeds, the array goes from its initial state to its final one in which the array is reversed.

One crucial point that should be noted is that the program stops as soon as it is finished (START>=FIN), i.e., as soon as the middle area vanishes. Were this not the case (e.g., if the loop was governed by the statement DO START=1 TO N),the program would proceed to interchange elements that had already been interchanged, negating the work previously done. This would, of course, make the program incorrect.

To summarize then, this method of proof is based on an invariant relation about the status of the system variables during execution of the loop. By noting the initial condi-

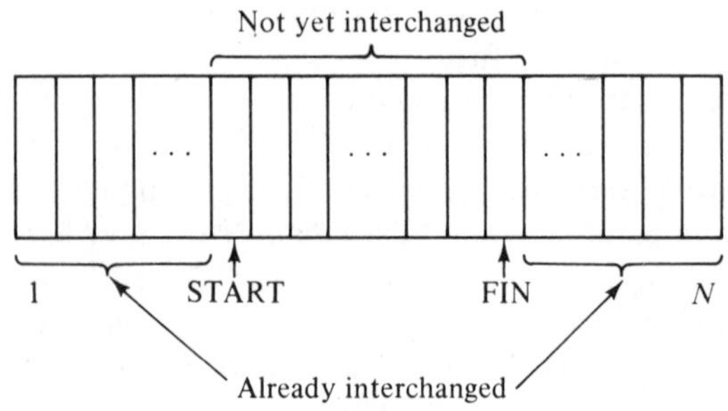

Figure 2.3.2. Reversing the elements of an array.

tions before the start of the loop and the conditions under which control leaves the loop, the actions of a program can be verified.

Invariant relationships always exist, but they are not necessarily easy to find. If the control structure of a loop is such that control may leave under any of 17 different alternate conditions and the body of the loop contains 137 statements including 18 nested loops, it is difficult to discover invariant statements about the loop. Even if one can be found, it is difficult to use in a proof because of the complexity of the initial and final conditions. Attempting a proof in such a case is probably a waste of time.

Thus we have discovered another argument for simplicity. In theory, one should be able to prove the correctness of every program submitted as correct. In reality, however, this is not always possible. If a program is kept short and simple, it is easier to analyze. Even if it is not possible to prove that a program is correct, it should be possible to justify intuitively the appropriateness of each portion of the program toward the final solution. These intuitive justifications properly belong as comments separating major segments of the program. These substitute for more formal proofs and should be paid as much attention as the coding itself. For if one cannot justify the individual portions of the program, the overall solution is very likely incorrect.

Testing and Debugging

Even after the logic of a program has been validated, the question remains whether the program does what it is supposed to. From a logical point of view an approach may indeed be correct, but the actual implementation of that approach as a program may be incorrect. There are many areas where a program can go wrong. It is the responsibility of the programmer to test his program to the point where he is reasonably certain that the code is correct. It may not always be clear just when the testing phase is complete enough to ensure validity, but some general guidelines are helpful.

Testing is the process of detecting errors or "bugs" in a program; ***debugging*** is the process of correcting the program in such a way that existing errors are removed without introducing new ones. In practice, the removal of errors in a way that does not affect other parts of a program is not at all easy.

An important distinction must be made between the symptom of an error and its cause. For example, suppose array A has upper bound 10 and an attempt is made to reference A(I) where I is 11. It may be possible to suppress the error and obtain output by rerunning the program with the upper bound of A changed to 11 and A(11) initialized to 0. However, such a modification rarely corrects the error; it merely eliminates its symptom. The actual cause of the error may be a loop that is executing once too often. The proper response is to modify the loop rather than the declaration. It is crucial that the programmer learn to recognize an indication of error for what it is—a symptom and not necessarily a cause. In all cases, debugging should aim at removing the cause and not the symptom. In the subsequent examples, we address our attention to the symptoms of errors and their possible causes. We do not consider the underlying logic of the problem because we consider only isolated program segments. However, the programmer should always be on the lookout for errors which stem from the method of problem solution rather than only from the program as written.

How can one tell that there are errors in a program? In general, there are three possibilities. Either there is some form of output indicating an error (e.g., a message indicating division by 0 or a system message indicating that the program has exceeded its time allocation), or there are no error messages but the output is obviously incorrect (for example, a program that is supposed to compute the sum of squares produces a negative number), or there may be no obvious indication that anything is wrong. In the first two cases there is clearly something wrong; it remains only to determine just what. This determination may not always be easy, but it is certainly easier than in the third case where the programmer has no idea that something is wrong. The most dangerous of all errors is the one which gives no indication of its presence. The fact that such an error can go undetected is a reflection that the testing phase was not sufficiently thorough. Unfortunately, there are many programs that "work" for long periods of time before a particular set of inputs uncovers an error "that was never there before." Although the programmer can rarely be absolutely certain that his program is correct, he should do all within his power to eliminate all possible errors.

We now consider several types of errors which frequently arise in programming.

Compilation and Execution Errors

Compilation errors are errors which are detected during program translation. They are usually easy to correct, unless they involve some little-used feature of the language. For example, statements which are syntactically incorrect are flagged by the compiler as such. Frequently the source of error is given. Some compilers (PL/C for example) even attempt to correct the error. These corrections should be studied carefully. Very often the correction that the compiler makes to a faulty statement gives the program a meaning that is entirely different from what the programmer had in mind. While blindly following the suggestions supplied by the compiler may eliminate the error message, it will probably not eliminate the error and may even introduce another. Thus, although such compiler messages are very helpful in pinpointing the existence of an error, the programmer should be the final judge of how to correct it.

Most of the errors that the programmer faces in debugging his program are execution errors–errors that occur during the actual running of the program. These errors are not always easy to pinpoint and are usually even more difficult to correct. We mention some of the most common execution errors in PL/I.

Invalid Data Type

Very often a variable in a program references a location in memory which contains data in incorrect format. (In the case of FIXED variables, this is sometimes called a ***data exception***.) Let us consider the possible causes for such an error.

Consider the following code:

```
DCL (X,Y)    FIXED;
Y=X+1;
```

The error is that X has not been given a value before it is used. The assignment statement does not execute properly because the computer expects to find a bit pattern at the location named X which can be interpreted as a FIXED number. If it so happens that the bit pattern at that location does not represent such a number, then the computer cannot perform the addition, and an error results. If the code is otherwise correct, then a proper initialization of X removes the error and the program would then execute properly. Of course, it is important to insert the initialization at the proper place in the program (the DECLARE statement, outside a loop, within a loop, etc.) in order to guarantee that the program solves the problem properly.

It may happen that although the programmer has not initialized X, the bit pattern which happens to be at that location does represent a FIXED number. Then the program will proceed without an error message, yet it will produce incorrect results. Nothing in the output indicates that the incorrect results are due to a failure to initialize X. Tracking down such an error is much more frustrating than tracking down an error for which an error message is produced. For this reason, some student compilers (such as PL/C) always produce an error message when a variable that has not been initialized is referenced.

A similar error occurs when a data area is referenced inadvertently. This often occurs in the case of array references where a memory address is computed by adding a base address to an offset determined by the value of the subscript (see Section 1.2). For example, consider the following program segment:

```
DCL A(10)   FIXED;
    . . .
    . . .
DO  I=1 TO 10;
    IF A(I)<A(I+1) THEN CALL SUB;
END;
```

The problem with this code is that when I equals 10, the comparison in the IF statement references A(11), which does not exist. The system attempts to access this element in the same way that it accesses any other element, that is, by referencing the address given by the base address of A plus (11–1)**esize* (where *esize* is the size of each element of A). Such a reference is to a location which is 1 beyond that occupied by the last element of A. Since the content of this data area probably does not satisfy the requirements for a FIXED number, a message that a field of invalid format has been encountered is probably printed. In this case, the error message has nothing to do with the actual error. The message is of course useful in indicating that there is something illegal in the reference, even though the actual message is incorrect.

Student compilers (such as PL/C) often provide automatic checking to ensure that every array reference is within the declared bounds of the array. When an array reference is made using a subscript which is out of bounds, a message is automatically printed identifying the array and the illegal subscript. However, such automatic checking severely decreases the efficiency of a program which uses arrays heavily. This is because such a check must be made during execution before every array reference. For this reason, production PL/I compilers do not include automatic subscript checking. However, they do include such checking as an option.

To activate this automatic checking option, the condition prefix

```
(SUBSCRIPTRANGE):
```

should be coded immediately before the statement for which the checking is desired. If this checking is desired for an entire procedure, then the condition prefix must precede the name of the procedure or program. To deactivate this checking capability, one codes

```
(NOSUBSCRIPTRANGE):
```

in the same manner. In this way, the programmer may exercise control over when the subscript checking features are used. For example, consider the following erroneous program:

```
(SUBSCRIPTRANGE):
        MN:  PROC OPTIONS(MAIN);
                DCL (A(10),I)          FIXED;
                DO I=1 TO 10;
                    GET LIST(A(I),A(I+1));
                    CALL SUB(I);
                END;

(NOSUBSCRIPTRANGE):
        SUB:  PROC(X);
                 DCL (X,I)             FIXED;
                 DO I=1 TO X;
                     PUT LIST(A(I));
                 END;
                END SUB;
             END MN;
```

All references to A within MN but outside SUB are checked for illegal subscripts, while all references to A within SUB are not. The SUBSCRIPTRANGE condition is said to be ***enabled*** in MN and ***disabled*** in SUB.

Although the system now tests for the legality of array references, the programmer must yet specify the action to be taken when an illegal reference is encountered. If the programmer does not specify the action to be taken, then the system will take "default" action, which depends on the particular implementation and installation. In many compilers the system action may be to merely halt execution, possibly printing some message first. However, it is a better idea for the programmer to specify his own actions upon encountering such a situation.

The set of actions to be taken upon the detection of such a condition is specified by an ON statement (see Section 2.1). For example, consider the following statement:

```
ON SUBSCRIPTRANGE BEGIN;
    PUT SKIP LIST('ARRAY OUT OF BOUNDS');
    STOP;
                      END;
```

If this statement is inserted immediately after the DECLARE statement in the program MN given above, then the programmer's error message is printed when the program attempts to read a value into A(11).

If it is appropriate to take corrective action, then statements to take such action should be placed in the BEGIN block. For example, let us reconsider the example of Section 2.1 in which it is desired to read a set of data cards, each of which contains two integers: an array subscript and a value to be inserted into that position of the array. The end of the data is signaled by a trailer card which contains a 0 as the first integer (and some irrelevant integer as the second so as not to raise the ENDFILE condition). The following program accomplishes this using the SUBSCRIPTRANGE condition:

```
(SUBSCRIPTRANGE):
        INPUT: PROC OPTIONS(MAIN);
                    DCL (A(100),POSITION,VALUE)    FIXED;
                    ON SUBSCRIPTRANGE GO TO OUT;
        LOOP:       DO WHILE('1'B);
                       GET LIST(POSITION,VALUE);
                       A(POSITION)=VALUE;
                    END LOOP;
        OUT:              /*   remainder of program   */
                 END INPUT;
```

When a 0 is read into the variable POSITION and is used to index the array A, the SUBSCRIPTRANGE condition is raised. The on-unit obtains control, and execution is directed to the statement labeled OUT.

Note that in this case, SUBSCRIPTRANGE is not being used for error detection. No error in the program execution occurs when the array is indexed improperly. Rather the condition is anticipated and the entire program is built around its occurrence.

As an example of how SUBSCRIPTRANGE can be used for execution error detection, consider the following. It is desired to read values into an array as in the previous example. However, instead of using a zero trailer card, the end of the input is signaled by the lack of any further data cards. Thus the ENDFILE condition is raised when no further values are to be read into the array. The danger of error is that some of the subscript values in the input might be out of bounds of the array. We would like to count the number of such errors and print the count at the end of the program. The program on page 128 does this.

After a SUBSCRIPTRANGE on-unit is executed, execution does not automatically resume with the statement following the statement which raised the condition. In this respect, the SUBSCRIPTRANGE condition differs from the ENDFILE condition. For this reason, the GO TO statement is required within the on-unit of the above program in order to continue processing the loop. If the GO TO statement were absent, execution would terminate.

When should the SUBSCRIPTRANGE condition be enabled? Clearly, it should be enabled during the development and testing phase of programming since it provides a high-powered method of early detection of serious errors which might otherwise remain undetected. However, what about after the program has passed the development stage,

```
(SUBSCRIPTRANGE):
  INPUT2: PROC OPTIONS(MAIN);
            DCL (A(100),POSITION,VALUE)    FIXED,
                 COUNT                     FIXED INIT(0);
            ON ENDFILE(SYSIN) GO TO OUT;
            ON SUBSCRIPTRANGE BEGIN;
                                   COUNT=COUNT+1;
                                   GO TO NEXT;
                                END;
  LOOP:     DO WHILE('1'B);
               GET LIST(POSITION,VALUE);
               A(POSITION)=VALUE;
  NEXT:     END LOOP;

  OUT:                /*    remainder of the program    */
            PUT SKIP LIST('THE NUMBER OF ILLEGAL SUBSCRIPTS IS:', COUNT);
         END INPUT2;
```

the final version of the program has been compiled, and its object code is being used for production purposes? The automatic checking feature provides constant vigilance over array references to make sure that they are legal. However, constant monitoring of every array reference during execution adds a tremendous overhead to the program. Every array reference is preceded by an execution-time check to make sure that the subscript value is within bounds. Such overhead undoubtedly retards the program execution speed. These considerations may be crucial in actual production runs which could last several hours.

In the above example, data values are used as array subscripts. Such a situation is a prime example of when subscript checking should be performed during execution. Testing can never ensure that such a program executes correctly for all inputs. Without a SUBSCRIPTRANGE on-unit, the program is not designed to execute for all inputs. It is only designed to execute on input containing subscripts within the array bounds. Whenever subscript values depend on external data, no amount of testing can guarantee the program will work for all data. In such cases, subscript checking during execution should be considered mandatory. However, when all subscript variables in a program take on values which can be determined from the program text, then subscript checking can be omitted in the interest of efficiency. Of course, a thorough testing procedure must be applied to such programs. During the testing phase, subscript checking should be used for all programs.

A similar error is referencing a nonexistent position of a bit or character string. For example, the statements

```
DCL STR    CHAR(4);
STR='ABCD';
X=SUBSTR(STR,2,4);
```

raise the STRINGRANGE condition because STR does not contain a fifth position. If the condition is enabled, the programmer can specify corrective action by using an ON STRINGRANGE statement.

Reusing Identifiers

Another common source of error in PL/I programs is the use of an identifier for more than one purpose. The simplest example of such an error occurs when a programmer mistakenly sets a variable equal to two distinct values. The programmer might mistakenly believe that the original value is no longer necessary, or the programmer might have overlooked the fact that the variable was already assigned a value in an earlier part of the program. There are several steps that can be taken to eliminate such oversights. First, the programmer should describe the purpose of each variable within the program. This description should be inserted as a comment in the declaration of the variable. Second, the programmer should make use of a cross-reference listing that may be obtained from most compiler outputs. This listing contains the statement numbers of all statements that reference each variable within the program. A careful check of this cross-reference should point to those statements in the program that should not be making reference to a particular variable.

There is a related problem that may not yield an error message although the results are almost certainly incorrect. This problem arises when a local variable within a subroutine is not declared. For example, consider a program to compute the amount of money which results if an amount, PRINC, is invested at a rate, RATE, for a period of years, YEARS, and the interest is compounded annually. Suppose this computation is to be repeated for 100 sets of inputs. A sample program might be as seen on page 130. Logically, the program is correct. However, the code as it stands is incorrect. The problem is that the identifier I in the subroutine FINAL refers to the same variable I that was declared in the main program. Thus, instead of processing input cards 1, 2, 3, . . . , 100, the program may demand an infinite amount of input. This is because when control returns from the subroutine to the main program, the value of I is the value of YEARS+1. Of course the value of YEARS is different for each input, so there is no control over the number of items to be processed. If the value of YEARS is always less than 99, then the value of I upon return from FINAL is always less than 100 and thus the loop LOOP is constantly repeated. This situation is an infinite loop. Also, if the value of YEARS exceeds 99 in one input set, then the loop is exited upon return from FINAL and the program is prematurely terminated.

The problem is that the variable I is not redeclared within the subroutine. Because of this, the value of I referenced within the subroutine is the value of I within the main program. The programmer intended that the loop in the main program execute 100 times and the loop in the subroutine execute YEARS times. By mistakenly using the same variable for both of these loops, we have the error indicated above. All variables should be declared in every routine in which the variable is used, unless it is specifically

```
PROG: PROC OPTIONS(MAIN);
            DCL (PRINC,RATE, AMT)  FLOAT,
                (YEARS,I)          FIXED;

LOOP:       DO I=1 TO 100;
                GET LIST(PRINC,RATE,YEARS);
                CALL FINAL(PRINC,RATE,YEARS,AMT);
                PUT SKIP EDIT(PRINC,RATE,YEARS,AMT)
                        (F(10,2),X(3), F(6,4), X(3), F(5), X(3), F(10,2));
            END LOOP;

FINAL:      PROC(PRINC,RATE,YEARS,AMT);
              DCL (PRINC,RATE,AMT)  FLOAT,
                  YEARS             FIXED;

              AMT=PRINC;
NEXT:         DO I=1 TO YEARS;
                  AMT=AMT*(1+RATE);
              END NEXT;
              RETURN;
            END FINAL;

          END PROG;
```

intended that the variable is global. It should be noted that the declaration of a variable does more than assign attributes; it also governs the allocation of memory to the variable. This subject will be discussed more fully in Chapters 3 and 6.

Counting Errors

Another type of error that often occurs is one that deals with counting. The usual case is that of a loop that is executed once too often (or once too seldom). This error may or may not yield an error message. But even if it does, the message probably has very little to do with the controls of the loop. As a simple example, consider the problem of reading elements into an array until there are none remaining and then finding the average of the elements. One might suggest the following:

```
         DCL (A(100),I,J)     FIXED,
             AVG              FIXED(7,2) INIT(0);
         ON ENDFILE(SYSIN) GO TO COMPUTE;
         GET LIST((A(I) DO I=1 TO 100));
COMPUTE: DO J=1 TO I;
             AVG=AVG+A(J);
         END COMPUTE;
         AVG=AVG/I;
```

From an aesthetic point of view there are several objections to this program segment. However, the major objection is that the program does not work. The error is that the index I is incremented before the next input element is read. For example, I is set to 5, then A(5) is read; then I is set to 6, then A(6) is read; etc. If there are twenty input numbers, I is set to 21 before the ENDFILE condition is raised in attempting to read A(21). Thus the value of I at the statement labeled COMPUTE is 21. The loop then attempts to add A(1) through A(21) when only 20 numbers exist.

It is not always adequate to start the index of the loop at a smaller value. For example, the following "correction" to the above makes things worse.

```
          DCL  (A(100),I,J)      FIXED,
                 AVG             FIXED(7,2) INIT(0);
          ON ENDFILE(SYSIN) GO TO COMPUTE;
          GET LIST((A(I) DO I=0 TO 99));
COMPUTE:  DO J=1 TO I;
            AVG=AVG+A(J);
          END COMPUTE;
          AVG=AVG/I;
```

The problem with this newer version is that while the final value of I seems to be equal to the actual number of input data items, the starting value of 0 causes a reference to A(0) which is out of bounds. It is not a good idea to patch the limits of the loop quickly without first ascertaining that the body of the loop remains correct.

A correct (and easier to understand) solution to the above is the following:

```
          DCL  (A(100),I,CNT)  FIXED,
                 AVG           FIXED(7,2) INIT(0);
          ON ENDFILE(SYSIN) GO TO COMPUTE;
INPUT:    DO I=1 TO 100;
            GET LIST(A(I));
            AVG=AVG+A(I);
          END INPUT;
COMPUTE:  CNT=I−1;
          AVG=AVG/CNT;
```

This program is clearer and also correct. Of course, the program could have been written using a statement such as

```
GET LIST((A(I+1) DO I=0 TO 99));
```

and would have worked correctly. The objection to such code (besides the lack of clarity) is that the limits of the loop should be adjusted to operations within the body rather than adjusting the body to artificial limits. For this reason the longer version is preferable.

There are no definite rules that will guarantee that counting errors of this sort do not occur. However, a good guideline is that the loop control structure mirror the desired effect of the loop and adjustments to counters be made after completion of the loop. The alternative is to control the loop in a clever manner using as many tricks as possible to avoid coding extra statements. As noted previously, such techniques usually cause more problems than they can possibly alleviate.

Accuracy of Numerical Results

Even after a program has been written and validated (even by the theoretical methods at the beginning of this section) and even after it has been established that the correct process is performed the proper number of times, there are still places where a program can go wrong. One of these is the reuse or misuse of identifiers for too many purposes, as discussed earlier in this section. A second area relates to the accuracy of the results. Consider, for example, the following program segment (the identifiers TOT and K are declared by default):

```
TOT=0;
DO K=1 TO 4;
   TOT=TOT + .1*K;
END
PUT SKIP LIST(TOT);
```

By executing the above program "by hand," one would expect that the answer should be 1. Try running the program and you will obtain a different answer. The error lies in the method used by PL/I to store the numbers internally. The computer produces results according to rigid rules of precision which do not always correspond to programmer intuition. In the above example, the value of .1 is stored in FIXED DECIMAL format, K is declared FIXED BINARY, and TOT is declared FLOAT by default. Because of conversion and precision rules the resulting intermediate values of the successive computations do not yield the required accuracy for the result. Similar problems frequently arise with division. For example, an attempt to compute the value of the expression 13+1/3 results in an error. (Try it.)

There are several things a programmer can do to improve the accuracy of a numerical result. One of these, of course, is to learn and understand the precision and conversion rules of the language and the compiler being used. For example, in PL/I whenever an operation involves a FIXED and FLOAT quantity, the FIXED quantity is first converted to FLOAT form and the result is FLOAT. Similarly, in an operation which involves a DECIMAL and a BINARY number, the DECIMAL number is first converted to BINARY. If TOT and K were both declared FIXED DECIMAL(3,1) or both declared FLOAT DECIMAL, the result of the first example would be correct. Additionally, FIXED division often yields truncated results. If the quantity 13+1/3 were written in floating-point form as 13E0+1E0/3E0, the expected result would be obtained.

On the other hand, there are instances where floating-point numbers should not be used. In problems where it is necessary to test for the exact equality of two values, floating-point numbers should be avoided. These cases also extend to controls on the number of times a loop is to be executed, as in the index of a DO loop. As an illustration of this, consider the following code:

```
          DCL  (X,S1,S2)          FLOAT,
                   I              FIXED;
          S1,S2=0;
    L1:   DO I=-20 TO 20 BY 2;
               S1=S1+1;
          END L1;

    L2:   DO  X=-2 TO 2 BY .2;
               S2=S2+1;
          END L2;
          PUT SKIP DATA(S1,S2);
```

One might expect that when the PUT statement is executed, the values of S1 and S2 are the same, since it appears that each loop is repeated the same number of times (21). Interestingly enough, the values are not the same. The first loop, of course, executes correctly, so the value of S1 is 21 (in floating-point form). The value of S2, however, is 20 (in floating-point form), indicating that L2 went through 20 iterations. The reason for this anomaly lies in the method used to represent floating-point numbers. The internal floating-point representation of a number may be a close approximation of its real value. For example, the number 5 may be represented by 4.99999. Sometimes, the difference can be ignored. In cases where a precise count is necessary, as in the above example, the floating-point approximation may yield an incorrect result. Floating-point numbers should not be used where the real intent of the solution is most clearly expressed by the use of fixed-point numbers.

Floating-point numbers should not be compared for exact equality. Instead, they should be tested for proximity, as in the statement

```
    IF ABS(X-Y) <= DELTA THEN . . .
```

DELTA can be made as small as desired, but should not be 0.

In general then, the use of floating-point numbers may be crucial in some cases and disastrous in others. It is the programmer's responsibility to make sure that the attributes of a particular variable are appropriate to the problem at hand.

Testing

For some of the errors mentioned above, the existence of an error is indicated on the printout in the form of error messages or warnings. In other cases, the program may just run out of time or space because it is in an infinite loop. In many cases, however, unless the programmer tests a program thoroughly, there may be errors in the program that go undetected until just the right combination of inputs is encountered. For this reason it is extremely important that a program be tested properly before it is put to serious use. While there exists no uniform method to guarantee that proper testing procedures are used, there are some general guidelines that uncover many of the errors mentioned above. By no means are these suggestions complete; each program requires test cases peculiar to its application.

Certainly, as a start, one should test the program for some simple inputs for which solutions can be easily computed by hand. If the program's solutions do not match those that have been calculated independently, then the program is clearly incorrect. However, since the correct answers are known, the temptation exists to adjust the program in the most expedient way so that it produces those correct answers. The most expedient method may not, however, be a valid one. The fact that correct answers are produced for certain inputs does not mean that the program has been corrected. It is necessary to trace the intermediate results of the program from start to finish and to determine which intermediate step is in error. Only when this has been done can a programmer be reasonably sure that he has located the source of error. In fact, even when initial tests indicate that the results for simple cases are correct, the intermediate results should be checked to be sure that correct actions are being taken at each point in the program.

Another set of test cases consisting of "boundary" values should be used. For example, suppose a tax law specifies that all people with income of less than $500.00 pay no tax, while those with income of $500.00 or above pay a rate of 4%. It is important to test the program for an income which is exactly $500.00 to verify that the proper tax is computed. In some cases, boundary cases can be verified by simply checking that the proper action is taken on equality. In others, it may be necessary to trace the actions of the program on boundary inputs to ascertain that those actions are correct. Besides testing some of these boundary values individually, it is also important to test them together to see how the program behaves on combinations of such inputs.

After the programmer is satisfied that the program behaves correctly on simple inputs and boundary values, the program should be tested on inputs that are known to be invalid. Very often a program's success depends on its ability to defend itself against invalid inputs as much as on its effects on valid inputs. Even if the user believes that all the input data is verified before submission to his program, there should be a basic amount of error detection within the program. If there exists a program to validate the input data, that fact should be stated, as a comment perhaps, at the outset of the program in question. This will at least absolve the programmer of any responsibility for the validity of the input. Yet, even when the input to a large program has been validated, the inputs to specific subroutines and processes must be validated. For this reason it is a good idea that each routine test that assumptions about its inputs hold. Also it is important to check that one or more bad items of input do not adversely impact computations on subsequent inputs.

Finally, the program should be tested for a large random sample of input values. In some cases, it may be possible to test the outputs against results from existing (but perhaps less efficient) programs. In cases where this is not feasible, some of these test cases should be followed through and checked by hand, laborious as this may be. Any time spent in testing the program from the start will probably pay off tenfold by eliminating errors during production runs.

Now that we have described the types of values for which to test the program, how should the testing proceed? If the program has been written in a top-down fashion, then the set of routines should be tested individually and as a single program. The routines may be tested in a top-down fashion; i.e., the main program is to be tested first, then the subroutines it calls, and finally the entire system as a whole. While testing a routine at a certain level, one assumes that the subroutines it calls already exist. In order to allow the program to run, the programmer has to code dummy routines. For example, consider the following routine:

```
ROUT: PROC(P1,P2);
          /*   group1 of statements    */
          CALL SUB1(P1,X);
          /*   group2 of statements    */
          RETURN;
      END ROUT;
```

The purpose of testing the above routine is to determine whether the statements included in *group1* and *group2* are correct. However, in order to allow the program to execute for testing purposes, a dummy routine for SUB1 must be coded, as in

```
SUB1: PROC(Q1,Q2);
          DCL (Q1,Q2)   FIXED;
          Q1=8;
          Q2=9;
          RETURN;
      END SUB1;
```

Before SUB1 is actually coded, the values "computed" by SUB1 in the dummy routine can be altered intentionally to cover all possible cases. In this way the actions of ROUT can be verified for all possibilities. Once ROUT has been tested, routines such as SUB1 can be coded and tested. This type of testing, in which routines at higher levels are tested before those at lower levels, is called ***top-down testing***.

Another type of testing, called ***bottom-up testing***, proceeds in the reverse order. From a logical point of view the program must be designed in a top-down fashion (one cannot know what a subroutine is to do before the program using that subroutine has been written). However, once all the routines have been designed, the ones at the lowest levels are written and tested before those at higher levels. This type of testing is easier, since whenever a program is being tested, all programs upon which it depends have already been tested. For this reason, many programmers prefer this technique. The only disadvantage to this method is that the calling programs may not be fully tested. For example, if a subroutine always returns positive numbers, the calling routine is never tested on negative numbers. If the subroutine is later modified so that negative numbers may be returned, a hitherto undiscovered error in the main routine may occur. However, both of these methods can be used effectively if the testing is done in a comprehensive manner.

Tracing the execution of a program is important in both general testing (so that intermediate results can be checked) and in detecting many types of errors. For example, programs that produce incorrect results for no apparent reason and those that appear to be in an infinite loop can best be debugged by tracing intermediate results. Probably the best way to trace a program is to force the printout of crucial variables at various intervals of execution. Each of these statements should identify the source of the output, as in

```
OUT:  PUT SKIP EDIT('AT LABEL OUT, X=',X) (A,F(8,2));
```

By following a sequence of such printouts, one can trace the order in which groups of statements are executed and the values of X as they are computed. By narrowing the error down to smaller and smaller segments of the program, the source of an error can be pinpointed precisely.

Tracing can also be done through the use of various compiler features (e.g., the CHECK option). These features can be very helpful. One of their disadvantages, however, is that they sometimes produce voluminous output. The danger of this is that some small, but important, detail goes undetected. Nevertheless they can be very effective in tracing errors.

Efficiency

Once it has been established that a program is correct, the program still cannot be considered reliable if it uses an inordinate amount of the machine's resources. For example, if only two hours of machine time or 2000 units of memory are available for a particular application and a program requires 25 hours or 25,000 units of memory, then the program is not acceptable. Of course, the program may be very efficient, but the facilities are simply saturated. However, it may be that rewriting the program would turn out a better product.

Good programmers should consider the efficiency of their product when the initial solution is planned. The selection of the overall solution to a program usually has significantly more effect on the efficiency of the resulting program than the actual form of the source statements. In the remainder of the text, a major part of our attention will be focused on efficient methods to solve problems.

However, there are some areas where an existing program can be made more efficient. For example, consider the following program segment:

```
L1:  DO I=1 TO 1000;
        GET LIST(A(I));
     END L1;
L2:  DO I=1 TO 1000;
        IF A(I)>0 THEN X=X+A(I);
     END L2;
```

The above code could be replaced by the much more efficient version:

```
L:    DO I=1 TO 1000;
          GET LIST(A(I));
          IF A(I)>0 THEN X=X+A(I);
      END L;
```

Implicit in every repetition of a loop is at least one branch, one test, and possibly the computation of other functions. In the above case, there is no reason to duplicate this effort needlessly by using the second loop to perform some action that could just as easily have been done in the first loop. There are other "obvious" places where programs can be improved. Programmers should review their code carefully to guarantee that it is as efficient as possible.

But there are also many nontrivial areas in which programs can be improved. For example, consider the following code:

```
        GET LIST(A,B);
LOOP:   DO WHILE('1'B);
            GET LIST(X,Y);
            W=(X+Y)**(A+B)/SQRT(10);
            PUT SKIP LIST(X,Y,W);
        END LOOP;
```

Each time through the loop, the value of the square root of 10 is recomputed. However, this value need be computed only once since its value does not change with each repetition of the loop. Similarly, the value of (A+B) does not change within the loop, so that it, too, may be computed once outside the loop. A more efficient version of the above code is:

```
        SQRTEN=SQRT(10);
        GET LIST(A,B);
        APLUSB=A+B;
LOOP:   DO WHILE('1'B);
            GET LIST(X,Y);
            W=(X+Y)**APLUSB/SQRTEN;
            PUT SKIP LIST(X,Y,W);
        END LOOP;
```

If the loop is repeated 1000 times (before being terminated by an ENDFILE condition), this revision saves 999 additions and 999 executions of the SQRT routine. In general, any computation which can be performed outside a loop should not appear within the loop.

Another example of local inefficiency is the following:

```
LOOP:  DO I=1 TO 100;
           GET LIST(X,Y);
           W=3*I*(X+Y);
           PUT SKIP LIST (X,Y,W);
       END LOOP;
```

In this example, I is multiplied by 3 each time through the loop. Thus, (X+Y) is multiplied by each of the values 3, 6, 9, . . . , 300. I is not used within the loop except at this point. The above code could therefore be performed more efficiently by the following:

```
LOOP:  DO I=3 TO 300 BY 3;
           GET LIST(X,Y);
           W=I*(X+Y);
           PUT SKIP LIST(X,Y,W);
       END LOOP;
```

This eliminates 100 multiplications.

Another way in which efficiency can be improved is by eliminating needless references to array elements. For example, consider the following code segment:

```
LOOP:  DO I=1 TO 100 BY 2;
           GET LIST(A(I),A(I+1));
           X=(A(I)+A(I+1))/2;
           Y=(A(I)–A(I+1))/2;
           A(I)=X;
           A(I+1)=Y;
       END LOOP;
```

Each time that an array element is referenced, a computation must be performed (add the base and offset). The above code involves 8*50 such computations. Contrast this with

```
LOOP:  DO I=1 TO 100 BY 2;
           GET LIST(X,Y);
           A(I)=(X+Y)/2;
           A(I+1)=(X–Y)/2;
       END LOOP;
```

This latter code involves only 2*50 address computations. (We are assuming that the values of X and Y are unused after leaving the loop.)

Unfortunately, it often happens that the process of making a program more efficient also makes the program less readable. Many of the techniques of good structure outlined in previous sections require more time to execute than other methods, so that when an entire program is constructed using these techniques, they may add to the overhead of the program. For this reason, some people argue that techniques of good structure should be abandoned if more efficient methods can be found to perform the same task.

This attitude does not promote the development of good programs. There is probably no more efficient method to perform many processes than to code the solution in assembly language and then optimize that code. However, the major purpose of high-level languages such as PL/I is to allow programmers to code solutions to problems without worrying about details of the lowest-level operations.

Once the decision to use a high-level language has been made, the programmer should exploit the features of that language that make the coding of the solution easier. When coding is done in PL/I, the rules of good structure outlined earlier in this chapter should be followed. These techniques produce programs that are easy to modify and adapt to changing needs.

There may be portions of a program that are inefficient. Before a decision is made to rewrite a portion of code, an important question must be answered: What percentage of the total execution time is spent in this section of code? If a particular portion of code represents only 5% of the total execution time of the program and a major rewriting operation can improve it so that it requires only half as much time to run, the net savings to the total program is not 50% but 2.5%.

In selecting an algorithm to solve a problem, efficiency should be the overriding factor after correctness is assured. Once that algorithm has been selected, the program should be coded and tested using the top-down structured approach. That program should be "speeded up" only if the improvement does not make the program less modifiable or if it can be established that the newer version produces a significant saving in the overall running time of the complete program.

Bibliography and References

Texts that emphasize structured programming in PL/I are (Conway and Gries, 1975) and (Shortt and Wilson, 1976). The SELECT statement, the DO UNTIL statement, and the LEAVE statement are described in (IBM, 1976). Programming style is discussed in (Kernighan and Plauger, 1970) and in (Yourdon, 1975). The latter book covers all the topics in this chapter. Also of interest is the December, 1974 issue of *Computing Surveys* on programming. Two other books of interest are (Dijkstra, 1972) and (Wirth, 1973). The bibliography at the end of this book contains many other references.

The prime number algorithms of Section 2.2 are discussed in (Chartres, 1967) and (Mairson, 1977). The latter contains another, more efficient algorithm.

Testing and debugging techniques are discussed in (Hetzel, 1972), (Huang, 1975), (Rustin, 1971), (Van Tassel, 1974), and (Yourdon, 1975). Efficiency considerations are discussed in PL/I manuals and in (Allen and Cocke, 1972). A discussion of proving program correctness may be found in (Hantler and King, 1976).

chapter 3

the stack

One of the most useful concepts in computer science is that of the stack. In this chapter, we shall examine this deceptively simple data structure and see why it plays such a prominent role in the areas of programming and programming languages. We shall define the abstract concept of a stack and show how that concept can be made into a concrete and valuable tool in problem solving.

3.1. Definition and Examples

A ***stack*** is an ordered set of items into which new items may be inserted and from which items may be deleted at one end, called the ***top*** of the stack.

Let us see what this definition means. Given any two items in a stack, one of them can be thought of as "higher" in the stack than the other. Thus we can picture a stack as in Fig. 3.1.1. Item F is higher in the stack than all the other items. Item D is higher than items A, B, and C but is lower than items E and F.

You may protest that if Fig. 3.1.1 were turned upside down a very similar picture would result, but A rather than F would be the highest element. If a stack were a static, unchanging object your objection would be quite correct. However, the definition of a stack provides for insertion and deletion of items so that a stack is really a dynamic, constantly changing object. Figure 3.1.1 is only a snapshot of a stack at a particular point

F
E
D
C
B
A

Figure 3.1.1. A stack containing six items.

in its continuing evolution. In order to have a true view of a stack, a motion picture is necessary.

The question therefore arises, how does a stack change? From the definition, note that a single end of the stack must be designated as the stack ***top***. New items may then be put on top of the stack (in which case the top of the stack moves upwards to correspond to the new highest element) or items which are at the top of the stack may be removed (in which case the top of the stack moves downwards to correspond to the new highest element). To answer the question "Which way is up?" we must decide which end of the stack is designated as its top—that is, at which end will items be added or deleted. By drawing Fig. 3.1.1 so that F is physically higher on the page than all the other items in the stack, we mean to imply that F is the current top element of the stack. If any new items are to be added to the stack, they will be placed on top of F, and if any items are to be deleted, F will be the first to be deleted. This is also indicated by the vertical lines which extend past the items of the stack in the direction of the stack top.

Of course stacks may be drawn in many different ways, as shown in Fig. 3.1.2, as long as it is clearly understood which end is the top of the stack. Ordinarily, we will illustrate stacks as in Fig. 3.1.1 with the stack top facing the top of the page.

Let us now view a motion picture of a stack to see how it expands and shrinks with the passage of time. Such a picture is given by Fig. 3.1.3. In Fig. 3.1.3(a) we see the stack as it exists at the time that the snapshot of Fig. 3.1.1 was taken. In Fig. 3.1.3(b), item G is added to the stack. According to the definition, there is only one place on the stack where it can be placed—on the top. The top element on the stack is now G. As the motion picture progresses through frames (c), (d), and (e), we see items H, I, and J successively added onto the stack. Notice that the last item inserted (in this case J) is at the top of the stack. Beginning with frame (f), however, the stack begins to shrink as first J, then I, H, G, and F are successively removed. At each point, the top element is removed since deletion can be made only from the top. Item G could not be removed from the stack before items J, I, and H were gone. This illustrates the most important attribute of a stack: that the last element inserted into a stack is the first element deleted. Thus J is deleted before I because J was inserted after I. For this reason a stack is sometimes called a ***last-in, first-out*** (or ***lifo***) ***queue***.

Between frames (j) and (k), the stack has stopped shrinking and begins to expand again as item K is added. However, this expansion is short-lived as the stack then shrinks to only three items in frame (n).

Note that there is no way to distinguish between frame (a) and frame (i) by looking at the stack's state at the two instances. In both cases, the stack contains the identical items in the same order and has the same stack top. No record is kept on the stack of the fact that four items had been inserted and deleted in the meantime. Similarly, there is no way to distinguish between frames (d) and (f) or (j) and (l). If a record is needed of the intermediate items having been on the stack, that record must be kept elsewhere; it does not exist within the stack itself.

In fact, we have actually taken an extended view of what is really observed in a stack. The true picture of a stack is given by a view from the top looking down, rather than from a side looking in. Thus, there is no perceptible difference between frames (h) and

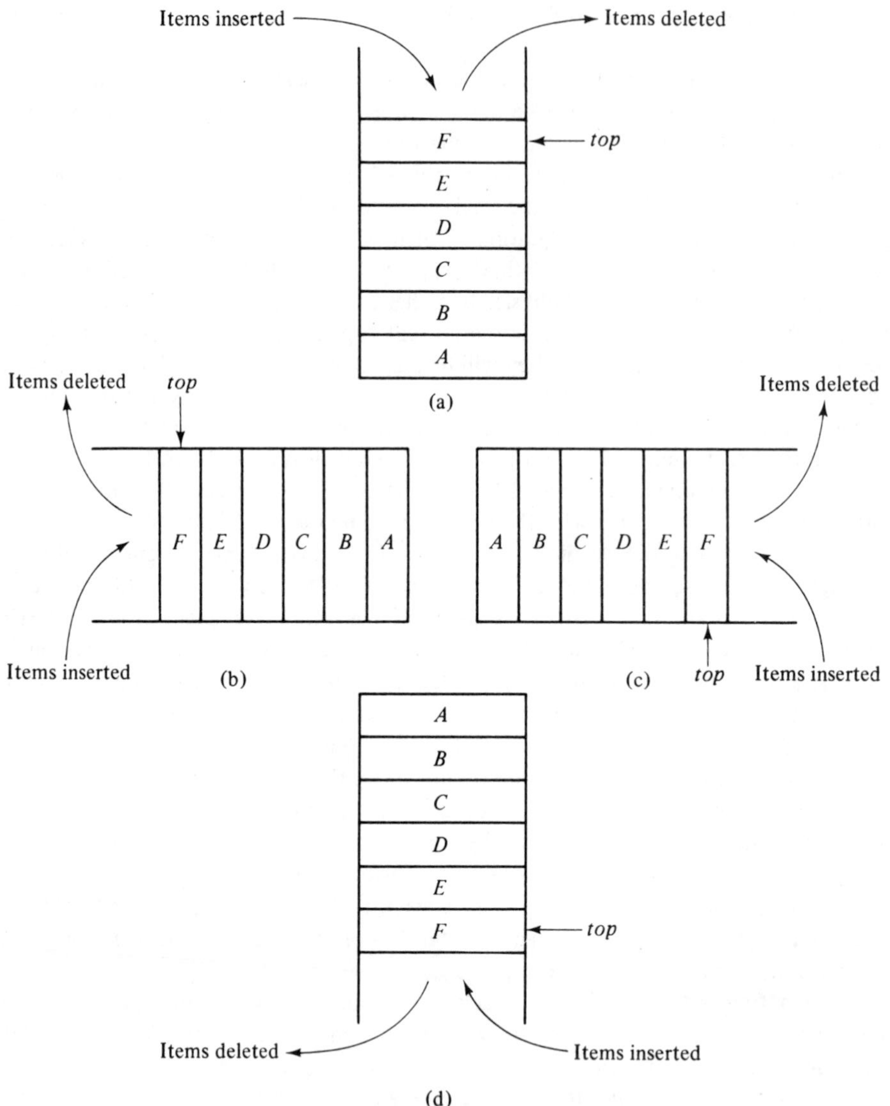

Figure 3.1.2. Four different views of the same stack.

(o) in Fig. 3.1.3. In each case the element at the top is G. While we know that the stack at (h) and the stack at (o) are not equal, the only way to determine this is to remove all the elements on both stacks and compare them individually. While we have been looking at cross sections of stacks to make our understanding clearer, you should remember that this is an added liberty and there is no real provision for taking such a picture.

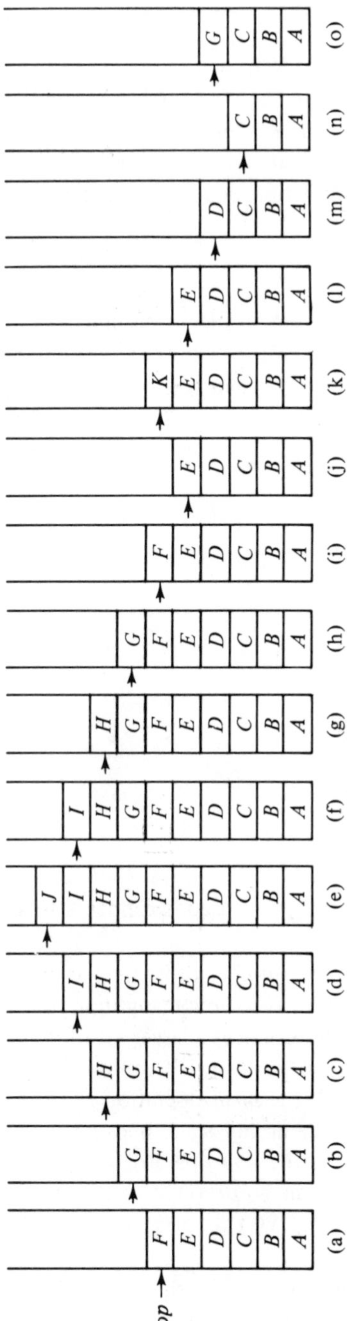

Figure 3.1.3. A motion picture of a stack.

Primitive Operations

The two changes which can be made to a stack are given special names. When an item is added to a stack, it is ***pushed*** onto the stack. Given a stack *s*, and an item *i*, performing the operation *push(s,i)* is defined as adding the item *i* to the top of stack *s*. Similarly, when an item is removed from the stack, it is ***popped***. The operation *pop(s)* removes the top element and returns it as a function value. Thus the assignment operation

i=pop(*s*)

removes the element at the top of *s* and assigns its value to *i*.

For example, if *s* is the stack of Fig. 3.1.3, we performed the operation *push(s,G)* in going from frame (a) to frame (b). We then performed, in turn, the operations:

push (*s,H*) (frame (c))
push (*s,I*) (frame (d))
push (*s,J*) (frame (e))
pop (*s*) (frame (f))
pop (*s*) (frame (g))
pop (*s*) (frame (h))
pop (*s*) (frame (i))
pop (*s*) (frame (j))
push (*s,K*) (frame (k))
pop (*s*) (frame (l))
pop (*s*) (frame (m))
pop (*s*) (frame (n))
push (*s,G*) (frame (o)).

Because of the push operation, which adds elements to a stack, a stack is sometimes called a ***pushdown queue***.

There is no upper limit on the number of items that may be kept in a stack since no mention was made in the definition as to how many items are allowed in the set. Pushing another item onto a stack merely produces a larger set of items. However, if a stack contains a single item and the stack is popped, the resulting stack contains no items and is called the ***empty stack***. Although the *push* operation is applicable to any stack, the *pop* operation cannot be applied to the empty stack because such a stack has no elements to delete. Therefore before applying the *pop* operator to a stack, we must ensure that the stack is not empty. The operation *empty*(*s*) determines whether or not a stack *s* is empty. If the stack is empty, *empty*(*s*) returns the value *true*, otherwise it returns the value *false*.

Another operation which can be performed on a stack is to determine what the top item on a stack is without removing it. This operation is written *top*(*s*) and returns as its value the top element of stack *s*. The operation *top*(*s*) is not really a new operation since it can be decomposed into a pop and a push.

```
x=top(s)
```

is equivalent to

```
x=pop (s)
push (s,x).
```

Like the operation *pop, top* is not defined for an empty stack. The result of an illegal attempt to pop an item from an empty stack is called ***underflow***. Underflow can be avoided by ensuring that *empty*(*s*) is *false* before attempting the operation *pop*(*s*) or *top*(*s*).

An Example

Now that we have defined a stack and have indicated the operations which can be performed on it, let us see how we may use the stack in problem solving. Suppose a mathematical expression is given which includes several sets of nested parentheses, for example,

```
7-((X *((X+Y) / (J-3)) + Y) /(4-2.5))
```

and we want to ensure that the parentheses are nested correctly. That is, we want to check that:

1. There are an equal number of right and left parentheses.
2. Every right parenthesis is preceded by a matching left parenthesis.

Expressions such as

```
((A+B)   or   A+B)
```

would violate condition 1, while

```
)A+B(-C   or   (A+B))-(C+D
```

would violate condition 2.

In order to solve this problem, think of each left parenthesis as opening a scope and each right parenthesis as closing a scope. The ***nesting depth*** at a particular point in an expression is the number of scopes which have been opened but not yet closed at that point. This is the same as the number of left parentheses encountered whose matching right parentheses have not yet been encountered. Let us define the ***parenthesis count*** at a particular point in an expression as the number of left parentheses minus the number of right parentheses which have been encountered in scanning the expression from its left end up to that particular point. If the parenthesis count is nonnegative, then it is the same as the nesting depth. The two conditions which must hold if the parentheses in an expression are to form an admissible pattern are:

1. The parenthesis count at the end of the expression is 0. This implies that no scopes have been left open or that exactly as many right parentheses as left parentheses have been found.
2. The parenthesis count at each point in the expression is nonnegative. This implies that no right parenthesis has been encountered for which a matching left parenthesis had not previously been encountered.

In Fig. 3.1.4, the count at each point in each of the previous five strings is given directly below that point. Since only the first string meets the above two conditions, it is the only one among the five with a correct parentheses pattern.

```
7 - ( ( X * ( ( X + Y ) / ( J - 3 ) ) + Y ) ( 4 - 2.5 ) )
0 0 1 2 2 2 3 4 4 4 4 3 3 4 4 4 4 3 2 2 2 1 2 2 2   2 1 0

( ( A + B )
1 2 2 2 2 1

A + B   )
0 0 0  -1

 )   A   +   B  ( - C
-1  -1  -1  -1  0 0 0

( A + B )   )    - ( C + D
1 1 1 1 0  -1   -1 0 0 0 0
```

Figure 3.1.4. Parenthesis count at various points of strings.

Let us now change the problem slightly and assume that three different types of scopes exist. These types are indicated by parentheses ((and)), brackets ([and]), and braces ({and}). A scope ender must be of the same type as its scope opener. Thus strings such as

(A+B], [(A+B]), {A–(B] }

are illegal.

It is necessary to keep track of not only how many scopes have been opened, but also of their types. This information is needed because when a scope ender is encountered, we must know the symbol with which the scope was opened in order to ensure that it is being closed properly.

A stack may be used to keep track of the types of scopes encountered. Whenever a scope opener is encountered, it is pushed onto the stack. Whenever a scope ender is encountered, the stack is examined. If the stack is empty, then the scope ender does not have a matching opener, so the string is invalid. If, however, the stack is nonempty, we pop the stack and check whether the popped item corresponds to the scope ender. If a match occurs, we continue. If it does not, then the string is invalid. When the end of the string is reached, we make sure that the stack is empty; otherwise, one or more scopes have been opened which have not been closed, making the string invalid. This procedure is outlined in Fig. 3.1.5. Figure 3.1.6 shows the state of the stack after reading in parts of the string $\{x+(y-[a+b])*c-[(d+e)]\}/(h-(j-(k-[l-n])))$.

```
Let s = the empty stack;
do while (we have not read the entire string);
    read the next symbol (symb) of the string;
    if symb = '(' or
      symb = '[' or
      symb = '{' then push (s, symb);
    if symb = ')' or
      symb = ']' or
      symb = '}' then do;
          if empty(s) then return ('invalid');
          i = pop(s);
          if i is not the matching opener for symb
               then return ('invalid');
                  end;
end;
if empty(s) then return ('valid');
          else return ('invalid');
```

Figure 3.1.5. An algorithm for matching parentheses.

Let us see why the solution to this problem calls for the use of a stack. The last scope to be opened must be the first to be closed. This is precisely simulated by a stack where the last element arriving is the first to leave. Each item on the stack represents a scope which has been opened but which has not yet been closed. Pushing an item onto the stack corresponds to the opening of a scope, and popping an item from the stack corresponds to the closing of a scope, leaving one less scope open.

Notice the correspondence between the number of elements on the stack in this example and the parenthesis count in the previous example. When the stack is empty (parenthesis count = 0) and a scope ender is encountered, an attempt is being made to close a scope which has never been opened, so that the parenthesis pattern is invalid. In the first example, this is indicated by a negative parenthesis count, and in the second example by an inability to pop the stack. The reason that a simple parenthesis count is inadequate for the second example is that we must keep track of the actual scope openers themselves. This can be done by use of a stack. Notice also that at any point we examine only the element at the top. The particular configuration of parentheses below the top element is irrelevant while we examine this top element. It is only after the top element has been popped that we concern ourselves with subsequent elements in a stack.

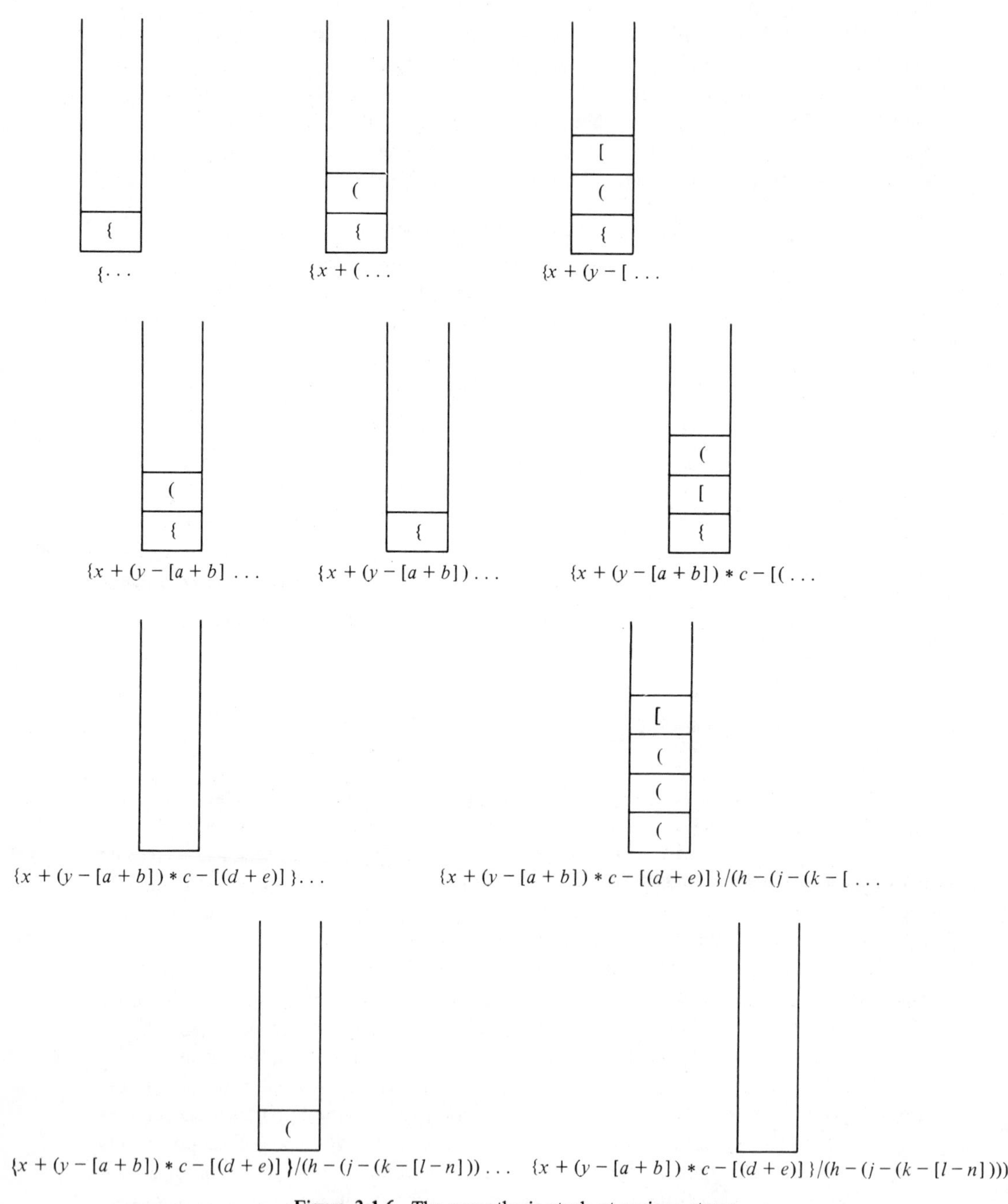

Figure 3.1.6. The parenthesis stack at various stages of processing.

In general, a stack can be used in any situation which calls for a last-in, first-out discipline or which displays a nesting pattern. We shall see more examples of the use of stacks in the remaining sections of this chapter and, indeed, throughout the text.

3.2. Representing Stacks in PL/I

Before programming a problem solution which calls for the use of a stack, we must decide how to represent a stack using the data structures which exist in our programming language. As we shall see, there are many ways to represent a stack in PL/I. We will now consider the simplest of these. As the chapter and the entire book progress, you will be introduced to other possible representations. Each of them, however, is merely an implementation of the concept introduced in Section 1 of this chapter. Each has its advantages and disadvantages in terms of how close it comes to mirroring the abstract concept of a stack and how much effort must be made by the programmer and the computer in using it.

A stack is a collection of ordered items and PL/I already contains a data structure which is a collection of ordered items—the array. Whenever a problem solution calls for use of a stack, therefore, it is tempting to begin a program by declaring an identifier STACK to be an array. Unfortunately, however, a stack and an array are two entirely different things. The number of elements in an array is fixed and is assigned by the declaration for the array. In general, the user cannot change this number. A stack, on the other hand, is fundamentally a dynamic object whose size is constantly changing as items are popped and pushed.

However, although an array cannot be a stack, it can be the home of a stack. That is, an array can be declared with a range which is large enough for the maximum size of the stack. During the course of program execution, the stack will grow and shrink within the space reserved for it. One end of the array will be the fixed bottom of the stack, while the top of the stack will constantly shift as items are popped and pushed. Thus, another variable is needed which, at each point during program execution, will keep track of the current position of the top of the stack.

A stack in PL/I may therefore be declared as a structure containing two objects: an array which will hold the elements of the stack, and a variable to indicate the position of the current stack top within the array. This may be done by the declaration

```
DCL 1  STACK,
       2 ITEM(100)  FIXED,
       2 TOP        FIXED;
```

Here we assume that the elements of the stack contained in the array ITEM are integers and that the stack will at no time contain more than 100 integers. There is, of course, no reason to restrict a stack to contain only integers; ITEM could just as easily be declared with the attributes CHAR(100) VAR or FLOAT or FIXED(10,5), or whatever other attributes we might wish to give to the elements of the stack. The identifier

TOP, however, must be declared as an integer since its value represents the position within the array ITEM of the topmost stack element. Thus, if the value of TOP is 5, there are five elements on the stack. These are ITEM(1), ITEM(2), ITEM(3), ITEM(4), and ITEM(5). When the stack is popped, the value of TOP must be changed to 4 to indicate that there are now only four elements on the stack and that ITEM(4) is the top element. On the other hand, if a new object is pushed onto the stack, the value of TOP must be increased by 1 to 6 and the new object inserted into ITEM(6).

The empty stack contains no elements and can therefore be indicated by TOP equaling 0. In order to initialize a stack to the empty state we may, at the start of execution, declare

```
DCL 1  STACK,
       2 ITEM(100)  FIXED,
       2 TOP        FIXED INIT(0);
```

To determine during the course of execution whether or not a stack is empty the condition TOP=0 may be tested by means of an IF statement as follows:

```
IF TOP=0 THEN /*     stack is empty     */;
         ELSE /*   stack is not empty   */;
```

This test corresponds to the operation *empty*(*s*) which was introduced in Section 1. Alternatively, we may write a function which returns *true* (or '1'B) if the stack is empty and *false* (or '0'B) if it is not empty. Such a function may be written as follows:

```
EMPTY:  PROC (STACK) RETURNS (BIT(1));
          DCL 1 STACK,
                  2 ITEM (*)   FIXED,
                  2 TOP        FIXED;
          IF TOP=0 THEN RETURN ('1'B);
                   ELSE RETURN ('0'B);
        END EMPTY;
```

Once this function exists, a test for the empty stack is implemented by the statement

```
IF EMPTY (STACK) THEN  /*     the stack is empty     */;
                 ELSE  /*   the stack is not empty   */;
```

You may wonder why we bother to define the function EMPTY when we could just as easily write IF TOP=0 each time that we want to test for the empty condition. The answer is that we wish to make our programs more comprehensible and to make the use of a stack independent of its implementation. Once we understand the stack concept, the phrase "EMPTY(STACK)" is more meaningful than the phrase "TOP=0." If we should later introduce a better implementation of a stack so that "TOP=0" becomes meaningless, we would have to change every reference to the variables TOP and ITEM throughout our entire program. On the other hand, the phrase "EMPTY(STACK)" would still retain its meaning, since it is an inherent attribute of the stack concept rather than of an implementation of that concept. All that would be required to revise our program to accommodate a new implementation of the stack would be a revision of the declaration of STACK in the main program and the rewriting of the function EMPTY. Aggregating the set of implementation-dependent trouble spots into small, easily identifiable units is an important asset in making a program more understandable and modifiable. This concept is known as ***modularization*** in which individual functions are isolated into low-level ***modules*** whose properties are easily provable. These low-level modules can then be used by more complex routines which do not have to concern themselves with the details of the low-level modules, but only with their function. The complex routines may then themselves be viewed as modules by still higher-level routines which use them independently of their internal details.

A programmer should always be concerned with the readability of the code he produces. Often a small amount of attention to clarity will save a large amount of time in debugging. Large- and medium-size programs will almost never be correct the first time they are run. If precautions are taken at the time that a program is written to ensure that it is easily modifiable and comprehensible, the total time needed to get the program to run correctly will be sharply reduced. For example, the IF statement in the EMPTY function could be replaced by the shorter, more efficient statement

```
RETURN (TOP=0);
```

The effect of this statement is precisely equivalent to the longer statement

```
IF TOP=0 THEN RETURN ('1'B);
         ELSE RETURN ('0'B);
```

This is because the value of the expression TOP=0 is '1'B if and only if the condition TOP=0 is true. However someone else who reads a program will probably be much more comfortable reading the IF statement. Often, you will find that if you use "tricks" of the language in writing programs, you will be unable to decipher your own programs after putting them aside for a day or two.

To implement the *pop* operation, the possibility of underflow must be taken into account since the user may inadvertently attempt to pop an element from an empty stack. Of course, such an attempt is illegal and should be avoided. However, if such an attempt should be made, the user should be informed of the underflow condition. We therefore introduce a function POP which performs the following three actions:

1. If the stack is empty, it prints a warning message and halts execution.
2. It removes the top element from the stack.
3. It returns this element to the calling program.

```
POP: PROC (STACK) RETURNS (FIXED);

          DCL 1 STACK,
                  2 ITEM(*)       FIXED,
                  2 TOP           FIXED,
                TOPITEM           FIXED;

          IF EMPTY(STACK) THEN DO;
                PUT SKIP LIST ('STACK UNDERFLOW');
                STOP;
                                      END;
          TOPITEM = ITEM(TOP);
          TOP = TOP–1;
          RETURN (TOPITEM);
     END POP;
```

Testing for Exceptional Conditions

Let us look at the POP function more closely. If the stack is not empty, the top element of the stack is saved in the variable TOPITEM. This element is then removed from the stack by the statement TOP=TOP–1;. Let us assume that when POP is called, TOP equals 87; that is, there are 87 items on the stack. The value of ITEM(87) is saved in TOPITEM and the value of TOP is changed to 86. Note that ITEM(87) still retains its old value; the array ITEM remains unchanged by the call to POP. However the stack is changed, since it now contains only 86 elements rather than 87. Recall that an array and a stack are two different objects. The array only provides a home for the stack. The stack itself contains only those elements between the first item of the array and the TOPth element. Thus, reducing the value of TOP by 1 effectively removes an element from the stack. This is true despite the fact that ITEM(87) retains its old value.

In order to use the POP function, the programmer can declare X FIXED and write:

```
X=POP(STACK);
```

X will then contain the value popped from the stack. If the intent of the POP function call was not to retrieve the element on the top of the stack, but only to remove it from the stack, X will not be used again in the program except perhaps to serve once more as the target of a POP function. Alternatively, the programmer could write CALL POP(STACK), which would invoke the routine POP but not save its returned value in the calling program for future use. Of course, the programmer should ensure that the stack is not empty when he calls the POP function. If he is unsure of the state of the stack, he may write

```
IF ¬EMPTY(STACK) THEN X=POP(STACK);
                      ELSE /*   take remedial action   */;
```

If the programmer unwittingly does call POP with an empty stack, the function will print out the error message 'STACK UNDERFLOW' and execution will halt. Although this is an unfortunate state of affairs, it is far better than what would occur had the IF statement in the POP routine been omitted entirely. In that case, the value of TOP would be 0 and an attempt would be made to access the nonexistent element ITEM(0). Depending on the PL/I compiler used, an error message would be printed pinpointing an attempt to access a nonexistent element in the statement TOPITEM=ITEM(TOP); or an error message would be printed without an indication of what caused it; or, what would be far worse, execution would continue with some extraneous value used for ITEM(0) without any error messages printed at all. This last possibility is the most dangerous of all since erroneous results would be produced by the program with no indication to the programmer that anything has gone wrong.

A programmer should always provide for the almost certain possibility of error. He should include his own diagnostics which are meaningful in the context of the problem. By doing so, if and when an error does occur, he will be able to immediately pinpoint its source and take corrective action.

However, within the context of a given problem, it may not be necessary to immediately halt execution upon the detection of underflow. Instead, it might be more desirable for the POP routine to signal the calling program that an underflow has occurred. The calling routine, upon detecting this signal, can take corrective action. Let us call the routine which pops the stack and returns an indication as to whether underflow has occurred, POPANDTEST.

```
POPANDTEST: PROC (STACK, X, UNDERFLOW);
                 DCL  1 STACK,
                           2 ITEM(*)        FIXED,
                           2 TOP            FIXED,
                         X                  FIXED,
                         UNDERFLOW          BIT(*);
                 IF EMPTY(STACK) THEN DO;
                           UNDERFLOW='1'B;
                           RETURN;
                                            END;
                 UNDERFLOW='0'B;
                 X= ITEM(TOP);
                 TOP=TOP-1;
                 RETURN;
              END POPANDTEST;
```

In the calling program the programmer would write

```
CALL POPANDTEST (STACK, X, UNDERFLOW);
IF UNDERFLOW THEN  /*          take corrective action          */;
            ELSE   /*  X is the element popped off the stack   */;
```

Implementing the push *Operation*

Let us now examine the *push* operation. It seems that this operation should be quite easy to implement using the array representation of a stack. A first attempt at a PUSH routine might be the following:

```
PUSH: PROC (STACK,X);
          DCL 1 STACK,
                2 ITEM(*)       FIXED,
                2 TOP           FIXED,
                X               FIXED;
          TOP=TOP+1;
          ITEM(TOP)= X;
          RETURN;
      END PUSH;
```

This routine makes room for the item X to be pushed onto the stack by incrementing TOP by 1, and then it inserts X into the array ITEM.

The routine directly implements the *push* operation, which was introduced in the last section. Yet, as it stands, it is quite incorrect. It allows a subtle error to creep in, caused by using the array representation of the stack. See if you can spot this error before reading further.

Recall that a stack is a dynamic structure which is constantly allowed to grow and shrink and thus change its size. An array, on the other hand, is a fixed object of predetermined size. Thus it is quite conceivable that a stack will outgrow the array which was set aside to contain it. This will occur when the array is full, that is, when the stack contains as many elements as the array, and an attempt is made to push yet another element onto the stack. The result of such an attempt is called an ***overflow***.

Assume that the array is full and that the PL/I PUSH routine is called. The full array is indicated by the condition TOP=100, so that the 100th (and last) element of the array is the current top of the stack. When PUSH is called, TOP is increased to 101 and an attempt is made to insert X into the 101st position of the array ITEM. Of course, ITEM contains only 100 elements, so that this attempt at insertion will result in an error and may (if the compiler is a good one or if the SUBSCRIPTRANGE condition has been enabled) produce an appropriate error message. This message is totally meaningless within the context of the original algorithm, since it does not indicate an error in the algorithm, but rather in the computer implementation of that algorithm. It would be far more desirable for the programmer to provide for the possibility of overflow and to print out a more meaningful message.

The PUSH routine may therefore be revised so that it reads as shown at the top of page 155.

Here, a check is made to determine whether the array is full before attempting to push another element onto the stack. The array will be full if TOP=HBOUND(ITEM,1). (The PL/I expression HBOUND(X,N), where X is an array name and N is an integer, gives the upper bound of the Nth dimension of array X. Thus, if X is a one-dimensional array, HBOUND(X,1) returns the largest allowable subscript of X.)

```
PUSH: PROC (STACK, X);

        DCL 1 STACK,
                2 ITEM(*)       FIXED,
                2 TOP           FIXED,
              X                 FIXED;

        IF TOP=HBOUND(ITEM,1) THEN DO;
               PUT SKIP LIST ('STACK OVERFLOW');
               STOP;
                                          END;
        TOP=TOP+1;
        ITEM(TOP) =X;
        RETURN;
      END PUSH;
```

You should again note that if and when the overflow condition is detected in PUSH, execution will halt immediately after the printing of an error message. This action, as in the case of POP, may not be the most desirable. It might, in some cases, make more sense for the calling routine to be able to invoke the push operation with the instructions:

```
CALL PUSHANDTEST (STACK, X, OVERFLOW);
IF OVERFLOW THEN  /*  overflow has been detected. X was not  */
                  /*  pushed on stack. take remedial action.  */;
            ELSE  /*   X was successfully pushed on stack     */
                  /*          continue processing             */;
```

This will allow the calling program to proceed after the call to PUSHANDTEST whether or not overflow was detected. The subroutine PUSHANDTEST is left as an exercise for the reader.

It is useful to compare this PUSH routine with the earlier POP function. Although the overflow and underflow conditions are handled similarly in the two routines, there is a fundamental difference between them. Underflow indicates that the POP operation cannot be performed on the stack and may indicate an error in the algorithm. No other implementation or representation of the stack will cure the underflow condition. Rather, the entire solution must be rethought. (Of course, it is possible that the programmer wishes an underflow to occur as a signal for ending one process and beginning another. However, in such a case, he would use the POPANDTEST routine rather than the POP function.)

Overflow, however, is not a condition which is applicable to a stack as an abstract data structure. As we saw in the last section, it is always possible to push an element onto a stack since a stack is just an ordered set and there is no limit to the number of elements such a set can contain. The possibility of an overflow is introduced when a stack is implemented by an array with only a finite number of elements, thereby prohibiting the growth of the stack beyond that number. It may very well be that the algorithm which the programmer used is correct; he just did not anticipate that his stack would become so large. Thus, in some cases, a possible way to correct an overflow condition is to change the declaration for the stack in the main program so that the array ITEM contains more elements.

The parameter STACK of the subroutines POP and PUSH was declared so that the array ITEM in the subroutine will contain exactly as many elements as the array ITEM in the main program. This is indicated by the asterisk in the declaration

```
DCL 1 STACK,
      2 ITEM(*)   FIXED,
      2 TOP       FIXED;
```

Therefore, the routines POP and PUSH will work correctly regardless of the number of elements allocated for the stack in the main program. If it is feasible to enlarge the array, only the upper bound in the main program need be changed. The two subroutines are independent of the maximum size of the array ITEM.

However, more often than not, an overflow does indicate an error in the program which cannot be attributed to a simple lack of space. The program may be in an infinite loop where things are constantly being pushed onto the stack and nothing is ever popped. Thus the stack will outgrow the array bound no matter how high that bound is set. The programmer should always check that this is not the case before indiscriminately raising the array bound. Often, the maximum stack size can easily be determined from the program and its inputs so that if the stack does overflow, there is probably something wrong with the algorithm which the program represents.

Let us now look at our last operation on stacks, *top*(*stack*), which returns the top element of a stack without removing it from the stack. As we noted in the last section, *top* is not really a primitive operation because it can be decomposed into the two operations

```
x= pop(stack)
push (stack,x)
```

This decomposition is the basis of the following function:

```
STACKTOP:  PROC(STACK) RETURNS (FIXED);
             DCL 1 STACK,
                     2 ITEM(*)   FIXED,
                     2 TOP       FIXED,
                   X             FIXED;
             X= POP(STACK);
             CALL PUSH (STACK,X);
             RETURN(X);
           END STACKTOP;
```

Notice that the function is not named TOP because the PL/I identifier TOP is already being used to refer to the top element of the stack.

However, this is a rather awkward way to retrieve the top element of a stack. Why not ignore the decomposition noted above and directly retrieve the proper value? Of course, a check for the empty stack and underflow must then be explicitly stated since the test is no longer handled by a call to POP.

The revised function is as follows:

```
STACKTOP:  PROC (STACK) RETURNS (FIXED);
             DCL 1  STACK,
                      2 ITEM(*)   FIXED,
                      2 TOP       FIXED;

             IF EMPTY(STACK) THEN DO;
                PUT SKIP LIST ('STACK UNDERFLOW');
                STOP;
                                         END;
             RETURN (ITEM(TOP));
           END STACKTOP;
```

You may wonder why we bother writing a separate routine STACKTOP. A reference to ITEM(TOP) would serve just as well. There are several reasons for this. First, the routine STACKTOP incorporates a test for underflow so that no mysterious errors will occur if the stack is empty. Second, it allows the programmer to use a stack without worrying about its internal makeup. Third, if a different implementation of a stack is introduced, the programmer need not comb through all the places where he referred to ITEM(TOP) in order to make those references compatible with the new implementation. He need only change the STACKTOP routine.

Armed with this set of PL/I routines, we can begin attacking problems which call for the use of stacks and presenting PL/I solutions. We shall do this in the succeeding sections before presenting other implementations of stacks.

3.3. An Example: PL/I Scope Nesting

Statement of Problem

To illustrate the usefulness of stacks, let us consider the rules for DO loop nesting in PL/I. A PL/I DO statement begins the scope of a loop, and an END statement ends that scope. If an END statement includes a label (as, for example, in the statement END LOOP;), then it ends the scope of the loop which begins with the DO statement which has the same label (as for example, LOOP: DO I=1 TO 10;). Any other scopes which have been opened past the DO statement so labeled but have not yet been closed are also ended by that same END statement. Thus scopes are closed in the reverse order that they are opened.

For an illustration of these rules, let us examine the program segment of Fig. 3.3.1. At line 1 of the program, the scope of the loop labeled LOOP1 is opened, and at line

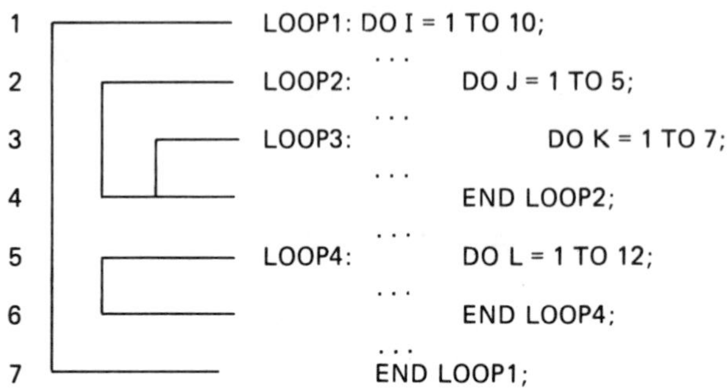

Figure 3.3.1. A PL/I program segment illustrating DO-LOOP nesting.

2, the scope of loop LOOP2 is opened. At line 3, yet another scope (of loop LOOP3) is opened, so that three scopes are open at that point. Line 4 indicates that the scope LOOP2 is to be closed. However in order to close LOOP2, LOOP3 must first be closed, since it was opened after LOOP2 and was not yet closed. Therefore, the END statement in line 4 closes both LOOP3 and LOOP2. Only a single scope (LOOP1) remains open. A new scope (LOOP4) is opened in line 5, so that two scopes (LOOP4 and LOOP1) are open. LOOP4 is closed in line 6, and LOOP1 is closed in line 7.

If an END statement does not include a label after the keyword END, then the END statement closes only a single scope. That scope is the most recently opened scope which has not yet been closed. For example, if statement 4 in Fig. 3.3.1 had been END; instead of END LOOP2;, a quite different pattern of scope nesting would be implied. This new pattern is illustrated in Fig. 3.3.2.

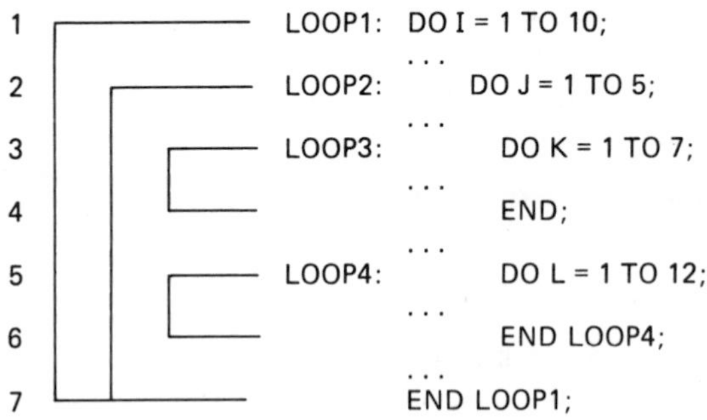

Figure 3.3.2. Another illustration of DO-LOOP nesting.

Notice that the END statement in line 4 now ends only a single scope (LOOP3) since LOOP3 is the last scope opened which has not yet been closed. When LOOP4 begins in line 5, LOOP2 is still open and is not ended until LOOP1 is ended in line 7.

It is good programming practice to always label DO statements and to refer to the label in the appropriate END statement. It is also a good idea never to use a single END statement to close the scope of more than one DO loop, but rather to include additional

END statements in order to make the program more readable. Indentation should be used to clarify which statements are in the scope of each loop. For example, line 5 is indented further in Fig. 3.3.2 than in Fig. 3.3.1 since it is included in the scope of LOOP2 in Fig. 3.3.1 but not in Fig. 3.3.2. While the compiler will ignore all indentation and will process a program solely based on the pattern of labels, DOs, and ENDs which appear, the human reader (including the programmer) will be better able to understand a program that is indented.

We wish to write a PL/I program which associates the END statement which closes a scope with the DO statement which opens it. In order to simplify the input process we will assume that the input consists of a deck of cards each of which is in one of the two forms

DO *label*

or

END *label*

where *label* is either a valid PL/I identifier or a blank. The label on a DO card should be thought of as the label of the DO statement so that a card of the form "DO *label*" corresponds to the PL/I statement

label: DO . . . ;

A card of the form "END *label*" corresponds to the PL/I statement

END *label*;

For example, an input deck corresponding to the DO loop structure of Fig. 3.3.2 is as follows:

```
DO   LOOP1     (first card)
DO   LOOP2
DO   LOOP3
END
DO   LOOP4
END  LOOP4
END  LOOP1     (last card)
```

The program should read a card and print it. If the card is a DO card with a label, it should print a message of the form

SCOPE *label* OPENED

If the DO card contains no label, the program should print

UNNAMED SCOPE OPENED

If the card is an END card, the program should print a series of messages of the form

SCOPE *label* CLOSED

or

UNNAMED SCOPE CLOSED

Of course, if an END card closes more than one scope, the order of the messages should indicate that the last scope opened is the first scope closed. For input corresponding to Fig. 3.3.2 the output should be

```
DO LOOP1
SCOPE LOOP1 OPENED
DO LOOP2
SCOPE LOOP2 OPENED
DO LOOP3
SCOPE LOOP3 OPENED
END
SCOPE LOOP3 CLOSED
DO LOOP4
SCOPE LOOP4 OPENED
END LOOP4
SCOPE LOOP4 CLOSED
END LOOP1
SCOPE LOOP2 CLOSED
SCOPE LOOP1 CLOSED
```

Note that the card END LOOP1 causes two messages to be printed, indicating that LOOP2 is closed before LOOP1.

Here is another example of output which might be printed by the program (this includes some unnamed scopes):

```
DO   LOOP1
SCOPE LOOP1 OPENED
DO   LOOP2
SCOPE LOOP2 OPENED
DO
UNNAMED SCOPE OPENED
END LOOP2
UNNAMED SCOPE CLOSED
SCOPE LOOP2 CLOSED
END
SCOPE LOOP1 CLOSED.
```

Algorithm for Solution

We can outline an algorithm as follows:

```
1     do while (there are more input cards);
2          read(card); print(card);
3          instr= the first word of card;
4          label=the second word of card;
5          if instr= 'DO' then do;
6               print an appropriate message;
7               store away label;
8                              end;
9          else if instr= 'END' then
10               if label= ' ' then
11                    print a message closing the last scope;
12               else print messages closing all scopes up
                                          to and including scope label;
13         else print an error message and perform
                         appropriate error recovery;
14    end;
```

This program outline is quite imprecise and cannot be immediately translated into a program. Rather, it is an attempt to mirror the specification statement (which is even more ambiguous) and to mold it into a framework around which a program can be written. In formulating such an outline, ambiguities in the specification are highlighted. (See if you can spot the ambiguities in specification that are illustrated by the outline example.) Once the outline has been written, each part of it can be isolated separately and refined until it has the precision necessary to be directly translatable into PL/I. During this refinement process you may find that certain parts of the specification have been omitted or must be made more precise. In that case, the outline must be revised, and the entire process reiterated. However, revision of the outline is a much simpler task than attempting to patch up a PL/I program which has been written directly from an English description. The relation between a PL/I statement and a specific English phrase in the specification is often very difficult to uncover since English and PL/I are so very different from each other. By using an outline as a bridge between the two languages, the path between them becomes more straightforward. This isolation and refinement process has become a very important tool in writing correct programs and has resulted in large savings of both machine time and programmer time.

Refining the Outline

Let us therefore begin refining the program outline. Line 1 begins a loop which will terminate when the input is exhausted. In PL/I, the end of an input file is indicated by the ENDFILE(SYSIN) condition, so that the main loop of the program may be written as

```
SCOPE:  PROC OPTIONS (MAIN);
            ON ENDFILE(SYSIN) GO TO FINISH;
INPUT:      DO WHILE ('1'B);
                GET EDIT (CARD) (A(80));
                PUT SKIP EDIT (CARD) (A(80));
                ...
            END INPUT;
FINISH: END SCOPE;
```

Of course, the variable CARD must be declared as CHAR(80). In lines 3 and 4 we are asked to extract the first and second "words" on the card. Since this is a possibly complicated operation (an arbitrary number of blanks may be interspersed among the words, or we may want to ensure that the words are valid PL/I identifiers), it is best left isolated in a subroutine of its own. We will therefore assume the existence of a function WORD which accepts two arguments: the first is a character string STR and the second is an integer N. WORD(STR,N) returns the Nth PL/I identifier in STR, or the null string if there is no Nth identifier.

We can therefore translate lines 3 and 4 of our outline into the two lines of code:

```
INSTR=WORD(CARD,1);
LAB=WORD(CARD,2);
```

Eventually the function WORD must be programmed in PL/I. However, by isolating it as a separate subprogram, we can postpone consideration of the details of character string extraction and focus instead on the main goals of the program. Later, when the program has been completed, we can fill in the details of the function WORD. This is a further step in the outline/refinement process in which programs are broken up into separately manageable modules.

Let us now turn our attention to lines 5 through 13 of the outline, which represent the heart of the program. Line 7 instructs us to "store away *label*." Note the deliberate vagueness of this instruction. Where are we to store this label? How are we to retrieve it? By the previous analysis, we have seen that DO loop scoping represents a last-in, first-out discipline; the last scope to be opened must be the first to be closed. Thus a stack is the natural data structure to use for this problem (hopefully, you had already realized that fact by now).

We will, therefore, declare a stack of character strings as follows:

```
DCL 1 STACK,
        2 LABELS(100)  CHAR(80) VAR,
        2 TOP FIXED    INIT (0);
```

We are assuming that no more than 100 scopes will be open simultaneously and that the maximum length of a label is 80 characters (this is imposed on us by the fact that a label must fit on a single card; indeed, if the labels of the input must be valid PL/I identifiers, they will be limited to the maximum length of an identifier in a particular PL/I implementation). Thus, "store away *label*" will be translated into "push *label* onto a stack."

Another point must yet be clarified before continuing with the program. Line 6 refers to an "appropriate message" to be printed upon opening a scope. By the original specification of the problem, this message depends on the label which names the scope. If the scope is labeled, the program must print

SCOPE *label* OPENED

Otherwise, the program prints

UNNAMED SCOPE OPENED

We can now translate lines 5 through 8 of the outline:

```
IF INSTR = 'DO' THEN DO;
   IF LAB=' ' THEN
      PUT SKIP LIST ('UNNAMED SCOPE OPENED');
               ELSE
      PUT SKIP EDIT ('SCOPE',LAB,'OPENED') (A,X(1),A,X(1),A);
   CALL PUSH (STACK, LAB);
                        END;
```

Note that even if LAB=' ', we must push LAB onto the stack. This is because at each point in the program, the stack contains the set of scopes which have been opened but not yet closed. Even if a scope is unnamed, it is, nevertheless, a valid scope and must be pushed onto the stack. Also note that the PUSH routine in this program segment must be different from the PUSH routine of Section 2. The PUSH subroutine of that section was written for a stack of integers, while this program uses a stack of character strings. Therefore, the DECLARE statement in the PUSH routine must be rewritten to conform to the attributes of the elements in the stack.

Let us now turn our attention to lines 9 through 11 of our outline. The message which is printed in line 11 must refer to the label of the last scope opened. This label can be retrieved by popping the stack. Thus the program continues:

```
ELSE  IF INSTR='END' THEN
           IF LAB=' ' THEN DO;
              LB=POP(STACK);
              IF LB=' 'THEN
                 PUT SKIP LIST ('UNNAMED SCOPE CLOSED');
                       ELSE
                 PUT SKIP EDIT('SCOPE',LB,'CLOSED') (A,X(1),A,X(1),A);
                             END;
```

Line 12 presents special problems. If an END statement refers to a label, that scope as well as all others which have been opened after it must be closed. Thus, the stack must be popped continuously, each scope being closed as it is popped from the stack until the desired label is reached. The translation of line 12 follows:

```
             ELSE DO;
                LB=POP(STACK);

CLOSELOOP:      DO WHILE(LB¬=LAB);
                   IF LB='' THEN PUT SKIP LIST
                                          ('UNNAMED SCOPE CLOSED');
                           ELSE PUT SKIP EDIT('SCOPE',LB,'CLOSED')
                                                (A,X(1),A,X(1),A);
                   LB=POP(STACK);
                END CLOSELOOP;
                PUT SKIP EDIT('SCOPE',LAB,'CLOSED') (A,X(1),A,X(1),A);
                   END;
```

We will see shortly why this code is inadequate, but let us first complete the program. Line 13 refers to the case where a card has been read whose instruction is neither DO nor END. We must decide what to print out to indicate the error and what to do once an error has been found. Perhaps the easiest thing to do is to print

```
ERROR. INSTRUCTION IS ILLEGAL, CARD IGNORED
```

and then ignore the card and continue processing as though it had never been encountered. This can be accomplished by the statement

```
ELSE PUT SKIP LIST ('ERROR. INSTRUCTION IS ILLEGAL,CARD IGNORED');
```

The Complete Program

Let us now put all the pieces together, add appropriate declarations, and examine the complete program.

```
SCOPE:   PROC OPTIONS(MAIN);
            DCL (INSTR,LAB,LB)    CHAR(80) VAR,
                CARD              CHAR(80),
                1  STACK,
                   2  LABELS(100) CHAR(80) VAR,
                   2  TOP         FIXED INIT (0);
            ON ENDFILE(SYSIN) GO TO FINISH;
INPUT:      DO WHILE('1'B);
               GET EDIT(CARD) (A(80));
               PUT SKIP EDIT (CARD) (A);
               INSTR=WORD(CARD,1);
               LAB=WORD(CARD,2);
```

```
                    IF INSTR='DO' THEN DO;
                      IF LAB=' 'THEN
                        PUT SKIP LIST('UNNAMED SCOPE OPENED');
                              ELSE
                        PUT SKIP EDIT('SCOPE',LAB,'OPENED')
                                    (A,X(1),A,X(1),A);
                      CALL PUSH (STACK,LAB);
                                     END;

                    ELSE IF INSTR='END' THEN
                      IF LAB=''THEN DO;
                        LB=POP(STACK);
                        IF LB=''THEN PUT SKIP LIST
                                         ('UNNAMED SCOPE CLOSED');
                              ELSE PUT SKIP EDIT
                                         ('SCOPE',LB,'CLOSED')
                                         (A,X(1),A,X(1),A);
                                   END;
                              ELSE DO;
                          LB=POP(STACK);
CLOSELOOP:                DO WHILE (LB¬=LAB);
                            IF LB=''THEN PUT SKIP LIST
                                              ('UNNAMED SCOPE CLOSED');
                                  ELSE PUT SKIP EDIT
                                              ('SCOPE',LB,'CLOSED')
                                              (A,X(1),A,X(1),A);
                            LB=POP(STACK);
                          END CLOSELOOP;
                          PUT SKIP EDIT('SCOPE',LAB,'CLOSED')
                                               (A,X(1),A,X(1),A);
                                  END;

                    ELSE PUT SKIP LIST
                        ('ERROR. INSTRUCTION IS ILLEGAL . . . . CARD IGNORED');
               END INPUT;
FINISH:  END SCOPE;
```

We must, of course, still supply the function WORD and appropriate versions of POP and PUSH which apply to stacks of character strings. We leave these as exercises for the student. The reader is urged to use the nesting structures of Figures 3.3.1 and 3.3.2 as input to the above program, and to note the following points:

1. The program produces the correct output for those inputs.
2. At each point of the program, the stack STACK contains the labels of scopes which have been opened but not yet closed.

We mentioned previously that the code developed for line 12 is inadequate. Upon reading an END statement which includes a label, the scope beginning at that label, as well as all unclosed scopes beginning after the label, must be closed. However, suppose the label included in the END statement has never been encountered previously? The loop CLOSELOOP is repeatedly executed, popping all the elements off the stack in a vain search for a nonexistent label. The loop will then be repeated once more (since LB is still not equal to LAB), and the program will execute the statement

```
LB=POP(STACK);
```

But at this point, the stack will be empty so that an underflow will occur and the program will halt.

To be sure, the input is incorrect, and some sort of error indication is called for. However, the message STACK UNDERFLOW which is printed by the POP routine upon detecting underflow is not very meaningful in the context of the original problem because it does not inform the user of the source of the error. In fact, the same error message would be printed for quite another reason if, for example, an END statement had been encountered while the stack was empty.

Another objection to the code for line 12 is that no error recovery has been incorporated into the program (except in the case of an illegal instruction). While we may want to halt program execution upon occurrence of an error, we more frequently would like to take some corrective action.

Therefore, instead of using the POP function, we will use the subroutine POPANDTEST, which tests for underflow but allows the calling program to detect its occurrence and take corrective action. We must decide what corrective action to take. Upon reading an END statement with no label which is not preceded by a DO statement, a reasonable course would be to simply ignore the END statement and continue processing. However, in the case of an END statement with a label which had not been previously encountered in a DO statement, underflow is not detected until after all open scopes have been closed. The best recovery that we can hope for is to print an error message and resume processing with no scopes remaining open.

Another error situation which can occur is for scopes to remain open after the input has been exhausted. This occurs when not enough END statements have been placed in the input to match the DO statements. A simple message at the end of the output, listing all unclosed scopes, should suffice to note this error.

The Program with Error Recovery

To incorporate these error recovery facilities, we present a second version of the program. Numbered arrows indicate portions of the program to which we will refer later.

```
SCOPE:      PROC OPTIONS (MAIN);
              DCL (INSTR, LAB, LB) CHAR(80) VAR,
                  CARD             CHAR(80),

                  UND              BIT(1),  /*  to detect underflow    */
                  1 STACK,
                    2 LABELS(100) CHAR (80) VAR,
                    2 TOP          FIXED INIT(0);
              ON ENDFILE(SYSIN) GO TO FINISH;

INPUT:        DO WHILE ('1'B);
                GET EDIT (CARD) (A(80));
                PUT SKIP EDIT (CARD) (A);
                INSTR= WORD(CARD,1);
                LAB=WORD(CARD,2);

                IF INSTR='DO' THEN DO;
                  IF LAB=' ' THEN
                    PUT SKIP LIST ('UNNAMED SCOPE OPENED');
                          ELSE
                    PUT SKIP EDIT ('SCOPE',LAB,'OPENED')
                                 (A,X(1),A,X(1),A);
                  CALL PUSH (STACK, LAB);
                                 END;

                ELSE IF INSTR='END' THEN

                  IF LAB=' ' THEN DO;
                    CALL POPANDTEST (STACK,LB,UND);
                    IF UND THEN DO;
                      /*  print message   */
                      PUT SKIP LIST ('ERROR—NO OPEN SCOPES');
                      PUT SKIP LIST ('END STATEMENT IGNORED');
                      /*  repeat the input loop    */
1——→                  GO TO OVER;
                              END;
                  IF LB=' ' THEN
                    PUT SKIP LIST ('UNNAMED SCOPE CLOSED');
                         ELSE
                    PUT SKIP EDIT('SCOPE',LB,'CLOSED') (A,X(1),A,X(1),A);
                            END;
                         ELSE DO;  /*  an end statement with a label    */
2——→                LB=' ';
                    CALL POPANDTEST(STACK, LB, UND);
CLOSELOOP:          DO WHILE (¬ UND & LB¬ =LAB);
                      IF LB=' ' THEN PUT SKIP LIST
                                           ('UNNAMED SCOPE CLOSED');
                             ELSE PUT SKIP EDIT('SCOPE',LB,'CLOSED')
                                                (A,X(1),A,X(1),A);
                      CALL POPANDTEST(STACK,LB,UND);
                    END CLOSELOOP;
```

```
3———→                IF UND THEN DO;
                        /*  print error message    */
                        PUT SKIP LIST ('INVALID LABEL IN END STATEMENT');
                        PUT SKIP LIST
                                ('ALL OPEN SCOPES HAVE BEEN CLOSED');
                                END;
                            ELSE PUT SKIP EDIT('SCOPE',LAB,'CLOSED')
                                            (A,X(1),A,X(1),A);
                            END;  /*  of DO above arrow 2   */
                ELSE PUT SKIP LIST
                    ('ERROR. INSTRUCTION IS ILLEGAL, CARD IGNORED.');
OVER:       END INPUT;

FINISH:     /*  check to see whether there are any unclosed scopes    */
            IF ¬EMPTY(STACK) THEN PUT SKIP LIST
                                ('THE FOLLOWING SCOPES REMAIN OPEN');
CLEANSTK:   DO WHILE (¬EMPTY(STACK));
                LB=POP(STACK);
                PUT SKIP LIST (LB);
            END CLEANSTK;

        END SCOPE;
```

Let us take a closer look at some features of this program. We use the subroutine POPANDTEST to pop an element from a stack and to set an underflow indicator UND to '1'B if underflow is detected. If the underflow condition is not detected, the second argument of this subroutine is set equal to the element popped from the stack. Since UND is a bit, we can test for underflow with the statement IF UND THEN . . . .

Note the GO TO statement at arrow number 1. Although it is usually a good idea to avoid GO TO statements because they make programs difficult to follow, in some situations they are a tremendous convenience. This example is a good case in point. An END statement with no label attached has been read. Upon attempting to pop the stack of opened scopes, an underflow occurs. This means that no scope is open and that the END statement is illegal. The program should print an error message and read the next card, ignoring the illegal END statement. The statement GO TO OVER; resumes the input loop in order to begin processing the next card. We could have omitted the GO TO OVER; statement and instead have inserted the word ELSE before the statement IF LB=' ' THEN . . . . However, we are already so deeply nested in IF statements and ELSE clauses that adding another such nesting would increase the complexity of the program structure to an unmanageable degree.

Another interesting point to note in this program is the DO statement at CLOSELOOP. An END statement with a label has been recognized, and we wish to close all scopes up to and including that label. POPANDTEST is called to pop the top label off the stack. One of three things can happen:

1. Underflow is detected, indicating that no scopes are on the stack.

2. A label matching the label on the END statement is popped off the top of the stack.

3. A label, other than the one on the END statement, is popped off the top of the stack.

In case 3 the scope opened by the popped label must be closed, and we must continue popping labels until either condition 1 or 2 occurs. Thus, as long as no underflow occurs and as long as the matching label is not reached, the loop must be repeated. Since LAB holds the label on the END statement, LB holds the label popped off the stack, and UND indicates overflow, the DO loop header is

```
DO WHILE (¬UND & LB¬=LAB);
```

However, if underflow does occur, LB is not given a value by POPANDTEST. The comparison LB¬=LAB may cause an error because LB is potentially undefined. (Despite the fact that the condition in the WHILE clause must be false because UND is '1'B, the computer will test whether LB¬=LAB before assigning a value to the entire expression and an error may occur. In an optimizing compiler, if the first operand of a conjunction is set to false, the second operand would not be evaluated and the entire conjunction becomes false. Thus, the above error is avoided. However, a programmer should attempt to program in a compiler-independent fashion.)

To avoid this possible error, a statement is inserted at arrow number 2 to set LB to the null string. If there is a label on the stack, POPANDTEST will reset LB to that label. However, if underflow occurs, LB will have a value (the null string) which can be compared with the value of LAB. Thus the DO statement will be executed properly, and the condition will be evaluated as false.

The loop CLOSELOOP may be exited as a result of one of two possible occurrences: either an underflow has occurred which calls for an error message, or LB=LAB, in which case the scope of LAB must be closed. We explicitly test for underflow at arrow number 3 to ensure that the correct action is taken.

More Error Recovery

However, there is still a reason to be dissatisfied with the program. When an END statement with a label is read and that label has never before been encountered, the current program will pop all labels until the underflow condition is detected and will then proceed to the next card. This may not be the best action to take. It may be desirable to simply ignore the erroneous END statement or to treat it as an END statement with no label, rather than to use it as a signal to close all open scopes. This would seem to be more sensible since such an error usually arises from a misspelling of a label in either a DO or END statement or from the omission of a DO statement. Leaving all open scopes (except possibly one) open allows a succeeding END statement to close all scopes up to a certain point and allows the remaining statements to be processed correctly.

For example, let us examine the effects of these three methods of error recovery if LOOP4 were misspelled in Fig. 3.3.1, line 6. As the program now stands, both LOOP4 and LOOP1 will be closed by the erroneous END statement. When we subsequently read

END LOOP1; an error message will again be printed, this time for a perfectly legitimate statement. Suppose that we ignored an incorrect label and treated the END statement as referencing no label. The statement would then close the last scope which was opened but not yet closed, which happens to be LOOP4. Thus the input would be processed correctly despite the error. This, of course, is the goal of a successful error recovery method. Further, such a method would tend to promote the recommended programming practice of ending each DO loop with its own END statement. If a programmer followed this practice, this method of error recovery would process his programs correctly despite any misspellings.

If we had decided to simply ignore all END statements with an unrecognizable label, and the programmer had misspelled LOOP4 in line 6 of Fig. 3.3.1, LOOP4 would remain open until closed by the statement END LOOP1. Such an action is probably preferable to ending both LOOP1 and LOOP4 at line 6. But if the programmer had inadvertently left out line 4, which begins scope LOOP4, this method of error recovery would ignore the END statement so that the structure of the remainder of the program is preserved. Thus we see that either of these methods of error recovery is preferable to the original method. The choice of which of the two error recovery schemes to select depends upon the type of error which is expected more frequently.

Let us focus our attention on the method which completely ignores an END statement with a previously unreferenced label. The other method, of taking the END statement as one with no label, presents the same programming problems and can easily be implemented by the reader after he has understood the subsequent discussion.

In order to print an error message and take corrective action, the program must first detect that an error has occurred. The only way of detecting that a label was not previously pushed onto the stack is by popping all the labels off the stack and recognizing that a particular label was not present. However, popping a label from a stack is equivalent to closing its scope. What is needed is some method of searching the elements of a stack without popping (and hence deleting) them from the stack.

A stack has been illustrated (see Fig. 3.1.1) by taking its cross section, so that it is apparent whether or not an element is on the stack. However, a stack is really meant to be viewed from above so that only its top element is recognizable. In order to tell whether some other element is on the stack, one must pop the top element, revealing a new top, then pop that element, etc., until the desired element or the empty stack is reached. The stack is defined by the operations which may be performed on it, and those operations (*pop* and *push*) only allow access to the top element.

Thus, in order to test for the presence of a particular label on the stack without popping and deleting all other labels, a method of saving the popped labels is needed. Such a method might be to create a temporary stack upon which to push the elements popped from the first stack as a search for the label proceeds. The original stack is popped and the popped element is pushed onto the temporary stack until one of two things occurs:

1. The stack is empty, in which case the desired label is not present.
2. The desired label is found at the top of the original stack.

An indicator FOUND can be set to an appropriate value depending upon whether condition 1 or 2 above arises. In any case, the labels of the temporary stack would then be popped and restored onto the original stack until the temporary stack is empty. This restores the original contents of STACK. Depending upon the value of FOUND, appropriate action may then be taken.

Alternatively, in order to test whether a given label is on the stack, we may retreat from an insistence on independence of implementation. Thus far, a stack has been manipulated only by using operations common to all implementations of a stack. Analogs of the POP and PUSH routines must be available for any implementation of stacks. However, we are now saying that we will cease using the data structure STACK as a pure stack and will examine its actual structure.

The data structure LABELS within STACK is really an array, and it is quite an easy matter to search an array. We can write a function SRCHSTK which searches the array representation of a stack for a given element and returns a result of *true* or *false* depending on whether the element has been found. This function may be written as follows:

```
SRCHSTK:    PROC(STACK,ELT) RETURNS (BIT(1));
               DCL 1 STACK,
                       2 ITEM(*)  CHAR(*) VAR,
                       2 TOP      FIXED,
                     ELT          CHAR(*) VAR,
                     I            FIXED;
SEARCH:        DO   I=1 TO TOP;
                  IF ITEM(I) =ELT THEN RETURN ('1'B);
               END SEARCH,
               RETURN ('0'B);
            END SRCHSTK;
```

Using the function SRCHSTK, we can rewrite the program so that an END card with a previously unknown label will be ignored. The program is identical to the previous version up to the ELSE preceding arrow number 2. We resume from there:

```
  ELSE   /*    an end statement with a label      */
   IF SRCHSTK(STACK,LAB) THEN DO;   /*    LAB exists on the stack     */
              LB=POP(STACK);
CLOSELOOP:  DO WHILE (LB¬=LAB);
                IF LB='' THEN PUT SKIP LIST ('UNNAMED SCOPE CLOSED');
                      ELSE PUT SKIP EDIT ('SCOPE',LB,'CLOSED')
                                              (A,X(1),A,X(1),A);
                LB=POP(STACK);
            END CLOSELOOP;
            PUT SKIP EDIT('SCOPE',LAB,'CLOSED') (A,X(1),A,X(1),A);
                                END;
```

```
            ELSE   /*   the label does not exist on the stack   */
                        PUT SKIP EDIT(LAB,
                            'IS A NONEXISTENT LABEL, STATEMENT IGNORED')
                                                  (A,X(1),A);
            IF (INSTR ¬= 'END') & (INSTR ¬= 'DO') THEN
               PUT SKIP LIST
                  ('ERROR,ILLEGAL INSTRUCTION, CARD IGNORED');
OVER: END INPUT;
FINISH: ...
```

By introducing and using the function SRCHSTK, the data structure STACK is no longer a true stack. However, we can use it as a stack when appropriate and as an array when that interpretation is more useful.

3.4. An Example: Infix, Postfix, and Prefix

Basic Definitions and Examples

In this section we shall examine a major application of stacks. While it is one of the most prominent applications, it is by no means the only one. The reason that we consider this application is that it illustrates so well the different types of stacks and the various operations and functions we have defined upon them. The example is also an important topic of computer science in its own right.

Before proceeding with the algorithms and programs of this section, it will be necessary to provide some groundwork. Consider the sum of A and B. We think of applying the ***operator*** "+" to the ***operands*** A and B and write the sum as A+B. This particular representation is called ***infix***. There are two alternative notations for expressing the sum of A and B using the symbols A, B, and +. These are

+ A B   ***prefix***

A B +   ***postfix***

The prefixes "pre," "post," and "in" refer to the relative position of the operator with respect to the two operands. In prefix notation the operator precedes the two operands, in postfix notation the operator follows the two operands, and in infix notation the operator is between the two operands. The prefix and postfix notations are not really as awkward to use as they might first appear. For example, if we were using a PL/I function to return the sum of the two arguments A and B, we might invoke it by ADD(A,B). The operator ADD precedes the operands A and B.

Let us now consider some additional examples. The evaluation of the expression A+B*C, as written in standard infix notation, requires knowledge of which of the two operations, + or *, is to be performed first. In the case of + and * we "know" that multiplication is to be done before addition (in the absence of parentheses to the contrary). Thus A+B*C is to be interpreted as A+(B*C) unless otherwise specified. We say that multiplication takes ***precedence*** over addition. Suppose we would now like to rewrite A+B*C in postfix. Applying the rules of precedence, we first convert the portion of the expression that is evaluated first, namely the multiplication. By doing this conversion in stages, we obtain

```
A+(B*C)     parentheses for emphasis
A+(BC*)     convert the multiplication
A(BC*)+     convert the addition
ABC*+       postfix form
```

The only rules to remember during the conversion process is that the operations with highest precedence are converted first and that after a portion of the expression has been converted to postfix it is to be treated as a single operand. Let us now consider the same example with the precedence of operators reversed by the deliberate insertion of parentheses.

```
(A+B)*C     infix form
(AB+)*C     convert the addition
(AB+)C*     convert the multiplication
AB+C*       postfix form
```

In the above example the addition was converted before the multiplication because of the parentheses. In going from (A+B)*C to (AB+)*C, A and B are the operands and + is the operator. In going from (AB+)*C to (AB+)C*, (AB+) and C are the operands and * is the operator. The rules for converting from infix to postfix are simple, providing you know the order of precedence. For binary operators the following is the order of precedence (highest to lowest):

```
exponentiation
multiplication/division
addition/subtraction
```

By using parentheses, we can override the default precedence. In the following examples we will denote exponentiation by the symbol $ rather than ** so as to eliminate confusion between two multiplication symbols and the exponentiation symbol. We give the following additional examples of converting from infix to postfix. Be sure that you understand each of these examples (and can do them on your own) before proceeding to the remainder of this section. We follow the PL/I convention that when unparenthesized operators of the same precedence are scanned, the order is assumed to be left to right except in the case of exponentiation, where the order is assumed to be from right to left. Thus A+B+C means (A+B)+C, while ABC means A$(B$C).

Infix	Postfix
A+B	AB+
A+B−C	AB+C−
(A+B)*(C−D)	AB+CD−*
A$B*C−D+E/F/(G+H)	AB$C*D−EF/GH+/+
((A+B)*C−(D−E))$(F+G)	AB+C*DE−−FG+$
A−B/(C*D$E)	ABCDE$*/−

The precedence rules for converting an expression from infix to prefix are identical. The only change from postfix conversion is that the operator is placed before the operands rather than after them. We present the prefix forms of the above expressions. Again, you should attempt to make the transformations on your own.

Infix	Prefix
A+B	+AB
A+B−C	−+ABC
(A+B)*(C−D)	*+AB−CD
A$B*C−D+E/F/(G+H)	+−*$ABCD//EF+GH
((A+B)*C−(D−E))$(F+G)	$−*+ABC−DE+FG
A−B/(C*D$E)	−A/B*C$DE

Note that the prefix form of a complex expression is not the mirror image of the postfix form, as can be seen from the second of the above examples, A+B−C. We will henceforth be concerned with the postfix transformations and will leave to the reader as exercises most of the work involving prefix.

One point immediately obvious about the postfix form of an expression is that it requires no parentheses. Let us consider the two expressions A+(B*C) and (A+B)*C. While the parentheses in one of the two expressions is superfluous (by convention A+B*C = A+(B*C)), the parentheses in the second expression is necessary to avoid confusion with the first. The postfix forms of these expressions are:

Infix	Postfix
A+(B*C)	ABC*+
(A+B)*C	AB+C*

There are no parentheses in either of the two transformed expressions. A close look tells us that the order of the operators in the postfix expressions determines the actual order of operations in evaluating the expression, making the use of parentheses unnecessary. In going from infix to postfix, we are sacrificing the ability to note at a glance the operands associated with a particular operator. We are gaining, however, an unambiguous form of the original expression without the use of cumbersome parentheses. In fact, you may argue that the postfix form of the original expression might look simpler were it not for the fact that it appears difficult to evaluate. For example, how do we know that letting A=3, B=4, and C=5 in the examples above, we have 3 4 5 * + =23 and 3 4 + 5 * =35?

Evaluating a Postfix Expression

The answer to this question lies in the development of an algorithm for evaluating expressions in postfix. Each operator in a postfix string refers to the previous two operands in the string. (Of course, one of these two operands may itself be the result of applying a previous operator.) Suppose that each time we read an operand we push it onto a stack. When we reach an operator, its operands will then be the top two elements on the stack. We can then pop these two elements, perform the indicated operation on them, and push the result on the stack so that it will be available for use as an operand of the next operator. The following algorithm evaluates an expression in postfix using this method.

```
Initialize a stack, opndstk, to be empty;
/*  scan the input string reading one element at a time into symb   */
do while (there are more characters in the input string);
    symb= next input character;
    if symb is an operand then push (opndstk, symb);
                          else /*  symb is an operator  */
                           do;
                 opnd2 = pop(opndstk);
                 opnd1 = pop(opndstk);
                 value=result of applying symb to opnd1 and opnd2;
                 push (opndstk, value);
                           end;
end;
result= pop(opndstk);
return (result);
```

Let us now consider an example. Suppose we are asked to evaluate the following expression in postfix:

6 2 3 + − 3 8 2 / + * 2 $ 3 +

We show the contents of the stack *opndstk* and the variables *symb, opnd1, opnd2,* and *value* after each successive iteration of the loop. The top of *opndstk* is to the right.

symb	*opnd1*	*opnd2*	*value*	*opndstk*
6				6
2				6,2
3				6,2,3
+	2	3	5	6,5
−	6	5	1	1
3	6	5	1	1,3
8	6	5	1	1,3,8
2	6	5	1	1,3,8,2
/	8	2	4	1,3,4
+	3	4	7	1,7
*	1	7	7	7
2	1	7	7	7,2
$	7	2	49	49
3	7	2	49	49,3
+	49	3	52	52

Let us make some observations about the above example which will aid us in translating the algorithm into a program. As its name implies, *opndstk* is a stack of operands. Each operand is pushed onto the stack when encountered. Therefore the maximum size of the stack is the number of operands which appear in the input expression. However, in dealing with most postfix expressions the actual size of the stack needed is less than this maximum since an operator removes operands from the stack. In the previous example the stack never contained more than four elements despite the fact that eight operands appeared in the postfix expression.

When an operator is encountered, the top two elements of the stack are popped and combined by the given operator. Suppose that an operator is encountered at a point where the stack contains fewer than two operands. This indicates an error in the original input string. We must decide whether our program should detect errors of this sort and, if so, what action it should take.

Finally, the result of the evaluated expression is the single remaining element on the stack when the input is exhausted. Suppose that more than one operand remains on the stack? Does this indicate an error? The answer is that it most assuredly does, and this error is a result of having too many operands and not enough operators. Again, there is an error in our input string.

Program to Evaluate a Postfix Expression

We are now prepared to plan our program to evaluate an expression in postfix notation. There are a number of questions we must consider before we can actually write the program. A primary consideration, as in all programs, is to define precisely the form and restrictions, if any, on the input. Usually the programmer is presented with the form of the input and is required to design his program to accommodate the given data. On the other hand, we are in the fortunate position of being able to choose the form of our input. This enables us to construct a program that is not overburdened with transformation problems that overshadow the actual intent of the routine. Had we been confronted with data in a form that is awkward and cumbersome to work with, we could relegate the transformations to various routines and use the output of these routines as input to our primary routine. In the "real world," recognition and transformation of input is a major concern.

Let us assume in this case that the input is in the form of a string of digits and operator symbols punched on a single data card. We will assume that operands are single nonnegative digits, e.g., 0, 1, 2, . . ., 8, 9. (as an exercise you may wish to consider a less restricted form of input.) Thus, for example, our input might look like 345*+ punched in the first five columns of a data card with the remaining columns left blank. We would like to write a program that reads data cards of this format, as long as there are any cards remaining, and prints out for each card the original input string and the result of the evaluated expression.

Taking a closer look at the algorithm, we indicate which portions of it are straightforward and which parts must undergo some transformation process. Since the symbols are read from the data cards as characters, we must find a method to convert the operand characters to numbers and the operator characters to operations. For example, we must have a method for converting the character string '5' to the number 5 and the character string '+' to the addition operation. The conversion of a character string to an integer can be handled in several ways. One method is to use the conversion facilities of PL/I; but this method depends on the particular PL/I compiler being used. We prefer to avoid such complications at this stage, although the student is encouraged to explore this method since conversions play an important role in PL/I programming. A second alternative is to assume a function CONVERT(STR) which accepts a character string STR of length 1 and returns the numerical value of that symbol, assuming that the symbol is a digit. To convert an operator symbol into the corresponding action, we use a function OPER which accepts an operator and two operands as input parameters. The function returns the value of the expression obtained by applying the operator to the two operands. The programming of these two routines is left as an exercise for the reader.

The body of the main routine might be the following:

```
         DCL EXPR CHAR(80);
         ON ENDFILE(SYSIN) STOP;
         PUT PAGE EDIT('ORIGINAL POSTFIX EXPRESSION', 'VALUE')
                        (A,COL(110),A);
         PUT SKIP;
INPUT:   DO WHILE ('1'B);
             /*  read in next expression   */
             GET EDIT (EXPR) (COL(1),A(80));
             PUT SKIP EDIT(EXPR, EVAL(EXPR))(A(100), F(15,4));
         END INPUT;
```

The main part of the program is, of course, the routine EVAL which is presented below. The routine is merely the PL/I implementation of the evaluation algorithm, taking into account the specific environment and format of the input data and calculated outputs. However, it tries to make the routine EVAL as independent of these features as possible, leaving conversions to the subroutines CONVERT and OPER. It also makes use of a function OPND which tests whether its argument is or is not an operand. If the argument is an operand, OPND returns '1'B; otherwise, it returns '0'B.

```
EVAL:  PROC(EXPR) RETURNS(FLOAT);
    /*  EVAL accepts a postfix expression as input    */
    /*     and returns the value of this expression   */
    /*           as a floating-point number           */

      DCL EXPR                    CHAR(*),
            1 OPNDSTK,
              2 OPRND(50)         FLOAT,
              2 OPRND_TOP         FIXED INIT(0),
    /*  the above INIT attribute initializes OPNDSTK    */
    /*              to empty on each call               */
```

```
          POSITION                    FIXED,
          VALUE                       FLOAT,
          SYMB                        CHAR(1),
          (OPND1,OPND2)               FLOAT,
       /*   POSITION is a pointer to the current position     */
       /*  of EXPR and SYMB will hold the current symbol      */

       /*    start scanning symbols until a blank is found    */
SCAN:     DO POSITION=1 TO 80 WHILE(SUBSTR(EXPR,POSITION,1) ¬=' ');
             SYMB=SUBSTR(EXPR,POSITION,1);
             IF OPND(SYMB) THEN CALL PUSH(OPNDSTK,CONVERT(SYMB));
                /*   we have found an operand so we push     */
                /*          its value on the stack           */
                          ELSE
                               OPERATOR: DO;
                    OPND2=POP(OPNDSTK);
                    OPND1=POP(OPNDSTK);
                    VALUE=OPER(SYMB,OPND1,OPND2);
                    CALL PUSH(OPNDSTK,VALUE);
                                          END OPERATOR;

          END SCAN;
          /*   we have now scanned the last character so we   */
          /*             return the top of the stack          */
          VALUE=POP(OPNDSTK);
          RETURN(VALUE);
       END EVAL;
```

The function EVAL calls upon the following functions and subroutines: POP, PUSH, CONVERT, OPND, and OPER. PUSH and POP were presented in Section 3.2, although they do require some modification (why?). The programming of the routines CONVERT and OPER is left as an exercise for the reader. OPND tests whether its argument is an operand or not, returning '1'B if it is and '0'B otherwise. A short version of this function follows:

```
OPND:  PROC(STR) RETURNS (BIT(1));
          DCL STR CHAR (*),
               NUMS CHAR (10) INIT ('1234567890');
          IF INDEX(NUMS, STR) =0 THEN RETURN ('0'B);
                                 ELSE RETURN ('1'B);
       END OPND;
```

By combining all these routines and supplying some data, you can now run a program to evaluate postfix expressions.

Limitations of the Program

Before we leave the program, we should note some of its deficiencies. Understanding what a program cannot do is as important as knowing what it can do. It should be obvious that attempting to use a program to solve a problem for which it was not intended will lead to chaos. Frequently an attempt is made to solve a problem with an incorrect program, only to have the program produce incorrect results, without the slightest trace of an error message. In these cases the programmer has no indication that the results are wrong, and may therefore make faulty judgments based on those results. For this reason, it is important for the programmer to understand the limitations of his program.

A major criticism of this program is that it does nothing in terms of error detection and recovery. Clearly, if the data on each input card is a correct postfix expression, then the program will work. Suppose, however, that one card has too many operators or operands or that they are not in a proper sequence. These problems could come about as a result of someone innocently using the program on a postfix expression that contains two-digit numbers, yielding an excessive number of operands. Or possibly the user of the program was under the impression that negative numbers could be handled by the program and that they are to be punched with the minus sign, the same sign that is used to represent subtraction. These minus signs will be treated as subtraction operators, resulting in an excess number of operators. Depending on the specific type of error, the computer may take one of several actions (e.g., halt execution, print erroneous results, etc.). Suppose that at the final statement of the program, the stack OPNDSTK is not empty. We will get no error messages (because we asked for none), and EVAL will return a numerical value for an expression that was probably incorrectly stated in the first place. Suppose one of the calls to the POP routine raises the underflow condition? Since we did not use the POPANDTEST routine to pop elements from the stack, our program will stop. This seems unreasonable since faulty data on one card should not prevent the processing of additional cards. By no means are these the only problems that could arise. As exercises you are asked to write programs that accommodate less restrictive inputs and some others that will test and detect some of the errors listed above.

The programmer who wishes to implement these routines will have to decide to what extent, if any, these routines should be modified. If he has already written a program TEST which merely tests for valid data (postfix form) and has already tested all the data cards with this routine, he can safely use the routine as given. If, on the other hand, there is a possibility of error on one or more input cards, he will have to decide which errors to test for and how to proceed if and when these conditions arise. Similarly, when the programmer gives a program to someone (his employer) with the statement that "it works," he should also make very clear for precisely what types of data it works, what the limitations of the program are, and what action the program will take upon receiving "bad" data. Only if a programmer specifies these limitations has he discharged his responsibility for writing the program.

Converting an Expression from Infix to Postfix

We have thus far presented routines to evaluate a postfix expression. Although we have discussed a method for transforming infix to postfix, we have not as yet presented an algorithm for doing so. It is to this task that we now direct our attention. Once such an algorithm has been constructed, we will have the capability of reading an infix expression and evaluating it by first converting it to postfix and then evaluating the postfix expression.

In our previous discussion, we mentioned that subexpressions within innermost parentheses must first be converted to postfix so that they can then be treated as single operands. In this fashion, parentheses can be successively eliminated until the entire expression is converted. The last pair of parentheses to be opened within a group of parentheses encloses the first subexpression within that group to be transformed. This last-in, first-out behavior should immediately suggest the use of a stack.

Consider the two infix expressions A+B*C and (A+B)*C and their respective postfix versions ABC*+ and AB+C*. In each case the order of the operands is the same as the order of the operands in the original infix expressions. In scanning the first expression, A+B*C, the first operand A can be immediately inserted into the postfix expression. Clearly the + symbol cannot be inserted until after its second operand, which has not yet been scanned, is inserted. Therefore, it must be stored away to be retrieved and inserted in its proper position. When the operand B is scanned, it is inserted immediately after A. Now, however, two operands have been scanned. What prevents the + symbol from being retrieved and inserted? The answer is, of course, the * symbol which follows and which has precedence over +. In the case of the second expression the closing parentheses indicate that the + operation should be performed first. Remember that in postfix, unlike infix, the operator which appears earlier in the string is the one which is applied first.

Since precedence plays such an important role in transforming infix to postfix, let us assume the existence of a function *prcd*(*op1*, *op2*), where *op1* and *op2* are characters representing operators. This function returns *true* if *op1* has precedence over *op2* whenever *op1* appears to the left of *op2* in an infix expression without parentheses. *prcd*(*op1*, *op2*) returns *false* otherwise. For example, *prcd*('*','+') and *prcd*('+','+') are *true*, while *prcd*('+','*') is *false*. Let us now present an outline of an algorithm to convert an infix string without parentheses into a postfix string. Since we are assuming no parentheses in our input string, the only governor of the order in which operators appear in the postfix string is precedence.

```
initialize the postfix string to '';
initialize the stack opstk to empty;
do while (there are more input symbols);
   read(symb);
   if symb is an operand then
             add symb to the postfix string;
                   else /*   the symbol is an operator    */
                      do;
        do while (¬empty(opstk) and prcd(top(opstk),symb));
         topsymb=pop(opstk);
         /*   topsymb has precedence over symb so    */
         /*    it can be added to the postfix string    */
         add topsymb to the postfix string;
        end;
```

```
          /*  At this point, either opstk is empty or symb       */
          /*  has precedence over top(opstk). We cannot          */
          /*  output symb into the postfix string until we       */
          /*  have read the next operator, which may have        */
          /*  precedence. We must therefore store symb.          */
13          push (opstk, symb);
14                              end;
15       end;

       /*  At this point, we have reached the end of the       */
       /*       string. We must output the operators           */
       /*       remaining on the stack into the postfix        */
       /*                  string.                             */
16       do while (¬empty(opstk));
17           topsymb= pop(opstk);
18           add topsymb to the postfix string;
19       end;
```

Simulate the algorithm with such infix strings as 'A∗B+C∗D' and 'A+B∗CDE' (where '$' represents exponentiation and *prcd*('$','$')=*false*) to convince yourself that it is correct. Note that at each point of the simulation, an operator on the stack has a lower precedence than all the operators above it. This is because the initial empty stack trivially satisfies this condition and an operator is pushed onto the stack (line 13) only if the operator currently on top of the stack has a lower precedence than the incoming operator.

You should also note the liberty which we have taken in line 9 in forming the condition

```
¬empty(optsk) and prcd(top(opstk),symb)
```

Make sure that you understand why such a condition should not be used in an actual program.

What modification must be made to this algorithm in order to accommodate parentheses? The answer is surprisingly little. When an opening parenthesis is read, it must be pushed onto the stack. This can be done by establishing the convention that *prcd*(*op*,'(')=*false* and *prcd*('(',*op*)=*false* for any operator symbol *op* other than a right parenthesis. This ensures that an operator symbol appearing after a left parenthesis will be pushed onto the stack.

When a closing parenthesis is read, all operators up to the first opening parenthesis must be popped from the stack into the postfix string. This can be done by setting *prcd*(*op*,')')=*true* for all operators *op* other than a left parenthesis. When these operators have been popped off the stack and the opening parenthesis is uncovered, special action must be taken. The opening parenthesis must be popped off the stack, and it and the closing parenthesis must be discarded rather than placed in the postfix string or on the stack. Let us set *prcd*('(',')') to *false*. This will ensure that upon reaching an opening parenthesis, the loop beginning at line 9 will be skipped so that the opening parenthesis will not be inserted into the postfix string. Execution will therefore proceed to line 13.

However since the closing parenthesis should not be pushed onto the stack, line 13 will be replaced with the statement

```
13      if empty(opstk) or symb¬=')' then push(opstk,symb);
                                      else topsymb= pop(opstk);
```

With the above conventions for the *prcd* function and the revision to line 13, the algorithm can be used to convert any infix string to postfix. We summarize the precedence rules for parentheses:

prcd('(',*op*)=*false* for any operator *op* including ')'
prcd(*op*,'(')=*false* for any operator *op* other than ')'
prcd(*op*,')')=*true* for any operator *op* other than '('
prcd(')',*op*)=*undefined* (an attempt to compare the two indicates an error).

We illustrate this algorithm on some examples:

Ex. 1: A+B*C

The contents of *symb*, the postfix string, and *opstk* are shown after scanning each symbol. *opstk* is shown with its top to the right.

	symb	postfix string	*opstk*
1	A	A	
2	+	A	+
3	B	AB	+
4	*	AB	+*
5	C	ABC	+*
6		ABC*	+
7		ABC*+	

Lines (1), (3), and (5) correspond to the scanning of an operand, so the symbol (*symb*) is immediately placed on the postfix string. In line (2) an operator was scanned and the stack was found to be empty, so the operator is placed on the stack. In line (4) the precedence of the new symbol (*) was greater than the precedence of the symbol on the top of the stack (+), so the new symbol is pushed onto the stack. In steps (6) and (7) the input string was empty, so the stack is popped and its contents placed on the postfix string.

Ex. 2: (A+B)*C

symb	postfix string	*opstk*
(		(
A	A	(
+	A	(+
B	AB	(+
)	AB+	
*	AB+	*
C	AB+C	*
	AB+C*	

In this example, when the right parenthesis is encountered, the stack is popped until a left parenthesis is encountered, at which point both parentheses are discarded. By using parentheses to force an order of precedence different than the default, the order of appearance of the operators in the postfix string is different than in Example 1.

Ex. 3: ((A–(B+C))*D)$(E+F)

symb	postfix string	*opstk*
(		(
(		((
A	A	((
–	A	((–
(	A	((–(
B	AB	((–(
+	AB	((–(+
C	ABC	((–(+
)	ABC+	((–
)	ABC+–	(
*	ABC+–	(*
D	ABC+–D	(*
)	ABC+–D*	
$	ABC+–D*	$
(	ABC+–D*	$(
E	ABC+–D*E	$(
+	ABC+–D*E	$(+
F	ABC+–D*EF	$(+
)	ABC+–D*EF+	$
	ABC+–D*EF+$	

Why does the conversion algorithm seem so involved and the evaluation algorithm seem so simple? The answer is that the former converts from one order of precedence (governed by the *prcd* function and the appearance of parentheses) to the natural order (i.e., the operation to be executed first appears first). Because of the many combinations of elements at the top of the stack (if not empty) and possible incoming symbol a large number of statements are necessary to cover each possibility. In the latter algorithm, on the other hand, the operators appear in precisely the order they are to be executed. For this reason the operands can be stacked until an operator is found, at which point the operation is performed immediately.

The motivation behind the conversion algorithm is the desire to output the operators in the order they are to be executed. In solving this problem by hand, we could follow vague instructions that require us to convert from the inside out. This works very well for humans doing a problem with pencil and paper (if they do not become confused or make a mistake). However, when writing a program or an algorithm, we must be more precise in our instructions. We cannot be sure that we have reached the innermost parentheses or the operator with the highest precedence until we have actually scanned all the symbols. At that time, we must backtrack to some previous point.

Rather than backtrack continuously, we make use of the stack to "remember" the operators encountered previously. If an incoming operator is of greater precedence than the one on top of the stack, then this new operator is pushed onto the stack. This means that when all the elements in the stack are finally popped, this new operator will precede the former top in the postfix string (which is correct since it has higher precedence). If, on the other hand, the precedence of the new operator is less than that of the top of the stack, then the operator at the top of the stack should be executed first. Therefore the top of the stack is popped, and the incoming symbol is compared with the new top, and so on. By including parentheses in our input string, we may override the order of operations. Thus when a left parenthesis is scanned, it is pushed on the stack. When its associated right parenthesis is found, all the operators between the two parentheses are placed on the output string because they are to be executed before any operators appearing after the parentheses.

Program to Convert an Expression from Infix to Postfix

There are two things that we must do before we actually start writing a program. The first is to define precisely the format of the input and output. The second is to construct, or at least define, those routines that the main routine depends upon. We will assume that our input will be a continuous stream of characters punched on data cards. The end of the string will be signaled by the occurrence of a blank. For the sake of simplicity, we will assume that all operands are single-character letters or digits. All operators and parentheses will be punched as themselves except that $ replaces ** for exponentiation. The output will be a character string. These conventions will make the output of the conversion process suitable for the evaluation process, provided that all the single-character operands in the initial infix string are digits.

In transforming the conversion algorithm into a PL/I program, we make use of several routines. Among these are EMPTY, POP, PUSH, and POPANDTEST, all suitably modified so that the elements on the stack are single-character strings. We also make use of the function OPND which returns '1'B if its argument is an operand and '0'B otherwise. This function must also be slightly modified from the version introduced in the program for the evaluation algorithm so that it recognizes a letter as well as a digit as an operand. These simple modifications are left to the reader.

Similarly, the PL/I PRCD function is left to the reader as an exercise. It accepts two single-character operator symbols as arguments and returns '1'B if the first has precedence over the second when it appears to the left of the second in an infix string and '0'B otherwise. The program should, of course, incorporate the parentheses conventions which we previously introduced.

Once these auxiliary subroutines and functions have been written, we can write the main routine that calls a conversion function POSTFIX and the function POSTFIX itself. We assume that the main routine reads in a card containing an expression in infix, calls the routine POSTFIX, and prints out the original string and the postfix string. The body of the main routine follows:

```
DCL IN_STRING              CHAR(80),
      POST_STRING          CHAR(80) VAR;
ON ENDFILE(SYSIN) STOP;
PUT SKIP EDIT('ORIGINAL INFIX STRING', 'POSTFIX STRING') (A(100),A);
```

```
LOOP:  DO WHILE ('1'B);
           GET EDIT(IN_STRING) (COL(1),A(80));
           POST_STRING= POSTFIX(IN_STRING);
           PUT SKIP EDIT(IN_STRING, POST_STRING) (A, COL(100), A);
       END LOOP;
```

The POSTFIX routine which implements the conversion appears below.

```
POSTFIX: PROC(INFIX) RETURNS(CHAR(80) VAR);
           /*  POSTFIX accepts a string in infix and returns   */
           /*       the postfix form of the original string    */

       DCL INFIX                     CHAR(*),
           OUT                       CHAR(80) VAR INIT(''),
           UND                       BIT(1),
           SYMB                      CHAR(1),
           TOPSYMB                   CHAR(1) INIT('+'),
           POSITION                  FIXED INIT(0),
           1 OPSTK,
             2 OPER(80)              CHAR(1),
             2 OPER_TOP              FIXED INIT(0);
       /*              stack is initially empty             */

       /*  begin scanning symbols until a blank is found   */
       /*        line 3 of the conversion algorithm         */
SCAN:  DO POSITION=1 BY 1 WHILE (SUBSTR(INFIX,POSITION,1)¬=' ');
           /*                  line 4                          */
           SYMB=SUBSTR(INFIX,POSITION,1);
           /*          check if SYMB is an operand             */
           /*                lines 5 and 6                     */
           IF OPND(SYMB) THEN OUT=OUT || SYMB;
                         ELSE OPERATOR: DO;
              CALL POPANDTEST(OPSTK, TOPSYMB, UND);

           /*              lines 9 through 12                  */
LOOP:         DO WHILE(¬ UND & PRCD(TOPSYMB, SYMB));
                  OUT=OUT||TOPSYMB;
                  CALL POPANDTEST(OPSTK, TOPSYMB, UND);
              END LOOP;
              IF ¬UND THEN CALL PUSH(OPSTK, TOPSYMB);

              /*  modified version of line 13   */
              IF UND|SYMB ¬=')'THEN CALL PUSH(OPSTK, SYMB);
                              ELSE TOPSYMB=POP(OPSTK);
                                          END OPERATOR;
       END SCAN;
```

```
                /*        lines 16 through 19        */
FINISH: DO WHILE(¬ EMPTY (OPSTK));
            OUT=OUT||POP(OPSTK);
        END FINISH;
        RETURN(OUT);
          END POSTFIX;
```

The program has one major flaw, in that it does not check that the input string is a valid infix expression. In fact, it would be instructive for you to examine the operation of this program when it is presented with a valid *postfix* string as input. As an exercise, you are asked to write a program which checks whether or not an input string is a valid infix expression.

It is useful for you to examine how lines 9 through 12 of the conversion algorithm were implemented. We could not simply code

```
DO WHILE(¬EMPTY (OPSTK) & PRCD(STACKTOP(OPSTK),SYMB));
```

because if OPSTK were empty, STACKTOP(OPSTK) would result in an underflow and halt program execution. Instead, we used POPANDTEST to both pop the top element and test for underflow simultaneously. However, if it turns out that the popped element (TOPSYMB) has lower precedence than the incoming symbol (SYMB), it must be restored to the stack. That is why we must add the statement

```
IF ¬ UND THEN CALL PUSH(OPSTK,TOPSYMB);
```

after the loop LOOP. Such a statement was unnecessary in the algorithm outline because there the top element of the stack is not popped until it is known that it has higher precedence than the incoming symbol.

One other point to make note of is the INIT attribute in the DECLARE statement for TOPSYMB:

```
TOPSYMB CHAR(1) INIT ('+').
```

The reason that TOPSYMB must be initialized is that the statement CALL POPANDTEST (OPSTK,TOPSYMB,UND); will be executed upon encountering the first operator. Since OPSTK is initially empty, TOPSYMB will not be changed by POPANDTEST. If TOPSYMB had no initial value, the call to PRCD(TOPSYMB, SYMB) in the DO WHILE statement would result in an error. This will occur in spite of the fact that it is the value of UND which will govern the algorithm's action in this case rather than the value of PRCD. By initializing TOPSYMB to some value, we are sure that PRCD will return a value on this call, although that value is irrelevant to further processing. It is details like the above that can often cause errors in program execution.

We can now write a program to read in an infix string and find its numerical value. If the original string consists of single-digit operands with no letter operands, the following sequence of statements will read in the original string and print out its value.

```
DCL (IN_STRING, OUT_STRING) CHAR(80),
    ANSWER                  FLOAT;
GET EDIT(IN_STRING) (COL(1),A(80));
OUT_STRING= POSTFIX(IN_STRING);
ANSWER= EVAL(OUT_STRING);
PUT SKIP EDIT(IN_STRING, ANSWER) (A,X(20),F(10,2));
```

The stack manipulation procedures (POP, PUSH, etc.) for the stack of character string operators (i.e., OPSTK) should be internal to POSTFIX, while the procedures for manipulating the stack of FLOAT operands (i.e., OPNDSTK) should be internal to EVAL. This is necessary to avoid any conflict between the two versions of each procedure.

Most of our attention in this section has been devoted to transformations involving postfix expressions. The algorithm to convert an infix expression into postfix scans characters from left to right, stacking and unstacking as necessary. If it were necessary to convert from infix to prefix, the infix string could be scanned from right to left and the appropriate symbols entered in the prefix string from right to left. Since most algebraic expressions are read from left to right, postfix is a more natural choice. It would be instructive for you to attempt to write algorithms and programs, similar to those presented in this section, to handle prefix notation.

The above programs are merely indicative of the type of routines one could write to manipulate and evaluate postfix expressions. They are by no means comprehensive or unique. There are many variations of the above routines that are equally acceptable. Some of the older high-level language compilers actually used routines such as EVAL and POSTFIX to handle algebraic expressions. Since that time, more sophisticated schemes have been developed to handle these problems.

3.5. The AUTOMATIC and CONTROLLED Storage Classes

In this section, we examine two features of PL/I which exhibit stack-like behavior. One of these features can be used as an alternative to the array implementation of stacks introduced in Section 2. Aside from their connection with stacks, however, these concepts form an important part of the PL/I language and are valuable weapons in the programmer's arsenal.

Each variable in a program represents a portion of the computer's memory where information can be stored. A variable whose identifier is declared FIXED BINARY represents a smaller portion of storage than a variable declared as an array or structure. However, declaring an identifier does not actually set aside storage for its variable. In fact, the PL/I DECLARE statement is nonexecutable; it only informs the compiler as to the attributes of the variable, a necessary prerequisite for the assignment of storage for that variable. The actual assignment of storage to a variable is called ***allocation*** and must be performed either immediately before the program begins execution (in which case, the storage is allocated ***statically***) or as part of the program execution (in which case. the storage is allocated ***dynamically***). Similarly, storage may be deallocated or ***freed*** from a variable. PL/I provides four different methods of allocating and freeing storage. The method used to allocate and free storage for a particular variable is called the ***storage class attribute*** of that variable and may be declared in a DECLARE statement, just as any other attribute. In this section we examine two of these storage classes, AUTOMATIC and CONTROLLED.

Blocks and the AUTOMATIC Storage Class

In order to declare an identifier X with the AUTOMATIC storage class attribute, you may code

```
DECLARE X AUTOMATIC;
```

or simply

```
DECLARE X;
```

The AUTOMATIC storage class is the default storage class; i.e., if no storage class attribute is declared explicitly, the variable is given the AUTOMATIC attribute by default. In fact, most (if not all) of the variables which you have been using in PL/I up to this point have been AUTOMATIC, since no storage class was declared for them. Of course, other attributes such as FIXED, CHAR(80) VAR, or FLOAT DECIMAL may be specified for a variable along with the AUTOMATIC attribute.

As indicated earlier, the DECLARE statement does not allocate storage; it only specifies the amount of storage to be allocated and the format of its contents. To understand how AUTOMATIC storage is allocated and freed in PL/I, we must first discuss the concept of a PL/I ***block***. There are two types of blocks in PL/I: BEGIN ***blocks*** and PROCEDURE ***blocks***. A BEGIN block is opened with the PL/I statement

```
BEGIN;
```

while a PROCEDURE block is opened with a PL/I PROCEDURE statement. Both types of blocks are closed with an END statement. The rules for block nesting and multiple closure of blocks are the same as for DO loops as presented in Section 3. During program execution, a BEGIN block is entered when the BEGIN statement is encountered in sequential execution or as the object of a GO TO statement or an ON statement. At that time, all AUTOMATIC variables declared within that block (but not within any contained block) are allocated. As long as control does not leave the BEGIN block, these variables remain allocated. When control leaves the BEGIN block (either by encountering its END statement in sequential execution or by executing a GO TO to a label outside the block), the storage for those variables is freed.

Let us present an example to illustrate this concept. Assume you have a list of numbers on data cards and you wish to print out these numbers in the reverse order in which they appear on the cards. However, you want your program to perform this task regardless of how many numbers appear in the list. Let us assume that preceding the list is a count of how many numbers appear in the list. Let us further assume that you have several such lists (each preceded by the count of elements in the list) and you wish your program to repeat the process for each list, as long as any input remains.

You cannot print the first number of a list until after you have read and printed all the other numbers. This exhibits a last-in, first-out behavior, and you may be tempted to use a stack. However, the problem is how large should the array which holds the elements of the stack be declared. If you do not declare the array large enough to contain the largest list, you will generate an overflow. Even after you have repeatedly tested your program successfully and certified it as correct, some user may submit an input to it which is larger than the array size. If on the other hand, you declare the array so large that you are confident that any reasonable input list can be contained within it, you are likely to be wasting storage most of the time.

The solution to this problem calls for allocating an array whose size equals the number of elements in each list (fortunately, according to our specifications this number appears at the head of the list). This can be done using a BEGIN block, as the following program illustrates:

```
EX1:      PROC OPTIONS(MAIN);
            DECLARE (N,I)              FIXED;
            ON ENDFILE (SYSIN) STOP;
REPEAT:     DO WHILE ('1'B);
               GET LIST (N);
BLOCK:         BEGIN;
                  DECLARE A(N)          FIXED;
                  GET LIST (A);
                  PUT SKIP(2) LIST ((A(I) DO I=N TO 1 BY -1));
               END BLOCK;
            END REPEAT;
          END EX1;
```

Storage for the variable N is allocated when the program begins execution since N is declared in the main (procedure) block of the program. Each time the REPEAT loop is repeated, a value for N is input and the BEGIN block is executed. Upon entry to the block (that is, upon execution of the BEGIN statement), storage for the array A is allocated. The amount of storage allocated for A depends upon the value of the variable N. Each time that the block is entered, the current value of N is used to determine the size of the array A to be allocated.

When the statement END BLOCK; is executed, the storage for A is freed and may be reused for some other variable. When the BEGIN block is reentered, storage for A is again allocated. Note, however, that the storage allocated for A the second time may be a totally different segment of storage than the area allocated for A the first time. This implies that the array A does not retain its previous values. Indeed, the array A does not exist between the time that it is freed and the time that it is reallocated. The first and second allocations of A are totally disjoint.

It is important to understand the distinction between the way in which the variables N and A change during the course of program execution. N is allocated only once at the start of program execution, and it exists until the program terminates. That is, N refers to a particular storage location throughout the program. It is only the *value* of N which changes as the loop is repeated; each time that the GET statement is executed, the content of that storage location is changed so that N receives a new value.

The change in the variable A is much greater, however. Not only do the values of A change, but the storage area which holds those values changes as A is allocated, freed, and then reallocated. The very nature of A changes, as it is first perhaps an array of only 3 elements and later an array of 1000 elements. A is constantly being destroyed and recreated as a different entity. Once A has been allocated, it can be assigned a value by the statement GET LIST (A);. This distinction between allocation and assignment is an important one, but one that beginning programmers often fail to realize.

The use of a BEGIN block to allocate storage ensures that:

1. Sufficient storage will be available for the largest set of data (providing, of course, that sufficient storage is available for your job).

2. No more storage than is actually needed will be used by your program during any iteration.

AUTOMATIC variables declared in a PROCEDURE block are also allocated upon entry to the block and freed upon exit. However, a PROCEDURE block cannot be entered by sequential program execution or as the object of a GO TO statement. If a procedure block appears in a program and the statement preceding that block is executed, the next statement to be executed will not be in the block, but rather the statement immediately following the END statement which closes the block. In order to enter a procedure, you must branch to it by means of a CALL statement (in the case of a subroutine) or by invoking it in an expression (in the case of a function). This mechanism should be familiar to you from previous experience in PL/I programming.

Just as in the case of a BEGIN block, AUTOMATIC storage is allocated upon entry to a PROCEDURE block and freed upon exit from that block, when the procedure returns to its calling program. Thus another method of programming the previous problem is as follows:

```
EX2:      PROC OPTIONS(MAIN);
            DECLARE N              FIXED;
            ON ENDFILE(SYSIN) STOP;
REPEAT:     DO WHILE ('1'B);
              GET LIST(N);
              CALL PROCESS(N);
            END REPEAT;
```

```
PROCESS:  PROCEDURE(N);
             DECLARE (N,I)          FIXED,
                     A(N)           FIXED;
             GET LIST(A);
             PUT SKIP(2) LIST ((A(I) DO I=N TO 1 BY -1));
             RETURN;
          END PROCESS;

       END EX2;
```

Be sure you understand how the above program works before pròceeding. Because storage for AUTOMATIC variables is allocated upon block entry, the actual location of the DECLARE statement within the block is irrelevant. In general, it is good programming practice to declare all variables at the beginning of a block. However, if a variable is declared at any point within the block (but not within any contained block), storage for that variable will still be allocated upon entry to the block. Thus both DECLARE statements in the following code segment will be applied before the GET statement:

```
DCL N               FIXED;
GET LIST(N);
DCL A(N)            FIXED;
```

It is for this reason that a BEGIN block is needed to ensure that these three statements are applied in sequence.

Blocks and Namescoping

Another feature of the PL/I language which is controlled by the block structure of a program is ***namescoping***. This refers to the manner by which variables may be referenced through identifiers in a PL/I program. An identifier which is declared within a block is known only within that block; it cannot be used outside the block to refer to its variable. Any identifier which is declared in an outer block is known within any contained block, unless it is redeclared. For example, let us examine the program EX1 which we introduced earlier. The identifier N was declared in the outer block as referring to a FIXED variable. Since N was not redeclared within the inner block BLOCK, it may be used within that block to refer to the same variable as in the main block. It is used in that way in two places: in the DECLARE statement to establish the bounds of array A and in the PUT statement where it governs the number of elements to be printed.

If a variable is declared in an inner block, it is called ***local*** to that block and can be referenced only from within that block. On the other hand, if the variable is declared in an outer block and not redeclared in an inner block, it is called a ***global*** variable and can be referenced both in the outer block and the inner block. By using a global variable, we can eliminate the parameter in the subroutine PROCESS in the program EX2 and allow the variable N to be accessed directly from within the subroutine. This modification produces the following program:

```
EX3:      PROC OPTIONS(MAIN);
            DECLARE N              FIXED;
            ON ENDFILE(SYSIN) STOP;
REPEAT:     DO WHILE ('1'B);
              GET LIST (N);
              CALL PROCESS;
            END REPEAT;

PROCESS:    PROC;
              DECLARE A(N)           FIXED;
              GET LIST (A);
              PUT SKIP(2) LIST ((A(I) DO I=N TO 1 BY -1));
              RETURN;
            END PROCESS;

          END EX3;
```

As another example, consider the identifier A which is declared in the BEGIN block EX1. That identifier has meaning only within that block. Suppose, however, that the identifier A is used outside the block, for example, if the statement GET LIST(A); were introduced immediately after the statement GET LIST(N);. The identifier A would not refer to an array at all. Rather, since it appears in the outer block where the identifier was not explicitly declared, it is implicitly declared by default to refer to a FLOAT DECIMAL variable, and a single number would be input by the statement GET LIST(A);. In that case, there would be two distinct variables with the same name A; one is FLOAT DECIMAL and can be referenced only in the outer block and the other is an array of FIXED numbers which can be referenced only in the inner block.

An identifier declared in an outer block may be redeclared in an inner block with completely different attributes. The result of such a redeclaration is that two variables exist, although they both have the same name. Within the outer block, outside the inner block, only the first variable can be referenced; within the inner block only the second can be referenced. This is because the first variable has no name within the inner block since its identifier has been reused for the name of a different variable. However, when the inner block is exited, the identifier once again refers to the first variable.

When a local variable is declared, it may be thought of as being pushed onto a stack of variables, each having the same identifier but referring to different objects. When the block in which the variable is declared is exited, the variable is popped off the stack, leaving the variable which was declared in the outer block on top of the stack. Only the variable at the top of the stack can be used at any particular point. To illustrate this, consider the example on page 193.

Let us trace this program's execution. In line 2, an AUTOMATIC variable I is declared FIXED. When program execution begins, that variable is allocated and given the initial value 4. At that point, there is a single object I declared in block EX4 on the stack, as shown in Fig. 3.5.1(a). Thus statement 3 causes the number 4 to be printed.

At line 4, BEGIN block L1 is entered. Since the identifier I is redeclared in that block

```
1    EX4:  PROC OPTIONS(MAIN);
2              DCL I                  FIXED INIT(4);
3              PUT LIST(I);
4    L1:       BEGIN;
5    IN:         PROC;
6                  DCL I              CHAR(5) INIT('ABCDE');
7    L2:           BEGIN;
8                    DCL I;
9                    I=2;
10   L3:             BEGIN;
11                     DCL I          FIXED INIT(0);
12                     PUT LIST(I);
13                   END L3;
14                   I=I+7;
15                   PUT LIST(I);
16                 END L2;
17                 PUT LIST(I);
18               END IN;

19               DCL I              FIXED INIT(10);
20               PUT LIST(I);
21               CALL IN;
22               I=I+6;
23               PUT LIST(I);
24               CALL IN;
25             END L1;
26             PUT LIST(I);
27         END EX4;
```

(line 19), a new variable is allocated and initialized to 10. The state of affairs after executing line 4 is illustrated in Fig. 3.5.1(b). A reference to I at this point is no longer to the variable declared in line 2, but rather to the variable declared in line 19. The I of block EX4 remains allocated (since we remain inside the block in which it was declared), but it cannot be referenced; it has no name in the current block.

The next statement after line 4 is a PROCEDURE statement (line 5), so that execution resumes with the next executable statement after its END (line 18). This next executable statement is at line 20, which causes the value of I at the top of the stack to be printed. Thus, the next number printed is 10. At line 21, the subroutine IN is called and the block IN is entered. Again, a local variable I is declared so that a new element must be pushed onto the stack. This time, however, I is declared not as an integer but as a character string. The same name may be used in different blocks of a program to refer to objects of radically differing attributes. The names are stacked and a reference to an identifier accesses the top element of the stack. At line 5, therefore, the stack is as shown in Fig. 3.5.1(c).

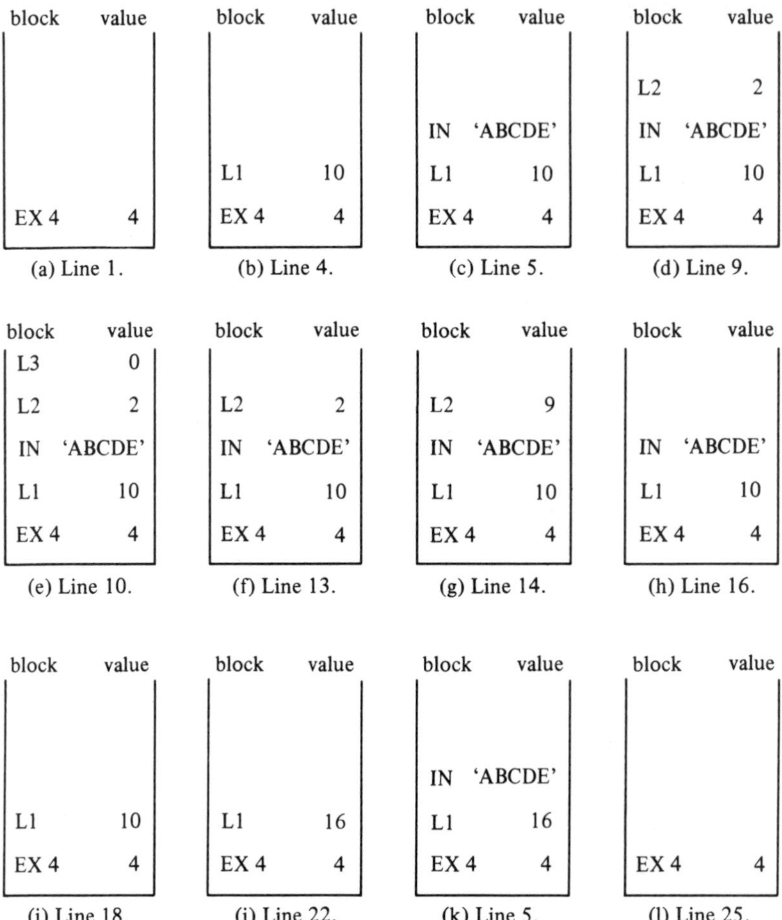

Figure 3.5.1. Successive views of the I stack for program EX4.

Trace through the remainder of the program yourself, following the stack as it is pushed and popped at the lines indicated. Convince yourself that the program prints the values 4,10,0,9,'ABCDE',16,0,9,'ABCDE',4.

The concepts of storage allocation and namescoping are often confused with each other because they are both controlled by the block structure of a program. The two concepts are, however, very different, and it is important to understand the difference. Namescoping refers to the position within the program text from which an identifier refers to a particular variable. Storage allocation refers to the moments of execution during which a given variable has storage allocated to it. You may be able to refer to a variable at a particular point, even though no storage has been allocated to it (although this is impossible with an AUTOMATIC variable in PL/I). Similarly, storage may be allocated to a variable even though you cannot refer to it (for example, an AUTOMATIC variable which is redeclared in an inner block). We will be able to understand this distinction more clearly when we examine another of the four storage classes of PL/I—the CONTROLLED storage class.

The CONTROLLED Storage Class

Users of PL/C should be warned that PL/C does not permit the use of the CONTROLLED storage class. The programs presented in the remainder of this section will therefore not execute properly in PL/C. However, the concept of dynamic user-controlled storage allocation is an important one, and the reader who has only the PL/C compiler available should nevertheless attempt to follow the discussion. It is recommended that sample programs using the CONTROLLED attribute be run on a full PL/I compiler.

A variable X may be declared to have the CONTROLLED storage class by the statement

```
DECLARE X CONTROLLED;
```

CTL may be used as an abbreviation for CONTROLLED. Of course, a controlled variable may be declared to have other attributes such as

```
DECLARE A FIXED(5,2) CTL;
```

or

```
DECLARE B(7,6) CHAR(10) VAR CTL;
```

Storage for a variable which has the CONTROLLED attribute is not allocated when the block in which it is declared is entered. Rather, the programmer must specifically allocate storage for the variable during execution by using the ALLOCATE statement. For example, storage for the variables declared above may be allocated by the statements

```
ALLOCATE X;
ALLOCATE A;
ALLOCATE B;
```

or by the single statement

```
ALLOCATE X,A,B;
```

Similarly, storage for CONTROLLED variables is not freed when the block in which the variables were declared is exited, but must be explicitly freed by use of the FREE statement, as in

```
FREE X;
```

or as in

```
FREE X,A,B;
```

If a CONTROLLED variable is referenced before it is allocated or after it is freed, an error will result, since no storage is allocated to it at that point.

The size of a CONTROLLED array may be specified either at declaration or at allocation. For example, if the array B is declared as above and the statement

```
ALLOCATE B;
```

is executed, enough storage for the 42 elements of the array B is allocated. However if the statement

```
ALLOCATE B(4,3);
```

is executed, only 12 elements are allocated and B is an array of dimension 4 by 3 rather than 7 by 6. This is because the bounds specified at allocation override the bounds specified at declaration. If an expression is used for the size, length, or bounds of a CONTROLLED variable, either in the DECLARE statement or ALLOCATE statement, that expression is evaluated at allocation to determine the size, length, or bounds. For example, if we declare

```
DCL A CHAR(N+1) CTL;
```

and then execute

```
N=10;
ALLOCATE A;
```

A refers to a character string of length 11.

Using this facility, the example of programs EX1, EX2, and EX3 can be reprogrammed using a CONTROLLED variable:

```
EX5:    PROC OPTIONS (MAIN);
          DCL N                    FIXED,
              A(N)                 FIXED CTL;
          ON ENDFILE(SYSIN) STOP;
REPEAT:   DO WHILE ('1'B);
             GET LIST(N);
             ALLOCATE A;
             GET LIST (A);
             PUT LIST ((A(I) DO I=N TO 1 BY -1));
             FREE A;
          END REPEAT;
        END EX5;
```

This method is more efficient than the methods of programs EX1, EX2, or EX3 because the overhead associated with block entry and exit is avoided; only the allocation and freeing is performed.

If a CONTROLLED variable is allocated and another ALLOCATE statement for the same variable is executed before the variable is freed, another segment of storage is allocated for the variable. This second segment of storage is called the second ***generation*** of the variable. The first generation is not freed but is kept on the bottom of a stack, and the second generation is pushed on top of it. Similarly, a third, fourth, etc. generation may be allocated; each is pushed onto a stack on top of the previous generation. The maximum size of this stack is governed by the amount of memory available to the job. Only the top of the stack may be accessed; that is, only the last generation of a variable may be referenced. When the variable is freed, its last generation is popped off the stack and no longer exists. Any reference to the variable will now be to the next-to-last generation, i.e., the new top item on the stack.

To illustrate this process let us look at yet another method of programming our example. Each time that a number is read, it is pushed onto the stack until all the numbers have been input. At that point, the stack is continually popped. Each element is printed as it is popped until the stack becomes empty. (Note that the array A was acting as a stack in the previous programs with items inserted from positions 1 to N and deleted in reverse order.) We need only a single elementary variable A rather than an array.

```
EX6:    PROC OPTIONS (MAIN);
          DCL N                    FIXED,
              A                    FIXED CTL;
          ON ENDFILE(SYSIN) STOP;
REPEAT:   DO WHILE ('1'B);
            GET LIST (N);
PUSH:       DO I=1 TO N;
              ALLOCATE A;
              GET LIST (A);
            END PUSH;
POP:        DO I=1 TO N;
              PUT LIST (A);
              FREE A;
            END POP;
          END REPEAT;
        END EX6;
```

Let us examine the action of program EX6 on the input 4,1,2,5,7,3,5,4,7, as shown in Fig. 3.5.2.

The first value of N that is input is 4. The loop PUSH is therefore executed four times. Initially no storage is allocated to the variable A. Upon execution of the ALLOCATE statement, a single storage area is allocated to A. Its value is set to 1 upon execution of the statement GET LIST (A);. When the loop is repeated, another segment of storage is allocated to A. There is now no way to refer to the first segment since the identifier A refers only to the latest generation. Thus when the value 2 is input, it is placed in this new segment, leaving the value of the first segment unchanged at the bottom of the stack. This process continues until all four values have been input and the stack is as shown in Fig. 3.5.2(d). The identifier A now refers to the top element of the stack, 7.

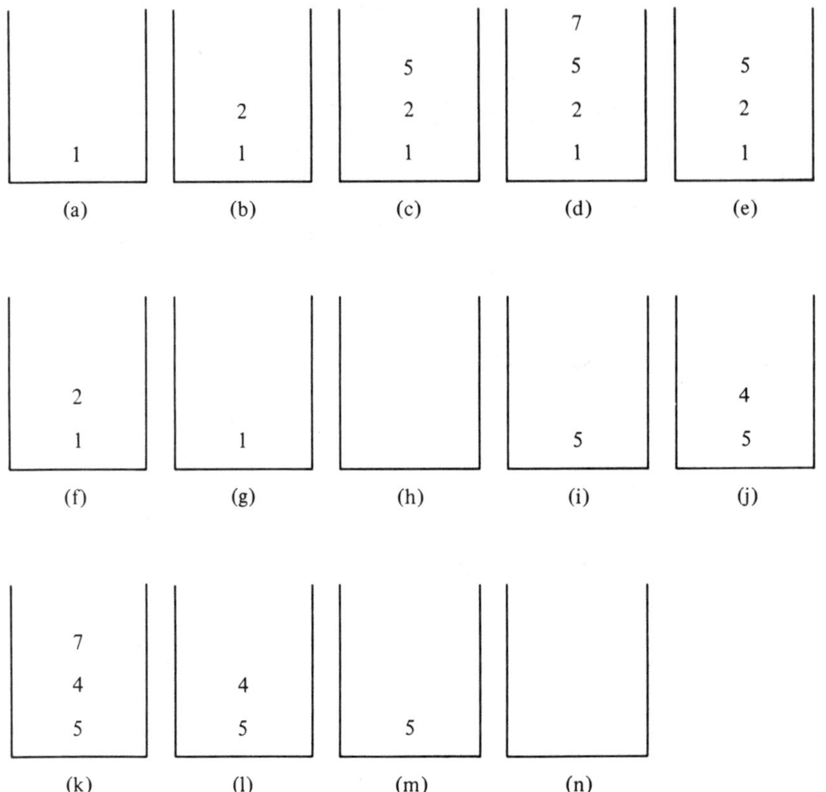

Figure 3.5.2. Successive views of the **A** stack for program EX6.

At this point, the POP loop is executed. The statement PUT LIST (A); prints out 7 since that is the value of the latest generation of A. The statement FREE A; frees this latest generation of A, so that the stack is popped and the next-to-last generation is at the top. Therefore, the identifier A now refers to the value 5 which is printed in the next execution of the loop. This process is repeated until all of the allocated storage is freed and the stack is empty, as in Fig. 3.5.2(h). The numbers printed are 7,5,2,1, which is the reverse of the order of their input.

Then the REPEAT loop is executed again, with the stack being pushed and popped as before, and the values 7,4,5 are printed.

CONTROLLED storage is not freed upon exit of the block in which it is declared, despite the fact that it can no longer be referenced outside that block. CONTROLLED storage can only be freed by executing a FREE statement or by termination of program execution.

Implementing Stacks Using the CONTROLLED Storage Class

A CONTROLLED variable may be used to implement a stack as an alternative to the array representation. We now present PUSH, POP, and EMPTY routines for such an implementation. A stack of integers may be declared by

```
DECLARE STACK FIXED CTL;
```

The PUSH routine simply allocates a new element and sets it to the proper value.

```
PUSH:  PROC (STACK,X);
          DCL STACK              FIXED CTL,
              X                  FIXED;
          ALLOCATE STACK;
          STACK=X;
          RETURN;
       END PUSH;
```

Note that under this implementation there is no way to test for stack overflow. However, overflow is a much rarer occurrence using a stack implemented by a CONTROLLED variable than with a stack implemented by an array. In a stack implemented using an array, overflow will occur if the stack grows beyond the bounds of the array. This may happen despite the fact that sufficient storage is available for the job. All that need be done to remedy the situation is to increase the bounds of the array. A CONTROLLED variable, however, has no bounds and therefore no limit on the number of generations which can be allocated. The only way that an overflow can occur is if the total storage allocated to the job is insufficient. In such a case, the program will halt with a system message indicating that this has occurred. The only solution (assuming program correctness) is to increase the storage allocated to the job.

In the PUSH routine, the parameter STACK was explicitly declared with the CONTROLLED attribute. This was necessary because a new generation of that variable was allocated within the subroutine. If a parameter is not declared CONTROLLED, even if the variable which is passed to it is declared CONTROLLED, no new generations of that variable may be allocated. Rather, the variable must have been already allocated upon call to the subroutine. The parameter's value throughout the subroutine (unless changed within the subroutine) will be the value assigned to its current generation at the point of call, and the parameter may not be used in an ALLOCATE or FREE statement.

In order to test whether a CONTROLLED stack is empty, we must determine whether storage is allocated to a PL/I CONTROLLED variable. For this purpose, PL/I provides the ALLOCATION built-in function. Unfortunately, this function is defined differently in different implementations of the language. In some implementations (e.g., IBM PL/I-F), the function is defined as returning a logical value, *true* or '1'B if its CONTROLLED variable argument is allocated and *false* or '0'B if its CONTROLLED variable argument is not allocated. In other implementations (e.g., the IBM Checkout/Optimizing compilers), the function returns an integer representing the number of generations of the variable which currently exist. In these implementations, the stack is empty if ALLOCATION(STACK)=0. However, because of the rules for conversion between integers and bit strings in PL/I, either of the following two versions of the EMPTY function will work correctly for both implementations. We indicate as preferable the version which does not require conversion.

```
EMPTY:   PROC(STACK) RETURNS (BIT(1));
           /*  Preferable if 'ALLOCATION' is defined as returning a  */
           /*                     bit string                         */

           DCL STACK              CTL FIXED;
           IF ALLOCATION(STACK) THEN RETURN ('0'B);
                                ELSE RETURN ('1'B);
         END EMPTY;
```

or

```
EMPTY:   PROC(STACK) RETURNS(BIT(1));
           /*  Preferable if 'ALLOCATION' is defined as returning  */
           /*                   an integer                         */

           DCL STACK          CTL FIXED;
           IF ALLOCATION(STACK)=0 THEN RETURN ('1'B);
                                  ELSE RETURN ('0'B);
         END EMPTY;
```

The function POP saves the current generation of the CONTROLLED variable so that it can be returned and then frees its storage, effectively popping the stack.

```
POP:   PROC(STACK) RETURNS (FIXED);
         DCL STACK                    FIXED CTL,
             X                        FIXED;
         IF EMPTY(STACK) THEN DO;
                PUT SKIP LIST('STACK UNDERFLOW');
                STOP;
                             END;
         X=STACK;
         FREE STACK;
         RETURN (X);
       END POP;
```

The routines STACKTOP and POPANDTEST are fairly straightforward and are left as exercises for the reader.

To illustrate the use of a CONTROLLED stack, consider the example presented in Section 3 of this chapter. The reader is urged to review that section if he is not familiar with it before proceeding further. The first two versions of the program SCOPE in that section are independent of the stack implementation (except in the declaration of the variable STACK). All that need be done in order for that program to execute correctly with stacks implemented using the CONTROLLED attribute is to modify the declaration

```
DCL  1 STACK,
        2 LABELS(100)          CHAR(80) VAR,
        2 TOP                  FIXED INIT (0);
```

to

```
DCL STACK                      CHAR(80) VAR CTL;
```

The pattern of stacking, unstacking, and testing the stack remains the same; it is only the implementation of the stack which changes. By making the above modification in the declaration and by supplying PUSH, POP, EMPTY, STACKTOP, and POPANDTEST routines for a CONTROLLED stack of character strings, the same program will run correctly. This is because the program was designed around the logical concept of a stack rather than a particular implementation.

However, if we attempt to execute the third version of the program SCOPE presented in Section 3, we run into a serious problem. Recall that we were dissatisfied with the second version because if an END statement with a nonexistent label were encountered, the entire stack of labels was popped before we realized that the label did not exist. To remedy this situation, we introduced a function SRCHSTK. Before any labels were popped, SRCHSTK searched the array in which the stack was kept to see if the label existed. This function, however, is dependent on the array implementation of the stack, since it searches through the elements of the array. In a pure stack, one cannot view an intermediate element on the stack without first popping the elements above it. Since a stack implemented using the CONTROLLED attribute does not allow access to any but the most recent generation of a CONTROLLED variable, it seems that the problem of Section 3 cannot be solved using such a stack.

This problem can be overcome by introducing a second CONTROLLED variable to act as an auxiliary stack. In searching for a particular label on the first stack, the labels must be popped. However, they can be saved on a second stack and restored to the first when either the desired label is found on the first stack or when the first stack becomes empty. Using this idea, we present a version of the function SRCHSTK for a CONTROLLED stack.

```
SRCHSTK:  PROC(STACK, ELT) RETURNS (BIT(1));
             DCL (STACK, AUXSTACK)        CTL CHAR(80) VAR,
                  (ELT, X)                CHAR(80) VAR,
                  UND                     BIT(1);

             X='';
             CALL POPANDTEST (STACK, X, UND);
SEARCH:      DO WHILE (¬UND & X¬=ELT);
                CALL PUSH(AUXSTACK, X);
                CALL POPANDTEST(STACK, X, UND);
             END SEARCH;
```

```
                 /*   At this point, if ELT exists on STACK, UND='0'B;   */
                 /*  otherwise UND='1'B. We now restore STACK to its     */
                 /*              original contents.                      */
                 IF ¬UND THEN CALL PUSH(STACK,X);
      RESTORE:   DO WHILE (¬EMPTY(AUXSTACK));
                    X=POP(AUXSTACK);
                    CALL PUSH(STACK, X);
                 END RESTORE;

                 /*  If UND='1'B, then STACK was emptied without finding   */
                 /*   ELT, so we wish to return '0'B; if UND='0'B, ELT was */
                 /*          found on STACK, so we return '1'B.            */
                 IF UND THEN RETURN ('0'B);
                        ELSE RETURN ('1'B);
              END SRCHSTK;
```

Using this version of SRCHSTK, the third and final version of the program in Section 3 will execute correctly. Note that this version of SRCHSTK works as well for the array implementation of the stack; the only modifications needed are in the declarations of STACK and AUXSTACK.

In the next section, we examine the advantages and disadvantages of the two implementations of a stack.

3.6. Efficiency of Stack Representations

In this section, we attempt to evaluate the two PL/I implementations of stacks and try to determine which the programmer should use in a particular case. In general, it cannot be said that one method is always "better" than the other; each has advantages and disadvantages which vary with the circumstances. However, it should be said that the determination of which implementation of stacks to use is usually a minor decision. Once this decision is made, the implementation selected should be easily replaceable by another. The important decision that a programmer must make is whether to use a stack in the first place or whether to use another data structure. Once the decision to use a stack has been made, the programmer must then decide how the stack is to be used and when to push, pop, and test.

After the programmer has made these decisions and created an algorithm, he must transform his algorithm into a program. This transformation implies translating a logical design into an exact specification within a given language, subject to all its rules, capabilities, exceptions, and pitfalls. This is not a trivial task. Many programmers have made the fatal error of assuming that an algorithm can be easily and directly translated into a program. In transforming an algorithm into a program, there are truly crucial decisions which the programmer must make. Along with these important decisions must come many minor ones. The programmer who attempts to make all decisions at the time that he starts writing the program is in for much trouble because of two factors. The first is that the earlier a decision is made, the more rigid the program becomes and the less susceptible it is to change. For example, a programmer may determine that process X must be performed at a certain point in the program and that method Y is a good way to perform it. He then proceeds to include method Y as an integral part of his program, interfacing it with numerous other processes and methods. He may later discover, however, that method Z is even better and more efficient than method Y. By that time, the dependence of the other parts of his program on the hooks and eyes of method Y is so great that replacing method Y with method Z requires rewriting the entire program.

The programmer's mistake in the above example is that he made two decisions at a time when only one was necessary. The decision to perform process X is a necessary one, but the details of how it is to be performed should have been left for a later time. The programmer should have assumed that process X would be accomplished somehow, and coded a line such as

```
CALL PROCESSX;
```

In designing the remainder of his program, he should have relied only on the fact that process X would be performed, but not on the method of its performance. In that way, he would have retained the flexibility of being able to later examine the various methods, Y and Z, of performing process X within the context of his program and to choose between them. The line CALL PROCESSX; may then be expanded into a loop or a large section of code, or parameters might be appended and a subroutine written so that it would be transformed into a true subroutine call.

The other factor which tends to favor decision postponement is the human factor. Until a genuine automatic programming system is developed, all programmers are human and subject to the same human frailties as athletes, doctors, or lawyers. Among these frailties are forgetfulness and a threshold of complexity which, while being greater in some individuals than in others, is nevertheless present in us all. The more interlocking decisions we make simultaneously, the more likely it is that one of them will be erroneous in either judgment or execution. By focusing on the top-level decisions only, we will have fewer decisions to make. Once we have made these major decisions, we can focus all our attention on each of the minor ones separately. This divide-and-conquer strategy has been an important factor in improving programmer efficiency.

Let us see how we have carried out this strategy in the examples of this chapter. We first examined each problem and determined that it exhibited a last-in, first-out behavior and therefore required a stack. We then determined the pattern of pushing, popping, and testing needed to solve the problem. Then we translated the solution outline into a program, taking careful note of such seemingly trivial items as the way in which PL/I executes a logical conjunction ("and"). We never needed to manipulate the stack within a program itself, because we always used the well-defined stack routines, PUSH, POP, POPANDTEST, STACKTOP, and EMPTY. Finally we presented two different methods of implementing these operations. Our success can be measured by the ease by which the program of Section 3 was modified to a different stack implementation in Section 5, requiring only small changes in some declarations and several key routines.

Having said all the foregoing, we must now focus on the primary topic of this section. Once a program has been fully specified, designed, and written, how do we make that last decision as to which implementation of stacks to use?

As stated previously, both the array and CONTROLLED implementations of stacks have advantages and disadvantages. The primary advantage of the CONTROLLED representation is that it does not waste storage. Only as many elements as are actually on the stack are allocated at any instant. In the array representation, it is necessary to preallocate as many storage locations as the maximum size of the stack. Often, one cannot tell in advance how large the stack may grow (e.g., it may depend on the input). Thus, space may be severely overallocated using the array representation. On the other hand, since the amount of space that is available for a stack is fixed, it may happen that space is underallocated, causing an overflow. An overflow cannot occur using the CONTROLLED representation unless the job truly did not request enough space.

The advantage of the array representation is in efficiency of execution. It is much faster to increase a variable by 1 and insert a value into an array than to request more storage space from the system. Each time that an ALLOCATE statement is executed, a request is issued to the system for another segment of storage. This request is handled by the operating system along with requests for a multitude of other functions which it must perform. The ALLOCATE statement, therefore, significantly increases execution time.

Often a compiler may implement CONTROLLED storage by allocating a pool of storage in one chunk for each CONTROLLED variable. Then the execution of an ALLOCATE statement means no more than enabling the use of an already allocated storage location. This is done to improve execution speed and to reduce the number of requests to the operating system. Such a method tends to even out the advantages between the array and CONTROLLED representations, since in both cases a PUSH operation is relatively quick and storage is overallocated for the stack. However, if the chunk first allocated is insufficient, the system will be called upon to provide another chunk, so that the basic differences between the two methods remain.

There is one other feature which can be argued as being both an advantage and a disadvantage of the two representations. This feature is the flexibility and added power inherent in the array representation. If the programmer desires, he need not restrict himself to using only the top element of the stack in the array representation. Rather, he can use the array as a true array with the capability of referencing any of its elements as easily as any other. In the CONTROLLED representation, on the other hand, one can only refer to the last generation of the variable; the previous generations are inaccessible until the later generations are freed. It can be argued that this is a significant advantage for the array representation. An illustration of this is the function SRCHSTK of Section 3, where we wished to examine whether a given element was on the stack. This is a relatively trivial operation in the array representation since one can simply search through the array elements without disturbing the stack. To accomplish the same thing in the CONTROLLED representation, one must resort to an auxiliary stack as illustrated in the version of SRCHSTK presented in Section 5. This is a rather awkward method of performing something as simple as searching for a particular element.

However, it may also be argued that this added flexibility is really a disadvantage. All it does is present more potential for programmer error because the programmer may utilize the stack incorrectly by indexing an element other than the top element. A stack is, by definition, a set of elements which can be accessed at only one end. Any other capabilities are imperfections in the representation of a stack. If the programmer wishes to use a stack, he should restrict himself to only those operations which are applicable to stacks. The counterargument, of course, is that we often wish to use an object in more ways than one.

Given these advantages and disadvantages, when should one use the array representation and when should one use the CONTROLLED representation? In general, if space is the important factor, the CONTROLLED representation should be used; if time is more important, the array representation should be used. For example, assume that a program calls for several potentially large stacks which grow and shrink independently. If the array representation were used, we would have to allocate a large array for each of the stacks. This may mean that the total storage requirements are too great. If the CONTROLLED representation is used, however, as one stack shrinks another growing stack can reuse the storage which the shrinking stack is giving up. Thus as long as the maximum total storage used by all the stacks together at any one instant is small enough, no problems will arise.

If, however, a program calls for several very active, moderately sized stacks, the array representation is preferable because the stacks are so active that the time spent on allocating and freeing under the CONTROLLED representation is prohibitively expensive.

In Chapter 5, yet another representation of stacks is introduced. The representation which should be used in a particular program depends upon the individual program and its environment. Another factor that should be remembered is that student jobs have quite different characteristics than production jobs in industry. Although time and space may not be significant factors for a student who is not paying for his use of the computer, they may indeed be significant for industrial programs which are run several thousand times and whose every run must be paid for.

Bibliography and References

Information on stacks may be found in any data structures text listed in the Bibliography. Most of these texts also discuss evaluating postfix expressions and translating from infix to postfix.

BEGIN blocks, scope nesting, and CONTROLLED storage are discussed in PL/I manuals and PL/I texts such as (Hughes, 1973) and (Pollack and Sterling, 1976).

chapter 4

recursion

This chapter introduces recursion, a programming tool which is one of the most powerful and one of the least understood by beginning students of programming. We define recursion, introduce its use in PL/I, and present several examples. We also examine an implementation of recursion using stacks. The programmer should be aware of how recursion is defined in his particular programming language because the lack of such knowledge will cause errors which may or may not be readily apparent. Finally, we discuss the advantages and disadvantages of using recursion in problem solving.

4.1. Recursive Definition and Processes

Many objects in mathematics are defined by presenting a process to produce that object. For example, π is defined as the ratio of the circumference of a circle to its diameter. This is equivalent to the set of instructions: Obtain the circumference of a circle and its diameter, divide the former by the latter, and call the result π. Clearly, the process specified must terminate with a definite result.

The Factorial Function

Another example of a definition specified by a process is that of the factorial function, a function which plays an important role in mathematics and statistics. Given a positive integer n, ***n factorial*** is defined as the product of all integers between n and 1. For example, 5 factorial is equal to 5∗4∗3∗2∗1=120, and 3 factorial equals 3∗2∗1=6; 0 factorial is defined as 1. In mathematics, the exclamation mark (!) is often used to denote the factorial function. We may therefore write the definition of this function as follows:

$$n!=1 \quad \text{if } n=0$$
$$n!=n*(n-1)*(n-2)*\cdots*1 \quad \text{if } n>0$$

Note that the three dots are really a shorthand for all the numbers between $n-3$ and 2 multiplied together. In order to avoid this shorthand in the definition of $n!$ we would have to list a formula for $n!$ for each value of n separately:

```
0!=1
1!=1
2!=2*1
3!=3*2*1
4!=4*3*2*1
...
```

Of course, we cannot hope to list a formula for the factorial of each integer. In order to avoid any shorthand and to avoid an infinite set of definitions, yet to define the function precisely, we may present an algorithm which accepts an integer n and returns the value of $n!$:

```
x=n;
prod=1;
do while (x>0);
   prod=x*prod;
   x=x-1;
end;
return (prod);
```

Such an algorithm is called ***iterative*** because it calls for the explicit repetition of some process until a certain condition is met. This algorithm can be readily translated into a PL/I function which returns $n!$ when n is input as a parameter. An algorithm may be thought of as a program for an "ideal" machine, without any of the practical limitations of a real computer, and therefore may be used to define a mathematical function. A PL/I function, however, cannot serve as the definition of the factorial function because of such limitations as precision and the finite size of a real machine.

Let us look more closely at the definition of $n!$ which lists a separate formula for each value of n. We may note, for example, that 4! equals 4*3*2*1, which equals 4*3!. In fact, for any $n>0$, we see that $n!$ equals $n*(n-1)!$. Multiplying n by the product of all integers from $n-1$ to 1 yields the product of all integers from n to 1. We may therefore define:

```
0!=1
1!=1*0!
2!=2*1!
3!=3*2!
4!=4*3!
...
```

or, using the mathematical notation used earlier:

```
n!=1          if n=0
n!=n*(n-1)! if n>0.
```

This definition may appear quite strange since it defines the factorial function in terms of itself. This seems to be a circular definition and totally unacceptable until we realize that the mathematical notation is only a concise way of writing out the infinite number of equations necessary to define $n!$ for each n. 0! is defined directly as 1. Once 0! has been defined, defining 1! as 1*0! is not circular at all. Similarly, once 1! has been defined, defining 2! as 2*1! is equally straightforward. It may be argued that the latter notation is more precise than the definition of $n!$ as $n*(n-1)*\cdots*1$ for $n>0$ because it does not resort to three dots to be filled in by the hopefully logical intuition of the reader. Such a definition, which defines an object in terms of a simpler case of itself, is called a ***recursive definition***.

Let us see how the recursive definition of the factorial function may be used to evaluate 5!. The definition states that 5! equals 5*4!. Thus, before we can evaluate 5!, we must first evaluate 4!. Using the definition once more, we find that 4!=4*3!. Therefore, we must evaluate 3!. Repeating this process, we have:

```
1.    5!=5*4!
2.         4!=4*3!
3.              3!=3*2!
4.                   2!=2*1!
5.                        1!=1*0!
6.                             0!=1
```

Each case is reduced to a simpler case until we reach the case of 0!, which is, of course, 1. At line 6 we have a value which is defined directly and not as the factorial of another number. We may therefore backtrack from line 6 to line 1, returning the value computed in one line to evaluate the result of the previous line. This produces:

```
6.    0!=1
5.    1!=1*0!=1*1=1
4.    2!=2*1!=2*1=2
3.    3!=3*2!=3*2=6
2.    4!=4*3!=4*6=24
1.    5!=5*4!=5*24=120
```

Let us attempt to incorporate this process into an algorithm. Again, we want the algorithm to input a nonnegative integer n and to return the nonnegative integer which is n factorial.

```
1.    if n=0 then return (1);
2.    x=n-1;
3.    find the value of x!. call it y.
4.    return (n*y);
```

This algorithm exhibits the process used to compute $n!$ by the recursive definition. The key to the algorithm is, of course, line 3 where we are told to "find the value of

$x!$." This requires reexecuting the algorithm with input x since the method for computing the factorial function is the algorithm itself. To see that the algorithm will eventually halt, note that at the start of line 3, x equals $n-1$. Each time that the algorithm is executed, its input is 1 less than the preceding time, so that (since the original input n was a nonnegative integer) 0 will eventually be input to the algorithm. At that point, the algorithm will simply return 1. This value is returned to line 3, which asked for the evaluation of $0!$. The multiplication of $y(=1)$ by $n(=1)$ is then executed, and the result is returned. This sequence of multiplications and returns continues until the original $n!$ has been evaluated. In the next section, we will see how to convert this algorithm into a PL/I program.

Of course, it is much simpler and more straightforward to use the iterative method for evaluating the factorial function. We present the recursive method as a simple example to introduce recursion, not as a more effective method of solving this particular problem. Indeed, all the problems in this section can be solved more efficiently by iteration. However, later in this chapter and in subsequent chapters, we will come across examples which are more easily solved by recursive methods.

Multiplication of Natural Numbers

Another example of a recursive definition is the definition of multiplication of natural numbers. The product $a*b$, where a and b are positive integers, may be defined as a added to itself b times. This is an iterative definition. An equivalent recursive definition is

$$a*b=a \quad \text{if } b=1$$
$$a*b=a*(b-1)+a \quad \text{if } b>1$$

In order to evaluate 6*3 by this definition, we must first evaluate 6*2 and then add 6. To evaluate 6*2, we must first evaluate 6*1 and add 6. But 6*1 equals 6 by the first part of the definition. Thus,

$$6*3=6*2+6=6*1+6+6=6+6+6=18$$

The reader is urged to convert the above definition into a recursive algorithm as a simple exercise.

Note the pattern which exists in recursive definitions. A simple case of the term to be defined is defined explicitly (in the case of the factorial, 0! is defined as 1; in the case of multiplication, $a*1=a$). The other cases are defined by applying some operation to the result of evaluating a simpler case. Thus, $n!$ is defined in terms of $(n-1)!$ and $a*b$ in terms of $a*(b-1)$. Successive simplifications of any particular case must eventually lead to the explicitly defined trivial case. In the case of the factorial function, successively subtracting 1 from n will eventually yield 0. In the case of multiplication, successively subtracting 1 from b will eventually yield 1. If this were not the case, the definition would be invalid. For example, if we defined

$$n! = \frac{(n+1)!}{n+1}$$

or

$$a*b=a*(b+1)-a$$

we would be unable to determine the values of 5! or 6*3. (You are invited to attempt to determine these values using the above definitions.) This is true despite the fact that the two equations are valid. Continually adding 1 to n or b does not eventually produce an explicitly defined case. Even if 100! were defined explicitly, how could the value of 101! be determined?

The Fibonacci Sequence

Let us examine a less familiar example. The ***Fibonacci sequence*** is the sequence of integers

0,1,1,2,3,5,8,13,21,34, . . .

Each element in this sequence is the sum of the two preceding elements (e.g., 0+1=1, 1+1=2, 1+2=3, 2+3=5, . . .). If we let *fib*(0)=0, *fib*(1)=1, etc., then we may define the Fibonacci sequence by the following recursive definition:

$$\begin{aligned} fib(n) &= n && \text{if } n=0 \text{ or } 1 \\ fib(n) &= fib(n-2)+fib(n-1) && \text{if } n>1 \end{aligned}$$

To compute *fib*(6), for example, we may apply the definition recursively to obtain

$fib(6) = fib(4)+fib(5) = fib(2)+fib(3)+fib(5)=$
$fib(0)+fib(1)+fib(3)+fib(5) = 0+1+fib(3)+fib(5) = 1+fib(1)+fib(2)+fib(5) =$
$1+1+fib(0)+fib(1)+fib(5) = 2+0+1+fib(5) = 3+fib(3)+fib(4) =$
$3+fib(1)+fib(2)+fib(4) = 3+1+fib(0)+fib(1)+fib(4) = 4+0+1+fib(2)+fib(3) =$
$5+fib(0)+fib(1)+fib(3) = 5+0+1+fib(1)+fib(2) = 6+1+fib(0)+fib(1) = 7+0+1 = 8$

Notice that the recursive definition of the Fibonacci numbers differs from the recursive definitions of the factorial function and multiplication. The recursive definition of *fib* refers to itself twice. For example, *fib*(6) = *fib*(4)+*fib*(5), so that in computing *fib*(6), *fib* must be applied recursively twice. However, part of the computation of *fib*(5) involves determining *fib*(4) so that a great deal of computational redundancy occurs in applying the definition. In the above example, *fib*(3) was recomputed three separate times. It would have been much more efficient to "remember" the value of *fib*(3) the first time that it was evaluated and reuse it each time that it was needed. An iterative method of computing *fib*(*n*) such as the following is much more efficient.

```
if n<=1 then return(n);
lofib=0;
hifib=1;
do i=2 to n by 1;
     x=lofib;
     lofib=hifib;
     hifib=x+lofib;
end;
return(hifib);
```

Essentially, this algorithm enumerates all the Fibonacci numbers in the successive values of the variable *hifib*.

Compare the number of additions (not including increments of the index variable *i*) which are performed in computing *fib*(6) by this algorithm and by using the recursive definition. In the case of the factorial function, the same number of multiplications must be performed in computing $n!$ by the recursive and iterative methods. The same is true of the number of additions in the two methods of computing multiplication. However in the case of the Fibonacci numbers, the recursive method is far more expensive than the iterative. We shall have more to say about the relative merits of the two methods in a later section.

The Binary Search

You may have received the erroneous impression that recursion is a very handy tool for defining mathematical functions but has no influence in more practical computing activities. The next example will illustrate an application of recursion to one of the most common activities in computing—that of searching.

Consider an array of elements in which objects have been placed in some order. For example, a dictionary or telephone book may be thought of as an array whose entries are in alphabetical order. A company payroll file may be in the order of employees' social security numbers. Suppose such an array exists and we wish to find a particular element in it. For example, we wish to look up a name in a telephone book, a word in a dictionary, or a particular employee in a personnel file. The process used to find such an entry is called a ***search***. Since searching is such a common activity in computing, it is desirable to find an efficient method for performing it. Perhaps the crudest search method is the ***sequential*** or ***linear*** search in which each item of the array is examined, in turn, and compared to the item being searched for until a match occurs. If the list is unordered and haphazardly constructed, the linear search may be the only way to find anything in it (unless, of course, the list is first rearranged). However, such a method would never be used in looking up a name in a telephone book. Rather, the book is opened to a random page and the names on that page are examined. Since the names are ordered alphabetically, such an examination would determine whether the search should proceed in the first or second part of the book.

Let us apply this idea to searching an array. If the array contains only one element, the problem is trivial. Otherwise, compare the item being searched for with the item at the middle of the array. If they are equal, the search has been completed successfully. If the middle element is greater than the item being searched for, the search process is repeated in the first half of the array (since if the item appears anywhere it must appear in the first half); otherwise, the process is repeated in the second half. Note that each time a comparison is made, the number of elements yet to be searched is cut in half. That is why this method is superior to the sequential search in which each comparison reduces the number of elements yet to be searched by only 1. Because of the division of the array to be searched into two equal parts, this search method is called the ***binary search***.

Notice that we have quite naturally defined a binary search recursively. If the item is not equal to the middle element, the instructions are to search a subarray using the same method. Thus the search method is defined in terms of itself with a smaller array as input. We are sure that the process will terminate because the input arrays grow smaller; and the search of a one-element array is defined nonrecursively since the middle element of such an array is its only element.

We now present a recursive algorithm to search a sorted array *a* for an element *x* between *a*(*low*) and *a*(*high*). The algorithm returns an *index* of *a* such that *a*(*index*)=*x*, if such an *index* exists between *low* and *high*. If *x* is not found in that portion of the array, the algorithm returns 0. We assume that *low* and *high* are either both greater or both less than 0 so that there is no element *a*(0). The reference to division in the following algorithm is to integer division, which returns only the integer part of the quotient. Thus, 5/2=2 and 19/2=9.

```
if low > high then return(0);
mid= (low + high)/2;
if x=a(mid) then return (mid);
if x < a(mid) then
                search for x in a(low) to a(mid-1);
        else
                search for x in a(mid+1) to a(high);
```

Since the possibility of an unsuccessful search is included (i.e., the element may not exist in the array), the trivial case has been altered somewhat. A search on a one-element array is not defined directly as returning that element. Instead that element is compared to the item being searched for. If the two items are not equal, the search continues in the "first" or "second" half–each of which contains no elements. This case is indicated by the condition *low*>*high*, and its result is defined directly as 0.

Let us apply this algorithm to an example. Suppose the array *a* contains the elements, 1, 3, 4, 5, 17, 18, 31, 33, in that order, and we wish to search for 17 (i.e., *x*=17) between item 1 and item 8 (i.e., *low*=1, *high*=8). Applying the algorithm, we have:

line 1: Is $low > high$? It is not, so continue.
line 2: $mid=(1+8)/2=4$
line 3: Is $x=a(4)$? 17 is not equal to 5, so continue.
line 4: Is $x<a(4)$? 17 is not less than 5, so perform the else clause at line 7.
line 7: Repeat the algorithm with $low=mid+1=5$ and $high=high=8$; i.e., search the upper half of the array.
line 1: Is $5 > 8$? No, so continue.
line 2: $mid= (5+8)/2= 6$
line 3: Is $x=a(6)$? 17 does not equal 18, so continue.
line 4: Is $x<a(6)$? Yes, since $17 < 18$, so execute the then clause.
line 5: Repeat the algorithm with $low= low= 5$ and $high= mid-1= 5$. We have isolated x between the fifth and the fifth elements of a.
line 1: Is $5 > 5$? No, so continue.
line 2: $mid= (5+5)/2= 5$.
line 3: Since $a(5)= 17$, return 5 as the answer. 17 is indeed the fifth element of the array.

Note the pattern of calls to and returns from the algorithm. A diagram tracing this pattern appears in Fig. 4.1.1. The solid arrows indicate the flow of control through the algorithm and the recursive calls. The dotted lines indicate returns. Since there are no steps to be executed in the algorithm after lines 5 or 7, the returned result is returned intact to the previous execution. Finally, when control returns to the original execution, the answer is returned to the caller.

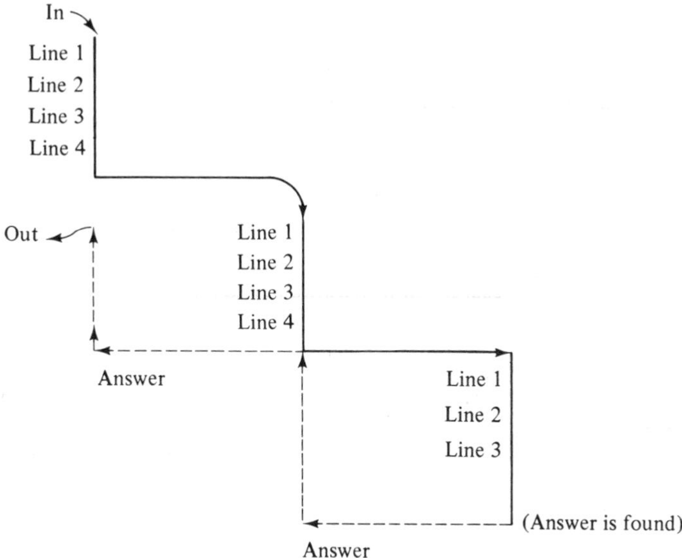

Figure 4.1.1. A diagrammatic representation of the binary search algorithm.

Let us examine how the algorithm works in searching for an item which does not appear in the array. Assume the array a as in the previous example and assume that we are searching for $x = 2$.

line 1: Is *low* > *high*? 1 is not greater than 8, so continue.
line 2: *mid*= (1+8)/2= 4
line 3: Is $x = a(4)$? 2 does not equal 5, so continue.
line 4: Is $x < a(4)$? Yes, 2 < 5, so perform the then clause.
line 5: Repeat the algorithm with *low*= *low*= 1 and *high*= *mid*−1= 3.
If 2 appears in the array, it must appear between $a(1)$ and $a(3)$ inclusive.
line 1: Is 1 > 3? No, continue.
line 2: *mid*= (1+3)/2= 2
line 3: Is $2 = a(2)$? No, continue.
line 4: Is $2 < a(2)$? Yes, since 2 < 3. Perform the then clause.
line 5: Repeat the algorithm with *low*= *low*= 1 and *high*= *mid*−1= 1.
If x exists in a, it must be the first element.
line 1: Is 1>1? No, continue.
line 2: *mid*= (1+1)/2= 1
line 3: Is $2 = a(1)$? No, continue.
line 4: Is $2 < a(1)$? 2 is not less than 1, so perform the else clause.
line 7: Repeat the algorithm with *low*= *mid*+1= 2 and *high*= *high*= 1.
line 1: Is *low* > *high*? 2 is greater than 1, so return 0. The item 2 does not exist in the array.

Properties of Recursive Definitions or Algorithms

Let us summarize what is involved in a recursive definition or algorithm. One important requirement for a recursive algorithm to be correct is that it not generate an infinite sequence of calls on itself. Clearly, any algorithm that does generate such a sequence will never terminate. For at least one argument or set of arguments, a recursive function f must be defined in terms that do not involve f. There must be a "way out" of the sequence of recursive calls. In the examples of this section the nonrecursive portions of the definitions were:

factorial:	$0! = 1$
multiplication:	$a*1 = a$
Fibonacci sequence:	$fib(0) = 0; fib(1) = 1$
binary search:	**if** *low* > *high* **then return** (0)
	if $x = a(mid)$ **then return** (*mid*)

Without such a nonrecursive exit, no recursive function can ever be computed. Any instance of a recursive definition or invocation of a recursive algorithm must eventually reduce to some manipulation of one or more simple, nonrecursive cases.

4.2. Recursion in PL/I

Factorial in PL/I

The PL/I language allows a programmer to write subroutines and functions which call themselves. Such routines are called ***recursive***. For example, the recursive algorithm to compute $n!$ may be directly translated into a PL/I function as follows:

```
FACT:  PROC (N) RECURSIVE RETURNS (FIXED(15));
             DCL  (N,X)         FIXED,
                    Y           FIXED(15);
             IF N=0 THEN RETURN (1);
             X=N-1;
             Y=FACT(X);
             RETURN(N*Y);
       END FACT;
```

The keyword RECURSIVE must appear in the PROCEDURE statement of a recursive PL/I procedure. In the statement Y=FACT(X); the function FACT calls itself. This is the essential ingredient of a recursive routine. The programmer assumes that the function he is computing has already been written and uses it in its own definition. However, he must ensure that this does not lead to an endless series of calls on itself.

Let us examine the execution of the above function when it is called by another program. For example, suppose the calling program contains the statement

```
PUT LIST (FACT(4));
```

When the calling routine calls FACT, the parameter N is set equal to 4. Since N is not 0, X is set equal to 3. At that point, FACT is called a second time with an argument of 3. Therefore, the block FACT is reentered and the local variables (X and Y) and parameter (N) of the block are reallocated. Since execution has not yet left the first call of FACT (by means of a RETURN, END, or GO TO statement), the first allocation of these variables remains. Thus there are two generations of each of these variables in existence simultaneously. From any point within the second execution of FACT, only the most recent copy of these variables can be referenced.

In general, each time the function FACT is entered recursively, a new set of local variables is allocated and only this new set may be referenced within that call of FACT. When a return from FACT to a point in a previous call takes place, the most recent allocation of these variables is freed and the previous copy is reactivated. This previous copy is the one which was allocated upon the original entry to the previous call and is local to that call.

This description suggests use of a stack to keep the successive generations of local variables. Each time that a recursive procedure is entered, a new allocation of its variables is pushed on top of the stack. Any reference to a local variable or parameter is through the current top of the stack. When the procedure returns, the stack is popped, the former top allocation is freed and the previous allocation becomes the current stack top to be used for referencing local variables. This mechanism will be examined more closely in a later section, but for now, let us see how it is applied in computing the factorial function.

Figure 4.2.1 contains a series of snapshots of the stacks for the variables N, X, and Y as execution of the FACT function proceeds. Initially, the stacks are empty as illustrated by Fig. 4.2.1(a). After the first call on FACT by the calling procedure, the situation is as shown in Fig. 4.2.1(b), with N=4. The variables X and Y are allocated but not initialized. Since N does not equal 0, X is set to 3 and FACT(3) is called (Fig. 4.2.1(c)). The new value of N does not equal 0, so X is set to 2 and FACT(2) is called (Fig. 4.2.1(d)). This continues until N equals 0 (Fig. 4.2.1(f)). At that point, the value 1 is returned from the call to FACT(0). Execution resumes from the point at which FACT(0) was called, which is the assignment of the returned value to the copy of Y declared in FACT(1). This is illustrated by the status of the stack shown in Fig. 4.2.1(g), where the variables allocated for FACT(0) have been freed and Y is set to 1.

The statement RETURN(N*Y) is then executed, multiplying the top values of N and Y to obtain 1, and returning this value to FACT(2) (Fig. 4.2.1(h)). This process is repeated twice more, until finally the value of Y in FACT(4) equals 6 (Fig. 4.2.1(j)). The statement RETURN(N*Y) is executed one more time. The product 24 is returned to the calling procedure, where it is printed by the statement

```
PUT LIST (FACT(4));
```

Note that each time that a recursive routine returns, it returns to the point immediately following the point from which it was called. Thus, the recursive call to FACT(3) returns to the assignment of the result to Y within FACT(4), but the call to FACT(4) returns to the PUT statement in the calling routine.

Let us transform some of the other recursive definitions and processes of the previous section into recursive PL/I programs. It is difficult to conceive of a PL/I programmer writing a function to compute the product of two nonnegative integers in terms of addition, since he can simply use an asterisk to perform the multiplication. Nevertheless, such a function can serve as another illustration of recursion in PL/I. Following closely the definition of multiplication in the previous section, we may write

```
MULT: PROC(A,B) RECURSIVE RETURNS(FIXED);
          DCL (A,B)           FIXED;
          IF B=1 THEN RETURN (A);
          RETURN(MULT(A,B-1)+A);
      END MULT;
```

Notice how similar this program is to the recursive definition of the last section. We leave it as an exercise for you to trace through the execution of this function when it is called with two positive integers. The use of stacks will be a great aid in this tracing process.

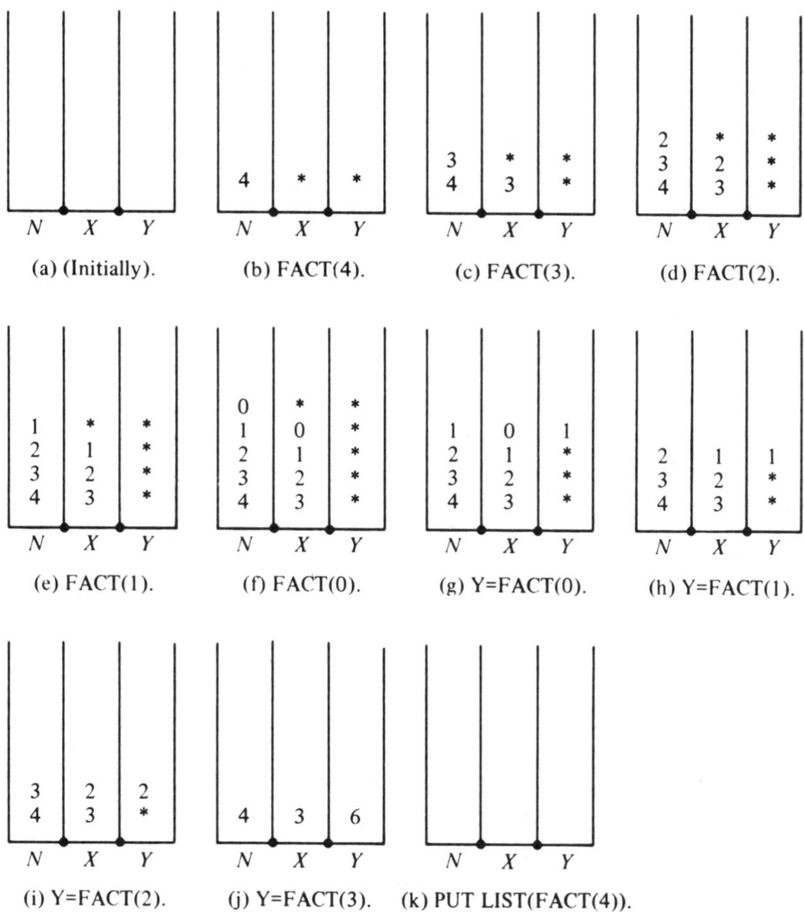

(a) (Initially). (b) FACT(4). (c) FACT(3). (d) FACT(2).

(e) FACT(1). (f) FACT(0). (g) Y=FACT(0). (h) Y=FACT(1).

(i) Y=FACT(2). (j) Y=FACT(3). (k) PUT LIST(FACT(4)).

Figure 4.2.1. The stack at various times during execution. (An asterisk indicates an uninitialized value.)

This example illustrates that a recursive function may invoke itself even within an expression appearing in a RETURN statement. Similarly, we could have written the recursive FACT function more compactly as

```
FACT:  PROC(N) RECURSIVE RETURNS(FIXED(15));
             DCL  N                  FIXED;
             IF N=0  THEN RETURN (1);
             RETURN(N*FACT(N-1));
       END FACT;
```

This avoids the explicit use of local variables X (to hold the value of N–1) and Y (to hold the value of FACT(X)). However, temporary locations are set aside anyway for these two values upon each invocation of the function. These temporaries are treated just as explicit local variables. Thus, in tracing the action of a recursive routine, it may be helpful to declare all temporary variables explicitly. See if it is any easier to trace the following more explicit version of MULT:

```
MULT:  PROC(A,B) RECURSIVE RETURNS(FIXED);
          DCL (A,B,C,D)          FIXED;
          IF B=1 THEN RETURN(A);
          C=B−1;
          D=MULT(A,C);
          RETURN(D+A);
       END MULT;
```

Another point which should be made is that it is particularly important to check for the validity of input parameters in a recursive routine. For example, let us examine the execution of the FACT routine when it is invoked by a statement such as

```
PUT LIST(FACT(−1));
```

Of course, the FACT function was not designed to produce a meaningful result for negative input. However one of the most important things for a programmer to learn is that a subroutine or function will invariably be presented at some time with invalid input and, unless provision is made for such input, the resultant error may be very difficult to trace. For example, when −1 is passed as a parameter to FACT, so that N=−1, X is set to −2 and −2 is passed to a recursive call on FACT. Another set of N, X, and Y is allocated, N is set to −2, and X becomes −3. This process continues until the program either runs out of time or space or the value of X becomes too small. No message indicating the true cause of the error is produced. If FACT were originally called with a complicated expression as its argument and the expression erroneously evaluated to a negative number, a programmer might spend hours searching for the cause of his error. The problem can be easily remedied by revising the FACT routine:

```
FACT:  PROC(N)  RECURSIVE RETURNS(FIXED(15));
          DCL  (N,X)          FIXED,
                 Y            FIXED(15);
          IF N<0 THEN DO;
                PUT SKIP LIST
          ('NEGATIVE NUMBER PASSED TO THE FACTORIAL FUNCTION');
                STOP;
                      END;
          IF N=0 THEN RETURN(1);
          X=N−1;
          Y=FACT(X);
          RETURN(N*Y);
       END FACT;
```

Similarly, the function MULT may be revised to guard against a nonpositive value in the second parameter. The revision is left to the reader.

The Fibonacci Numbers in PL/I

We now turn our attention to the Fibonacci sequence. A PL/I program to compute the Nth Fibonacci number can be modeled closely after the recursive definition:

```
FIB:    PROC(N)  RECURSIVE RETURNS(FIXED);
          DCL     (N,X,Y)            FIXED;
          IF N<0 THEN DO;
                   PUT SKIP LIST
                   ('NEGATIVE ARGUMENT TO THE FIBONACCI FUNCTION');
                   STOP;
                         END;
          IF N<=1 THEN RETURN(N);
          X=FIB(N-1);
          Y=FIB(N-2);
          RETURN(X+Y);
        END FIB;
```

Let us trace through the action of the above function in computing the sixth Fibonacci number. You may compare the action of the routine with the manual computation we performed in the last section to compute FIB(6). The stacking process is illustrated in Fig. 4.2.2. When the program is first called, the variables N, X, and Y are allocated and N is set to 6 (Fig. 4.2.2(a)). Since N>1, N–1 is evaluated and FIB is called recursively. A new set of N, X, and Y is allocated and N is set to 5 (Fig. 4.2.2(b)). This process continues (Figs. 4.2.2(c)-(f)) with each successive value of N equalling 1 less than its predecessor, until FIB is called with N=1. The sixth call to FIB returns 1 to its caller so the fifth allocation of X is set to 1 (Fig. 4.2.2(g)).

The next sequential statement Y=FIB(N–2); is then executed. The value of N which is used is the most recently allocated one, which is 2. Thus we again call on FIB with an argument of 0 (Fig. 4.2.2(h)). The value of 0 is immediately returned so that Y in FIB(2) is set to 0 (Fig. 4.2.2(i)). Note that each recursive call results in a return to the point of call so that the call of FIB(1) returns to the assignment to X, while the call of FIB(0) returns to the assignment to Y. The next statement to be executed in FIB(2) is the RETURN statement, which returns X+Y = 1+0 = 1 to the point at which FIB(2) is called from within FIB(3). This is the assignment to X, so that X in FIB(3) is given the value FIB(2)=1 (Fig. 4.2.2(j)). The process of calling and pushing and returning and popping continues until finally the routine returns for the last time to the main program with the value 8. Figure 4.2.2 shows the stack up to the point where FIB(5) calls on FIB(3) so that its value can be assigned to Y. The reader is urged to complete the picture by drawing the stack states for the remainder of the program execution.

This program illustrates that a recursive routine may call itself a number of times with different arguments. In fact, as long as a recursive routine uses only local variables, the programmer can use the routine just as he uses any other and assume that it performs

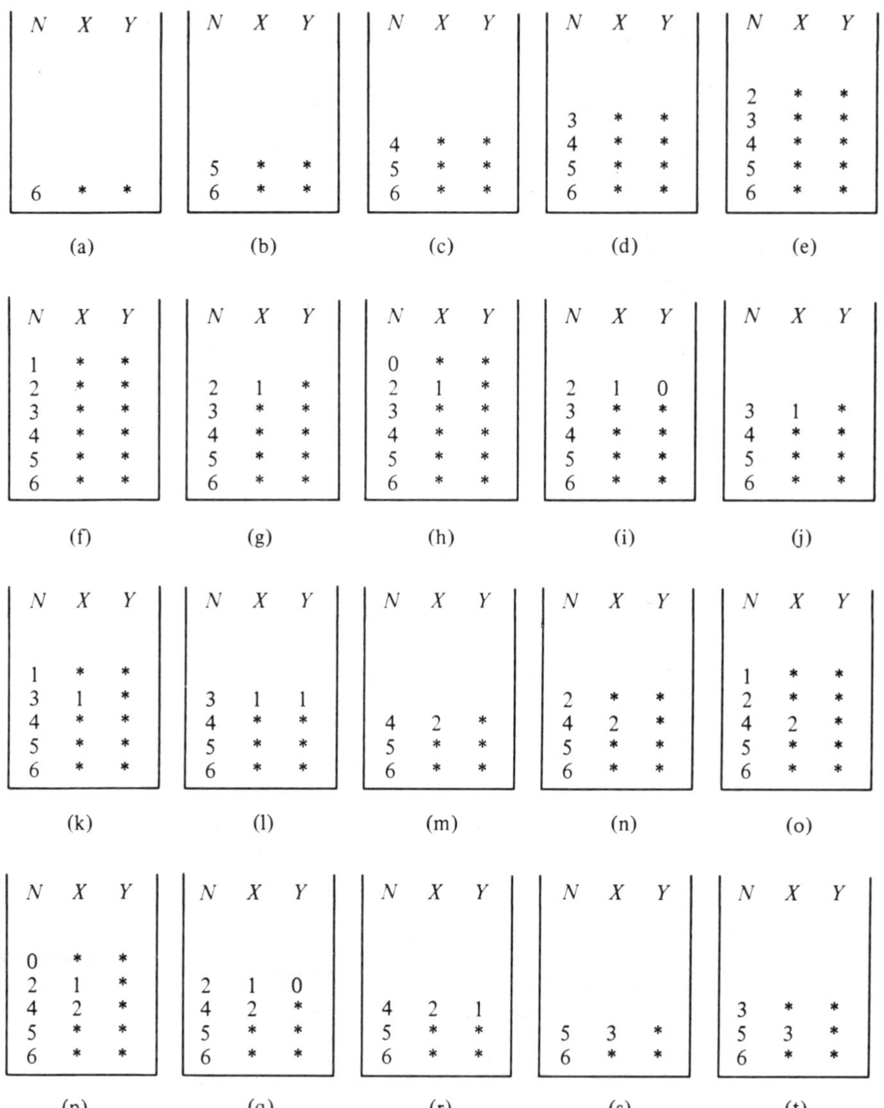

Figure 4.2.2. The recursion stack of the Fibonacci function.

its function and produces the desired value. He need not worry about the underlying stacking mechanism.

The Binary Search in PL/I

Let us now present a PL/I program for the binary search. A function to do this would accept an array A and an element X as input and would return the index I in A such that

A(I)=X, or 0 if no such I existed. Thus, the function BINSRCH might be invoked in a statement such as

```
I=BINSRCH(A,X);
```

However, in looking at the binary search algorithm of Section 4.1 as a model for a recursive PL/I routine, we note that two other parameters are passed in the recursive calls. Lines 5 and 7 of that algorithm call for a binary search on only part of the array. Thus, in order for the function to be recursive, the bounds between which the array is to be searched must also be specified. Thus the routine is written as follows:

```
BINSRCH:   PROC(A,X,LOW,HIGH) RECURSIVE RETURNS(FIXED);
                DCL (A(*),X,LOW,HIGH,MID) FIXED;
                IF LOW > HIGH THEN RETURN (0);
                MID=(LOW+HIGH)/2;
                IF X=A(MID) THEN RETURN(MID);
                IF X < A(MID)   THEN RETURN(BINSRCH(A,X,LOW,MID-1));
                                ELSE RETURN(BINSRCH(A,X,MID+1,HIGH));
           END BINSRCH;
```

When BINSRCH is first called from another routine to search for X in an array declared by

```
DCL A(N) FIXED;
```

it would be called by the statement

```
I=BINSRCH(A,X,1,N);
```

You are urged to trace the execution of this routine and follow the stacking and unstacking using the example of the last section where A is an array of 8 elements (N=8) containing 1,3,4,5,17,18,31,33, in that order. The value being searched for is 17 (X=17). Note that the array A is stacked for each recursive call. (This is not strictly correct. Since A is a parameter which has the same attributes as its argument, only the address of A is passed to BINSRCH and the original array is used to access the values of A. The address of A is stacked on each recursive call. If, however, an array is declared as a local variable in a recursive routine, space for the entire array must be reallocated at each recursive call and the entire array is stacked.)

In the course of tracing through the BINSRCH routine, you may have noticed that the values of the two parameters A and X do not change throughout its execution. Each time that BINSRCH is called, the same array is searched for the same element: it is only the upper and lower bounds of the search which change. It therefore seems wasteful to stack and unstack the addresses of these two parameters each time that the routine is called recursively.

One solution is to allow A and X to be global variables, declared in the calling routine which includes the function BINSRCH as a subblock. In this case these variables are declared in the surrounding block by

```
DCL (A(N),X) FIXED;
```

and the first two statements of BINSRCH are replaced by

```
BINSRCH: PROC(LOW,HIGH) RECURSIVE RETURNS(FIXED);
                  DCL (LOW,HIGH,MID)    FIXED;
```

The routine would be called by a statement such as

```
I = BINSRCH (1,N);
```

In this case, all references to A and X are to the single copy which is declared in the outer block but also known in the inner block. This saves the allocation and freeing of multiple copies of these two variables.

However, this solution has some serious drawbacks. The variable X must always be set in the calling routine to the variable whose value is being searched for. Further, the routine can only be used to search an array A which is declared within the outer block to have a fixed size. The routine cannot be used to search two different arrays with different sizes unless the array A is reallocated each time with different bounds. Another serious objection is one based on logical and aesthetic design factors. Logically, the two parameters to a search function should be the set which is being searched and the object being searched for, in our case A and X. However, in the current version of BINSRCH, neither of these appears as a parameter. Instead the two parameters which do appear—the upper and lower bounds—relate to the internal workings of the algorithm and not with the problem specification.

To remedy all these problems, we may rewrite the BINSRCH function as a nonrecursive routine with parameters A and X which calls on an internal auxiliary recursive routine AUXSRCH with parameters LOW and HIGH, as follows:

```
BINSRCH: PROC(A,X) RETURNS(FIXED);
            DCL (A(*),X,N)      FIXED;
            N=HBOUND(A,1);
            RETURN(AUXSRCH(1,N));

        AUXSRCH:    PROC(LOW,HIGH) RECURSIVE RETURNS(FIXED);
                        DCL (LOW,HIGH,MID)    FIXED;
                        IF LOW > HIGH THEN RETURN (0);
                        MID=(LOW+HIGH)/2;
                        IF X=A(MID) THEN RETURN(MID);
                        IF X<A (MID) THEN RETURN (AUXSRCH(LOW,MID–1));
                                      ELSE RETURN (AUXSRCH(MID+1,HIGH));
                    END AUXSRCH;

         END BINSRCH;
```

Using this scheme, the variables A and X are passed to the binary search routine, as they should be. A and X do not change their values and are not stacked. The work of stacking, unstacking, and altering the values of LOW and HIGH is left to the internal recursive routine AUXSRCH. The programmer wishing to make use of BINSRCH in this program need not even be aware of the existence of LOW and HIGH. He merely invokes the routine with a statement such as

```
I=BINSRCH(A,X);
```

Recursive Chains

A recursive procedure need not call itself directly. Rather, it may call itself indirectly as in the following example:

```
A: PROC RECURSIVE;               B: PROC RECURSIVE;
          .                                .
          .                                .
          .                                .
       CALL B;                          CALL A;
          .                                .
    END A;                           END B;
```

In this example procedure A calls B, which may in turn call A, which may again call B. Thus both A and B are recursive since they indirectly call on themselves. However, the fact that they are recursive is not evident from examining the body of either of the routines individually. The routine A seems to be calling a separate routine B, and it is impossible to determine by examining A alone that it will indirectly call itself.

More than two routines may participate in a ***recursive chain***. Thus a routine A may call B which calls C . . . which calls Z which calls A. Each routine in the chain may potentially call itself and is therefore recursive. Of course, the programmer must ensure that his program does not generate an infinte sequence of recursive calls.

Recursive Definition of Algebraic Expressions

As an example of such a recursive chain, consider the following recursive set of definitions:

1. An ***expression*** is a *term* followed by a *plus sign* followed by a *term*, or a *term* alone.

2. A ***term*** is a *factor* followed by an *asterisk* followed by a *factor*, or a *factor* alone.

3. A ***factor*** is either a *letter* or an *expression* enclosed in *parentheses*.

Before looking at some examples, note that none of the above three items is defined directly in terms of itself. However, each is defined in terms of itself indirectly. An expression is defined in terms of a term, a term in terms of a factor, and a factor in terms of an expression. Similarly, a factor is defined in terms of an expression, which is defined in terms of a term, which is defined in terms of a factor. Thus the entire set of definitions forms a recursive chain.

Let us now give some examples. The simplest form of a factor is a letter. Thus *A, B, C, Q, Z, M* are all factors. They are also terms since a term may be a factor alone. They are also expressions since an expression may be a term alone. Since *A* is an expression, (*A*) is a factor and therefore a term as well as an expression. *A*+*B* is an example of an expression which is neither a term nor a factor. (*A*+*B*), however, is all three. *A***B* is a term and therefore an expression, but it is not a factor. *A***B*+*C* is an expression which is neither a term nor a factor. *A**(*B*+*C*) is a term and an expression but not a factor.

Each of the above examples is a valid expression. This can be shown by applying the definition of an expression to each of them. Consider, however, the string *A*+**B*. It is neither an expression, term, nor factor. It would be instructive for you to attempt to apply the definitions of expression, term and factor to see that none of them describe the string *A*+**B*. Similarly, (*A*+*B**)*C* and *A*+*B*+*C* are not valid expressions according to the above definitions.

Let us write a program which reads a character string from a card, prints it out, and then prints VALID if it is a valid expression and INVALID if it is not. We will use three functions to recognize expressions, terms, and factors respectively. We first, however, present an auxiliary function GETSYMB which operates on two global variables: STR and POS. The first of these variables, STR, is the input character string. The second of these variables, POS, is the position in STR from which we wish to read a character. If POS≤LENGTH(STR), then GETSYMB returns the character at position POS of STR and increments POS by 1. If POS>LENGTH(STR), then GETSYMB simply returns the null string.

```
GETSYMB:   PROC RETURNS (CHAR(1) VAR);
                DCL     C     CHAR(1) VAR;
                IF POS>LENGTH(STR) THEN C = '';
                                         ELSE C=SUBSTR(STR,POS,1);
                POS=POS+1;
                RETURN(C);
           END GETSYMB;
```

The function which recognizes an expression is called EXPR. It too has no arguments and uses STR and POS as global variables. It returns '1'B (true) if a valid expression begins at position POS of STR and '0'B (false) otherwise. It also resets POS to the position following the longest expression it can find. Having described the function EXPR, we can write the main routine which calls it.

```
FINDEXP: PROC OPTIONS(MAIN);
                 DCL STR                  CHAR(100) VAR,
                     POS                  FIXED BIN INIT(1),
                     OK                   BIT(1);
```

```
        GET LIST(STR);
        PUT SKIP LIST(STR);
        OK=EXPR;
        IF OK & POS> LENGTH(STR) THEN
                    PUT SKIP LIST ('VALID');
                                 ELSE
                    PUT SKIP LIST ('INVALID');

        /*      The condition can fail for one (or both) of two       */
        /*          reasons. If ¬ OK, then there is no valid          */
        /*   expression beginning at POS. If POS<=LENGTH(STR),        */
        /*      there may be a valid expression starting at POS,      */
        /*          but it does not occupy the entire string.         */
    END FINDEXP;
```

The functions EXPR, GETSYMB, FACTOR, and TERM (the latter two will be explained shortly) are inserted immediately before the statement END FINDEXP; so that they can access the global variables STR and POS.

The functions FACTOR and TERM are much like EXPR except that they are responsible for recognizing factors and terms respectively. They also reposition POS to the position following the longest factor or term within the string STR that they can find.

The code for these routines adheres closely to the definitions given earlier. Each of the routines attempts to satisfy one of the criteria for the entity being recognized. If one of these criteria is satisfied, then '1'B is returned. If none of these criteria are satisfied, then '0'B is returned.

```
EXPR:  PROC RECURSIVE RETURNS(BIT(1));
          DCL  OK                   BIT(1),
                C                   CHAR(1) VAR;

          /*           look for a term            */
          OK=TERM;
          IF ¬OK THEN      /*   no expression exists   */
                     RETURN('0'B);

          /*        look at the next symbol        */
          C=GETSYMB;
          IF C¬='+' THEN DO;
          /*  We have found the longest expression  */
          /*    (a single term). Reposition POS so   */
          /*   it refers to the position immediately */
          /*            after the expression.        */
              POS=POS-1;
              RETURN('1'B);
                     END;
```

```
          /*    At this point, we have found a term     */
          /*     and a plus sign. We must look for      */
          /*              another term.                 */
        OK=TERM;
        IF OK   THEN RETURN ('1'B);
                ELSE RETURN ('0'B);

      END EXPR;
```

The routine TERM which recognizes terms is very similar, and we present it without comments:

```
   TERM:  PROC RECURSIVE RETURNS(BIT(1));
             DCL  OK          BIT(1),
                  C           CHAR(1)   VAR;
             OK=FACTOR;
             IF ¬OK THEN RETURN ('0'B);
             C=GETSYMB;
             IF C¬='*'  THEN DO;
                            POS=POS-1;
                            RETURN('1'B);
                                  END;
             OK=FACTOR;
             IF OK    THEN RETURN ('1'B);
                      ELSE RETURN ('0'B);
          END TERM;
```

The function FACTOR recognizes factors and should now be fairly straightforward.

```
FACTOR:  PROC RECURSIVE RETURNS(BIT(1));
            DCL  OK      BIT(1),
                 C       CHAR(1)   VAR,
                 ALPH    CHAR(26)  INIT
                                   ('ABCDEFGHIJKLMNOPQRSTUVWXYZ');
            C=GETSYMB;

            IF C¬='('THEN      /*   check for a letter    */
                  IF INDEX(ALPH,C)=0   THEN RETURN ('0'B);
                                       ELSE RETURN ('1'B);

              /*   the factor is a parenthesized expression     */
            OK=EXPR;
            IF ¬OK THEN RETURN ('0'B);
            C=GETSYMB;
            IF C¬=')'  THEN RETURN ('0'B);
                       ELSE RETURN ('1'B);
       END FACTOR;
```

All three routines must be specified RECURSIVE since each may call itself indirectly. For example, if you trace through the actions of the program FINDEXP for the input string '(A*B+C*D)+(E*(F)+G)', you will find that each of the routines EXPR, TERM, and FACTOR calls on itself.

4.3. Writing Recursive Programs

In the last section we saw how to take a recursive definition or algorithm and transform it into a PL/I program. It is a much more difficult task to develop a recursive PL/I solution to a problem specification whose algorithm is not supplied. It is not only the program but also the original definitions and algorithms that must be developed. In general, when faced with the task of writing a program to solve a problem, there is no reason to look for a recursive solution. Most problems can be solved in a straightforward manner using nonrecursive methods. We shall have more to say about these "efficiency" considerations in later sections. However, some problems can be solved logically and most elegantly by recursion. In this section we shall try to identify those problems which can be solved recursively, develop a technique for finding recursive solutions, and present some examples.

Let us reexamine the factorial function. Factorial is probably a prime example of a problem which should not be solved recursively since the iterative solution is so direct and simple. However, let us examine the elements which make the recursive solution work. First of all, we can recognize a large number of distinct cases to solve. That is, we want to write a program to compute 0!, 1!, 2!, etc. We can also identify a "trivial" case for which a nonrecursive solution is directly obtainable. This is the case of 0!, which is defined as 1. The next step is to find a method of solving a "complex" case in terms of a "simpler" case. This will allow reduction of a complex problem to a simpler problem. The transformation of the complex case to the simpler case should eventually result in the trivial case. This would mean that the complex case is ultimately defined in terms of the trivial case.

Let us examine what this means when applied to the factorial function. 4! is a more "complex" case than 3!. The transformation which is applied to the number 4 to obtain the number 3 is simply the subtraction of 1. Repeatedly subtracting 1 from 4 eventually results in 0, which is a "trivial" case. Thus if we are able to define 4! in terms of 3!, and in general $n!$ in terms of $(n-1)!$, we will be able to compute 4! by first working our way down to 0! and then working our way back up to 4! using the definition of $n!$ in terms of $(n-1)!$. In the case of the factorial function we have such a definition, since

$$n! = n * (n-1)!$$

Thus 4! =4*3! =4*3*2! =4*3*2*1! =4*3*2*1*0! =4*3*2*1*1 =24.

These are the essential ingredients of a recursive routine: being able to define a "complex" case in terms of a "simpler" case and having a directly solvable (nonrecursive) "trivial" case. Once this has been done, one can develop a solution using the assumption that the simpler case has already been solved. The PL/I version of the factorial function assumes that (N−1)! is defined and uses that quantity in computing N!.

Let us see how these ideas apply to other examples of the previous sections. In defining $a*b$, the case of $b=1$ is trivial since in that case, $a*b$ is defined as a. In general, $a*b$ may be defined in terms of $a*(b-1)$ by the definition $a*b = a*(b-1) + a$. Again the complex case is transformed into a simpler case by subtracting 1, eventually leading to the trivial case of $b=1$. Here the recursion is based on the second parameter b alone.

In the case of the Fibonacci function, two trivial cases were defined: $fib(0) = 0$ and $fib(1) = 1$. A complex case, $fib(n)$, is then reduced to two simpler cases $fib(n-1)$ and $fib(n-2)$. It is because of the definition of $fib(n)$ as $fib(n-1) + fib(n-2)$ that two trivial cases directly defined are necessary. $fib(1)$ cannot be defined as $fib(0) + fib(-1)$ because the Fibonacci function is not defined for negative numbers.

The binary search function is an interesting case of recursion. The recursion is based on the number of elements in the array which must be searched. Each time the routine is called recursively, the number of elements to be searched is halved (approximately). The trivial case is the one in which there are either no elements to be searched or the element being searched for is at the middle of the array. If $low>high$, then the first of these two conditions holds and 0 is returned. If $x=a(mid)$, the second condition holds and *mid* is returned as the answer. In the more complex case of $high-low+1$ elements to be searched, the search is reduced to taking place in one of two subregions.

1. the lower half of the array from *low* to $mid-1$
2. the upper half of the array from $mid+1$ to *high*

Thus a complex case (a large area to be searched) is reduced to a simpler case (an area to be searched of approximately half the size of the original area). This eventually reduces to a comparison with a single element ($a(mid)$) or a search among an array of no elements.

The Towers of Hanoi Problem

Thus far we have been looking at recursive definitions and examining how they fit the pattern we have established. Let us now look at a problem which is not specified in terms of recursion and see how we can use recursive techniques to produce a logical and elegant solution. The problem is the Towers of Hanoi problem, whose initial setup is shown in Fig. 4.3.1. Three pegs, *A*, *B*, and *C*, exist. Five disks of differing diameters are placed on peg *A* so that a larger disk is always below a smaller disk. The object is to move the five disks to peg *C* using peg *B* as auxiliary. Only the top disk on any peg may be moved to any other peg, and a larger disk may never rest on a smaller one. See if you can produce a solution. Indeed it is not even apparent that a solution exists.

Let us see if we can develop a solution. Instead of focusing our attention on a solution for five disks, let us consider the general case of n disks. Suppose we had a solution for $n-1$ disks and we could state a solution for n disks in terms of the solution for $n-1$ disks. Then the problem would be solved. This is true because in the trivial case of one disk (continually subtracting 1 from n will eventually produce 1), the solution is simple: merely move the single disk from peg *A* to peg *C*. Therefore, we will have developed a recursive solution if we can state a solution for n disks in terms of $n-1$. See if you can find such a relationship. In particular, for the case of five disks, suppose we knew how to

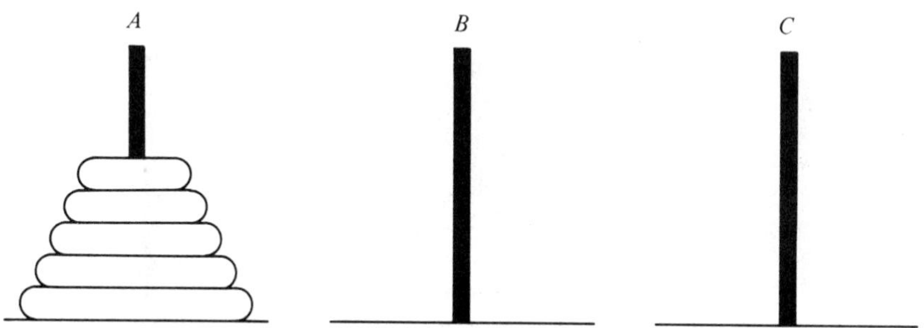

Figure 4.3.1. The initial setup of the Towers of Hanoi.

move the top four disks from peg A to another peg according to the rules. How could we then complete the job of moving all five? Recall that there are three pegs available.

Suppose we could move four disks from peg A to peg C. Then we could just as easily move them to B, using C as auxiliary. This would result in the situation depicted in Fig. 4.3.2(a). We could then move the largest disk from A to C (Fig. 4.3.2(b)) and finally again apply the solution for four disks to move the four disks from B to C, using the now empty peg A as an auxiliary (Fig. 4.3.2(c)). Thus we may state a recursive solution to the Towers of Hanoi problem as follows:

To move n disks from A to C, using B as auxiliary:

1. If $n=1$, then move the single disk from A to C and stop.
2. Move the top $n-1$ disks from A to B, using C as auxiliary.
3. Move the remaining disk from A to C.
4. Move the $n-1$ disks from B to C, using A as auxiliary.

We are sure that this algorithm will produce a correct solution for any value of n. If $n=1$, step 1 will result in the correct solution. If $n=2$, we know that we already have a solution for $n-1=1$, so that steps 2 and 4 will perform correctly. Similarly, when $n=3$, we already have produced a solution for $n-1=2$, so that steps 2 and 4 can be performed. In this fashion, we can show that the solution works for $n=1, 2, 3, 4, 5, \ldots$ up to any value for which we desire a solution. Notice that we developed the solution by identifying a trivial case ($n=1$) and a solution for a general complex case (n) in terms of a simpler case ($n-1$).

How can this solution be converted into a PL/I program? We are no longer dealing with a mathematical function such as factorial, but rather with concrete actions such as "move a disk." How are we to represent such actions in the computer? The problem is not completely specified. What are the inputs to the program? What are its outputs to be? Whenever you are told to write a program, you must receive specific instructions as to exactly what the program is expected to do. A problem statement such as "solve the Towers of Hanoi problem" is quite insufficient. What is usually meant when such a problem is specified is that not only the program but also the inputs and outputs must be designed so that they reasonably correspond to the problem description. The design of inputs and outputs is an important phase of a solution and should be given as much attention as the rest of a program. There are two reasons for this. The first is that the

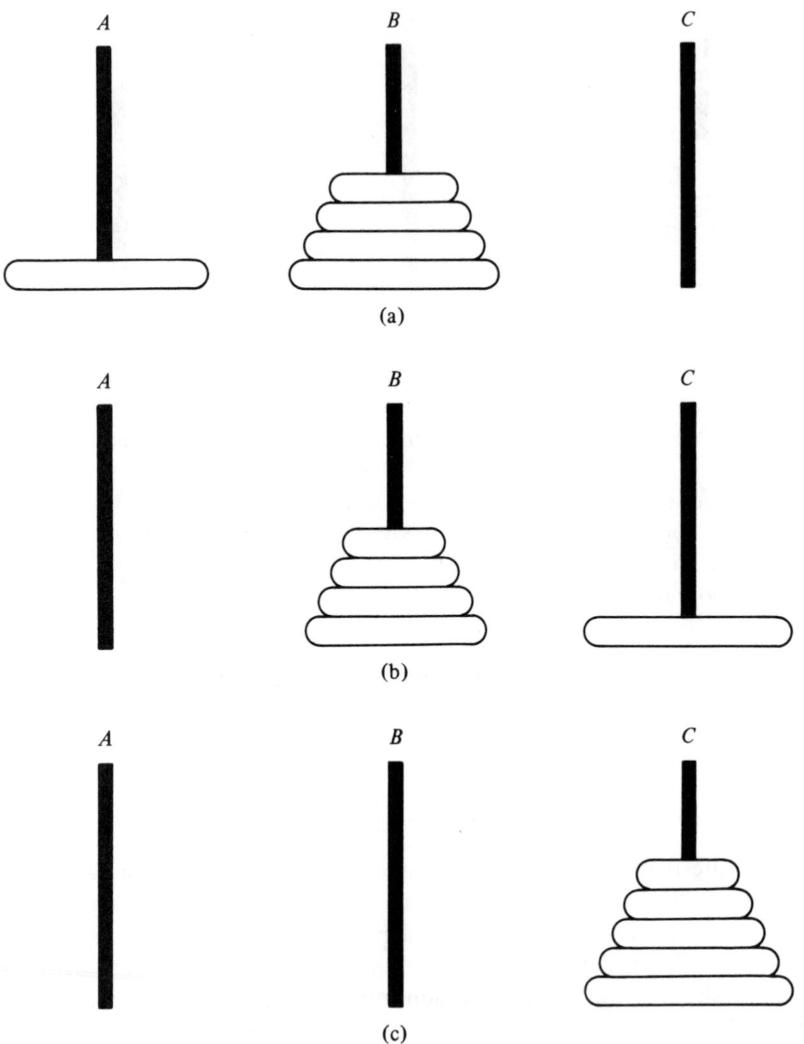

Figure 4.3.2. Recursive solution to the Towers of Hanoi.

user (who must ultimately evaluate and pass judgment on your work) will not see the elegant method you incorporated in your program, but will struggle mightily to decipher the output or to adapt his input data to your particular input conventions. The failure to agree early on input and output details has been the cause of much grief to programmers and users alike. The second reason is that a slight change in the input or output format may make the program much simpler to design. Thus the programmer can make his job much easier if he is able to design an input or output format compatible with his algorithm. Of course these two considerations, convenience to the user and convenience to the programmer, often conflict sharply, and some happy medium must be found.

However, the user as well as the programmer must be a full participant in the decisions on input and output formats.

Let us, then, proceed to design the inputs and outputs for this program. The only input needed is the value of N, the number of disks. At least, that may be the programmer's view. The user may want the names of the disks (such as "red," "blue," "green," etc.) and perhaps the names of the pegs (such as "left," "right," and "middle") as well. The programmer can probably convince the user that naming the disks 1, 2, 3, . . . , N and the pegs *A, B, C* is just as convenient. If the user is adamant, the programmer can write a small function to convert the user's names to his own and vice versa.

A reasonable form for the output would be a list of statements such as

```
MOVE DISK xxx FROM PEG yyy TO PEG zzz
```

where *xxx* is the number of the disk to be moved and *yyy* and *zzz* are the names of the pegs involved. The action to be taken for a solution would be to perform each of the output statements in the order that they appear in the output.

The programmer then decides to write a subroutine TOWERS (he is purposely vague about the parameters at this point) to print the above output. His main program would be

```
RESULT: PROC OPTIONS(MAIN);
          DCL N    FIXED;
          GET LIST(N);  /*  read in number of disks    */
          CALL TOWERS(parameters);
        END RESULT;
```

Let us assume that the user will be satisfied to name the disks 1, 2, 3, . . . , N and the pegs *A, B,* and *C*. What should the parameters to TOWERS be? Clearly, they should include N, the number of disks to be moved. This not only includes information about how many disks there are but also what their names are. The programmer then notices that in the recursive algorithm, he will have to move N–1 disks using a recursive call to TOWERS. Thus, on the recursive call, the first parameter to TOWERS will be N–1. But this implies that the top N–1 disks are numbered 1, 2, 3, . . . , N–1 and that the smallest disk is numbered 1. This is a good example of programming convenience determining problem representation. There is no *a priori* reason for labeling the smallest disk 1; logically the largest disk could have been labeled 1 and the smallest disk N. However, since it leads to a simpler and more direct program, we will choose to label our disks so that the smallest disk has the smallest number.

What are the other parameters to TOWERS? At first glance, it might appear that no additional parameters are necessary since the pegs are named *A, B,* and *C* by default. However, a closer look at the recursive solution leads us to the realization that on the recursive calls disks will not be moved from *A* to *C* using *B* as auxiliary but rather from *A* to *B* using *C* (step 2) or from *B* to *C* using *A* (step 4). We therefore include three more parameters in TOWERS. The first, FROM, represents the peg from which we are removing disks; the second, TO, represents the peg to which we will take the disks; and the third, AUX, represents the auxiliary peg. This situation is one which is quite typical of recursive routines; additional parameters are necessary to handle the recursive call situation. We already saw one example of this in the binary search program where the parameters LOW and HIGH were necessary.

The complete program to solve the Towers of Hanoi problem, closely following the recursive solution, may be written as follows:

```
RESULT: PROC OPTIONS(MAIN);
          DCL N      FIXED;
          GET LIST(N);  /*   read number of disks      */
          CALL TOWERS(N, 'A','C','B');

 TOWERS: PROC(N,FROM,TO,AUX) RECURSIVE;
            DCL N                  FIXED,
                (FROM,TO,AUX)     CHAR(*);

          /*    if only one disk, make the move and return     */
             IF N=1 THEN DO;
                PUT SKIP EDIT('MOVE DISK 1 FROM PEG',FROM,
                              'TO PEG',TO)  (A,X(1));
                RETURN;
                        END;

          /*    move top N-1 disks from A to B, using C as     */
          /*                 auxiliary                          */
             CALL TOWERS(N-1,FROM,AUX,TO);

          /*      move remaining disk from A to C         */
             PUT SKIP EDIT('MOVE DISK',N,'FROM PEG',FROM,
                           'TO PEG',TO)
                           (A,F(2), 4 (X(1),A));

          /*    move N-1 disks from B to C, using A as    */
          /*                auxiliary                     */
             CALL TOWERS(N-1,AUX,TO,FROM);
             RETURN;
          END TOWERS;

        END RESULT;
```

A note of caution for PL/C programmers is necessary. The keyword 'TO' is a reserved word in PL/C, so a different identifier must be used.

TOWERS is our first example of a recursive routine which is not a function. It is called by using the CALL statement, exactly as any other subroutine would be called.

Trace the actions of the above program when it reads in the value 5 for N. Be careful to keep track of the changing values of the parameters FROM, AUX, and TO. Verify that it produces the following output:

```
MOVE DISK 1 FROM PEG A TO PEG C
MOVE DISK 2 FROM PEG A TO PEG B
MOVE DISK 1 FROM PEG C TO PEG B
MOVE DISK 3 FROM PEG A TO PEG C
MOVE DISK 1 FROM PEG B TO PEG A
MOVE DISK 2 FROM PEG B TO PEG C
MOVE DISK 1 FROM PEG A TO PEG C
MOVE DISK 4 FROM PEG A TO PEG B
MOVE DISK 1 FROM PEG C TO PEG B
MOVE DISK 2 FROM PEG C TO PEG A
MOVE DISK 1 FROM PEG B TO PEG A
MOVE DISK 3 FROM PEG C TO PEG B
MOVE DISK 1 FROM PEG A TO PEG C
MOVE DISK 2 FROM PEG A TO PEG B
MOVE DISK 1 FROM PEG C TO PEG B
MOVE DISK 5 FROM PEG A TO PEG C
MOVE DISK 1 FROM PEG B TO PEG A
MOVE DISK 2 FROM PEG B TO PEG C
MOVE DISK 1 FROM PEG A TO PEG C
MOVE DISK 3 FROM PEG B TO PEG A
MOVE DISK 1 FROM PEG C TO PEG B
MOVE DISK 2 FROM PEG C TO PEG A
MOVE DISK 1 FROM PEG B TO PEG A
MOVE DISK 4 FROM PEG B TO PEG C
MOVE DISK 1 FROM PEG A TO PEG C
MOVE DISK 2 FROM PEG A TO PEG B
MOVE DISK 1 FROM PEG C TO PEG B
MOVE DISK 3 FROM PEG A TO PEG C
MOVE DISK 1 FROM PEG B TO PEG A
MOVE DISK 2 FROM PEG B TO PEG C
MOVE DISK 1 FROM PEG A TO PEG C
```

Verify that the above solution actually works and does not violate any of the rules.

Translation from Prefix to Postfix Using Recursion

Let us examine another problem for which the recursive solution is the most direct and elegant one. This is the problem of converting a prefix expression to postfix. Prefix and postfix notation were discussed in the last chapter. Briefly, prefix and postfix notations are methods of writing mathematical expressions without parentheses. In prefix notation each operator immediately precedes its operands. In postfix notation each operator immediately follows its operands. To refresh your memory, here are a few conventional (infix) mathematical expressions with their prefix and postfix equivalents:

Infix	Prefix	Postfix
A+B	+AB	AB+
A+B*C	+A*BC	ABC*+
A*(B+C)	*A+BC	ABC+*
A*B+C	+*ABC	AB*C+
A+B*C+D−E*F	−++A*BCD*EF	ABC*+D+EF*−
(A+B)*(C+D−E)*F	**+AB−+CDEF	AB+CD+E−*F*

The most convenient way to define postfix and prefix is by using recursion. Assuming no constants and using only single letters as variables, we see that a prefix expression is a single letter, or an operator followed by two prefix expressions. A postfix expression may be similarly defined as a single letter, or as an operator preceded by two postfix expressions. The above definitions assume that all operations are binary–i.e., each requires two operands. Examples of such operations are addition, subtraction, multiplication, division, and exponentiation. It is easy to extend the above definitions of prefix and postfix to include unary operations such as negation or factorial, but in the interest of simplicity we will not do so here. Verify that each of the above prefix and postfix expressions are valid by showing that they satisfy the definitions and make sure that you can identify the two operands of each operator.

We will put these recursive definitions to use in a moment, but first let us return to our problem. Given a prefix expression, how can we convert it into a postfix expression? We can immediately identify a trivial case: if a prefix expression consists of only a single variable, then that expression is its own postfix equivalent. That is, an expression such as *A* is valid as both a prefix and a postfix expression.

Now consider a longer prefix string. If we knew how to convert any shorter prefix string to postfix, could we convert this longer prefix string? The answer is yes, with one proviso. Every prefix string longer than a single variable contains an operator, a first operand, and a second operand (remember we are assuming binary operators only). Assume we are able to identify the first and second operands, which are necessarily shorter than the original string. We can then convert the long prefix string to postfix by first converting the first operand to postfix, then converting the second operand to postfix and appending it to the end of the first converted operand, and finally appending the initial operator to the end of the resultant string. Thus we have developed a recursive algorithm for converting a prefix string to postfix with the single provision that we must specify a method for identifying the operands in a prefix expression. We can summarize our algorithm as follows:

1. If the prefix string is a single variable, return it as the postfix equivalent.

2. Let *op* be the first operator of the prefix string.

3. Find the first operand *opnd1* of the string. Convert it to postfix and call it *post1*.

4. Find the second operand *opnd2* of the string. Convert it to postfix and call it *post2*.

5. Return (*post1* || *post2* || *op*).

Before transforming this algorithm into a PL/I program, let us examine its inputs and outputs. We wish to write a function CONVERT which accepts a varying-length character string as input. This character string represents a prefix expression in which all variables are single letters and the allowable operators are '+', '–', '*', and '/'. The function returns a varying-length character string which is the postfix equivalent of the prefix parameter.

Assume the existence of a function FIND which accepts a varying-length character string and returns an integer which is the length of the longest prefix expression contained within the input string which starts at the beginning of that string. For example, FIND('A+CD') returns 1, since 'A' is the longest prefix string starting at the beginning of 'A+CD'. FIND('+*ABCD+GH') returns 5 since '+*ABC' is the longest prefix string starting at the beginning of '+*ABCD+GH'. If no such prefix string exists within the input string starting at the beginning of the input string, FIND returns 0. (For example, FIND('*+AB') returns 0.) This function is used to identify the first and second operands of a prefix operator. Assuming the existence of the function FIND, a conversion routine may be written as follows:

```
CONVERT:  PROC(PREFIX) RECURSIVE RETURNS(CHAR(256) VAR);
            DCL PREFIX          CHAR(*) VAR,
                (POSTFIX,OPND1,OPND2,TEMP)
                                CHAR(256) VAR,
                OPS             CHAR(4) INIT('+-*/'),
                ALPH            CHAR(26)
                           INIT('ABCDEFGHIJKLMNOPQRSTUVWXYZ'),
                OP              CHAR(1),
                (M,N)           FIXED;

            IF LENGTH(PREFIX)=1 THEN
                      /*   check for variable   */
                IF INDEX(ALPH,PREFIX)¬=0 THEN DO;
                    POSTFIX=PREFIX;
                    RETURN(POSTFIX);
                                                END;
                                          ELSE DO;
                    PUT SKIP LIST('ILLEGAL PREFIX STRING');
                    STOP;
                                               END;
```

```
    /*        the prefix string is longer than        */
    /*              a single character                */
    /*        extract the operator and check          */
    /*                  for validity                  */
OP=SUBSTR(PREFIX,1,1);
IF INDEX(OPS,OP)=0 THEN DO;
    PUT SKIP LIST('ILLEGAL PREFIX STRING');
    STOP;
                                END;

    /*          extract the first operand             */
TEMP=SUBSTR(PREFIX,2);
N=FIND(TEMP);
IF N=0 THEN DO;
    PUT SKIP LIST('ILLEGAL PREFIX STRING');
    STOP;
                END;
OPND1=SUBSTR(PREFIX,2,N);

    /*         extract the second operand             */
TEMP=SUBSTR(PREFIX,N+2);
M=FIND(TEMP);
IF M=0 THEN DO;
    PUT SKIP LIST('ILLEGAL PREFIX STRING');
    STOP;
                END;
OPND2=SUBSTR(PREFIX,N+2,M);

    /*    check that the second operand ends          */
    /*       at the end of the prefix string          */
IF N+M+1¬=LENGTH(PREFIX) THEN DO;
    PUT SKIP LIST('ILLEGAL PREFIX STRING');
    STOP;
                                        END;

    /*    convert the two operands to postfix         */
    /*          and append the operator               */
POSTFIX=CONVERT(OPND1) || CONVERT(OPND2) || OP;
RETURN(POSTFIX);
END CONVERT;
```

Note that several checks have been incorporated into CONVERT to ensure that the parameter is a valid prefix string. One of the most difficult classes of errors to detect are those resulting from invalid inputs and the programmer's neglect to check for validity.

We now turn our attention to the function FIND which is given a character string and returns the length of the longest prefix string which is contained in that input string starting at its first character. The word "longest" in this definition is superfluous since there is at most one substring starting at the beginning of a given string which is a valid prefix expression. To see this, note that it is trivially true in a string of length 1. Assume it is true for a short string. Then a long string which contains a prefix expression as an initial substring must begin with either a variable, in which case that variable is the desired substring, or with an operator. Deleting the initial operator, the remaining string is shorter than the original string and can therefore have at most a single initial prefix expression. This expression is the first operand of the initial operator. Similarly, the remaining substring (after deleting the first operand) can only have a single initial substring which is a prefix expression. This expression must be the second operand. Therefore, we have uniquely identified the operator and operands of the prefix expression starting at the first character of an arbitrary string, if such an expression exists.

Notice that this proof has given us a recursive method for finding the initial prefix expression in a string. We now incorporate this method into a function FIND:

```
FIND: PROC(STR) RECURSIVE RETURNS(FIXED);
         DCL STR        CHAR(*) VAR,
             TEMP       CHAR(256) VAR,
             ALPH       CHAR(26)
               INIT('ABCDEFGHIJKLMNOPQRSTUVWXYZ'),
             (M,N)      FIXED,
             FIRST      CHAR(1);

         IF LENGTH(STR)=0 THEN RETURN(0);
         FIRST=SUBSTR(STR,1,1);
         IF INDEX(ALPH,FIRST)¬=0 THEN
      /*  First character is a letter. That letter   */
      /*           is the initial substring.          */
                                              RETURN(1);

      /*     otherwise find the first operand         */
         IF LENGTH(STR)<2 THEN RETURN(0);
         TEMP=SUBSTR(STR,2);
         M=FIND(TEMP);
         IF M=0 THEN RETURN (0);
         IF LENGTH(STR)=M+1 THEN
      /*            no second operand                 */
                                         RETURN(0);
         TEMP=SUBSTR(STR,M+2);
         N=FIND(TEMP);
         IF N=0 THEN RETURN(0);
         RETURN(M+N+1);
      END FIND;
```

Make sure that you understand how these routines work by tracing their actions on both valid and invalid prefix expressions. More important, make sure that you understand how they were developed and how logical analysis led to a natural recursive solution which was directly translatable into a PL/I program.

4.4. Simulating Recursion

In this section we shall examine more closely some of the mechanisms used to implement recursion so that we can simulate these mechanisms using nonrecursive techniques. This activity is important for several reasons. First of all, many commonly used programming languages (such as FORTAN, COBOL, and most machine languages) do not allow recursive programs. Problems such as the Towers of Hanoi and prefix to postfix conversion whose solutions can be derived and stated quite simply using recursive techniques can be programmed in these languages by simulating the recursive solution using more elementary operations. If we know that the recursive solution is correct (and it is often fairly easy to prove such a solution correct) and we have established techniques for converting a recursive solution to a nonrecursive one, then we can create a correct solution in a nonrecursive language. It is not an uncommon occurrence for a programmer to be able to state a solution to a problem in the form of a recursive algorithm. The ability to generate a nonrecursive solution from this algorithm is indispensable if he is using a compiler that does not support recursion.

Another reason for examining the implementation of recursion is that it will allow us to understand the implications of recursion and some of its hidden pitfalls. While these pitfalls do not exist in mathematical definitions that employ recursion, they seem to be an inevitable accompaniment of an implementation in a real language on a real machine.

Finally, even in a language such as PL/I which does support recursion, a recursive solution to a problem is usually more expensive than a nonrecursive solution, both in terms of time and space. Frequently, this expense is a small price to pay for the logical simplicity and self-documentation of the recursive solution. However, in a production program (such as a compiler, for example) which may be run thousands of times, the recurrent expense is a heavy burden on the system's limited resources. Thus a program may be designed to incorporate a recursive solution in order to reduce the expense of design and certification, and then carefully converted to a nonrecursive version to be put into actual day-to-day use. As we shall see, in performing such a conversion it is often possible to identify parts of the implementation of recursion which are superfluous in a particular application and thereby significantly reduce the amount of work that the program must perform.

Before examining the actions of a recursive subroutine, let us take a step back and examine the action of a nonrecursive routine. We will then be able to see what mechanisms must be added to support recursion. Before proceeding, we adopt the following convention. Suppose we have the statement

```
CALL ROUT(X);
```

where ROUT is defined as a procedure by the statement

```
ROUT: PROC(A);
```

X will be referred to as an ***argument*** (of the calling routine) and A will be referred to as a ***parameter*** (of the called routine).

What happens when a subroutine is called? The action of calling a subroutine may be divided into three parts:

1. passing parameters
2. allocating and initializing local variables
3. transferring control to the subroutine

Let us examine each of these three steps in turn.

1. Passing Parameters:

Call by Reference

There are many different methods of passing parameters that have been used in a wide variety of programming languages. Each of these implements the basic idea that a parameter of a subroutine assumes the value of the argument passed to it by the calling routine. However, there are many ways in which this concept can be implemented, each having different implications for the compilation and execution of the program. We will discuss three such methods in connection with PL/I and the simulation of recursive routines. The simplest case of passing a parameter occurs when the argument of the calling routine is an identifier whose attributes match exactly those of the corresponding parameter of the called routine. In such a case, PL/I uses a ***call by reference*** in which the variable which appears as a parameter refers to the same storage location as the argument. This implies that storage need not be allocated within the subroutine's data area for the parameter, since the parameter refers to an already existing location in the calling routine's data area. All that must be allocated within the subroutine is a location to hold the address of the argument so that the subroutine may access that address. For this reason, call by reference is also known as ***call by address***. Because a reference to a parameter within the subroutine is actually a reference to the storage location of its corresponding argument, a change in the value of the parameter in the subroutine will produce precisely the same change in the original argument.

In call by reference a parameter may be used as an ***output parameter***; i.e., it may be used to return a value to the calling program. For example, in the routine POPANDTEST of the last chapter, the parameters X and UND were used to communicate to the calling routine the value popped off the stack and whether or not an underflow had occurred. Similarly, the stack itself was a parameter which was modified by POP, PUSH, and POPANDTEST. An argument which is passed by reference need not be initialized in the calling routine since its value is never used in the passing mechanism; only its address is passed. Of course, if the corresponding parameter's value is used within the subroutine, it must first be initialized in either the calling routine or in the subroutine. The term "output parameter" is really a description of the use of the parameter rather than a syntactic classification. It is the use of a parameter (and argument within the calling routine) that will determine which of the terms input parameter, output parameter, or input-output parameter apply.

Call by Dummy Argument

If the attributes of an argument do not match those of its corresponding parameter, so that conversion must be performed, or if an argument is a constant or an expression, PL/I uses a ***dummy argument***. This means that an additional storage area possessing the attributes of the parameter is allocated within the data area of the calling program. It is the address of this storage area which is passed to the subroutine. Before this address is passed, the content of the storage area is initialized to the converted value of the argument specified. (In some compilers, e.g., the IBM Optimizing and Checkout compilers, conversion is done automatically for internal subroutines. For external subroutines (and in other compilers for internal subroutines as well) conversion is specified by using the ENTRY attribute.)

Creation of a dummy argument means that the parameter cannot be used as an output parameter since any changes applied to the parameter in the subroutine are reflected in the dummy argument only; the original argument remains unchanged. The use of a dummy argument also implies that the argument must have been properly initialized before effecting the subroutine call since in creating the dummy argument, the calling procedure uses that value of initialization. No extra storage (except for one location holding an address) need be allocated in the called procedure since only an address is being passed. The dummy argument is a part of the calling routine's data area. In essence then, a call by dummy argument behaves exactly as a call by reference, except that if the attributes of the argument and those of the parameter do not match, the address passed to the subroutine is that of the "dummy" area rather than that of the original area.

Call by Value

A third type of calling mechanism which is used in some languages (but not in PL/I) is ***call by value***. In this scheme, a copy of the argument is made locally within the subroutine, and any changes to the parameter are made to that local copy. The effect of this scheme is the same as that of dummy arguments since the original input parameters cannot be altered. However, in this method, storage for the parameters is allocated within the data area of the subroutine.

If no assignment (including input) is made to a parameter within a subroutine, the three methods will appear identical to the user and it should be of no concern to him which of the methods is being used. We shall return to this point later.

Examples of Subroutine Calls

If, however, changes are made to the parameter from within a subroutine, the particular type of call being used will have an effect on the program's results. Let us consider as an example the routine INCR given below:

```
INCR:  PROC(X);
          DCL X FIXED;
          X=X+1;
          RETURN;
       END INCR;
```

Suppose we are operating in an environment using a call by reference and we execute the following sequence of instructions:

```
DCL A     FIXED INIT(8);
PUT LIST(A);
CALL INCR(A);
PUT LIST(A);
```

The output of the above program would be

```
8    9
```

A diagram of main storage before and after execution of the statement X=X+1; is given in Fig. 4.4.1. Notice that any change to X within INCR will change the value in the data area to which A refers.

Let us now consider the effect of the following:

```
DCL A     FLOAT INIT(8);
PUT LIST(A);
CALL INCR(A);
PUT LIST(A);
```

If we are operating under a system of call by reference, an attempt to execute X=X+1; will result in an error (why?). However, if we are using a dummy argument, the output will be

```
8    8
```

An illustration of what occurs in a call by dummy argument is given in Fig. 4.4.2. Observe that the value of 8 is copied to a dummy data area in a form in which its attributes match those of the parameter X (FIXED). The instruction X=X+1; operates on this dummy area.

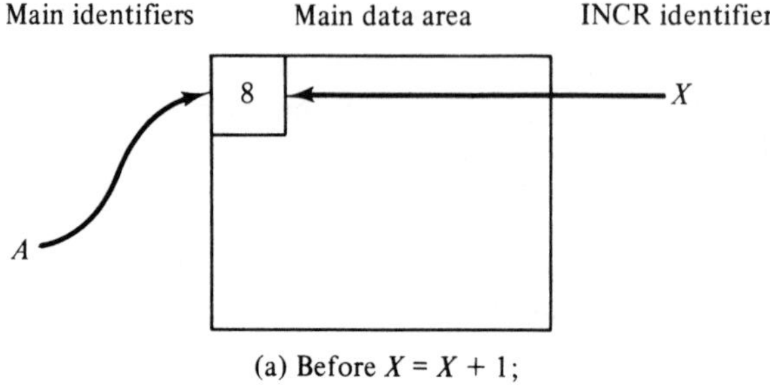

(a) Before $X = X + 1$;

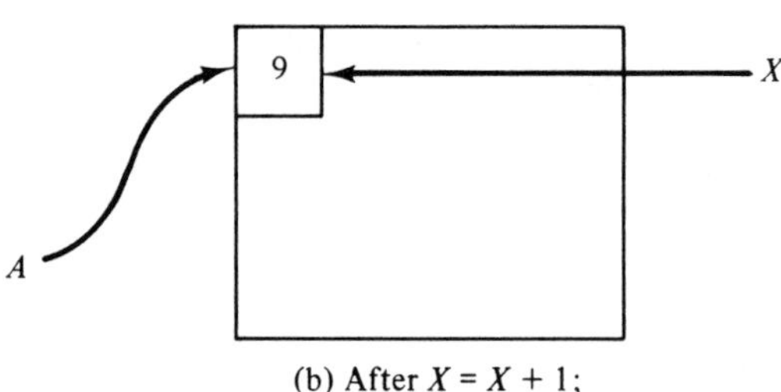

(b) After $X = X + 1$;

Figure 4.4.1. An illustration of call by reference.

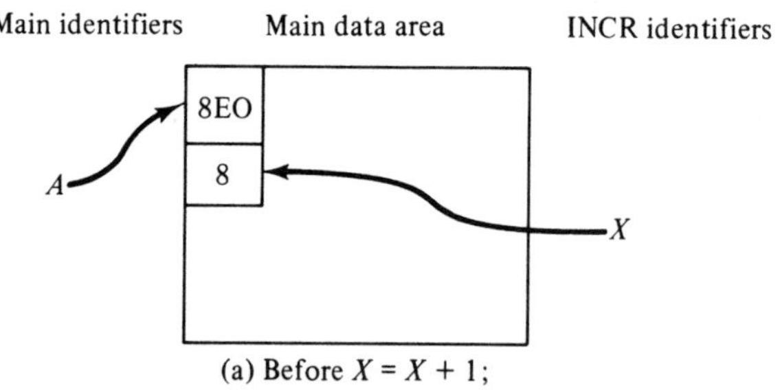

(a) Before $X = X + 1$;

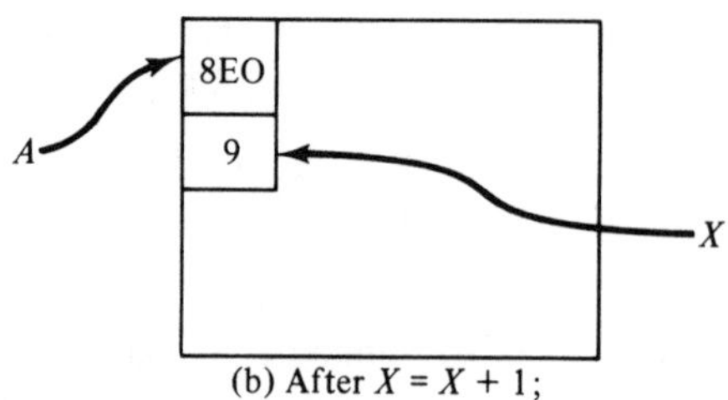

(b) After $X = X + 1$;

Figure 4.4.2. An illustration of use of dummy argument.

Finally, let us assume a call by value scheme that accepts

```
DCL A FIXED INIT(8);
PUT LIST(A);
CALL INCR(A);
PUT LIST(A);
```

In this case, even though the identifiers A and X have the same attributes, the output will be

```
8   8
```

This is illustrated in Fig. 4.4.3. Notice that in a call by value scheme the value of A is first copied into the data area of the subroutine and it is this area that is referenced by X.

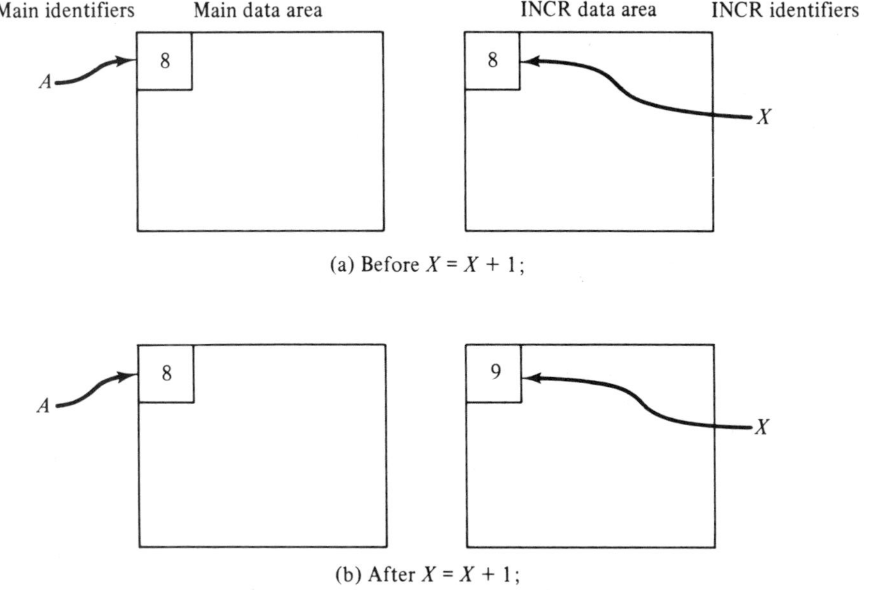

(a) Before $X = X + 1$;

(b) After $X = X + 1$;

Figure 4.4.3. An illustration of call by value.

In PL/I a subroutine call is implemented by reference if the argument is a simple variable whose attributes match exactly those of the corresponding parameter. If the argument is either a constant, expression, or a variable with attributes different than those of the corresponding parameter, the call uses dummy arguments.

2. Allocating and Initializing Local Variables:

After parameters have been passed, the local AUTOMATIC variables of the subroutine are allocated. These local variables include all those declared directly in the procedure block to have the AUTOMATIC attribute either by default or explicitly. They also include any temporaries which must be created during the course of execution. For example, in evaluating the expression

```
X + Y + Z
```

a storage location must be set aside to hold the value of X+Y so that Z can be added to it. Another storage location must be set aside to hold the value of the entire expression after it has been evaluated. Such locations are called ***temporaries*** since they are needed only temporarily during the course of execution. Similarly, in a statement such as

```
X=FACT(N);
```

a temporary must be set aside to hold the value of FACT(N) before that value can be assigned to X. (The assignment may require conversion from the attributes of the value returned.) Any local variable declared in the PROCEDURE block to have the INITIAL attribute is initialized at this time.

3. Transferring Control to the Subroutine:

At this point control may still not be passed to the subroutine because provision has not yet been made for saving the ***return address***. If a subroutine is given control, it must eventually restore control to the calling routine by means of a branch. However, it cannot execute that branch unless it knows the location to which it must return. Since this location is within the calling routine and not within the subroutine, the only way that the subroutine can know this address is to have it passed as a parameter. This is exactly what happens. Aside from the explicit parameters specified by the programmer, there are also a set of implicit parameters which contain information necessary for the subroutine to execute and return correctly. Chief among these implicit parameters is the return address. The subroutine stores this address within its own data area. When it is ready to return control to the calling program, the subroutine retrieves the return address and branches to that location.

Once the parameters and the return address have been passed, control may be transferred to the subroutine, since everything required has been done to ensure that the subroutine will operate on the appropriate data and then return to the calling routine safely.

Return from a Subroutine

When a subroutine returns, three actions are performed. First, the return address is retrieved and stored in a safe location. Second, the subroutine's data area is freed. This data area contains all local variables, temporaries, argument addresses (in the case of a call by reference), and the return address. Finally, a branch is taken to the return address which had been previously saved. This restores control to the calling program at the point immediately after the instruction that initiated the call. In addition, if the subprogram is a function, the value returned is placed in a secure location from which the calling program may retrieve it. Usually this location is a hardware register which is set aside for this purpose.

Suppose a main procedure has called a subroutine B which has called C which has in turn called D. This is illustrated in Fig. 4.4.4(a), where we indicate that control currently resides somewhere within D. Within each subroutine, there is a location set aside for the return address. Thus the return address area of D contains the address of the instruction in C immediately following CALL D;. Figure 4.4.4(b) shows the situation immediately following D's return to C. The return address within D has been retrieved and control transferred to that address.

You may have noticed that the string of return addresses forms a stack; i.e., the most recent address to be added to the chain is the first to be removed. At any point, we can only access the return address from within the subroutine that is currently executing, which represents the top of the stack. When the stack is popped (i.e., when the subroutine returns), a new top is revealed within the calling routine. Calling a subroutine has the effect of pushing an element on the stack, and returning pops the stack.

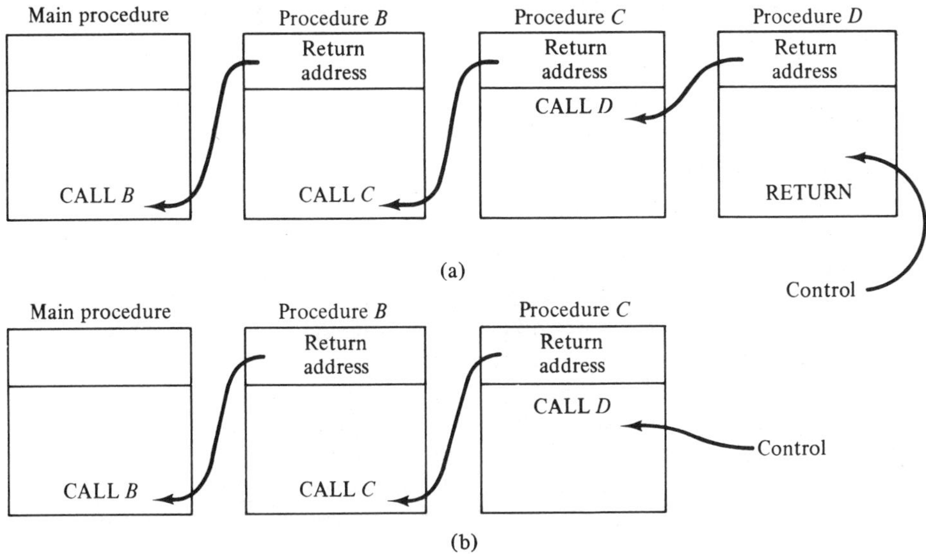

Figure 4.4.4. A series of procedures calling one another.

Implementing Recursive Routines

What must be added to this description in the case of a recursive routine? The answer is: surprisingly little. Each time a recursive routine calls itself, an entirely new data area for that particular call must be allocated. As before, this data area contains all argument addresses, local AUTOMATIC variables, temporaries, and a return address. The point to remember is that in recursion a data area is associated not with a subroutine alone, but with a particular call to that subroutine. Each call causes a new data area to be allocated, and each reference to an item in the subroutine's data area is to the data area of the most recent call. Similarly, each return causes the current data area to be freed, and the data area allocated immediately prior to the current area becomes current. This behavior, of course, suggests the use of a stack.

Simulation of Factorial

In Section 2, where we described the action of the recursive factorial function, we used a set of stacks to represent the successive allocations of each of the local variables and parameters. These stacks may be thought of as separate stacks, one for each local variable. Alternatively, and closer to reality, we may think of all these stacks as a single large stack. Each element of this large stack is an entire data area containing subparts representing the individual local variables or parameters. Each time that the recursive routine is called, a new data area is allocated. The parameters within this data area are initialized to refer to their corresponding arguments (either actual or dummy). The return address within the data area is initialized to the address following the call instruction. Any reference to local variables or parameters are via the current data area. When the recursive routine returns, the returned value (in the case of a function) and the return address are saved, the data area is freed, and a branch to the return address is executed. The calling routine retrieves the returned value (if any), resumes execution, and refers to its own data area, which is now on top of the stack.

Let us now examine how we can simulate the actions of a recursive procedure. We will need a stack of data areas declared by

```
DCL 1 STACK,
      2 TOP              FIXED,
      2 DATA_AREA . . .
```

The DATA_AREA is itself a structure containing the various items which exist in a data area. Since we do not yet know how to manipulate addresses in PL/I, we cannot simulate the mechanism of a call by reference. However, if we replace a call by reference with a call by value, no harm will result as long as parameters are not changed within the subroutine. Since all of the recursive routines we have looked at in this chapter satisfy this property, we will simulate a call by value mechanism for recursive routines.

Let us look at a specific example, the factorial function. We repeat the code for that function:

```
FACT:  PROC (N)  RECURSIVE RETURNS(FIXED(15));
             DCL     (N,X)            FIXED,
                       Y              FIXED(15);
             IF N=0  THEN RETURN(1);
             X=N-1;
             Y=FACT(X);
             RETURN(N*Y);
       END FACT;
```

How are we to declare the data area for this routine? It must contain the parameter N (since we are simulating a call by value, this parameter contains the value of N rather than the address of the argument) and the local variables X and Y. As we shall see, no temporaries are needed. The data area must also contain a return address. In this case, there are two possible points to which we might want to return: the assignment of FACT(X) to Y and the main program which called FACT. Suppose we declare an array of two labels by

```
DCL L(2) LABEL;
```

and we let L(2) be the label of a section of code

```
L(2): Y = RESULT;
```

within the simulating program. Let L(1) be the label of a statement

```
L(1): RETURN(RESULT);
```

This reflects a convention that the variable RESULT contains the value to be returned by an invocation of the FACT function. The return address will be stored as an integer I (equal to either 1 or 2). Upon returning from a recursive call, the statement

```
GO TO L(I);
```

is used to simulate a return. Thus if I=1, a return is executed to the main program which called FACT, and if I=2, a return is simulated to the assignment of the returned value to Y in the previous execution of FACT.

Thus the data area stack for this example can be declared as follows:

```
DCL 1 STACK,
      2 TOP                  FIXED  INIT(0),
      2 DATA_AREA(50),
        3 PARAM              FIXED,
        3 X                  FIXED,
        3 Y                  FIXED(15),
        3 RETADDR            FIXED;
```

We choose to call the simulated parameter PARAM rather than N so as to avoid confusion with the parameter N passed to the simulating routine. We also declare a current data area to hold the values of the variables in the simulated "current" call on the recursive routine. The declaration is

```
DCL 1 CURR_AREA,
      2 CURR_PARAM           FIXED,
      2 CURR_X               FIXED,
      2 CURR_Y               FIXED(15),
      2 CURR_RETADDR         FIXED;
```

In addition, we declare a single variable RESULT by

```
DCL RESULT   FIXED (15);
```

This variable is used to communicate the returned value of FACT from one recursive call of FACT to its caller, and from FACT to the outside calling routine. Since the elements on the stack of data areas are structures and a PL/I function cannot return a structure, we cannot use a function POP to pop a data area from STACK. Instead, we must write a subroutine POPSUB called by

```
CALL POPSUB(STACK,AREA);
```

where STACK is the stack of data areas and AREA is a structure representing a data area. POPSUB pops the stack and sets AREA to the structure. We leave the details as an exercise.

A return from FACT is simulated by the code

```
RESULT=value to be returned;
I= CURR_RETADDR;
CALL POPSUB (STACK,CURR_AREA);
GO TO L(I);
```

A recursive call to FACT is simulated by pushing the current data area on the stack, reinitializing the variables CURR_PARAM and CURR_RETADDR to the parameter and return address of this call respectively, and then transferring to the start of the simulated routine. The code to accomplish this is as follows. (Recall that X holds the value of N–1, which is to be the new parameter. Recall also that on a recursive call we wish to eventually return to L(2).)

```
CALL PUSH(STACK,CURR_AREA);
CURR_PARAM= CURR_X;
CURR_RETADDR=2;
GO TO START;
```

Of course, the POPSUB and PUSH routines must be written so that they pop and push entire structures of data areas rather than simple variables. (Another imposition of the PL/I implementation of stacks is that the variable CURR_Y must be initialized to some value or an error will result in the PUSH routine upon assignment of CURR_Y to Y.)

When the simulation first begins, the current area must be initialized so that CURR_PARAM equals N and CURR_RETADDR equals 1 (indicating a return to the calling routine). A dummy data area must be pushed onto the stack so that when POPSUB is executed in returning to the main routine, an underflow does not occur. This dummy data area must also be initialized so as not to cause an error in the PUSH routine (see the comment in parentheses at the end of the last paragraph). Thus the simulated version of the recursive FACT routine is as follows:

```
SIMFACT: PROC(N)  RETURNS(FIXED(15));
               DCL      (N,I)                    FIXED,
                        RESULT                   FIXED(15);
               DCL      1 STACK,
                          2 TOP                  FIXED INIT(0),
                          2 DATA_AREA(50),
                            3 PARAM              FIXED,
                            3 X                  FIXED,
                            3 Y                  FIXED(15),
                            3 RETADDR            FIXED;
               DCL      1 CURR_AREA,
                          2 CURR_PARAM           FIXED,
                          2 CURR_X               FIXED,
                          2 CURR_Y               FIXED(15),
                          2 CURR_RETADDR         FIXED;
               DCL      L(2)                     LABEL;

               /*   initialization    */
               CURR_PARAM=0;
               CURR_X=0;
               CURR_Y=0;
               CURR_RETADDR=0;

          /*     push the dummy data area onto the stack        */
               CALL PUSH(STACK,CURR_AREA);

          /*     set the parameter and the return address of    */
          /*     the current data area to their proper values   */
               CURR_PARAM=N;
               CURR_RETADDR=1;

     START:    /*  this is the beginning of the simulated  */
               /*              factorial routine           */
                IF CURR_PARAM=0 THEN
               /*        simulation of RETURN(1)           */
                                        DO;
                    RESULT=1;
                    I=CURR_RETADDR;
                    CALL POPSUB(STACK,CURR_AREA);
                    GO TO L(I);
                                        END;
               CURR_X=CURR_PARAM-1;
```

```
        /*    simulation of recursive call to FACT     */
        CALL PUSH(STACK,CURR_AREA);
        CURR_PARAM=CURR_X;
        CURR_RETADDR=2;
        GO TO START;

L(2):   /*    this is the point to which we return     */
        /*      from the recursive call. Set Y to      */
        /*             returned value.                 */
        CURR_Y=RESULT;

        /*    simulation of RETURN(N*Y)        */
        RESULT=CURR_PARAM*CURR_Y;
        I=CURR_RETADDR;
        CALL POPSUB(STACK,CURR_AREA);
        GO TO L(I);

L(1):   /*    at this point we return to the main routine    */
        RETURN(RESULT);
      END SIMFACT;
```

Trace through the execution of this program for N=5, and be sure that you understand what the program does and how it does it.

Notice that no space was reserved in the data area for temporaries, since they need not be saved for later use. The temporary location which holds the value of N*Y in the original recursive routine is simulated by the temporary for CURR_PARAM*CURR_Y in the simulating routine. This is not the case in general. For example, if a recursive routine FUNCT contained a statement such as

```
X = A*FUNCT(B) + C*FUNCT(D);
```

the temporary for A*FUNCT(B) must be saved during the recursive call on FUNCT(D). However, in the example of the factorial function it is not required to stack the temporary.

Improving the Simulated Routine

This leads, naturally, to the question of whether all of the local variables really need to be stacked at all. A variable must be saved on the stack only if its value at the point of initiation of a recursive call must be reused after return from that call. Let us examine whether the variables N, X, and Y meet this requirement. Clearly N does have to be stacked. In the statement

```
Y=N*FACT(X);
```

the old value of N must be used in the multiplication after return from the recursive call on FACT. However, this is not the case for X and Y. In fact, the value of Y is not even defined at the point of the recursive call, so clearly it need not be stacked. Similarly, although X is defined at the point of call, it is never used again after returning, so why bother saving it?

This point can be illustrated even more sharply by the following realization. If X and Y were not declared within the recursive function FACT, but rather were declared as global variables, the routine would work just as well. Thus the automatic stacking and unstacking action performed by recursion for the local variables X and Y is unnecessary.

Another interesting question to consider is whether the return address is really needed on the stack. Since there is only one textual recursive call to FACT, there is only one return address within FACT. The other return address is to the main routine which originally called FACT. But suppose a dummy data area had not been stacked upon initialization of the simulation. Then a data area is placed on the stack only in simulating a recursive call. When the stack is popped in returning from a recursive call, that area is removed from the stack. However, when an attempt is made to pop the stack in simulating a return to the main procedure, an underflow will occur. We can test for this underflow by using POPANDTEST rather than POPSUB, and when it does occur, we can return directly to the outside calling routine rather than through a local label. This means that one of the return addresses can be eliminated. Since this leaves only a single possible return address, it need not be placed on the stack.

Thus the data area has been reduced to contain the parameter alone, and the stack may be declared by

```
DCL 1 STACK,
      2 TOP          FIXED INIT(0),
      2 PARAM(50)    FIXED;
```

The current data area is reduced to a single variable declared by

```
DCL CURR_PARAM FIXED;
```

The program is now quite compact and comprehensible.

```
SIMFACT: PROC(N)  RETURNS(FIXED(15));
            DCL (N,X,CURR_PARAM)        FIXED,
                (RESULT,Y)              FIXED(15);
            DCL 1 STACK,
                  2 TOP                 FIXED INIT(0),
                  2 PARAM(50)           FIXED;
            DCL UND                     BIT(1);

                /*  initialization   */
            CURR_PARAM=N;
```

```
START:          /*    beginning of simulated routine    */
            IF CURR_PARAM=0 THEN
                /*      simulation of RETURN(1)      */
                                        DO;
                RESULT=1;
                CALL POPANDTEST(STACK,CURR_PARAM,UND);
                IF UND THEN
            /*        return to main routine         */
                            RETURN(RESULT);
                        ELSE
            /*      return from recursive call       */
                            GO TO L2;
                                        END;
            X=CURR_PARAM-1;

                /*    simulation of recursive call    */
            CALL PUSH(STACK,CURR_PARAM);
            CURR_PARAM=X;
            GO TO START;

L2:         /*    we return to this point from the simulated    */
            /*                 recursive call                   */
            Y=RESULT;

            /*          simulation of RETURN(N*Y)               */
            RESULT=CURR_PARAM*Y;
            CALL POPANDTEST(STACK,CURR_PARAM,UND);
            IF UND THEN  /*   return to main routine   */
                         RETURN(RESULT);
                   ELSE  /*   return to recursive call  */
                         GO TO L2;
        END SIMFACT;
```

Eliminating GOTOs

Although the above program is certainly simpler than the previous one, it is still far from an "ideal" program. If you were to look at the program without having seen its derivation, it is probably doubtful that you could identify it as computing the factorial function. The statements

```
GO TO START;
```

and

```
GO TO L2;
```

are particularly irritating since they interrupt the flow of thought at a time that one might otherwise come to an understanding of what is happening. Let us see if we can transform this program into a still more readable version.

Several transformations are immediately apparent. First of all, the code beginning with

```
CALL POPANDTEST(STACK,CURR_PARAM,UND);
```

and ending with

```
GO TO L2;
```

is repeated twice for the two cases CURR_PARAM=0 and CURR_PARAM≠0. The two sections can easily be combined into one. A further observation is that the two variables X and CURR_PARAM are assigned values from each other and are never in use simultaneously, so they may be combined and referred to as one variable X. A similar statement may be made about the variables RESULT and Y, which may be combined and referred to as the single variable Y.

Performing these transformations leads to the following version of SIMFACT:

```
SIMFACT: PROC(N)  RETURNS(FIXED(15));
            DCL       (N,X)              FIXED,
                      Y                  FIXED(15),
                      UND                BIT(1);
            DCL        1 STACK,
                         2  TOP          FIXED INIT(0),
                         2  PARAM(50)    FIXED;
            X=N;
START:      IF X=0  THEN Y=1;
                    ELSE DO;
                              CALL PUSH(STACK,X);
                              X=X-1;
                              GO TO START;
                         END;
L1:         CALL POPANDTEST(STACK,X,UND);
            IF UND THEN RETURN(Y);
L2:         Y=X*Y;
            GO TO L1;
         END SIMFACT;
```

We are now beginning to approach a readable program. Note that the program consists of two loops:

1. The START loop which consists of the entire IF statement labeled START. This loop is exited when X=0, at which point Y is set to 1 and execution proceeds to L1.

2. The L1 loop which begins at L1 and ends with the statement GO TO L1;. This loop is exited when the stack has been emptied and underflow occurs, at which point a return is executed.

These loops can easily be transformed into explicit DO loops as follows:

```
START:   DO  WHILE (X¬=0);
             CALL PUSH(STACK,X);
             X=X−1;
         END START;
         CALL POPANDTEST(STACK,X,UND);
L1:      DO  WHILE (¬UND);
             Y=X*Y;
             CALL POPANDTEST(STACK,X,UND);
         END L1;
         RETURN(Y);
```

Let us examine these two loops more closely. X starts off at the value of the input parameter N and is reduced by 1 each time that the START loop is repeated. Each time X is set to a new value, the old value of X is saved on the stack. This continues until X is 0. Thus after the START loop has been executed, the stack contains, from top to bottom, the integers 1 to N.

The L1 loop merely removes each of these values from the stack and sets Y to the product of the popped value and the old value of Y. Since we know what the stack contains at the start of L1, why bother popping the stack? We can use these values directly. We can eliminate the stack and the START loop entirely and replace the L1 loop with a loop which multiplies Y by each of the integers from 1 to N in turn. The resulting program is:

```
SIMFACT:   PROC(N)  RETURNS(FIXED(15));
             DCL    (N,X)         FIXED,
                      Y           FIXED(15) INIT(1);
L1:          DO   X=1 TO N;
                  Y=Y*X;
             END L1;
             RETURN(Y);
           END SIMFACT;
```

But this program is a direct PL/I implementation of the iterative version of the factorial function as presented in Section 1. The only change is that X varies from 1 to N rather than from N to 1.

Simulating the Towers of Hanoi

We have shown that successive transformations of a nonrecursive simulation of a recursive routine may lead to a simpler program for solving a problem. Let us now look at a more complex example of recursion, the Towers of Hanoi problem presented in Section 3. We will simulate its recursion and attempt to simplify the simulation to produce a nonrecursive solution. We present again the recursive program of Section 3.

```
TOWERS:     PROC(N,FROM,TO,AUX)    RECURSIVE;
              DCL     N                     FIXED,
                      (FROM,TO,AUX)         CHAR(1);
              IF N=1 THEN DO;
                 PUT SKIP EDIT
                    ('MOVE DISK 1 FROM PEG',FROM,'TO PEG',TO) (A,X(1));
                 RETURN;
                            END;
              CALL TOWERS (N-1,FROM,AUX,TO);
              PUT SKIP EDIT
                    ('MOVE DISK',N,'FROM PEG',FROM,'TO PEG',TO)
                                            (A,F(2), 4(X(1),A));
              CALL TOWERS(N-1,AUX,TO,FROM);
              RETURN;
            END TOWERS;
```

Make sure that you understand the problem and the recursive solution before proceeding. If you do not, reread Section 3.

There are four parameters in this subroutine, each of which is subject to change in a recursive call. Therefore, the data area must contain elements representing all four. There are no AUTOMATIC local variables. There is a single temporary which is needed to hold the value of N–1, but this can be represented by a similar temporary in the simulating program and does not have to be stacked. There are three possible points to which the subroutine returns on various calls: the calling program and the two points following the recursive calls. Therefore, an array of three labels

```
DCL L(3)   LABEL;
```

is needed. The return address will be encoded as an integer (either 1, 2, or 3) within each data area.

Consider the following nonrecursive simulation of TOWERS:

```
SIMTOWERS:    PROC(N,FROM,TO,AUX);
                DCL N                        FIXED.
                     (FROM,TO,AUX)           CHAR(*);
                DCL 1   STACK,
                        2 TOP                FIXED INIT(0),
                        2 DATA_AREA(50),
                           3 NPARAM          FIXED,
                          (3 FROMPARAM,
                           3 TOPARAM,
                           3 AUXPARAM)       CHAR(1),
                           3 RETADDR         FIXED;
```

```
        DCL 1   CURR_AREA,
                 2 CURR_N             FIXED,
                (2 CURR_FROM,
                 2 CURR_TO,
                 2 CURR_AUX)          CHAR(1),
                 2 CURR_RETADDR       FIXED;
        DCL L(3)                      LABEL;
        DCL TEMP                      CHAR(1);
        DCL I                         FIXED;

        /*    initialization    */

         CURR_N=0;
         CURR_FROM='';
         CURR_TO='';
         CURR_AUX='';
         CURR_RETADDR=0;

      /*   push dummy data area onto stack   */
         CALL PUSH (STACK,CURR_AREA);


      /*   set the parameters and the return   */
      /*    address of the current data area   */
      /*          to their proper values       */

          CURR_N=N;
          CURR_FROM=FROM;
          CURR_TO=TO;
          CURR_AUX=AUX;
          CURR_RETADDR=1;

START:  /*   this is the beginning of the simulated   */
        /*                 routine                    */
              IF CURR_N=1       THEN DO;
                    PUT SKIP EDIT('MOVE DISK 1 FROM PEG',
                       FROM,'TO PEG',TO) (A,X(1));
                    I=CURR_RETADDR;
                    CALL POPSUB(STACK,CURR_AREA);
                    GO TO L(I);
                                        END;

        /*   this is the first recursive call   */
              CALL PUSH(STACK,CURR_AREA);
              CURR_N=CURR_N-1;
```

```
                TEMP=CURR_AUX;
                CURR_AUX=CURR_TO;
                CURR_TO=TEMP;
                CURR_RETADDR=2;
                GO TO START;

L(2):                 /*   we return to this point from    */
                      /*      the first recursive call     */
                PUT SKIP EDIT('MOVE DISK',CURR_N,'FROM PEG',
                      CURR_FROM,'TO PEG',CURR_TO)
                      (A,F(2),(4)(X(1),A));

             /*     this is the second recursive call      */
                CALL PUSH(STACK,CURR_AREA);
                CURR_N=CURR_N-1;
                TEMP=CURR_FROM;
                CURR_FROM=CURR_AUX;
                CURR_AUX=TEMP;
                CURR_RETADDR=3;
                GO TO START;

L(3):               /*   return to this point from    */
                    /*   the second recursive call    */
                I=CURR_RETADDR;
                CALL POPSUB(STACK,CURR_AREA);
                GO TO L(I);

L(1):           RETURN;          /*    return to calling program    */
             END SIMTOWERS;
```

Let us attempt to simplify the above program. First, notice that three labels were used for return addresses: two for each of the recursive calls and one for the return to the main program. However, the return to the main program can be signaled by an underflow in the stack, exactly as in the second version of SIMFACT. This leaves two return labels. If we could eliminate one more such label, it would no longer be necessary to stack the return address, since there would be only one point remaining to which control may be passed if the stack is popped successfully. We focus our attention on the second recursive call and the following statements:

```
CALL TOWERS(N-1,AUX,TO,FROM);
RETURN;
```

The actions that occur in simulating this call are:

1. Push the current data area *a1* onto the stack.

2. Set the parameters in the new current data area *a2* to their respective values, N–1, AUX, TO, and FROM.

3. Set the return label in the current data area *a2* to the address of the RETURN statement immediately following the call.

4. Branch to the beginning of the simulated routine.

After the simulated routine has completed, it is ready to return. The following actions occur:

5. Save the return label *l* from the current data area *a2*.

6. Pop the stack and set the current data area to the popped data area *a1*.

7. Branch to *l*.

But *l* is the label of the RETURN statement. Thus, the next step is to pop the stack again and return once more. We never again make use of the information in the current data area *a1*, since it is immediately destroyed by popping the stack as soon as it has been restored. Since there is no reason to use this data area again, there is no reason to save it on the stack in simulating the call. Data need be saved on the stack only if it is to be reused. Therefore, in this case, the call may be simulated simply by:

1. Changing the parameters in the current data area to their respective values.

2. Branching to the beginning of the simulated routine

When the simulated routine returns, it can return directly to the routine which called the current version. There is no reason to execute a return to the current version, only to return immediately to the previous version. Since there is only one possible return address left, it is unnecessary to keep it in the data area, to be pushed and popped with the rest of the data. Whenever the stack is popped successfully, there is only one address to which a branch can be executed: the statement following the first call. If an underflow is encountered, the routine returns to the calling routine.

Our revised nonrecursive simulation of TOWERS follows:

```
SIMTOWERS:  PROC(N,FROM,TO,AUX);
                  DCL N                         FIXED,
                        (FROM,TO,AUX)           CHAR(*);
                  DCL 1  STACK,
                           2  TOP               FIXED INIT(0),
                           2  DATA_AREA(50),
                              3  NPARAM         FIXED,
                             (3  FROMPARAM,
                              3  TOPARAM,
                              3  AUXPARAM)      CHAR(1);
```

```
              DCL 1  CURR_AREA,
                       2  CURR_N              FIXED,
                      (2  CURR_FROM,
                       2  CURR_TO,
                       2  CURR_AUX)           CHAR(1);
              DCL  UND                        BIT(1),
                   TEMP                       CHAR(1);

              /*   initialization    */
              CURR_N=N;
              CURR_FROM=FROM;
              CURR_TO=TO;
              CURR_AUX=AUX;

START:        /*   the simulated routine begins here    */
              IF CURR_N=1   THEN   DO;
                   PUT SKIP EDIT('MOVE DISK 1 FROM PEG',
                      CURR_FROM,'TO PEG',CURR_TO) (A,X(1));
              /*              simulate return              */
                   CALL POPANDTEST(STACK,CURR_AREA,
                                                        UND);
                   IF UND THEN    /*   return to main routine   */
                                  RETURN;
              /*    otherwise, go to point after the recursive    */
              /*                        call                      */
                   GO TO RETADDR;
                                   END;

              /*        simulation of first recursive call        */
              CALL PUSH(STACK,CURR_AREA);
              CURR_N=CURR_N-1;
              TEMP=CURR_TO;
              CURR_TO=CURR_AUX;
              CURR_AUX=TEMP;
              GO TO START;

RETADDR:         /*   this is the point of return from   */
                 /*            the recursive call        */
              PUT SKIP EDIT ('MOVE DISK',CURR_N,
                 'FROM PEG', CURR_FROM,'TO PEG',
                                                     CURR_TO)
                 (A,F(2),(4) (X(1),A));
```

```
            /*      simulation of second recursive call      */
            CURR_N=CURR_N-1;
            TEMP=CURR_FROM;
            CURR_FROM=CURR_AUX;
            CURR_AUX=TEMP;
            GO TO START;
        END SIMTOWERS;
```

Examining the structure of the program, we see that it can easily be reorganized into a simpler format. We begin from the label START.

```
START:   DO WHILE('1'B);
LOOP1:      DO WHILE(CURR_N¬=1);
                 CALL PUSH(STACK,CURR_AREA);
                 CURR_N=CURR_N-1;
                 TEMP=CURR_TO;
                 CURR_TO=CURR_AUX;
                 CURR_AUX=TEMP;
            END LOOP1;
            PUT SKIP EDIT('MOVE DISK 1 FROM PEG',CURR_FROM,
                                  'TO PEG',CURR_TO) (A,X(1));
            CALL POPANDTEST(STACK,CURR_AREA,UND);
            IF UND THEN RETURN;
            PUT SKIP EDIT ('MOVE DISK',CURR_N,'FROM PEG',
                                  CURR_FROM,'TO PEG',CURR_TO)
                       (A,F(2),(4) (X(1),A));
            CURR_N=CURR_N-1;
            TEMP=CURR_FROM;
            CURR_FROM=CURR_AUX;
            CURR_AUX=TEMP;
         END START;
```

Trace through the actions of this program and see how it reflects the actions of the original recursive version.

4.5. Efficiency of Recursion

In general, a nonrecursive version of a program will execute more efficiently in terms of time and space than a recursive version. This is because the overhead involved in entering and exiting a block is avoided in the nonrecursive version. As we have seen, it is often possible to identify a good number of local variables and temporaries which do not have to be saved and restored through the use of a stack. In a nonrecursive program this needless stacking activity can be eliminated. However, in a recursive procedure the compiler is usually unable to identify such variables, and they are therefore stacked and unstacked to ensure that no problems arise.

However, we have also seen that sometimes a recursive solution is the most natural and logical way of solving a problem. It is doubtful whether a programmer could have developed the nonrecursive solution to the Towers of Hanoi problem directly from the problem statement. A similar comment may be made about the problem of converting prefix to postfix, where the recursive solution flows directly from the definitions. A nonrecursive solution involving stacks is much more difficult to develop and more prone to error.

Thus we have a conflict between machine efficiency and programmer efficiency. With the cost of programming increasing steadily, and the cost of computation decreasing, we have reached the point where in most cases it is not worth a programmer's time to laboriously construct a nonrecursive solution to a problem which is most naturally solved recursively. Of course an incompetent, overly clever programmer may come up with a complicated recursive solution to a simple problem which can be solved directly by nonrecursive methods. (An example of this is the factorial function or even the binary search.) However, if a competent programmer identifies a recursive solution as being the simplest and most straightforward method for solving a particular problem, it is probably not worth the time and effort to discover a more efficient method.

However, this is not always the case. If a program is to be run very frequently (often, entire computers are dedicated to continually running the same program) so that increased efficiency in execution speed significantly increases throughput, then the extra investment in programming time is worthwhile. Even in such cases, it is probably better to create a nonrecursive version by simulating and transforming the recursive solution than by attempting to create a nonrecursive solution from the problem statement.

To do this most efficiently, what is required is to first write the recursive routine and then its simulated version, including all stacks and temporaries. After this has been done, eliminate all stacks and variables that are superfluous. The final version is a refinement of the original program, and is certainly more efficient. Clearly, the elimination of each superfluous and redundant operation will improve the efficiency of the resulting program. However, every transformation applied to a program is another opening through which an unanticipated error may creep in.

The ideas and transformations that we have put forward in presenting the factorial function and in the Towers of Hanoi problem can be applied to more complex problems whose nonrecursive solution is not readily apparent. The extent to which a recursive solution (actual or simulated) can be transformed into a direct solution will depend in large measure on the particular problem and the ingenuity of the programmer.

Bibliography and References

Recursion is discussed in (Barron, 1968) and most of the texts in the Bibliography which deal with algorithms or data structures. Recursion in PL/I is discussed in many PL/I manuals and texts such as (Conway and Gries, 1975). The stack implementation of recursion is presented in (Gries, 1971), (Maurer, 1977), and (Tremblay and Sorenson, 1975) among others. The removal of recursion is discussed in (Auslander and Strong, 1978), (Bird, 1977), and (Knuth, 1974).

The method of backtracking mentioned in the Supplementary Exercise Manual in the Exercises of Section 4.3 is discussed in (Bitner and Reingold, 1975), (Golomb and Baumert, 1965), (Goodman and Hedetniemi, 1977), and (Reingold, Nievergelt, and Deo, 1977).

Methods of passing parameters are discussed in (Gries, 1971) and (Pratt, 1975). Exercises 4.4.13 through 4.4.17 in the Exercise Manual are adapted from (Bird, 1977).

chapter 5

queues and lists

This chapter introduces the queue, an important data structure which is often used to simulate real-world situations. The concepts of the stack and queue are then extended to a new structure, the list. Various forms of lists and their associated operations are examined, and several applications are presented.

5.1. The Queue and Its Sequential Representation

A ***queue*** is an ordered set of items from which items may be deleted at one end (called the ***front*** of the queue) and into which items may be inserted at the other end (called the ***rear*** of the queue).

Figure 5.1.1(a) illustrates a queue containing three elements *A, B,* and *C*. *A* is at the front of the queue, and *C* is at the rear. In Fig. 5.1.1(b), an element is deleted from the queue. Since elements may be deleted only from the front of the queue, *A* is removed and *B* is now at the front. In Fig. 5.1.1(c), when items *D* and *E* are inserted, they must be inserted at the rear of the queue.

Since *D* has been inserted into the queue before *E*, it will be removed earlier. The first element inserted into a queue is the first element to be removed. For this reason a queue is sometimes called a ***fifo*** (first-in, first-out) list, as opposed to a stack which is a ***lifo*** (last-in, first-out) list. Examples of a queue abound in the real world. A line at a bank or at a bus stop, and a batch of jobs waiting to be read by a card reader are all familiar examples of queues.

There are three primitive operations which can be applied to a queue. The operation *insert*(*queue*,*x*) inserts item *x* at the rear of the queue *queue*. The operation *x*=*remove* (*queue*) deletes the front element from the queue *queue* and sets *x* to its contents. The third operation, *empty*(*queue*) returns *false* or *true* depending on whether or not the queue contains any elements. The queue in Fig. 5.1.1 can be obtained by the following sequence of operations. We assume that the queue is initially empty.

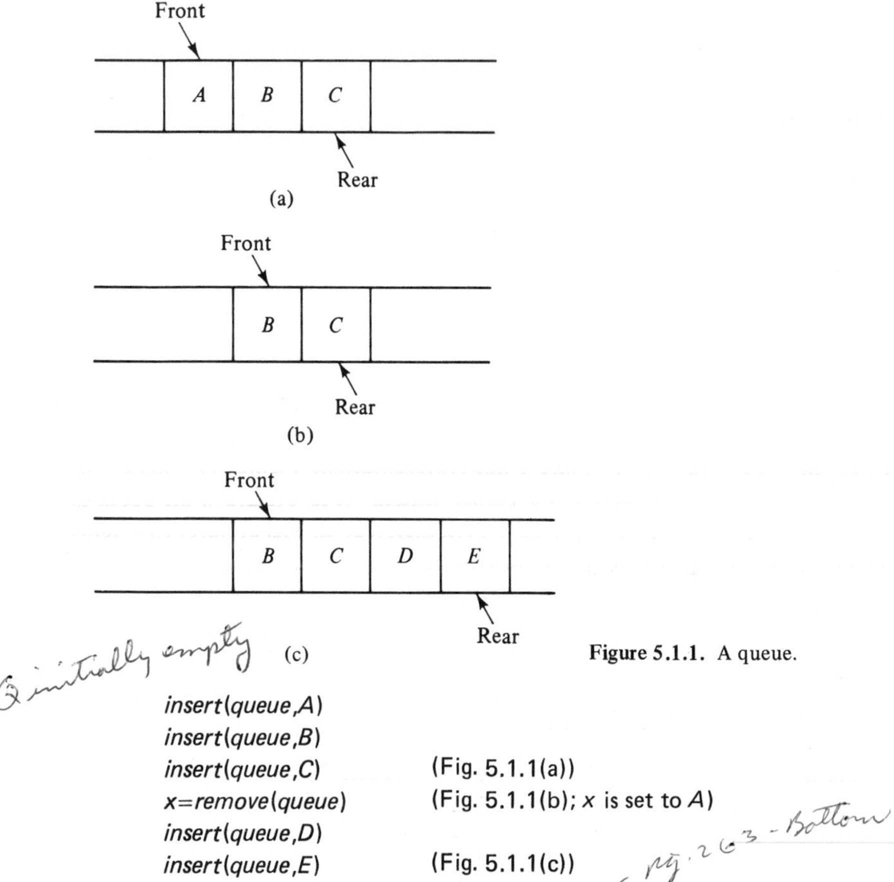

Figure 5.1.1. A queue.

```
insert(queue,A)
insert(queue,B)
insert(queue,C)          (Fig. 5.1.1(a))
x=remove(queue)          (Fig. 5.1.1(b); x is set to A)
insert(queue,D)
insert(queue,E)          (Fig. 5.1.1(c))
```

The *insert* operation can always be performed since there is no limit to the number of elements a queue may contain. The *remove* operation, however, can be applied only if the queue is nonempty—there is no way to remove an element from a queue which contains no elements. The result of an illegal attempt to remove an element from an empty queue is called ***underflow***. The *empty* operation is, of course, always applicable.

How shall a queue be represented in PL/I? An idea which comes immediately to mind is to use an array to hold the elements of the queue and to use two variables, FRONT and REAR, to hold the positions within the array of the first and last elements of the queue. Thus a queue of intergers might be declared by

```
DCL 1 QUEUE,
        2 ITEMS (100)    FIXED,
        2 FRONT          FIXED,
        2 REAR           FIXED;
```

Of course, using an array to hold a queue introduces the possibility of overflow if the queue contains more elements than were allocated for the array. Ignoring the possibility of underflow and overflow for the moment, the operation *insert(queue, x)* could be implemented by the PL/I statements

```
REAR = REAR + 1;
ITEMS(REAR) = X;
```

and the operation *x* = *remove(queue)* could be implemented by

```
X=ITEMS(FRONT);
FRONT=FRONT+1;
```

Initially, REAR is set to 0 and FRONT is set to 1, and the queue is empty whenever REAR<FRONT. The number of elements in the queue at any time is equal to the value of REAR–FRONT+1.

Let us examine what might happen under this representation. Figure 5.1.2 illustrates an array of five elements used to represent a queue. Initially (Fig. 5.1.2(a)), the queue is empty. In Fig. 5.1.2(b) items *A, B,* and *C* have been inserted. In Fig. 5.1.2(c) two items have been deleted, and in Fig. 5.1.2(d) two new items *D* and *E* have been inserted. The value of FRONT is 3 and the value of REAR is 5, so that there are only 5–3+1=3 elements in the queue. Since the array contains five elements, there should be room for the queue to expand without the worry of overflow. However, to insert *F* into the queue, REAR must be increased by 1 to 6 and ITEMS(6) must be set to the value of *F*. But ITEMS is an array of only five elements, so that the insertion cannot be made.

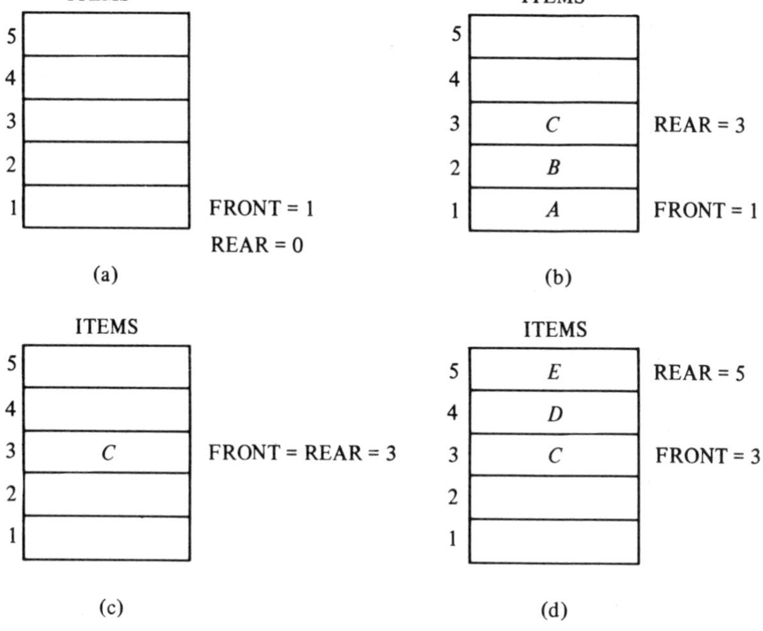

Figure 5.1.2.

It is possible to reach the absurd situation where the queue is empty yet no new element can be inserted (see if you can come up with a sequence of insertions and deletions to reach that situation). Clearly, the array representation as outlined above is unacceptable.

One solution is to modify the *remove* operation so that when an item is deleted, the entire queue is shifted to the beginning of the array. The operation x = *remove*(*queue*) would then be implemented (again, ignoring the possiblity of underflow) by:

```
X=ITEMS(1);
DO I=1 TO REAR−1;
     ITEMS(I)=ITEMS(I+1);
END;
REAR=REAR−1;
```

The variable FRONT need no longer be specified as part of the queue, since the first element of the array is always at the front of the queue. The empty queue is represented by the queue in which REAR equals 0. Figure 5.1.3 shows the queue of Fig. 5.1.2 under this new representation.

This method, however, is too inefficient to be satisfactory. Each deletion involves moving every remaining element of the queue. If a queue contains 500 or 1000 elements, this is clearly too high a price to pay. Further, the operation of removing an element from a queue logically involves manipulation of only one element—the one currently at the front of the queue. The implementation of that operation should reflect this and should not involve a host of extraneous operations. (For a somewhat more efficient alternative, see Exercise 4 in the Exercise Manual.)

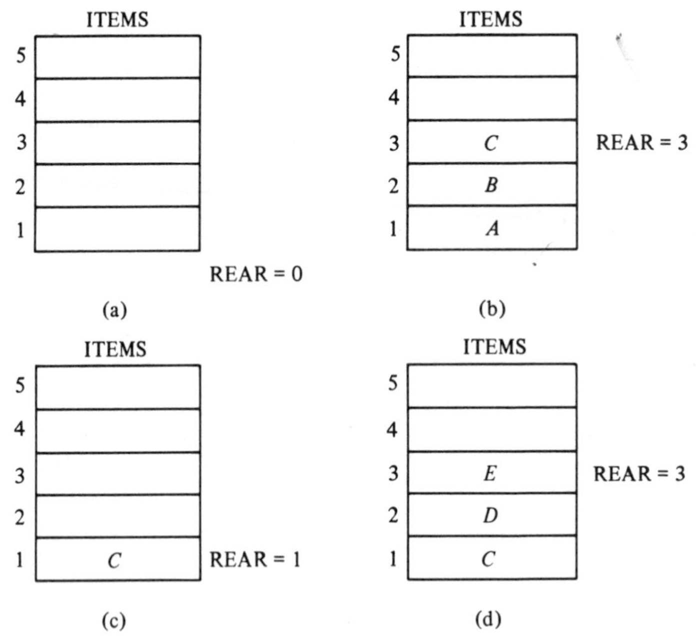

Figure 5.1.3.

Another solution is to treat the array which holds the queue as a circle rather than as a straight line. That is, we imagine the first element of the array as immediately following its last element. This implies that even if the last element is occupied, a new value can be inserted behind it in the first element of the array as long as that first element is empty.

Let us look at an example. Assume that a queue contains three items in positions 3, 4, and 5 of a five-element array. This is the situation of Fig. 5.1.2(d) reproduced as Fig. 5.1.4(a). Although the array is not full, the last element of the array is occupied. If an attempt is now made to insert item *F* into the queue, it can be placed in position 1 of the array, as shown in Fig. 5.1.4(b). The first item of the queue is in ITEMS(3), which is followed in the queue by ITEMS(4), ITEMS(5), and ITEMS(1). Figures 5.1.4(c), (d), and (e) show the status of the queue as first two items *C* and *D* are deleted, then *G* is inserted, and finally *E* is deleted.

Unfortunately, it is difficult under this representation to determine when the queue

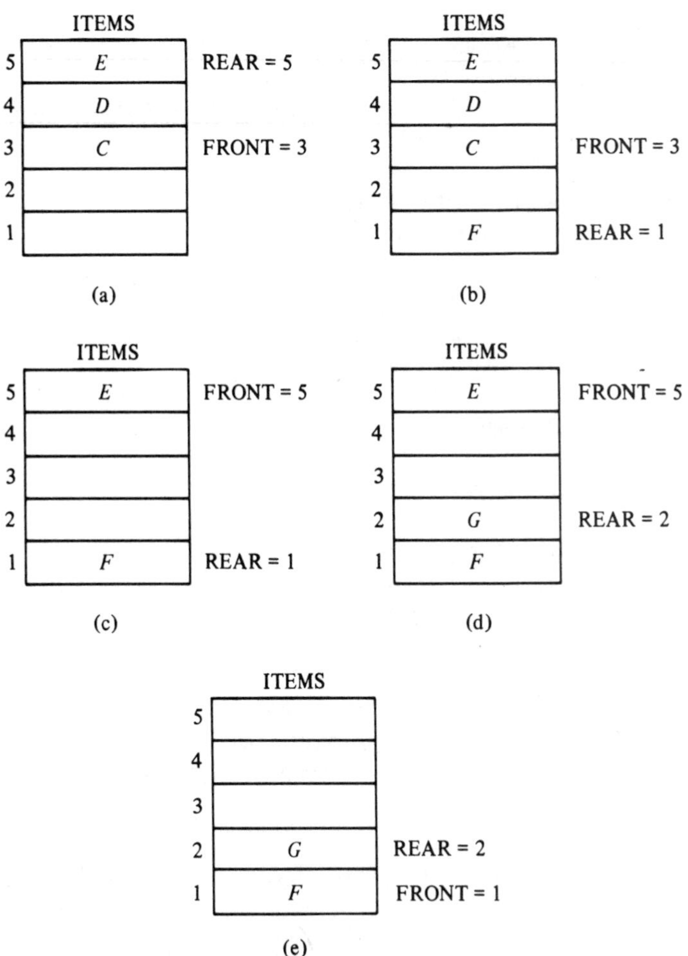

Figure 5.1.4.

is empty. The condition REAR<FRONT is no longer valid as a test for the empty queue since Figs. 5.1.4(b), (c), and (d) all illustrate situations in which the condition is true yet the queue is not empty.

One way of solving this problem is to establish the convention that the value of FRONT is the index of the array element immediately preceding the first element of the queue rather than the index of the first element itself. Thus since REAR contains the index of the last element of the queue, the condition FRONT=REAR implies that the queue is empty.

A queue of integers may therefore be declared by

```
DCL 1 QUEUE,
      2 ITEMS (100)      FIXED,
      2 FRONT            FIXED INIT(100),
      2 REAR             FIXED INIT(100);
```

Note that FRONT and REAR are initialized to the last index of the array, rather than 0 or 1, because the last element of the array immediately precedes the first one within the queue under this representation. Since REAR=FRONT, the queue is initially empty.

The *empty* function may be coded as:

```
EMPTY:   PROC(QUEUE)  RETURNS(BIT(1));
            DCL 1  QUEUE,
                  (2  ITEMS(*),
                   2  FRONT,
                   2  REAR)         FIXED;
            IF FRONT=REAR  THEN RETURN ('1'B);
                                ELSE RETURN ('0'B);
         END EMPTY;
```

The operation *remove*(*queue*) may be coded as:

```
REMOVE: PROC(QUEUE)  RETURNS(FIXED);
            DCL 1  QUEUE,
                  (2  ITEMS(*),
                   2  FRONT,
                   2  REAR)         FIXED,
                X                   FIXED;
            IF EMPTY(QUEUE) THEN DO;
                                PUT SKIP LIST('QUEUE UNDERFLOW');
                                STOP;
                                     END;
            IF FRONT=HBOUND(ITEMS,1)   THEN FRONT=1;
                                       ELSE FRONT=FRONT+1;
            X=ITEMS(FRONT);
            RETURN(X);
         END REMOVE;
```

Note that FRONT must be updated before an element is extracted.

Of course, often an underflow condition is meaningful and serves as a signal for a new phase of processing. We may wish to use a subroutine REMVANDTEST which would be called by the statement

```
CALL REMVANDTEST(QUEUE, X, UND);
```

This routine sets UND to '0'B and X to the element removed from the queue if the queue is nonempty, and sets UND to '1'B if underflow occurs. The coding of such a routine is left to the reader.

The insert *Operation*

The *insert* operation involves the detection of overflow. Overflow occurs when the entire array is occupied by items of the queue and an attempt is made to insert yet another element into the queue. For example, consider the queue of Fig. 5.1.5(a). There are three elements in the queue: *C, D,* and *E* in ITEMS(3), ITEMS(4), and ITEMS(5) respectively. Since the last item of the queue occupies ITEMS(5), REAR equals 5. Since the first element of the queue is in ITEMS(3), FRONT equals 2. In Figs. 5.1.5(b) and (c), items *F* and *G* are inserted into the queue and the value of REAR is changed accordingly. At that point, the array is full and an attempt to perform any more insertions will cause an overflow. But this is indicated by the fact that FRONT=REAR, which is precisely the indication for underflow. It seems that there is no way to distinguish between the empty queue and the full queue under this implementation. Such a situation is clearly unsatisfactory.

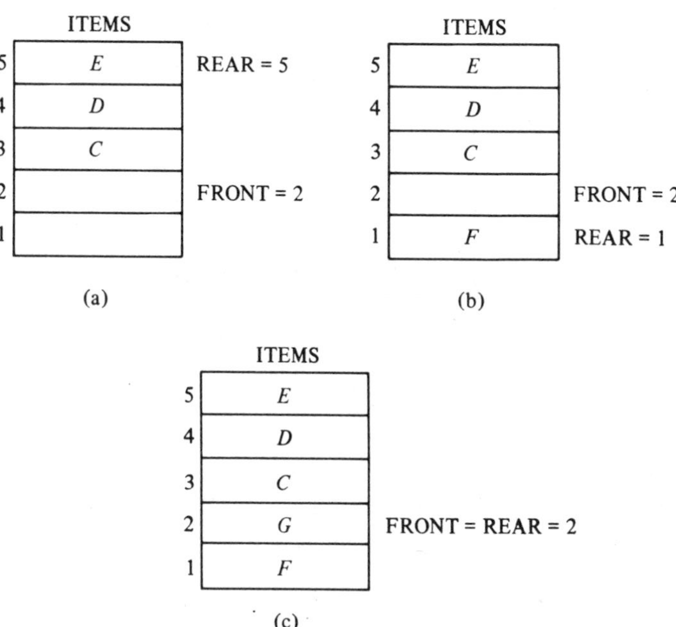

Figure 5.1.5

Convention

One solution is to sacrifice one element of the array and to allow a queue to grow only as large as 1 less than the size of the array. Thus, if an array of 100 elements is declared as a queue, the queue may have up to 99 members. An attempt to insert a hundredth element into the queue will cause an overflow. The INSERT routine may then be written as follows:

```
INSERT:  PROC(QUEUE,X);
           DCL 1 QUEUE,
                  (2 ITEMS(*),
                   2 FRONT,
                   2 REAR)       FIXED,
                 X               FIXED;
           /*   make room for new element    */
           IF REAR=HBOUND(ITEMS,1) THEN REAR=1;
                                   ELSE REAR=REAR+1;
           /*        check for overflow        */
           IF REAR=FRONT THEN DO;
                             PUT SKIP LIST('QUEUE OVERFLOW');
                             STOP;
                          END;
           /*        insert the element        */
           ITEMS(REAR)=X;
           RETURN;
        END INSERT;
```

The test for overflow in INSERT occurs after REAR has been adjusted, while the test for underflow in REMOVE occurs immediately upon entering the routine, before FRONT is updated.

5.2. Linked Lists

What are the drawbacks of using sequential storage to represent stacks and queues? One major drawback is that a fixed amount of storage remains allocated to the stack or queue even when the structure is actually using a smaller amount or possibly no storage at all. Further, no more than that fixed amount of storage may be allocated, thus introducing the possibility of overflow.

Assume that a program uses two stacks implemented in two separate arrays ITEMS1 and ITEMS2. Further, assume that each of these arrays has 100 elements. Then despite the fact that 200 elements are available for the two stacks, neither can grow beyond 100 items. Even if the first stack contains only 25 items, the second cannot contain more than 100. One solution to this problem is to allocate a single array ITEMS of 200 elements. The first stack will occupy ITEMS(1), ITEMS(2), . . . , ITEMS(TOP1), while the second stack will be allocated from the other end of the array, occupying ITEMS(200),

ITEMS(199), . . . , ITEMS(TOP2). Thus, when one of the stacks is not occupying storage, the other stack may make use of that storage. Of course, two distinct sets of POP, PUSH, and EMPTY routines are necessary for the two stacks since one grows by increasing TOP1 while the other grows by decreasing TOP2.

Unfortunately, while such a scheme allows two stacks to share a common area, no such simple solution exists for three or more stacks or even for two queues. Instead, one must keep track of the tops and bottoms (or fronts and rears) of all structures sharing a single large array. Each time that the growth of one structure is about to impinge on the storage currently being used by another, all the structures must be shifted within the single array to allow for the growth. (See Exercises 3.2.18 through 3.2.20 in the Exercise Manual.)

In a sequential representation, the items of a stack or queue are implicitly ordered by the sequential order of storage. Thus, if ITEMS(X) represents an element of a queue, the next element will be ITEMS(X+1) (or if X=N, ITEMS(1)). Suppose that the items of a stack or a queue were explicitly ordered, that is, each item contained within itself the address of the next item. Such an explicit ordering gives rise to a data structure pictured in Fig. 5.2.1, which is known as a ***linear linked list***. Each item in the list is called a ***node*** and contains two fields, an ***information*** field and a ***next address*** field. The information field holds the actual element on the list. The next address field contains the address of the next node in the list. Such an address, which is used to access a particular node, is known as a ***pointer***. The entire linked list is accessed from an external pointer *list* which points to (contains the address of) the first node in the list. (By an "external" pointer, we mean one that is not included within a node. Rather its value can be accessed directly by referencing a variable.) The next address field of the last node in the list contains a special value, known as ***null***, which is not a valid address. This ***null pointer*** is used to signal the end of a list.

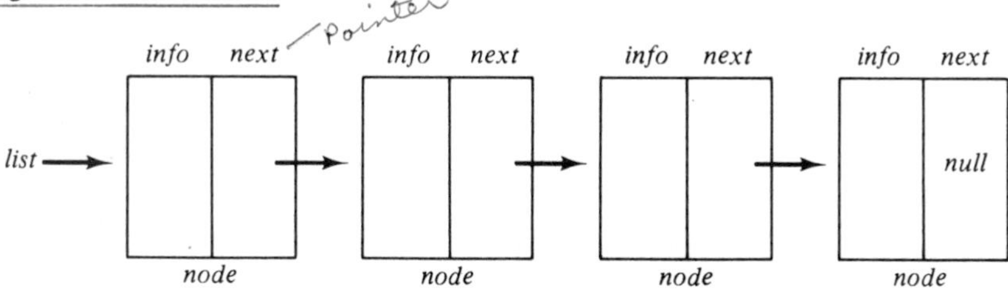

Figure 5.2.1. A linear linked list.

The list with no nodes on it is called the ***empty list*** or the ***null list***. The value of the external pointer *list* to such a list is the null pointer. Thus a list can be initialized to the empty list by the operation *list=null.*

Notation

We now introduce some notation. If p is a pointer to a node, *node*(p) refers to the node pointed to by p, *info*(p) refers to the information portion of that node, and *next*(p) refers to the next address portion and is therefore a pointer. Thus, if *next*(p) is not *null*, *info*(*next*(p)) refers to the information portion of the node which follows *node*(p) in the list.

Adding and Removing Nodes from a List

A list is a dynamic data structure. The number of nodes on a list may vary dramatically as elements are inserted and removed. For example, suppose we are given a list of integegers, as illustrated in Fig. 5.2.2(a) and we desire to add the integer 6 to the front of that list. That is, we wish to change the list so that it appears as in Fig. 5.2.2(f).

Example

The first step is to obtain a node in which to house the additional integer. If a list is to grow and shrink, there must be some mechanism for obtaining empty nodes to be added onto the list. Note that, unlike an array, a list does not come with a presupplied set of storage locations into which elements can be placed.

Let us assume the existence of a mechanism for obtaining empty nodes. The operation

```
p=getnode
```

obtains an empty node and sets the contents of a variable named *p* to the address of that node. This means that *p* is a pointer to this newly allocated node. Figure 5.2.2(b) illustrates the list and the new node after performing the *getnode* operation. The details of how this operation works will be explained shortly. The results of the *getnode* operation are similar to the results of the ALLOCATE statement for PL/I CONTROLLED storage, where a new storage location is obtained by calling upon the system to make such a location available for use. (However, see Exercise 42 of the Exercise Manual for an important distinction.)

The next step is to insert the integer 6 into the *info* portion of the newly allocated node. This is done by the operation

```
info(p)=6
```

The result of this operation is illustrated in Fig. 5.2.2(c).

After setting the *info* portion of *node*(*p*), it is necessary to set the *next* portion of that node. Since *node*(*p*) is to be inserted at the front of the list, the node which follows should be the current first node on the list. Since the variable *list* contains the address of that first node, *node*(*p*) can be added to the list by performing the operation

```
next(p)=list
```

This operation places the value of *list* (which is the address of the first node on the list) into the *next* field of *node*(*p*). Figure 5.2.2(d) illustrates the result of this operation.

At this point, *p* points to the list with the additional item included. However, since *list* is the external pointer to the desired list, its value must be modified to the address of the new first node of the list. This can be done by performing the operation

```
list=p
```

which changes the value of *list* to the value of *p*. Figure 5.2.2(e) illustrates the result of this operation. Note that Figs. 5.2.2(e) and (f) are identical except that the value of *p* is not shown in Fig. 5.2.2(f). This is because *p* is used as an auxiliary variable during the process of modifying the list, but its value is irrelevant to the status of the list before and after the process. Once the above operations have been performed, the value of *p* may be changed without affecting the list.

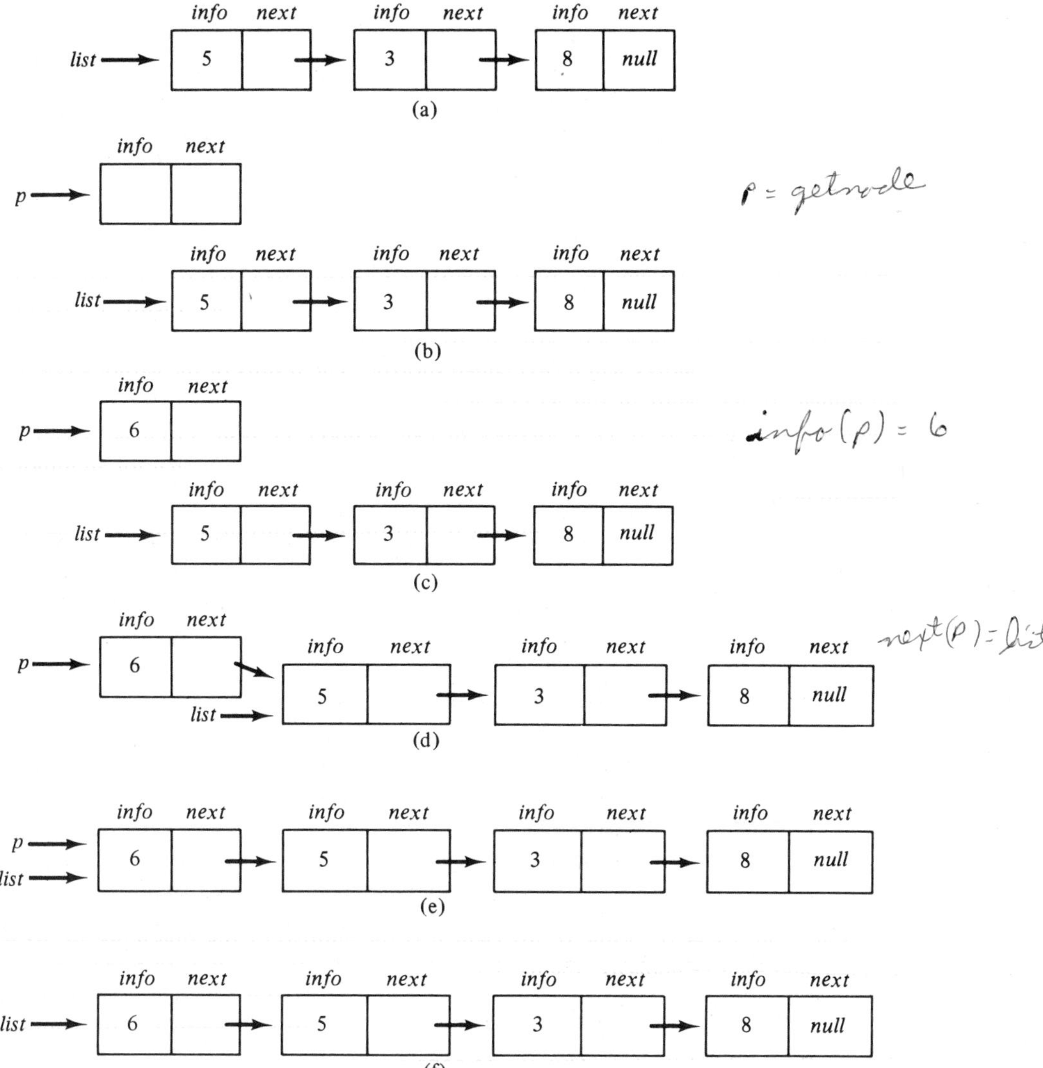

Figure 5.2.2. Adding an element to the front of a list.

Putting all the steps together, we have an algorithm for adding the integer 6 to the front of the list *list*:

```
p=getnode;
info(p)=6;
next(p)=list;
list=p;
```

The algorithm can obviously be generalized so that it adds any object x to the front of a list *list* by replacing the operation *info*(*p*)=6 with *info*(*p*)=*x*. Convince yourself that the algorithm works correctly, even if the list is initially empty (*list*=*null*).

Figure 5.2.3 illustrates the process of removing the first node of a nonempty list and storing the value of its *info* field into a variable x. The initial configuration is shown in Fig. 5.2.3(a), and the final configuration is shown in Fig. 5.2.3(f). The process itself is almost the exact opposite of the process of adding a node to the front of a list. To obtain Fig. 5.2.3(d) from Fig. 5.2.3(a), the following operations (whose actions should be clear) are performed:

```
p=list;             (Fig. 5.2.3(b))
list=next(p);       (Fig. 5.2.3(c))
x=info(p);          (Fig. 5.2.3(d))
```

At this point, the algorithm has accomplished what it was supposed to do: the first node has been removed from *list*, and x has been set to the desired value. However, the algorithm is not yet complete. In Fig. 5.2.3(d), p still points to the node which was formerly first on the list. However, that node is currently useless because it is no longer on the list and its information has been stored in x. (The node is not considered to be on the list despite the fact that *next*(*p*) points to a node on the list, since there is no way to reach *node*(*p*) from the external pointer *list*.) The variable p was used as an auxiliary variable during the process of removing the first node from the list. The starting and ending configurations of the list make no reference to p. It is therefore reasonable to expect that p will be used for some other purpose in a short while after this operation has been performed. But once the value of p is changed, there is no way to access the node at all, since neither an external pointer nor a *next* field contains its address. Therefore, the node is currently useless and cannot be reused, yet it is taking up valuable storage.

It would be desirable to have some mechanism for making *node*(*p*) available for reuse even if the value of the pointer p is changed. The operation which does this is

```
freenode(p)        (Fig. 5.2.3(e))
```

Once this operation has been performed, it becomes illegal to reference *node*(*p*) since the node is no longer allocated. Since the value of p is a pointer to a node which has been freed, any reference to that value is also illegal.

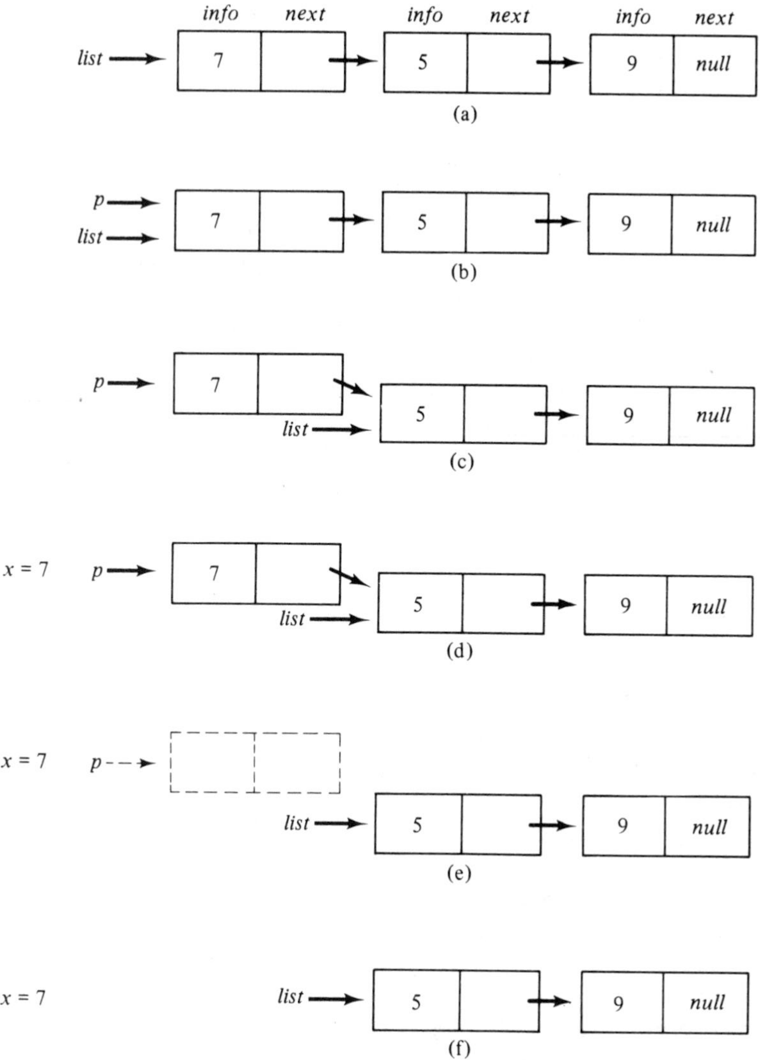

Figure 5.2.3. Removing a node from the front of a list.

However, the node might be reallocated and a pointer to it reassigned to *p* by the operation *p=getnode*. Note that we say that the node "might be" reallocated, since the *getnode* operation returns a pointer to some newly allocated node. There is no guarantee that this new node is the same as the one which has just been freed.

Another way of thinking of *getnode* and *freenode* is that *getnode* creates a new node, while *freenode* destroys a node. Under this view, nodes are not used and reused but are rather created and destroyed. We shall say more about the two operations *getnode* and *freenode* and about the concepts they represent in a moment, but first we make the following interesting observation.

Linked Implementation of Stacks

The operation of adding an element to the front of a linked list is quite similar to that of pushing an element onto a stack. In both cases, a new item is added as the only immediately accessible item in a set. A stack can be accessed only through its top element, and a list can be accessed only from the pointer to its first element. Similarly, the operation of removing the first element from a linked list is analogous to popping a stack. In both cases, the only immediately accessible item of a set is removed from that set, and the next item becomes immediately accessible.

Thus we have discovered yet another way of implementing a stack. A stack may be represented by a linear linked list. The first node of the list is the top of the stack. If an external pointer *stack* points to such a linked list, the operation *push*(*stack*,*x*) may be implemented by

```
p=getnode;
info(p)=x;
next(p)=stack;
stack=p;
```

The operation *empty*(*stack*) is merely a test as to whether *stack* equals *null*.

The operation *x*=*pop*(*stack*) is the operation of removing the first node from a nonempty list and signaling underflow if the list is empty.

```
if empty(stack) then do;
                  print ('underflow');
                  stop;
                     end;
p=stack;
stack=next(p);
x=info(p):
freenode(p);
```

Figure 5.2.4(a) illustrates a stack implemented as a linked list, and Fig. 5.2.4(b) illustrates the same stack after another element has been pushed onto it.

The getnode *and* freenode *Operations*

We now return to a discussion of the *getnode* and *freenode* operations. In an abstract, idealized world it is possible to postulate an infinite number of unused nodes available for use by abstract algorithms. The *getnode* operation finds one such node and makes it available to the algorithm. Alternatively, the *getnode* operation may be conceived as a machine which manufactures nodes and never breaks down. Thus, each time that *getnode* is invoked, it presents its caller with a brand new node, different from all the nodes previously in use.

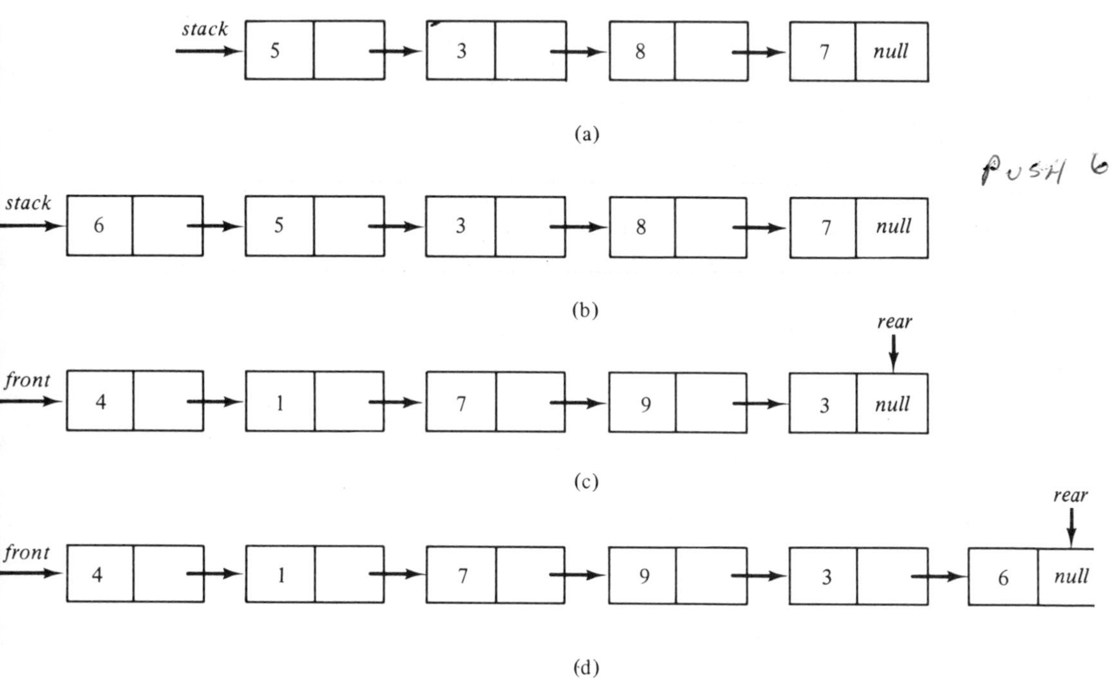

Figure 5.2.4. A stack and a queue as linked lists.

In such an ideal world, the *freenode* operation would be unnecessary to make a node available for reuse. Why use an old second-hand node when a simple call to *getnode* can produce a new, never before used node? The only harm which an unused node can do is to reduce the number of nodes which can possibly be used, but if an infinite supply of nodes is available, then such a reduction is meaningless.

Unfortunately, we live in a real world. Computers do not have an infinite amount of storage and cannot manufacture more storage for immediate utilization (at least, not yet). Therefore, there are a finite number of nodes available, and it is impossible to use more than that number at any given instant. If it is desired to use more than that number over a given period of time, then some nodes must be reused. The function of *freenode* is to make a node which is no longer being used in its current context available for reuse in a different context.

We might think of a finite pool of empty nodes existing initially. This pool cannot be accessed by the programmer except through the *getnode* and *freenode* operations. *getnode* removes a node from the pool, while *freenode* returns a node to the pool. Since any unused node is as good as any other, it makes no difference which node is retrieved by *getnode* or where within the pool a node is placed by *freenode*.

The most natural form for this pool to take is that of a linked list acting as a stack. The list is linked together by the *next* field in each node. The *getnode* operation removes the first node from this list and makes it available for use. The *freenode* operation adds a node to the front of the list, making it available for reallocation by the next *getnode*. The list of available nodes is called the ***available list.***

What happens when the available list is empty? This means that all nodes are currently in use and it is impossible to allocate any more. If a program calls on *getnode* when the available list is empty, then the amount of storage assigned for that program's data structures is too small. Therefore, overflow occurs. This is similar to the situation of a stack implemented in an array overflowing the array bounds.

As long as data structures are abstract, theoretical concepts in a world of infinite space, there is no possibility of overflow. It is only when they are implemented as real objects in a finite area that the possibility of overflow arises.

Let us assume that the external pointer ***avail*** points to the list of available nodes. Then the operation

```
p=getnode
```

is implemented as follows:

```
if avail=null then do;
                        print ('overflow');
                        stop;
                   end;
p=avail;
avail=next(avail);
```

Since the possibility of overflow is accounted for in the *getnode* operation, it need not be mentioned in the list implementation of *push*. If a stack is about to overflow all available nodes, the instruction *p=getnode*; within the *push* operation will result in an overflow.

The implementation of *freenode*(*p*) is straightforward:

```
next(p)=avail;
avail=p;
```

The advantage of the list implementation of stacks is that all the stacks being used by a program can share the same available list. When any stack needs a node, it can obtain it from the single available list. When any stack no longer needs a node, it returns the node to that same available list. As long as the total amount of space needed by all the stacks is less than the amount of space initially available to them all, each stack is able to grow and shrink to any size. No space has been preallocated to any single stack, and no stack is using space which it does not need. Furthermore, other data structures such as queues may also share the same set of nodes.

Linked Implementation of Queues

Let us now examine how to represent a queue as a linked list. Recall that items are deleted from the front of a queue and inserted at the rear. Let the list pointer which points to the first element of a list represent the front of the queue. Another pointer to the last element of the list represents the rear of the queue, as shown in Fig. 5.2.4(c). Figure 5.2.4(d) illustrates the same queue after a new item has been inserted.

If we let *queue* consist of a list and two pointers, *front* and *rear*, then the operations *empty(queue)* and *x=remove(queue)* are completely analogous to *empty(stack)* and *x=pop(stack)* with the pointer *front* replacing *stack*. However, special attention must be paid to the case in which the last element is removed from a queue. In this case, *rear* must also be set to *null* since in an empty queue both *front* and *rear* are *null*. The algorithm for *x=remove(queue)* is therefore as follows:

```
if empty(queue) then do;
                        print ('underflow');
                        stop;
                     end;
p=front;
x=info(p);
front=next(p);
if front = null then rear=null;
freenode(p);
return(x);
```

The operation *insert(queue,x)* can be implemented by:

```
p=getnode;
info(p)=x;
next(p)=null;
if rear=null then front=p;
             else next(rear)=p;
rear=p;
```

What are the disadvantages of representing a stack or queue by a linked list? Clearly, a node in a linked list occupies more storage than a corresponding element in an array since two pieces of information are necessary in a list node for each item (*info* and *next*) while only one piece of information is needed in the array implementation. However the space used for a list node is usually not twice the space used by an array element since the elements in such a list usually consist of entire structures with many subparts. For example if each element on a stack were a structure occupying 10 words, the addition of an eleventh word to contain a pointer increases the space requirement by only 10%. Further, in many machine languages it is possible to compress information and a pointer into a single word so that there is no space degradation.

Another disadvantage is the additional time which must be spent in managing the available list. Each addition and deletion of an element from a stack or a queue involves a corresponding deletion or addition to the available list.

The advantage of using linked lists is that all the stacks and queues of a program have access to the same free list of nodes. Nodes which are unused by one stack may be used by another, as long as the total number of nodes in use is not greater than the total number of nodes available.

The Linked List as a Data Structure

Linked lists are important not only as a means of implementing stacks and queues, but as data structures in their own right. An item is accessed in a linked list by traversing the list from its beginning. An array implementation allows access to the *n*th item in a group using a single operation, while a list implementation requires *n* operations. It is necessary to pass through each of the first $n-1$ elements before reaching the *n*th element because there is no relation between the memory location occupied by an element of a list and its position within that list.

The advantage of a list over an array occurs when it is necessary to insert or delete an element in the middle of a group of other elements. For example, suppose we wish to insert an element *x* between the third and fourth elements in an array of size 10 which currently contains seven items. Items 7 through 4 must first be moved one slot and the new element inserted in the newly available position 4. This process is illustrated by Fig. 5.2.5(a). In this case insertion of one item involves moving four items in addition to the insertion itself. If the array contained 500 or 1000 elements, a correspondingly larger number of elements would have to be moved. Similarly, to delete an element from an array, all the elements past the element deleted must be moved one position.

On the other hand, if the items are stored as a list, inserting a new element involves allocating a node, inserting the information and adjusting two pointers. The amount of work required is independent of the size of the list. This is illustrated in Fig. 5.2.5(b).

Let *insafter(p,x)* denote the operation of inserting an item *x* into a list after a node pointed to by *p*. This operation may be implemented as follows:

```
q=getnode;
info(q)=x;
next(q)=next(p);
next(p)=q;
```

An item can only be inserted after a given node, not before the node. This is because there is no way to proceed from a given node to its predecessor in a linear list without traversing the list from its beginning. To insert an item before *node(p)*, the *next* field of its predecessor must be changed to point to a newly allocated node. But, given *p*, there is no way to find that predecessor.

Similarly, to delete a node from a linear list it is insufficient to be given a pointer to that node. This is because the *next* field of the node's predecessor must be changed to point to the node's successor and there is no direct way of reaching the predecessor of a given node. The best that can be done is to delete a node following a given node. Let *delafter* (*p*,*x*) denote the operation of deleting the node following *node*(*p*) and assigning its contents to the variable *x*. This operation may be implemented as follows:

```
q=next(p);
x=info(q);
next(p)=next(q);
freenode(q);
```

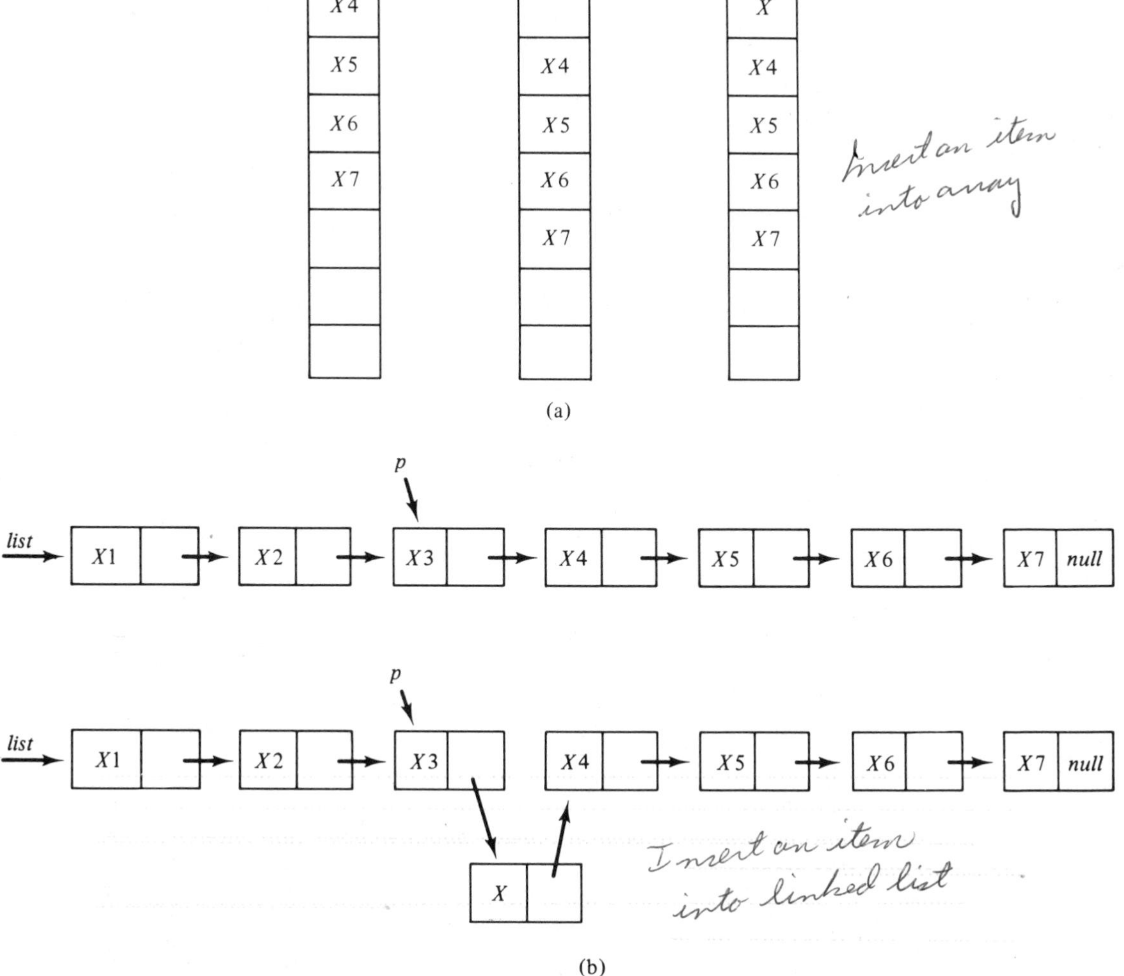

Figure 5.2.5.

The freed node is placed back onto the available list so that it may be reused in the future.

Examples of List Operations

We illustrate these two operations as well as the *push* and *pop* operations for lists with some simple examples. The first example is to delete all occurrences of the number 4 from a list *list*. The list is traversed in a search for nodes which contain 4 in their *info* fields. Each such node must be deleted from the list. But in order to delete a node from a list, its predecessor must be known. For this reason, two pointers, *p* and *q*, are used. *p* is used to traverse the list, and *q* always points to the predecessor of *p*. The algorithm makes use of the *pop* operation to remove nodes from the beginning of the list and the *delafter* operation to remove nodes from the middle of the list.

```
q=null;
p=list;
do while (p¬=null);
   if info(p)=4 then

      if q=null then /*    remove first node of list     */
                    do;
                 x=pop(list);
                 p=list;
                    end;
                 else /*   move up p and delete the      */
                    /*            node after q           */
                    do;
                 p=next(p);
                 delafter(q,x);
                    end;

      else /*   continue traversing the list     */
           do; /*   advance p and q    */
              q=p;
              p=next(p);
           end;
end;
```

The practice of using two pointers, one following the other, is a common one in working with lists. This technique is used in the next example as well. Assume that a list *list* is ordered so that smaller items precede larger ones. It is desired to insert an item *x* into this list in its proper place. The algorithm to do so makes use of the *push* operation to add a node to the front of the list and the *insafter* operation to add a node in the middle of the list.

Ordered List Example

```
q=null;
p=list;
do while (p¬=null  & x >info(p));
         q=p;
         p=next(p);
end;
```

```
/*  at this point a node containing x must be inserted       */
if q=null then   /* insert x at the head of the list         */
              push(list,x);
        else insafter (q,x);
```

This is a very common operation and will be denoted by *place(list,x)*.

Lists in PL/I

How can linear lists be represented in PL/I? Since a list is simply a collection of nodes, an array of nodes immediately suggests itself. However the nodes cannot be ordered by the array ordering; each must contain within itself a pointer to its successor. Thus a group of nodes might be declared as follows:

```
DCL     1 NODE(500),
          2 INFO        FIXED,
          2 NEXT        FIXED;
```

In this scheme, a pointer is an integer between 1 and 500 which references a particular element of the array NODE and the null pointer is represented by the integer 0.

Let the variable LIST represent a pointer to a list. Suppose LIST has the value 7. Then NODE(7) is the first node on the list, so that NODE(7).INFO (or simply INFO(7)) is the first data item on the list. The second node of the list is given by NODE (7).NEXT (or NEXT(7)). Suppose NEXT(7) equals 385. Then INFO(385) is the second data item on the list and NEXT(385) points to the third node. The nodes of a list may be scattered throughout the array NODE in any arbitrary order. Each node carries within itself the address of its successor except for the last node in the list whose NEXT field contains 0, which is the null pointer. There is no relation between the contents of a node and the pointer to it. The pointer P to a node merely specifies which element of the array NODE is being referenced; it is NODE(P).INFO which represents the information contained within that node.

Figure 5.2.6 illustrates a potion of an array NODE which contains four linked lists. The list LIST1 starts at NODE(17) and contains the integers 3, 7, 14, 6, 5, 37, 12. The nodes which contain these integers in their INFO fields are scattered throughout the array. The NEXT field of each node contains the index within the array of the node containing the next element of the list. The last node on the list is NODE(24), which contains the integer 12 in its INFO field and the null pointer (zero) in its NEXT field to indicate that it is last on the list. Similarly, LIST2 begins at NODE(5) and contains the integers 17 and 26, LIST3 begins at NODE(12) and contains the integers 31, 19, and 32, and LIST4 begins at NODE(4) and contains the integers 1, 18, 13, 11, 4, and 15. The variables LIST1, LIST2, LIST3, and LIST4 are integers representing external pointers to the four lists. Thus the fact that the variable LIST2 has the value 5 represents the fact that the list to which it points begins at NODE(5).

Initially, all nodes are unused since no lists have yet been formed. Therefore, they

	INFO	NEXT
1	26	0
2	11	10
3	5	16
LIST4 = 4	1	25
LIST2 = 5	17	1
6	13	2
7		
8	19	19
9	14	13
10	4	22
11		
LIST3 = 12	31	8
13	6	3
14		
15		
16	37	24
LIST1 = 17	3	21
18		
19	32	0
20		
21	7	9
22	15	0
23		
24	12	0
25	18	6
26		
27		

Figure 5.2.6. An array of nodes containing four linked lists.

must all be placed on the available list. If the global variable AVAIL is used to point to the available list, we may initially organize that list as follows:

```
AVAIL=1;
DO I=1 TO 499;
   NEXT(I)=I+1;
END;
NEXT(500)=0;
```

The 500 nodes are initially linked in their natural order, so that NODE(I) points to NODE(I+1). Thus NODE(1) is the first node on the available list, NODE(2) is the second, etc. NODE(500) is the last node on the list since NEXT(500) equals 0. There is no reason other than convenience for initially ordering the nodes in this fashion. We could just as well have set NEXT(1) to 500, NEXT(500) to 2, NEXT(2) to 499, etc., until NEXT(250) is set to 251 and NEXT(251) to 0. The important point is that the ordering is explicit within the nodes themselves and is not implied by some other underlying structure.

For the remaining subroutines in this section, we assume that the variables NODE and AVAIL are global and can, therefore, be used by any routine.

When a node is needed for use in a particular list, it is obtained from the available list. Similarly, when a node is no longer necessary, it is returned to the available list. These two operations are implemented by the PL/I routines GETNODE and FREENODE. GETNODE is a function which removes a node from the available list and returns a pointer to it.

```
GETNODE:    PROC RETURNS(FIXED);
                 DCL P                  FIXED;
                 IF AVAIL=0 THEN DO;
                           PUT SKIP  LIST ('OVERFLOW');
                           STOP;
                                    END;
                 P=AVAIL;
                 AVAIL=NEXT(AVAIL);
                 RETURN(P);
            END GETNODE;
```

If AVAIL equals 0 when this function is called, there are no nodes available. This means that the list structures of a particular program have overflowed the available space.

The subroutine FREENODE accepts a pointer to a node and returns that node to the available list.

```
FREENODE:   PROC(P);
                 DCL P                  FIXED;
                 NEXT(P)=AVAIL;
                 AVAIL=P;
                 RETURN;
            END FREENODE;
```

The primitive operations for lists are straightforward PL/I versions of the corresponding algorithms. The routine INSAFTER accepts a pointer P to a node and an item X as parameters. It first ensures that P is not null and then inserts X into a node following the node pointed to by P.

```
INSAFTER:   PROC(P,X);
                 DCL (P,Q,X)          FIXED;
                 IF  P=0 THEN DO;
                     PUT SKIP LIST ('VOID INSERTION');
                     RETURN;
                                  END;
                 Q=GETNODE;
                 INFO(Q)=X;
                 NEXT(Q)=NEXT(P);
                 NEXT(P)=Q;
                 RETURN;
            END INSAFTER;
```

The routine DELAFTER(P,X) deletes the NODE following NODE(P) and stores its contents in X.

```
DELAFTER:  PROC(P,X);
               DCL (P,Q,X)        FIXED;
               IF P=0 THEN DO;
                  PUT SKIP LIST ('VOID DELETION');
                  RETURN;
                             END;
               IF NEXT(P)=0 THEN DO;
                  PUT SKIP LIST ('VOID DELETION');
                  RETURN;
                                   END;
               Q=NEXT(P);
               X=INFO(Q);
               NEXT(P)=NEXT(Q);
               CALL FREENODE(Q);
               RETURN;
           END DELAFTER;
```

Before calling INSAFTER, we must be sure that P is not null. Before calling DELAFTER, we must be sure that neither P nor NEXT(P) is null.

Queues as Lists in PL/I

We now present algorithms for manipulating a queue represented as a linear list, leaving algorithms for manipulating a stack as exercises for the reader. A queue is represented as a structure:

```
DCL  1 QUEUE,
       2 FRONT          FIXED,
       2 REAR           FIXED;
```

FRONT and REAR are pointers to the first and last nodes of a queue represented as a list. The empty queue will be represented by FRONT and REAR both equaling 0, the null pointer. The function EMPTY need check only one of these pointers, since in a nonempty queue neither FRONT nor REAR will be 0.

```
EMPTY:     PROC(QUEUE) RETURNS(BIT(1));
               DCL  1 QUEUE,
                      (2 FRONT,
                       2 REAR)         FIXED;
               IF FRONT=0 THEN RETURN ('1'B);
                          ELSE RETURN ('0'B);
           END EMPTY;
```

The routine to insert an element into a queue may be written as follows:

```
INSERT:     PROC(QUEUE,X);
                DCL   1 QUEUE,
                         (2 FRONT,
                          2 REAR)          FIXED,
                      (P,X)                FIXED;
                P=GETNODE;
                INFO(P)=X;
                NEXT(P)=0;
                IF REAR=0   THEN FRONT=P;
                            ELSE NEXT(REAR)=P;
                REAR=P;
                RETURN;
            END INSERT;
```

The function REMOVE which deletes the first element from a queue and returns its value may be written as follows:

```
REMOVE:     PROC(QUEUE) RETURNS(FIXED);
                DCL   1 QUEUE,
                         (2 FRONT,
                          2 REAR)          FIXED,
                      (X,P)                FIXED;
                IF EMPTY (QUEUE) THEN DO;
                         PUT SKIP LIST('QUEUE UNDERFLOW');
                         STOP;
                                           END;
                P=FRONT;
                X=INFO(P);
                FRONT=NEXT(P);
                IF FRONT=0 THEN REAR=0;
                CALL FREENODE(P);
                RETURN(X);
            END REMOVE;
```

Example of a List Operation in PL/I

Let us look at a somewhat more complex list operation implemented in PL/I. We have defined the operation *place*(*list*,*x*), where *list* points to a sorted linear list and *x* is an element to be inserted into its proper position within the list. Ordinarily, the algorithm for performing that operation could be translated directly into PL/I. However, that algorithm contains the line

```
do while (p¬=null & x>info(p));
```

A direct translation of this line into PL/I is

```
DO WHILE(P¬=0 & X>INFO(P));
```

But if P is equal to 0 (which is the null pointer under this PL/I implementation of lists), then INFO(P) is undefined and a reference to it will cause an error. Thus we want to avoid the evaluation of INFO(P) in the case that P equals 0. We assume that we have already implemented the stack routine PUSH. The code to implement the *place* operation follows:

```
PLACE:    PROC(LIST,X);
             DCL (P,LIST,Q,X)                FIXED;
             P=LIST;
             Q=0;
SEARCH:      DO WHILE (P¬=0);
                IF X<=INFO(P) THEN GO TO FOUND;
                Q=P;
                P=NEXT(P);
             END SEARCH;

FOUND:       IF Q=0 THEN   /*  insert X at the head of the list  */
                           CALL PUSH(LIST,X);
                      ELSE CALL INSAFTER(Q,X);
             RETURN;
          END PLACE;
```

Some PL/I compilers allow the use of a REPEAT clause in the DO statement. For example, the statement

```
DO I = 3 REPEAT 2*I WHILE(I<100);
```

repeats a loop for the six values of I: 3, 6, 12, 24, 48, and 96. The loop variable is set to an initial value for the first execution of the loop body and is reset to the value of the expression following the word REPEAT in each subsequent repetition of the loop. Such a capability is very useful in traversing a linked list. For example, the SEARCH loop in the above program can be rewritten as:

```
SEARCH:      DO P=LIST REPEAT NEXT(P) WHILE(P¬=0);
                IF X<=INFO(P) THEN GO TO FOUND;
                Q=P;
             END SEARCH;
```

This eliminates two other statements (P=LIST; outside the loop, and P=NEXT(P); within the loop). However, many PL/I compilers do not allow the REPEAT clause, so the examples in this text do not use it.

Noninteger Lists

Of course, a node on a list need not represent an integer. For example, to represent a stack of character strings by a linked list, nodes containing character strings in their INFO fields are needed. Such nodes could be declared by

```
DCL    1    NODE(500),
            2    INFO                    CHAR(256) VAR,
            2    NEXT                    FIXED;
```

A particular application may call for nodes containing more than one item of information. For example, each student in a list of students may have the following information stored about him: his name, college identification number, address, grade point index, major, etc. Nodes for such an application may be declared as follows:

```
DCL    1 STUDENTNODE(500),
          2 INFO,
            3 NAME                 CHAR(256) VAR,
            3 ID                   CHAR(9),
            3 ADDRESS              CHAR(256) VAR,
            3 GPINDX               FIXED(4,3),
            3 MAJOR                CHAR(20) VAR,
                          . . .
          2 NEXT                   FIXED;
```

A separate set of PL/I routines must be written to manipulate lists containing each type of node.

Header Nodes

Sometimes it is desirable to keep an extra node at the front of a list. Such a node does not represent an item in the list and is called a ***header node*** or a ***list header***. The *info* portion of such a header node might be unused, as illustrated in Fig. 5.2.7(a). More often, the *info* portion of such a node could be used to keep global information about the entire list. For example, Fig. 5.2.7(b) illustrates a list in which the *info* portion of the header node contains the number of nodes (not including the header) in the list. In such a data structure more work is needed to add or delete an item from the list since the count in the header node must be adjusted properly. However, the number of items in the list may be obtained directly from the header node so that the entire list need not be traversed.

Another example of the use of header nodes is the following. Suppose a factory assembles machinery out of smaller units. A particular machine (inventory number *A746*) might be made up of a various number of different parts (numbers *B841*, *K321*, *A087*, *J492*, *G593*). This assembly could be represented by a list such as the one illustrated in Fig. 5.2.7(c), where each item on the list represents a subpart and where the header node represents the entire assembly.

The empty list would no longer be represented by the null pointer, but rather by a list with a single header node, as in Fig. 5.2.7(d).

Of course, routines such as EMPTY, PUSH, POP, INSERT, and REMOVE must be rewritten to account for the presence of a header node. Most of the routines become a bit more complex, but some, like INSERT, become simpler since an external list pointer is never null. We leave the rewriting of the routines as an exercise for the reader. The routines INSAFTER and DELAFTER need not be changed at all. In fact, INSAFTER and DELAFTER can be used in place of PUSH and POP since the first item in such a list appears in the node which follows the header node, rather than in the first node on the list.

If the *info* portion of a node can contain a pointer (as is true in our PL/I implementation of a list of integers where a pointer is represented by an integer), then additional possibilities for the use of a header node present themselves. For example, the *info* portion of a list header might contain a pointer to the last node in the list, as in Fig. 5.2.7(e).

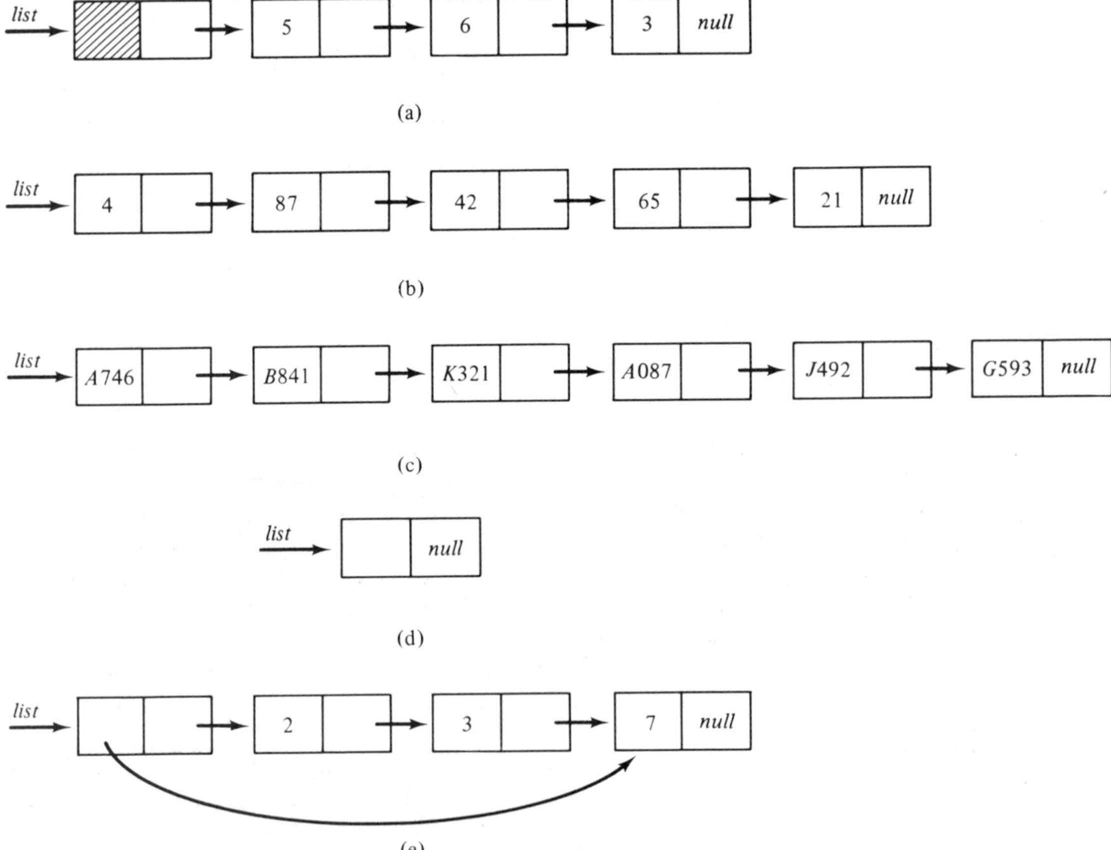

Figure 5.2.7. Lists with header nodes.

Such an implementation would simplify the representation of a queue. Until now two external pointers, *front* and *rear*, were necessary for a list to represent a queue. However, now only a single external pointer *queue* to the header node of the list is necessary. *next*(*queue*) would point to the front of the queue and *info*(*queue*) to its rear.

Another possibility for the use of the *info* portion of a list header is as a pointer to a "current" node in the list during a traversal process. This would eliminate the need for an external pointer during traversal. All of these possibilities are explored further in the Exercise Manual.

5.3. An Example: Simulation Using Linked Lists

One of the most useful applications of queues and linked lists is in ***simulation.*** A simulation program is one which attempts to model a real-world situation in order to learn something about it. Each object and action in the real situation has its counterpart in the program. If the simulation is accurate, that is, if the program successfully mirrors the real world, then the result of the program should mirror the result of the actual actions being simulated. Thus it is possible to understand what occurs in the real-world situation without actually observing its occurrence.

Let us look at an example. Suppose there is a bank with four tellers. A customer enters the bank at a specific time *t*1, desiring to conduct a transaction with any teller. The transaction may be expected to take a certain period of time *t*2 before it is completed. If a teller is free, the customer can begin his transaction immediately and will leave the bank as soon as his transaction has been completed, at time *t*1+*t*2. The total time that he has spent in the bank is exactly equal to the duration of his transaction, *t*2.

However, it is possible that none of the tellers are free; they are all servicing customers who arrived previously. In that case, there is a line waiting at each teller's window. The line for a particular teller may consist of a single person, the one currently transacting his business with the teller, or it may be a very long line. The customer proceeds to the back of the shortest line and waits until all the customers who precede him on the line have completed their transactions and have left the bank. At that time, he may transact his business. The customer leaves the bank at *t*2 time units after he has reached the front of his teller's line. In this case the time spent in the bank is *t*2 plus the time spent waiting on line.

Given such a system, we would like to compute the average time spent by a customer in the bank. One way of doing so is to stand in the bank doorway, ask departing customers the time of their arrival and record the time of their departure, subtract the first from the second and take the average over all customers. However, this would not be very practical. It would be difficult to ensure that no customer is overlooked leaving the bank. Furthermore, it is doubtful that most customers would remember the exact time of arrival.

Instead, we write a program to simulate the customer actions. Each part of the real-world situation has its analogue in the program. The input to the program is a deck of cards, each representing a customer. The real-world action of a customer arriving is modeled by a card being read in. As each customer arrives, two facts are known; the time of his arrival and the duration of his transaction (since, presumably the customer knows when he arrives what he wishes to do at the bank). Thus each card contains two numbers: the time (in minutes since the bank opened) of the customer's arrival and the amount of time (again, in minutes) necessary for his transaction. These input cards are ordered by increasing arrival time.

The four lines in the bank are represented by four queues. Each node of the queues represents a customer waiting on a line, and the node at the front of a queue represents the customer currently being serviced by a teller.

Suppose that at a given instant of time the four lines each contain a specific number of customers. What can happen to alter the status of the lines? Either a new customer enters the bank, in which case one of the lines will have an additional customer, or the first customer on one of the four lines completes his transaction, in which case that line will have one less customer. Thus there are a total of five actions (a customer entering plus four cases of a customer leaving) which can change the status of the lines. Each of these five actions is called an ***event***.

The simulation proceeds by finding the next event to occur and effecting the change in the queues which mirrors the change in the lines at the bank due to that event. In order to keep track of events, the program uses an ***event list***. This list contains at most five nodes, each representing the next occurrence of one of the five types of event. Thus the event list contains one node representing the next customer arriving and four nodes representing each of the four customers at the head of a line completing his transaction and leaving the bank. Of course, it is possible that one or more of the lines in the bank are empty, or that the doors of the bank have been closed for the day so that no more customers are arriving. In such cases, the event list contains fewer than five nodes.

An event node representing a customer's arrival is called an ***arrival node***, and a node representing a departure is called a ***departure node***. At each point in the simulation, it is necessary to know the next event to occur. For this reason, the event list is ordered by increasing time of event occurrence, so that the first event node on the list represents the next event to occur.

The first event to occur is the arrival of the first customer. The event list is therefore initialized by reading the first card and placing an arrival node representing the first customer's arrival on the event list. Initially, of course, all four queues are empty. The simulation then proceeds as follows: The first node is removed from the event list, and the changes which that event causes are made to the queues. As we shall soon see, these changes may also cause additional events to be placed on the event list. The process of removing the first node from the event list and effecting the changes which it causes is repeated until the event list is empty.

When an arrival node is removed from the event list, a node representing the arriving customer is placed on the shortest of the queues representing the four lines. If that customer is the only one on his queue, a node representing his departure is also placed on the event list, since he is at the front of his queue. At the same time, the next card is read and an arrival node representing the next customer to arrive is placed on the event list. Thus there always will be an arrival node on the event list (as long as the input is not exhausted, at which point no more customers arrive) since as soon as one arrival node is removed, another is added.

When a departure node is removed from the event list, the node representing the departing customer is removed from the front of one of the four queues. At that point, the amount of time which the departing customer has spent in the bank is computed and added to a total. At the end of the simulation, this total will be divided by the number of customers to yield the average time spent by all customers. After a customer node has been deleted from the front of its queue, the next customer on the queue (if any) becomes the one being serviced by that teller and a departure node for that next customer is added to the event list.

This process continues until the event list is empty, at which point the average time is computed and printed. Note that the event list itself does not mirror any part of the real-world situation. It is used as part of the program to control the entire process. A simulation such as this one, which proceeds by changing the simulated situation in response to the occurrence of one of several events, is called an ***event-driven simulation***.

We now examine the data structures which are necessary for this program. The nodes on the queues represent customers, and therefore must contain fields representing the arrival time and the transaction duration in addition to a NEXT field to link the nodes in a list. The nodes on the event list represent events, and therefore must contain the time that the event occurs, the type of the event, and any other information associated with that event, as well as a NEXT field. Thus it would seem that two separate node pools are needed for the two different types of node. This would entail two GETNODE and FREENODE routines and two sets of list manipulation routines. To avoid this cumbersome set of duplicate routines, let us try to use a single type of node for both events and customers.

After some thought, we realize that we can declare such a pool of nodes as follows:

```
DCL 1 NODE(500),
      2 INFO,
        (3 TIME,
         3 DURATION,
         3 TYPE)                FIXED,
      2 NEXT                    FIXED;
```

For a customer, TIME is the customer's arrival time and DURATION is his transaction's duration. TYPE is unused in a customer node. NEXT is used as a pointer to link the queue together. For an event node, TIME is used to hold the time of the event's occurrence; DURATION is used for the transaction duration of the arriving customer in an arrival node and is unused in a departure node. TYPE is an integer between 0 and 4, depending on whether the event is an arrival (TYPE=0) or a departure from line 1, 2, 3, or 4 (TYPE=1, 2, 3, or 4). NEXT holds a pointer linking the event list together.

The four queues are declared as an array by the declaration:

```
DCL 1 Q(4),
      (2 FRONT,
       2 REAR)                FIXED;
```

In addition, an array NUM(4) holds the number of customers on each line. The variable EVLIST points to the front of the event list. The variable TOTTIME is used to keep track of the total time spent by all customers, and COUNT keeps count of the number of customers. An auxiliary variable AUXINFO is used to store temporarily the information portion of a node. This variable is declared by

```
DCL 1 AUXINFO,
      (2 AUXTIME,
       2 AUXDUR,
       2 AUXTYPE)             FIXED;
```

The main routine declares all the global variables mentioned above, initializes all lists and queues, and repeatedly removes the next node from the event list to drive the simulation until the event list is empty. It calls on the routine PLACE(EVLIST, AUXINFO) to insert a node whose information is given by AUXINFO in its proper place in the event list. The event list is ordered by increasing value of the TIME field, and the AUXTIME field is used to place the new node in its proper position. The main routine also calls on POPSUB(EVLIST, AUXINFO) to remove the first node from the event list and place its information in AUXINFO. These two PL/I routines must be suitably modified from the examples given in the last section in order to handle this type of node.

The main routine also calls on routines ARRIVE and DEPART which effect the changes in the event list and the queues caused by an arrival and a departure. Specifically, ARRIVE(ATIME,DUR) reflects the arrival of a customer at time ATIME with a transaction of duration DUR, and DEPART(QINDX,DTIME) reflects the departure of the first customer from queue Q(QINDX) at time DTIME. The coding of these routines will be given shortly.

```
BANK:  PROC OPTIONS(MAIN);
         DCL 1 NODE(500),
                 2 INFO,
                   (3 TIME,
                    3 DURATION,
                    3 TYPE)             FIXED,
                 2 NEXT                 FIXED,
               1 AUXINFO,
                 (2 AUXTIME,
                  2 AUXDUR,
                  2 AUXTYPE)            FIXED,
```

```
            1 Q(4),
              (2 FRONT,
               2 REAR)                    FIXED,
            (AVAIL,NUM(4))                FIXED,
            (EVLIST,COUNT,TOTTIME)        FIXED INIT(0),
            (ATIME,DUR,QINDX,DTIME,I)     FIXED;

                /*   initialize available list   */
        AVAIL=1;
        DO I=1 TO 499;
            NEXT(I)=I+1;
        END;
        NEXT(500)=0;

                /*      initialize queues        */
        Q=0;
        NUM=0;

              /*   initialize the event list   */
              /*     with the first arrival    */
        ON ENDFILE(SYSIN) GO TO LOOP;
        GET LIST(AUXTIME,AUXDUR);
        AUXTYPE=0;
        CALL PLACE(EVLIST,AUXINFO);

              /*    begin the event-driven     */
              /*          simulation           */
LOOP:   DO WHILE(EVLIST¬=0);
            CALL POPSUB(EVLIST,AUXINFO);

              /*   check if the next event     */
              /*      is an arrival or a       */
              /*          departure            */
            IF AUXTYPE=0 THEN DO;
                                ATIME=AUXTIME;
                                DUR=AUXDUR;
                                CALL ARRIVE(ATIME,DUR);
                             END;
                        ELSE DO;
                                QINDX=AUXTYPE;
                                DTIME=AUXTIME;
                                CALL DEPART(QINDX,DTIME);
                             END;
        END LOOP;
```

```
        PUT SKIP EDIT('AVERAGE TIME IS',TOTTIME/COUNT)
                      (A,F(4,1));

                    /* the routines ARRIVE and  */
                    /* DEPART are inserted here */
     END BANK;
```

The routine ARRIVE(ATIME,DUR) modifies the queues and the event list to reflect a new arrival at time ATIME with a transaction of duration DUR. It inserts a new customer node at the rear of the shortest queue by calling the subroutine INSERT(QUEUE, AUXINFO), which must be suitably modified to handle the type of node in this example. If the customer is the only one on his queue, a node representing his departure is added to the event list by calling on the subroutine PLACE(EVLIST,AUXINFO). Then, the next card is read and an arrival node is placed on the event list to replace the arrival which has just been processed. If there are no more cards, then the ENDFILE condition is raised. In that case, the ON statement in the main program causes the remaining events on the event list to be processed.

```
ARRIVE:      PROC(ATIME,DUR);
               DCL (ATIME,                 /*      arrival time         */
                    DUR,                   /*  transaction duration     */
                    SMALL,I,J)  FIXED;     /*   auxiliary variables     */

                    /*   find the shortest queue    */
               J=1;
               SMALL=NUM(1);
FINDSHORT:     DO I=2 TO 4;
                  IF NUM(I)<SMALL THEN DO;
                                          SMALL=NUM(I);
                                          J=I;
                                       END;
               END FINDSHORT;

                    /*    Queue J is the shortest. Insert a new     */
                    /*     node representing the new arrival        */
               AUXTIME=ATIME;
               AUXDUR=DUR;
               AUXTYPE=J;
               CALL INSERT(Q(J),AUXINFO);
               NUM(J)=NUM(J)+1;

                    /*    Check if this is the only node on the     */
                    /*        queue. If it is, the customer's       */
                    /*   departure must be placed on the event      */
                    /*                   list.                      */
```

```
   IF NUM(J)=1 THEN DO;
                          AUXTIME=ATIME+DUR;
                          CALL PLACE(EVLIST,AUXINFO);
                      END;

          /*      Read the new arrival card. Place the      */
          /*             arrival on the event list.          */
   GET LIST(AUXTIME,AUXDUR);
   AUXTYPE=0;
   CALL PLACE(EVLIST,AUXINFO);
   RETURN;
 END ARRIVE;
```

The routine DEPART(QINDX,DTIME) modifies the queue Q(QINDX) and the event list to reflect the departure of the first customer on the queue at time DTIME. The customer is removed from his queue by a call to REMOVE(QUEUE,AUXINFO), which must be suitably modified to handle the type of node in this example. The departure node of the next customer on the queue (if any) replaces the departure node which has just been removed from the event list.

```
DEPART:  PROC(QINDX,DTIME);
           DCL  (QINDX,                /*    the queue index      */
                 DTIME,                /*    time of departure    */
                 P)             FIXED; /*    auxiliary variable   */

           /*    remove the customer node from the queue      */
           /*                and gather statistics             */
           CALL REMOVE(Q(QINDX),AUXINFO);
           NUM(QINDX)=NUM(QINDX)-1;
           TOTTIME=TOTTIME+(DTIME-AUXTIME);
           COUNT=COUNT+1;

           /*      if there are any more customers on the     */
           /*      queue, place the departure of the next     */
           /*         customer onto the event list after      */
           /*            computing its departure time         */
           IF NUM(QINDX)>0 THEN DO;
                                   P=FRONT(QINDX);
                                   AUXTIME=DTIME+DURATION(P);
                                   AUXTYPE=QINDX;
                                   CALL PLACE(EVLIST,AUXINFO);
                                END;
           RETURN;
        END DEPART;
```

Simulation programs are rich in their use of list structures. The reader is urged to explore the use of PL/I for simulation and the use of special purpose simulation languages.

5.4. Other List Structures

Although a linked linear list is a rather useful data structure, it has several shortcomings. In this section we shall present other methods of organizing a list and show how they can be used to overcome these shortcomings.

Circular Lists

One of the shortcomings of linear lists is that given a pointer *p* to a node in such a list, we cannot reach any of the nodes that precede *node*(*p*). If a list is traversed, the original pointer to the beginning of the list must be preserved in order to be able to reference the list again.

Suppose a small change is made to the structure of a linear list so that the *next* field in the last node contains a pointer back to the first node rather than the null pointer. Such a list is called a ***circular list*** and is illustrated in Fig. 5.4.1. From any point in such a list it is possible to reach any other point in the list. If we begin at a given node and traverse the entire list, we ultimately end up at the starting point. Note that a circular list

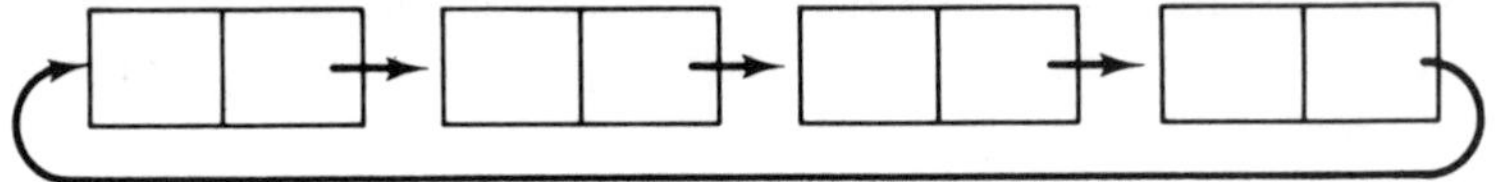

Figure 5.4.1. A circular list.

does not have a natural "first" or "last" node. We must, therefore, establish a first and last node by convention. One useful convention is to let the external pointer to the circular list point to the last node and to allow the following node to be the first node, as illustrated in Fig. 5.4.2. We also establish the convention that a null pointer represents an empty circular list.

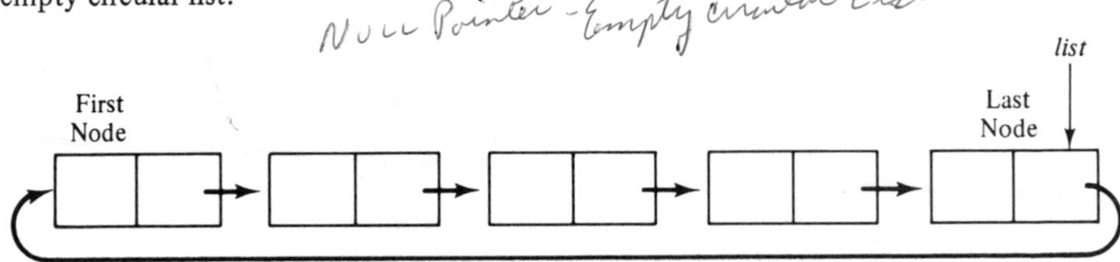

Figure 5.4.2. The first and last nodes of a circular list.

The Stack as a Circular List

A circular list can be used to represent a stack or a queue. Let STACK be a pointer to the last node of a circular list, and let us adopt the convention that the first node is the top of the stack. The following is a PL/I routine to push an integer X onto the stack, assuming a set of NODEs and an auxiliary routine GETNODE as presented in the last section. The PUSH routine calls on the function EMPTY which tests whether its parameter is 0.

Push Circular

```
PUSH:  PROC(STACK,X);
          DCL (STACK,X,P)          FIXED;
          P=GETNODE;
          INFO(P)=X;
          IF EMPTY(STACK) THEN STACK=P;
                              ELSE NEXT(P) =NEXT(STACK);
          NEXT(STACK) =P;
          RETURN;
       END PUSH;
```

Note that the PUSH routine is a bit more complex for circular lists than it is for linear lists.

The PL/I POP function for a stack implemented as a circular list is as follows:

Pop Circular

```
POP:   PROC(STACK)RETURNS(FIXED);
          DCL(STACK,X,P)           FIXED;
          IF EMPTY(STACK) THEN DO;
                  PUT SKIP LIST('STACK UNDERFLOW');
                  STOP;
                                  END;
          P=NEXT(STACK);
          X=INFO(P);
          IF P=STACK THEN  /*   only one node on the stack    */
                              STACK=0;
                        ELSE NEXT(STACK)=NEXT(P);
          CALL FREENODE(P);
          RETURN(X);
       END POP;
```

The Queue as a Circular List

It is easier to represent a queue as a circular list than as a linear list. As a linear list, a queue is specified by two pointers, one to the front of the list and the other to its rear. However, by using a circular list, a queue may be specified by a single pointer QUEUE to that list. NODE(QUEUE) is the rear of the queue, and the following node is its front. The routine REMOVE(QUEUE) is identical to POP(STACK) except that all references to STACK are replaced by QUEUE. The PL/I routine INSERT may be coded as follows:

Insert

```
INSERT:  PROC(QUEUE,X);
            DCL(QUEUE,X,P)      FIXED;
            P=GETNODE;
            INFO(P)=X;
            IF EMPTY(QUEUE) THEN QUEUE=P;
                                ELSE NEXT(P)=NEXT(QUEUE);
```

```
        NEXT(QUEUE)=P;
        QUEUE=P;
        RETURN;
      END INSERT;
```

Note that this is equivalent to the code

```
CALL PUSH(QUEUE,X);
QUEUE=NEXT(QUEUE);
```

That is, to insert an element into the rear of a circular queue, the element is inserted into the front of the queue and the queue pointer is then advanced one element, so that the new element becomes the rear.

Primitive Operations on Circular Lists

The routine INSAFTER(P,X) for a circular list, which inserts a node containing X after NODE(P), is identical to the routine for linear lists as presented in Section 5.2. Let us now consider the routine DELAFTER(P,X), which deletes the node following NODE(P) and stores its contents in X. Looking at the corresponding routine for linear lists as presented in Section 5.2, we note one additional consideration in the case of a circular list. Suppose P points to the only node in the list. In a linear list, NEXT(P) is null in that case, making the deletion invalid. In the case of a circular list, however, NEXT(P) points to NODE(P) so that NODE(P) follows itself. The question is whether or not it is desirable to delete NODE(P) from the list in this case. It is unlikely that we would want to do so, since the operation DELAFTER is usually invoked when pointers to each of two nodes are given, one immediately following another, and it is desired to delete the second. DELAFTER for circular lists is implemented as follows:

```
DELAFTER: PROC(P,X);
            DCL(P,Q,X)          FIXED;

            IF P=0 THEN  /*  an empty list    */
                   DO;
                      PUT SKIP LIST('VOID DELETION');
                      RETURN;
                   END;

            IF P=NEXT(P) THEN  /*   the list contains   */
                               /*   only a single node  */
                      DO;
                        PUT SKIP LIST('VOID DELETION');
                        RETURN;
                      END;
```

```
        Q=NEXT(P);
        X=INFO(Q);
        NEXT(P)=NEXT(Q);
        CALL FREENODE(Q);
        RETURN;
     END DELAFTER;
```

It is also easier to free an entire circular list than to free a linear list. In the case of a linear list, the entire list must be traversed, as one node at a time is returned to the available list. For a circular list, we can write a routine FREELIST which effectively frees an entire list.

```
FREELIST:  PROC(LIST);
              DCL (P,LIST)          FIXED;
              P=NEXT(LIST);
              NEXT(LIST)=AVAIL;
              AVAIL=P;
              LIST=0;
              RETURN;
           END FREELIST;
```

Similarly, we may write a routine CONCAT(L1,L2) which concatenates two lists; that is, it appends the circular list pointed to by L2 to the end of the circular list pointed to by L1.

```
CONCAT:    PROC(L1,L2);
              DCL (L1,L2,P)         FIXED;
              IF L2=0 THEN RETURN;
              IF L1=0 THEN DO;
                                 L1=L2;
                                 RETURN;
                           END;
              P=NEXT(L1);
              NEXT(L1) =NEXT(L2);
              NEXT(L2) =P;
              L1=L2;
              RETURN;
           END CONCAT;
```

The Josephus Problem

Let us consider a problem which can be solved in a straightforward manner by using a circular list. The problem is known as the Josephus problem and postulates a group of soldiers surrounded by an overwhelming enemy force. There is no hope for victory without reinforcements, but there is only a single horse available for escape. The soldiers agree to a pact to determine which of them is to escape and summon help. They form a circle, and a number n is picked from a hat. One of their names is also picked from a hat. Beginning with the soldier whose name is picked, they begin to count clockwise around the circle. When the count reaches n, that soldier is removed from the circle, and the count begins again with the next man. The process continues so that each time the count reaches n, a man is removed from the circle. Once a soldier is removed from the circle, of course, he is no longer counted. The last soldier remaining is to take the horse and escape. The problem is: given a number n, the ordering of the men in the circle, and the man from whom the count begins, to determine the order in which men are eliminated from the circle and which man escapes.

The input to the program is the number n and a list of names which is the clockwise ordering of the men in the circle, beginning with the man from whom the count is to start. The program should print out the names of the men in the order that they are eliminated and the name of the man who escapes.

For example, suppose n equals 3 and there are five men named A, B, C, D, and E. We count three men starting at A, so that C is eliminated first. We then begin at D and count D, E, and back to A, so that A is eliminated next. Then we count B, D, and E (C has already been eliminated) and finally B, D, and B, so that D is the man who escapes.

Clearly a circular list in which each node represents one man is a natural data structure to use in solving this problem. It is possible to reach any node from any other by counting around the circle. To represent the removal of a man from the circle, his node is deleted from the circular list. Finally, when only one node remains on the list, the result is determined.

An outline of the program might be the following:

```
read n;
do while (there is more data);
   read name;
   insert name on the circular list;
end;
do while (there is more than one node on the list);
   count through n−1 nodes on the list;
   print the name in the nth node;
   delete the nth node;
end;
print the name of the only node on the list;
```

We will assume that a set of nodes has been declared in a main program by

```
DCL 1 NODE(500),
      2 INFO      CHAR(30) VAR,
      2 NEXT      FIXED;
```

and that an available list has been initialized. We also assume at least one name in the input. The program uses the routines INSERT, DELAFTER, and FREENODE.

```
JOSEPHUS:  PROC;
             DCL NAME          CHAR(30) VAR,
                 (N,I)         FIXED,
                 LIST          FIXED INIT(0);
             GET LIST(N);

               /*     read in the names, placing each at the     */
               /*                rear of the list                 */
             ON ENDFILE(SYSIN) GO TO COUNT;
FORMLIST:    DO WHILE('1'B);
                GET LIST(NAME);
                CALL INSERT(LIST,NAME);
             END FORMLIST;

COUNT:         /*     continue counting as long as more than     */
               /*          one node remains on the list           */
             DO WHILE(LIST¬=NEXT(LIST));
               DO I=1 to N-1;
                  LIST=NEXT(LIST);
                  /*      at this point LIST points to the        */
                  /*                   Ith node                   */
               END;
               /*     NEXT(LIST) points to the Nth node           */
               CALL DELAFTER(LIST,NAME);
               PUT SKIP LIST(NAME);
             END COUNT;

               /*      print the only name on the list and       */
               /*                 free its node                   */
             PUT SKIP EDIT('THE MAN WHO ESCAPES IS:',INFO(LIST))
                                          (A,X(1));
             CALL FREENODE(LIST);
             RETURN;
           END JOSEPHUS;
```

Header Nodes

Suppose we wish to traverse a circular list. This can be done by repeatedly executing p=$next(p)$; where p is initially a pointer to the beginning of the list. However, since the list is circular, we will not know when the entire list has been traversed unless another pointer *list* points to the first node and a test is made for the condition p=*list*.

An alternate method is to place a header node as the first node of a circular list. This list header may be recognized by a special value in its *info* field which cannot be the valid contents of a list node in the context of the problem, or it may contain a flag (a separate bit) marking it as a header. The list can then be traversed using a single pointer, with the traversal halting when the header node is reached. The external pointer to the list is to its header node, as illustrated in Fig. 5.4.3. This means that a node cannot easily be added onto the rear of such a circular list, as could be done when the external pointer was to the last node of the list. Of course, it is possible to keep a pointer to the last node of a circular list even when a header node is being used.

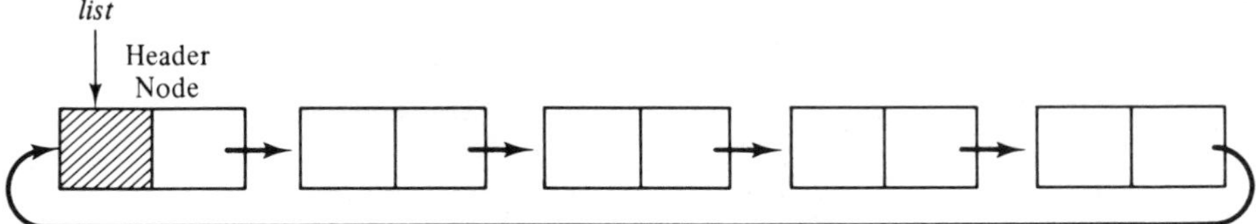

Figure 5.4.3. A circular list with a header node.

If a stationary external pointer to a circular list is present in addition to the pointer used for traversal, then the header node need not contain a special code, but can be used in much the same way as a header node of a linear list to contain global information about the list. The end of a traversal would be signaled by the equality of the traversing pointer and the external stationary pointer.

Addition of Long Positive Integers Using Circular Lists

We now present an example of an application which uses circular lists with header nodes. The hardware of most computers allows integers of only a specific maximum length. Suppose we wish to represent positive integers of arbitrary length and to write a function which returns the sum of two such integers. To add two integers, their digits are traversed from right to left and corresponding digits and a possible carry from the previous digits' sum are added. This suggests representing long integers by storing their digits from right to left in a list so that the first node on the list contains the least significant digit (rightmost) and the last node contains the most significant (leftmost). However, in order to save space, we will keep five digits in each node. (The default precision for FIXED DECIMAL is (5,0).) We may declare the set of nodes by

```
DCL 1 NODE(500),
        2 INFO       FIXED,
        2 NEXT       FIXED;
```

Since we wish to traverse the lists during the addition but wish to eventually restore the list pointers to their original values, we use circular lists with headers. The header node is distinguished by an INFO value of −1. For example, the integer 459763497210698463 is represented by the list illustrated in Fig. 5.4.4.

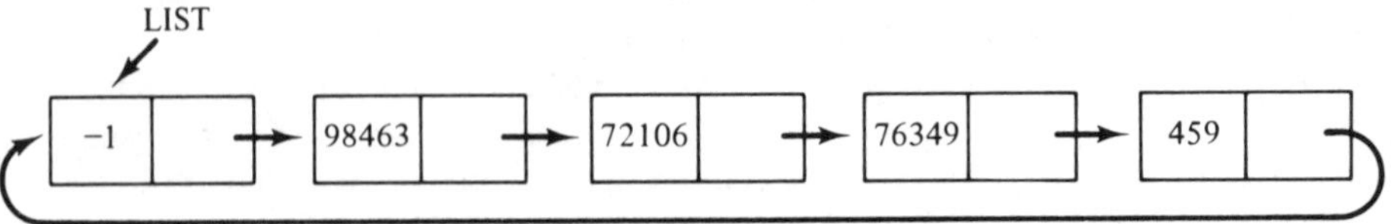

Figure 5.4.4. A large integer as a circular list.

Now let us write a function ADDINT which accepts pointers to two such lists representing integers, creates a list representing the sum of the integers, and returns a pointer to the sum list. Both lists are traversed in parallel, and five digits are added at a time. If the sum of two five-digit numbers is X, the low-order five digits of X can be extracted by the expression MOD(X,100000), which yields the remainder of X on division by 100,000. The carry can be computed by truncating X/100000 to an integer. When the end of one list is reached, the carry is propagated to the remaining digits of the other list. The function follows and uses the routines GETNODE and INSAFTER.

```
ADDINT:  PROC(P,Q) RETURNS(FIXED);
            DCL (P,Q,S,CARRY,NUMBER)      FIXED,
                 TOTAL                    FIXED(6),
                 HUNTHOU                  FIXED(6) INIT(100000);

         /*    move P and Q to the nodes following the headers    */
            P=NEXT(P);
            Q=NEXT(Q);

         /*             set up header node for the sum            */
            S=GETNODE;
            INFO(S) =-1;
            NEXT(S) =S;

         /*               initially there is no carry             */
            CARRY=0;

TRAVERSE:   DO WHILE(INFO(P) ¬=-1 & INFO(Q) ¬=-1);

              /*    add the INFO of two nodes and previous carry     */
                 TOTAL=INFO(P) +INFO(Q) +CARRY;

              /*      Determine the low-order five digits of sum.    */
              /*      Insert into the list. Advance the traversals.  */
                 NUMBER=MOD (TOTAL,HUNTHOU);
                 CALL INSAFTER(S,NUMBER);
                 S=NEXT(S);
                 P=NEXT(P);
                 Q=NEXT(Q);

              /*           determine whether there is a carry         */
                 CARRY=TOTAL/HUNTHOU;
            END TRAVERSE;

         /*    at this point there may be nodes left in one of    */
         /*                       P or Q                           */
```

```
TRAVP:      DO WHILE(INFO(P) ¬=-1);
               TOTAL=INFO(P) +CARRY;
               NUMBER=MOD (TOTAL,HUNTHOU);
               CALL INSAFTER(S,NUMBER);
               CARRY=TOTAL/HUNTHOU;
               S=NEXT(S);
               P=NEXT(P);
            END TRAVP;

TRAVQ:      DO WHILE(INFO(Q) ¬=-1);
               TOTAL=INFO(Q) +CARRY;
               NUMBER=MOD(TOTAL,HUNTHOU);
               CALL INSAFTER(S,NUMBER);
               CARRY=TOTAL/HUNTHOU;
               S=NEXT(S);
               Q=NEXT(Q);
            END TRAVQ;

         /*    check if there is an extra carry from first five     */
         /*                        digits                           */
            IF CARRY=1 THEN DO;
                  CALL INSAFTER(S,CARRY);
                  S=NEXT(S);
                                  END;

         /*    S points to the last node in the sum. NEXT(S)        */
         /*                  points to its header.                  */
            RETURN(NEXT(S));
         END ADDINT;
```

Doubly Linked Lists

Although a circularly linked list has advantages over a linear list, it still has several drawbacks. One cannot traverse such a list backwards, nor can a given node be deleted from a circularly linked list given only a pointer to that node. In cases where these facilities are required, the appropriate data structure is a ***doubly linked list***. Each node in such a list contains two pointers, one to its predecessor and another to its successor. In fact, in the context of doubly linked lists, the terms predecessor and successor are meaningless, since the list is entirely symmetric. Doubly linked lists may be either linear or circular and may or may not contain a header node, as illustrated in Fig. 5.4.5.

We may consider the nodes on a doubly linked list to consist of three fields: an *info* field which contains the information stored in the node and *left* and *right* fields which contain pointers to the nodes on either side. We may declare a set of such nodes in PL/I by

```
DCL 1 NODE(500),
        2 INFO    FIXED,
        2 LEFT    FIXED,
        2 RIGHT   FIXED;
```

Note that the available list for such a set of nodes need not be doubly linked, since it is not traversed bidirectionally. The available list may be linked together by using either the LEFT or RIGHT pointer. Of course, appropriate GETNODE and FREENODE routines must be written.

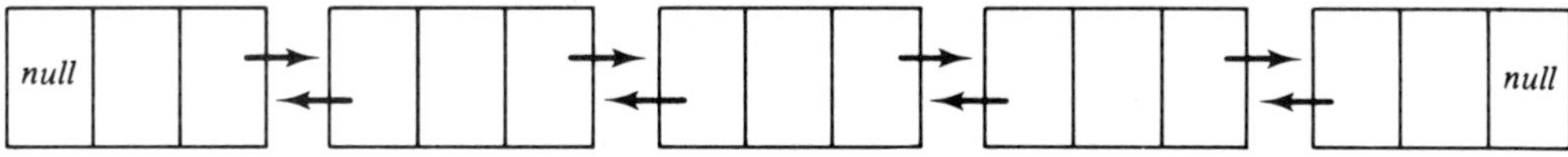

(a) A linear doubly linked list.

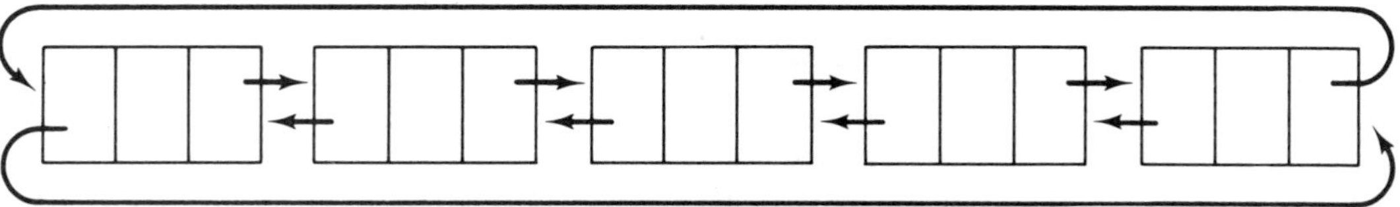

(b) A circular doubly linked list without a header.

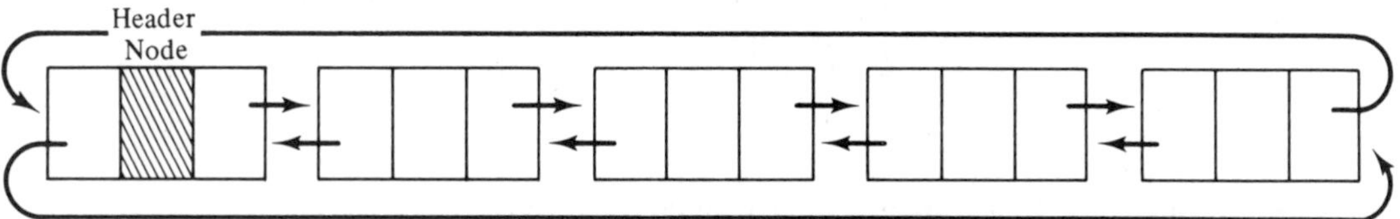

(c) A circular doubly linked list with a header.

Figure 5.4.5. Doubly linked lists.

We now present routines to operate on doubly linked circular lists. A convenient property of such a list is that if p is a pointer to any node in a doubly linked list, then

$$left(right(p)) = p = right(left(p))$$

One operation which can be performed on doubly linked lists but not on ordinary linked lists is to delete a given node. The following PL/I routine deletes the node pointed to by P from a doubly linked list and stores its contents in X.

```
DELETE:  PROC(P,X);
           DCL (P,X,Q)        FIXED;
           IF P=0 THEN DO;
                 PUT SKIP LIST('VOID DELETION');
                 RETURN;
                        END;
```

```
        X=INFO(P);
        Q=LEFT(P);
        RIGHT(Q) =RIGHT(P);
        LEFT(RIGHT(P)) =Q;
        CALL FREENODE(P);
        RETURN;
    END DELETE;
```

The routine INSERTRIGHT inserts a node with information field X to the right of NODE(P) in a doubly linked list.

```
INSERTRIGHT:  PROC(P,X);
                DCL (P,X,Q,R)        FIXED;
                IF P=0 THEN DO;
                   PUT SKIP LIST('VOID INSERTION');
                   RETURN;
                               END;
                Q=GETNODE;
                INFO(Q) =X;
                R=RIGHT(P);
                LEFT(R) =Q;
                RIGHT(Q) =R;
                LEFT(Q) =P;
                RIGHT(P) =Q;
                RETURN;
              END INSERTRIGHT;
```

A routine INSERTLEFT to insert a node with information field X to the left of NODE(P) in a doubly linked list is similar and is left as an exercise for the reader.

Addition of Long Integers Using Doubly Linked Lists

As an illustration of the use of doubly linked lists, let us consider extending the implementation of long integers to include negative as well as positive integers. The header node of a circular list representing a long integer will contain an indication of whether the integer is positive or negative. When we wanted to add two positive integers, we traversed the integers from the least significant digit to the most significant. However, in order to add a positive and a negative integer, the smaller absolute value must be subtracted from the larger absolute value and the result must be given the sign of the integer with the larger absolute value. Thus some method is needed for testing which of two integers represented as circular lists has the larger absolute value.

The first criterion which may be used to identify the integer with the larger absolute value is the length of the integers (assuming that they do not contain leading 0s). Thus we can count the number of nodes in each list. The list which has more nodes represents the integer with the larger absolute value. However, this count involves an extra traversal of the list. Instead of counting the number of nodes, the count could be kept as part of the header node and referred to as needed.

However, if both lists have the same number of nodes, then it is necessary to traverse the lists from the most significant digit to the least significant digit to determine which number is larger. Note that this traversal is in the opposite direction of the traversal which must be used in actually adding two integers. For this reason, doubly linked lists are used to represent such integers.

Consider the format of the header node. In addition to a right and left pointer, the header must contain the length of the list and an indication of whether the number is positive or negative. These two pieces of information can be combined into a single FIXED number whose absolute value is the length of the list and whose sign is the sign of the integer. However, in doing so, the ability to identify the header node by examining the sign of its INFO field is destroyed. When a positive integer was represented as a singly linked circular list, an INFO field of –1 indicated a header node. Under the new representation, however, a header node may contain an INFO field such as 5 which is a valid INFO field for any other node in the list.

There are several ways to remedy this problem. One way is to add another field to each node to indicate whether or not it is a header node. Such a field could be a single bit with a value if '1'B if the node is a header and '0'B if it is not. This means, of course, that each node would require more space. Alternatively, the count could be eliminated from the header node and an INFO field of –1 would indicate a postive number and –2 a negative number. A header node could then be identified by its negative INFO field. However, this would increase the time needed to compare two numbers since it would be necessary to count the number of nodes in each list. Such space/time tradeoffs are very common in computing, and a decision must be made as to which efficiency should be sacrificed and which retained. In our case, we choose yet a third option which is to retain an external pointer to the list header. A pointer P can be identified as pointing to a header if it is equal to the original external pointer; otherwise the node to which P points is not a header.

Figure 5.4.6 indicates a sample node and the representation of three integers as doubly linked lists. Note that the least significant digits are to the right of the header, and that the counts in the header nodes do not include the header node itself.

Using the above representation, we present a function COMPABS which compares the absolute value of two integers represented as doubly linked lists. Its two parameters are pointers to the list headers, and it returns 1 if the first has the greater absolute value, –1 if the second has the greater absolute value, and 0 if the absolute values of the two integers are equal.

```
COMPABS:  PROC(P,Q) RETURNS(FIXED);
               DCL (P,Q,R,S)              FIXED;
                    /*   compare the counts   */
               IF ABS(INFO(P)) > ABS(INFO(Q)) THEN RETURN(1);
               IF ABS(INFO(P)) < ABS(INFO(Q)) THEN RETURN(-1);
          /*              the counts are equal              */
```

```
                  R=LEFT(P);
                  S=LEFT(Q);
              /*  traverse the list from most significant digit     */
    TRAVERSE:     DO WHILE(R¬=P);
                     IF INFO(R) > INFO(S) THEN RETURN(1);
                     IF INFO(R) < INFO(S) THEN RETURN(-1);
                     R=LEFT(R);
                     S=LEFT(S);
                  END TRAVERSE;
              /*        the absolute values are equal               */
                  RETURN(0);
               END COMPABS;
```

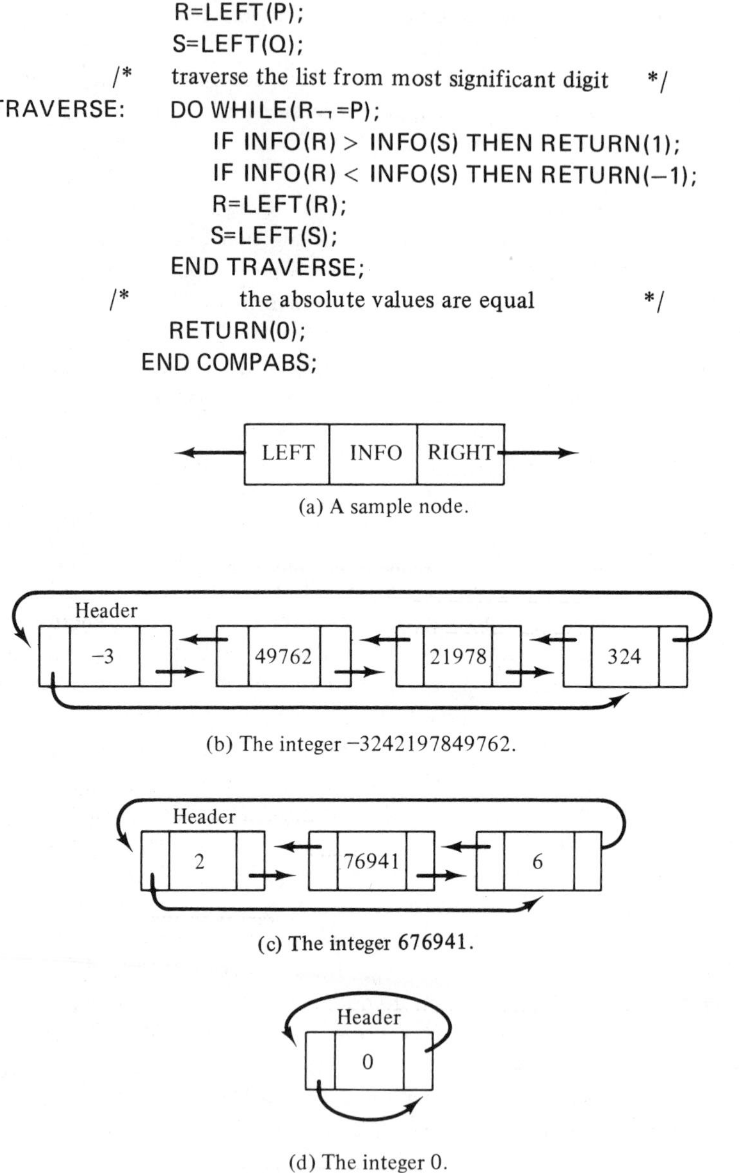

(a) A sample node.

(b) The integer −3242197849762.

(c) The integer 676941.

(d) The integer 0.

Figure 5.4.6. Integers as doubly linked lists.

We are now ready to write a function ADDIFF which accepts two pointers to lists representing long integers of differing sign where the absolute value of the first is not less than that of the second, and which returns a pointer to a list representing the sum of the integers. We must, of course, be careful to eliminate leading 0s from the sum. To do this, we keep a pointer ZEROPTR to the first node of a consecutive set of leading zero nodes and a flag ZEROFLAG which is '1'B if and only if the last node of the sum generated so far is 0.

In this function P points to the number with the larger absolute value and Q points to the number with the smaller absolute value. The values of these variables do not change. Auxiliary variables PPTR and QPTR are used to traverse the lists. The sum is formed in a list pointed to by the variable R.

```
ADDIFF:  PROC(P,Q) RETURNS(FIXED);
           DCL(P,Q,R,S,ZEROPTR,DIFF)     FIXED,
              (PPTR,QPTR)                FIXED,
              HUNTHOU                    FIXED(6)    INIT(100000),
              (COUNT,BORROW)             FIXED       INIT(0),
              ZEROFLAG                   BIT(1)      INIT('0'B);

         /*     generate a header node for the sum          */
           R=GETNODE;
           LEFT(R),RIGHT(R) =R;

         /*          traverse the two lists                 */
           PPTR=RIGHT(P);
           QPTR=RIGHT(Q);
TRAVERSE:  DO WHILE(QPTR ¬=Q);
             DIFF=INFO(PPTR) -BORROW-INFO(QPTR);
             IF DIFF>=0 THEN BORROW=0;
                     ELSE DO;
                            DIFF=DIFF+HUNTHOU;
                            BORROW=1;
                          END;

         /*     generate a node and insert it to the        */
         /*          left of header in the sum              */
             CALL INSERTLEFT(R,DIFF);
             COUNT=COUNT+1;

         /*          test for zero node                     */
             IF DIFF=0 THEN DO;
                     IF ¬ZEROFLAG THEN ZEROPTR=LEFT(R);
                     ZEROFLAG='1'B;
                          END;
                     ELSE ZEROFLAG='0'B;
             PPTR=RIGHT(PPTR);
             QPTR=RIGHT(QPTR);
           END TRAVERSE;

         /*       traverse remainder of P list              */
PTRAV:     DO WHILE(PPTR ¬=P);
             DIFF=INFO(PPTR) -BORROW;
```

```
    IF DIFF>=0 THEN BORROW=0;
               ELSE DO;
                       DIFF=DIFF+HUNTHOU;
                       BORROW=1;
                    END;
    CALL INSERTLEFT(R,DIFF);
    COUNT=COUNT+1;
       IF DIFF=0 THEN DO;
              IF ¬ ZEROFLAG THEN ZEROPTR=LEFT(R);
              ZEROFLAG='1'B;
                           END;
                     ELSE ZEROFLAG='0'B;
    PPTR=RIGHT(PPTR);
  END PTRAV;

  IF ZEROFLAG THEN /*    delete leading zeros        */
        DO WHILE(ZEROPTR ¬=R);
           S=ZEROPTR;
           ZEROPTR=RIGHT(ZEROPTR);
           CALL DELETE(S,DIFF);
           COUNT=COUNT-1;
        END;

  /*        insert COUNT and sign into header           */
  IF INFO(P)>0 THEN INFO(R) =COUNT;
              ELSE INFO (R) =-COUNT;
  RETURN(R);
END ADDIFF;
```

We can also write a function ADDSAME which adds two numbers with like signs. This is very similar to the function ADDINT of the previous implementation, except that it deals with a doubly linked list and must keep track of the number of nodes in the sum.

Using these routines, we can write a new version of ADDINT which adds two integers represented by doubly linked lists.

```
ADDINT:  PROC(P,Q) RETURNS(FIXED);
           DCL (P,Q)                  FIXED;
         /*         check if integers are of like sign          */
           IF INFO(P)*INFO(Q) >0 THEN RETURN(ADDSAME(P,Q));
         /*    check which has the greater absolute value     */
           IF COMPABS(P,Q) >0 THEN RETURN(ADDIFF(P,Q));
                                ELSE RETURN(ADDIFF(Q,P));
         END ADDINT;
```

Bibliography and References

Queues and lists are discussed in all the texts marked with a D in the Bibliography at the back of this book. Elementary simulation techniques may be found in (Goodman and Hedetneimi, 1977) and (Tremblay and Sorenson, 1976). More extensive treatments are in (Fishman, 1973), (Gordon, 1969), and (Kleinrock, 1975).

chapter 6

pl/I list processing

This chapter discusses the list processing facilities available in PL/I. Under these techniques, a pointer is the actual address of an item. Since address manipulation facilities are heavily dependent on the language, they cannot be carried over easily from one language to another. The examples and techniques of this chapter are therefore restricted to the PL/I language and are not applicable to other programming languages. Users of PL/C should be warned that most of the features introduced in this chapter are not available in that language.

6.1. Pointers and the BASED Storage Class

PL/I allows the programmer to access memory by referring to the absolute address of some location. A variable whose contents are interpreted as an address in memory is called a POINTER variable. Such a variable may be declared by

```
DECLARE P POINTER;
```

(PTR may be used as an abbreviation of the keyword POINTER.) The built-in function ADDR accepts a single argument and returns the address of its argument. Thus the statement

```
P=ADDR(X);
```

sets the value of the pointer variable P to the address of the variable X. Note that the value of P is not equal to the value of X; it is equal to the address of the location where the value of X may be found.

Assume that three structures A, B, and C, each containing large amounts of information, have been identically declared. Suppose each of the three structures has a FIXED elementary item named NUM and we wish to identify the structure whose NUM value is the largest of the three. One way of doing this is by declaring a new structure X with the same subfields as A, B, and C and coding

```
IF A.NUM>B.NUM THEN X=A;
                ELSE X=B;
IF C.NUM>X.NUM THEN X=C;
```

However, each time that one structure is assigned to another, large amounts of information must be moved. We would like to have some method of identifying the structure with the largest NUM field without moving extensive amounts of information. The use of pointers allows us to do this as follows:

```
DCL P PTR;
IF A.NUM>B.NUM THEN P=ADDR(A);
                ELSE P=ADDR(B);
IF C.NUM>MAX(A.NUM, B.NUM)
                THEN P=ADDR(C);
```

The above code sets P to the address of the structure with the largest NUM field, without expensive assignments of the structures themselves.

We notice an important difference between the above two portions of code. In the first, A.NUM and B.NUM are compared only once, after which X.NUM is set to the larger of the two values. In the second IF statement it is unnecessary to determine once again the larger of A.NUM and B.NUM since X.NUM already holds that value. The second version, however, does not save the actual larger value, but only a pointer to the structure which contains that value. Thus in order to compare C.NUM to the actual value, the value must be recomputed using the MAX function.

We also face a related problem. Once the address of the structure that we are interested in (which is in P) has been found, how do we get to the structure itself? We do not know whether P points to A, B, or C. What good is an address if it cannot be used to obtain a value?

The BASED Storage Class

The answer lies in the PL/I BASED storage class. The declaration

```
DCL Y FIXED BASED(P);
```

does not cause any storage to be allocated to the variable Y upon entry to the block in which it appears. Rather, Y is to be used as a pattern or template through which the information at the location given by the pointer P is to be interpreted. As explained in Section 1.1, information in a computer is simply a sequence of bits which can be interpreted in many different ways. For example, a specific bit pattern may be interpreted as the character 'A' or as the number 193. It is the *attributes* of the variable used to access a particular location in memory which determine how the information contained therein is to be interpreted. The above declaration states that the variable Y refers to the FIXED number whose address is stored in the pointer P. If we were to declare

```
DCL C CHAR(10) BASED (Q);
```

then C would refer to the character string of length 10 at location Q. P and Q need not be declared separately as pointers; their appearance in the BASED attribute contextually declares them as such.

For example, consider the following program segment:

```
1    DCL X FIXED BASED(P),
2        Y FIXED INIT(0);
3    P=ADDR(Y);
4    X=8;
5    PUT LIST(Y);
```

At line 1, X is declared to refer to the location in memory specified by pointer P. At line 2, Y is declared to have the AUTOMATIC storage class by default and is therefore allocated storage and is initialized to 0 when the surrounding block is entered. At line 3, P is set to the address of Y. Therefore, the reference to X in line 4 is a reference to the FIXED variable at address P, which is a reference to Y. The assignment statement at line 4 therefore changes the value of Y to 8, and line 5 prints the number 8.

Let us now return to the example in which we wanted to identify the structure A, B, or C which has the largest NUM field. Suppose an auxiliary structure X is declared as follows:

```
DCL 1 X BASED (P),
      2 NUM FIXED,
      2 /*   remainder of declaration    */
        /*   identical to A, B, and C    */
```

We may then code the solution as follows:

```
IF A.NUM>B.NUM THEN P=ADDR(A);
               ELSE P=ADDR(B);
IF C.NUM>X.NUM THEN P=ADDR(C);
```

It is no longer necessary to invoke the MAX function in the second IF statement. After the first IF statement, P points to the structure A or B with the larger NUM field. Since X is declared identically to A and B and is based on P, no storage is allocated to X and a reference to X will be to whichever of A or B has the larger NUM field. Similarly, once both IF statements have been executed, P points to the structure with the largest NUM field and X may be used to reference its value.

Let us now suppose that we wished to find both the structure with the smallest NUM field and the one with the largest. One solution is to use two pointers, P and Q, and two BASED variables, X and Y, declared by

```
DCL 1 X BASED(P),
        2 NUM FIXED,
        2 /*    remainder of declaration     */
          /*     identical to A, B, and C    */;
DCL 1 Y BASED(Q),
        2 NUM FIXED,
        2 /*    remainder of declaration     */
          /*     identical to A, B, and C    */;
```

and then code

```
IF A.NUM>B.NUM THEN DO;
                        P=ADDR(A);
                        Q=ADDR(B);
                          END;
                     ELSE DO;
                        P=ADDR(B);
                        Q=ADDR(A);
                          END;
IF C.NUM>X.NUM THEN P=ADDR(C);
IF C.NUM<Y.NUM THEN Q=ADDR(C);
```

In the above example, X and Y are both used as patterns for a variable, structured according to the declarations of A, B, and C. X is used to reference the structure pointed to by P, and Y is used to reference the structure pointed to by Q. After the first IF statement, X refers to the structure A or B with the larger NUM field and Y to the structure with the smaller NUM field. If C.NUM is larger than both A.NUM and B.NUM the second IF statement resets X (by changing the value of P) to C. If C.NUM is smaller than both A.NUM and B.NUM, the third IF resets Y (by changing the value of Q) to C.

Note that the BASED attribute must be declared for an entire structure or array and cannot be specified for a subelement of an aggregate item.

Pointer Qualification

PL/I allows the use of a BASED variable to reference the contents of a location even though the pointer upon which the variable is based does not point to that location. This may be done by explicitly ***qualifying*** the variable. The expression

```
P->X
```

where X is a BASED variable and P is a pointer, refers to the information stored at location P interpreted as having the attributes of X. P is said to ***qualify*** X. However, X need not be based on P. If it so happens that X is based on P, then the expressions P—>X and

X mean the same thing. (The symbol "->" is written as a minus sign followed by a "greater than" symbol with no intervening blanks.)

Thus we can dispense with the declaration of Y in the above example and code:

```
IF A.NUM>B.NUM THEN DO;
                     P=ADDR(A);
                     Q=ADDR(B);
                              END;
                      ELSE DO;
                     Q=ADDR(A);
                     P=ADDR(B);
                              END;
IF C.NUM > P->X.NUM THEN P=ADDR(C);
IF C.NUM < Q->X.NUM THEN Q=ADDR(C);
```

The second IF could have been written in a slightly shorter form as

```
IF C.NUM>X.NUM THEN P=ADDR(C);
```

since X was declared BASED(P). However, it is a good idea to always qualify a variable explicitly, even if the qualification is done by the pointer on which the variable is based. Note also that if the declaration of Y is eliminated, Q must be explicitly declared as a pointer.

Types of Addressing in PL/I

Now that we have discussed pointers in PL/I, let us review the methods of addressing storage in the language. Any reference to an address is a reference to a location in memory. PL/I allows the programmer three forms of referencing memory: ***symbolic***, ***relative***, and ***absolute***. We discuss each of these in turn.

SYMBOLIC ADDRESSING: A symbolic address is a reference to a valid PL/I identifier which represents a location in memory. For example,

```
X=Y+1;
```

is an instruction which directs that the contents of the location at the address specified by the symbol X is to be replaced by the sum of the contents of the location specified by the symbol Y and the constant 1. (The *constant* "1" is merely a reference to some location in memory which holds the *value* 1.) In this example X and Y are symbolic addresses which are translated into actual addresses by the compiler. There is no relationship between the address specified by the symbol X and the address specified by the symbol Y (or the symbol "1" for that matter). By using symbolic addressing, the programmer is freed from all the burdens (and advantages) of knowing something about actual addresses.

For example, consider a function BIG which returns the value of the largest of eight fixed-point numbers (ignoring the built-in MAX function):

```
BIG1:   PROC(X1,X2,X3,X4,X5,X6,X7,X8) RETURNS(FIXED);

             DCL (X1,X2,X3,X4,X5,X6,X7,X8, LARGE)  FIXED;
             LARGE=X1;
             IF X2>LARGE THEN LARGE=X2;
             IF X3>LARGE THEN LARGE=X3;
             IF X4>LARGE THEN LARGE=X4;
             IF X5>LARGE THEN LARGE=X5;
             IF X6>LARGE THEN LARGE=X6;
             IF X7>LARGE THEN LARGE=X7;
             IF X8>LARGE THEN LARGE=X8;
             RETURN(LARGE);

        END BIG1;
```

The assignment statement ANS=BIG1(A1,A2,A3,A4,A5,A6,A7,A8); will set ANS to the value of the largest of the eight variables A1, A2, A3, A4, A5, A6, A7, and A8. The names of the eight variables do not affect the method by which they are stored or accessed. They might as well have been assigned the names JOE, JILL, MIKE, MACK, JANE, GEORGE, HARRY, and PETE as long as they are declared to have the FIXED attribute.

Clearly, routines such as the one above are unacceptable. The amount of coding required is entirely too much for the small amount of computing that is done. More important, however, is the lack of generality of the function BIG1. If the programmer required the largest of seven or nine or any other number of numbers (other than eight), he would have to code separate routines for each of them. For these reasons symbolic addressing is not always sufficient.

RELATIVE ADDRESSING: If a competent programmer were asked to code a solution to the problem of computing the largest of eight numbers, he would probably make a major change in the manner in which the input data is stored. Instead of storing the original numbers in eight separate (and separately named) locations, they can be stored in an array declared by

```
DCL A(8) FIXED;
```

In this fashion the programmer can reference A(1),A(2),. . .,A(8): the first, second,. . ., eighth element of the array. The reference A(I) is to the Ith element of the array. As explained in Section 1.2, the array A is stored sequentially in main storage as shown in Fig. 6.1.1. Suppose the array A is stored in successive locations starting at location 100 in main storage. (We ignore for the moment that each element of A may actually require more than one location.) Then A(1) is at location 100, A(2) at location 101, and A(I) at location 100+I–1. A reference to A(I) is really a reference to an address that consists of two parts: 100 is the ***base*** for the entire array A, and I–1 is the ***offset*** of the Ith element within the area assigned to A. For each reference to an element of A the

100	101	102	103	104	105	106	107
$A(1)$	$A(2)$	$A(3)$	$A(4)$	$A(5)$	$A(6)$	$A(7)$	$A(8)$

Figure 6.1.1. Sequential representation of an array.

base of 100 is constant while the computation of I–1 changes for each value of I. The statement

```
A(I) = A(J)+1;
```

involves the computation of two addresses: those of A(I) and A(J). The address of A(I) is 100+I–1, while the address of A(J) is 100+J–1. The values of I and J during the execution of the above statement will determine the actual locations referenced.

The above addressing scheme is called ***relative addressing*** because the address of the desired element is computed relative to the starting address of the first element of the array. The advantage in using such a scheme is that it permits referencing different elements of the array in different executions of the same statement. For example, we present an alternative version of BIG1 as follows:

```
BIG2:   PROC(X) RETURNS(FIXED);
          DCL (X(*), LARGE,I)        FIXED;
          LARGE= X(1);
TEST:     DO I=2 TO HBOUND(X,1);
             IF X(I)> LARGE THEN LARGE=X(I);
          END TEST;
          RETURN(LARGE);
        END BIG2;
```

The above routine is clearly more compact than BIG1. In addition, the routine BIG2 does not expand or contract with the number of elements passed to it. This routine can be invoked by passing the entire array to it and coding

```
ANS= BIG2(A);
```

Before proceeding, we should ask if there are any disadvantages to relative addressing. While relative addressing does yield simpler programs, there is the disadvantage that the area reserved for A must be in contiguous (sequential) locations. In the case of symbolic addressing there is no relation between the address of A1 and that of A2. In the case of array storage, however, the address of A(2) is computed from the starting address of the array. It is therefore crucial that A(2) immediately follow A(1) in main storage. Thus in order to use indirect addressing it is necessary to reserve storage for all the elements of an array as a single large block rather than as individual storage locations strewn about memory. This may cause problems. For example, if 10,000 locations were required in memory, it is possible that these locations could be found in various parts of memory. At the same time, however, it may not be possible to produce 10,000 contiguous locations. In such a case we would have to call upon some higher-level memory management routine or find some other method for solving the given problem. Another disadvantage of relative addressing is the time which is involved in computing the address of a referenced object, given the base address of the array and the value of the subscript. We shall examine some of these considerations in Chapter 10.

ABSOLUTE ADDRESSING: In symbolic addressing, the name of a variable refers to that variable's location. In absolute addressing, an object's location may be specified by the contents of another location. As we have seen, a POINTER variable contains an address which can be used in conjunction with a BASED variable to reference a memory location. Since the value of a POINTER variable may change, and since a BASED variable may be used to interpret any location in memory according to given attributes, the object which is referenced by a given POINTER-BASED variable pair may change during execution.

Let us attempt to rewrite the routine to find the largest of eight numbers, using absolute addresses. The routine BIG3 accepts an array of pointers P, where P(1) contains the address of the first number, P(2) the address of the second, etc.

```
BIG3:   PROC(P) RETURNS(FIXED);
            DCL (P(*),Q)           PTR,
                 X                 FIXED BASED(R),
                 I                 FIXED;
            R=P(1); /*   R contains the first address     */
                    /*  therefore X is the value of the   */
                    /*          first number              */
LOOP:       DO I=2 TO HBOUND(P,1);
               Q=P(I);
               IF Q->X > R->X THEN R=Q;
            END LOOP;
            RETURN(R->X);
        END BIG3;
```

Let us examine the sequence of statements

```
Q=P(I);
IF Q->X > R->X THEN R=Q;
```

The first assigns the address of the Ith number to Q. The value Q->X is then compared to the value of R->X. Q->X is the value of the Ith element, and R->X is a reference to the element in memory pointed to by R. R contains the address of the largest of all the elements that have been examined at any point in the program's execution. The program scans successive elements, changing R when it finds a new "largest" element. Each time that R changes, R–>X refers to a new element. After leaving the loop, R contains the address of the largest of the numbers, so that

```
RETURN(R->X);
```

returns this largest value.

Let us now consider how the function BIG3 could be invoked from a calling routine. Obviously, an array of addresses, rather than the numbers themselves, must be passed to the function. First, let us consider the case where the items are contained in an array A. We could then code

```
DCL (A(8),ANS,I)          FIXED,
     P(8)                 PTR;
GET LIST(A);
DO   I=1 TO 8;
     P(I)=ADDR(A(I));
END;
ANS=BIG3(P);
```

The loop places the address of each of the eight numbers into a successive element of the array P.

Suppose the items were not declared as an array but rather as separately named variables. We could then code

```
DCL (A1,A2,A3,A4,A5,A6,A7,A8,ANS)  FIXED,
     P(8)                          PTR;
GET LIST(A1,A2,A3,A4,A5,A6,A7,A8,);
P(1)=ADDR(A1);
P(2)=ADDR(A2);
P(3)=ADDR(A3);
P(4)=ADDR(A4);
P(5)=ADDR(A5);
P(6)=ADDR(A6);
P(7)=ADDR(A7);
P(8)=ADDR(A8);
ANS=BIG3(P);
```

Again the addresses of the items are put into the array P, so that P can be passed to the function BIG3.

Comparing the Different Addressing Schemes

Summarizing, we have three versions of BIG. The function BIG1 assumes that the data is stored in arbitrary locations and operates on actual values. It is necessary to pass each of the items to the subroutine separately. Even if the items were stored sequentially, the subroutine makes no use of this information.

The function BIG2 assumes that the data is stored in an array. The subroutine makes use of this fact in the way it accesses the data. Of course, if the data in the original program is not stored as an array, it will be necessary to declare an array of proper size and copy the original data into the array in order to use BIG2.

The function BIG3 makes no assumption about the organization of the original data. In fact, the values of the original data are not passed to the subroutine at all. It is an array of addresses that is passed to the subroutine. Because the subroutine operates on the array of addresses and not on the original data, it is irrelevant to the execution of the subroutine whether or not the original numbers are stored as an array. It is simpler to assign the addresses to the array P if the numbers are stored in an array. However, even if the original numbers are not stored in an array, once the assignment of addresses has been made, the execution of the subroutine proceeds correctly.

We should now address the question of which of the three functions is "better." Before we do this, however, a word of caution is in order. There are virtually no cases in which one method of doing something is unequivocally "better" than another. There are always instances and cases in which there are redeeming features even for a generally poor method. Returning to our example, the first version is clearly unacceptable, if only for the reason that it must be rewritten depending on the number of parameters being passed to it. The second version is more general than the first because it can operate on any number of arguments. However, its limitation is that it imposes a restriction on the organization of the data. It is not always feasible or desirable to store the original data items in an array, especially if each item is a large structure. However, if a programmer knows that he will only be concerned with arrays and never deal with data that is noncontiguous, then BIG2 is the best choice.

There will undoubtedly be some cases in which a programmer will be faced with the problem of writing a subroutine which may be applied to either contiguous or noncontiguous data. One alternative is to write a separate routine for each case. The other alternative is to write a routine such as BIG3, which operates on an array of pointers containing the addresses of the data. The subroutine will operate on the data at the addresses passed to it, and will assume no relationship among the addresses themselves. Such a routine could be used if the original structure of the inputs is in the form of an array, but could also be used in the case where the input elements are not in array format. In those cases where a programmer must process data that is both contiguous and noncontiguous, it would be worth his while to consider using POINTER variables as parameters to a subroutine. On the other hand, it may be simpler to deal directly with the data at hand rather than to first transfer the addresses of the data to an array of pointers. The real advantage of the array of pointers is in the case where the data is spread out over main storage but the number of data items varies.

Another advantage of using an array of pointers, even in the case when the data is stored in an array, is when each element of the array is large and considerable movement of data would take place if the array were passed. Since considerable movement of data (which significantly increases the execution time of the program) is necessary, it may be more efficient to perform this movement on single addresses rather than on huge structures. As usual, each case must be evaluated on its own merits as to whether the extra saving of time is worth the additional coding required in using POINTER variables.

Another Example

Let us consider another example. We wish to write a function AVG which accepts as input an array of pointers to a set of numbers whose average is to be computed. We assume that a very large array of pointers is declared in the calling routine to be passed to the subroutine but the entire array is not full. Since some of the entries in the array may be dummies (not pointing to valid data), the HBOUND function cannot be used for the limit of a loop. We introduce the PL/I built-in function NULL which accepts no parameters and returns a pointer with a special "null" value which is not the address of any real location in memory. (In some PL/I compilers, a built-in function with no arguments must be declared explicitly. We do not adopt this convention here.)

We give the code for the calling routine and the function AVG.

```
        DCL  (NUMB(100),I)     FIXED,
                P(100)         PTR;
        ON ENDFILE(SYSIN)    GO TO PRINT;
        P=NULL;  /*    the entire array of pointers is    */
                 /*          initialized to NULL          */
                 /*              in memory                */
        /*  if an entry in NUMB contains a valid number, its   */
        /*  address is assigned to the corresponding entry in P  */
READ:   DO I=1 TO 100;
           GET LIST(NUMB(I));
           P(I)=ADDR(NUMB(I));
        END READ;

PRINT:  PUT SKIP LIST(AVG(P));
        STOP;

AVG:    PROC(P)        RETURNS(FLOAT);
          DCL     (P(*),Q)          PTR,
                  AVER              FLOAT INIT(0),
                  X                 FIXED BASED(Q),
                  (I,N)             FIXED;

LOOP:     DO I=1 TO HBOUND(P,1) WHILE (P(I) ¬= NULL);
             /*   process each number until entry in P is NULL    */
             Q=P(I);
             AVER=AVER + Q->X;  /*    add next number to average     */
          END LOOP;
          N=I-1;  /*   N is count of numbers    */
          IF N¬=0 THEN AVER=AVER/N;
          RETURN(AVER);
        END AVG;
```

Pointers and BASED Variables in Subroutines

Before concluding this section, we should make note of one of the implications of using POINTER and BASED variables in subroutines. A subroutine may alter local variables, global variables, and parameters. Local variables are those declared in the subroutine and are known locally only to the subroutine. Global variables are declared in a surrounding block and may be known to both the calling program and to the subroutine. Parameters, of course, are passed from the calling program to the subroutine. From a practical point of view, a programmer should use as few global variables as possible. By eliminating the use of global variables entirely, a programmer can ensure that a subroutine will not change the value of any variable declared outside the routine, unless that variable is explicitly passed as an argument. Thus in debugging a program, he need not consider the effects of a subroutine on any variables that are global to it. Once the actions of such a subroutine have been tested and verified independently of the program in which it will eventually be inserted, only its effects on its inputs need be considered.

A program that contains subroutines which modify global variables is considerably more difficult to debug. Since a call to such a subroutine may affect any of the variables that are global to it, there are many more interrelationships among the variables that must be explored before all errors can be removed. To the extent that modules of a program can be isolated from one another by removing global variables, the number of these relationships can be significantly reduced, and a program that is easier to debug can be produced.

In programs that do not use BASED variables, one can determine which global variables are accessed by a subroutine by referring to a table of cross references which may be obtained from the compiler output. Programs that use BASED variables, on the other hand, have an additional liability in that a subroutine may reference variables without giving any indication of the fact. A check of the variable names used by such a subroutine may turn up only local variables and parameters. However, if one of these parameters is a pointer, then the use of a BASED variable local to the subroutine may in fact result in the access of some global location. This is because a BASED variable only specifies a pattern for the location pointed to by the pointer which qualifies it (either by default or explicitly). If this pointer is a parameter (or if it is assigned from a parameter), then a reference to this BASED variable is actually a reference to a location within the calling program. In effect then, we are dealing with a global variable. For example, the function AVG given above does not explicitly mention the variable NUMB. Yet, since P is an array of pointers to the elements of NUMB and is used within AVG, the function does reference the array NUMB. This is not necessarily a disadvantage. It is merely a feature that a programmer should be aware of in programming and debugging.

6.2. Implementing Lists Using BASED Storage

Allocating and Freeing Copies of a BASED Variable

In the last section we saw how to manipulate addresses using the PL/I POINTER attribute. In each of the examples of that section, however, it was necessary to first declare and allocate storage for an AUTOMATIC variable and then assign the address of that variable to a POINTER variable. There is another method of setting a POINTER variable to reference a location. It is possible to allocate portions of storage explicitly and assign their addresses to POINTER variables. Suppose a variable X is declared by

```
DCL X BASED(P) FIXED;
```

and Q is declared by

```
DCL Q PTR;
```

The following statements may be used to allocate and free portions of storage:

ALLOCATE X;	allocates a FIXED location and sets the POINTER variable P to the address of this location
ALLOCATE X SET(Q);	allocates a FIXED location but places the address of the location in Q rather than P
FREE X;	frees the FIXED location currently pointed to by P (the pointer on which X is based)
FREE Q−>X;	frees the FIXED location currently pointed to by the POINTER variable Q

Consider the following example:

```
1     DCL X BASED(P) FIXED,
2           (P,Q,R)        PTR;
3     ALLOCATE X;
4     X=3;
5     Q=P;
6     ALLOCATE X;
7     X=8;
8     ALLOCATE X SET(R);
9     R->X=10;
10    PUT LIST(Q->X, X, R->X);
```

The above statements have the effect of first allocating a location with the attributes of X, placing its address in P, setting its value to 3 and setting Q to the address of that location (lines 3 through 5), then allocating an additional location with the attributes of X and placing its address in P, setting its value to 8 (lines 6 through 7), and finally allocating a third location with the attributes of X, setting R to its address and setting its value to 10 (lines 8 through 9). The effect of these statements is illustrated in Fig. 6.2.1. Thus the PUT LIST statement in line 10 will print

```
3     8     10
```

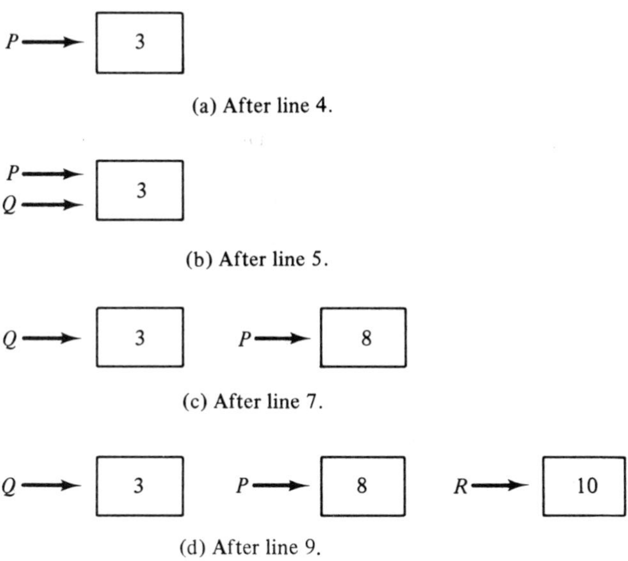

(a) After line 4.

(b) After line 5.

(c) After line 7.

(d) After line 9.

Figure 6.2.1.

Suppose we then execute the additional statements:

```
11        FREE Q->X;
12        Q=R;
13        FREE X;
14        ALLOCATE X SET(R);
15        R->X=5;
16        PUT LIST(R->X, Q->X);
```

The effect of these statements is illustrated in Fig. 6.2.2. The PUT LIST statement in line 16 will print

```
5    10
```

An attempt to execute PUT LIST(X); at this point is an error since an unqualified reference to X is to P–>X but P does not point to an allocated portion of storage. Note that if two ALLOCATE statements are executed one after the other, as in

```
ALLOCATE X;   X=5;
ALLOCATE X;   X=6;
```

the first copy of X is lost since its address was not saved. Since the space allocated for these variables is not known by any other name (as in the examples of the previous section), unless the address of the first copy is saved it will be lost. In fact, it cannot even be freed since there is no way to refer to it in a FREE statement. It would be an example of a memory location which is allocated but cannot be referenced.

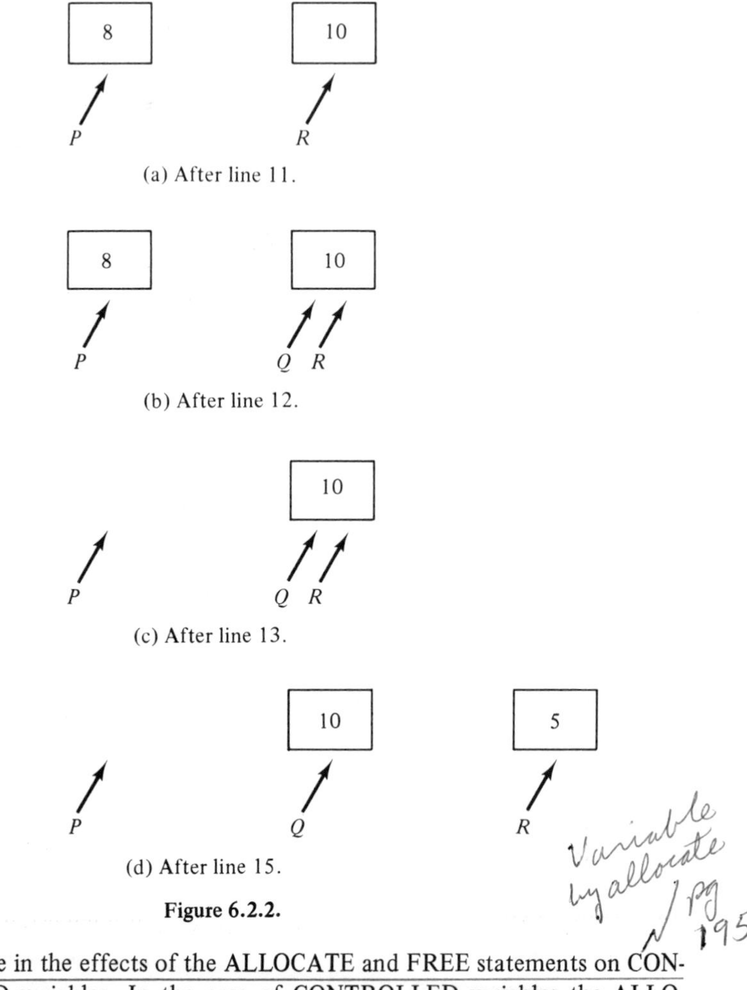

(a) After line 11.

(b) After line 12.

(c) After line 13.

(d) After line 15.

Figure 6.2.2.

Note the difference in the effects of the ALLOCATE and FREE statements on CONTROLLED and BASED variables. In the case of CONTROLLED variables the ALLOCATE and FREE statements behave as *push* and *pop* operations on a stack. Using the CONTROLLED variable, it is impossible to access any element in a set except the one at the top. BASED variables, on the other hand, allow the programmer to access any element in the set, providing its address is stored in some POINTER variable.

Linked Lists Using BASED Variables

Now that we have the capability of allocating and freeing copies of a BASED variable, let us see how BASED variables can be used to implement linked lists. Recall that a linked list consists of a set of nodes, each of which has two fields: an information field and a pointer to the next node in the list. In addition there is an external pointer to the first node in the list We will use POINTER variables to implement list pointers. We would declare a single node by

```
DCL 1 NODE,
      2 INFO      FIXED,
      2 NEXT      PTR;
```

Such a node is identical to the nodes of Section 5.2, except that the NEXT field now has the POINTER attribute (pointing to the absolute address of the next node in a list) rather than the FIXED attribute (pointing to the index within an array where the next node in the list is kept). We must now decide how to construct a list and implement the primitive operations as in Section 5.2. One way of doing this is to use an array and code:

```
DCL 1 NODE(100),
      2 INFO      FIXED,
      2 NEXT      PTR;
```

The contents of NEXT(I) would be the address of NODE(J) if NODE(J) follows NODE(I) in the list. Such an implementation is, of course, ridiculous. It is simpler to reference NODE(J) by its index J within the array rather than to first compute its address. We are merely imposing an artificial layer of complexity in using POINTER variables for the field NEXT. We leave the completion of this variation of the array implementation as an exercise for the reader.

Let us rather employ the dynamic allocation features of BASED storage to implement linked lists. Instead of declaring an array to represent an aggregate collection of nodes, we declare a node to be BASED and allocate and free copies when necessary. Thus we declare

```
DCL 1 NODE BASED(NDPTR),
      2 INFO      FIXED,
      2 NEXT      PTR;
```

The variable NODE is global to all subroutines which reference it. When the block containing this declaration is entered, no storage is allocated; rather a structure is defined whose fields can be used providing NDPTR has been properly initialized. Suppose, in addition, we declare

```
DCL P PTR;
```

An execution of the statement

```
P = GETNODE;
```

should place the address of an available node into P. We present the routine GETNODE:

```
GETNODE: PROC RETURNS(PTR);
         DCL P PTR;
         ALLOCATE NODE SET(P);
         RETURN(P);
      END GETNODE;
```

Similarly an execution of the statement

```
CALL FREENODE(P);
```

should return the node whose address is at P to available storage. We present the routine FREENODE.

```
FREENODE:  PROC(P);
               DCL   P   PTR;
               FREE P->NODE;
               RETURN;
           END FREENODE;
```

The programmer need not be concerned with managing available storage. In fact, there is no longer a need for the pointer AVAIL (pointing to the first available node) since it is the PL/I system that governs the allocating and freeing of nodes and it is the system that keeps track of the first available node. Note also that there is no test in GETNODE for determining whether overflow has occurred. This is because such a condition will be detected during the execution of the ALLOCATE statement and is system-dependent.

Since the routines GETNODE and FREENODE are so simple under this implementation, they are often replaced by the in-line statements ALLOCATE NODE SET(P); and FREE P->NODE;.

In writing programs dealing with pointer and BASED variables, it is a good idea to pointer-qualify each reference to a BASED variable and not rely upon the current value of the POINTER variable on which it is based. This helps eliminate errors which might occur when routines are combined with others that use the POINTER variable upon which a node is based.

The routines INSAFTER(P,X) and DELAFTER(P,X) are presented using the BASED storage implementation of a linked list. Assume LIST is a POINTER variable which points to the first node of a list (if any) and is equal to NULL in the case of an empty list.

```
INSAFTER:  PROC(P,X);
               DCL   (P,Q)    PTR,
                       X      FIXED;
               IF P=NULL THEN DO;
                              PUT SKIP LIST('VOID INSERTION');
                              RETURN;
                                 END;
               Q=GETNODE;
               Q->INFO=X;
               Q->NEXT=P->NEXT;
               P->NEXT=Q;
               RETURN;
           END INSAFTER;
```

```
DELAFTER: PROC(P,X);
              DCL    (P,Q)   PTR,
                      X       FIXED;
              IF P=NULL THEN DO;
                       PUT SKIP LIST('VOID DELETION');
                       RETURN;
                            END;
              IF P–>NEXT=NULL THEN DO;
                       PUT SKIP LIST('VOID DELETION');
                       RETURN;
                                      END;
              Q=P–>NEXT;
              X=Q–>INFO;
              P–>NEXT=Q–>NEXT;
              CALL FREENODE(Q);
              RETURN;
            END DELAFTER;
```

Notice the striking similarity between the above routines and those of the second half of Section 5.2. Both are implementations of the algorithms of the first half of that section. In fact, the only difference between the two versions is in the manner in which the list pointers are specified.

Stacks and queues can also be implemented using this new implementation of linked lists. We leave these as exercises for the reader.

List Operations Using the BASED Implementation

We now present several small examples to illustrate some features of list manipulation in PL/I. In each of these we assume that the following appears in a surrounding routine:

```
DCL 1  NODE   BASED(NDPTR),
       2 INFO          FIXED,
       2 NEXT          PTR;
DCL  LIST              PTR;
LIST=NULL;
```

The variable LIST is initialized to NULL indicating that the list is initially empty. Of course various statements may subsequently insert and delete elements from the list.

First let us write a routine INSEND(LIST,X) to insert the element X at the end of a list LIST.

```
INSEND:  PROC(LIST,X);
           DCL  (LIST,P,Q)        PTR,
                   X              FIXED;
```

```
            P=GETNODE;
            P->INFO=X;
            P->NEXT=NULL;
            IF LIST=NULL THEN LIST=P;
            /*    search for last node    */
                        ELSE DO;
                               Q=LIST;
                               DO WHILE(Q->NEXT ¬= NULL);
                                    Q=Q->NEXT;
                               END;
                               Q->NEXT=P;
                             END;
            RETURN;
          END INSEND;
```

We now present a function SEARCH(LIST,X) which returns a pointer to the first occurrence of X within the list LIST, and the null pointer if X does not occur in the list.

```
SEARCH:   PROC(LIST,X) RETURNS(PTR);
            DCL  (LIST,P)          PTR,
                  X                FIXED;
            P=LIST;
            DO WHILE (P¬=NULL);
                 IF P->INFO = X THEN RETURN(P);
                 P=P->NEXT;
            END;
            RETURN(P);
          END SEARCH;
```

The next routine deletes all nodes whose INFO field contains the value X.

```
REMVX:    PROC(LIST,X);
            DCL   (LIST,P,Q)   PTR,
                  (X,Y)        FIXED;
            Q=NULL;
            P=LIST;
            DO WHILE (P¬=NULL);
              IF P->INFO=X THEN
                IF Q=NULL THEN DO;
                /*        remove first node of LIST        */
                              LIST=LIST->NEXT;
                              CALL FREENODE(P);
                              P=LIST;
                                 END;
```

```
                        ELSE DO;
                  /*     advance P and remove node after Q      */
                          P=P->NEXT;
                          CALL DELAFTER(Q,Y);
                            END;

                ELSE  /*     advance to next node of LIST        */
                      DO;
                        Q=P;
                        P=P->NEXT;
                      END;
             END;
             RETURN;
           END REMVX;
```

Users of a PL/I compiler which includes the REPEAT option (see Section 5.2) can simplify list traversals in the BASED implementation. For example, the loop in the routine SEARCH can be rewritten as follows:

```
DO P=LIST REPEAT P->NEXT WHILE(P¬=NULL);
    IF P->INFO=X THEN RETURN(P);
END;
```

The DO group in the ELSE clause within INSEND can be rewritten as follows:

```
ELSE DO;
         DO Q=LIST REPEAT Q->NEXT WHILE(Q->NEXT¬=NULL);
         END;
         Q->NEXT=P;
     END;
```

Comparing the BASED and Array Implementations of Lists

It is instructive to examine the advantages and disadvantages of the BASED and array implementations of linked lists. The major disadvantage of the BASED implementation is that it is more time consuming to call upon the system to ALLOCATE and FREE storage than to manipulate a programmer-managed available list. Its major advantage is that a set of nodes is not reserved in advance for use by a particular group of lists. For example, suppose a program uses two types of lists: lists of integers and lists of character strings. Under the array representation, two arrays of fixed size would be immediately allocated. If one group of lists overflows its array, the program cannot continue. Under the BASED representation, two BASED variables are declared at the outset, but no storage is allocated for either until needed. As nodes are needed, the system is called upon to provide them. Any storage not used for one type of node may be used for another. Thus as long as sufficient storage is available for the nodes actually present in the list, no overflow will occur.

Another advantage of the BASED implementation is that a reference to P—>NODE does not involve the address computation which is necessary in computing the address of NODE(P). To compute the address of NODE(P), the contents of P must be added to the base address of the array NODE, while the address of P—>NODE is given by the contents of P directly.

6.3. Examples

In this section we consider some examples involving linked allocation which use the BASED storage implementation of linked lists. The programs could be written equally well using the array representation of Chapter 5. As exercises you are asked to implement these programs using the methods of Chapter 5.

Example 6.3.1: An Airline Reservation System

Consider the problem of programming an airline reservation system. The input consists of a control deck containing flight data used to initialize the system, followed by a passenger deck containing data on passenger reservations. The control deck consists of a card containing a single number (representing the number of flights available that day) followed by a set of cards (one for each flight), each of which contains a flight number in columns 1 through 3 and the seating capacity for that flight in columns 5 through 7. A sample control deck is illustrated in Fig. 6.3.1.1(a).

Once this control deck has been read, a separate card is read for each passenger request for service. The requests may be of three types: reservation, cancellation, or inquiry. The type of each request is indicated by the word RESERVE, CANCEL, or INQUIRE beginning in column 1. A request for a reservation or a cancellation is accompanied by a passenger name beginning in column 15 and a flight number beginning in column 50. An inquiry is accompanied by a passenger name only. (We assume that a passenger inquires about all of the flights on a particular journey but may cancel one particular leg of the journey.) A sample set of data for a passenger request deck is shown in Fig. 6.3.1.1(b).

We are to write a program that processes these two decks of cards. For each passenger service request card, a message describing the action taken is to be printed.

Before designing a program, the requirements of the problem must be defined more precisely. In particular, it must be determined what action is to be taken for each of the possible passenger requests. In the case of a reservation the passenger is to be placed on a flight list for the flight, if the flight is not full. If the flight is full, the passenger is to be placed on a waiting list so that he will be placed on the flight if there are any cancellations. In the case of a cancellation, the passenger is to be deleted from the flight list if he is currently booked on the flight, and the first passenger from the waiting list (if any) is to be placed on the flight list. If the cancelled passenger is on the waiting list, he must be removed from it. Finally, in the case of an inquiry, a list of all flights on which the passenger is booked or waiting is to be printed.

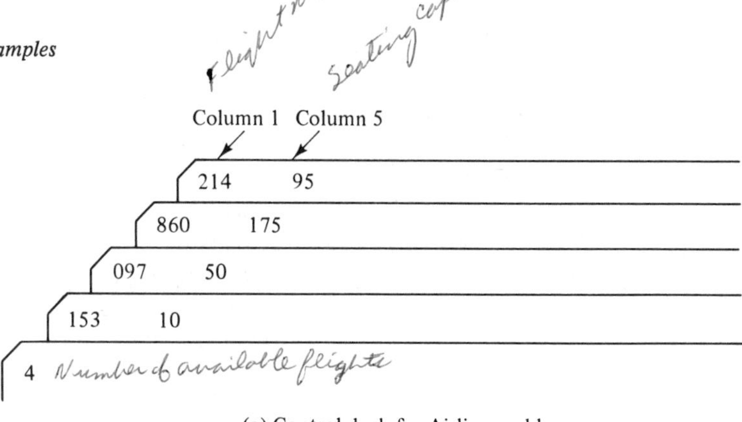

(a) Control deck for Airline problem.

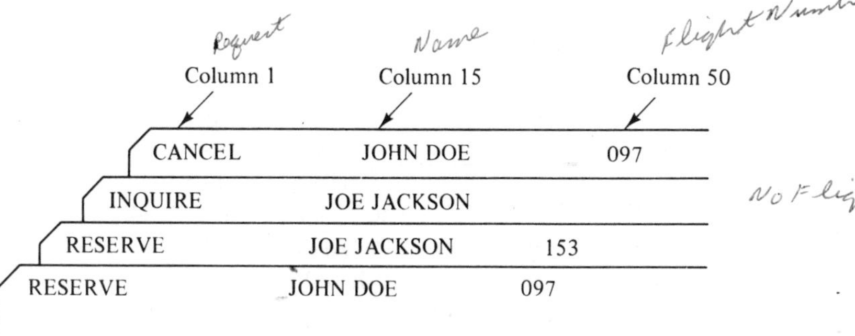

(b) Passenger request deck for Airline problem.

Figure 6.3.1.1.

Now that we have defined the actions to be taken for the various requests, we may consider the data structures which will be necessary. Clearly, two lists are required for each flight: a list of passengers currently booked on the flight and a waiting list for the flight. The passenger list has no restrictions as to where a passenger may be inserted or deleted. The waiting list, however, should be a queue so that if a cancellation occurs the first person on the waiting list will be the first to be given a seat on the flight. However, we must also have the capability of deleting a passenger from the middle of the waiting list (in case of a cancellation). It will also be necessary to keep a record of the capacity of each flight and of the number of people currently on the flight. We can thus declare the data structures for this program as follows:

```
DCL #FLIGHTS FIXED;

/*   structure for nodes in each of the lists   */
DCL 1 PASS_NODE BASED(P),
      2 NAME     CHAR(20),
      2 NEXT     PTR;
GET LIST(#FLIGHTS);
```

```
BLOCK:   BEGIN; /*   we declare a separate structure    */
                /*        for each of the flights       */
         DCL 1  FLIGHT(#FLIGHTS),
                2 FLTNO     CHAR(3),  /*    flight number        */
                2 CPCTY     FIXED,    /*    capacity of flight   */
                2 COUNT     FIXED,    /*    number of people     */
                                      /*    currently on flight  */
                2 FLTHD     PTR,      /*    pointer to first     */
                                      /*    passenger on flight  */
                                      /*         list            */
                2 WAITLIST,
                  (3 FRONT,           /*      queue for          */
                  3 REAR)   PTR;      /*    waiting list         */
```

Before proceeding to the program, let us consider what routines will be required for manipulating the lists. First, it is necessary to be able to locate the index of the structure representing the flight within the array FLIGHT given its flight number. We call the function which does this FIND and leave its coding as an exercise for the reader. The function accepts a three-character flight number as a parameter and returns the index in the array FLIGHT of the structure representing that flight. We will also need the routines INSERT and REMOVE to insert and remove an element from a queue. However, we will see shortly that these routines must be somewhat modified. Since elements will be eliminated from positions other than the front of the waiting queues and also from the flight lists, the DELAFTER routine will also be required.

The final decision that must be made relates to the structure of the passenger list. Since deletions can be made from either end or from within the list, our choice of a data structure should depend upon the ease with which other operations can be performed. Aside from deleting an element, the only operations needed are insertion and searching for a name within the list. Keeping the list in order by name will make searching more efficient in the case where a name is not present on the list (why?). However, keeping a sorted list will reduce the efficiency of every insertion.

We choose to make all insertions at the head of the list. The following additional routines are therefore needed: a routine SEARCH(LISTHD,NAME,PRED,FOUND) which accepts a pointer to the head of a list and the name of a passenger. Upon returning, PRED contains a pointer to the predecessor of the node containing the name NAME if the name is present in the list, and FOUND will be '1'B. If NAME is not present, then FOUND will be '0'B. A dummy node is stored at the beginning of each passenger list, so that the output parameter PRED of SEARCH can be used as an input argument to DELAFTER even if the desired node is first on the list. Such a technique is frequently used to make subroutines applicable to special cases. Similarly, a dummy node is stored at the head of each waiting list so that DELAFTER may be used to delete the first passenger on the waiting list. This means that the REMOVE routine for the queue must be altered since FRONT points to a node before the actual front of the queue. The EMPTY function for queues must also be modified to allow for a dummy node. The routine INSAFTER is also used. We now present the main program and the subroutine for the CANCEL request. The routines to handle reservations and inquiries are left as exercises for the reader.

```
AIRLINE:    PROC OPTIONS(MAIN);
                DCL #FLIGHTS            FIXED;
                DCL 1 PASS_NODE         BASED(P),
                      2 NAME            CHAR(30),
                      2 NEXT            PTR;
                DCL I                   FIXED,
                    COMMAND             CHAR(10)VAR,
                    NAM                 CHAR(30),
                    PRED                PTR,
                    (FOUND,FLAG)        BIT(1),
                    FLT                 CHAR(3);
                GET LIST(#FLIGHTS);

BLOCK:          BEGIN; /*   declare a separate structure for   */
                       /*            each flight               */
                DCL 1   FLIGHT(#FLIGHTS),
                        2 FLTNO             CHAR(3),
                        2 CPCTY             FIXED,
                        2 COUNT             FIXED,
                        2 FLTHD             PTR,
                        2 WAITLIST,
                          (3 FRONT,
                           3 REAR)          PTR;

                /*   initialize variables and lists    */
INITIALIZE:     DO I=1 TO #FLIGHTS;
                    GET EDIT(FLTNO(I),CPCTY(I))(COL(1),A(3),X(1),F(3));
                    /*   flight initially empty    */
                    COUNT(I)=0;
                    /*      insert dummy at head of each list      */
                    ALLOCATE PASS_NODE SET(PRED);
                    FLTHD(I)=PRED;
                    PRED->NAME='';
                    PRED->NEXT=NULL;

                    /*   insert dummy at front of each queue     */
                    ALLOCATE PASS_NODE SET(PRED);
                    FRONT(I),REAR(I)=PRED;
                    PRED->NAME='';
                    PRED->NEXT=NULL;
                END INITIALIZE;
                ON ENDFILE(SYSIN) STOP;
```

```
                /*      process requests from customers        */

CUSTOMER: DO WHILE('1'B);
                GET EDIT(COMMAND) (COL(1),A(10));
                PUT SKIP EDIT(COMMAND)(A);
                IF COMMAND='INQUIRE' THEN CALL INQUIRE;
                   ELSE IF COMMAND='RESERVE' THEN CALL RESERVE;
                      ELSE IF COMMAND='CANCEL' THEN CALL CANCEL;
                         ELSE PUT SKIP LIST('INVALID COMMAND');
          END CUSTOMER;


CANCEL:   PROC;
                DCL  I                        FIXED;
                GET EDIT(NAM,FLT)(COL(15),A(30),COL(50),A(3));
                PUT EDIT(NAM,FLT)(A,X(2));
                I=FIND(FLT);
                IF I=0 THEN DO;
                         PUT SKIP EDIT(FLT,'INVALID FLIGHT')
                                        (A,X(2));
                         RETURN;
                              END;
                CALL SEARCH(FLTHD(I),NAM,PRED,FOUND);

                IF FOUND THEN  /*   remove from flight list     */
                      DO;
                           CALL DELAFTER(PRED,NAM);
                           PUT  SKIP EDIT(NAM,
                                     'DELETED FROM FLIGHT',FLTNO(I))
                                                            (A,X(2));
                           IF ¬EMPTY(WAITLIST(I)) THEN
                /*   remove first passenger from queue       */
                /*            and place on flight            */
                                                        DO;
                                 NAM=REMOVE(WAITLIST(I));
                                 CALL INSAFTER(FLTHD(I),NAM);
                                 PUT SKIP EDIT(NAM,
                                       'NOW BOOKED ON FLIGHT',FLTNO(I))
                                                            (A,X(2));
                                                        END;
                                                 ELSE
                                 COUNT(I)=COUNT(I)-1;
                           RETURN;
                      END;
                CALL SEARCH(FRONT(I),NAM,PRED,FOUND);
```

```
        IF FOUND THEN /*   remove from waiting list   */
                DO;
                 CALL DELAFTER(PRED,NAM);
                 PUT SKIP EDIT
                   (NAM,'DELETED FROM WAITING LIST OF FLIGHT',
                                          FLTNO(I)) (A,X(2));
                END;
        RETURN;
     END CANCEL;

     /*  routines RESERVE and INQUIRE go here   */

     END BLOCK;
  END AIRLINE;
```

We leave the coding of the two other major routines, INQUIRE and RESERVE, as exercises for the reader. There are more efficient ways of programming the above example so that not so much time is spent in searching for names on lists. Some of these techniques will be examined in Section 9.4.

Example 6.3.2: Sparse Matrices

We now consider a second application of linked allocation using BASED and POINTER variables. As in the previous section, the main emphasis is on linked lists. Its implementation using BASED variables is of secondary importance. As exercises you are asked to implement the routines presented here using the array method of Chapter 5.

A ***matrix*** is a two-dimensional array. Figure 6.3.2.1 illustrates some matrices. Each matrix in that figure is a two dimensional array with m rows and n columns. The values of m and n for each matrix are shown. Matrices are used in many fields, including mathematics, economics, computer science, etc. For example, if a company has m customers and produces n items, the entry in row i column j could be used to represent the amount of item j to be shipped to customer i. There are a number of recognized operations defined on matrices, some of which will be illustrated in this section, and others in the exercises of the Exercise Manual.

Suppose we are programming a problem whose solution calls for the use of matrices. How can a matrix be represented in memory? The simplest and most obvious answer is, of course, to use a two-dimensional array. For example, we might code

```
     DCL (M,N)          FIXED;
     GET LIST(M,N);
  P: BEGIN;
        DCL A(M,N)      FIXED;
```

When the BEGIN block P is entered, storage for a two-dimensional array of M rows and N columns is allocated. Any element in the array can be referenced by A(I,J), where

$$A = \begin{bmatrix} 5 \end{bmatrix} \qquad m = 1, \; n = 1$$

(a)

$$B = \begin{bmatrix} 1 & 0 & 2 \\ -1 & 4 & 6 \end{bmatrix} \qquad m = 2, \; n = 3$$

(b)

$$C = \begin{bmatrix} 1 & 3 & 7 & 5 \end{bmatrix} \qquad m = 1, \; n = 4$$

(c)

$$D = \begin{bmatrix} 8 & 7 \\ 2 & 5 \\ 1 & 4 \end{bmatrix} \qquad m = 3, \; n = 2$$

(d)

$$E = \begin{bmatrix} 1 & 0 & 0 & 3 & 0 & 0 & 0 & 0 & 0 \\ 0 & 2 & 0 & 0 & 0 & 0 & 0 & 2 & 0 \\ 0 & 0 & 0 & 0 & 0 & 0 & 0 & 0 & 0 \\ 0 & 0 & 0 & 0 & 0 & 0 & 0 & 0 & 0 \\ 0 & 0 & 0 & -1 & 4 & 0 & 0 & 0 & 0 \\ 0 & 0 & 0 & 8 & 0 & 0 & 2 & 0 & 0 \\ 0 & 0 & 0 & 0 & 1 & 0 & 0 & 0 & 0 \end{bmatrix} \qquad m = 7, \; n = 9$$

(e)

Figure 6.3.2.1. Examples of matrices.

I represents the row number and J the column number of the element. Notice that nothing is assumed about the actual contents of the array except that they are FIXED numbers. M*N is the number of elements allocated. We say the matrix is of size M by N (sometimes written as M X N).

The representation of a matrix by an array is certainly satisfactory for small matrices. Very often, however, we deal with a matrix such as the one in Fig. 6.3.2.1(e), which contains mostly 0s. A matrix which is filled with mostly 0s is called a ***sparse matrix***. The actual amount of nonzero data is small compared with the amount of storage set aside for the matrix. Suppose that the matrix of Fig. 6.3.2.1(e) were 700 by 900 rather than 7 by 9, and the additional rows and columns were all 0. Such a matrix, if represented as a two-dimensional array, would exceed the storage capacity of most computers existing today. Yet since there are only nine nonzero data items in this matrix, there is surely some method of representing the matrix in fewer than 630,000 units of storage.

Let us see how a sparse matrix can be represented using linked allocation. We will keep in memory a list of only those elements which are nonzero, linked to each other in a way that describes their position in the large matrix. Thus if a position of the matrix is represented in the list, its value is given within a list node. If a position is not represented in the list, its value is 0. How should this list be organized? One way is as a single linear linked list consisting of all the nonzero elements of the first row, followed by all the nonzero elements of the second row, etc. Of course, since not every column is represented in a particular row, each node will also include an indication of the column in which the element appears. It will also be necessary to keep an indication of where a particular row ends. (This indication can consist of a special flag in the last node of each row, or an extra node at the end of each row with a zero value field.) This method has the drawback that the entire list would have to be searched each time a particular element is to be accessed. Also while an entire row can be accessed once its first element has been located, accessing a column is an entirely different matter. To access a column the entire list must be traversed until that column position is encountered in the last row. This is clearly inefficient. In addition, it does not mirror the two-dimensional nature of a matrix which implies that either a row or a column can be traversed once its first element has been accessed.

One possible solution is to keep a separate list for each row. This would certainly reduce the time necessary to access a particular element, since only a single smaller list (that of the row in question) would have to be searched, rather than a list of all the matrix elements. However, the problem of accessing a column remains. Keeping the matrix in column order rather than row order would merely transfer the problem from that of accessing a column to that of accessing a row.

To allow easy access to any row or column of the matrix, we let each nonzero matrix element appear on two lists, one for its row and one for its column. Thus, each node contains two pointers, one to the next element in its row and one to the next element in its column. In addition, each node contains fields for the row number, column number, and the value of its element. Thus a node is declared by

```
DCL 1 NODE        BASED(ND),
      2 ROW       FIXED,
      2 COL       FIXED,
      2 VAL       FIXED,
      2 NEXTROW   PTR,     /*  to next element in same column   */
      2 NEXTCOL   PTR;     /*    to next element in same row    */
```

Figure 6.3.2.2(a) depicts the fields of a sample node. Figure 6.3.2.2(c) illustrates the representation of the matrix of Fig. 6.3.2.2(b).

As with any linked list, some method of accessing the first element of each list in the matrix representation is required. This can be done in either of two ways. One method would be to keep two arrays of pointers, ROWFIRST and COLFIRST, where ROWFIRST(I) points to the first node in row I, and COLFIRST(I) points to the first node in column I.

An alternate method is to keep a dummy column (column 0) containing as many elements as there are rows. Each element in this dummy column points to the first element of its respective row. Similarly, a dummy row (row 0) exists containing as many elements as there are columns. Each element in this dummy row points to the first element of its respective column. Each node in these dummy lists serves as a header node for a row list or a column list. These header nodes may be recognized by a zero value in the column or row field respectively. Since each row and column has a header, they are

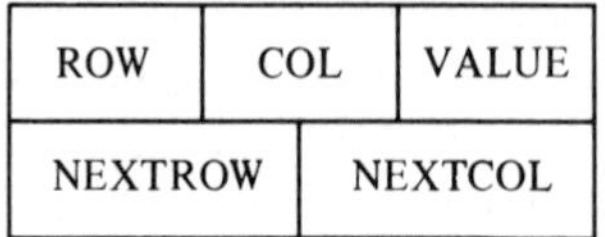

(a) Fields of a sample node.

$$\begin{pmatrix} 3 & 0 & 2 \\ -1 & 0 & 0 \\ 0 & 0 & 5 \end{pmatrix}$$

(b) Matrix in array format.

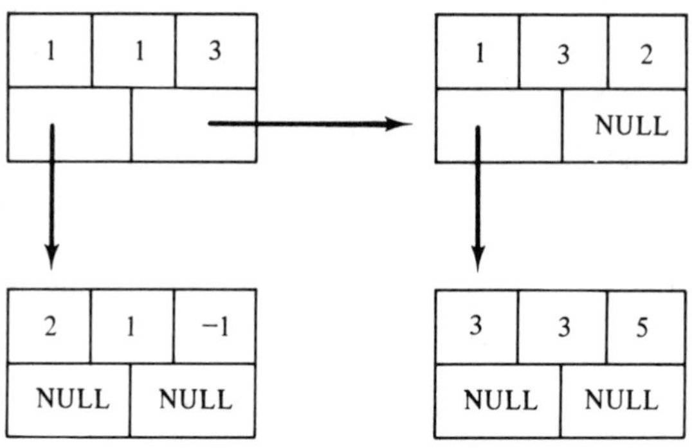

(c) Matrix using linked allocation.

Figure 6.3.2.2.

kept as circular lists. An external pointer points to a dummy element at row 0, column 0. Figure 6.3.2.3 illustrates this scheme. Figure 6.3.2.3(a) illustrates a 4 × 4 matrix and Fig. 6.3.2.3(b) illustrates its linked representation. Notice the dummy column on the left and the dummy row on the top, each element of which points to the first nonzero element of a row or column. Since row 1 consists of only 0s, it contains only the dummy node whose NEXTCOL field points to itself. Note also that the element pointed to by A serves as the header node of the matrix. Given A, it is possible to reach any node in the matrix. A structure in which nodes appear on more than one list and contain more than one pointer is called a ***multi-linked list***.

Before proceeding with some applications of this method, some comments on its use are appropriate. If the matrix of Fig. 6.3.2.3(a) were to be stored as a two-dimensional array, it would require 16 nodes of storage, each consisting of one field. Using the linked method depicted in Fig. 6.3.2.3(b), we require 16 nodes of storage, each consisting of five fields. By no stretch of the imagination could this latter method be considered more efficient than the former. Moreover, if we use the array method, a particular element can be accessed merely by referencing it; to access that same element in the linked method requires a rather elaborate traversal procedure, as we shall see shortly. Thus only

$$\begin{pmatrix} 0 & 0 & 0 & 0 \\ 0 & 2 & 0 & 3 \\ -2 & 4 & 0 & 0 \\ 0 & 0 & -1 & 8 \end{pmatrix}$$

(a) Matrix using array format.

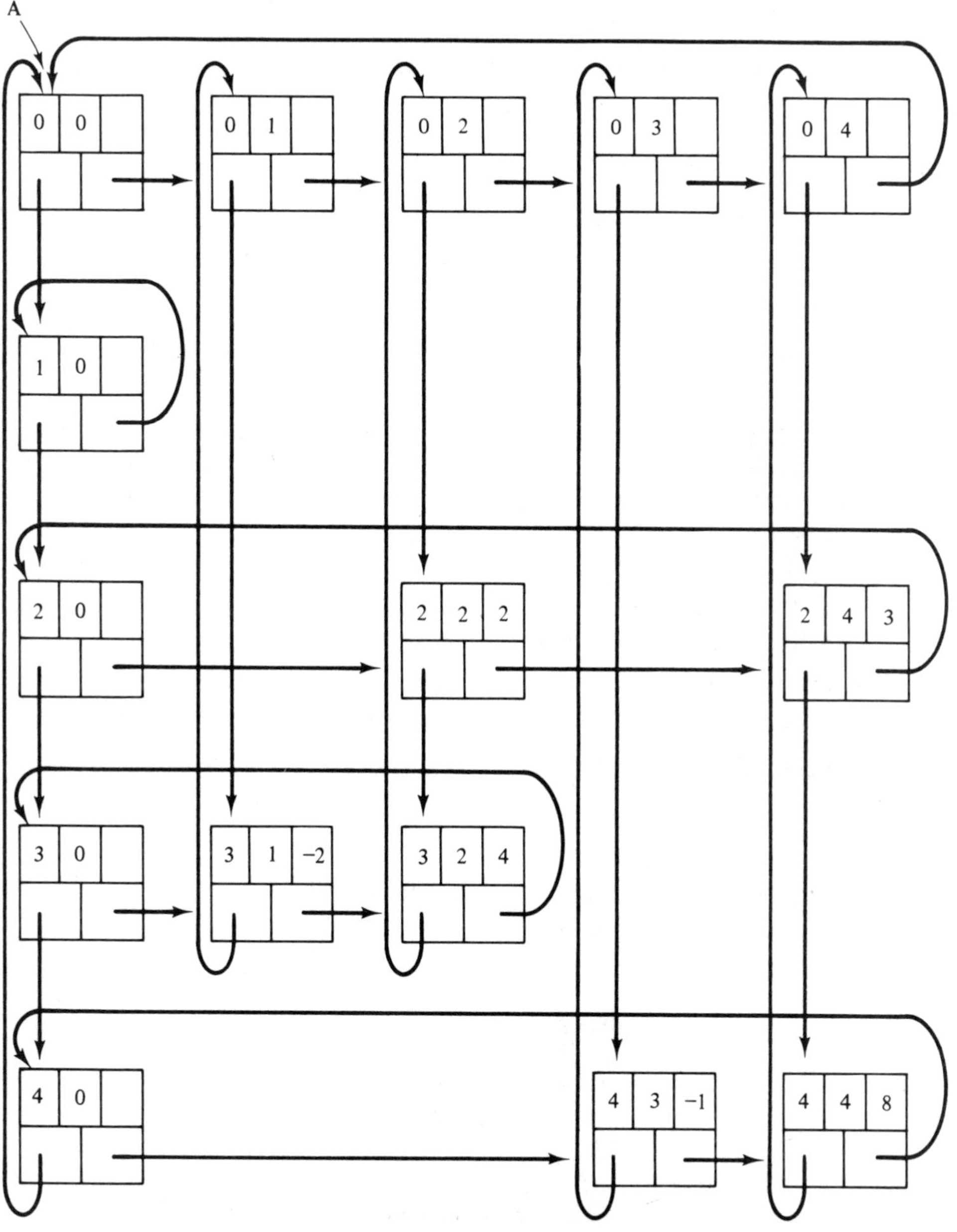

(b) Matrix using linked allocation.

Figure 6.3.2.3.

where the matrices are very large and sparse (relatively few nonzero entries) is it more efficient to use the linked allocation rather than the array implementation. All the routines written below are simpler to code when the matrix is stored as an array. Thus, while the methods and examples of this section apply to matrices of any size and any number of nonzero elements, applying them to the wrong types of matrices will seriously affect the speed and storage efficiency of the programs involved.

Let us now consider some transformations on matrices. An ***elementary row operation*** is defined as one of the following:

1. multiplying any row by a nonzero constant
2. interchanging any two rows
3. adding a multiple of one row to another

We consider each of these three operations in turn, and assume the following routines:

FINDABOVE(A,R,C). This routine accepts a pointer A to a matrix, a row number R, and a column number C. The function returns a pointer to the node in column C which immediately precedes the position where a node at row R and column C would be if it were present in the matrix.

INSERTAFTER(P,Q,X). This routine inserts a new node with value X into the same row as P–>NODE and the same column as Q–>NODE, immediately following P–>NODE in its row and Q–>NODE in its column.

DELETEAFTER(P,Q,X). This routine deletes the node pointed to by both P–>NEXTCOL and Q–>NEXTROW and places its value into X.

We present the routine FINDABOVE and leave the coding of the other two as exercises.

```
FINDABOVE: PROC(A,R,C)    RETURNS(PTR);
              DCL (A,P,Q,Z)          PTR,
                  (R,C)              FIXED;

           /*  find pointer to dummy node of column C  */
              P=A;
              DO WHILE(P->COL<C);
                  P=P->NEXTCOL;
              END;

          /*  P now points to dummy node of column C   */
          /*   advance P through column C until row R  */
          /*              is reached or passed         */
              Q=P;
              Z=P->NEXTROW;
```

```
      DO WHILE(P->ROW<R & Z->ROW ¬=0);
      Q=P;
      P=P->NEXTROW;
      Z=P->NEXTROW;
    END;

    IF P->ROW>=R THEN RETURN(Q);
                 ELSE RETURN(P);
  END FINDABOVE;
```

1. *Multiplying a row by a nonzero constant.*

If the array representation is used, the routine is trivial. We intentionally do not use array cross sections in these routines so that the looping process is made explicit.

```
MULT:   PROC(A,ROW,CONST);
            /*   multiply row number ROW by    */
            /*      the constant CONST ¬=0     */
          DCL (A(*,*) ,ROW,CONST,J)    FIXED;
LOOP:     DO J=1 TO HBOUND(A,2);
            A(ROW,J)=A(ROW,J)*CONST;
          END LOOP;
          RETURN;
        END MULT;
```

If the linked representation is used, then there are some minor changes necessary in the looping mechanism.

```
MULT2:  PROC(A,ROW,CONST);
          DCL (A,ABOVE,Q)              PTR,
              (ROW,CONST)              FIXED;

            /*        A points to the head of the matrix     */
          ABOVE=FINDABOVE(A,ROW,0);
            /*       ABOVE points to the element above       */
            /*          row ROW in the dummy column          */
          Q=ABOVE->NEXTROW;
          Q=Q->NEXTCOL; /*  Q is first nonzero entry in      */
                        /*               row ROW             */

LOOP:     DO WHILE(Q->COL>0); /* test for end of row         */
            /*                 multiply element              */
            Q->VAL=Q->VAL * CONST;
            /*              advance to next column           */
            Q=Q->NEXTCOL;
          END LOOP;
          RETURN;
        END MULT2;
```

Notice that there are no insertions or deletions in MULT2, since multiplying by a nonzero constant cannot change a nonzero entry to 0 or vice versa. Suppose we wished to multiply a row by 0. No changes are necessary in MULT (except that the operation is no longer an elementary row operation). MULT2, however, must be modified considerably since an entire row now becomes 0 and each of its elements must therefore be removed from the list. We could code MULT0 as follows:

```
MULT0:  PROC(A,ROW);  /*   since CONST is 0, it need not    */
                      /*         be a parameter             */
          DCL (A,ABOVE,Q,P)                     PTR,
              (ROW,X)                           FIXED;
          ABOVE=FINDABOVE(A,ROW,0);
          Q=ABOVE->NEXTROW;
          P=Q->NEXTCOL;
LOOP:     DO WHILE(P->COL>0);
             ABOVE=FINDABOVE(A,ROW,P->COL);
          /*  no multiplication is necessary; delete the element.  */
              CALL DELETEAFTER(Q,ABOVE,X);
              P=P->NEXTCOL;
          END LOOP;
          RETURN;
        END MULT0;
```

Of course MULT2 and MULT0 could be combined into a single routine.

2. *Interchanging two rows.*

If a matrix is stored as a two-dimensional array, a routine to interchange two rows is straightforward:

```
INT:    PROC(A,ROW1,ROW2);
          DCL (A(*,*), ROW1,ROW2,J,HOLD)   FIXED;
LOOP      DO J=1 TO HBOUND(A,2);
              HOLD=A(ROW1,J);
              A(ROW1,J)=A(ROW2,J);
              A(ROW2,J) =HOLD;
          END LOOP;
          RETURN;
        END INT;
```

Storing the matrix as a multi-linked list requires a choice between two options. Nodes in ROW1 and ROW2 could actually be allocated and freed as necessary so that the interchange is made. A second option is to keep the two rows intact, adjusting the column pointers to reflect the interchange. We select this second option. Since interchanging two rows is a symmetric operation, we will assume without loss of generality that ROW1 < ROW2.

The rows ROW1 and ROW2 are traversed in parallel. As the algorithm proceeds from one column to the next in each of ROW1 and ROW2, one of three conditions may occur:

(a) There is an element in a particular column of ROW2, but the corresponding element in ROW1 is 0. The element must be moved from ROW2 to ROW1.

(b) There is an element in a particular column of ROW1, but the corresponding element in ROW2 is 0. The element must be moved from ROW1 to ROW2.

(c) There are elements in a particular column of both ROW1 and ROW2. The element of ROW1 must be interchanged with that of ROW2.

Figures 6.3.2.4(a), (b), and (c) depict (for an arbitrary column J) the situations after the appropriate action is taken. In Figure 6.3.2.4(a) the notation (ROW1=>) means that a nonzero element of ROW1 and column J would belong between two elements of column J at the point indicated, and similarly for the notation (ROW2=>) in Fig. 6.3.2.4(b). (Note that because complete rows are being moved, there is no need to adjust the NEXTCOL fields. We begin our loop at the first nonzero column and halt when we reach the dummy column.)

```
INT2:       PROC(A,ROW1,ROW2);
              DCL (A,ABOVE1,ABOVE2,R1,R2,TEMP,T) PTR,
                  (ROW1,ROW2,J)                  FIXED;
              R1=FINDABOVE(A,ROW1,0);
              R1=R1->NEXTROW;
              R2= FINDABOVE(A,ROW2,0);
              R2=R2->NEXTROW;
              R1=R1->NEXTCOL;
              R2=R2->NEXTCOL;

         /*   R1 and R2 now point to the first nonzero elements in      */
         /*        their respective rows (ROW1 and ROW2)                */
LOOP:         DO WHILE('1'B); /*  test for completion inside loop       */
ONEZERO:        DO WHILE(R1->COL¬=R2->COL);
                /*   we have at least one zero     */
                  IF (R1->COL<R2->COL) & (R1->COL>0)    |
                      /*    ROW1 is nonzero and ROW2 is zero            */
                    R2->COL=0      /*    reached end of ROW2            */
                                 THEN DO;
                TEMP=RI->NEXTROW;
                IF (TEMP->ROW< ROW2)&(TEMP->ROW 0)
                                            THEN SWAP1:DO;
                   /*         If R1 and R2 are not adjacent, then          */
                   /*  move element at R1 to R2. See Fig. 6.3.2.4(b)       */
                       J=R1->COL;
                       ABOVE1=FINDABOVE(A,ROW1,J);
                       ABOVE2=FINDABOVE(A,ROW2,J);
                       ABOVE1->NEXTROW=R1->NEXTROW;
                       R1->NEXTROW=ABOVE2->NEXTROW;
                       ABOVE2->NEXTROW=R1;
                                                   END SWAP1;
                     R1->ROW=ROW2;
```

```
     /*   advance R1 to next column     */
        R1=R1->NEXTCOL;
                                           END;
                                    ELSE  DO;
        J=R2->COL;
        ABOVE1=FINDABOVE(A,ROW1,J);
        TEMP=ABOVE1->NEXTROW;
        IF TEMP->ROW<ROW2 THEN SWAP2: DO;
   /*       If R1 and R2 are not adjacent, then          */
   /*  move element at R2 to R1. See Fig. 6.3.2.4(a).  */
           ABOVE2=FINDABOVE(A,ROW2,J);
           ABOVE2->NEXTROW=R2->NEXTROW;
           R2->NEXTROW=ABOVE1->NEXTROW;
           ABOVE1->NEXTROW=R2;
                                              END SWAP2;
        R2->ROW=ROW1;
        /*   advance R2 to next column     */
        R2=R2->NEXTCOL;
                                            END;
   END ONEZERO;
    /*    at this point R1 and R2 point to the same column   */
    /*                  swap R1 with R2                       */
    /*                  see Fig. 6.3.2.4(c)                   */
   J=R1->COL;
   ABOVE1=FINDABOVE(A,ROW1,J);
   ABOVE2=FINDABOVE(A,ROW2,J);
   TEMP=R2->NEXTROW;
   ABOVE1->NEXTROW=R2;
   T=R1->NEXTROW;
   IF T->ROW<ROW2
            /*   rows are not adjacent    */
                          R2->NEXTROW=R1->NEXTROW;
                     ELSE R2->NEXTROW=R1;
   ABOVE2->NEXTROW=R1;
   R1->NEXTROW=TEMP;
   R1->ROW=ROW2;
   R2->ROW=ROW1;
/*                  check if finished                       */
   IF R1->COL=0        /*  R1 and R2 both point to    */
                       /*       dummy column          */
                  THEN RETURN;
/*                  advance R1 and R2                       */
   R1=R1->NEXTCOL;
   R2=R2->NEXTCOL;
  END LOOP;
END INT2;
```

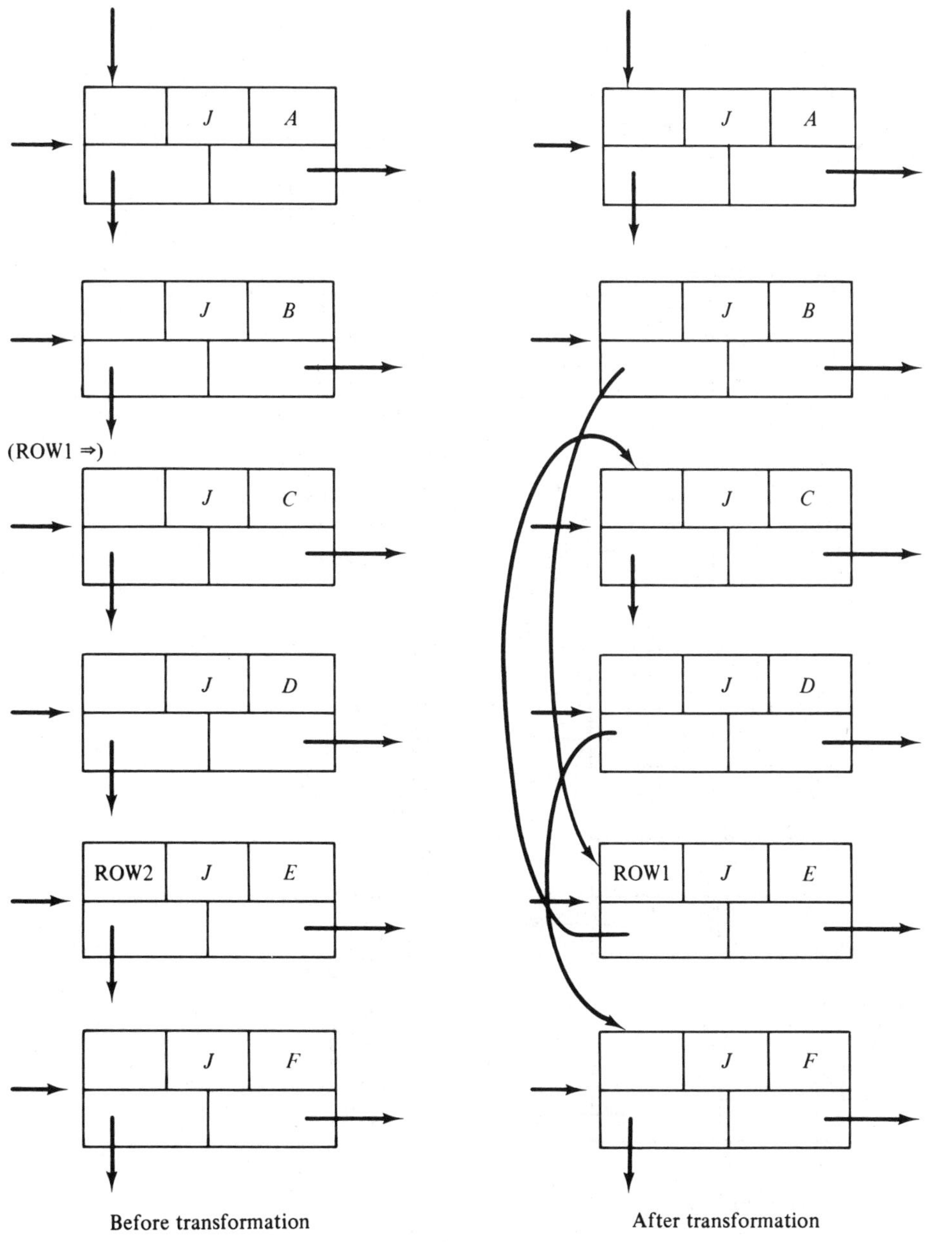

(a) ROW1 = 0 and ROW 2 ≠ 0.

Figure 6.3.2.4.

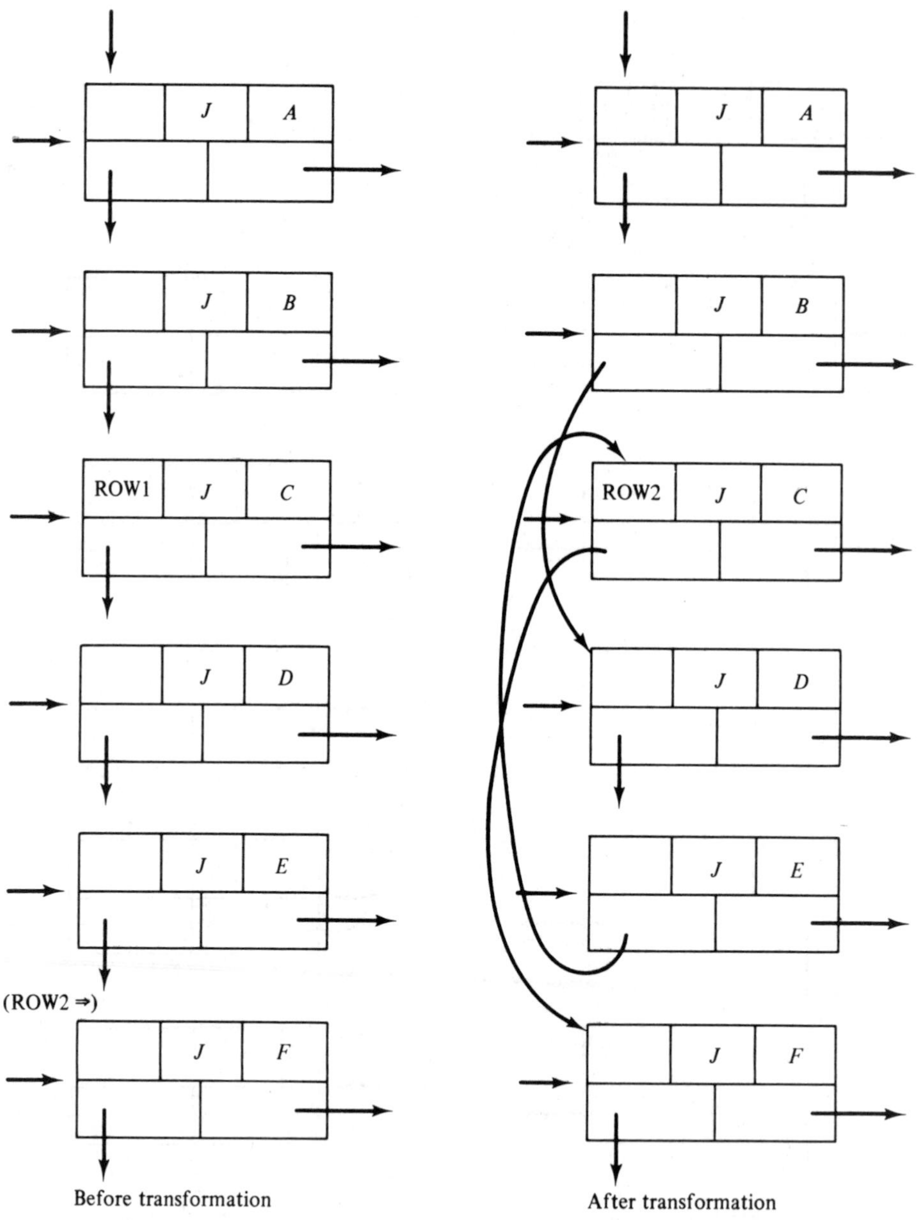

(b) ROW2 = 0, ROW1 ≠ 0.

Figure 6.3.2.4. *(cont.)*

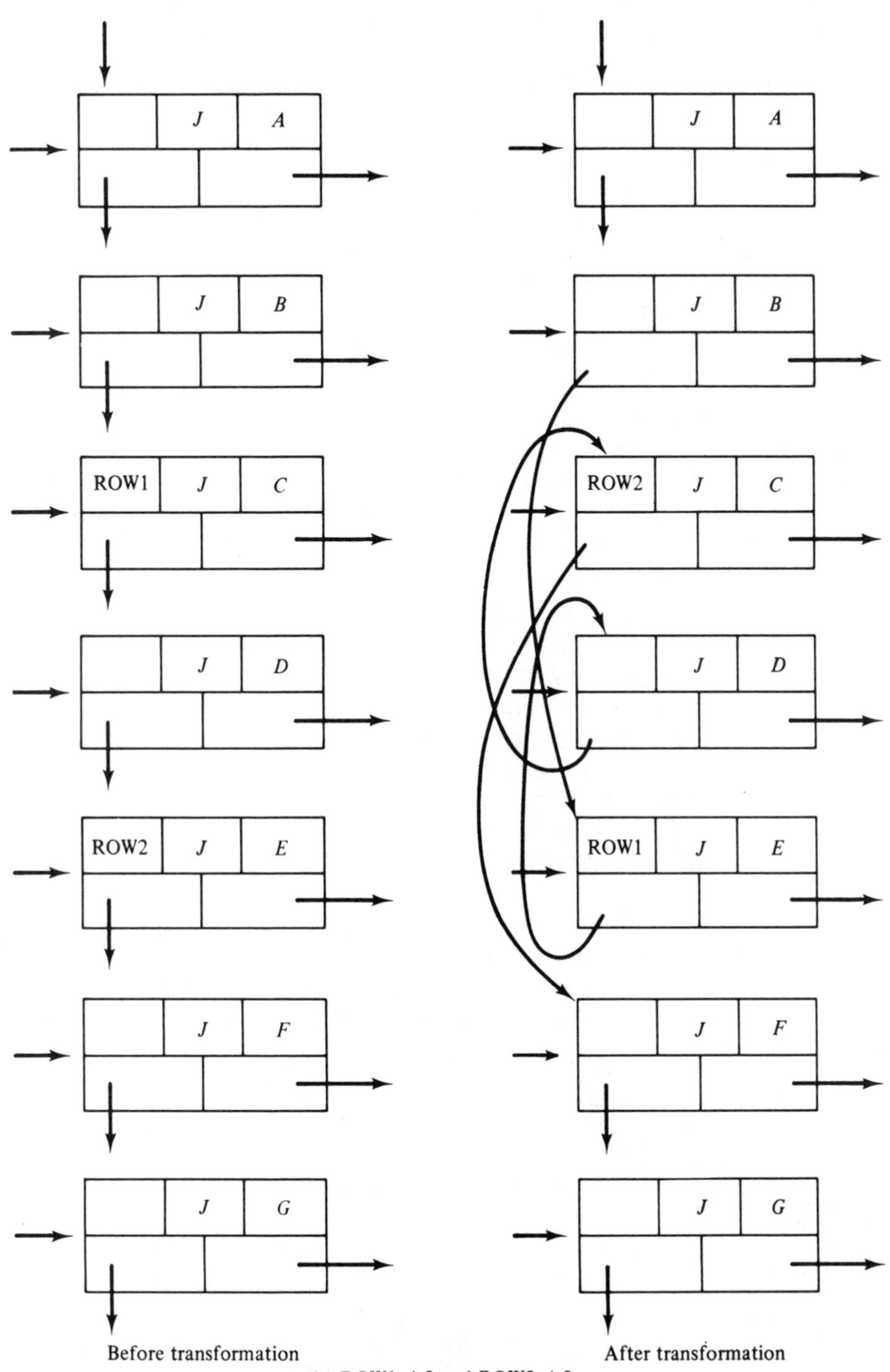

Before transformation After transformation

(c) ROW1 ≠ 0 and ROW2 ≠ 0.

Figure 6.3.2.4. (*cont.*)

3. *Adding a multiple of one row to another*

The routine which handles the case where the matrix is stored as an array is straightforward.

```
MULTPLE:  PROC(A,ROW1,ROW2,CONST);
          /*  replace ROW1 by ROW1+CONST*ROW2     */
             DCL (A(*,*),ROW1,ROW2,CONST,J)      FIXED;
LOOP:        DO J=1 TO HBOUND(A,2);
                A(ROW1,J) =A(ROW1,J)  +  CONST*A(ROW2,J);
             END LOOP;
             RETURN;
          END MULTPLE;
```

In the case of the matrix stored as a multi-linked list, both rows are again traversed in parallel. As each element of ROW2 is reached, R1 is advanced to the corresponding column in ROW1. If such an element exists, its value is adjusted; and if it now becomes 0, it is deleted from the list. If such a column element does not exist, a new node with the appropriate value is created.

```
MULTPLE2:  PROC(A,ROW1,ROW2,CONST);
              DCL (A,R1,R2,Q,ABOVE)             PTR,
                    (ROW1,ROW2,CONST,X)         FIXED;
              IF CONST=0 THEN RETURN;
              R1=FINDABOVE(A,ROW1,0);
              R2=FINDABOVE(A,ROW2,0);
              Q=R1–>NEXTROW;
              R1=Q–>NEXTCOL;
              R2=R2–>NEXTROW;
              R2=R2–>NEXTCOL;

           /*  traverse ROW2   */

LOOP:         DO WHILE(R2–>COL > 0);
                 DO WHILE(R1–>COL < R2–>COL  &  R1–>COL ¬=0);
                   /*   corresponding element of ROW2 is 0    */
                   /*                advance R1               */
                    Q=R1;
                    R1=R1–>NEXTCOL;
                 END;

                 IF R1–>COL=R2–>COL THEN  /*  matching columns   */
MATCHCOL:                   DO;
                    R1–>VAL=R1–>VAL  +  CONST*R2–>VAL;
                    IF R1–>VAL=0 THEN      /*     delete node      */
                                        DO;
                          ABOVE=FINDABOVE(A,ROW1, R1–>COL);
                          CALL DELETEAFTER(Q,ABOVE,X);
                                        END;
```

```
                    /*  update R1 and R2    */
                    R1=Q->NEXTCOL;
                    R2=R2->NEXTCOL;
                        END MATCHCOL;
                                        ELSE   /*  insert new element   */
NEWELT:                 DO;
                    ABOVE=FINDABOVE(A,ROW1,R2->COL);
                    CALL INSERTAFTER(Q,ABOVE,R2->VAL*CONST);
                    Q=Q->NEXTCOL;
                    R1=Q->NEXTCOL;
                    R2=R2->NEXTCOL;
                        END NEWELT;

            END LOOP;
            RETURN;
          END MULTPLE2;
```

6.4. Summary of Storage Classes in PL/I

In this section we review the highlighting features of the various storage classes of PL/I. Recall from Chapter 3 that namescoping and storage class of a variable are distinct issues. ***Namescoping*** refers to those points within a program in which a name may be referenced. The rules for namescoping may be summarized by the following:

1. If A is declared in a block, then the scope of A is that block.
2. If the outermost block in which A is used contains no declaration for A, then the scope of A is the outermost block of the external routine in which A appears.

Once a scope for A is opened in a block, A may be referenced from any point within that block, or from any other block which is internal to it. Of course, an internal block may open a new scope for A, in which case the old scope is stacked. A scope is closed when the block in which it was opened is exited. Reread Section 3.4 for a more complete discussion of the rules of namescoping.

Within a variable's namescope, various attributes are assigned to it, either explicitly or by default. One of these attributes is the ***storage class attribute***, which governs the method by which storage is allocated to the variable. This is a completely distinct concept from that of namescoping. Storage may not exist for a variable although it may be possible to refer to the variable. Similarly, storage may exist for a variable, yet a reference to it may be illegal.

There are two types of storage classes: ***static*** and ***dynamic***. The storage class of a variable is said to be ***static*** if storage is allocated before program execution begins and freed after program execution ends. If storage is allocated and freed from a variable during program execution, the variable's storage class is ***dynamic***. PL/I allows variables to have static storage (called STATIC) or one of three types of dynamic storage (called AUTOMATIC, CONTROLLED, and BASED). We consider each of these in turn.

A variable A may be given the STATIC storage class attribute by a statement such as

```
DCL  A  STATIC  FIXED;
```

In this case storage is allocated to A before the start of program execution and is not freed until the completion of program execution. If the above declaration appears in a subroutine, A is a local variable of that subroutine and can be referenced only from within the subroutine, although its storage will remain allocated and it will retain its value between calls. A STATIC variable declared with the INITIAL attribute will be initialized only once, at the start of program execution when storage is allocated to it. Even if its declaration appears in a subroutine, a STATIC variable will not be reinitialized on each call to the subroutine.

Consider the following example: A ***random number generator*** is a routine which computes a set of numbers which are randomly distributed between specific bounds. The initial input to this routine is called the ***seed***. Suppose we wish to write a random number generator to return a random number between 0 and 99,999. For the first call a seed is input to the generator; each subsequent call uses the previous random number as its seed. The method used in the following example is known as the ***mid-square method***, which squares the seed and extracts the middle five digits.

```
RANDOM: PROC RETURNS(FIXED);
            DCL X   STATIC   FIXED INIT(-1),
                Y            FIXED(10);
            IF   X=-1  THEN GET LIST(X);
            Y=X*X;      /*        square X          */
            Y=Y/1000;   /*   delete 3 trailing digits  */
            Y=MOD(Y,100000);
                        /*   delete 2 leading digits   */
            X=Y;
            RETURN(X);
        END RANDOM;
```

In the above example the function would be invoked by J=RANDOM;. Before the start of program execution, storage is allocated to X and is initialized to –1. Upon the first call to RANDOM the value of X is –1, so that X is read from a data card. This transmits the initial seed to the function. After the seed has been transmitted, the function proceeds with its recomputation of X based on this seed value. On each subsequent call, however, the test of X=–1 fails because X retains its value from the previous call. Thus no data is read and X is recomputed based on its previous value. However, by the rules for namescoping, X may be referenced only from within RANDOM.

In addition to the STATIC storage class, PL/I supports three dynamic storage classes. A variable is given the AUTOMATIC storage class either by default or by a statement such as

```
DCL A AUTOMATIC FIXED;
```

Storage for A is allocated upon entry to the block which opens the scope for A and is freed when that block is exited.

Let us reconsider the following example from Section 3.5. Suppose we wish to allocate space for an array of size N, where N is to be read from a data card. The code

```
DCL N  FIXED;
GET LIST(N);
DCL A(N) FIXED;
```

will produce an error. Because the two declarations are in the same block and because both N and A have the AUTOMATIC storage class, storage will be allocated to both N and A upon entry to the containing block. At that point, however, no value has yet been assigned to N. The correct version is

```
     DCL  N FIXED;
     GET  LIST(N);
B:  BEGIN;
       DCL  A(N)  FIXED;
```

Here again, both N and A have the AUTOMATIC storage class. However, storage is allocated to N before storage is allocated to A since the block which opens the scope for N is entered before the block which opens the scope for A. Thus storage for N will be allocated, and the GET LIST statement will be executed. When the block B is entered, storage will be allocated to A. But at this point the variable N has already been initialized, so that the proper number of elements are allocated to A.

Because a reference to an undeclared variable in an internal block is a reference to a variable declared in a surrounding block, it is usually a good idea to declare all local variables in subroutines so that subroutine calls do not affect the values of variables in the calling procedure unless they are explicitly passed as parameters.

The AUTOMATIC storage class is usually used for variables which are local to a block and hence are declared in that block.

A variable may be given the CONTROLLED storage class by a statement such as

```
DCL A CONTROLLED  FIXED;
```

or

```
DCL A CTL              FIXED;
```

Storage for A is allocated by the statement

```
ALLOCATE A;
```

and is freed by the statement

```
FREE A;
```

If upon allocation a previous copy of A already exists, that copy is pushed onto a stack and the new allocation of A becomes the current copy. Similarly, when the current copy of A is freed, the copy of A on top of the stack (if any) is popped and becomes the current copy. The ALLOCATION function can be used to determine if any (and, under some implementations, how many) copies of A exist.

If A is to be an array, then the bounds can be specified in the DECLARE statement as in

```
DCL  A(10) CTL     FIXED;
ALLOCATE  A;
```

or in the ALLOCATE statement as in

```
DCL  A(*)  CTL     FIXED;
GET LIST(N);
ALLOCATE A(N);
```

As mentioned in Section 3.5, the CONTROLLED storage class is merely an implementation of a stack. Reread the section for the details.

A variable is given the BASED storage class by a statement such as

```
DCL  A  BASED(P)  FIXED;
```

An unqualified reference to A is a reference to the location specified by the POINTER variable P. A is a template for the storage area being referenced. The POINTER variable P can obtain its value either by assigning the address of some other variable to it (e.g., the ADDR function) or by a statement such as ALLOCATE A SET(P); in which a specific area in memory is allocated and its address assigned to P. The BASED storage class is frequently used in list processing applications and in those cases where the overhead of moving data is significant. For the details of the BASED storage class, reread Sections 6.1 and 6.2.

Bibliography and References

BASED storage is discussed in PL/I manuals and texts such as (Bates and Douglas, 1975), (Hughes, 1973), and (Pollack and Sterling, 1976). List processing using BASED storage is also discussed in (Tremblay and Sorenson, 1976), (IBM, 1971), (IBM, 1972A), and (IBM, 1972B).

Methods for storing sparse matrices and algorithms for manipulating them may be found in (Knuth, 1973A) and (Pfaltz, 1977).

chapter 7

trees and graphs

In this chapter we focus our attention on two data structures which have been found to be extremely useful in many applications: trees and graphs. We shall define these data structures and show how they can be represented in PL/I and how they can be applied to solving a wide variety of problems.

7.1. Binary Trees

A ***binary tree*** is a finite set of elements which is either empty or contains a single element called the ***root*** of the tree and whose remaining elements are partitioned into two disjoint subsets, each of which is itself a binary tree. These two subsets are called the ***left*** and ***right subtrees*** of the original tree. Each element of a binary tree is called a ***node*** of the tree.

A conventional method of picturing a binary tree is shown in Fig. 7.1.1. This tree consists of nine nodes with A as its root. Its left subtree is rooted at B, and its right subtree is rooted at C. This is indicated by the two branches emanating from A, to B on the left and to C on the right. The absence of a branch indicates an empty subtree. For example, the left subtree of the binary tree rooted at C and the right subtree of the binary tree rooted at E are both empty. The binary trees rooted at D, G, H, and I have empty right and left subtrees.

Figure 7.1.2 illustrates some structures which are not binary trees. Be sure that you understand why each of them is not a binary tree as defined above.

If *n1* is the root of a binary tree and *n2* is the root of its left or right subtree, then *n1* is said to be the ***father*** of *n2* and *n2* is said to be the ***left*** or ***right son*** of *n1*. A node which has no sons (such as D, G, H, or I of Fig. 7.1.1) is called a ***leaf***. Node *n1* is an ***ancestor*** of node *n2* (and *n2* is a ***descendant*** of *n1*) if *n1* is either the father of *n2* or the father of some ancestor of *n2*. For example, in the tree of Fig. 7.1.1, A is an ancestor of G and H is a descendant of C but E is neither an ancestor nor a descendant of C. A node *n2* is a ***left descendant*** of node *n1* if *n2* is either the left son of *n1* or a descendant of the left son of *n1*. A ***right descendant*** may be similarly defined. Two nodes are ***brothers*** if they are left and right sons of the same father.

The ***level*** of a node in a binary tree may be defined as follows: The root of the tree

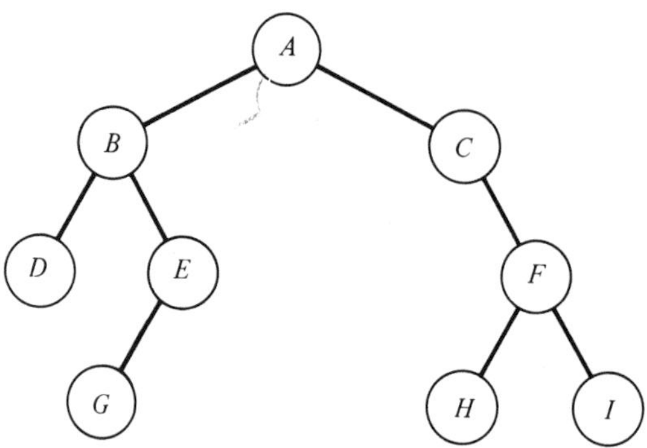

Figure 7.1.1. A binary tree.

has level 0 and the level of any other node in the tree is 1 more than the level of its father. For example, in the binary tree of Fig. 7.1.1, node E is at level 2 and H is at level 3. A ***complete binary tree of level n*** is one in which each node of level n is a leaf and in which each node of level less than n has nonempty left and right subtrees. Figure 7.1.3 illustrates a complete binary tree of level 3. (Other texts define the term "complete binary tree" differently to refer to a type of tree which we introduce in Section 7.3.2. However, we use this definition consistently in this text.)

One method of viewing a binary tree is to regard each node as having three elementary fields. *info*(*node*) references the information which is stored in a particular node, while *left*(*node*) and *right*(*node*) reference pointers to the roots of the left and right subtrees of the binary tree rooted at *node*. Of course if a left or right subtree is empty, the corresponding pointer is null.

In constructing a binary tree, the operations *maketree, setleft*, and *setright* are useful. *maketree*(x) creates a new binary tree consisting of a single node with information field x. An algorithm for this function is the following:

```
p=getnode;
info(p) =x;
left(p) =null;
right(p) =null;
return(p);
```

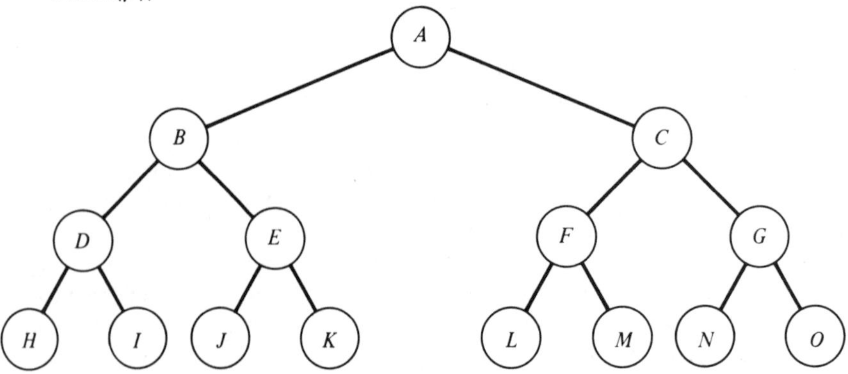

Figure 7.1.3. A complete binary tree of level 3.

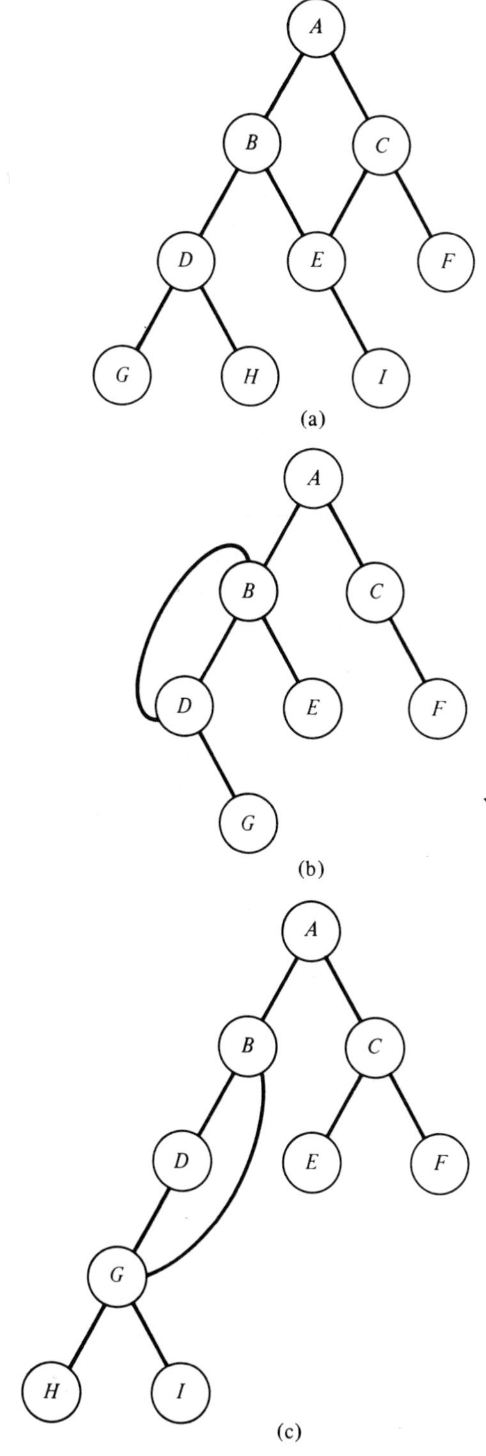

Figure 7.1.2. Structures which are not binary trees.

setleft(p,x) accepts a pointer *p* to a binary tree node with no left son. It creates a new left son of *node(p)* with information field *x*. An algorithm for *setleft* follows.

```
if left(p)¬=null then do;
   print('illegal setleft operation');
   stop;
                  end;
q=maketree(x);
left(p)=q;
```

setright(p,x) is analogous to *setleft* except that it creates a right son of *node(p)*.

Applications of Binary Trees

A binary tree is a useful data structure when two-way decisions must be made at each point in a process. For example, suppose we wanted to find all duplicates in a list of numbers. One way of doing this is to compare each number with all those that precede it. However, this involves a large number of comparisons. The number of comparisons can be reduced by using a binary tree. The first number is read and placed in a node which is established as the root of a binary tree with empty left and right subtrees. Each successive number in the list is then compared to the number in the root. If it matches, we have a duplicate. If it is smaller, the process is repeated with the left subtree, and if it is larger, the process is repeated with the right subtree. This continues until either a duplicate is found or an empty subtree is reached. The number is then placed into a new node at that position in the tree. An algorithm for doing this follows.

```
   /*    read the first number and insert it into    */
   /*          a single-node binary tree             */
read (number);
tree=maketree(number);
do while (there are numbers left in the input);
   read (number);
   p,q=tree;
   do while (number¬=info(p) & q¬=null);
      p=q;
      if number<info(p) then q=left(p);
                        else q=right(p);
   end;
   if number=info(p) then print (number,'is a duplicate');
   /*    insert number to the right or left of p     */
         else if number<info(p) then setleft(p,number);
                                else setright(p,number);
end;
```

Figure 7.1.4 illustrates the tree which would be constructed from the input

14 15 4 9 7 18 3 5 16 4 20 17 9 14 5

The output would indicate that 4, 9, 14, and 5 are duplicates.

Another common operation is to ***traverse*** a binary tree, that is, to pass through the tree, enumerating each of its nodes once. We may simply wish to print the contents of each node as we enumerate it, or we may wish to process it in some other fashion. In either case, we speak of ***visiting*** the nodes of a binary tree.

The order in which the nodes of a linear list are visited is clearly from first to last. However, there is no such "natural" linear order for the nodes of a tree. Thus different orderings are used for traversal in different cases. We shall define three of these traversal methods. The methods will all be defined recursively so that traversing a binary tree involves visiting the root and traversing its left and right subtrees. The only difference among the methods is the order in which these three operations are performed. In each of these methods, nothing need be done to traverse an empty binary tree.

To traverse a nonempty binary tree in ***preorder*** (also known as ***depth-first order***), we perform the following three operations:

1. Visit the root.
2. Traverse the left subtree in preorder.
3. Traverse the right subtree in preorder.

To traverse a nonempty binary tree in ***inorder*** or ***symmetric order***:

1. Traverse the left subtree in inorder.
2. Visit the root.
3. Traverse the right subtree in inorder.

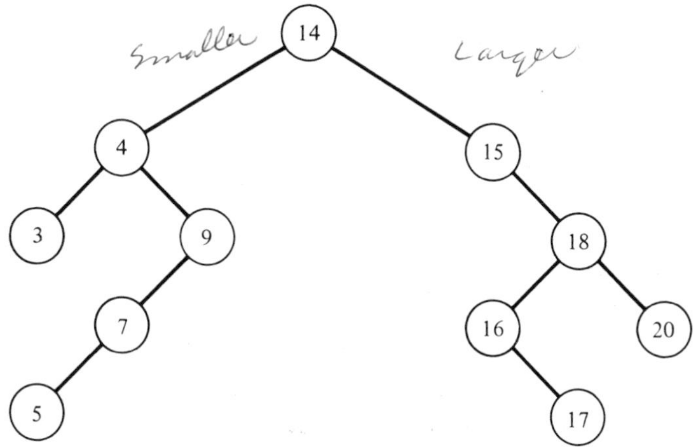

Figure 7.1.4. A binary tree constructed for finding duplicates.

To traverse a nonempty binary tree in ***postorder***:

1. Traverse the left subtree in postorder.
2. Traverse the right subtree in postorder.
3. Visit the root.

Figure 7.1.5 illustrates two binary trees and their traversals in preorder, inorder, and postorder.

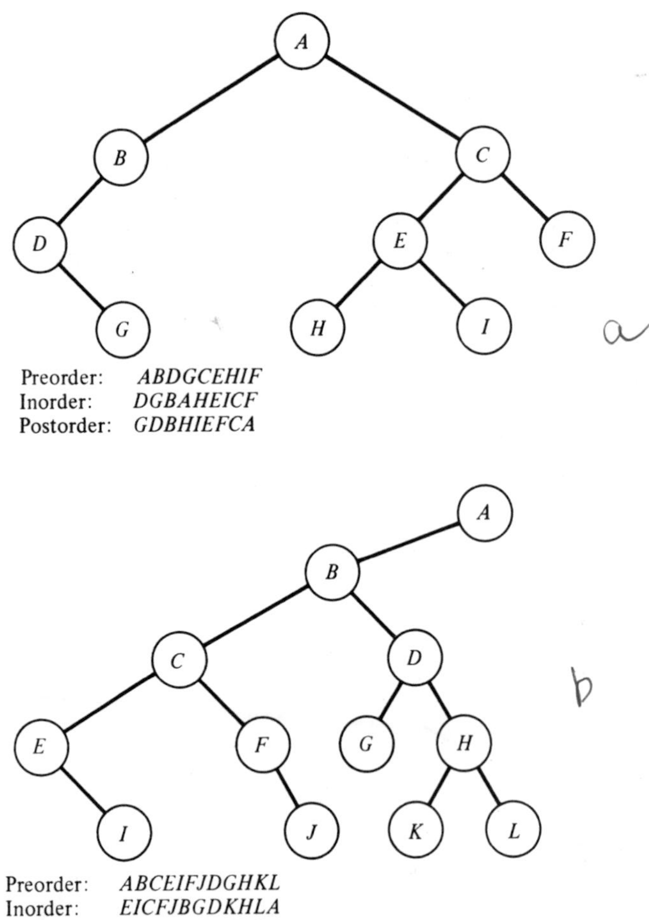

Figure 7.1.5. Binary trees and their traversals.

Most algorithms or processes which use binary trees proceed in two phases. The first phase builds a binary tree, and the second traverses the tree. As an example of such an algorithm, consider the following sorting method. Given a list of numbers punched on cards, we wish to print them in ascending order. As we read the numbers, they can be inserted into a binary tree such as the one of Fig. 7.1.4. However, unlike the previous algorithm which was used to find duplicates, duplicate values are also placed in the tree. When a number is compared to the contents of a node in the tree, a left branch is taken if the number is smaller than the contents of the node and a right branch if it is greater than or equal to the contents of the node. Thus if the input list is

14,15,4,9,7,18,3,5,16,4,20,17,9,14,5

the binary tree of Fig. 7.1.6 is produced. Such a binary tree has the property that the contents of each node in the left subtree of a node *n* are less than the contents of *n* and the contents of each node in the right subtree of *n* are greater than or equal to the contents of *n*. Thus, if the tree is traversed in inorder (left, root, right), the numbers are printed in ascending order. (You are asked to prove this as an exercise.) The use of binary trees in sorting and searching will be discussed further in Chapters 8 and 9.

Let us denote the operation of traversing a binary tree in inorder and printing the contents of each of its nodes by *intrav*(*tree*). Then the sorting algorithm may be written as follows:

```
read (number);
tree=maketree(number);
do while (there are numbers left in the input);
   read (number);
   p,q=tree;
   do while (q ¬= null);
      p=q;
      if number < info(p) then q=left(p);
                          else q=right(p);
   end;
   if number < info(p) then setleft(p,number);
                       else setright(p,number);
end;
      /*   traverse the tree   */
intrav(tree);
```

As another application of binary trees, consider the following method of representing an expression containing operands and binary operators. Let the root of a binary tree contain an operator which is to be applied to the results of evaluating the expressions represented by the left and right subtrees. A node representing an operator has two nonempty subtrees, while a node representing an operand has two empty subtrees. Figure 7.1.7. illustrates some expressions and their tree representations. (The character '$' is again used to represent exponentiation.)

Let us see what happens when these binary trees are traversed. Traversing such a tree in preorder means that the operator (the root) will precede its two operands (the subtrees). Thus, a preorder traversal should yield the prefix form of the expression. (For definitions of the prefix and postfix forms of an arithmetic expression, see Sections 3.4

14,15, 4,9,7,18, 3,5, 16,4,20, 17,9,14,5

Smaller ^ Larger or =

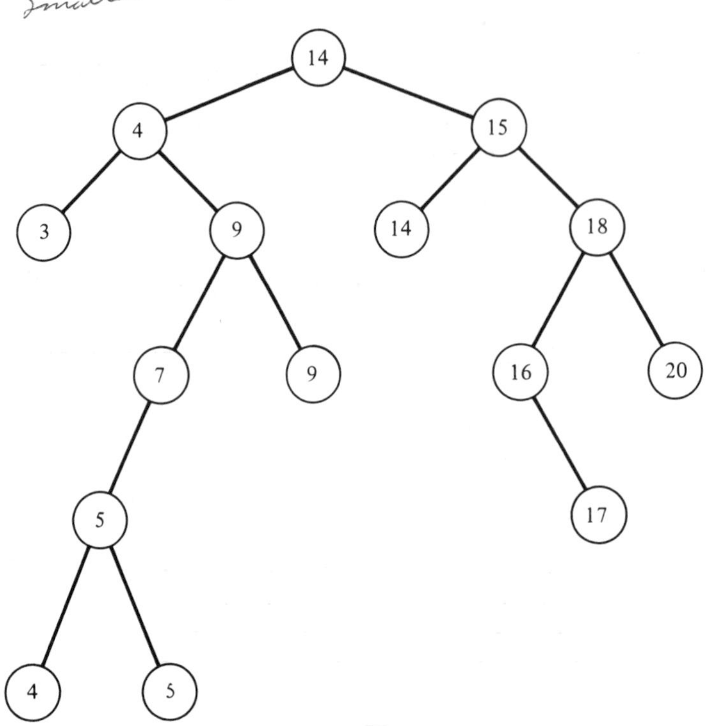

Figure 7.1.6. A binary tree constructed for sorting.

and 4.3.) This is indeed the case. Traversing the binary trees of Fig. 7.1.7 in preorder yields the prefix forms

```
+A*BC           (Fig. 7.1.7(a))
*+ABC           (Fig. 7.1.7(b))
+A*-BC$D*EF     (Fig. 7.1.7(c))
$+A*BC*+ABC     (Fig. 7.1.7(d))
```

Similarly, traversing such a binary tree in postorder places the operator after its two operands so that a postorder traversal produces the postfix form of the expression. The postorder traversals of the binary trees of Fig. 7.1.7 yield the postfix forms

```
ABC*+           (Fig. 7.1.7(a))
AB+C*           (Fig. 7.1.7(b))
ABC-DEF*$*+     (Fig. 7.1.7(c))
ABC*+AB+C*$     (Fig. 7.1.7(d))
```

What happens when such binary trees are traversed in inorder? Since the root (operator) is visited after the nodes of the left subtree and before the nodes of the right subtree (the two operands), we might expect an inorder traversal to yield the infix form of the expression. Indeed if the binary tree of Fig. 7.1.7(a) is traversed, the infix expres-

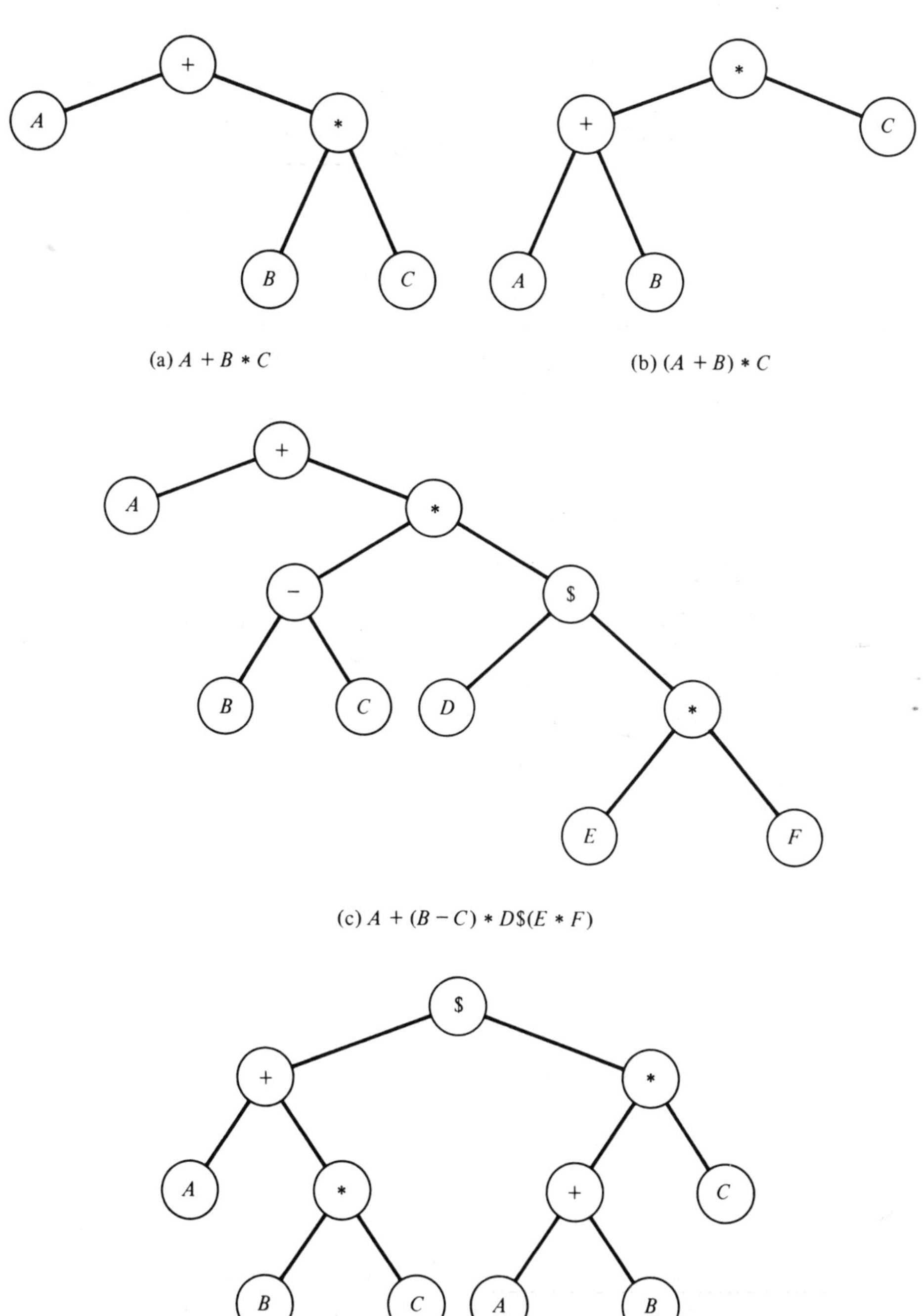

(a) $A + B * C$

(b) $(A + B) * C$

(c) $A + (B - C) * D\$(E * F)$

(d) $(A + B * C)\ \$\ ((A + B) * C)$

Figure 7.1.7. Expressions and their binary tree representation.

sion $A+B*C$ is obtained. However, the binary tree does not contain parentheses since the ordering of the operations is implied by the structure of the tree. Thus an expression whose infix form requires parentheses to override explicitly the conventional precedence rules cannot be retrieved by a simple inorder traversal. The inorder traversals of the trees of Fig. 7.1.7 yield the expressions

```
A+B*C           (Fig. 7.1.7(a))
A+B*C           (Fig. 7.1.7(b))
A+B-C*D$E*F     (Fig. 7.1.7(c))
A+B*C$A+B*C     (Fig. 7.1.7(d))
```

which are correct except for parentheses.

7.2. Binary Tree Representations

In this section we examine various methods of implementing binary trees in PL/I and present routines which build, traverse, and apply binary trees.

As in the case with list nodes, tree nodes may be implemented as array elements or as allocations of a BASED variable. Each node must contain INFO, LEFT, and RIGHT fields. The LEFT and RIGHT fields of a node point to the roots of its left and right subtrees respectively. Using the array implementation, we may declare

```
DCL 1 NODE(500),
        2 INFO          FIXED,
        2 LEFT          FIXED,
        2 RIGHT         FIXED;
```

and create an available list by

```
DCL AVAIL               FIXED INIT(1);
DO I=1 TO 499;
    LEFT(I)=I+1;
END;
LEFT(500) =0;
```

The routines GETNODE and FREENODE are straightforward and are left as exercises. Note that the available list is not a binary tree but a linear list whose nodes are linked together by the LEFT field.

Under the array implementation, the following function implements the *maketree* operation which allocates a node and sets it as the root of a binary tree with empty right and left subtrees.

```
MAKETREE: PROC(X) RETURNS(FIXED);
            DCL (P,X)          FIXED;
            P=GETNODE;
            INFO(P) =X;
            LEFT(P),RIGHT(P) =0;
            RETURN(P);
          END MAKETREE;
```

The routine SETLEFT(P,X) sets a node with contents X as the left son of NODE(P).

```
SETLEFT:  PROC(P,X);
            DCL (P,Q,X)       FIXED;
            IF P = 0 THEN DO;
                  PUT SKIP LIST('VOID INSERTION');
                  STOP;
                              END;
            IF LEFT(P) ¬= 0 THEN DO;
                           PUT SKIP LIST('INVALID INSERTION');
                           STOP;
                                      END;
            Q=MAKETREE(X);
            LEFT(P) =Q;
            RETURN;
          END SETLEFT;
```

The routine SETRIGHT(P,X) which creates a right son of NODE(P) with contents X is similar and is left as an exercise for the reader.

The following program uses a binary tree to find duplicate numbers in an input list. It closely follows the algorithm of Section 7.1.

```
DUP:    PROC OPTIONS(MAIN);
          DCL  (P,Q,TREE,NUMBER,I)        FIXED,
                 1  NODE(500),
                    2 INFO                FIXED,
                    2 LEFT                FIXED,
                    2 RIGHT               FIXED,
                 AVAIL                    FIXED INIT(1);
          DO  I=1 TO 499;
               LEFT(I) = I+1;
          END;
          LEFT(500) = 0;
          ON ENDFILE(SYSIN) GO TO DONE;

          GET LIST(NUMBER);
          TREE=MAKETREE(NUMBER);
```

```
LOOP:    DO WHILE('1'B);
               GET LIST(NUMBER);
               P,Q=TREE;


INSNUMB:       DO WHILE(NUMBER¬=INFO(P) & Q¬=0);
                  P=Q;
                  IF NUMBER < INFO(P) THEN Q=LEFT(P);
                                      ELSE Q=RIGHT(P);
               END INSNUMB;

               IF NUMBER=INFO(P) THEN PUT SKIP EDIT
                                      (NUMBER,'IS A DUPLICATE') (F(5),X(2),A);
                    ELSE IF NUMBER < INFO(P) THEN CALL SETLEFT(P,NUMBER);
                                             ELSE CALL SETRIGHT(P,NUMBER);
         END LOOP;

DONE:  END DUP;
```

Alternatively, the identifier NODE may be declared by

```
DCL 1 NODE BASED(NDPTR),
        2 INFO      FIXED,
        2 LEFT      PTR,
        2 RIGHT     PTR;
```

Under this implementation, an explicit available list is not needed. The routines GETNODE and FREENODE simply allocate and free a copy of the BASED variable NODE. The MAKETREE function may be written as follows:

```
MAKETREE:  PROC(X) RETURNS(PTR);
             DCL X          FIXED,
                 P          PTR;
             P=GETNODE;
             P->INFO=X;
             P->LEFT,P->RIGHT=NULL;
             RETURN(P);
           END MAKETREE;
```

The SETLEFT routine is also straightforward.

```
SETLEFT:  PROC(P,X);
                DCL   (P,Q)    PTR,
                      X        FIXED;
                IF P=NULL THEN DO;
                      PUT SKIP LIST('VOID INSERTION');
                      STOP;
                                END;

                IF P->LEFT¬=NULL THEN DO;
                      PUT SKIP LIST('INVALID INSERTION');
                      STOP;
                                          END;

                Q=MAKETREE(X);
                P->LEFT=Q;
                RETURN;
          END SETLEFT;
```

We use the array implementation in subsequent examples—the BASED implementation versions are straightforward modifications of the programs we present, and we leave them as exercises for the reader.

Binary Tree Traversals in PL/I

We may implement the traversal of binary trees in PL/I by recursive routines which mirror the traversal definitions. The three PL/I routines PRETRAV, INTRAV, and POSTTRAV print out the contents of a binary tree in preorder, inorder, and postorder respectively. The parameter to each routine is a pointer to the root node of a binary tree.

```
PRETRAV:  PROC(TREE) RECURSIVE;
             DCL TREE    FIXED;
             IF TREE=0 THEN RETURN;
                /*          visit the root          */
             PUT SKIP LIST(INFO(TREE));
                /*       traverse left subtree      */
             CALL PRETRAV(LEFT(TREE));
                /*      traverse right subtree      */
             CALL PRETRAV(RIGHT(TREE));
             RETURN;
          END PRETRAV;
```

```
INTRAV:     PROC(TREE) RECURSIVE;
              DCL TREE    FIXED;
              IF TREE=0 THEN RETURN;
                 /*     traverse left subtree       */
              CALL INTRAV(LEFT(TREE));
                 /*         visit the root          */
              PUT SKIP LIST(INFO(TREE));
                 /*     traverse right subtree      */
              CALL INTRAV(RIGHT(TREE));
              RETURN;
            END INTRAV;

POSTTRAV:   PROC(TREE) RECURSIVE;
              DCL TREE    FIXED;
              IF TREE=0 THEN RETURN;
                 /*     traverse left subtree       */
              CALL POSTTRAV(LEFT(TREE));
                 /*     traverse right subtree      */
              CALL POSTTRAV(RIGHT(TREE));
                 /*         visit the root          */
              PUT SKIP LIST(INFO(TREE));
              RETURN;
            END POSTTRAV;
```

The reader is invited to simulate the actions of these routines on the trees of Figs. 7.1.5 and 7.1.6.

Of course, more efficient routines could be written to perform these traversals which explicitly perform the necessary stacking and unstacking. For example, a nonrecursive routine to traverse a binary tree in inorder may be written as follows:

```
INTRAV2:    PROC(TREE);
              DCL TREE                  FIXED,
                    1 STACK,
                      2 TOP             FIXED INIT(0),
                      2 ITEMS(100)      FIXED,
                    P                   FIXED;

              P=TREE;
LOOP:         DO WHILE('1'B);
                 /*   travel down left hand branches as far as    */
                 /*   possible, saving pointers to nodes passed   */
```

```
LEFTRAV:        DO WHILE(P¬=0);
                   CALL PUSH(STACK,P);
                   P=LEFT(P);
                END LEFTRAV;
                /*              check if finished                    */
                IF EMPTY(STACK) THEN RETURN;
                /*    at this point the left subtree is empty        */
                /*                visit the root                     */
                P=POP(STACK);
                PUT SKIP LIST(INFO(P));
                /*           traverse right subtree                  */
                P=RIGHT(P);
             END LOOP;
          END INTRAV2;
```

Threaded Binary Trees

Similar nonrecursive routines can be written to implement preorder and postorder traversals. However, since traversing a binary tree is such a common operation, it would be helpful to find a more efficient method to perform the operation. Let us examine the routine INTRAV2 to discover the reason that a stack is needed. The stack is popped when P equals the null pointer (0 under the array implementation). This happens in one of two cases: one case is when the loop LEFTRAV is exited after having been executed one or more times. This implies that the program has traveled down left branches until it reached a null pointer, stacking each node as it was passed. Thus the top element of the stack is the value of P before it became null. If an auxiliary pointer Q is kept one step behind P, the value of Q can be used directly and need not be popped.

The other case in which P is null is when the LEFTRAV loop is skipped entirely. This occurs after reaching a node with an empty right subtree, executing the statement P=RIGHT(P); and returning to repeat the loop LOOP. At this point, we would have lost our way were it not for the stack whose top points to the node whose left subtree was just traversed. Suppose, however, that instead of containing a null pointer, a node with an empty right subtree contained a pointer to the node which would be on top of the stack at that point in the algorithm. Then there would no longer be a need for the stack since the node directly points to its inorder successor. Such a pointer is called a ***thread*** and must be differentiable from a tree pointer which is used to link a node to its left or right subtrees. Figure 7.2.1 shows the binary trees of Fig. 7.1.5 with threads replacing null pointers in nodes with empty right subtrees. The threads are drawn with dotted lines to differentiate them from tree pointers. Note that the rightmost node in each tree still has a null right pointer since it has no inorder successor. Such trees are called ***right in-threaded*** binary trees.

How can threads be represented in the PL/I implementation of binary trees? In the array implementation, a thread can be represented by a negative value of RIGHT(P).

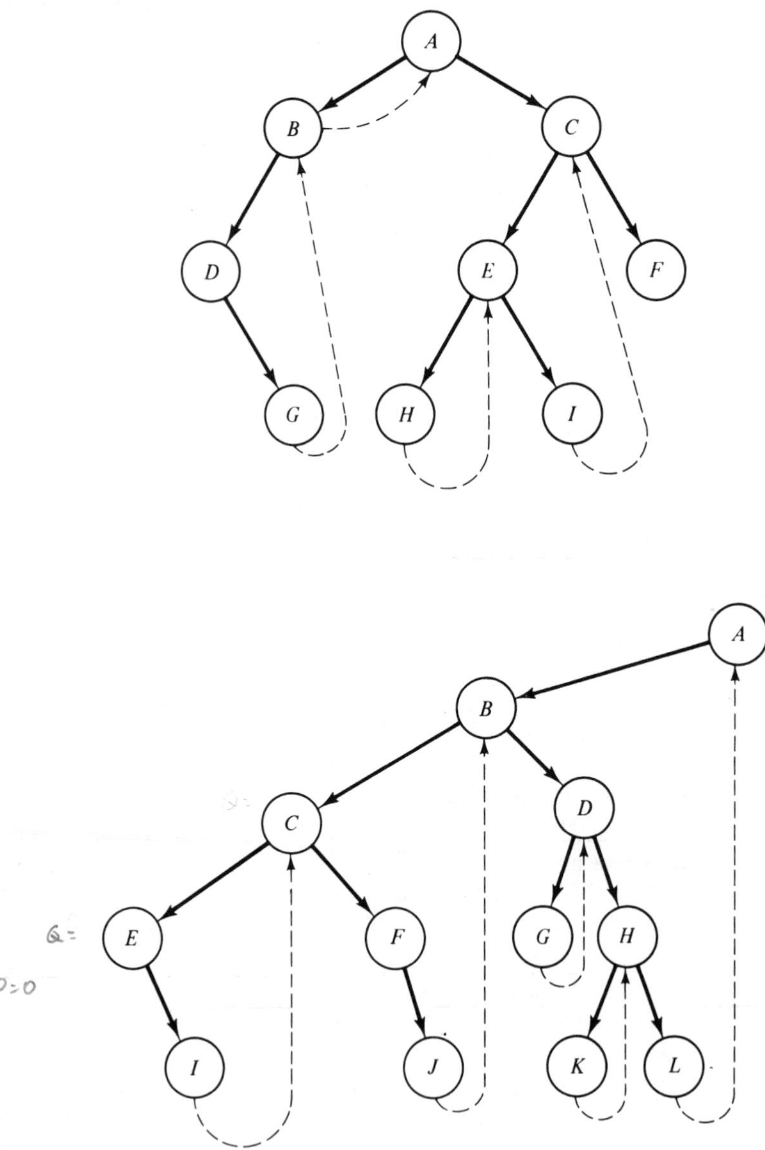

Figure 7.2.1. Right in-threaded binary trees.

If RIGHT(P)<0, the absolute value of RIGHT(P) is the index in the array NODE of the inorder successor of NODE(P). The sign of RIGHT(P) indicates whether its absolute value represents a thread (minus) or a pointer to a nonempty subtree (plus).

Under this implementation, the following routine traverses a right in-threaded binary tree in inorder.

```
INTRAV3:   PROC(TREE);
             DCL (P,Q,TREE)   FIXED;
             P=TREE;
LOOP:        DO WHILE('1'B);
             /*     travel down left links keeping Q behind P     */
               Q=0;
LEFTRAV:       DO WHILE(P¬=0);
                 Q=P;
                 P=LEFT(P);
               END LEFTRAV;

             /*              check if finished                    */
               IF Q=0 THEN RETURN;
               PUT SKIP LIST(INFO(Q));
               P=RIGHT(Q);

BACKUP:        DO WHILE(P<0);
                 Q=-P;
                 PUT SKIP LIST(INFO(Q));
                 P=RIGHT(Q);
               END BACKUP;

             /*            traverse right subtree                 */
             END LOOP;
           END INTRAV3;
```

In a right in-threaded binary tree, the inorder successor of any node can be found efficiently. Such a tree can also be constructed in a straightforward manner. The function MAKETREE remains unchanged. The routines SETLEFT and SETRIGHT are straightforward:

```
SETLEFT:   PROC(P,X);
             DCL (P,X,Q)      FIXED;
             IF P=0 THEN DO;
                   PUT SKIP LIST('VOID INSERTION');
                   STOP;
                          END;
```

```
        IF LEFT(P) ¬=0 THEN DO;
              PUT SKIP LIST('INVALID INSERTION');
              STOP;
                                   END;
        Q=GETNODE;
        INFO(Q) =X;
        LEFT(P) =Q;
           /*   the inorder successor of NODE(Q) is NODE(P)   */
        RIGHT(Q) =–P;
        LEFT(Q) =0;
        RETURN;
     END SETLEFT;



SETRIGHT:  PROC(P,X);
        DCL (P,X,Q,R)   FIXED;
        IF P=0 THEN DO;
              PUT SKIP LIST('VOID INSERTION');
              STOP;
                       END;
        IF RIGHT(P)>0 THEN DO;
              PUT SKIP LIST('INVALID INSERTION');
              STOP;
                                   END:
        Q=GETNODE;
        INFO(Q) =X;

           /*       save the inorder successor of NODE(P)        */
        R=RIGHT(P);
        RIGHT(P) =Q;
        LEFT(Q) =0;
           /*        the inorder successor of NODE(Q) is          */
           /*        the previous successor of NODE(P)            */
        RIGHT(Q) =R:
        RETURN;
     END SETRIGHT;
```

To implement a right in-threaded binary tree under the BASED implementation for nodes of a binary tree, an extra bit must be added to each node to indicate whether or not its right pointer is a thread. Thus, a node would be declared as follows:

```
DCL 1 NODE BASED(NDPTR),
      2 INFO       FIXED,
      2 LEFT       PTR,
      2 RIGHT      PTR,
      2 RTHREAD    BIT(1);  /*  '1'B if RIGHT is a   */
                            /*   non-null thread     */
```

We present a routine to implement an inorder traversal.

```
INTRAV4:    PROC(TREE);
               DCL (P,Q,TREE)      PTR;
               P=TREE;
LOOP:          DO WHILE('1'B);
                  Q=NULL;
LEFTRAV:          DO WHILE(P¬=NULL);
                     Q=P;
                     P=P->LEFT;
                  END LEFTRAV;

                  IF Q=NULL THEN RETURN;
                  PUT SKIP LIST(Q->INFO);
                  P=Q->RIGHT;

BACKUP:           DO WHILE(Q->RTHREAD);
                     PUT SKIP LIST(P->INFO);
                     Q=P;
                     P=Q->RIGHT;
                  END BACKUP;

               END LOOP;
            END INTRAV4;
```

We leave to the reader to provide appropriate MAKETREE, SETLEFT, and SETRIGHT routines for right in-threaded binary trees under this implementation.

A ***left in-threaded*** binary tree may be similarly defined as one in which each null left pointer is altered to contain a thread to that node's inorder predecessor, and an ***in-threaded*** binary tree may be defined as a binary tree which is both left in-threaded and right in-threaded. However, left in-threading does not yield the advantages of right in-threading. We may also define right and left ***pre-threaded*** binary trees in which null right and left pointers of nodes are set to their preorder successors and predecessors respectively. A right pre-threaded binary tree may be traversed efficiently in preorder without the use of a stack. A right in-threaded binary tree may also be traversed in preorder without the use of a stack. The traversal algorithms are left as exercises for the reader.

Heterogeneous Binary Trees

Often, the information contained in different nodes of a binary tree do not all have the same attributes. For example, in representing a binary expression with constant numerical operands we may wish to use a binary tree whose leafs contain numbers but whose nonleaf nodes contain character strings representing operators. Figure 7.2.2(a) illustrates such a binary tree. To represent such a tree in PL/I, we may place a pointer in the information portion of each node. This pointer may then point to an object having the appropriate attributes for that node. Figure 7.2.2(b) shows such a representation of the binary tree in Fig. 7.2.2(a). Tree nodes are indicated by circles, and information nodes by rectangles. Of course, each tree node must contain within itself an indication of the type of object to which its INFO field points. In this example, we can determine whether the INFO field points to a number or a character string by checking if the node has an empty left (or right) subtree. If the left subtree of a node is empty, then the node is a leaf and therefore represents an operand; otherwise, it represents an operator. Thus in this case an extra field is not needed in each node and we may declare

```
DCL 1 NODE BASED(NDPTR),
        2 INFO      PTR,
        2 LEFT      PTR,
        2 RIGHT     PTR;
DCL OPERAND         FLOAT  BASED(OPNDPTR),
    OPERATOR        CHAR(1)  BASED(OPTRPTR);
```

Let us write a PL/I function EVALBINTREE which accepts a pointer to such a tree and returns the value of the expression represented by the tree. The function recursively evaluates the left and right subtrees and then applies the operator of the root to the two results. We use the auxiliary function OPER(SYMB,OPND1,OPND2) introduced in Section 3.4. The first parameter of OPER is a character string representing an operator, and the last two parameters are floating-point numbers which are two operands. The function OPER returns the result of applying the operator to the two operands. The function EVALBINTREE may then be written as follows (the variables NODE, OPERAND, and OPERATOR are global):

```
EVALBINTREE:   PROC(TREE) RECURSIVE  RETURNS(FLOAT);
                 DCL  (TREE,P,Q,R)      PTR,
                      SYMB              CHAR(1),
                      (OPND1,OPND2)     FLOAT;
                 P=TREE->LEFT;
                 IF P=NULL THEN        /*   the expression is a    */
                                       /*     single operand       */
                                     DO;
                                       Q=TREE->INFO;
                                       RETURN(Q->OPERAND);
                                     END;
```

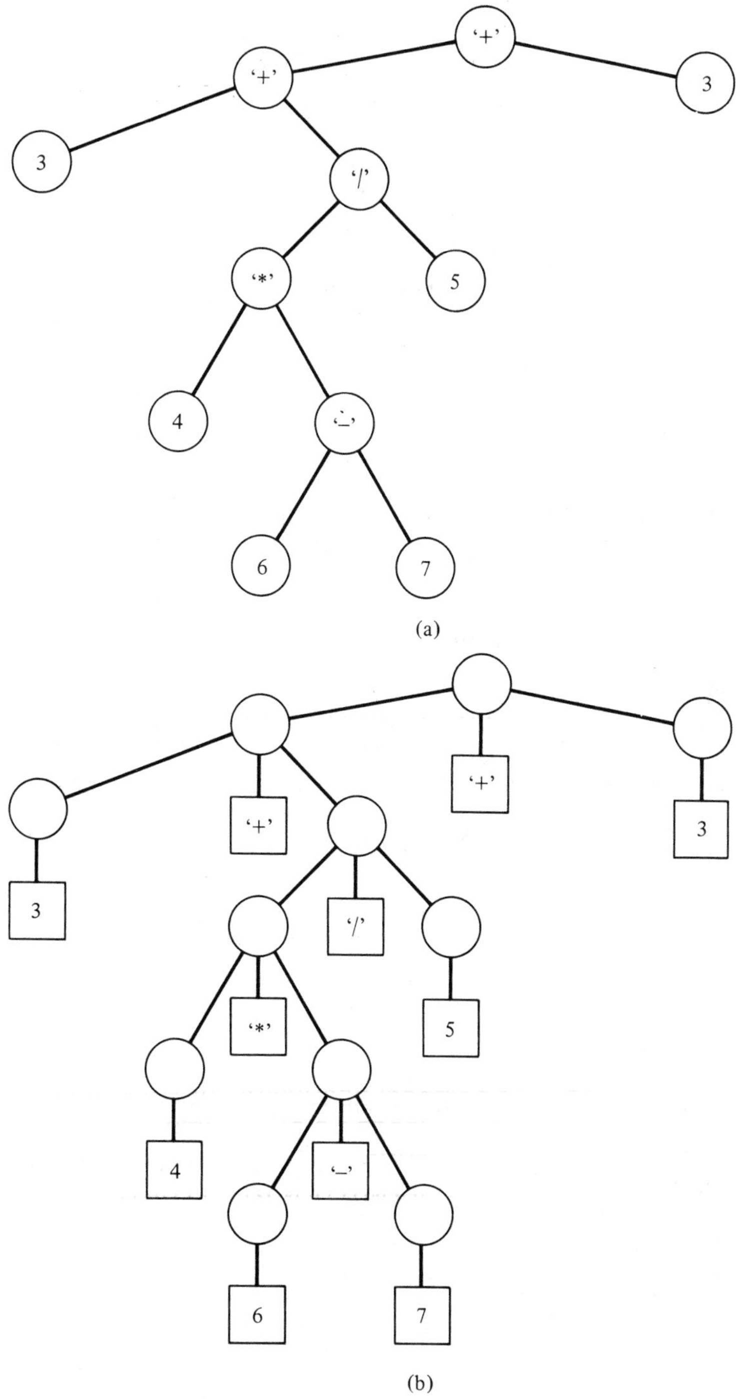

Figure 7.2.2. Binary tree representing 3 + 4 * (6−7)/5 + 3.

```
    /*          evaluate the left subtree          */
    OPND1=EVALBINTREE(P);
    /*          evaluate the right subtree         */
    Q=TREE->RIGHT:
    OPND2=EVALBINTREE(Q);
    /*          extract the operator               */
    R=TREE->INFO;
    SYMB=R->OPERATOR;
    /*   apply the operator and return result      */
    RETURN(OPER(SYMB,OPND1,OPND2));
END EVALBINTREE;
```

7.3. Other Representations and Applications

There are other representations of binary trees, each suited for the efficient performance of specific operations. In this section we examine some of these representations and their applications.

Example 7.3.1: The Huffman Algorithm

Consider the following problem. Suppose we have an alphabet of n symbols and a long message consisting of symbols from this alphabet. We wish to encode this message as a long bit string by assigning a bit string code to each symbol of the alphabet and concatenating the individual codes of the symbols making up the message to produce an encoding for the message. For example, suppose the alphabet consists of the four symbols A, B, C, D and codes are assigned to these symbols as follows:

Symbol	Code
A	'010'B
B	'100'B
C	'000'B
D	'111'B

The message *ABACCDA* would then be encoded as '010100010000000111010'B. However, such an encoding would be inefficient since three bits are used for each symbol, so that 21 bits are needed to encode the entire message. Suppose a two-bit code is assigned to each symbol, as follows:

Symbol	Code
A	'00'B
B	'01'B
C	'10'B
D	'11'B

Then the code for the message would be '00010010101100'B, which requires only 14 bits. We wish to find a code which minimizes the length of the encoded message.

Let us reexamine the above example. The letters B and D each appear only once in the message, while the letter A appears three times. Thus if a code is chosen in which the letter A is assigned a shorter bit string than the letters B and D, then the length of the encoded message would be small. This is because the short code (representing the letter A) would appear more frequently than the long code. Indeed, codes can be assigned as follows:

Symbol	Code
A	'0'B
B	'110'B
C	'10'B
D	'111'B

Using this code, the message *ABACCDA* is encoded as '0110010101110'B, which requires only 13 bits. In very long messages that contain symbols which appear very infrequently, the savings are substantial. Note that the code for one symbol may not be a prefix of the code for another. This must be true if the decoding is to proceed from left to right. If the code for a symbol x, $c(x)$, were a prefix of the code of a symbol y, $c(y)$, then when $c(x)$ is encountered, it is unclear whether $c(x)$ represents the symbol x or whether it is the first part of $c(y)$.

In our example the bit string is scanned from left to right. If a 0 is encountered as the first bit, the symbol is an A; otherwise, it is a B, C, or D and the next bit is examined. If the second bit is a 0, then the symbol is a C; otherwise, it must be a B or a D and the third bit must be examined. If the third bit is a 0, the symbol is a B; if it is a 1, the symbol is a D. As soon as the first symbol has been identified, the process is repeated starting at the next bit to find the second symbol.

This suggests a method for developing an optimal encoding scheme given the frequency of occurrence of each symbol in a message. Find the two symbols which appear least frequently. In our example, these are B and D. The last bit of their codes will differentiate between them: 0 for B and 1 for D. Combine these two symbols into the single symbol *BD* whose code represents the knowledge that a symbol is either a B or a D. The frequency of occurrence of this new symbol is the sum of the frequencies of its two constituent symbols. Thus the frequency of *BD* is 2. There are now three symbols: A (frequency 3), C (frequency 2), and *BD* (frequency 2). Again choose the two symbols with smallest frequency: C and *BD*. The last bit of their codes will differentiate between them: 0 for C and 1 for *BD*. The two symbols are then combined into the single symbol *CBD* with frequency 4. There are now only two symbols remaining: A and *CBD*. These are combined into the single symbol *ACBD*. The last bits of the codes for A and *CBD* will differentiate between them: 0 for A and 1 for *CBD*.

The symbol *ACBD* now contains the entire alphabet; it is assigned the null bit string, ''B, as its code. This means that at the start of the decoding, before any bits have been examined, it is certain that any symbol is contained in *ACBD*. The two symbols which comprise *ACBD* (*A* and *CBD*) are assigned the codes '0'B and '1'B respectively. If a 0 is encountered, the encoded symbol is an *A*; if a 1 is encountered, it is a *C*, *B*, or *D*. Similarly, the two symbols which constitute *CBD* (*C* and *BD*) are assigned the codes '10'B and '11'B respectively. The first bit indicates that the symbol is one of the constituents of *CBD*, and the second bit indicates whether it is a *C* or a *BD*. The symbols which comprise *BD* (*B* and *D*) are then assigned the codes '110'B and '111'B. By this process, symbols which appear frequently in the message are assigned shorter codes than symbols which appear infrequently.

The action of combining two symbols into one suggests the use of a binary tree. Each nonleaf node of the tree represents a symbol and the leafs represent the symbols of the original alphabet. Figure 7.3.1.1(a) shows the binary tree constructed using the previous example. Each node in the illustration contains a symbol and its frequency. Figure 7.3.1.1(b) shows the binary tree constructed by this method for the alphabet and frequency table of Fig. 7.3.1.1(c). Such trees are called ***Huffman trees*** after the discoverer of this encoding method.

Once the Huffman tree is constructed, the code of any symbol in the alphabet can be determined by starting at the leaf which represents that symbol and climbing up to the root. The code is initialized to ''B. Each time that a left branch is climbed, a 0 is appended to the left of the code; each time that a right branch is climbed, a 1 is appended to the left of the code.

Note that in constructing the tree and obtaining the codes, it is only necessary to keep links from each node to its father and an indication of whether each node is a left or right son; links from a father to either of his two sons are unnecessary. Each node contains three fields: *father*, *type*, and *freq*. *father* is a pointer to the node's father. If the node is the root, then its *father* field is null. *type* is 'L' or 'R' depending on whether the node is a left or right son. *freq* is the frequency of occurrence of the symbol represented by that node. The inputs to the algorithm are *n*, the number of symbols in the original alphabet, and *frequency*, an array of size *n* such that *frequency*(*i*) is the relative frequency of the *i*th symbol. The algorithm is to assign values to an array *code* of size *n* so that *code*(*i*) contains the code for the *i*th symbol. The algorithm also constructs an array *position* of size *n* such that *position*(*i*) points to the node representing the *i*th symbol.

We may outline Huffman's algorithm as follows:

```
           /*   initialize the set of root nodes      */
rootnodes= the empty set;

           /*   construct a node for each symbol      */
do i= 1 to n;
     p=getnode;
     freq(p)=frequency(i);
     position(i)=p;
     add p to rootnodes;
end;
```

```
do while (rootnodes contains more than one item);
      p1=the element in rootnodes with smallest freq value;
      remove p1 from rootnodes;
      p2=the element in rootnodes with smallest freq value;
      remove p2 from rootnodes;

      /*      combine p1 and p2 as branches of a single tree       */
      p=getnode;
      father(p1)=p;
      type(p1)='L';
      father(p2)=p;
      type(p2)='R';
      freq(p)=freq(p1)+freq(p2);
      add p to rootnodes;
end;

      /*      the tree is now constructed; use it to find codes.      */
root=the single element of rootnodes;
do i=1 to n;
      p=position(i);
      code(i)= ''B;
      do while (p¬=root);
                          /*  travel up the tree  */
         if type(p)='L' then code(i)='0'B||code(i);
                        else code(i)='1'B||code(i);
         p=father(p);
      end;
end;
```

Note that every nonleaf node in a Huffman tree has nonempty right and left subtrees. Such a tree is called a ***strictly binary tree***. The trees used to represent binary expressions in the last section are also strictly binary. It can be shown that a strictly binary tree with n leafs has $2n-1$ nodes (this is left as an exercise for the reader). Since the leafs of a Huffman tree represent the symbols of the original alphabet, the total number of nodes in the tree can be computed from the number of symbols in the alphabet. Thus if there are n symbols in the alphabet, the Huffman tree can be represented by an array of nodes of size $2n-1$.

Let us write a program to encode a message using Huffman's algorithm. Ordinarily, codes are not constructed on the basis of the frequency of the occurrence of characters within a single message, but rather on the basis of their frequency within a whole set of messages, and the same code set is used for each message. For example, if messages consist of English words, then the known relative frequency of occurrence of the letters of the alphabet in the English language could be used. The input to the program consists of a number N which is the number of symbols in the alphabet followed by a set of N

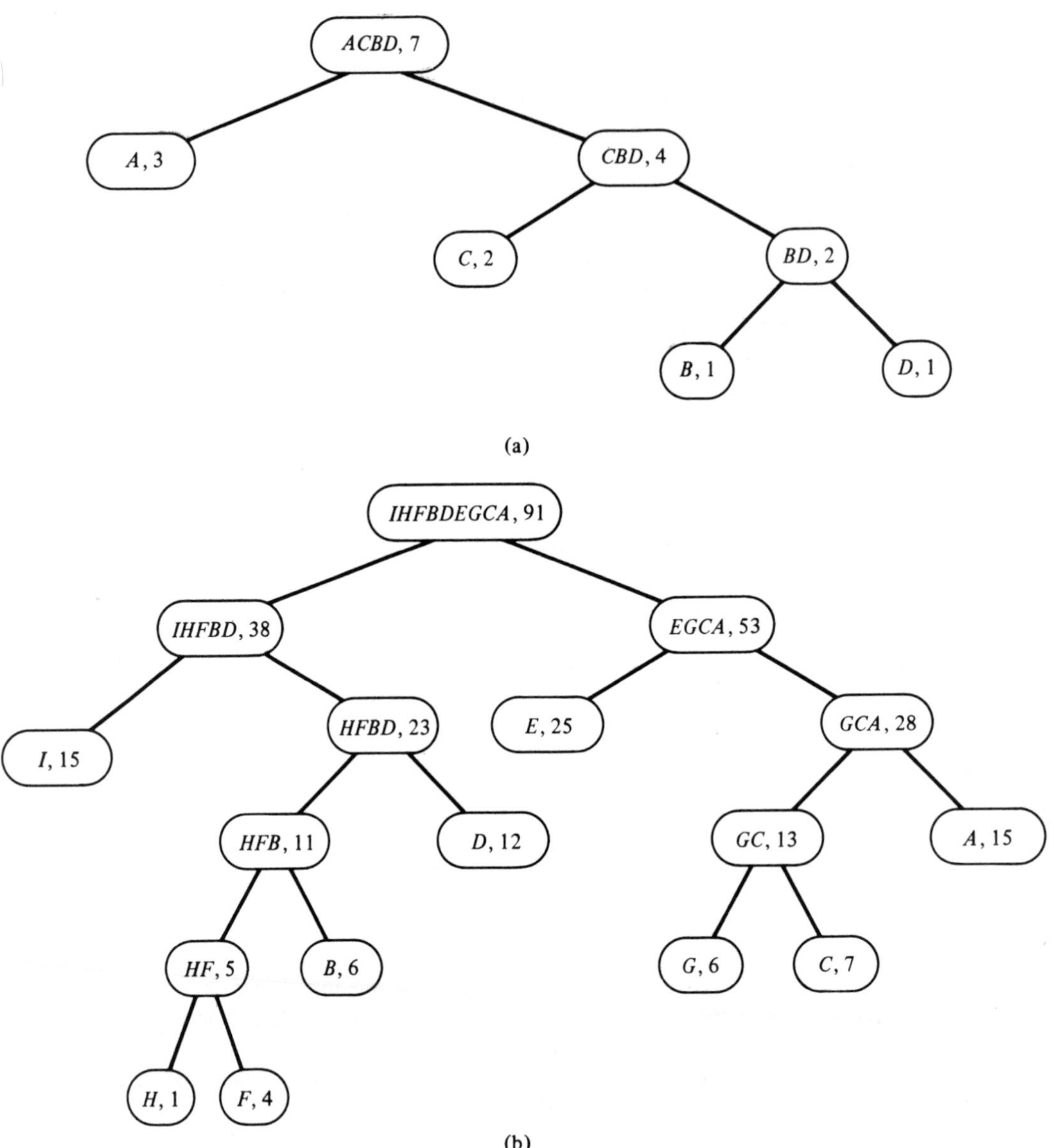

(a)

(b)

Symbol	Frequency	Code	Symbol	Frequency	Code	Symbol	Frequency	Code
A	15	'111'B	*D*	12	'011'B	*G*	6	'1100'B
B	6	'0101'B	*E*	25	'10'B	*H*	1	'01000'B
C	7	'1101'B	*F*	4	'01001'B	*I*	15	'00'B

(c)

Figure 7.3.1.1. Huffman trees.

pairs, each of which consists of a symbol and its relative frequency. The program constructs a string ALPH which consists of all the symbols in the alphabet and an array CODE such that CODE(I) is the code assigned to the Ith symbol in ALPH. It uses two auxiliary arrays: FATHER and FREQ. Each of these arrays is of size 2*N–1. FATHER(I) is negative if the node of the tree represented by I is a left son, and it is positive if the node is a right son. The absolute value of FATHER(I) is a pointer to the father of node I. If node I is the root of a tree, then FATHER(I) is equal to 0. FREQ(I) is used to contain the frequency of the symbol represented by node I.

```
FINDCODE:  PROC OPTIONS(MAIN);
             DCL (I,J,N,MAXFREQ,N1,N2,
                   SMALL1,SMALL2)          FIXED,
                   SYMB                    CHAR(1),
                   CD                      BIT(100) VAR;
             GET LIST(N);
BLOCK:       BEGIN;
                 /*  initialize arrays  */
                 DCL CODE(N)               BIT(100) VAR,
                     ALPH                  CHAR(N) VAR INIT(''),
                     FATHER(2*N-1)         FIXED,
                     FREQ(2*N-1)           FIXED;
                 FATHER=0;
                 FREQ=0;
                 CODE=''B;

                 /*      initialize alphabet and frequencies      */
SETUPALPH:       DO I=1 TO N;
                   GET LIST(SYMB,FREQ(I));
                   ALPH=ALPH||SYMB;
                 END SETUPALPH;

                 /*   MAXFREQ holds a number larger than   */
                 /*             any frequency              */
                 MAXFREQ=SUM(FREQ)+1;


BUILDTREE:       DO I=N+1 TO 2*N-1;

                        /*    I is the next available node. Search    */
                        /*    all previous nodes for the two root     */
                        /*      nodes N1 and N2 with smallest         */
                        /*               frequences.                  */
                     N1,N2=0;
                     SMALL1,SMALL2=MAXFREQ;
```

```
SEARCH:              DO J=1 TO I-1;
                        IF FATHER(J)=0 THEN    /*   J is a root node    */
                           IF FREQ(J)<SMALL1 THEN DO;
                                        SMALL2=SMALL1;
                                        SMALL1=FREQ(J);
                                        N2=N1;
                                        N1=J;
                                                    END;
                           ELSE IF FREQ(J)<SMALL2 THEN DO;
                                        SMALL2=FREQ(J);
                                        N2=J;
                                                         END;
                     END SEARCH;

                        /*     set N1 to the left subtree of I and      */
                        /*          N2 to the right subtree             */
                     FATHER(N1)=-I;
                     FATHER(N2)=I;
                     FREQ(I)=FREQ(N1)+FREQ(N2);
               END BUILDTREE;

                     /*   extract the codes from the tree    */
EXTCODE:       DO  I=1 TO N;
                  J=I;
                  CD=''B;
UPTREE:           DO WHILE(FATHER(J)¬=0);
                   IF FATHER(J)<0 THEN   /*   left son    */
                                         CD='0'B||CD;
                                  ELSE   /*   right son   */
                                         CD='1'B||CD;


                   J=ABS(FATHER(J));
                  END UPTREE;
                  CODE(I)=CD;
               END EXTCODE;

                  /*   print results   */
PRINT:         DO I=1 TO N;
                  PUT SKIP LIST(SUBSTR(ALPH,I,1),FREQ(I),CODE(I));
               END PRINT;

             END BLOCK;
          END FINDCODE;
```

The reader is referred to Section 9.4 which suggests further improvements to the above program. We leave to the reader the coding of the function ENCODE(ALPH,CODE,MSGE). This function accepts the string ALPH and the array CODE constructed in the above program and a message MSGE and returns the bit string encoding of the message.

Given the encoding of a message and the Huffman tree used in constructing the code, the original message can be recovered as follows: Begin at the root of the tree. Each time that a 0 is encountered, move down a left branch, and each time that a 1 is encountered, move down a right branch. Repeat this process until a leaf is encountered. The next character of the original message is the symbol that corresponds to that leaf. See if you can decode '1110100010111011'B using the Huffman tree of Fig. 7.3.1.1(b).

In order to decode, it is necessary to travel from the root of the tree down to its leafs. This means that instead of an array FATHER, two arrays LEFT and RIGHT are needed to hold the left and right sons of a particular node. It is straightforward to construct the arrays LEFT and RIGHT from the array FATHER. Alternatively, the arrays LEFT and RIGHT can be constructed directly from the frequency information for the symbols of the alphabet using an approach similar to that used in constructing the array FATHER. (Of course, if the trees are to be identical, the symbol/frequency pairs must be presented in the same order under the two methods.) We leave these algorithms, as well as the decoding algorithm, as exercises for the reader.

This section presented an example which illustrates two distinct concepts. This first is that of a strictly binary tree. Such a binary tree is one in which each nonleaf node has both left and right sons. If the number of leafs in such a tree is n, then the total number of nodes is $2n-1$. The significance of this fact is that the amount of storage that such a tree needs is known and may be allocated in advance.

The other concept is that there are many ways to represent a binary tree. For example, a node could contain pointers to its left and right sons (as in the last section), or a pointer to its father (as in this section), or a pointer to its brother, or any combination of these. It is up to the programmer to select the representation which makes his particular application most efficient in terms of time, space, and ease of programming.

Example 7.3.2: The Josephus Problem Revisited

All the representations of binary trees which we have discussed so far specified the links among the nodes explicitly by using either an array *father* or *left* and *right* arrays. For a certain class of strictly binary trees this explicit specification can be eliminated. Define an ***almost complete binary tree*** as a strictly binary tree for which there is a nonnegative integer k such that:

1. Every leaf in the tree is at level k or at level $k+1$.

2. If a node in the tree has a right descendant at level $k+1$, then all its left descendants which are leafs are also at level $k+1$.

The binary tree of Fig. 7.3.1.1(a) is not almost complete since it contains leafs at levels 1, 2, and 3, thus violating condition 1. Similarly, the binary tree of Fig. 7.3.1.1(b) is not almost complete since it contains leafs at levels 2, 3, 4, and 5. The strictly binary tree of Fig. 7.3.2.1(a) satisfies condition 1 since every leaf is either at level 2 or at level 3. However, condition 2 is violated since *A* has a right descendant at level 3 (*J*) but also has a left descendant which is a leaf at level 2 (*E*). The binary tree of Fig. 7.3.2.1(b) satisfies both conditions 1 and 2 and is therefore an almost complete binary tree.

The nodes of an almost complete binary tree can be numbered in such a way that the number assigned a left son is twice the number assigned its father and the number assigned a right son is 1 more than twice the number assigned its father. Figure 7.3.2.1(c) illustrated the numbering of the nodes of the tree of Fig. 7.3.2.1(b). To represent an almost complete binary tree, we do not need *father*, *left*, or *right* links. Instead, node *n* is the implicit father of nodes $2n$ and $2n+1$. (We should note that many texts refer to such a tree as a "complete binary tree" rather than as an "almost complete binary tree." Still other texts use the term "complete" to refer to the concept which we call "strictly binary." We prefer to use the term "complete" as it was introduced in Section 7.1.)

As an example of the use of such a tree representation let us reconsider the Josephus problem of Section 5.4. The reader should reread the statement of the problem. The solution presented in that section uses a circular list containing names. Each time that *n* people are counted, the step

```
LIST=NEXT(LIST);
```

is performed $n-1$ times.

We can use an almost complete strictly binary tree to represent the Josephus problem as follows. Let the initial number of people be *total*. Then the binary tree has *total* leafs representing people and therefore $2total-1$ nodes. Each node of the tree contains an integer which is the number of leafs in the subtree rooted at that node. In addition, each leaf contains the name of the person whom it represents. Figure 7.3.2.2(a) illustrates the initial binary tree for the Josephus problem with $total=9$. (Leafs are shown as squares, nonleafs as circles.) The names are represented by the identifiers *N1* through *N9*. The dashed arrows in that figure will be explained shortly.

Let *n* be the number to be counted around the circle in choosing the next man to be eliminated. To illustrate the algorithm we use $n=13$. The process proceeds in two phases. The first phase finds the root of a subtree which is known to contain the leaf representing the next man to be eliminated. Initially, this is the root of the tree. The next phase travels down the tree to find that leaf and eliminates it. Since $n=13$ is greater than the count in the tree root (9), the fourth man in the circle must be found (since counting the first nine only returns us to the beginning). Proceed to the left son of the root. Since the count in that left son (5) is greater than the number which remains to be counted (4), the next man to be eliminated is in that subtree. Again proceed to the left son of that node. Now, however, the count in that left son (3) is less than the number to be counted (4). This means that the next man is not in the left subtree, but in the right subtree. Therefore, move to the right subtree and reduce the number remaining to be counted by the number of men represented by the left subtree. Three men have been counted, and one man remains to be counted. The left son is a leaf representing the next man to be eliminated. The dashed lines in Fig. 7.3.2.2(a) represent the path taken to this leaf.

To eliminate this man, reduce the count in that node and all of its ancestors by 1.

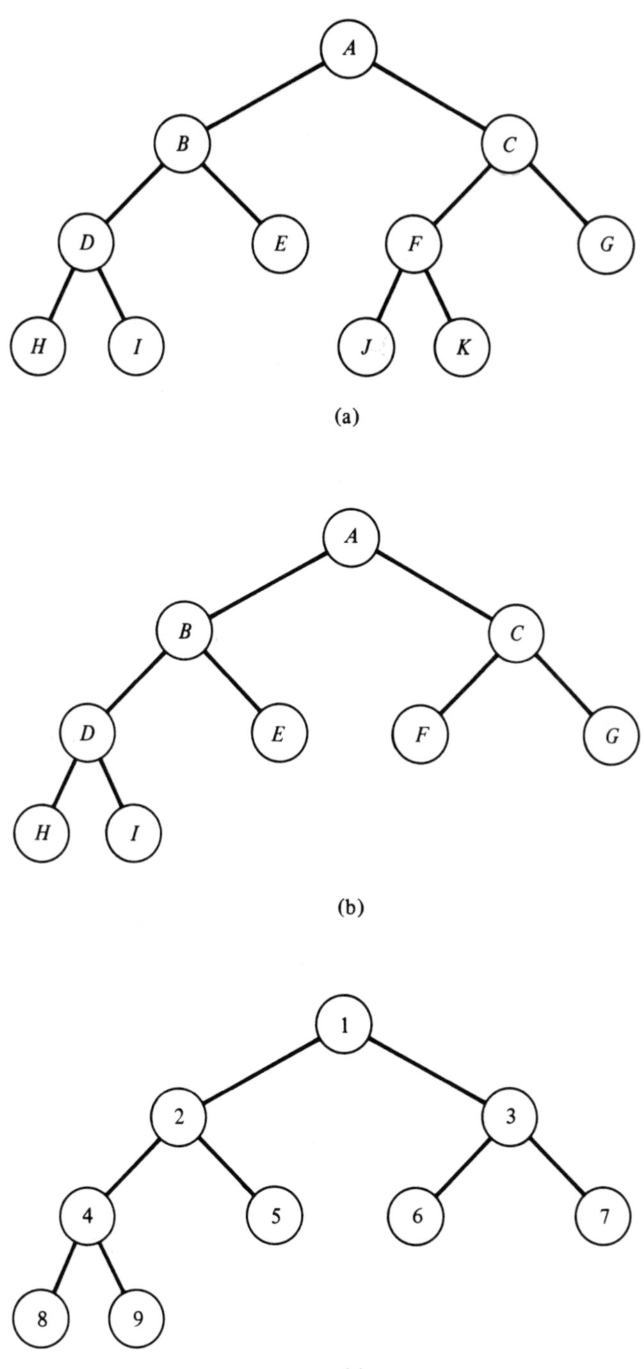

Figure 7.3.2.1.

Also, transfer the name in its right brother to its father. The father now becomes a leaf in the tree, representing the man previously represented by the right son. The new tree is shown in Fig. 7.3.2.2(b).

The process executes the first phase and climbs back up the tree. The number of men remaining to be counted is set to *n*, which is 13. In moving up the tree, it starts at the node representing the man just eliminated and repeats the following process:

1. At a left son, advance to its right brother.
2. At a right son, subtract the count in that node from the number of people remaining to be counted and move up the tree until a left son is encountered.

Note that the first time this process is executed the number subtracted from the remaining count will be 0 (if the man just eliminated was a right son) or 1 (if the man just eliminated was a left son). The process continues until it reaches either the root of the tree or a right son whose count is greater than the number of people remaining to be counted. At that point, the next man to be eliminated is in the subtree rooted at that node, so the second phase is executed once again.

The dashed lines in Fig. 7.3.2.2(b) illustrate this process. Figures 7.3.2.2(c) and (d) illustrate the entire process being performed once again. The value of the remaining number of men to be counted is illustrated at certain nodes.

The algorithm for the Josephus problem follows. *count*(*p*) is the number of men represented by the subtree rooted at *node*(*p*), *father*(*p*) is the father of *node*(*p*), *left*(*p*) is its left son, *rbro*(*p*) is its right brother, and *name*(*p*) is the name of the man represented by *node*(*p*) if it is a leaf. We assume that all of these quantities have been suitably initialized to represent an almost complete binary tree with *total* leaves. *n* represents the number of men to be counted.

```
   /*                    initialization                          */
p=tree;
   /*    remain is the number of men remaining to be counted     */
   /*     eliminate complete traversals of the tree from this    */
   /*                          count                             */
remain = mod(n-1,count(p))+1;
do while(count(tree)¬=1);
   /*      Repeat the process as long as more than one man       */
   /*           remains. At this point, p always points to       */
   /*        a node which is the root of a subtree known to      */
   /*         contain the next man to be eliminated. Move        */
   /*                down the tree to find that man.             */
   do while (count(p)>1);
      p=left(p);
      if remain>count(p) then do;
                 remain=remain-count(p);
                 p=rbro(p);
                          end;
   end;
```

```
   /*     at this point p points to the next man to be eliminated      */
q=p;
print (name(p));
do while(q¬=null);
   /*            reduce the count of each ancestor of p              */
   count(q)=count(q)-1;
   /*            move up the name of q's son if necessary            */
   if count(q)=1 then
          if count(left(q))=1 then name(q)=name(left(q));
                               else name(q)=name(right(q));
   q=father(q);
end;

   /*              reset remain and move up the tree                 */
remain=n;
if p points to a left son then p=rbro(p);
   /*                    p points to a right son                     */
do while (remain>count(p) & p¬=tree);
   remain=remain-count(p);
   do while(p is a right son);
      p=father(p);
   end;
   if p¬=tree then   /*   p points to a left son   */
                  p=rbro(p);
end;

   if p=tree then remain=mod(remain-1,count(tree))+1;
end;

  /*    at this point count(tree)=1, so name(tree) is the last man     */
print(name(tree));
```

In implementing this algorithm in PL/I, we can take advantage of the fact that the original tree is almost complete. The tree with TOTAL leafs is represented by two arrays, COUNT and NAME, each of size 2∗TOTAL–1. A pointer to a node is therefore an integer between 1 and 2∗TOTAL–1. The root of the tree will be at position 1, so that TREE=1. The left son of the node at position P is at position 2∗P+1. Thus *left(p)* may be translated into 2∗P and *rbro(p)* into P+1. *father(p)* may be computed by truncating the value of P/2 to an integer. P points to a left son if and only if it is a multiple of 2. Thus the test for whether P points to a left son is a check whether or not MOD(P,2) equals 0.

To set up the original tree we must face the problem of initializing the arrays COUNT and NAME. Initially, only the leafs have names assigned to them. These leafs occupy positions TOTAL through 2∗TOTAL–1 in the array, so that NAME(I) may be set equal to the null string for I<TOTAL. However, in looking at the tree of Fig. 7.3.2.2(a) we note that the TOTAL names do not appear sequentially in positions

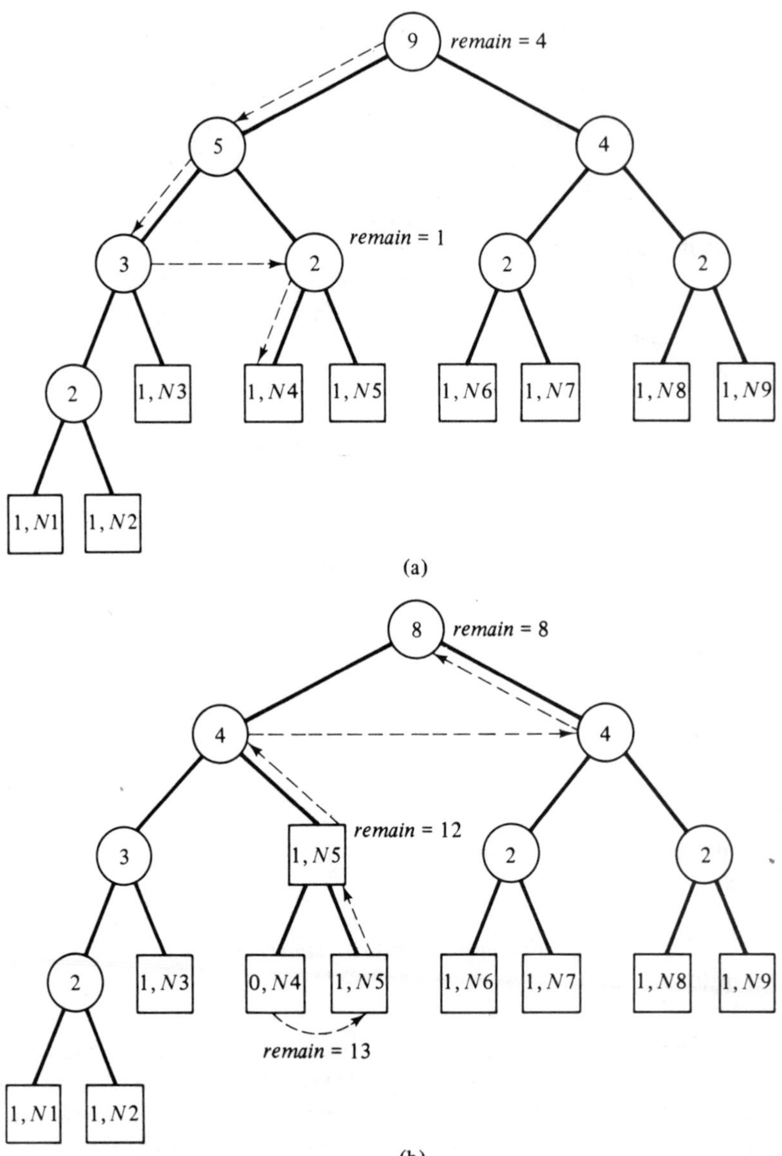

Figure 7.3.2.2. The Josephus problem (TOTAL = 9, $N = 13$).

TOTAL through 2*TOTAL–1. Rather, in that example, the first two names appear in positions 16 and 17 and the remaining names in positions 8 through 15. It can be shown that the leftmost node at level J in an almost complete binary tree occupies position 2**J. Thus if I is the ***depth*** (maximum level) of such a binary tree, the first names are assigned to positions 2**I through 2*TOTAL–1 and the remainder (if any) to posi-

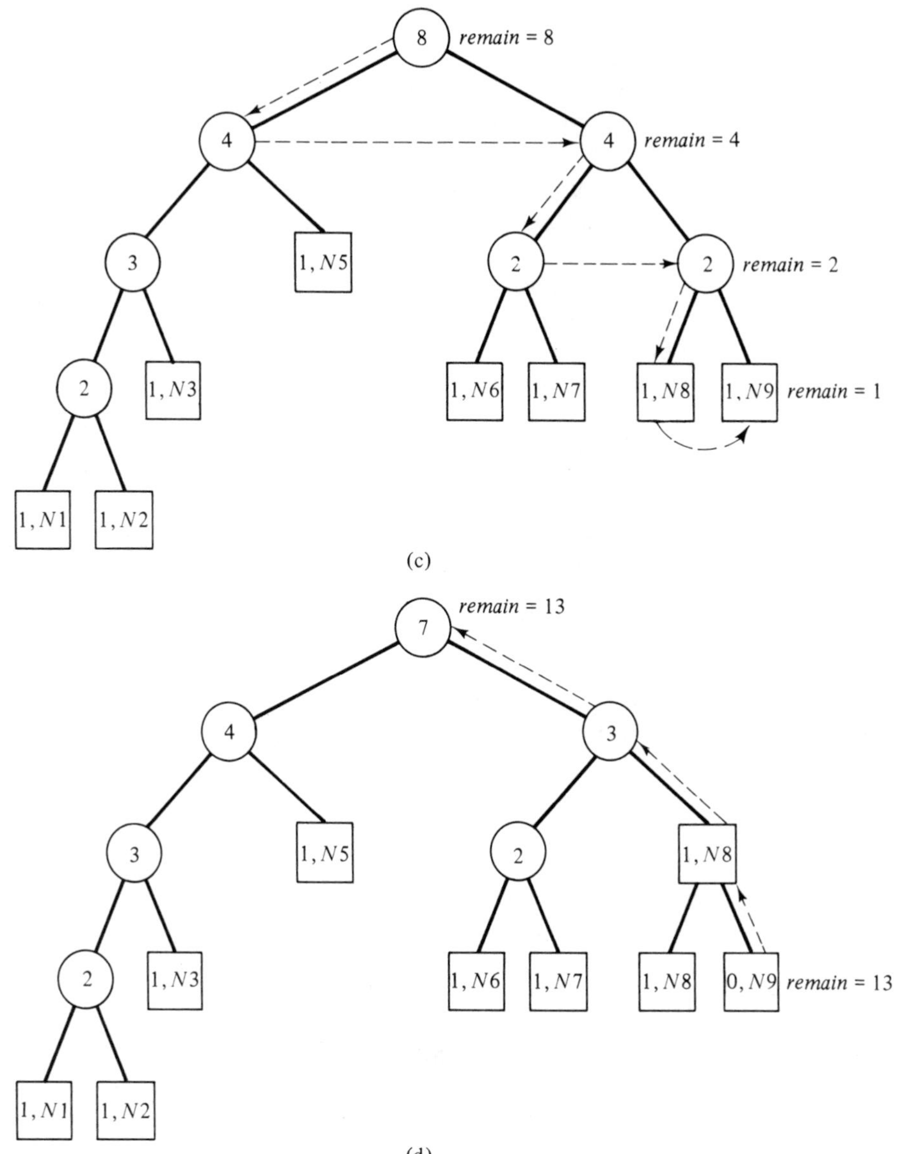

Figure 7.3.2.2. *(cont.)*

tions TOTAL through 2**I–1. The maximum level in an almost complete binary tree is the smallest integer J such that 2**J is greater than or equal to the number of leafs.

We may now write a PL/I program to read the number of people in the circle (TOTAL), followed by the count used in eliminating people (N), followed by the names of the people in the circle. The program then prints out the order in which the people are eliminated from the circle.

```
JOSEPHUS:   PROC OPTIONS(MAIN);
               DCL (I,N,P,Q,
                    REMAIN,TOTAL,TWOTOMAX)   FIXED;
               GET LIST(TOTAL,N);
BLOCK:         BEGIN;
                  DCL COUNT(2*TOTAL-1)          FIXED,
                       NAME(2*TOTAL-1)          CHAR(30) VAR;

          /*             initialize the tree                */
          /*        find the maximum level minus 1          */
                  TWOTOMAX=1;
FINDMAX:          DO WHILE(TWOTOMAX<TOTAL);
                     TWOTOMAX=2*TWOTOMAX;
                  END FINDMAX;

          /*           assign names and counts              */
READNAMES:        DO I=TWOTOMAX TO 2*TOTAL-1, TOTAL TO TWOTOMAX-1;
                     GET LIST(NAME(I));
                     COUNT(I)=1;
                  END READNAMES;
SETCOUNT:         DO I=TOTAL-1 TO 1 BY -1;
                     COUNT(I)=COUNT(2*I)+COUNT(2*I+1);
                  END SETCOUNT:

          /*             follow the algorithm               */
                  P=1;
                  REMAIN=MOD(N-1,COUNT(P))+1;
          /*   repeat as long as more than one man remains  */
LOOP:             DO WHILE(COUNT(1)¬=1);
            /*  P points to root of subtree containing next man  */
MOVEDOWN:            DO WHILE(COUNT(P)>1);
                       P=2*P;
                       IF REMAIN>COUNT(P) THEN DO;
                             REMAIN=REMAIN-COUNT(P);
                             P=P+1;
                                                  END;
                     END MOVEDOWN;

            /*      P points to next man to be eliminated        */
                     PUT SKIP LIST(NAME(P));
                     Q=P;
REMOVE:              DO WHILE(Q¬=0);
          /*           reduce count of each ancestor         */
                        COUNT(Q)=COUNT(Q)-1;
               /*       move up name of son of Q, if necessary        */
```

```
                 IF COUNT(Q)=1 THEN
                    IF COUNT(2*Q)=1 THEN NAME (Q)=NAME(2*Q);
                                     ELSE NAME(Q)=NAME(2*Q+1);
                 Q=Q/2;
              END REMOVE;

          /*          reset REMAIN and move up the tree           */
              REMAIN=N;
              IF MOD(P,2)=0 THEN P=P+1;
          /*          P points to a right son            */
MOVEUP:       DO WHILE(REMAIN>COUNT(P) & P¬=1);
                 REMAIN=REMAIN–COUNT(P);
                 DO WHILE (MOD(P,2)=1 & P¬=1);
                    P=P/2;
                 END;
                 IF P¬=1 THEN   /*   P points to a left son    */
                            P=P+1;
              END MOVEUP;

              IF P=1 THEN REMAIN=MOD(REMAIN–1,COUNT(P))+1;
          END LOOP;
          PUT SKIP LIST(NAME(1));
       END BLOCK;
    END JOSEPHUS;
```

7.4. Trees and Their Applications

In this section, we consider general trees and their representations. We also investigate some of their uses in problem solving.

7.4.1. Trees

A ***tree*** is a finite nonempty set of elements. One of these elements is called the ***root*** and the remaining elements are partitioned into $m \geqslant 0$ disjoint subsets, each of which is itself a tree. Each element in a tree is called a ***node*** of the tree.

Figure 7.4.1.1 illustrates some trees. Each node may be the root of a tree with zero or more subtrees. A node with no subtrees is a ***leaf***. We use the terms ***father***, ***son***, ***ancestor***, ***descendant***, and ***level*** in the same sense that we used them for binary trees. Two nodes which have the same father are ***brothers***. We also define the ***degree*** of a node in a tree as the number of its sons. Thus in Fig. 7.4.1.1(a), node C has degree 0 (and is therefore a leaf), node D has degree 1, node B has degree 2 and node A has degree 3. There is no upper limit on the degree of a node.

Let us compare the trees of Figs. 7.4.1.1(a) and (c). They are equivalent as trees. Each has A as its root and three subtrees. One of those subtrees has root C with no subtrees, another has root D with a single subtree rooted at G, and the third has root B with two subtrees rooted at E and F. The only difference between the two illustrations is the

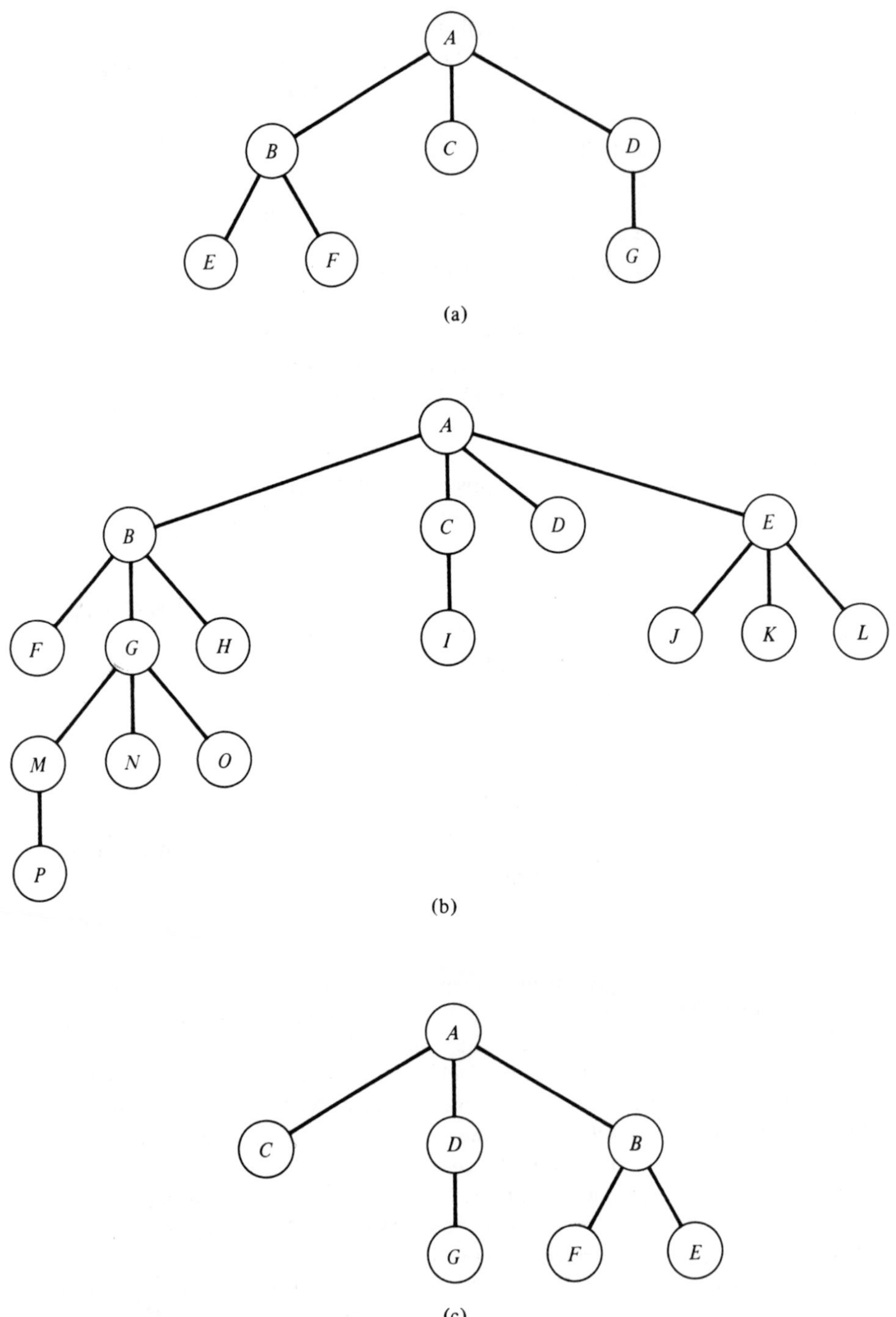

Figure 7.4.1.1. Examples of trees.

order in which the subtrees are arranged. The definition of a tree makes no distinction among subtrees of a general tree as in the case of a binary tree, where a distinction is made between the left and right subtrees. An ***ordered tree*** is defined as a tree in which the subtrees of each node form an ordered set. Thus, in an ordered tree, we may speak of the first, second, or last son of a particular node. The first son of a node in an ordered tree is often called the ***oldest*** son of that node, and the last son is called the ***youngest***. Although the trees of Figs. 7.4.1.1(a) and (c) are equivalent as unordered trees, they are different as ordered trees. In the remainder of this chapter we use the word "tree" to refer to "ordered tree." A ***forest*** is an ordered set of ordered trees.

The question arises as to whether a binary tree is a tree. Every binary tree except for the empty binary tree is indeed a tree. However, not every tree is binary since a tree node may have more than two sons while a binary tree node may not. Even a tree whose nodes have at most two sons is not necessarily a binary tree. This is because an only son in a general tree is not designated as being a "left" or a "right" son and in a binary tree every son must be either a "left" son or a "right" son. In fact, although a nonempty binary tree is a tree, the designation of left and right have no meaning within the context of a tree (except perhaps to order the two subtrees of those nodes with two sons). A nonempty binary tree is a tree each of whose nodes has a maximum of two subtrees which have the added designation of "left" or "right".

PL/I Representations of Trees

How can an ordered tree be represented in PL/I? Two alternatives immediately come to mind: an array of tree nodes is declared or a BASED variable is allocated for each node created. However, what should the structure of each individual node be? In the representation of a binary tree, each node contains an information field and two pointers to its two sons. But how many pointers should a tree node contain? The number of sons of a node is variable and may be as large or as small as desired. If we arbitrarily declare

```
DCL 1 NODE(500),
        2 INFO          FIXED,
        2 SONS(20)      FIXED;
```

then we are restricting the number of sons a node may have to a maximum of 20. Although it is true that, in most cases, this will be sufficient, it is inadequate when it is necessary to create dynamically a node with 21 or 100 sons. Far worse than this remote possibility is the fact that 20 units of storage are reserved for each node in the tree even though a node may actually have only 1 or 2 (or even 0) sons. This is a tremendous waste of space.

One alternative is to link all the sons of a node together in a linear list. Thus the set of available nodes (using the array implementation) might be declared as follows:

```
DCL 1 NODE(500),
        2 INFO          FIXED,
        2 SON           FIXED,
        2 NEXT          FIXED;
```

SON(P) points to the oldest son of NODE(P) and NEXT(P) points to the next younger brother of NODE(P). Alternatively, a node may be declared as a BASED variable:

```
DCL 1 NODE BASED(P),
      2 INFO          FIXED,
      2 SON           PTR,
      2 NEXT          PTR;
```

Figure 7.4.1.2 illustrates the representations of the trees of Figs. 7.4.1.1 under these methods.

Note that under this implementation, each tree node contains two pointers, SON and NEXT. If we think of SON as corresponding to the LEFT pointer of a binary tree node and NEXT as corresponding to its RIGHT pointer, then this method actually represents a general ordered tree by a binary tree. We may picture this binary tree as the original tree tilted 45° with all father-son links removed except for those between a node and its oldest son, and with links added between each node and its next younger brother. Figure 7.4.1.3 illustrates the binary trees corresponding to the trees of Fig. 7.4.1.1.

In fact, a binary tree may be used to represent an entire forest since the NEXT pointer in the root of a tree can be used to point to the next tree of the forest. Figure 7.4.1.4 illustrates a forest and its corresponding binary tree.

Tree Traversals

The traversal methods for binary trees induce traversal methods for forests. The preorder, inorder, or postorder traversals of a forest may be defined as the preorder, inorder, or postorder traversals of its corresponding binary tree. If a forest is represented as a set of BASED variable nodes with SON and NEXT pointers as given above, a PL/I routine to print out the contents of its nodes in inorder may be written as follows:

```
INTRAV: PROC(P)RECURSIVE;
           DCL P PTR;
           IF P=NULL THEN RETURN;
           CALL INTRAV(P->SON);
           PUT SKIP LIST(P->INFO);
           CALL INTRAV(P->NEXT);
           RETURN;
        END INTRAV;
```

Routines for preorder and postorder traversals are similar.

These traversals of a forest may also be defined directly as follows:

Preorder

1. Visit the root of the first tree in the forest.
2. Traverse in preorder the forest formed by the subtrees of the first tree, if any.
3. Traverse in preorder the forest formed by the remaining trees in the forest, if any.

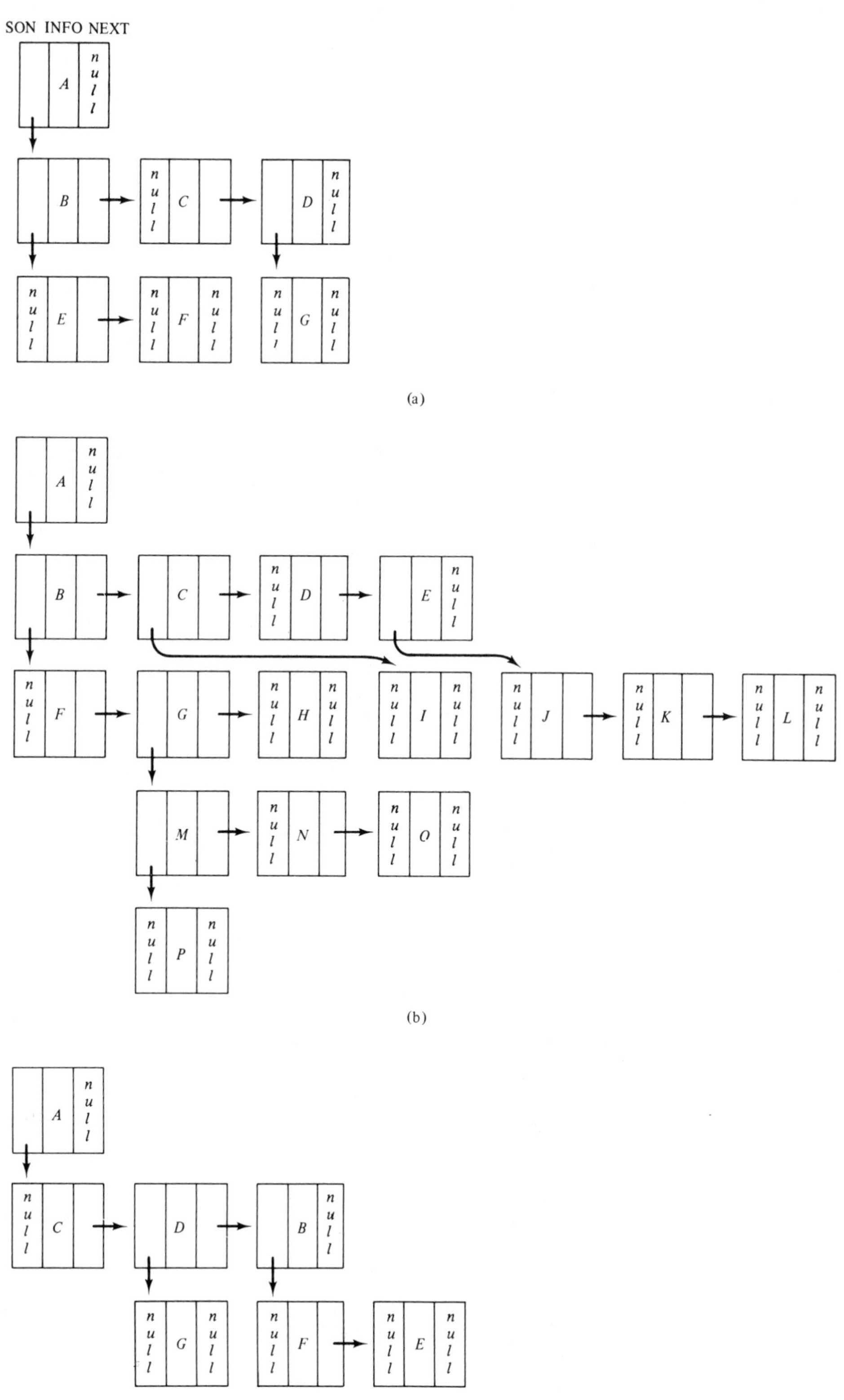

Figure 7.4.1.2. Tree representations.

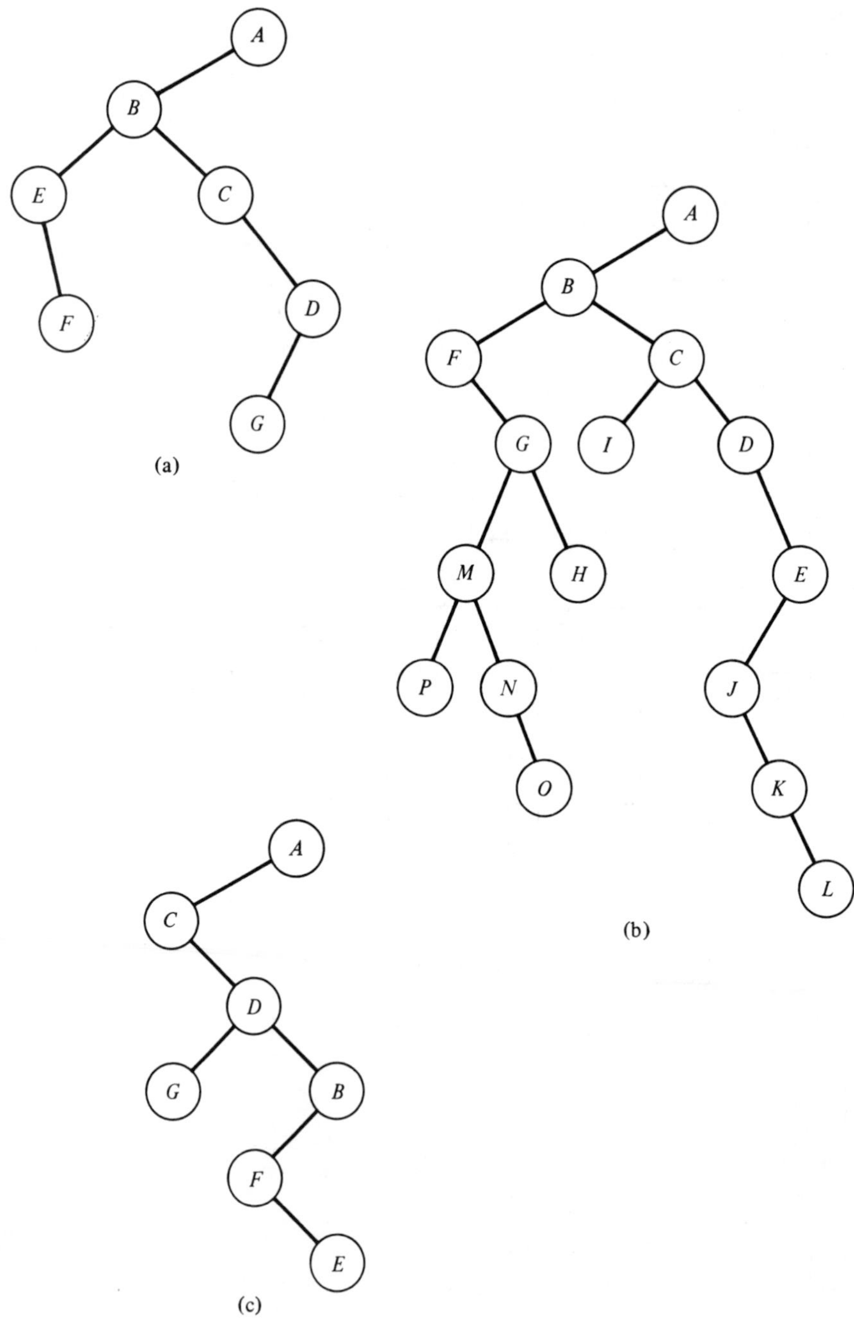

Figure 7.4.1.3. Binary trees corresponding to trees of Fig. 7.4.1.1.

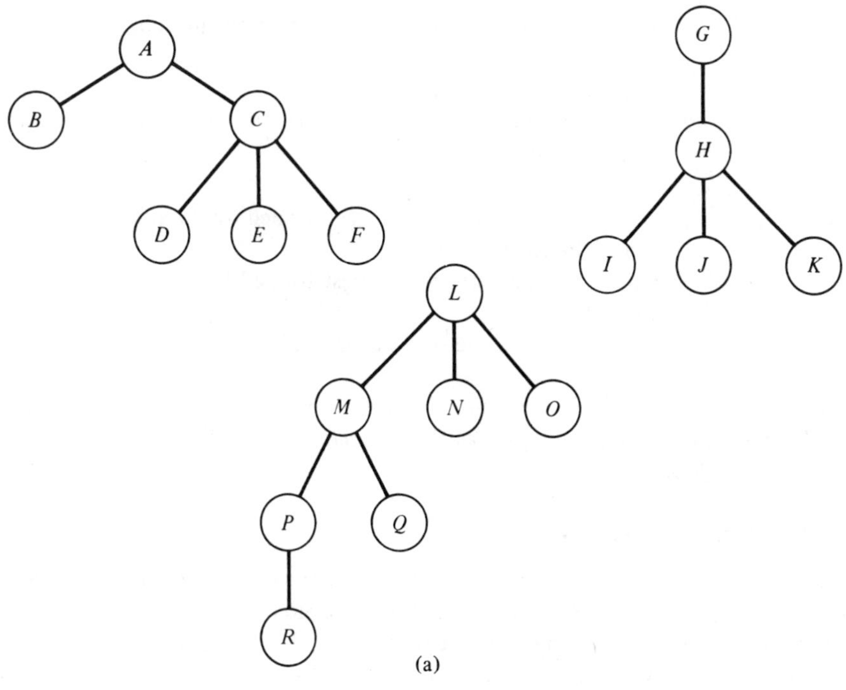

(a)

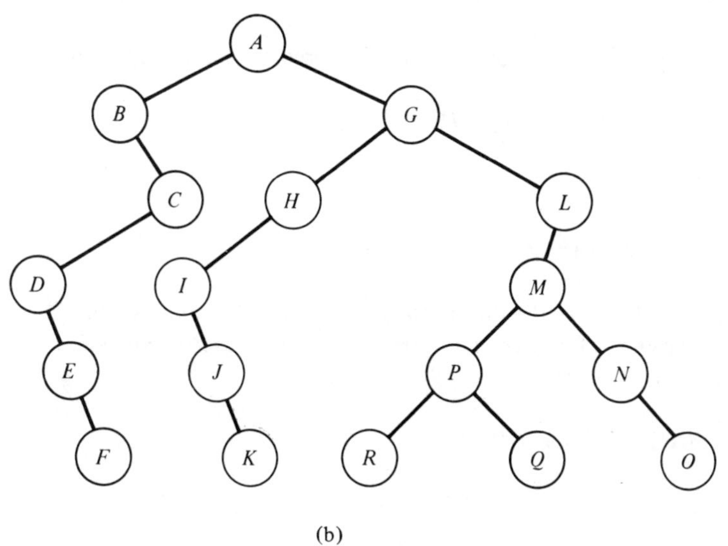

(b)

Figure 7.4.1.4. A forest and its corresponding binary tree.

Inorder
1. Traverse in inorder the forest formed by the subtrees of the first tree in the forest, if any.
2. Visit the root of the first tree.
3. Traverse in inorder the forest formed by the remaining trees in the forest, if any.

Postorder
1. Traverse in postorder the forest formed by the subtrees of the first tree in the forest, if any.
2. Traverse in postorder the forest formed by the remaining trees in the forest, if any.
3. Visit the root of the first tree in the forest.

The nodes of the forest in Fig. 7.4.1.4(a) may be listed in preorder as *ABCDEFGHIJKLMPRQNO*, in inorder as *BDEFCAIJKHGRPQMNOL*, and in postorder as *FEDCBKJIHRQPONMLGA*.

General Expressions as Trees

An ordered tree may be used to represent a general expression in much the same way that a binary tree may be used to represent a binary expression. Since a node may have any number of sons, nonleaf nodes need not represent only binary operators but can represent operators with any number of operands. Figure 7.4.1.5 illustrates two expressions and their tree representations. The symbol "%" is used to represent unary negation to avoid confusing it with binary subtraction, which is represented by a minus sign. A function reference such as *f*(*G*,*H*,*I*,*J*) is viewed as the operator *f* applied to the operands *G*, *H*, *I*, and *J*.

A traversal of the trees of Fig. 7.4.1.5 in preorder results in the strings

∗%+AB−+Clog+D!EfGHIJ

and

q+ABsinC∗X+YZ

respectively. These are the prefix versions of those two expressions. Thus we see that a preorder traversal of an expression tree produces its prefix expression. Inorder traversal yields the respective strings

AB+%CDE!+log+GHIJf−∗

and

AB+CsinXYZ+∗q,

which are the postfix versions of the two expressions. The fact that an inorder traversal

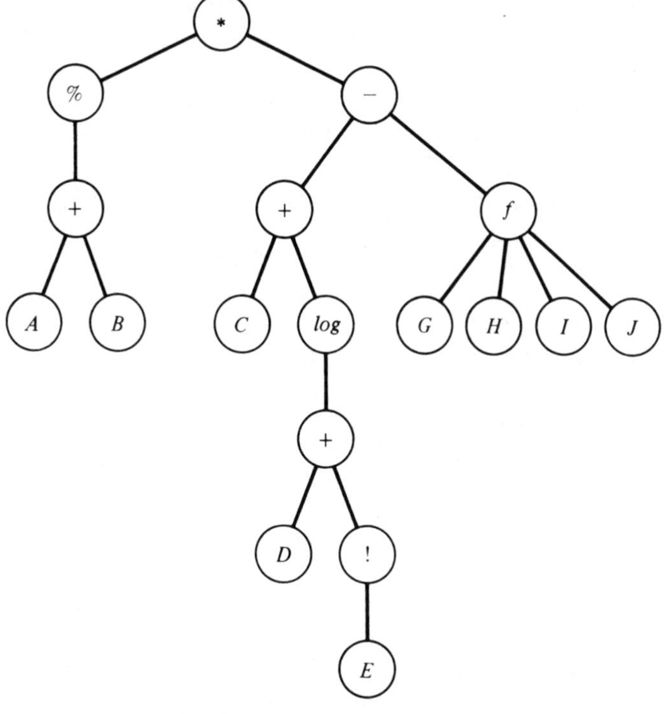

(a) $-(A + B) * (C + log(D + E!) - f(G, H, I, J))$

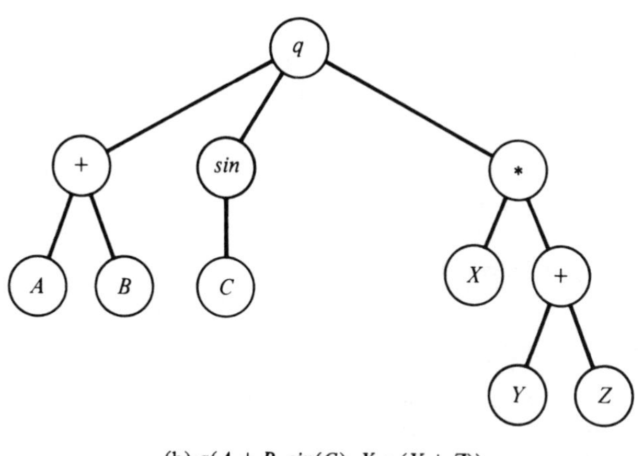

(b) $q(A + B, sin(C), X * (Y + Z))$

Figure 7.4.1.5. Tree representation of an arithmetic expression.

yields a postfix expression might be surprising at first glance. However, the reason for it becomes clear upon examination of the transformation which takes place when a general ordered tree is represented by a binary tree.

Consider an ordered tree in which each node has zero or two sons. Such a tree is shown in Fig. 7.4.1.6(a), and its binary tree equivalent is shown in Fig. 7.4.1.6(b). Traversing the binary tree of Fig. 7.4.1.6(b) is the same as traversing the ordered tree of Fig. 7.4.1.6(a). However, a tree such as the one in Fig. 7.4.1.6(a) may be considered as a binary tree in its own right, rather than as an ordered tree. Thus it is possible to perform a binary tree traversal directly on the tree of Fig. 7.4.1.6(a). Beneath that figure are the binary traversals of that tree, while beneath Fig. 7.4.1.6(b) are the binary traversals of the tree in that figure which are the same as the traversals of the tree of Fig. 7.4.1.6(a) if it is considered as an ordered tree.

Note that the preorder traversals of the two binary trees are the same. Thus if a preorder traversal on a binary tree representing a binary expression yields the prefix of the expression, then that traversal on an ordered tree representing a general expression which happens to have only binary operators yields prefix as well. However, the postorder traversals of the two binary trees are not the same. Instead, the inorder traversal of the second (which is the same as the inorder traversal of the first, if it is considered as an ordered tree) is the same as the postorder traversal of the first. Thus, the inorder traversal of an ordered tree representing a binary expression is equivalent to the postorder traversal of the binary tree representing that expression, which yields postfix.

Suppose that it is desired to evaluate an expression whose operands are all numerical constants. Such an expression can be represented in PL/I by a tree each of whose nodes is declared by:

```
DCL 1 NODE BASED(NDPTR),
      2 INFO      PTR,
      2 SON       PTR,
      2 NEXT      PTR;
```

The SON and NEXT pointers are used to link together the nodes of a tree as previously illustrated. Since a node may contain information which may be either a number (operand) or a character string (operator), INFO is a POINTER (as in Section 7.2) which points to either an operator or an operand declared by

```
DCL   OPERATOR CHAR(10)     BASED(TPTR),
      OPERAND  FLOAT        BASED(NPTR);
```

We wish to write a PL/I function EVALTREE(P) which accepts a pointer to such a tree and returns the value of the expression represented by that tree. The routine EVALBINTREE presented in Section 7.2 performs a similar function for binary expressions. EVALBINTREE utilizes a function OPER which accepts an operator symbol and two numerical operands and returns the numerical result of applying the operator to the operands. However, in the case of a general expression we cannot use such a function since the number of operands (and hence the number of arguments) varies with the

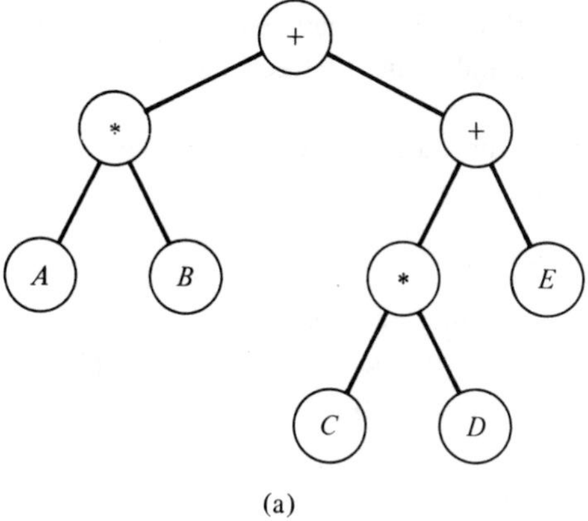

(a)

Preorder: $+ * AB + * CDE$
Inorder: $A * B + C * D + E$
Postorder: $AB * CD * E + +$

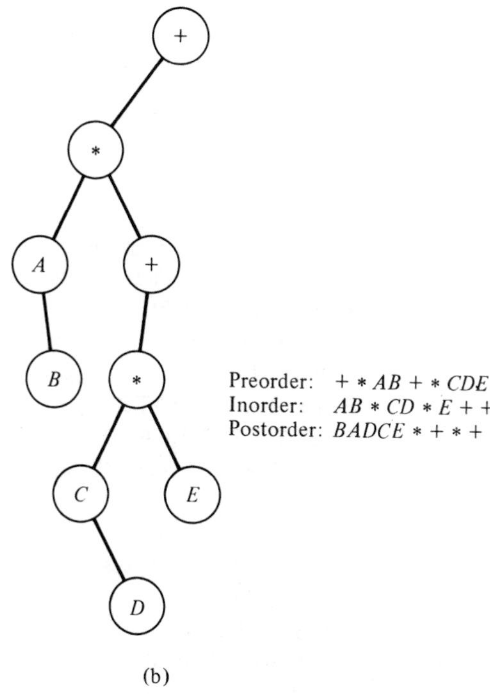

(b)

Figure 7.4.1.6.

operator. We therefore introduce a new function APPLY(P) which accepts a pointer to an expression tree which contains a single operator and its numerical operands, and returns the result of applying the operator to its operands. For example, the result of calling the function APPLY with parameter P pointing to the tree in Fig. 7.4.1.7 is 24. Thus if the root of the tree which is passed to EVALTREE represents an operator, each of its subtrees must be replaced by tree nodes representing the numerical results of their evaluation so that the function APPLY may be called. As the expression is evaluated, the tree nodes representing operands must be freed and operator nodes must be converted to operand nodes.

We present a recursive subroutine REPLACE which accepts a pointer to an expression tree and replaces the tree with a tree node representing the numerical result of its evaluation.

```
REPLACE:   PROC(P) RECURSIVE;
             DCL (P,Q,R,S)          PTR,
                 VALUE              FLOAT;

             IF P->SON=NULL THEN /*   the tree represents   */
                                 /*    a single operand     */
                                 RETURN;
             Q=P->SON;

OPNDLOOP:    DO WHILE(Q¬=NULL);
                /*   replace each of its subtrees by operands   */
                CALL REPLACE(Q);
                Q=Q->NEXT;
             END OPNDLOOP;

             /*   apply the operator in the root of the   */
             /*          operands in the subtrees         */
             VALUE=APPLY(P);
             /*   replace the operator by the result   */
             Q=P->INFO;
             FREE Q->OPERATOR;
             ALLOCATE OPERAND SET(Q);
             Q->OPERAND=VALUE;
             P->INFO=Q;

             /*   free all the subtrees   */
             Q=P->SON;
             P->SON=NULL;
FREELOOP:    DO WHILE(Q¬=NULL);
                R=Q;
                Q=Q->NEXT;
                S=R->INFO;
                FREE S->OPERAND;
                FREE R->NODE;
             END FREELOOP;

             RETURN;
           END REPLACE;
```

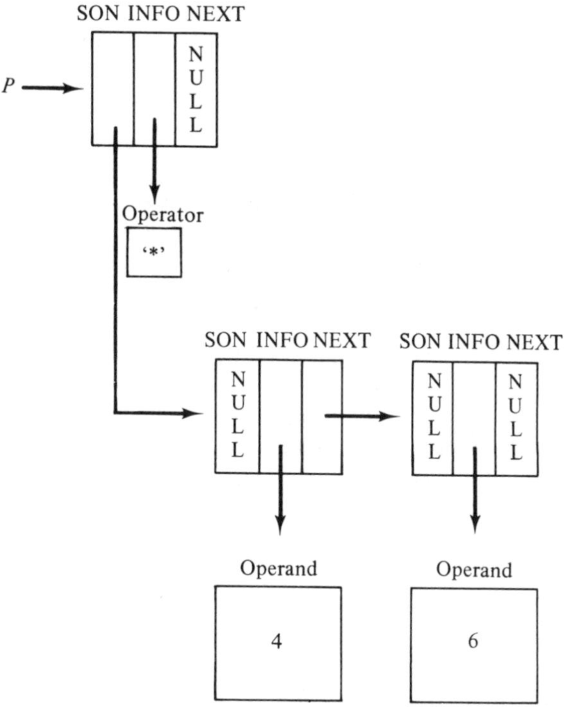

Figure 7.4.1.7. An expression tree.

The function EVALTREE may now be written as follows:

```
EVALTREE: PROC(P) RETURNS(FLOAT);
             DCL  (P,Q)          PTR,
                  VALUE          FLOAT;
             CALL REPLACE(P);
             Q=P–>INFO;
             VALUE=Q–>OPERAND;
             FREE Q–>OPERAND;
             FREE P–>NODE;
             RETURN(VALUE);
          END EVALTREE;
```

Note that after calling EVALTREE(P) the tree is destroyed and the value of P is meaningless. This is a case of a ***dangling pointer*** in which a pointer variable contains an address of a variable which has been freed. PL/I programmers who use BASED storage should be very careful to recognize such pointers and not to use them subsequently.

Other Tree Operations

In constructing a tree there are several operations which are frequently used. One of these is *setsons* which accepts a node of a tree that has no sons and a linear list of nodes linked together through the *next* field. *setsons* establishes the nodes in the list as the sons of the node in the tree. The PL/I routine to implement this operation is straightforward (we use the array of nodes implementation).

```
SETSONS: PROC(P,LIST);
          /*          P points to a tree node,          */
          /*       LIST to a list of nodes linked       */
          /*  together through their NEXT fields        */
          DCL(P,LIST)         FIXED;
          IF P=0 THEN DO;
               PUT SKIP LIST ('INVALID INSERTION');
               STOP;
                          END;
          IF SON(P) ¬= 0 THEN DO;
               PUT SKIP LIST('INVALID INSERTION');
               STOP;
                                        END;
          SON(P) =LIST;
          RETURN;
     END SETSONS;
```

Another common operation is *addson*(p,x) where p points to a node in a tree and it is desired to add a node containing x as the youngest son of *node*(p). The PL/I routine to implement *addson* is as follows. The routine calls the auxiliary function GETNODE which removes a node from the available list and returns a pointer to it.

```
ADDSON:     PROC(P,X);
              DCL (P,Q,R,X)        FIXED;
              IF P=0 THEN DO;
                   PUT SKIP LIST ('INVALID INSERTION');
                   STOP;
                            END;
              /*      The pointer Q traverses the list of       */
              /*      sons of P.  R is one node behind.         */
              R=0;
              Q=SON(P);

TRAVERSE:     DO WHILE (Q¬=0);
                   R=Q;
                   Q=NEXT(Q);
              END TRAVERSE;

              /*  at this point, R points to the youngest       */
              /*    son of P or is null if P has no sons        */
```

```
        Q=GETNODE;
        INFO(Q) =X;
        NEXT(Q) =0;
        IF R=0 THEN  /*    P has no sons    */
                  SON(P) =Q;
             ELSE NEXT(R) =Q;
        RETURN;
      END ADDSON;
```

Note that in order to add a new son to a node, the list of existing sons must be traversed. Since adding a son is a common operation, a representation is often used which makes this operation more efficient. Under this alternate representation, the list of sons is ordered from youngest to oldest rather than vice versa. Thus SON(P) points to the youngest son of NODE(P), and NEXT(P) points to its next older brother. Under this representation the routine ADDSON may be written as follows:

```
ADDSON: PROC(P,X);
          DCL(P,Q,X) FIXED;
          IF P=0 THEN DO;
                          PUT SKIP LIST ('INVALID INSERTION');
                          STOP;
                      END;
          Q=GETNODE;
          INFO(Q) =X;
          NEXT(Q) =SON(P);
          SON(P) =Q;
          RETURN;
        END ADDSON;
```

Another variation in representing a tree is to allow the NEXT field of the last son of a node to point back to its father, rather than to hold the value NULL. This allows a node to be reached from any of its descendants. Of course, there must be an indication within a node as to whether its NEXT field points to a brother or a father. Under the implementation which uses an array of nodes this can be accomplished by representing a pointer to the father by a negative number, much in the same way that threads were represented in binary trees.

Alternatively, a FATHER field can be included in each node so that it is possible to proceed directly from a node to its father without having to first traverse a possibly long list of brothers.

Example 7.4.2: Game Trees

One application of trees is to game playing by computer. We illustrate this application by writing a PL/I program to determine the "best" move in tic-tac-toe from a given board position. Assume that there is a function EVALUATE which accepts a board position and either the character 'X' or 'O' and returns a numerical value which represents how "good" the position seems to be for that player (the larger the value returned by EVALUATE, the better the position). Of course, a winning position yields the largest possible value, and a losing position yields the smallest. An example of such an evaluation function for tic-tac-toe is the number of rows, columns, and diagonals remaining open for one player minus the number remaining open for his opponent (except that the value 9 would be returned for a position that wins, and −9 for a position that loses). This function does not "look ahead" to consider any possible board positions which might result from the current position–it merely evaluates a static board position.

Given a board position, the best next move could be determined by considering all possible moves and resulting positions. That move which results in the board position with the highest evaluation should be selected. However, such an analysis does not necessarily yield the best move, as can be seen from Fig. 7.4.2.1. This figure illustrates a position and the five possible moves which X can make from that position. Applying the evaluation function described above to the five resulting positions yields the values shown. Four moves yield the same maximum evaluation, although three of them are distinctly inferior to the fourth. (The fourth position yields a certain victory for X, while the other three can be drawn by O.) In fact, the move which yields the smallest evaluation is as good or better than the moves which yield a higher evaluation. One reason for this is that the above static evaluation function is not good enough to predict the outcome of the game. While a better evaluation function could easily be produced for the game of tic-tac-toe (even if it were by the brute force method of listing all positions and the appropriate response), most games are too complex for static evaluators to determine the best response.

Suppose it were possible to look ahead several moves. Then the choice of a move could be improved considerably. Define the ***look-ahead level*** as the number of future moves to be considered. Starting at any position, it is possible to construct a tree of the possible board positions which may result from each move. Such a tree is called a ***game tree***. The game tree for the opening tic-tac-toe position with a look-ahead level of 2 is illustrated in Fig. 7.4.2.2. (Actually other positions do exist, but because of symmetry considerations, these are effectively the same as the positions shown.) Note that the maximum level (called the ***depth***) of the nodes in such a tree is equal to the look-ahead level.

Let us designate the player who must move at the root's game position as ***plus*** and his opponent as ***minus***. We attempt to find the best move for plus from the root's game position. The remaining nodes of the tree may be designated as ***plus nodes*** or ***minus nodes*** depending upon which player must move from that node's position. Each node of Fig. 7.4.2.2 is marked as a plus or minus node.

Suppose the game positions of all the sons of a plus node have been evaluated for player plus. Then clearly, plus should choose the move which yields the maximum evaluation. Thus, the value of a plus node to player plus is the maximum of the values of its sons. On the other hand, once plus has made his move, minus will select the move which yields the minimum evaluation for player plus. Thus the value of a minus node to player plus is the minimum of the values of its sons.

Therefore in order to decide the best move for player plus from the root, the positions in the leaves must be evaluated for player plus using a static evaluation function.

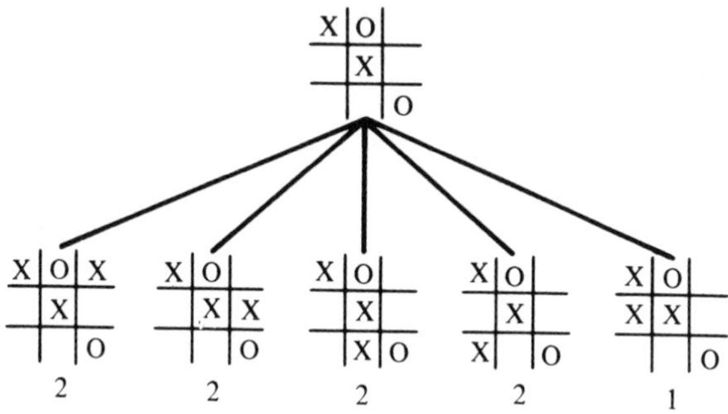

Figure 7.4.2.1.

These values are then moved up the game tree by assigning to each plus node the maximum of its sons' values and to each minus node the minimum of its sons' values on the assumption that minus will select the move that is worst for plus. The value assigned to each node of Fig. 7.4.2.2 by this process is indicated in that figure immediately below the node. The move which plus should select, given the board position in the root node, is the one which maximizes its value. Thus the opening move for *X* should be the middle square as illustrated in Fig. 7.4.2.2. Figure 7.4.2.3 illustrates the determination of *O*'s best reply. Note that the designation of "plus" and "minus" depends on whose move is being calculated. Thus, in Fig. 7.4.2.2, *X* is designated as plus, while in Fig. 7.4.2.3, *O* is designated as plus. In applying the static evaluation function to a board position, the value of the position to whichever player is designated as plus is computed. This method is called the ***minimax method*** since, as the tree is climbed, the maximum and minimum functions are applied alternately.

The best move for a player from a given position may be determined by first constructing the game tree and applying a static evaluation function to the leafs. These values are then moved up the tree by applying the minimum and maximum at minus and plus nodes respectively. Each node of the game tree must include a representation of the board and an indication of whether the node is a plus node or a minus node. An array of nodes is therefore declared by

```
DCL 1 NODE(500),
        2 BOARD(3,3)        CHAR(1),
        2 TURN              FIXED,
        2 SON               FIXED,
        2 NEXT              FIXED;
```

BOARD(P,I,J) has the value 'X', 'O', or ' ' depending on whether the square in row I and column J of NODE(P) is occupied by either of the players or is unoccupied. TURN(P) has the value 1 or −1 depending on whether NODE(P) is a plus or minus node respectively. The remaining two fields of NODE are used to position the node within the tree. SON(P) points to the oldest son of NODE(P), while NEXT(P) points to its next younger brother. We assume that the above declaration is global, that an available list of nodes has been established, and that appropriate GETNODE and FREENODE routines have been written.

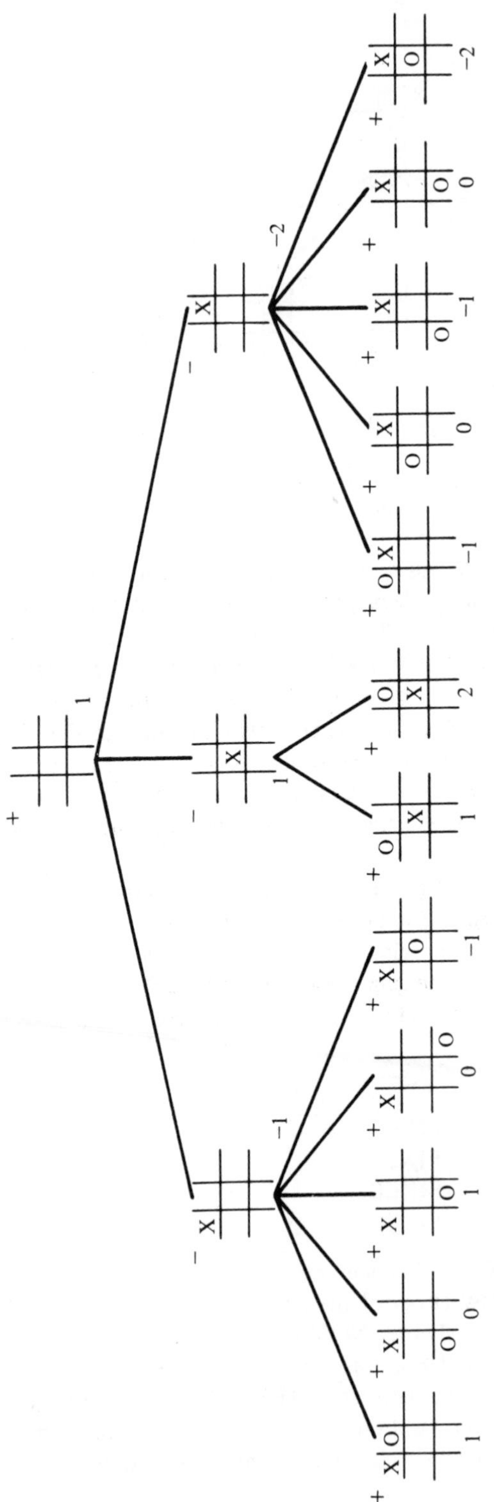

Figure 7.4.2.2. A game tree for tic-tac-toe.

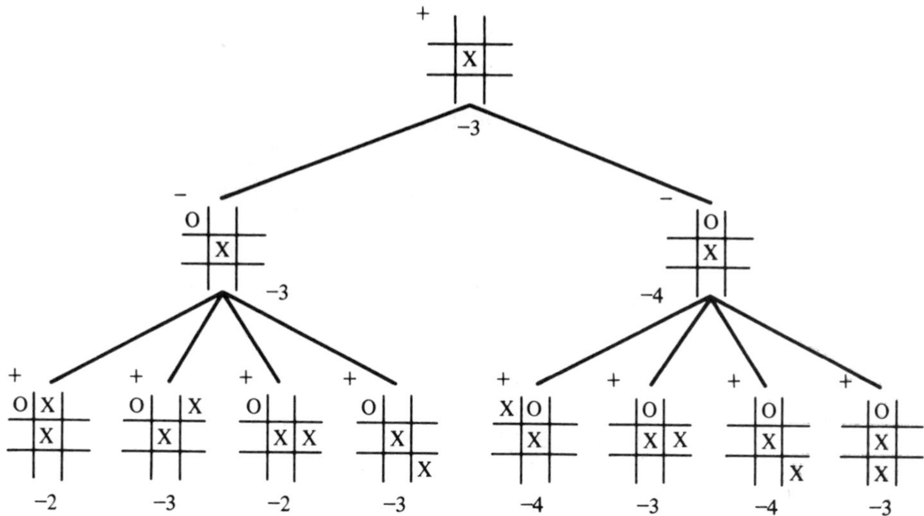

Figure 7.4.2.3. Computing O's reply.

The PL/I routine NEXTMOVE(BRD,PLAYER,LOOKLEVEL,NEWBRD) computes the best next move. BRD is a 3 by 3 array representing the current board position, PLAYER is 'X' or 'O' depending on whose move is being computed (note that in tic-tac-toe the value of PLAYER could be computed from BRD, so that this parameter is not strictly necessary), and LOOKLEVEL is the look-ahead level used in constructing the tree. NEWBRD is an output parameter which represents the best board position that can be achieved by PLAYER from position BRD. NEXTMOVE uses two auxiliary routines, BUILDTREE and BESTBRANCH. The function BUILDTREE builds the game tree and returns a pointer to its root. The subroutine BESTBRANCH computes the value of two output parameters: BEST, which is a pointer to the tree node representing the best move, and VALUE, which is the evaluation of that move using the minimax technique.

```
NEXTMOVE: PROC(BRD,PLAYER,LOOKLEVEL,NEWBRD);
             DCL (BRD,NEWBRD) (*,*)                   CHAR(*),
                 PLAYER                               CHAR(*),
                 (TREE, BEST, VALUE, LOOKLEVEL)       FIXED;
             TREE=BUILDTREE(BRD, LOOKLEVEL);
             CALL BESTBRANCH(TREE, PLAYER, BEST, VALUE);
             NEWBRD=BOARD(BEST,*,*);
             RETURN;
          END NEXTMOVE;
```

The function BUILDTREE returns a pointer to the root of a game tree. It uses the auxiliary function GETNODE which removes a node from the available list and returns a pointer to it. It also uses a routine EXPAND(P,PLEVEL,DEPTH) in which P is a pointer to a node in a game tree, PLEVEL is its level, and DEPTH is the depth of the game tree which is to be constructed. EXPAND produces the subtree rooted at P to the proper depth.

```
BUILDTREE:  PROC(BRD,LOOKLEVEL) RETURNS(FIXED);
               DCL BRD(*,*)                  CHAR(*),
                    (LOOKLEVEL,TREE)         FIXED;

               /*   create the root of the tree and initialize it   */
               TREE=GETNODE;
               BOARD(TREE,*,*) =BRD;

               /*   the root is a plus node by definition   */
               TURN(TREE) =1;
               SON(TREE),NEXT(TREE) =0;

               /*   create the rest of the game tree   */
               CALL EXPAND(TREE,0,LOOKLEVEL);
               RETURN(TREE);
            END BUILDTREE;
```

EXPAND may be implemented by generating all board positions which may be obtained from the board position of NODE(P) and establishing them as the sons of P in the game tree. EXPAND then calls itself recursively using these sons as parameters until the desired depth is reached. EXPAND uses an auxiliary function GENERATE which accepts a board position BRD and returns a pointer to a list of nodes containing the board positions which can be obtained from BRD. This list is linked together by the NEXT field. We leave the coding of GENERATE as an exercise for the reader.

```
EXPAND:     PROC(P,PLEVEL,DEPTH) RECURSIVE;
               DCL (P,PLEVEL,DEPTH,Q)        FIXED;
               IF PLEVEL=DEPTH THEN
                  /*   P is already at the maximum level   */
                                          RETURN;
               Q=GENERATE(BOARD(P,*,*));
               SON(P) =Q;

               /*   traverse the list of nodes   */
SONLOOP:       DO WHILE(Q¬=0);
                  TURN(Q) = -TURN(P);
                  SON(Q) =0;
                  CALL EXPAND(Q,PLEVEL+1,DEPTH);
                  Q=NEXT(Q);
               END SONLOOP;

               RETURN;
            END EXPAND;
```

Once the game tree has been created, BESTBRANCH evaluates the nodes of the tree. When a pointer to a leaf is passed to BESTBRANCH, it calls a function EVALUATE which statically evaluates the board position of that leaf for the player whose move we are determining. The coding of EVALUATE is left as an exercise. When a pointer to a nonleaf is passed to BESTBRANCH, the routine calls itself recursively on each of its sons and then assigns the maximum of its sons' values to the nonleaf if it is a plus node, and the minimum if it is a minus node. BESTBRANCH also keeps track of which son yielded this minimum or maximum value.

If TURN(P) = −1, then NODE(P) is a minus node and it is to be assigned the minimum of the values assigned to its sons. If, however, TURN(P) is 1, NODE(P) is a plus node and its value should be the maximum of the values assigned to the sons of NODE(P). Since MIN(X,Y) =−MAX(−X,−Y) (you are invited to prove this as a trivial exercise), the correct maximum or minimum can be found by multiplying the values of each of the sons by TURN(P), taking the maximum, and then multiplying by TURN(P) once more. These ideas are incorporated into BESTBRANCH. The output parameters BEST and VALUE are, respectively, a pointer to that son of the tree's root which maximizes its value and the value of that son which has now been assigned to the root.

```
BESTBRANCH:  PROC(ND,PLAYER,BEST,VALUE) RECURSIVE;
               DCL (ND,BEST,VALUE,P,PBEST,VAL)          FIXED,
                   PLAYER                               CHAR(*);
               IF SON (ND) =0  THEN
                     /*   the node is a leaf    */
                     DO;
                        VALUE=EVALUATE(BOARD(ND,*,* ),PLAYER);
                        BEST=ND;
                        RETURN;
                     END;

               /*   the node is not a leaf    */
               /*   traverse the list of sons    */
               P=SON(ND);
               CALL BESTBRANCH(P,PLAYER,BEST,VALUE);
               /*   if ND is a minus node, multiply by −1   */
               VALUE=TURN(ND) * VALUE;
               BEST=P
               P=NEXT(P);
SONLOOP:       DO WHILE (P¬=0);
                     CALL BESTBRANCH(P,PLAYER,PBEST,VAL);
                     VAL=TURN(ND)*VAL;
                     IF VAL > VALUE THEN DO;
                                     VALUE=VAL;
                                     BEST=P;
                                          END;

                     P=NEXT(P);
               END SONLOOP;
```

```
      /*   if ND is a minus node, multiply by -1   */
      /*         to obtain the minimum             */
      VALUE=TURN(ND) * VALUE;
      RETURN;
   END BESTBRANCH;
```

7.5. Graphs and Their Applications

In this section, we consider a new data structure: the graph. We define some of the terms associated with graphs and show how to implement them in PL/I. We also present several applications of graphs.

7.5.1. Graphs

A ***graph*** consists of a set of ***nodes*** (or ***vertices***) and a set of ***arcs***. Each arc in a graph is specified by a pair of nodes. Figure 7.5.1.1(a) illustrates a graph. The set of nodes is $\{A,B,C,D,E,F,G,H\}$, and the set of arcs is $\{(A,B),(A,C),(A,D),(C,D),(C,F),(E,G),(A,A)\}$. If the pairs of nodes which make up the arcs are ordered pairs, then the graph is said to be a ***directed graph*** (or ***digraph***). Figures 7.5.1.1(b), (c), and (d) illustrate three digraphs. The arrows between nodes represent arcs. The head of each arrow represents the second node in the ordered pair of nodes making up an arc, while the tail of each arrow represents the first node in the pair. The set of arcs for the graph of Fig. 7.5.1.1(b) is $\{\langle A,B\rangle,\langle A,C\rangle,\langle A,D\rangle,\langle C,D\rangle,\langle F,C\rangle,\langle E,G\rangle,\langle A,A\rangle\}$. We use parentheses to indicate an unordered pair and angled brackets to indicate an ordered pair. In the remainder of this chapter we restrict our attention to digraphs.

Note that a graph need not be a tree (Figure 7.5.1.1(a,b,d)) but that a tree must be a graph (Fig. 7.5.1.1(c)). Note also that a node need not have any arcs associated with it (node H in Figs. 7.5.1.1(a) and (b)).

A node n is ***incident*** to an arc x if n is one of the two nodes in the ordered pair of nodes which comprise x. (We also say that x is incident to n.) The ***degree*** of a node is the number of arcs incident to it. The ***indegree*** of a node n is the number of arcs which have n as the head, and the ***outdegree*** of n is the number of arcs which have n as the tail. For example, node A in Fig. 7.5.1.1(d) has indegree 1, outdegree 2, and degree 3. A node n is ***adjacent*** to a node m if there is an arc from m to n.

A ***relation*** R on a set S is a set of ordered pairs of elements of S. For example, if $S=\{3,5,6,8,10,17\}$, then the set $R=\{\langle 3,10\rangle,\langle 5,6\rangle,\langle 5,8\rangle,\langle 6,17\rangle,\langle 8,17\rangle,\langle 10,17\rangle\}$ is a relation. If $\langle x,y\rangle$ is a member of a relation R, then x is said to be ***related*** to y in R. The above relation R may be described by saying that x is related to y if x is less than y and the remainder obtained by dividing y by x is odd. $\langle 8,17\rangle$ is a member of this relation since 8 is smaller than 17 and the remainder on dividing 17 by 8 is 1 which is odd. A relation may be represented by a graph in which the nodes represent the underlying set and the arcs represent the ordered pairs of the relation. Figure 7.5.1.2(a) illustrates the graph representing the above relation. A number may be associated with each arc of a graph as in Fig. 7.5.1.2(b). In that figure, the number associated with each arc is the remainder obtained by dividing the integer at the head of the arc by the integer at the tail. Such a

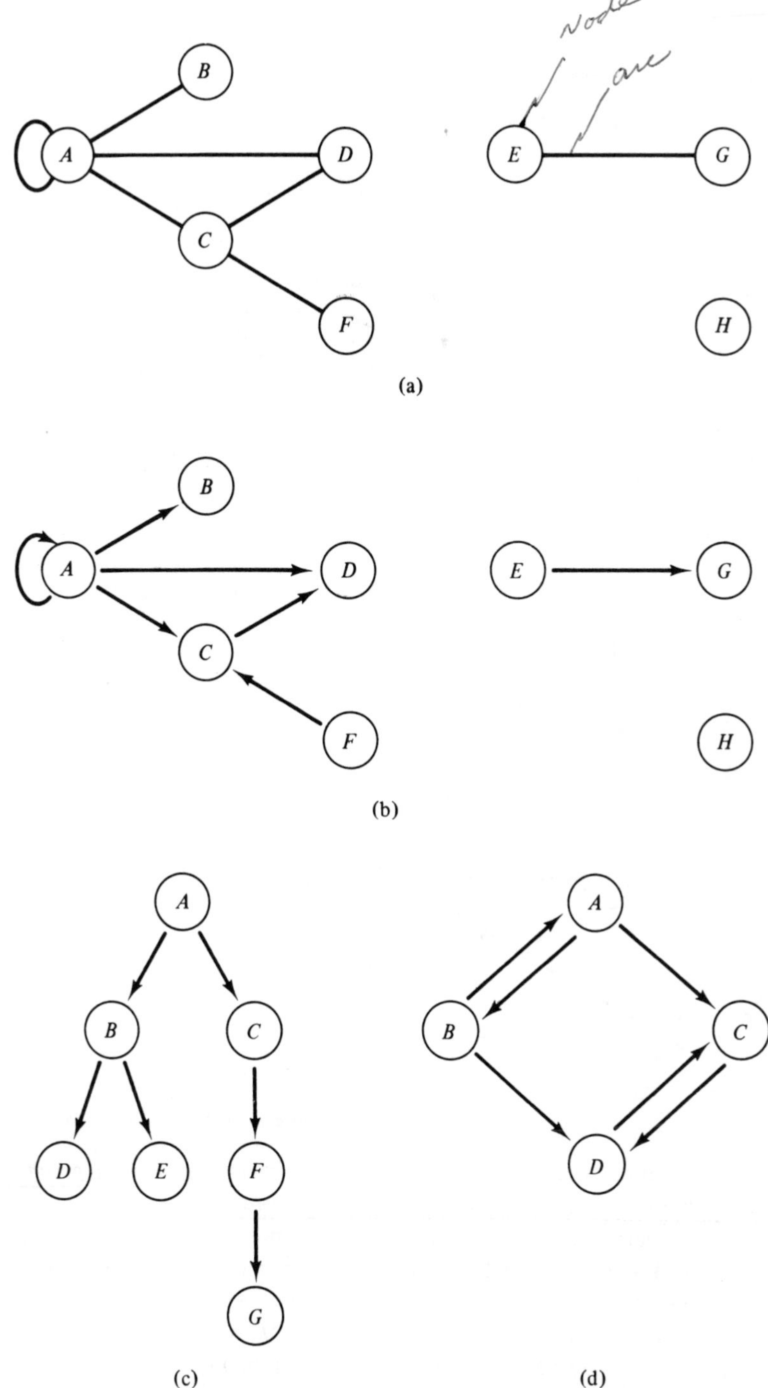

Figure 7.5.1.1. Examples of graphs.

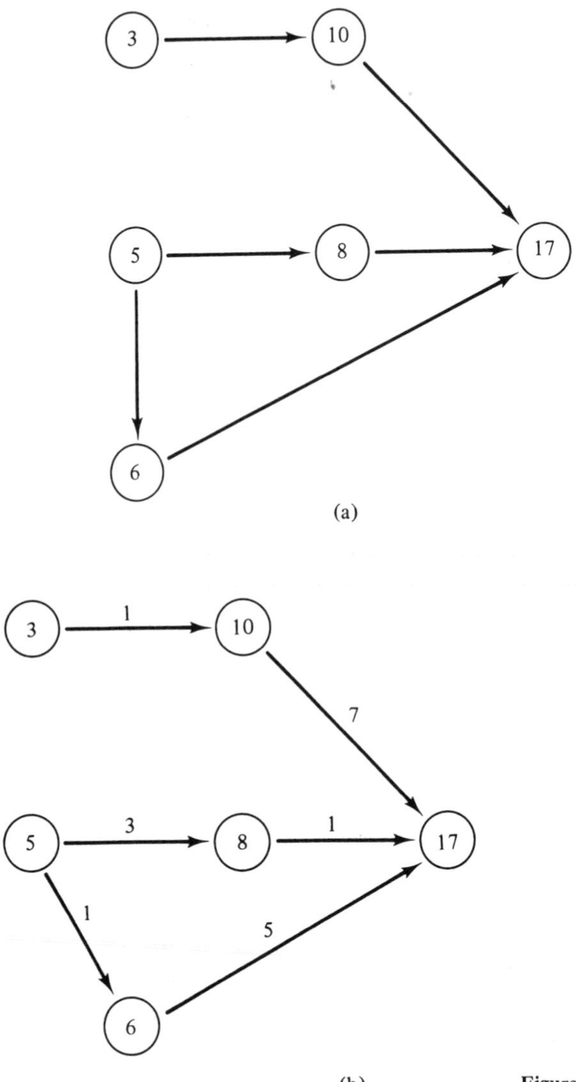

Figure 7.5.1.2. Relations and graphs.

graph, in which a number is associated with each arc, is called a ***weighted graph*** or a ***network***. The number associated with an arc is called its ***weight.***

We identify several primitive operations which are useful in dealing with graphs. The operation *join*(*a*,*b*) adds an arc from node *a* to node *b* if one does not already exist. *joinwt*(*a*,*b*,*x*) adds an arc from *a* to *b* with weight *x* in a weighted graph. *remv*(*a*,*b*) and *remvwt*(*a*,*b*,*x*) remove an arc from *a* to *b* if one exists (*remvwt* also sets *x* to its weight). While we may also want to add or delete nodes from a graph, we postpone a discussion of these possibilities until a later section. The function *adjacent*(*a*,*b*) returns *true* if *b* is adjacent to *a*, and *false* otherwise.

A ***path of length k*** from node a to node b is defined as a sequence of k+1 nodes $n_1,n_2,\ldots,n_{k+1}$ such that $n_1 = a$, $n_{k+1} = b$ and *adjacent*(n_i,n_{i+1}) is *true* for all i between 1 and k. If for some integer k, a path of length k exists between a and b, then there is a ***path*** from a to b. A path from a node to itself is called a ***cycle***. If a graph contains a cycle, it is ***cyclic***; otherwise, it is ***acyclic***.

Consider the graph of Fig. 7.5.1.3. There is a path of length 1 from A to C, two paths of length 2 from B to G, and a path of length 3 from A to F. There is no path from B to C. There are cycles from B to B, from H to H, and from G to G. Be sure that you can find all paths of length less than 9 and all cycles in the figure.

An Application of Graphs

We now consider an example. Consider input consisting of a card containing four integers followed by any number of cards with two integers each. The first integer on the first card, n, represents a number of cities which for simplicity are numbered from 1 to n. The second and third integers on that card are between 1 and n and represent two cities, A and B. It is desired to travel from city A to city B using exactly *nr* roads, where *nr* is the fourth integer on the first card. Each subsequent card contains two integers representing two cities. This indicates that there is a road from the first city to the second. The problem is to determine whether there is a path of required length by which one can travel from city A to city B.

A plan for solution is the following: Create a graph with the cities as nodes and the roads as arcs. To find a path of length *nr* from node A to node B, look for a node C such that an arc exists from A to C and a path of length *nr*–1 exists from C to B. If these conditions are satisfied for some node C, then the desired path exists. If the conditions are not satisfied for any node C, then the desired path does not exist. The algorithm uses an auxiliary recursive function *findpath*(k, a, b). This function returns *true* if there is a path

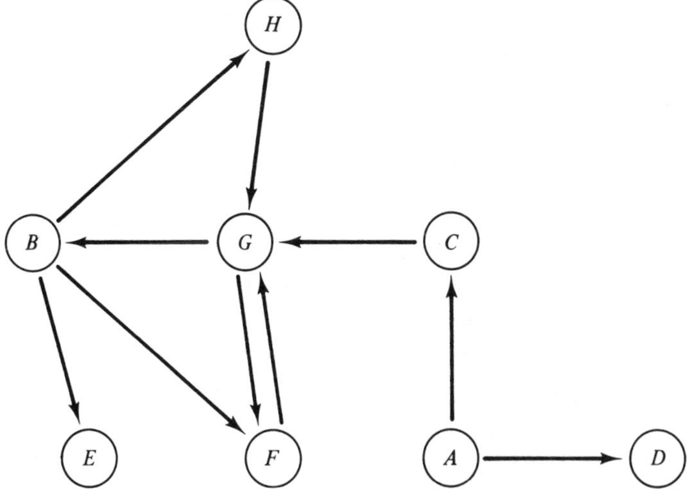

Figure 7.5.1.3.

of length *k* from *a* to *b* and *false* otherwise. The algorithms for the program and the function follow:

```
read (n);           /*          number of cities              */
create n nodes and label them from 1 to n;
read (a,b);         /*        seek path from a to b           */
read (nr);          /*  desired number of roads to take       */
do while (there is more input);
   read (city1, city 2);
   join (city1, city2);
end
if findpath(nr,a,b)  then print ('a path exists from ',a,'to',b,'in',nr,'steps');
                     else print  ('no path exists from ',a,'to',b,'in',nr,'steps');
```

The algorithm for the function *findpath*(*k*,*a*,*b*) follows:

```
if k=1  then    /*   search for path of length 1      */
        if adjacent(a,b)  then return(true);
                          else return(false);
do c=1 to n;    /*   check each city as intermediate      */
          if adjacent(a,c) then
                                    if   findpath(k−1,c,b)   then return(true);
end;
/*   no valid path found     */
return(false);
```

While the above algorithm is a solution to the problem, it has several deficiencies. Many paths are investigated several times during the recursive process. Also, while the algorithm must actually check each possible path, the final result merely ascertains whether a desired path exists; it does not produce the path itself. More likely than not, it is desirable to find the nodes of the path in addition to knowing whether or not a path exists. Also, the algorithm does not test for the existence of a path regardless of length; it only tests for a path of specific length. We explore solutions to some of these problems later in this chapter and in the Exercise Manual.

PL/I Representation of Graphs

Let us now turn to the question of representing graphs in PL/I. Suppose that the number of nodes in the graph is constant; i.e., arcs may be added or deleted, but nodes are not. A graph with N nodes could then be declared as follows:

```
DCL 1 GRAPH,
        2 NODE(N),
          3  /*     information associated with each node        */
        2 ARC(N,N),
          3 ADJ    BIT(1),
          3 /*        information associated with each           */
            /*                    existing arc                   */
```

The array NODE(N) represents the N nodes with appropriate information assigned to each node. The array ARC(N,N) is a two-dimensional array representing every possible ordered pair of nodes. The value of ADJ(I,J) is either '1'B or '0'B depending upon whether or not node J is adjacent to node I. The array ADJ is called an ***adjacency matrix***. In the case of a weighted graph each arc can also be assigned information.

Frequently the nodes of a graph are numbered from 1 to N and no information is assigned to them. Also, we may be interested in the existence of arcs but not in any weights or other information about them. In such cases the graph could be declared simply by

```
DCL ADJ(N,N)    BIT(1);
```

In effect, the graph is totally described by its adjacency matrix. We present the code for the primitive operations described above in the case where a graph is described by its adjacency matrix.

```
JOIN:       PROC(ADJ,NODE1,NODE2);
              /*        adds an arc from NODE1 to NODE2          */
              DCL ADJ(*,*)                BIT(*),
                  (NODE1,NODE2)           FIXED;
              ADJ(NODE1,NODE2) = '1'B;
              RETURN;
            END JOIN;

REMV:       PROC(ADJ,NODE1,NODE2);
              /* deletes arc from NODE1 to NODE2 if one exists   */
              DCL ADJ(*,*)                BIT(*),
                  (NODE1,NODE2)           FIXED;
              ADJ(NODE1,NODE2) = '0'B;
              RETURN;
            END REMV;

ADJACENT:   PROC(ADJ,NODE1,NODE2) RETURNS (BIT(1));
              /*        tests whether there is an arc from       */
              /*               NODE 1 to NODE2                   */
              DCL ADJ(*,*)                BIT(*),
                  (NODE1,NODE2)           FIXED;
              IF ADJ(NODE1,NODE2) THEN RETURN ('1'B);
                                  ELSE RETURN ('0'B);
            END ADJACENT;
```

A weighted graph with a fixed number of nodes may be declared by

```
DCL 1 ARC(N,N),
      2 ADJ        BIT(1),
      2 WEIGHT     FIXED;
```

The routine JOINWT which adds an arc from NODE1 to NODE2 with a given weight WT may be coded as follows:

```
JOINWT: PROC(ARC,NODE1,NODE2,WT);
          DCL 1  ARC(*,*)
                   2 ADJ                BIT(*),
                   2 WEIGHT             FIXED,
                (WT,NODE1,NODE2)        FIXED;
          ADJ(NODE1,NODE2) = '1'B;
          WEIGHT(NODE1,NODE2) = WT;
          RETURN;
        END JOINWT;
```

The routine REMVWT is left to the reader as an exercise.

Transitive Closure

Let us assume that a graph is completely described by its adjacency matrix, *adj* (i.e., no data is associated with the nodes, and the graph is not weighted). Consider the logical expression *adj*(*i*,*k*) & *adj*(*k*,*j*). Its value is *true* if and only if the values of both *adj*(*i*,*k*) and *adj*(*k*,*j*) are *true*, which implies that there is an arc from node *i* to node *k* and an arc from node *k* to node *j*. Thus *adj*(*i*,*k*) & *adj*(*k*,*j*) equals *true* if and only if there is a path of length 2 from *i* to *j* passing through *k*.

Now consider the expression

$$(adj(i,1)\&adj(1,j))\ |\ (adj(i,2)\&adj(2,j))\ |\ \ldots\ |\ (adj(i,n)\&adj(n,j)).$$

The value of this expression is *true* only if there is a path of length 2 from node *i* to node *j* either through node 1, or through node 2, . . . , or through node *n*. This is the same as saying that the expression evaluates to *true* if and only if there is some path of length 2 from node *i* to node *j*. Consider an array adj_2 such that $adj_2(i,j)$ is the value of the above expression. adj_2 is called the ***path matrix of length 2***. $adj_2(i,j)$ indicates whether or not there is a path of length 2 between *i* and *j*. If you are familiar with matrix multiplication, note that adj_2 is the product of *adj* with itself, with numerical multiplication replaced by conjunction (the *and* operation) and addition replaced by disjunction (the *or* operation). adj_2 is said to be the ***Boolean product** of adj* with itself.

Figure 7.5.1.4 illustrates this process. Figure 7.5.1.4(a) depicts a graph and its adjacency matrix. Figure 7.5.1.4(b) is the Boolean product of that matrix with itself, and thus is the path matrix of length 2 for the graph. Convince yourself that a 1 appears in row *i*, column *j* of the matrix of Fig. 7.5.1.4(b) if and only if there is a path of length 2 from node *i* to node *j* in the graph.

Similarly, define adj_3, the path matrix of length 3, as the Boolean product of adj_2 with *adj*. $adj_3(i,j)$ equals *true* if and only if there is a path of length 3 from *i* to *j*. In general, to compute the path matrix of length *l*, form the Boolean product of the path matrix of length *l*–1 with the adjacency matrix. Figure 7.5.1.5 illustrates the matrices adj_3 and adj_4 of the graph in Figure 7.5.1.4(a).

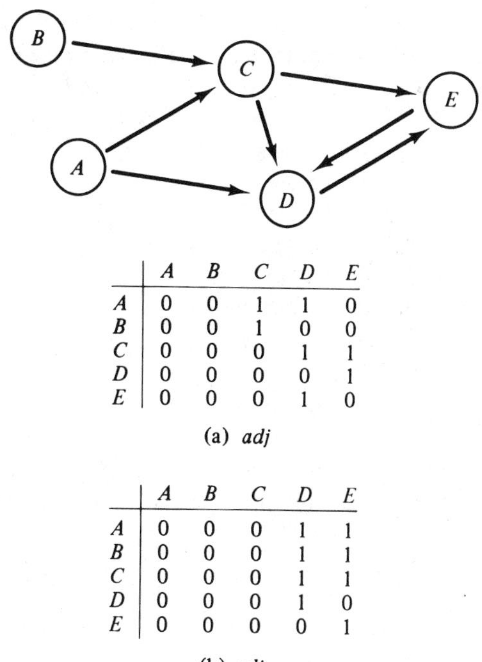

	A	B	C	D	E
A	0	0	1	1	0
B	0	0	1	0	0
C	0	0	0	1	1
D	0	0	0	0	1
E	0	0	0	1	0

(a) *adj*

	A	B	C	D	E
A	0	0	0	1	1
B	0	0	0	1	1
C	0	0	0	1	1
D	0	0	0	1	0
E	0	0	0	0	1

Figure 7.5.1.4. (b) adj_2

	A	B	C	D	E
A	0	0	0	1	1
B	0	0	0	1	1
C	0	0	0	1	1
D	0	0	0	0	1
E	0	0	0	1	0

(a) adj_3

	A	B	C	D	E
A	0	0	0	1	1
B	0	0	0	1	1
C	0	0	0	1	1
D	0	0	0	1	0
E	0	0	0	0	1

Figure 7.5.1.5. (b) adj_4

Assume we want to know whether a path of length 3 or less exists between two nodes of a graph. If such a path exists between nodes *i* and *j*, then it must be of length 1, 2, or 3. If there is a path of length 3 or less between nodes *i* and *j*, then the value of

$$adj(i,j) \mid adj_2(i,j) \mid adj_3(i,j)$$

must be *true*. Figure 7.5.1.6 shows the matrix formed by *or*ing the matrices *adj*, adj_2 and adj_3. This matrix contains a 1 in row *i*, column *j*, if and only if there is a path of length 3 or less from node *i* to node *j*.

Suppose we wish to construct a matrix *path* such that *path(i,j)* is *true* if and only if there is some path from node *i* to node *j* (of any length). Clearly,

$$path(i,j) = adj(i,j) \mid adj_2(i,j) \mid \ldots$$

However, the above equation cannot be used in computing *path* since the process that it describes is an infinite one. However, if the graph has *n* nodes, it must be true that

$$path(i,j) = adj(i,j) \mid adj_2(i,j) \mid \ldots \mid adj_n(i,j).$$

This is because if there is a path of length $m>n$ from *i* to *j*, then there must be another path from *i* to *j* of length less than or equal to *n*. To see this, note that since there are only *n* nodes in the graph, at least one node *k* must appear in the path of length *m* twice. The path can be shortened by removing the cycle from *k* to *k*. This process is repeated until no two nodes in the path (except possibly *i* and *j*) are equal and therefore the path is of length *n* or less. Figure 7.5.1.7 illustrates the matrix *path* for the graph of Fig. 7.5.1.4(a). The matrix *path* is often called the ***transitive closure*** of the matrix *adj*.

We may write a PL/I routine which accepts an adjacency matrix ADJ and computes its transitive closure PATH. This routine uses an auxiliary routine PROD(A,B,C) which sets the array C equal to the Boolean product of A and B.

	A	*B*	*C*	*D*	*E*
A	0	0	1	1	1
B	0	0	1	1	1
C	0	0	0	1	1
D	0	0	0	1	1
E	0	0	0	1	1

Figure 7.5.1.6.

	A	*B*	*C*	*D*	*E*
A	0	0	1	1	1
B	0	0	1	1	1
C	0	0	0	1	1
D	0	0	0	1	1
E	0	0	0	1	1

Figure 7.5.1.7. $path = adj \mid adj_2 \mid adj_3 \mid adj_4 \mid adj_5$.

```
TRANSCLOSE: PROC(ADJ,PATH);
          DCL  (ADJ,PATH) (*,*)                              BIT(*),
               (NEWPROD,ADJPROD) (HBOUND(ADJ,1),HBOUND(ADJ,2))BIT(1),
               I                                             FIXED;
          IF HBOUND(ADJ,1)¬=HBOUND(ADJ,2)THEN
               /*          the adjacency matrix is not square          */
               DO;
                  PUT SKIP LIST('INVALID ADJACENCY MATRIX');
                  STOP;
               END;
          ADJPROD,PATH=ADJ;
NXTPOWER: DO   I=1 TO HBOUND(ADJ,1)-1;
               /*      I represents the number of times ADJ has        */
               /*          been multipled by itself to obtain          */
               /*      ADJPROD. At this point PATH represents          */
               /*              all paths of length I or less           */
               CALL PROD(ADJPROD,ADJ,NEWPROD);
               PATH=PATH | NEWPROD;
               ADJPROD=NEWPROD;
          END NXTPOWER;
          RETURN;
        END TRANSCLOSE;
```

The routine PROD may be written as follows:

```
PROD:       PROC(A,B,C);
               DCL (A,B,C) (*,*)                    BIT(*),
                   VAL                              BIT(1),
                   (I,J,K)                          FIXED;
               IF HBOUND(A,2)¬=  HBOUND(B,1) THEN DO;
                  PUT SKIP LIST('PRODUCT CANNOT BE FORMED');
                  STOP;
                                                    END;
ROWLOOP:       DO I=1 TO HBOUND(A,1);
COLLOOP:          DO J=1 TO HBOUND(B,2);
                     /*        compute C(I,J)          */
                     VAL= '0'B;
PRODLOOP:            DO K=1 TO HBOUND(A,2);
                        VAL=VAL | (A(I,K) & B(K,J));
                     END PRODLOOP;
                     C(I,J)=VAL;
                  END COLLOOP;
               END ROWLOOP;
               RETURN;
            END PROD;
```

Warshall's Algorithm

The above method is quite inefficient. Let us see if a more efficient method to compute *path* can be produced. Let us define the matrix $path_k$ such that $path_k(i,j)$ is *true* if and only if there is a path from node i to node j which does not pass through any nodes numbered higher than k (except, possibly, for i and j themselves). How can the value of $path_{k+1}(i,j)$ be obtained from $path_k$? Clearly for any i and j such that $path_k(i,j)$=*true*, $path_{k+1}(i,j)$ must be *true* (why?). The only situation in which $path_{k+1}(i,j)$ can be *true* while $path_k(i,j)$ is *false* is if there is a path from i to j passing through node k+1 but there is no path from i to j passing through only nodes 1 through k. But this means that there must be a path from i to k+1 passing through only nodes 1 through k and a similar path from k+1 to j. Thus $path_{k+1}(i,j)$=*true* if and only if one of the following two conditions holds:

1. $path_k(i,j)$=*true*
2. $path_k(i,k+1)$=*true* and $path_k(k+1,j)$=*true*.

This means that $path_{k+1}(i,j)=path_k(i,j) \mid (path_k(i,k+1)\ \&\ path_k(k+1,j))$. An algorithm to obtain the matrix $path_k$ from the matrix $path_{k-1}$ based on this observation follows:

```
do i=1 to n;
   do j=1 to n;
      pathk(i,j)=pathk-1(i,j)| (pathk-1(i,k) & pathk-1(k,j));
   end;
end;
```

This may be logically simplified and made more efficient as follows:

```
pathk=pathk-1
do  i=1 to n;
     if pathk-1(i,k) then
              do j =1 to n;
                 pathk(i,j)=pathk-1(i,j) | pathk-1(k,j);
              end;
end;
```

Clearly, $path_0(i,j)$=*adj* since the only way to go from node i to node j without passing through any other nodes is to go directly from i to j. Further, $path_n(i,j)$=*path* since if a path may pass through any nodes numbered from 1 to n, then any path from node i to node j may be selected. The following PL/I routine may therefore be used to compute the transitive closure.

```
TRANSCLOSE: PROC(ADJ,PATH);
               DCL (ADJ,PATH) (*,*)                     BIT(*),
                    (N,I,J,K)                           FIXED;
               N=HBOUND(ADJ,1);
               IF N¬= HBOUND(ADJ,2) THEN DO;

                  PUT SKIP LIST ('INVALID ADJACENCY MATRIX');
                  STOP;
                                                  END;

               PATH=ADJ;  /*   PATH starts off as ADJ      */
PATHKLOOP:     DO K=1 TO N;
                  /*   compute successive values of PATH   */
ROWLOOP:          DO I=1 TO N;
                     IF PATH(I,K) THEN
COLLOOP:                DO J=1 TO N;
                           PATH(I,J)=PATH(I,J) | PATH(K,J);
                        END COLLOOP;
                  END ROWLOOP;

               END PATHKLOOP;
               RETURN;
            END TRANSCLOSE;
```

This method of finding the transitive closure is often called ***Warshall's algorithm***, after its discoverer.

7.5.2. A Flow Problem

In this section we consider a real-world problem and illustrate a solution which uses a weighted graph. There are a number of formulations of this problem whose solutions carry over to a wide range of applications. We present one such formulation here and refer the reader to the literature for alternate versions.

Assume a water pipe system as in Fig. 7.5.2.1(a). Each arc represents a pipe, and the number above each arc represents the capacity of that pipe in gallons per minute. The nodes represent points at which pipes are joined and water is transferred from one pipe to another. Two nodes, S and T are designated as a ***source*** of water and a ***user*** of water (or a ***sink***) respectively. This means that water originating at S must be carried through the pipe system to T. Water may flow through a pipe in only one direction (pressure-sensitive valves may be used to prevent water from flowing backwards) and there are no pipes entering S or leaving T. Thus, a weighted directed graph, as in Fig. 7.5.2.1(a), is an ideal data structure to model the situation.

We would like to maximize the amount of water flowing from the source to the sink. Although the source may be able to produce water at a prodigious rate and the sink may be able to consume water at a comparable rate, the pipe system may not have the capacity to carry it all to the sink. Thus the limiting factor of the entire system is the pipe capacity. Many other real-world problems are similar in nature. The system could be an electrical network, a railway system, a communications network, or any other distribution system in which one wants to maximize the amount of an item being delivered from one point to another.

Define a ***capacity function***, $c(a,b)$, where a and b are nodes, as follows: If *adjacent*(a,b) (i.e. if there is a pipe from a to b), then $c(a,b)$ is the capacity of the pipe from a to b. If there is no pipe from a to b, then $c(a,b)=0$. At any point in the operation of the system, a given amount of water (possibly 0) flows through each pipe. Define a ***flow function***, $f(a,b)$, where a and b are nodes, as 0 if b is not adjacent to a, and as the amount of water flowing through the pipe from a to b otherwise. Clearly, $f(a,b) \geq 0$ for all nodes a and b. Furthermore, $f(a,b) \leq c(a,b)$ for all nodes a and b since a pipe may not carry more water than its capacity. Let v be the amount of water which flows through the system from S to T. Then the amount of water leaving S through all pipes equals the amount of water entering T through all pipes, and both these amounts equal v. This can be stated by the equality:

$$\sum_{x \in nodes} f(S,x) = v = \sum_{x \in nodes} f(x,T)$$

No node other than S can produce water, and no node other than T can absorb water. Thus the amount of water leaving any node other than S or T is equal to the amount of water entering that node. This can be stated by

$$\sum_{y \in nodes} f(x,y) = \sum_{y \in nodes} f(y,x) \quad \text{for all nodes } x \neq S,T$$

Define the ***inflow*** of a node x as the total flow entering x and the ***outflow*** as the total flow leaving x. The above conditions may be rewritten as

$$outflow(S) = inflow(T) = v$$
$$inflow(x) = outflow(x) \quad \text{for all } x \neq S,T$$

Several flow functions may exist for a given graph and capacity function. Figures 7.5.2.1(b) and (c) illustrate two possible flow functions for the graph of Fig. 7.5.2.1(a). Make sure that you understand why both of them are valid flow functions and why both satisfy the above equations and inequalities.

We wish to find a flow function which maximizes the value of v, the amount of water going from S to T. Such a flow function is called ***optimal***. Clearly, the flow function of Fig. 7.5.2.1(b) is better than the one of Fig. 7.5.2.1(c) since v equals 7 in the former but only 5 in the latter. See if you can find a flow function which is better than the one in Fig. 7.5.2.1(b).

One valid flow function can be achieved by setting $f(a,b)$ to 0 for all nodes a and b. Of course this flow function is least optimal since no water flows from S to T. Given a

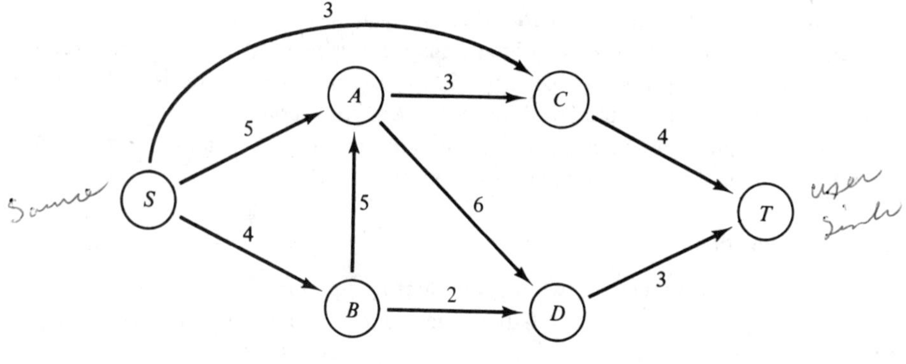

(a) A flow problem.

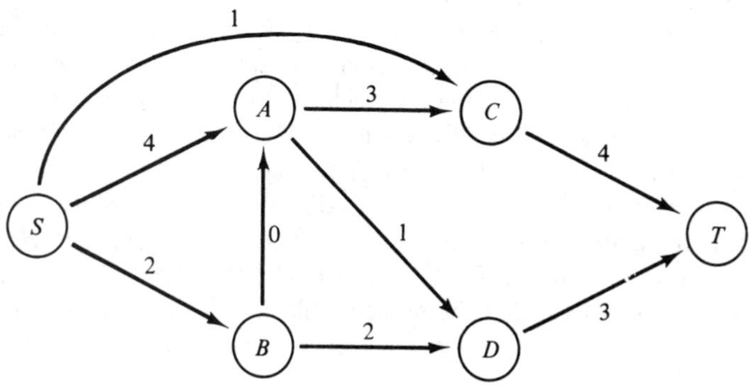

(b) A flow function.

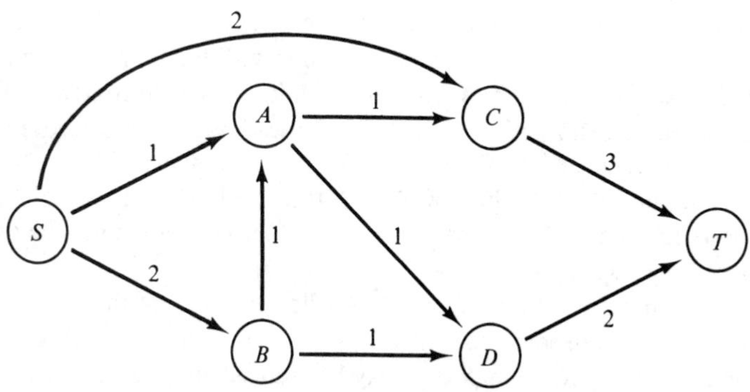

(c) A flow function.

Figure 7.5.2.1.

flow function, it can be improved so that the flow from S to T is increased. However, the improved version must satisfy all the conditions for a valid flow function. In particular, if the flow entering any node (except for S or T) is increased or decreased, the flow leaving that node must be increased or decreased correspondingly. The strategy for producing an optimal flow function is to begin with the zero flow function and to successively improve upon it until an optimal flow function is produced.

Improving a Flow Function

Given a flow function f there are two ways to improve upon it. One way consists of finding a path $S=x_1,x_2, \ldots ,x_n=T$ from S to T such that the flow along each arc in the path is strictly less than the capacity (i.e., $f(x_{k-1},x_k) < c(x_{k-1},x_k)$ for all k between 2 and n). The flow can be increased on each arc in such a path by the minimum value of $c(x_{k-1},x_k) - f(x_{k-1},x_k)$ for all k between 2 and n (so that when the flow has been increased along the entire path there is at least one arc $\langle x_{k-1},x_k\rangle$ in the path for which $f(x_{k-1},x_k) = c(x_{k-1},x_k)$ and through which the flow may not be increased).

This may be illustrated by the graph of Fig. 7.5.2.2(a) which gives the capacity and the current flow respectively for each arc. There are two paths from S to T with positive flow ((S,A,C,T) and (S,B,D,T)). However each of these paths contains one arc ($\langle A,C\rangle$ and $\langle B,D\rangle$) in which the flow equals the capacity. Thus the flow along these paths may not be improved. However, the path (S,A,D,T) is such that the capacity of each arc in the path is greater than its current flow. The maximum amount by which the flow can be increased along this path is 1 since the flow along arc $\langle D,T\rangle$ cannot exceed 3. The resulting flow function is shown in Fig. 7.5.2.2(b). The total flow from S to T has been increased from 5 to 6. To see that the result is still a valid flow function, note that for each node (except T) whose inflow is increased, the outflow is increased by the same amount.

Are there any other paths whose flow can be improved? In this example, you should satisfy yourself that there are not. However, given the graph of Fig. 7.5.2.2(a) we could have chosen to improve the path (S,B,A,D,T). The resulting flow function is illustrated in Fig. 7.5.2.2(c). This function also provides for a net flow of 6 from S to T and is therefore neither better nor worse than the flow function of Fig. 7.5.2.2(b).

Even if there is no path whose flow may be improved, there may be another method of improving the net flow from the source to the sink. This is illustrated by Fig. 7.5.2.3. In Fig. 7.5.2.3(a) there is no path from S to T whose flow may be improved. But if the flow from X to Y is reduced, the flow from X to T can be increased. To compensate for the decrease in the inflow of Y, the flow from S to Y could be increased. The flow from X to Y can be redirected to T as shown in Fig. 7.5.2.3(b), and the net flow from S to T can thereby be increased from 4 to 7.

We may generalize this second method as follows: Suppose there is a path from S to some node y, a path from some node x to T, and a path from x to y with positive flow. Then the flow along the path from x to y may be reduced and the flows from x to T and from S to y may be increased by the same amount. This amount is the minimum of the flow from x to y and the differences between capacity and flow in the paths from S to y and x to T.

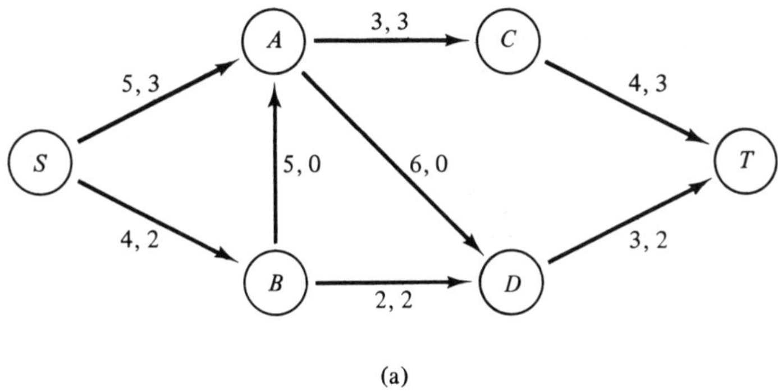

(a)

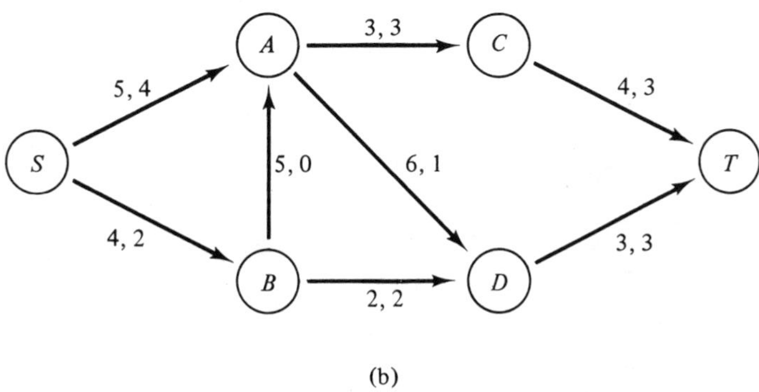

(b)

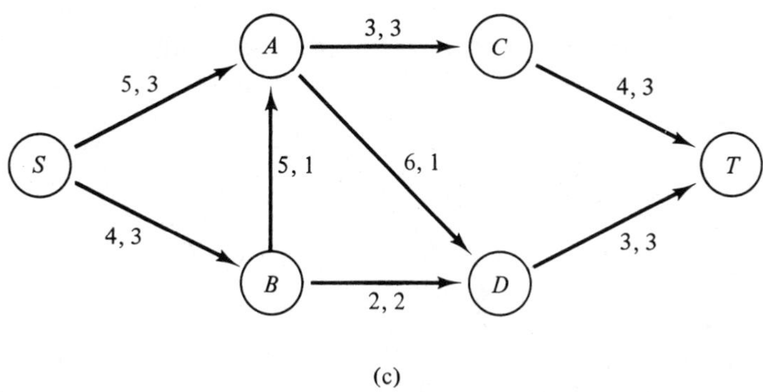

(c)

Figure 7.5.2.2. Increasing the flow in a graph.

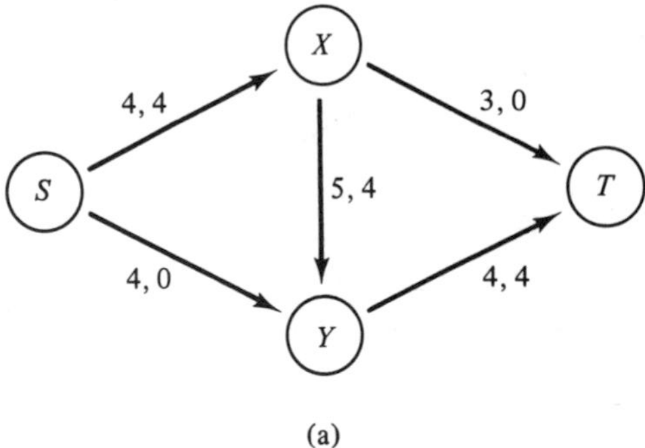

(a)

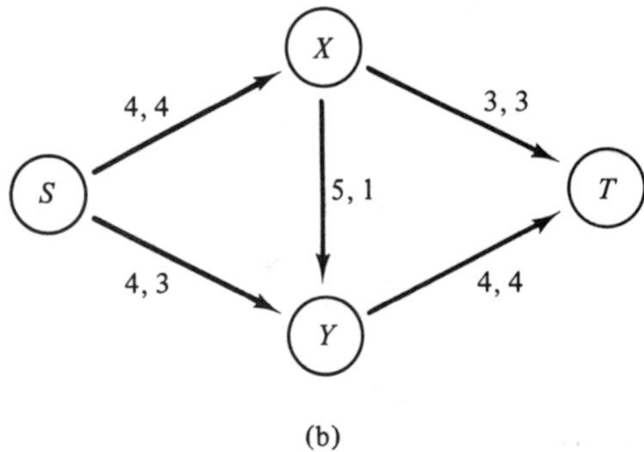

(b)

Figure 7.5.2.3. Increasing the flow in a graph.

These two methods may be combined by proceeding through the graph from S to T as follows: The amount of water emanating from S towards T can be increased by any amount (since we have assumed no limit on the amount which can be produced by the source) only if the pipes from S to T can carry the increase. Suppose the pipe capacity from S to x allows the amount of water entering x to be increased by an amount a. If the pipe capacity to carry the increase from x to T exists, then the increase can be made. Then if a node y is adjacent to x (i.e., there is an arc $\langle x,y \rangle$), the amount of water emanating from y towards T can be increased by the minimum of a and the unused capacity of arc $\langle x,y \rangle$. This is an application of the first method. Similarly, if node x is adjacent to some node y (i.e., there is an arc $\langle y,x \rangle$), then the amount of water emanating from y towards T can be increased by the minimum of a and the existing flow from y to x. This can be done by reducing the flow from y to x as in the second method. Proceeding in this fashion from S to T, the amount by which the flow to T may be increased can be determined.

Define a ***semipath*** from S to T as a sequence of nodes $S = x_1, x_2, \ldots, x_n = T$ such that, for all $1<i<=n$, either $\langle x_{i-1}, x_i \rangle$ or $\langle x_i, x_{i-1} \rangle$ is an arc. Using the above technique, we may describe an algorithm to discover a semipath from S to T such that the flow to each node in the semipath may be increased. This is done by building upon already discovered partial semipaths from S. If the last node in a discovered partial semipath from S is a, the algorithm considers extending it to any node b such that either $\langle a,b \rangle$ or $\langle b,a \rangle$ is an arc.

The partial semipath is extended to b only if the extension can be made in such a way that the inflow to b can be increased. Once a partial semipath has been extended to a node b, that node is removed from consideration as an extension of some other partial semipath. (This is because at this point we are trying to discover a single semipath from S to T.) The algorithm of course keeps track of the amount by which the inflow to b may be increased and whether its increase is due to consideration of the arc $\langle a,b \rangle$ or $\langle b,a \rangle$.

This process continues until some partial semipath from S has been completed by extending it to T. The algorithm then proceeds backwards along the semipath adjusting all flows until S is reached. (This will be illustrated shortly with an example.) The entire process is then repeated in an attempt to discover yet another such semipath from S to T. When no partial semipath may be successfully extended, then the flow cannot be increased and the existing flow is optimal. (You are asked to prove this as an exercise.)

An Example

Let us illustrate this process with an example. Consider the arcs and capacities of the weighted graph of Fig. 7.5.2.4. We begin by assuming a flow of 0, and we attempt to discover an optimal flow. Figure 7.5.2.4(a) illustrates the initial situation. The two numbers above each arc represent the capacity and current flow respectively. We may extend a semipath from S to (S,X) and (S,Z) respectively. The flow from S to X may be increased by 4 and the flow from S to Z may be increased by 6. The semipath (S,X) may be extended to (S,X,W) and (S,X,Y) with corresponding increases of flow to W and Y of 3 and 4 respectively. The semipath (S,X,Y) may be extended to (S,X,Y,T) with an increase of flow to T of 4. (Note that at this point we could have chosen to extend (S,X,W) to (S,X,W,T). Similarly we could have extended (S,Z) to (S,Z,Y) rather than (S,X) to (S,X,W) and (S,X,Y). These decisions are arbitrary.)

Since we have reached T by the semipath (S,X,Y,T) with a net increase of 4, we increase the flow along each forward arc of the semipath by this amount. The results are depicted in Fig. 7.5.2.4(b).

We now repeat the above process with the flow of Fig. 7.5.2.4(b). (S) may be extended to (S,Z) only since the flow in arc $\langle S,X \rangle$ is already at capacity. The net increase to Z through this semipath is 6. (S,Z) may be extended to (S,Z,Y), yielding a net increase of 4 to Y. (S,Z,Y) cannot be extended to (S,Z,Y,T) since the flow in arc $\langle Y,T \rangle$ is at capacity. However, it can be entended to (S,Z,Y,X) with a net increase to node X of 4. Note that since this semipath includes a backwards arc $\langle Y,X \rangle$, it implies a reduction in the flow from X to Y of 4. The semipath (S,Z,Y,X) may be extended to (S,Z,Y,X,W) with a net increase of 3 (the unused capacity of $\langle X,W \rangle$) to W. This semipath may then be extended to (S,Z,Y,X,W,T) with a net increase of 3 in the flow to T. Since we have reached T with an increase of 3, we proceed backwards along this semipath. Since $\langle W,T \rangle$ and $\langle X,W \rangle$ are forward arcs, their flow may each be increased by 3. Since $\langle Y,X \rangle$ is a backwards arc, the flow along $\langle X,Y \rangle$ is reduced by 3. Since $\langle Z,Y \rangle$ and $\langle S,Z \rangle$ are forward arcs, their flow may be increased by 3. This results in the flow shown in Fig. 7.5.2.4(c).

We then attempt to repeat the process. (S) may be extended to (S,Z) with an

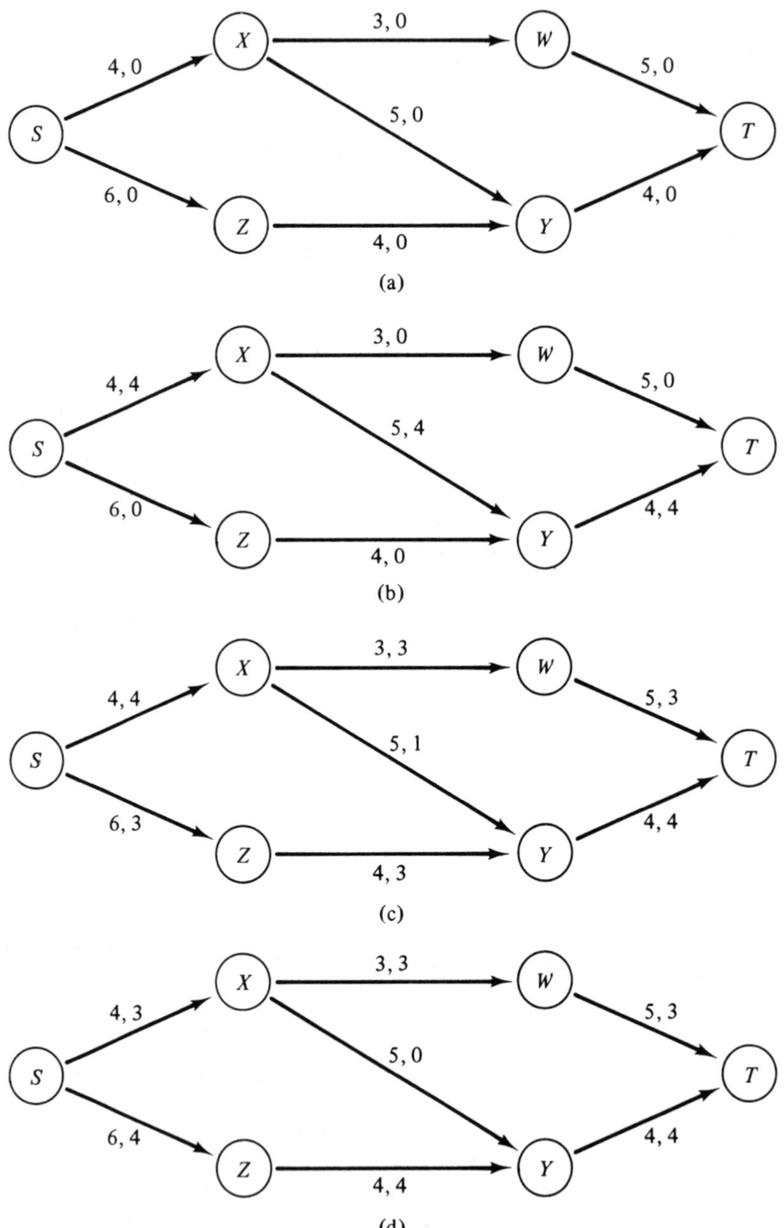

Figure 7.5.2.4. Producing an optimum flow.

increase of 3 to Z, (S,Z) may be extended to (S,Z,Y) with an increase of 1 to Y, and (S,Z,Y) may be extended to (S,Z,Y,X) with an increase of 1 to X. However since arcs $\langle S,X\rangle$, $\langle Y,T\rangle$, and $\langle X,W\rangle$ are at capacity, no semipath may be extended further and an optimum flow has been found. Note that this optimum flow need not be unique. Figure 7.5.2.4(d) illustrates another optimum flow for the same graph which was obtained from Fig. 7.5.2.4(a) by considering the semipaths (S,X,W,T) and (S,Z,Y,T).

The Algorithm and Program

Given a weighted graph (an adjacency matrix and a capacity matrix) with a source S and a sink T, the algorithm to produce an optimum flow function for that graph may be outlined as follows:

```
1   initialize the flow function to 0 at each arc;
2   do while(true);
3       attempt to find a semipath from S to T which increases the
                                                flow to T by a > 0;
4       if a semipath cannot be found then return;
5       increase the flow to each node (except S) in the semipath by a;
6   end;
```

Of course, the heart of the algorithm lies in line 3. Once a node has been placed on a partial semipath, it can no longer be used to extend a different semipath. Thus the algorithm uses a logical value *onpath*(*node*) which indicates whether or not *node* is on some semipath. It also needs an indication of which nodes are at the ends of partial semipaths so that such partial semipaths can be extended by adding adjacent nodes. The bit *endpath*(*node*) indicates whether or not *node* is at the end of a partial semipath. For each node on a semipath the algorithm must keep track of what node precedes it on that semipath and the direction of the arc. *precede*(*node*) points to the node which precedes *node* on its semipath, and *forward*(*node*) has the value *true* if and only if the arc is from *precede*(*node*) to *node*. *improve*(*node*) indicates the amount by which the flow to *node* may be increased along its semipath. The algorithm which attempts to find a semipath from S to T along which the flow may be increased may be written as follows. (We assume that $c(a,b)$ contains the capacity of the pipe from a to b and that $f(a,b)$ contains the current flow from a to b.)

```
set endpath(node), onpath(node) to false for all nodes;
endpath(S)=true;
onpath(S) =true;


/*   compute maximum flow from S which pipes can carry     */
improve(S)=sum of c(S,node) over all nodes node;
do while (¬onpath(T) & there exists a node nd such that endpath(nd));
    endpath(nd)=false;
    do while (there exists a node i such that
                         ¬onpath(i) & f(nd,i)<c(nd,i) & adjacent (nd,i));
```

```
            /*   the flow from nd to i may be increased      */
            /*           place i on the semipath              */
                            onpath(i)   = true;
                            endpath(i)  = true;
                            precede(i)  = nd;
                            forward(i)  = true;
                            improve(i)  = min(improve(nd),c(nd,i)-f(nd,i));
      end;


      do while (there exists a node i such that
                         ¬onpath(i) & f(i,nd)>0 & adjacent(i,nd));
            /*   the flow from i to nd may be decreased      */
            /*           place i on the semipath              */
                            onpath(i)   = true;
                            endpath(i)  = true;
                            precede(i)  = nd;
                            forward(i)  = false;
                            improve(i)  = min(improve(nd),f(i,nd));
      end;
   end;
   if onpath(T) then we have found a semipath from S to T;
             else the flow is already optimum;
```

Once a semipath from S to T has been found, the flow may be increased along that semipath (line 5 above) by the following algorithm:

```
a=improve(T);
nd=T;
do while (nd¬=S);
   pred = precede(nd);
   if forward(nd) then f(pred,nd)=f(pred,nd)+a;
                  else f(nd,pred)=f(nd,pred)-a;
   nd=pred;
end;
```

This method of solving the flow problem is known as the ***Ford-Fulkerson algorithm*** after its discoverers.

Let us now convert these algorithms into a PL/I subroutine MAXFLOW(CAP,S,T,FLOW,TOTFLOW), where CAP is an input parameter representing a capacity function defined on a weighted graph and declared by

```
DCL CAP(*,*)    FIXED;
```

S and T are input parameters representing the source and sink, FLOW is an output parameter representing the maximum flow function, and TOTFLOW is the amount of flow from S to T under the flow function FLOW.

The previous algorithms may be converted easily into PL/I programs. Two single-bit arrays ENDPATH and ONPATH and two integer arrays PRECEDE and IMPROVE are required. The array *forward* of the algorithm may be combined with the array *precede* to produce the PL/I array PRECEDE in which PRECEDE(ND) is positive or negative depending on whether *forward(nd)* is *true* or *false* in the algorithm. The absolute value of PRECEDE(ND) is the node which precedes ND on a semipath. Similarly, the question of whether J is adjacent to I can be answered by checking whether or not CAP(I,J)=0.

We present the routine here as a straightforward implementation of the algorithms. ANY is a built-in PL/I function which accepts an array of bits and returns '1'B if any element of the array is '1'B. If none of the elements equals '1'B, then ANY returns '0'B.

```
MAXFLOW:  PROC(CAP,S,T,FLOW,TOTFLOW);
            DCL  (CAP(*,*),
                    S,T,TOTFLOW,N,X,PRED,ND,I,
                    FLOW(*,*))                        FIXED;
            /*    determine number of nodes    */
            N=HBOUND(CAP,1);

BLOCK:      BEGIN;
            DCL (PRECEDE,IMPROVE) (N)           FIXED,
                 (ENDPATH,ONPATH) (N)           BIT(1);
            /*   initialize    */
            FLOW=0;
            TOTFLOW=0;

LOOP:       DO WHILE('1'B);
               /*    attempt to find a semipath from S to T    */
               ENDPATH,ONPATH='0'B;
               ENDPATH(S),ONPATH(S)='1'B;
               IMPROVE(S)=SUM(CAP(S,*));

EXTEND:        DO WHILE (¬ONPATH(T)  &  ANY (ENDPATH));
                  DO ND=1 TO N WHILE (¬ENDPATH(ND));
                  END;
                  ENDPATH(ND)='0'B;
```

```
NEXTNODE:       DO I=1 TO N;
                  IF (FLOW(ND,I)<CAP(ND,I)) &
                    (¬ONPATH(I)) THEN DO;
                           ONPATH(I)='1'B;
                           ENDPATH(I)='1'B;
                           PRECEDE(I)=ND;
                           IMPROVE(I)=MIN(IMPROVE(ND),
                                        CAP(ND,I)−FLOW(ND,I));
                                    END;
                  IF (FLOW(I,ND)>0) &
                    (¬ONPATH(I)) THEN DO;
                           ONPATH(I)='1'B;
                           ENDPATH(I)='1'B;
                           PRECEDE(I)=−ND;
                           IMPROVE(I)=MIN(IMPROVE(ND),
                                                  FLOW(I,ND));
                                    END;
                END NEXTNODE;
              END EXTEND;

              IF ¬ONPATH(T) THEN   /*  flow is optimum  */   RETURN;
              /*  increase the flow along the semipath  */
              X=IMPROVE(T);
              TOTFLOW=TOTFLOW+X;
              ND=T;

BACK:         DO WHILE(ND¬=S);
                PRED=PRECEDE(ND);
                IF PRED>0 THEN  /*  increase flow from PRED  */
                       FLOW(PRED,ND)=FLOW(PRED,ND)+X;
                         ELSE   /*  decrease flow to PRED   */
                       FLOW(ND,−PRED)=FLOW(ND,−PRED)−X;
                ND=ABS(PRED);
              END BACK;
            END LOOP;
            END BLOCK;
          END MAXFLOW;
```

For large graphs with many nodes, the arrays IMPROVE and ENDPATH may be prohibitively expensive in terms of space. Furthermore, a search through all nodes to find one such that ENDPATH(ND) = '1'B may be very inefficient in terms of time. An alternate solution might be to note that the value of IMPROVE is required only for those nodes ND such that ENDPATH(ND)='1'B. Those graph nodes which are at the end of semipaths may be kept in a list whose nodes are declared by

```
DCL 1 LISTNODE(100),
      2 GRAPHNODE    FIXED,
      2 IMPROVE      FIXED,
      2 NEXT         FIXED;
```

When a node which is at the end of a semipath is required, remove the first element from the list. We can similarly dispense with the array PRECEDE by maintaining a separate list of nodes for each semipath. However, this suggestion is of dubious value since almost all nodes will be on some semipath. You are invited to write the routine MAXFLOW as an exercise using these suggestions to save time and space.

7.6. The Linked Representation of Graphs

The adjacency matrix representation of a graph is frequently inadequate because it requires advance knowledge of the number of nodes. If a graph must be constructed in the course of solving a problem, or if it must be dynamically updated as the program proceeds, a new matrix must be created for each addition or deletion of a node. This is prohibitively inefficient, especially in a real-world situation where a graph may have a hundred or more nodes. Further, even if a graph has very few arcs so that the adjacency matrix (and the weight matrix for a weighted graph) is sparse, space must be reserved for every possible arc between two nodes whether or not such an arc exists. If the graph contains n nodes, a total of n^2 locations must be used.

As you might expect, the remedy is to use a linked structure, allocating and freeing nodes from an available pool. This is similar to the methods used to represent dynamic binary and general trees. In the linked representation of trees, each allocated node corresponds to a tree node. This is possible because each tree node is the son of only one other tree node and is therefore contained in only a single list of sons. However, in a graph an arc may exist between any two graph nodes. It is possible to keep an adjacency list for every node in a graph (such a list contains all nodes adjacent to a given node), and a node might find itself on many different adjacency lists (one for each node to which it is adjacent). But this requires that each allocated node contain a variable number of pointers, depending on the number of nodes to which it is adjacent. This solution is clearly impractical as we saw in attempting to represent general trees with nodes containing pointers to each of its sons.

An alternative is to construct a multi-linked structure in the following way. The nodes of the graph (hereafter referred to as ***graph nodes***) are represented by a linked list of ***header nodes***. Each such header node contains three fields: *info*, *nextnode*, and *arcptr*. If p points to a header node representing a graph node A, then *info*(p) contains any information associated with graph node A. *nextnode*(p) is a pointer to the header node representing the next graph node, if any. Each header node is at the head of a list of nodes of a second type called ***list nodes***. This list is called the ***adjacency list***. Each node on an adjacency list represents an arc of the graph. *arcptr*(p) points to the adjacency list of nodes representing the arcs emanating from the graph node A.

Each adjacency list node contains two fields: *ndptr* and *nextarc*. If q points to a list node representing an arc $\langle A,B \rangle$, *ndptr*(q) is a pointer to the header node representing the graph node *B*. *nextarc*(*q*) points to a list node representing the next arc emanating from graph node *A*, if any. Each list node is contained in a single adjacency list representing all arcs emanating from a given graph node. The term ***allocated nodes*** is used to refer to both header and list nodes of a multilinked structure representing a graph. We also refer to an adjacency list node as an ***arc node***.

Figure 7.6.1 illustrates this representation. If each graph node carries some information but (since the graph is not weighted) the arcs do not, then two types of allocated nodes are needed: one for header nodes (graph nodes) and the other for adjacency list nodes (arcs). These are illustrated in Fig. 7.6.1(a). Each header node contains an *info* field and two pointers. The first of these is to the adjacency list of arcs emanating from the graph node, and the second is to the next header node in the graph. Each arc node contains two pointers, one to the next arc node in the adjacency list and the other to the header node representing the graph node which terminates the arc. Figure 7.6.1(b) depicts a graph, and Fig. 7.6.1(c) its linked representation.

Note that header nodes and list nodes have different formats and must be represented by different PL/I structures. This necessitates keeping two distinct available lists. Even in the case of a weighted graph in which each list node contains an *info* field to hold the weight of an arc, two different structures may be necessary if the information in the header nodes is not an integer. For simplicity we make the assumption that both header and list nodes have the same format and contain two pointers and a single FIXED information field. These nodes are declared using the array implementation by:

```
DCL 1 NODE(500),
      2 INFO          FIXED,
      2 POINT         FIXED,
      2 NEXT          FIXED;
```

In the case of a header node, NODE(P) represents a graph node *A*, INFO(P) represents the information associated with the graph node *A*, NEXT(P) points to the next graph node, and POINT(P) points to the first list node representing an arc emanating from *A*. In the case of a list node, NODE(P) represents an arc ⟨*A*,*B*⟩, INFO(P) represents the weight of the arc, NEXT(P) points to the next arc emanating from *A*, and POINT(P) points to the header node representing the graph node *B*. Using the BASED implementation, the nodes may be declared as

```
DCL 1 NODE BASED(NDPTR),
      2 INFO            FIXED,
      2 POINT           PTR,
      2 NEXT            PTR;
```

We use the array implementation in the remainder of this section and assume the existence of routines GETNODE and FREENODE.

We now present the implementation of the primitive graph operations using the linked representation. The routine JOINWT(P,Q,WT) accepts two pointers P and Q to

arcptr	info	nextnode

A sample header node representing a graph node.

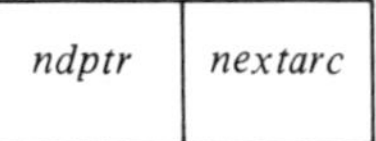

A sample list node representing an arc.

(a)

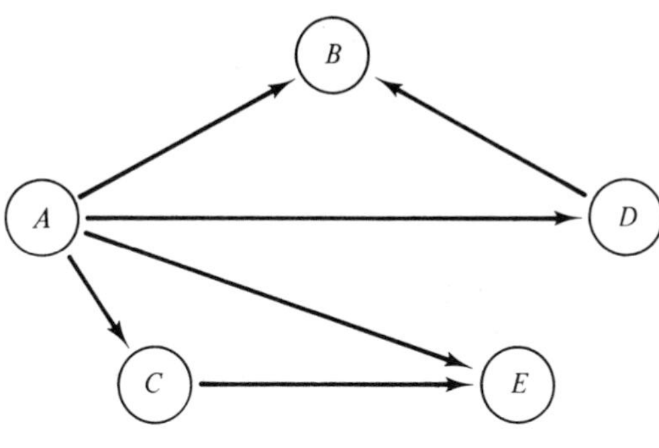

(b) A graph.

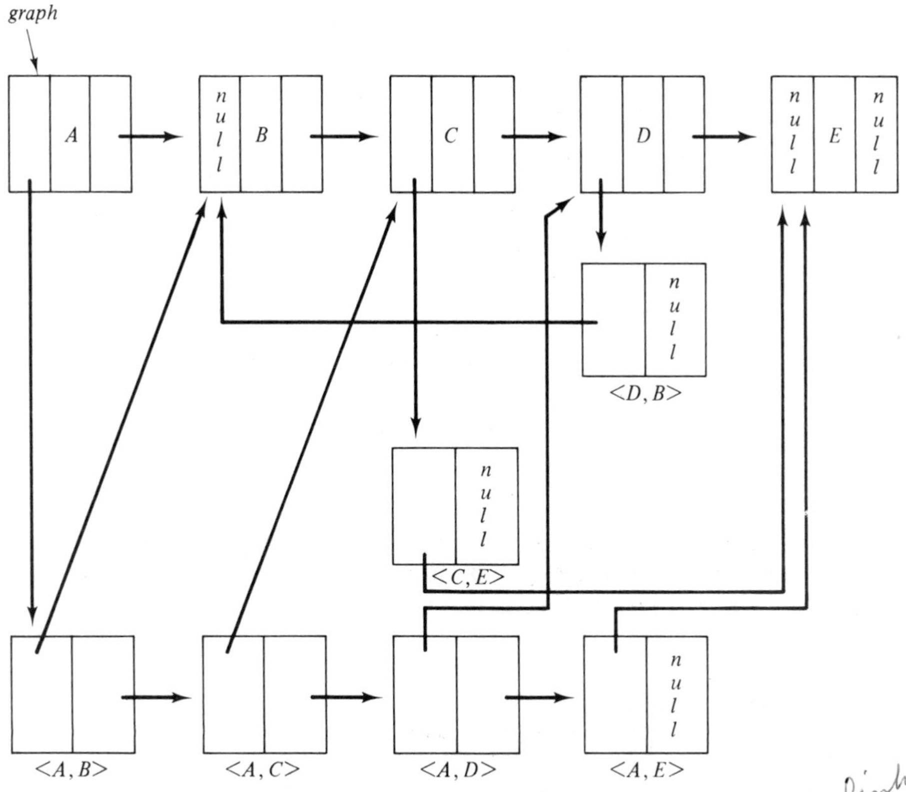

(c) Linked representation of a graph.

Figure 7.6.1. Linked representation of a graph.

two header nodes and creates an arc between them with weight WT. If an arc already exists between them, that arc's weight is set to WT. The array NODE is declared globally.

```
JOINWT:  PROC(P,Q,WT);
           DCL (P,Q,WT,R,R2)     FIXED;
           /*  search the list of arcs emanating from NODE(P)   */
           /*                 for an arc to NODE(Q)              */
           R2=0;
           R=POINT(P);

SEARCH:    DO WHILE(R¬=0);
             IF POINT(R)=Q THEN DO;
                          /*  NODE(R) represents an arc from   */
                          /*       NODE(P) to NODE(Q)          */
                                     INFO(R)=WT;
                                     RETURN;
                                 END;
             R2=R;
             R=NEXT(R);
           END SEARCH;
           /*  an arc from NODE(P) to NODE(Q) does not exist   */
           /*              such an arc must be created          */
           R=GETNODE;
           POINT(R)=Q;
           NEXT(R)=0;
           INFO(R)=WT;
           IF R2=0 THEN POINT(P)=R;
                   ELSE NEXT(R2)=R;
           RETURN;
         END JOINWT;
```

We leave the implementation of the operation *join* for an unweighted graph as an exercise for the reader. The routine REMV(P,Q) accepts pointers to two header nodes and removes the arc between them, if one exists.

```
REMV:    PROC(P,Q);
           DCL (P,Q,R,R2)     FIXED;
           R2=0;
           R=POINT(P);
```

```
SEARCH:    DO WHILE(R¬=0);
              IF POINT(R)=Q THEN DO;
                            /*  R points to an arc from NODE(P)  */
                            /*              to NODE(Q)           */
                              IF R2=0 THEN POINT(P)=NEXT(R);
                                    ELSE NEXT(R2)=NEXT(R);
                              CALL FREENODE(R);
                              RETURN;
                                  END;
              R2=R;
              R=NEXT(R);
           END SEARCH;
           /*   no arc exists from NODE(P) to NODE(Q)    */
           RETURN;
         END REMV;
```

We leave the implementation of the operation *remvwt*(p,q,x) which sets x equal to the weight of the arc $\langle p,q \rangle$ in a weighted graph and then removes the arc from the graph as an exercise for the reader.

The function ADJACENT(P,Q) accepts pointers to two header nodes and determines whether NODE(Q) is adjacent to NODE(P).

```
ADJACENT:  PROC(P,Q) RETURNS(BIT(1));
              DCL (P,Q,R)             FIXED;
              R=POINT(P);
SEARCH:       DO WHILE(R¬=0);
                 IF POINT(R)=Q THEN RETURN ('1'B);
                 R=NEXT(R);
              END SEARCH;
              RETURN ('0'B);
           END ADJACENT;
```

Another useful function is FINDNODE(GRAPH,X) which returns a pointer to a header node with information field X if such a header node exists, and returns the null pointer otherwise.

```
FINDNODE:  PROC(GRAPH,X) RETURNS(FIXED);
              DCL (GRAPH,X,P)           FIXED;
              P=GRAPH;
SEARCH:       DO WHILE(P¬=0);
                 IF INFO(P) =X THEN RETURN(P);
                 P=NEXT(P);
              END SEARCH;
              RETURN(0);
           END FINDNODE;
```

The function ADDNODE(GRAPH,X) adds a node with information field X to a graph and returns a pointer to that node.

```
ADDNODE:  PROC(GRAPH,X) RETURNS(FIXED);
            DCL (GRAPH,X,P)            FIXED;
            P=GETNODE;
            INFO(P)=X;
            POINT(P)=0;
            NEXT(P)=GRAPH;
            GRAPH=P;
            RETURN(P);
          END ADDNODE;
```

The reader should be aware of another important difference between the adjacency matrix representation and the linked representation of graphs. Implicit in the matrix representation is the ability to traverse a row or column of the matrix. Traversing a row is equivalent to identifying all arcs emanating from a given node. This can be done efficiently in the linked representation by traversing the list of arc nodes starting at a given header node. Traversing a column of an adjacency matrix, however, is equivalent to identifying all arcs which terminate at a given node; there is no corresponding method for accomplishing this under the linked representation. Of course, the linked representation could be modified to include two lists emanating from each header node: one for the arcs emanating from the graph node and the other for the arcs terminating at the graph node. However, this would require allocating two nodes for each arc, thus increasing the complexity of adding or deleting an arc. Alternatively, each arc node could be placed on two lists. In this case, an arc node would contain four pointers: one to the next arc emanating from the same node, one to the next arc terminating at the same node, one to the header node at which it terminates, and one to the header node from which it emanates. Header nodes would contain three pointers: one to the next header node, one to the list of arcs emanating from it, and one to the list of arcs terminating at it. The programmer must, of course, choose from among these represenatations by examining the needs of his specific problem and considering both time and storage efficiency. We invite the reader to write a routine REMVNODE(GRAPH,P) which removes a header node pointed to by P from a graph pointed to by GRAPH using the various graph represenatations which we have outlined above. Of course, when a node is removed from a graph, all arcs emanating and terminating at that node must also be removed. In the linked representation which we have presented, there is no easy way of removing a node from a graph since the arcs terminating at the node cannot be obtained directly.

An Application to Scheduling

Let us now consider an application using the linked representation of graphs. Suppose a chef in a diner receives an order for a fried egg. The job of frying an egg can be decomposed into a number of distinct subtasks:

Get egg	Crack egg	Get grease
Grease pan	Heat grease	Pour egg into pan
Wait until egg is done		Remove egg

Some of these tasks must precede other (e.g., "get egg" must precede "crack egg"). Others may be done simultaneously (e.g., "get egg" and "heat grease"). The chef wishes to provide the quickest service possible and is assumed to have an unlimited number of assistants. The problem is to assign tasks to the assistants so as to complete the job in the least possible time.

Although this example may seem frivolous, it is typical of many real-world scheduling problems. A computer system may wish to schedule jobs to minimize turnaround time; a compiler may wish to schedule machine language operations to minimize execution time; a plant manager may wish to organize an assembly line to minimize production time, etc. All these problems are closely related and can be solved by the use of graphs.

Let us represent the above problem as a graph. Each node of the graph represents a subtask, and each arc $\langle x,y \rangle$ represents the requirement that subtask y cannot be performed until subtask x has been completed. This graph G is shown in Fig. 7.6.2.

Consider the transitive closure of G. The transitive closure is the graph T such that $\langle x,y \rangle$ is an arc of T if and only if there is a path from x to y in G. This transitive closure is shown in Fig. 7.6.3.

In the graph T, an arc exists from node x to node y if and only if subtask x must be performed before subtask y. Note that neither G nor T can contain a cycle since if a cycle from node x to itself existed, then subtask x could not be performed until after subtask x had been completed. This is clearly an impossible situation in the context of the problem.

Since G does not contain a cycle, there must be at least one node in G which has no predecessors. To see this, suppose that every node in the graph did have a predecessor. In particular, let us choose a node z which has a predecessor y. y cannot equal z, or the graph would have a cycle from z to itself. Since every node has a predecessor, y must also have a predecessor x which is not equal to either y or z. Continuing in this fashion, a sequence of distinct nodes

$$z,y,x,w,v,u, \ldots$$

is obtained. If any two nodes in this sequence were equal, a cycle would exist from that node to itself. However, the graph contains only a finite number of nodes so that, eventually, two of the nodes must be equal. This is a contradiction. Thus there must be at least one node without a predecessor.

In the graphs of Figs. 7.6.2 and 7.6.3, the nodes A and F do not have predecessors. Since they have no predecessors, the subtasks which they represent may be performed immediately and simultaneously without waiting for any other subtasks to be completed. Once these two subtasks have been performed, their nodes can be removed from the graph. Note that the resulting graph does not contain any cycles since nodes and arcs

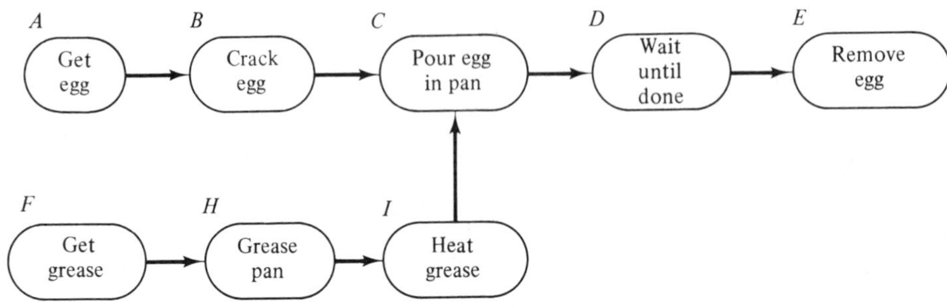

Figure 7.6.2.

have been removed from a graph which originally contained no cycles. Therefore the resulting graph must also contain at least one node with no predecessors. In the example, B and H are two such nodes. Thus the subtasks B and H may be performed simultaneously in the second time period.

Continuing in this fashion, we find that the minimum time in which the egg can be fried is six time periods (assuming that every subtask takes exactly one time period) and that a maximum of two assistants need be employed, as follows:

Time period	Assistant 1	Assistant 2
1	Get egg	Get grease
2	Crack egg	Grease pan
3	Heat grease	
4	Pour egg into pan	
5	Wait until done	
6	Remove egg	

The above process can be outlined as follows:

1. Read in precedences and construct the graph.
2. Use the graph to determine subtasks which can be done simultaneously.

Let us refine each of these two steps. Two crucial decisions must be made in refining step 1. The first is to decide the format of the input; the second is to decide on the representation of the graph. Clearly, the input must contain indications of which subtasks must precede others. The most convenient way to represent these requirements is by ordered pairs of subtasks; each data card contains the names of two subtasks, where the first subtask on a card must precede the second. Of course, the data must be valid in the sense that no subtask may precede itself (no cycles are permitted in the graph). Only those precedences which are implied by the data and the transitive closure of the resulting graph are assumed to hold. A subtask may be represented by a character string such as 'GET EGG' or by a number. We choose to represent subtasks by character strings in order that the input data reflect the real-world situation as closely as possible. If the number of subtasks at the start of execution is known, an adjacency bit matrix, where each bit is initialized to '0'B, could be used to represent the graph. As each precedence is read in, a '1'B could be inserted in the matrix at an appropriate position. However, let us assume that this information is unavailable at the start of execution and it is necessary to provide for an arbitrary number of nodes. For this reason the linked representation of a graph is used.

What information should be kept with each node of the graph? Clearly, the name of the subtask that the node represents is needed for output purposes. The remaining information depends on how the graph is used. This will become apparent only after step 2 is refined. Here is a good example of how the various parts of a program outline interact with each other to produce a single unit.

Step 2 can be refined into the following algorithm:

```
do while (the graph is not empty);
   determine which nodes have no predecessors;
   output this group of nodes with an indication that they can be
                              performed simultaneously in the next time period;
   remove these nodes and their incident arcs from the graph;
end;
```

How can it be determined which nodes have no predecessors? One method is to maintain a *count* field in each node containing the number of nodes which precede it. Note that we are not interested in which nodes precede a given node—only in how many. If the *count* of a node is 0, then that node is known to have no predecessors and may be placed on an ouput list. Each time a node x is output, its adjacency list of arcs must be traversed and the *count* field decremented in every node adjacent to x. During each simulated time period, the list of nodes remaining in the graphs is traversed, in a search for

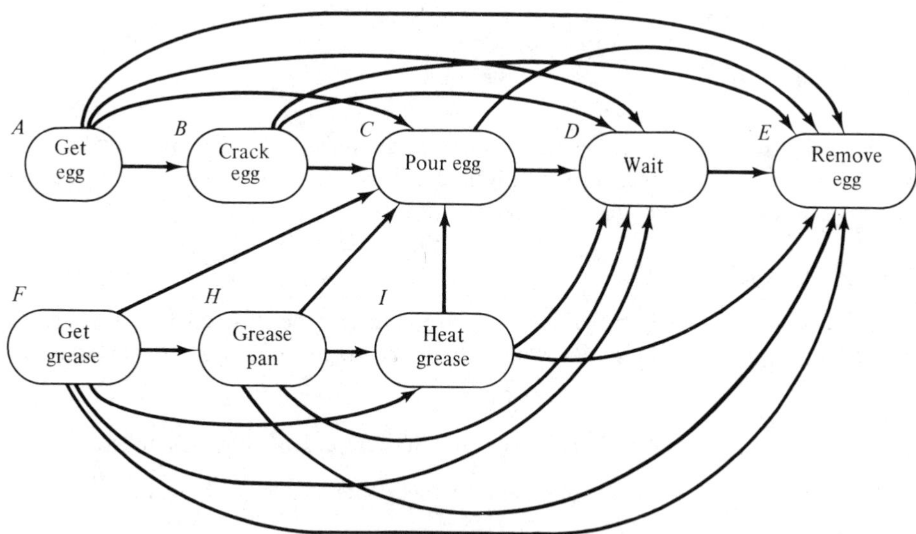

Figure 7.6.3.

those whose *count* field is 0 and which may now be output. Thus the refinement of step 2 may be rewritten as follows:

```
do period=1 by 1 while(graph¬=null);
   /*        initialize the output list to empty         */
   output=null;
   /*     traverse the graph, searching for nodes        */
   /*    which may be placed on the output list          */
   p=graph;
   do while(p¬=null);
      if count(p)=0 then remove node(p) from the list of graph nodes
                                          and place it on the output list;
      set p to the next graph node;
   end;

   if output=null then error—every node in the graph has a predecessor
                                  and therefore the graph contains a cycle;
   /*              traverse the output list              */
   p=output;
   do while(p¬=null);
      print(info(p));
      traverse the list of arcs emanating from node(p), reducing the
               count of each terminating node by one.  Free each
               arc node as it is encountered;
      q=next node in output list;
      free node(p);
      p=q;
   end;
end;
```

Note that it is possible to delete nodes from the linked representation in the above example efficiently only because the only nodes deleted are those with no predecessors. Thus deleted nodes have no arcs terminating in them.

The PL/I Program

At this point in the refinement of step 2, we can indicate the structure of the nodes that we shall need. The header nodes which represent graph nodes contain the following fields:

INFO	holds the name of the subtask represented by this node.
COUNT	holds the number of predecessors of this graph node.
ARCPTR	a pointer to the list of arcs emanating from this node.
NEXTNODE	a pointer to the next node in the graph or in the output list.

Each list node representing an arc contains two pointers:

NODEPTR a pointer to its terminating node.

NEXTARC a pointer to the next arc in the adjacency list.

Thus two types of nodes are required: one to represent graph nodes and one to represent arcs. Using the array representation of lists, these may be declared by

```
DCL 1 GRAPHNODE(500),
      2 INFO        CHAR(20) VAR,
      2 COUNT       FIXED,
      2 ARCPTR      FIXED,
      2 NEXTNODE    FIXED,
    1 ARC(500),
      2 NODEPTR     FIXED,
      2 NEXTARC     FIXED;
```

Of course, there are two available lists (pointed to by AVAILNODE and AVAILARC) and two sets of routines (GETNODE, FREENODE and GETARC, FREEARC) to allocate and free allocated nodes. We also assume the existence of a function FIND(GRAPH,INF) which searches a list of graph nodes pointed to by GRAPH for one such node whose INFO field equals INF. If no such graph node exists, FIND allocates a new graph node ND and sets INFO(ND) to INF and COUNT(ND) and ARCPTR(ND) to 0. FIND then adds ND to the list of graph nodes. In either case, FIND returns a pointer to the graph node containing INF. The routine JOIN described above is also used.

We may now write a PL/I scheduling program:

```
SCHEDULE:   PROC OPTIONS(MAIN);
              DCL 1 GRAPHNODE(500),
                      2 INFO                        CHAR(20) VAR,
                     (2 COUNT,
                      2 ARCPTR,
                      2 NEXTNODE)                   FIXED,
                    1 ARC(500),
                     (2 NODEPTR,
                      2 NEXTARC)                    FIXED,
                    GRAPH                           FIXED INIT(0),
                    (AVAILNODE,AVAILARC)            FIXED INIT(1),
                    (INF1,INF2)                     CHAR(20) VAR,
                    (P,Q,PERIOD,R,T,OUTPUT)         FIXED;
```

```
                /*          initialize the available lists          */
INITAV:         DO I=1 TO 499;
                   NEXTNODE(I),NEXTARC(I)=I+1;
                END INITAV;
                NEXTNODE(500),NEXTARC(500)=0;
                ON ENDFILE(SYSIN) GO TO STEP2;
                COUNT=0;

                /*             construct the graph                  */
INPUT:          DO WHILE('1'B);
                /*      read a precedence and place the arc         */
                /*         representing it into the graph           */
                   GET LIST(INF1,INF2);
                   P=FIND(GRAPH,INF1);
                   Q=FIND(GRAPH,INF2);
                   CALL JOIN(P,Q);

                /*   increment the count of the terminal node       */
                   COUNT(Q)=COUNT(Q)+1;
                END INPUT:

                /*        the graph has been constructed            */
STEP2:          DO PERIOD=1 BY 1 WHILE(GRAPH¬=0);
                    OUTPUT=0;
                    P=GRAPH;
                    Q=0; /*   Q remains one node behind P during    */
                         /*               traversal                 */
TRAVGRAPH:          DO WHILE(P¬=0);
                       R=NEXTNODE(P);
                       IF COUNT(P)=0 THEN DO;
                       /*   remove GRAPHNODE(P) from the graph      */
                          IF Q=0 THEN GRAPH=R;
                                 ELSE NEXTNODE(Q)=R;
                       /*      place GRAPHNODE(P) on output list    */
                          NEXTNODE(P)=OUTPUT;
                          OUTPUT=P;
                                              END:
                                       ELSE Q=P;
                       P=R;
                    END TRAVGRAPH;

                    IF OUTPUT=0 THEN DO;
                          PUT SKIP LIST(
                             'ERROR IN INPUT—GRAPH CONTAINS A CYCLE');
                          STOP;
                                         END;
                    PUT SKIP(2) DATA (PERIOD);
```

```
                /*            traverse the output list            */
                P=OUTPUT;
PRINTOUT:       DO WHILE(P¬=0);
                      PUT SKIP LIST(INFO(P));

                 /*   traverse arcs emanating from GRAPHNODE(P)   */
                      Q=ARCPTR(P);
TRAVARCS:             DO WHILE(Q¬=0);
                         T=NODEPTR(Q);
                         COUNT(T)=COUNT(T)-1;
                         R=NEXTARC(Q);
                         CALL FREEARC(Q);
                         Q=R;
                      END TRAVARCS;

                      R=NEXTNODE(P);
                      CALL FREENODE(P);
                      P=R;
                END PRINTOUT;
            END STEP2;
        END SCHEDULE;
```

Improving the Program

Although the above program is correct, it is highly inefficient. See if you can spot the reason for this before reading further. Consider the fact that, in a typical real-world situation, there may be hundreds of subtasks, yet no more than three or four of them can be performed in a single time period. Thus the entire job may require 100 or more time periods to complete. This means that the loop labeled STEP2 is repeated many times. Each time it is repeated, the entire list of 100 graph nodes (on the average) must be traversed in the loop labeled TRAVGRAPH in order to locate the few whose COUNT field is 0. (This average of 100 assumes that the graph initially has 200 nodes. Justify this estimate as an exercise.) This is very inefficient.

As each time period is simulated, those nodes whose subtasks can be performed in the next time period can be identified. This can be done when the COUNT in a node is reduced by 1 and the COUNT becomes 0. At that point, why not remove the node from the list of graph nodes and place it on a new list of those nodes which can be output in the next time period? Then, in the next time period, this new list can be traversed to produce the output, so that the entire graph need not be searched for nodes with a COUNT field of 0.

The reader is encouraged at this point to discover the reason for not using this seemingly simple system. Once he has discovered the problem, he is also encouraged to find a solution.

Consider the method which would be used to remove a node from the list of graph nodes. Since this list is a linked linear list, we cannot remove a node from it unless we have a pointer to its predecessor on the list. However, when we identify a node with zero count from the arc which it terminates, we have a pointer only to that node itself and not to its predecessor on the list of graph nodes. In order to reach the predecessor we have to traverse the list from its beginning, which is the source of the original inefficiency.

There are several possible solutions to this problem. One possible solution is deferred to Section 9.4.2, where we introduce the concepts necessary for its implementation. Another solution, which the thoughtful reader should have discovered, is to link the graph nodes in a doubly linked list rather than in a singly linked linear list, so that a node's predecessor may be reached directly from the node itself, instead of through a traversal of the entire list from its beginning.

Although the graph nodes are linked in a doubly linked list, the output list may remain a singly linked linear list since it actually behaves like a stack, for which a linear list is sufficient. After performing step 1, which creates the graph, the doubly linked list of graph nodes is traversed once in order to initialize the output list to contain those graph nodes which initially have no predecessors. As each time period is subsequently simulated, the output list created in the previous time period is traversed, the subtask represented by each node in the list is output, the counts in the graph nodes adjacent to each node in the output list are reduced, and if the count in an adjacent node becomes zero, that adjacent node is placed in the output list for the next period. This means that two output lists are needed: one for the current period, which was created in the previous period and is now being traversed; and one which is being created in the current period and will be traversed in the next.

The refinement of step 2 under this implementation may be outlined as follows:

```
  /*    traverse the list of graph nodes and place all those     */
  /*      nodes with zero count on the initial output list       */
p=graph;
output=null;
do while(p¬=null);
   q=nextnode(p);
   if count(p)=0 then do;
               remove node(p) from the graph list;
               place node(p) on the output list;
                      end;
   p=q;
end;
   /*              simulate the time periods                     */
do period=1 by 1 while(output¬=null);
   print(period);
   /*        initialize the next period's output list            */
   nextout=null;
   /*               traverse the output list                     */
   p=output;
```

```
        do while(p¬=null);
           print(info(p));
     /*    traverse the list of arcs emanating from node(p)        */
        r=arcptr(p);
        do while(r¬=null);
           s=nextarc(r);
     /*        reduce the count in the terminating node            */
           t=nodeptr(r);
           count(t)=count(t)-1;
           if count(t)=0 then do;
                       remove node(t) from the graph;
     /*                add node(t) to the nextout list           */
                       nextnode(t)=nextout;
                       nextout=t;
                                  end;
           freearc(r);
           r=s;
        end;
        q=nextnode(p);
        freenode(p);
        p=q;
     end;
     output=nextout;
  end;
  if graph¬=null then error—there is a cycle in the graph;
```

In order to accommodate the pointers of the doubly linked list, the graph nodes must include an extra field BACKNODE containing a pointer to the previous graph node in the list. Thus GRAPHNODE is declared by

```
DCL 1  GRAPHNODE(500),
         2 INFO                    CHAR(20) VAR,
        (2 COUNT,
         2 ARCPTR,
         2 BACKNODE,
         2 NEXTNODE)               FIXED;
```

The available list of graph nodes and the two output lists need not be doubly linked, so that the contents of BACKNODE are irrelevant for nodes on these lists. The procedure FIND must be suitably modified to accommodate doubly linked lists. The routine JOIN is also used. Having dispensed with these preliminaries, we may write a PL/I scheduling program as follows:

```
SCHEDULE:  PROC OPTIONS(MAIN);
              DCL 1  GRAPHNODE(500),
                       2 INFO                          CHAR(20) VAR,
                      (2 COUNT,
                       2 ARCPTR,
                       2 BACKNODE,
                       2 NEXTNODE)                     FIXED,
                    1  ARC(500),
                      (2 NODEPTR,
                       2 NEXTARC)                      FIXED,
                    (GRAPH,OUTPUT)                     FIXED INIT(0),
                    (AVAILNODE,AVAILARC)               FIXED INIT(1),
                    (INF1,INF2)                        CHAR(20) VAR,
                    (P,Q,R,PERIOD,NEXTOUT,S,T,I,V,W)   FIXED;
              /*   initialize the available lists   */
INITAV:       DO I=1 TO 499;
                 NEXTNODE(I),NEXTARC(I)=I+1;
              END INITAV;
              NEXTNODE(500),NEXTARC(500)=0;
              ON ENDFILE(SYSIN) GO TO STEP2;
              COUNT=0;
              /*   construct the graph   */
INPUT:        DO WHILE('1'B);
                 GET LIST(INF1,INF2);
           /*    the function FIND will adjust all necessary      */
           /*    forward and backward pointers in adding a        */
           /*    graph node with INFO field INF1 or INF2 to       */
           /*         the doubly linked list of graph nodes       */
                 P=FIND(GRAPH,INF1);
                 Q=FIND(GRAPH,INF2);
                 CALL JOIN(P,Q);
                 COUNT(Q)=COUNT(Q)+1;
              END INPUT;
STEP2:        /*    traverse the list of graph nodes and place    */
              /*     all graph nodes with zero count on the       */
              /*                  output list                     */
              P=GRAPH;
INITOUT:      DO WHILE(P¬=0);
                 Q=NEXTNODE(P);
                 IF COUNT(P)=0 THEN DO;
              /*   remove GRAPHNODE(P) from the graph list   */
                       R=BACKNODE(P);
                       IF Q¬=0 THEN BACKNODE(Q)=R;
                       IF R¬=0 THEN NEXTNODE(R)=Q;
                                ELSE GRAPH=Q;
```

```
            /*      place GRAPHNODE(P) on the output list       */
                        NEXTNODE(P)=OUTPUT;
                        OUTPUT=P;
                                              END;
              P=Q;
            END INITOUT;

            /*                simulate the time periods             */
SIMTIME:    DO PERIOD =1 BY 1 WHILE(OUTPUT¬=0);
              PUT SKIP(2) DATA(PERIOD);
            /*       initialize next output list, and traverse      */
              NEXTOUT=0;
              P=OUTPUT;
TRAVOUT:      DO WHILE(P¬=0);
                PUT SKIP LIST(INFO(P));
            /*  traverse arcs emanating from GRAPHNODE(P)   */
                R=ARCPTR(P);
TRAVARC:        DO WHILE(R¬=0);
                  S=NEXTARC(R);

                /*  reduce count in the terminating node    */
                  T=NODEPTR(R);
                  COUNT(T)=COUNT(T)-1;
                  IF COUNT(T)=0 THEN DO;
                       /*       once the subtask represented       */
                       /*       by GRAPHNODE(P) has been           */
                       /*           performed, the subtask         */
                       /*     represented by GRAPHNODE(T)          */
                       /*             may be performed             */
                       /*    remove GRAPHNODE(T) from the          */
                       /*                 graph list               */
                       V=NEXTNODE(T);
                       W=BACKNODE(T);
                       IF V¬=0 THEN BACKNODE(V)=W;
                       IF W¬=0 THEN NEXTNODE(W)=V;
                              ELSE GRAPH=V;
                       /*   place GRAPHNODE(T) on the new          */
                       /*                output list               */
                       NEXTNODE(T)=NEXTOUT;
                       NEXTOUT=T;
                                        END;
                  CALL FREEARC(R)

                  R=S;
                END TRAVARC;
```

```
/*      continue traversing the output list        */
    Q=NEXTNODE(P);
    CALL FREENODE(P);
    P=Q;
 END TRAVOUT;

 /*  reset the output list for the next period    */
 OUTPUT =NEXTOUT;
END SIMTIME;
IF GRAPH¬=0 THEN DO;
    PUT SKIP LIST(
        'ERROR IN INPUT— GRAPH CONTAINS A CYCLE');
    STOP;
                END;

END SCHEDULE;
```

Bibliography and References

Any text on data structures (marked with a D in the Bibliography at the end of the text) contains information on trees. The Huffman algorithm is from (Huffman, 1952) and is discussed in (Knuth, 1973A), (Maurer, 1977), and (Tremblay and Sorenson, 1976). The tree solution to the Josephus problem is in (Harrison, 1973). Game trees are discussed in (Horowitz and Sahni, 1975) and in (Nilsson, 1971).

Texts on the mathematics of graph theory are (Berge, 1961), (Harary, 1969), and (Ore, 1962). Material on the adjacency matrix representation of graphs and relations may be found in (Berztiss, 1977), (Stanat and McAllister, 1977), and (Tremblay and Manohar, 1975). Warshall's algorithm is in (Warshall, 1962). Other references which discuss the computation of the transitive closure are (O'Neil and O'Neil, 1973) and (Warren, 1975). Graph algorithms may be found in (Aho, Hopcroft, and Ullman, 1974), (Berztiss, 1977), (Even, 1978), and (Reingold, Nievergelt, and Deo, 1977).

The linked representation of graphs is discussed in (Berztiss, 1977), (Pfaltz, 1977), and (Tremblay and Sorenson, 1976). Topological sorting is found in (Knuth, 1973A) and (Pfaltz, 1977). The flow algorithm is from (Fulkerson, 1977) and is discussed in (Even, 1978). PERT networks are discussed in (Berztiss, 1977), (Lockyer, 1964), (Lockyer, 1966), (Pfaltz, 1977), and (Tremblay and Sorenson, 1976).

A short word on terminology is in order. The terms "complete binary tree," "almost complete binary tree," and "strictly binary tree" as used in this text are not standard. The reason for this is that a consensus has not yet been reached within the computer science community on the terminology used to refer to these particular types of trees. Thus, different authors define terms such as "complete binary tree," "full binary tree," "fully binary tree," etc. to mean different things. We have chosen a terminology which we believe to be descriptive and reasonable, but the reader should be prepared for alternate terminology in other sources.

chapter **8**

sorting

Sorting and searching are among the most common programming processes. In the first section of this chapter we discuss some of the overall considerations involved in sorting. In the remainder of the chapter we discuss some of the more common sorting techniques. In the next chapter we discuss searching and some applications.

8.1. General Background

The concept of an ordered set of elements is one which has considerable impact on our daily lives. Consider, for example, the process of finding a telephone number in a telephone directory. This process, called a ***search***, is simplified considerably by the fact that the names in the directory are listed in alphabetical order. Consider the trouble you might have in attempting to locate a telephone number if the names were listed in the order in which the customers placed their phone orders with the telephone company. In such a case, the names might as well have been entered in random order. Since the entries are sorted in alphabetical rather than in chronological order, the process of searching is simplified. Or consider the case of someone searching for a book in a library. Because the books are shelved in a specific order (Library of Congress, Dewey System, etc.), each book is assigned a specific position relative to the others and can be retrieved in a reasonable amount of time (if it is there). Or consider a set of numbers sorted sequentially in a computer's memory. As we shall see in the next chapter, it is usually easier to find a particular element of that set if the numbers are sorted. In general, a set of items is kept sorted in order to either produce a report (to simplify manual retrieval of information, as in a telephone book or a library shelf) or to make machine access to data more efficient.

We now present some basic terminology. A ***file*** of size n is a sequence of n items $r(1), r(2), \ldots, r(n)$. Each item in the file is called a ***record***. A ***key*** $k(i)$ is assoicated with each record $r(i)$. The key is usually (but not always) a subfield of the entire record. The file is said to be ***sorted on the key*** if $i<j$ implies that $k(i)$ precedes $k(j)$ in some ordering on the keys. In the example of the telephone book, the file consists of all the entries in the book. Each entry is a record. The key upon which the file is sorted is the name field of the record. Each record also contains fields for an address and a telephone number.

A sort can be classified as being ***internal*** if the records that it is sorting are in main memory or ***external*** if some of the records that it is sorting are in auxiliary storage. We restrict our attention to internal sorts.

It is possible for two records in a file to have the same key. A sorting technique is called ***stable*** if for all records i and j such that $k(i)=k(j)$, if $r(i)$ precedes $r(j)$ in the original file, then $r(i)$ precedes $r(j)$ in the sorted file.

A sort takes place either on the records themselves or on an auxiliary table of pointers (called ***sorting by address***). For example, consider Fig. 8.1.1(a) in which a file of five records is shown. If the file is sorted in increasing order on the numeric key shown, then the resulting file is as shown in Fig. 8.1.1(b). In this case the actual records themselves have been sorted.

Suppose, however, that the amount of data stored in each of the records in the file of Fig. 8.1.1(a) is so large that the overhead involved in moving the actual data is prohibitive. In this case an auxiliary table of pointers may be used so that these pointers are moved instead of the actual data. This is shown in Fig. 8.1.2. The table in the center is the file, and the table at the left is the initial table of pointers. The entry in position j in the table of pointers points to record j. During the sorting process, the entries in the pointer table are adjusted so that the final table is as shown at the right. Originally the first pointer was to the first entry in the file; upon completion the first pointer is to the third entry in the table. Note that none of the original file entries are moved. In most of the programs in this chapter we illustrate techniques of sorting actual records; the extension of these techniques to sorting by address is straightforward and will, in general, be left as an exercise for the reader.

	Key	Other fields
Record 1	4	*DDD*
Record 2	2	*BBB*
Record 3	1	*AAA*
Record 4	5	*EEE*
Record 5	3	*CCC*

File

(a) Original file.

1	*AAA*
2	*BBB*
3	*CCC*
4	*DDD*
5	*EEE*

File

(b) Sorted file.

Figure 8.1.1. Sorting actual records.

Because of the relationship between sorting and searching, the first question to ask in any application is whether or not it pays to sort. Sometimes, there is less work involved in searching a set of elements for a particular one than to first sort the entire set and to then extract the desired element. On the other hand, if frequent use of the file is required for the purpose of retrieving specific elements, then it might be more efficient to sort the file. This is because the overhead of successive searches may far exceed the overhead involved in first sorting the file and subsequently retrieving elements from the sorted

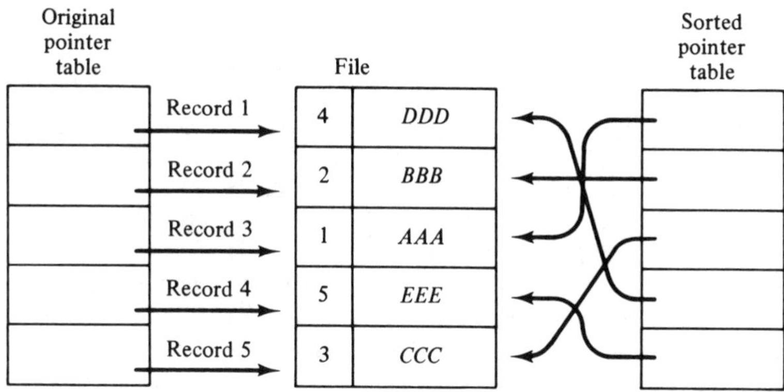

Figure 8.1.2. Sorting by using an auxiliary table of pointers.

file. Thus it cannot be said that it is more efficient either to sort or not to sort. The programmer must make a decision based on individual circumstances. Once a decision to sort has been made, other decisions must be made including what is to be sorted and what methods are to be used. There is no one sorting method that is universally superior to all others. The programmer must carefully examine the problem and the desired results before deciding these very important questions.

Efficiency Considerations

As we shall see in this chapter, there are a great number of methods which can be used to sort a file. The programmer must be aware of several interrelated efficiency considerations so that he can intelligently choose which sorting method is most appropriate to his particular problem. Three of the most important of these considerations include: the length of time which must be spent by the programmer in coding a particular sorting program, the amount of machine time necessary for running the program, and the amount of space necessary for the program.

If a file is small, sophisticated sorting techniques designed to minimize space and time requirements are usually worse or only marginally better in achieving efficiencies than simpler, generally less efficient methods. Similarly, if a particular sorting program is to be run only once and there is sufficient machine time and space in which to run it, it would be ludicrous for a programmer to spend days investigating the best methods of obtaining the last ounce of efficiency. In such cases, the amount of time which must be spent by the programmer is properly the overriding consideration in determining which sorting method to use. However, a strong word of caution must be inserted. Programming time is never a valid excuse for using an incorrect program. A sort which is run only once may be able to afford the luxury of an inefficient technique, but it cannot afford an incorrect one. The presumably sorted data may be used in an application in which the assumption of ordered data is crucial.

A programmer must be able to recognize the fact that a particular sort is inefficient and must be able to justify its use in a particular situation. Too often, programmers take the easy way out and code an inefficient sort which is then incorporated into a larger system in which the sort is a key component. The designers and planners of the system are then surprised at the inadequacy of their creation. In order to maximize his own efficiency, a programmer must be knowledgeable of a wide range of sorting techniques and be cognizant of the advantages and disadvantages of each, so that when the need for a sort arises, he can supply the one which is most appropriate for the particular situation.

This brings us to the other two efficiency considerations: time and space. As in most computer applications, the programmer must often optimize one of these at the expense of the other. In considering the time necessary to sort a file of size n, we do not concern ourselves with actual time units, as these will vary from one machine to another, from one program to another, and from one set of data to another. Rather, we are interested in the change in the amount of time required to sort a file induced by a change in the file size n. Let us see if we can make this concept more precise. We say that y is ***proportional*** to x if multiplying x by a constant multiplies y by that same constant. Thus if y is proportional to x, doubling x will double y and multiplying x by 10 multiplies y by 10. Similarly, if y is proportional to x^2, then doubling x multiplies y by 4 and multiplying x by 10 multiplies y by 100.

There are two ways to determine the time requirements of a sort, neither of which yields results that are applicable to all cases. One method is to go through a sometimes intricate and involved mathematical analysis of various cases (e.g., best case, worst case, average case). The result of this analysis is usually a formula giving the average time required for a particular sort as a function of the file size n. Suppose that such a mathematical analysis on a particular sorting program results in the conclusion that the program takes $.01n^2 + 10n$ time units to execute. Figure 8.1.3 shows the time needed by the sort for various values of n. You will notice that for small values of n, the quantity $10n$ overwhelms the quantity $.01n^2$. This is because the difference between n^2 and n is small for small values of n and is more than compensated for by the difference between 10 and .01. Thus, for small values of n, an increase in n by a factor of 2 (e.g., from 50 to 100) increases the time needed for sorting by approximately that same factor of 2 (from 525 to 1100). Similarly, an increase in n by a factor of 5 (e.g., from 10 to 50), increases the sorting time by approximately 5 (from 110 to 515). However, as n becomes larger, the difference between n^2 and n increases so quickly that it eventually more than makes up for the difference between 10 and .01. Thus when n equals 1000, the two terms contribute equally to the amount of time needed by the program. As n becomes even larger, the term $.01n^2$ overwhelms the term $10n$ and the contribution of the term $10n$ becomes almost insignificant. Thus, for large values of n, an increase in n by a factor of 2 (e.g., from 50,000 to 100,000) causes an increase in sorting time of approximately a factor of 4 (from 25.5 million to 101 million) and an increase in n by a factor of 5 (e.g., from 10,000 to 50,000) increases the sorting time by approximately a factor of 25 (from 1.1 million to 25.5 million). Indeed, as n becomes larger and larger, the sorting time becomes more and more closely proportional to n^2, as is clearly illustrated by the last column of Fig. 8.1.3. Because of this, we say that the time for the sort is on the ***order of*** n^2, written $O(n^2)$. Thus for large n the time required by the sort is almost proportional to n^2. Of course, for small values of n, the sort may exhibit drastically different behavior (as in Fig. 8.1.3), a situation which must be taken into account in analyzing its efficiency.

n	$a = 0.01n^2$	$b = 10n$	$a + b$	$\frac{(a+b)}{n^2}$
10	1	100	101	1.01
50	25	500	525	0.21
100	100	1,000	1,100	0.11
500	2,500	5,000	7,500	0.03
1,000	10,000	10,000	20,000	0.02
5,000	250,000	50,000	300,000	0.01
10,000	1,000,000	100,000	1,100,000	0.01
50,000	25,000,000	500,000	25,500,000	0.01
100,000	100,000,000	1,000,000	101,000,000	0.01
500,000	2,500,000,000	5,000,000	2,505,000,000	0.01

Figure 8.1.3.

Using this concept of the order of a sort, we can compare various sorting techniques and classify them as being "good" or "bad" in specific cases. One might hope to discover the "optimal" sort which is $O(n)$; unfortunately, however, it can be shown that no such sort exists. Most of the classical sorts we shall consider have time requirements which range from $O(n \log n)$ to $O(n^2)$. (You are asked to show as an exercise that the base of the logarithm is irrelevant in determining the order of the sort.) In the former, multiplying the file size by 100 will multiply the sorting time by less than 200 (if the base of the logarithm is 10); in the latter, multiplying the file size by 100 multiplies the sorting time by a factor of 10,000. Figure 8.1.4 shows the comparison of $n \log n$ with n^2 for a range of values of n. It can be seen from the figure that for large n, as n increases, n^2 increases at a much more rapid rate than $n \log n$. However, a sort should not be selected simply because it is $O(n \log n)$. The relation of the file size n and the other terms comprising the actual sorting time must be known. In particular, terms which play an insignificant role for large n may play a very dominant role for small n. All of these considerations must be taken into account before an intelligent sort selection can be made.

n	$n \log_{10} n$	n^2
1×10^1	1.0×10^1	1.0×10^2
5×10^1	8.5×10^1	2.5×10^3
1×10^2	2.0×10^2	1.0×10^4
5×10^2	1.3×10^3	2.5×10^5
1×10^3	3.0×10^3	1.0×10^6
5×10^3	1.8×10^4	2.5×10^7
1×10^4	4.0×10^4	1.0×10^8
5×10^4	2.3×10^5	2.5×10^9
1×10^5	5.0×10^5	1.0×10^{10}
5×10^5	2.8×10^6	2.5×10^{11}
1×10^6	6.0×10^6	1.0×10^{12}
5×10^6	3.3×10^7	2.5×10^{13}
1×10^7	7.0×10^7	1.0×10^{14}

Figure 8.1.4. A comparison of $n \log n$ and n^2 for various value of n.

A second method of determining time requirements of a sorting technique is to actually run a program and measure its efficiency (either by measuring absolute time units or the number of operations performed). In order to use such results in measuring the efficiency of a sort, the test must be run on "many" sample files. Even when such statistics have been gathered, the application of that sort to a specific file need not yield results which follow the general pattern. Peculiar attributes of the file in question may make the sorting speed deviate significantly. In the sorts of the subsequent sections we shall give an intuitive explanation as to why a particular sort is classified as $O(n^2)$ or $O(n \log n)$; we leave mathematical analysis and sophisticated testing of empirical data as exercises for the ambitious reader.

In most cases, the time needed by a sort depends upon the original sequence of the data. For some sorts, input data which is almost in sorted order can be completely sorted in time $O(n)$, while input data which is in reverse order needs time which is $O(n^2)$. For other sorts the time required is $O(n \log n)$ regardless of the original order of the data. Thus if we have some knowledge about the original data, we can make a more intelligent decision as to which sorting method to select. On the other hand, if we have no such knowledge, we may wish to select a sort based on the worst possible case or based on the "average" case. In any event, the only general comment that can be made about sorting techniques is that there is no "best" general sorting technique. The choice of a sort must, of necessity, depend on the specific circumstances.

Once a particular sorting technique has been selected, the programmer should do his best to make the program as efficient as possible. In many programming applications it is often necessary to sacrifice efficiency for the sake of clarity. With sorting, the situation is usually the opposite. Once a sorting program has been written and tested, the programmer's chief goal is to improve its speed, even if it becomes less readable. The reason for this is that a sort may account for the major part of a program's efficiency, so that any improvement in sorting time significantly affects overall efficiency. Another reason is that a sort is often used quite frequently, so that a small improvement in its execution speed saves a great deal of computer time. It is usually a good idea to remove subroutine calls, especially from inner loops, and replace them with the code of the subroutine in line, since the call-return mechanism of a language can be prohibitively expensive in terms of time. In many of the programs we do not do this so as not to obfuscate the intent of the program with huge blocks of code. But before using the following programs on large files the reader would do well to replace subroutine calls with code in line.

Space constraints are usually less important than time considerations. One of the reasons for this is that for most sorting programs the amount of space needed is closer to $O(n)$ than to $O(n^2)$. A second reason is that if more space is required it can almost always be found in auxiliary storage. Of course the usual relationship between time and space holds for sorting algorithms, i.e., those programs that require less time usually require more space, and vice versa.

In the remaining sections we investigate some of the more popular sorting techniques and indicate some of their advantages and disadvantages.

8.2. Exchange Sorts

Bubble Sort

The first sort we present is probably the most widely known among beginning students of programming: the ***bubble sort***. One of the characteristics of this sort is that it is easy to understand and program. Yet, of all the sorts we shall consider, it is probably the least efficient.

In each of the subsequent examples, an array of integers X of size N is to be sorted so that $X(I) \leqslant X(J)$ for $1 \leqslant I < J \leqslant N$. It is straightforward to extend this simple format to one which is used in sorting N records, each with a subfield key K.

The basic idea underlying the bubble sort is to pass through the file sequentially several times. Each pass consists of comparing each element in the file with its successor (X(J) with X(J+1)) and interchanging the two elements if they are not in proper order. Consider the following file:

25 57 48 37 12 92 86 33

The following comparisons are made on the first pass:

X(1)	with	X(2)	(25 with 57)	no interchange
X(2)	with	X(3)	(57 with 48)	interchange
X(3)	with	X(4)	(57 with 37)	interchange
X(4)	with	X(5)	(57 with 12)	interchange
X(5)	with	X(6)	(57 with 92)	no interchange
X(6)	with	X(7)	(92 with 86)	interchange
X(7)	with	X(8)	(92 with 33)	interchange

Thus, after the first pass, the file is in the order

25 48 37 12 57 86 33 92

Notice that after this first pass, the largest element (in this case 92) is in its proper position within the array. In general, X(N–I+1) will be in its proper position after iteration I. The method is called the bubble sort because each number slowly "bubbles" up to its proper position. After the second pass the file is

25 37 12 48 57 33 86 92

Notice that 86 has now found its way to the second highest position. Since each iteration places a new element into its proper position, a file of N elements requires no more than N–1 iterations.

The complete set of iterations is the following:

iteration 0 (original file)	25	57	48	37	12	92	86	33
iteration 1	25	48	37	12	57	86	33	92
iteration 2	25	37	12	48	57	33	86	92
iteration 3	25	12	37	48	33	57	86	92
iteration 4	12	25	37	33	48	57	86	92
iteration 5	12	25	33	37	48	57	86	92
iteration 6	12	25	33	37	48	57	86	92
iteration 7	12	25	33	37	48	57	86	92

On the basis of the above discussion we could proceed to code the bubble sort. However, there are some obvious improvements to the above method. First, since all of the elements in positions greater than or equal to N–I+1 are already in proper position after iteration I, they need not be compared in succeeding iterations. Thus on the first pass N–1 comparisons are made, on the second pass N–2 comparisons, and on the (N–1)th pass only one comparison is made (between X(1) and X(2)). Therefore, the process speeds up as it proceeds through successive passes.

We have shown that N–1 passes are sufficient to sort a file of size N. However, in the above sample file of eight elements, the file was sorted after five iterations, making the last two iterations unnecessary. In order to eliminate unnecessary passes, we must be able to detect the fact that the file is already sorted. But this is a simple task since in a sorted file no interchanges are made on any pass. By keeping a record of whether or not any interchanges are made in a given pass, we can determine whether any further passes are necessary. Under this method, if the file can be sorted in less than N–1 passes, then the final pass makes no interchanges.

Using these improvements, we present the routine BUBBLE which accepts two parameters X and N. X is an array of FIXED numbers and N is the number of elements to be sorted. (N may be less than the upper bound of X.)

```
BUBBLE:    PROC(X,N);
             DCL (X(*),N,PASS,J,HOLD)                 FIXED,
                  INTCHNGE                            BIT(1)   INIT('1'B);

LOOP:        DO PASS=1 TO N–1 WHILE (INTCHNGE);
             /*    outer loop controls the number of passes     */
                 INTCHNGE='0'B;  /*  initially no interchanges have  */
                                 /*     been made on this pass       */

EACHPASS:        DO J=1 TO N–PASS;
                 /*   inner loop governs each individual pass    */
                    IF X(J)>X(J+1) THEN  /*  elements out of order   */
                      DO;
                        /*          an interchange is necessary          */
                        INTCHNGE='1'B;
                        HOLD=X(J);
                        X(J)=X(J+1);
                        X(J+1)=HOLD;
                      END;
               END EACHPASS;
             END LOOP;
             RETURN;
           END BUBBLE;
```

What can be said about the efficiency of the bubble sort? In the case of a sort that does not include the two improvements outlined above, the analysis is simple. There are

$N-1$ passes and $N-1$ comparisons on each pass. Thus the total number of comparisons is $(N-1)*(N-1)=N^2-2N+1$, which is $O(N^2)$. Of course, the number of interchanges depends on the original order of the file. However, the number of interchanges cannot be greater than the number of comparisons. It is likely that it is the number of interchanges rather than the number of comparisons which takes up the most time in the algorithm's execution.

Let us see how the improvements which we introduced affect the speed of the bubble sort. The number of comparisons on iteration I is $N-I$. Thus, if there are K iterations, the total number of comparisons is $(N-1)+(N-2)+(N-3)+ \ldots +(N-K)$, which equals $(2KN-K^2-K)/2$. It can be shown that the average number of iterations, K, is $O(N)$, so that the entire formula is still $O(N^2)$, although the constant multiplier is smaller than before. However, there is additional overhead involved in testing and initializing the bit INTCHNGE (one per pass) and setting it to '1'B (once for every interchange).

The only redeeming features of the bubble sort are that it requires little additional space (one memory location to hold the temporary value for interchanging) and that it is $O(N)$ in the case that the file is completely sorted (or almost completely sorted). This follows from the observation that only one pass of $N-1$ comparisons (and no interchanges) is necessary to establish that a sorted file is sorted.

There are some other ways to improve the bubble sort. One of these is to observe that the number of passes necessary before the file is sorted is the largest distance by which a number must move "down" in the array. In our example, for instance, 33, which starts at position 8 in the array, ultimately finds its way to position 3 after five iterations. The bubble sort can be speeded up by having successive passes go in opposite directions so that the number of passes is reduced. This version and others are considered in the Exercise Manual.

Quicksort

The next sort we consider is the ***partition exchange sort*** (or ***quicksort***). Let x be an array to be sorted and n the number of elements in the array. Choose an element a from a specific position within the array (for example, a can be chosen as the first element so that $a=x(1)$). Suppose the elements of x are rearranged so that a is placed into position j and the following conditions hold:

1. Each of the elements in positions 1 through $j-1$ is less than or equal to a.

2. Each of the elements in positions $j+1$ through n is greater than or equal to a.

Notice that if these two conditions hold for a particular a and j, then a remains in position j when the array is completely sorted. (You are asked to prove this fact as an exercise.) If the above process is repeated with the subarrays $x(1)$ through $x(j-1)$ and $x(j+1)$ through $x(n)$ and any subarrays created by the process in successive iterations, the final result is a sorted file.

Let us illustrate the quicksort with an example. If an initial array is given as

```
25  57  48  37  12  92  86  33
```

and the first element (25) is placed in its proper position, then the resulting array is

```
12  25  57  48  37  92  86  33
```

At this point, 25 is in its proper position in the array ($x(2)$), each element below that position (12) is less than or equal to 25, and each element above that position (57, 48, 37, 92, 86, and 33) is greater than or equal to 25. Since 25 is in its final position, the original problem has been decomposed into the problem of sorting the two subarrays

```
(12)  and  (57  48  37  92  86  33)
```

Nothing need be done to sort the first of these subarrays: a file of one element is already sorted. To sort the second subarray the process is repeated and the subarray is further subdivided. The entire array may now be viewed as

```
12  25  (57  48  37  92  86  33)
```

where parentheses enclose the subarrays which are yet to be sorted. Repeating the process on the subarray $x(3)$ through $x(8)$ yields

```
12  25  (48  37  33)  57  (92  86)
```

and further repetitions yield

```
12  25  (37   33)  48  57  (92  86)
12  25  (33)  37   48  57  (92  86)
12  25   33   37   48  57  (92  86)
12  25   33   37   48  57  (86) 92
12  25   33   37   48  57   86  92
```

Note that the final array is sorted.

By this time you should have noticed that the quicksort may be defined most conveniently as a recursive procedure. We may outline an algorithm *quick(lb,ub)* to sort all elements in an array *x* between $x(lb)$ and $x(ub)$ (*lb* is the lower bound, *ub* the upper bound) as follows:

```
if lb>=ub then return;    /*        array is sorted              */

rearrange (lb,ub,j);      /*  rearrange the elements of the     */
                          /*  subarray such that one of the     */
                          /*  elements (possibly x(lb)) is      */
                          /*  now at x(j) (j is an output       */
                          /*      parameter) and:               */
                          /*   1. x(i) <= x(j) for lb<=i<j      */
                          /*   2. x(i) >= x(j) for j<i<=ub      */
                          /*   x(j) is now at its final         */
                          /*         position                   */

quick(lb,j-1);            /*  sort the subarray between         */
                          /*     x(lb) and x(j-1)               */

quick(j+1,ub);            /*  sort the subarray between         */
                          /*     x(j+1) and x(ub)               */
```

The only remaining problem is to describe a mechanism to implement *rearrange* which allows a specific element to find its proper position with respect to the others in the subarray. Note that the way in which this rearrangement is implemented is irrelevant to the sorting method. All that is required by the sort is that the elements are partitioned properly. In the above example, the elements in each of the two subfiles remain in the same relative order as they appear in the original file. However, such a rearrangement method is relatively inefficient.

One way to effect a rearrangement efficiently is the following: Let a=$x(lb)$ be the element whose final position is sought. (There is no appreciable efficiency gained by selecting the first element of the subarray as the one which is inserted into its proper position; it merely makes some of the programs easier to code.) Two pointers, *up* and *down*, are initialized to the upper and lower bounds of the subarray respectively. At any point during execution, each element in a position above *up* is greater than or equal to a and each element in a position below *down* is less than or equal to a. The two pointers *up* and *down* are alternately moved towards each other. Execution begins by decreasing the pointer *up* one position at a time until $x(up) < a$. At that point $x(up)$ and $x(down)$ are interchanged. (Note that after the interchange the value of $x(up)$ is a.) The algorithm then proceeds in the opposite direction and increments the pointer *down* one position at a time until $x(down) > a$. When this happens, $x(up)$ and $x(down)$ are interchanged and scanning resumes in the opposite direction. (Note that after this interchange the value of $x(down)$ is a.) The process halts when *up*=*down*, at which point j=*up*, $x(j)$=a, and each element in a position above j is greater than or equal to $x(j)$ and each element in a position below j is less than or equal to $x(j)$.

We illustrate this process on the sample file, showing the positions of *up* and *down* as they are adjusted. The direction of the scan is indicated by an arrow at the pointer being moved. An asterisk indicates that an interchange is made.

```
a = x(lb) = 25

down                                                 <--up
25     57     48     37     12     92     86     33

down                                          <--up
25     57     48     37     12     92     86     33

down                                   <--up
25     57     48     37     12     92     86     33

down                        up
25     57     48     37     12     92     86     33   *

down-->                     up
12     57     48     37     25     92     86     33

       down                 up
12     57     48     37     25     92     86     33   *

       down              <--up
12     25     48     37     57     92     86     33

       down       <--up
12     25     48     37     57     92     86     33

       down  <--up
12     25     48     37     57     92     86     33

      down=up
12     25     48     37     57     92     86     33
```

At this point 25 is in its proper position (position 2) and every element to its left is less than or equal to 25 and every element to its right is greater than or equal to 25. We could now proceed to sort the two subarrays (12) and (48 37 57 92 86 33) by applying the same method.

An algorithm to implement *rearrange* is as follows: *lb* and *ub* are input parameters, and *j* is an output parameter.

```
a = x(lb);          /*  a is the element whose final   */
                    /*      position is sought          */
j = lb;             /*  j will be set to the final position  */
                    /*            of a                  */
up = ub;
down = lb;
```

```
do while (true);
   move_down: do while (up > down & x(up) >= a);
                  up = up -1;
              end move_down;
              j = up;
              if up = down then return;
              interchange x (up) and x(down);
   move_up:   do while (down < up & x(down) <= a);
                  down = down+1;
              end move_up;
              j = down;
              if down = up then return;
              interchange x (down) and x (up);
end;
```

Before writing a program to implement *rearrange*, we can make one improvement. Each time *x*(*up*) and *x*(*down*) are interchanged, *a* is inserted into a new position, which is only temporary if an additional interchange is necessary. Instead of actually inserting *a* into this position, let us simply remember the position in a pointer variable *j* (which we must do anyway). Should additional "interchanges" be necessary, then the new element can be inserted into *x*(*j*) and *j* is set to the former position of this element. Before returning, we must, of course, insert *a* into *x*(*j*).

A program for *rearrange* follows:

```
REARRANGE:  PROC(LB,UB,J);
               DCL (LB,UB,J,UP,DOWN,A)      FIXED;
               A=X(LB);
               J=LB;
               UP=UB;
               DOWN=LB;
LOOP:          DO WHILE('1'B);
                  /*   move down the array    */
MOVE_DOWN:        DO WHILE(UP>DOWN & X(UP)>=A);
                     UP=UP-1;
                  END MOVE_DOWN;
                  J=UP;
                  IF UP=DOWN THEN GO TO DONE;
                  X(DOWN)=X(UP);
                  /*   move up the array    */
MOVE_UP:          DO WHILE(DOWN<UP & X(DOWN)<=A);
                     DOWN=DOWN+1;
                  END MOVE_UP;
                  J=DOWN;
                  IF DOWN=UP THEN GO TO DONE;
                  X(UP)=X(DOWN);
               END LOOP;
```

```
DONE:           X(J)=A;
                RETURN;
             END REARRANGE;
```

The routine can be made slightly more efficient by eliminating some of the redundant tests. You are asked to do this as an exercise.

We may now code a program to implement the quicksort. As in the case of BUBBLE, the parameters are the array X and the number of elements of X we wish to sort, N. Since the algorithm requires the sorting of two subarrays, we write an internal recursive routine QUICK whose parameters are the lower and upper bounds of the array between which we wish to sort.

```
QUICKSRT:     PROC(X,N);
                DCL  (X(*),N)                 FIXED;
                CALL QUICK(1,N);
                RETURN;

QUICK:        PROC(LB,UB) RECURSIVE;
                DCL (LB,UB,J)                 FIXED;
                IF LB>=UB THEN RETURN;
                CALL REARRANGE(LB,UB,J);
                CALL QUICK(LB,J-1);
                CALL QUICK(J+1,UB);
                RETURN;
              END QUICK;

              END QUICKSRT;
```

Improving the Program

While the above programs are concise in terms of what they accomplish and how they do it, the overhead of subroutine calls (and especially recursive subroutine calls) should be avoided in programs such as sorts, where execution efficiency is a significant consideration. The recursive calls to QUICK can easily be eliminated by using a stack as in Chapter 4. Once REARRANGE has been executed, the current parameters to QUICK are no longer needed, except in computing the arguments to the two subsequent recursive calls. Thus instead of stacking the current parameters upon each recursive call, we can compute and stack the new parameters for each of the two recursive calls. Under this approach, the stack at any point contains the lower and upper bounds of all subarrays which must yet be sorted. Furthermore, since the second recursive call immediately precedes the RETURN statement (as in the Towers of Hanoi problem), it may be eliminated entirely and replaced with a branch. Finally, since the order in which the two recursive calls are made is irrelevant in this problem, we elect in each case to stack the larger subarray and process the smaller subarray immediately. You are asked to show as an exercise that this keeps the size of the stack to a minimum. With the above improvements in mind we code the routine QUICKSRT2:

```
QUICKSRT2:   PROC(X,N);
               DCL (X(*),N,I,J)              FIXED;
                   1 STACK,
                     2 TOP                   FIXED INIT(0),
                     2 BOUNDS(N),
                       (3 LOWER,
                        3 UPPER)             FIXED,
                   1 NEWBNDS,
                     (2 LB,
                      2 UB)                  FIXED;
               LB=1;
               UB=N;
               CALL PUSH(STACK,NEWBNDS);
             /*   repeat as long as there are any unsorted subarrays   */
             /*                     on the stack                        */
REPEAT:        DO WHILE(¬ EMPTY(STACK));
                  CALL POPSUB(STACK,NEWBNDS);
AGAIN:            DO WHILE(UB>LB);
                     /*    process next subarray     */
                     CALL REARRANGE(LB,UB,J);
                     /*    stack the larger subarray    */
                     IF J-LB > UB-J THEN  /*   stack lower subarray    */
                             DO;
                                I=UB;
                                UB=J-1;
                                CALL PUSH(STACK,NEWBNDS);
                                 /*   process upper subarray    */
                                LB=J+1;
                                UB=I;
                             END;
                                ELSE /*   stack upper subarray    */
                           DO;
                                I=LB;
                                LB=J+1;
                                CALL PUSH(STACK,NEWBNDS);
                                   /*   process lower subarray    */
                                LB=I;
                                UB=J-1;
                           END;
                  END AGAIN;
               END REPEAT;
               RETURN;
             END QUICKSRT2;
```

Of course the routines REARRANGE, EMPTY, POPSUB, and PUSH must be supplied and should be inserted in line for maximum efficiency. Trace the action of QUICKSRT2 on the sample file.

Efficiency of Quicksort

How efficient is the quicksort? Assume that the file size n is a power of 2, say $n=2^m$ so that $m = \log_2 n$. Assume also that the proper position for $x(lb)$ always turns out to be the exact middle of the subarray. In that case there will be approximately n comparisons (actually $n-1$) on the first pass, after which the file is split into two subfiles, each of size $n/2$ approximately. For each of these two files there are approximately $n/2$ comparisons, and a total of four files each of size $n/4$ are formed. Each of these files requires $n/4$ comparisons, yielding a total of 8 subfiles. After halving the subfiles m times, there are n files of size 1. Thus the total number of comparisons for the entire sort is approximately

$$n + 2(n/2) + 4(n/4) + 8(n/8) + \ldots + n(n/n)$$

or

$$n + n + n + n + \ldots + n \quad (m \text{ terms})$$

comparisons. There are m terms because the file is subdivided m times. Thus the total number of comparisons is $O(nm)$ or $O(n \log n)$ (recall that $m=\log_2 n$). Thus if the above properties describe the file, then the quicksort is $O(n \log n)$, which is relatively efficient.

The above analysis assumes that the original array and all the resulting subarrays are unsorted in such a way that $x(lb)$ always find its proper position at the middle of the subarray. Suppose the above conditions do not hold and the original array is sorted (or almost sorted). If, for example, $x(lb)$ is in its correct position, then the original file is split into subfiles of sizes 0 and $n-1$. If this process continues, then a total of $n-1$ subfiles are sorted, the first of size n, the second of size $n-1$, the third of size $n-2$, etc. Assuming k comparisons in rearranging a file of size k, the total number of comparisons to sort the entire file is

$$n + (n-1) + (n-2) + \ldots + 2$$

which is $O(n^2)$. Similarly, if the original file is sorted in descending order, the final position of $x(lb)$ is ub and the file is again split into two subfiles which are heavily unbalanced (sizes $n-1$ and 0). Thus the quicksort has the seemingly absurd property that it works best for files which are completely unsorted and worst for files which are completely sorted. The situation is precisely the opposite for the bubble sort, which works best for sorted files and worst for unsorted files. The analysis for the case where the file size is not an integral power of 2 is similar but slightly more complex; the results, however, remain the same. It can be shown, however, that on the average (over all files of size n), the quicksort makes $O(n \log n)$ comparisons.

The space requirements for the quicksort depend upon the number of nested recursive calls or on the size of the stack. Clearly the stack can never grow larger than the number of elements in the original file. How much smaller than *n* the stack grows depends upon the number of subfiles generated and on their sizes. The size of the stack can be somewhat contained by always stacking the larger of the two subarrays and applying the routine to the smaller of the two. This guarantees that all smaller subarrays are subdivided before larger subarrays, giving the net effect of having fewer elements on the stack at any given time. The reason for this is that a smaller subarray can be divided fewer times than a larger subarray. Of course, the larger subarray will ultimately be processed and subdivided, but this will occur after the smaller subarrays have already been sorted.

8.3. Selection and Tree Sorting

Straight Selection Sort

A ***selection sort*** is one in which successive elements are selected from the file and placed in proper position. The following program is an example of a ***straight selection sort***. The largest number is first placed in the Nth position, the next largest is placed in position N–1, etc.

```
SELECT:    PROC(X,N);
             DCL  (X(*) ,N,I,J,INDX,LARGE)         FIXED;

NEXT:        DO I=N TO 2 BY-1;
               /*   place the largest number of X(1) through    */
               /*   X(I) into LARGE and its index into INDX     */
               LARGE = X(1);
               INDX = 1;

FINDLRGE:      DO J = 2 TO I;
                  IF X(J) > LARGE THEN DO;
                                          LARGE = X(J);
                                          INDX = J;
                                       END;
               END FINDLRGE;

               /*   place LARGE into position I   */
               X(INDX) =X(I);
               X(I) =LARGE;
             END NEXT;
             RETURN;
           END SELECT;
```

This sort is also known as the ***push-down sort***.

Analysis of the straight selection sort is straightforward. The first pass makes $N{-}1$ comparisons, the second pass makes $N{-}2$, etc. Therefore, there is a total of

$$(N-1) + (N-2) + (N-3) + \ldots + 1 = N*(N-1)/2$$

comparisons, which is $O(N^2)$. The number of interchanges is always $N-1$ (unless a test is added to prevent the interchanging of an element with itself). There is little additional storage required (except to hold a few temporary variables). The sort may therefore be categorized as $O(N^2)$ although it is faster than the bubble sort. There is no improvement if the input file is completely sorted or unsorted since the testing proceeds to completion without regard to the makeup of the file. Despite the fact that it is simple to code, it is unlikely that the straight selection sort would be used on any files but those for which N is small.

Binary Tree Sorts

In the remainder of this section we illustrate several selection sorts which utilize binary trees. Before we do that, however, let us analyze the binary tree sort of Section 7.1. The reader is advised to review that sort before proceeding further.

The method involves scanning each element of the input file and placing it in its proper position in a binary tree. To find the proper position of an element y, a left or right branch is taken at each node depending upon whether y is less than the element in the node or greater than or equal to it. Once each input element is in its proper position in the tree, the sorted file can be retrieved by an inorder traversal of the tree. We present the algorithm for this sort, modifying it to accommodate the input as a preexisting array.

```
/*     establish the first element as root      */
tree=maketree (x(1));
/*     repeat for each successive element       */
do i=2 to n;
   y=x(i);
   q,p=tree;
/*     travel down the tree until a leaf is reached        */
   do while (p¬=null);
      q=p;
      if y<info(p) then p=left(p);
                   else p=right(p);
   end;
   if y < info(q)  then setleft(q,y);
                   else setright(q,y);
end;
/*     the tree is built, traverse it in inorder      */
intrav(tree);
```

In order to convert the above algorithm into a subroutine to sort an array, it is necessary to revise INTRAV so that visiting a node involves placing the contents of the node into the next position of the original array.

The relative efficiency of this method depends upon the original order of the data. If the original array is completely sorted (or sorted in reverse order), then the resulting tree appears as a sequence of only right (or left) links as in Fig. 8.3.1. In this case the inser-

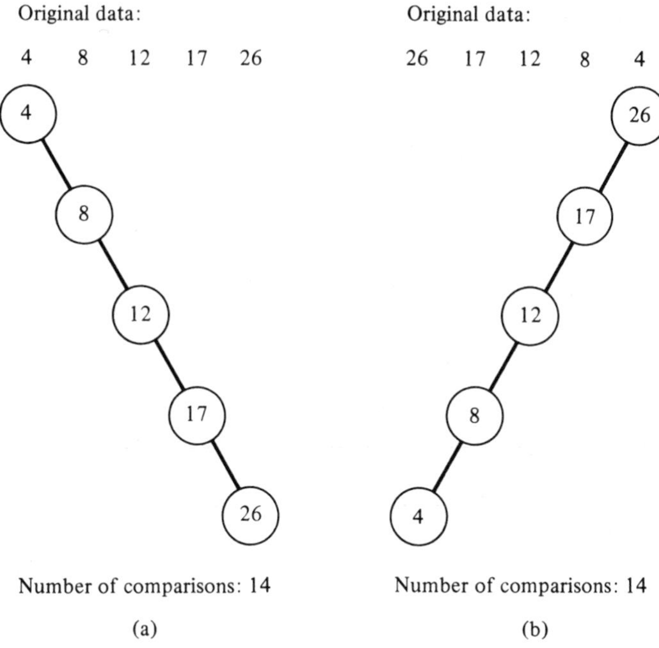

Figure 8.3.1.

tion of the first node requires no comparisons, the second node requires two comparisons, the third node three comparisons, etc. Thus the total number of comparisons is

$$2 + 3 + \ldots + n = n\ (n+1)/2 - 1$$

which is $O(n^2)$.

On the other hand, if the data in the original array is organized so that approximately half the numbers following any given number a in the array are less than a and half are greater than a, then trees such as those in Fig. 8.3.2 result. In such a case, the depth of the resulting binary tree is the smallest integer d greater than or equal to $\log_2 (n+1) - 1$. The number of nodes at any level l (except possibly for the last) is 2^l, and the number of comparisons necessary to place a node at level l (except when l=0) is l+1. Thus, the total number of comparisons is between

$$d + \sum_{l=1}^{d-1} 2^l (l+1) \text{ and } \sum_{l=1}^{d} 2^l (l+1)$$

It can be shown (mathematically inclined readers might be interested in proving this fact as an exercise) that the resulting sums are $O(n \log n)$.

Of course, once the tree has been created, time is expended in traversing it. (Note that if the tree is threaded as it is created, then the traversal time is sharply reduced.)

This sort requires that one tree node be reserved for each array element. Depending

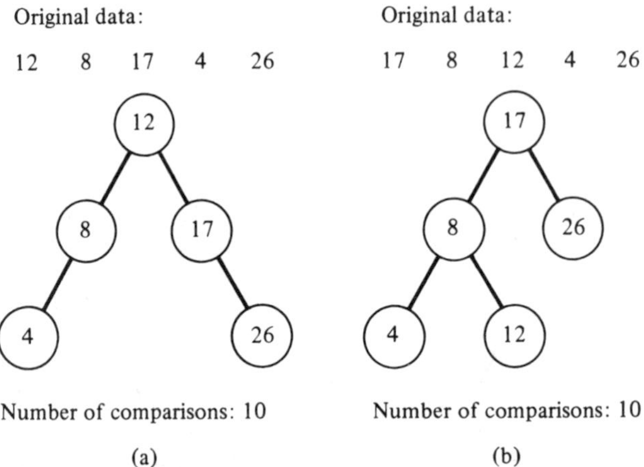

Figure 8.3.2.

on the method used to implement the tree, space may be required for tree pointers and threads, if any.

Tournament Sort

The next tree sort we consider is frequently called the ***tournament sort*** because its actions mirror those of a tournament where participants play each other to determine the best player. (This sort is also called the ***tree selection sort***.) Consider a tournament which determines the best player from the set {Ed, Gail, Keith, George, Jack, Pat, Barbara, Frank}. The outcome of the tournament can be represented by a binary tree as in Fig. 8.3.3. Each leaf of the tree represents a player in the tournament. Each nonleaf node represents the results of a game between the players represented by its two sons. In the diagram of Fig. 8.3.3(a) it is clear that Gail is the tournament champion.

But suppose it is also desired to determine the second best player. Pat is not necessarily the second best player despite the fact that he played Gail in the championship game. To determine the second best player, it would be necessary for Keith (who lost to Gail in the quarter finals) to play George (who lost to Gail in the semifinals) and the winner of that match to play Pat.

Let us indicate that a player has been declared a winner by placing an asterisk in the leaf node corresponding to that player. Clearly, if a node is marked with an asterisk, its player does not participate in any future runoffs. If both sons of a node contain an asterisk, then those sons both represent players who have completed the tournament and therefore the father node is also marked with an asterisk and no longer participates in any further runoffs. If only one son of a node is marked with an asterisk, then the player represented by the other son is moved up to the father node. For example, when the leaf containing Gail in Fig. 8.3.3(a) is marked with an asterisk, the name Keith is moved up to replace Gail in the father of that leaf. The tournament is then replayed from that point, with George playing Keith (George wins), and George playing Pat (Pat wins), thus yielding the tree of Fig. 8.3.3(b). Pat is indeed the second best player. This process may

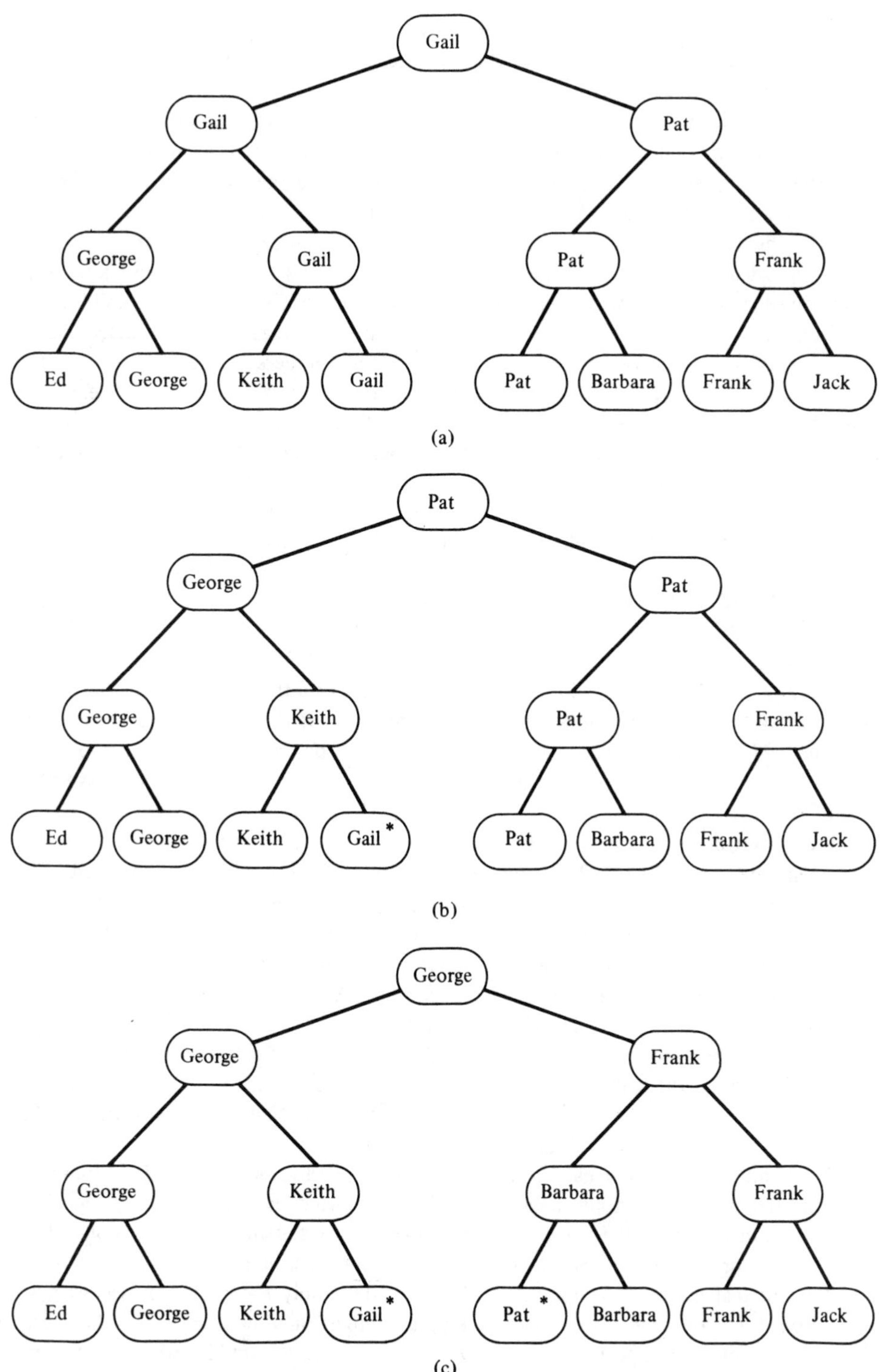

Figure 8.3.3. A tournament.

be continued (Fig. 8.3.3(c) illustrates that George is third best) until all the nodes of the tree are marked with asterisks.

The same technique is used in the tournament sort. Each of the original elements is assigned to a leaf node of a binary tree. The tree is constructed in bottom-up fashion from the leaf nodes to the root as follows: Choose two leaf nodes and establish them as the sons of a newly created father node. The content of the father node is set to the larger of the two numbers represented by its sons. This process is repeated until either one or zero leafs remain. If one remains, move the node itself up to the previous level. Now repeat this process with the newly created father nodes (plus the possible node which had no partner in the previous repetition) until the largest number is placed in the root node of a binary tree whose leafs contain all the numbers of the original file. The contents of this root node may then be output as the largest element. The leaf node containing the value at the root is then replaced with a number smaller than any in the original file (this corresponds to marking it with an asterisk). The contents of all its ancestors are then recomputed from the leafs to the root. This process is repeated until all the original elements have been output.

Figure 8.3.4(a) shows the initial tree using the file presented in the last section

25 57 48 37 12 92 86 33

After 92 is output, the tree is transformed as in Fig. 8.3.4(b), where 92 has been replaced by −1 and 86 is moved up to the root position. Note that it is necessary to recompute the contents of those nodes which were ancestors of the original leaf node which contained 92. Figure 8.3.4(c) shows the tree after 57 has moved up to the root. The reader is asked to complete the process until all the elements of the original file have been output.

Before writing a program to implement the tournament sort, we must decide how to implement the tree in PL/I. The linked representation of Section 7.2 could be used. The efficiency of the program can be improved by using the representation of Section 7.3, in which an almost complete binary tree is represented as an array. In this representation, if index I references a node, then LEFT(I) is referenced by index 2*I, RIGHT(I) is referenced by 2*I+1, and FATHER(I) is referenced by the integer part of I/2. In order to simplify the coding, we use a complete binary tree. In such a tree, only those nodes at the maximum level are leafs. Such a tree with eight leafs is illustrated in Fig. 8.3.4. In general, the number of leafs in a complete binary tree is a power of 2. If the original file is of size N which is not a power of 2, then the number of leafs is the smallest power of 2 greater than N and the extra leafs are initialized to −1.

A second question is: What should the contents of the tree nodes be? Suppose we allow the tree nodes to contain the actual items to be sorted, as in Fig. 8.3.4. Then when the root is output, the leaf node corresponding to that root element must be replaced by a very small number and the contents of all its ancestors must be readjusted. But in order to locate the leaf node corresponding to the root, given only the root, it is necessary to travel from the root down to the leaf, making a comparison at each level. Furthermore, this process must be repeated for each new root node. It would certainly be more efficient if it were possible to proceed directly from the root to the leaf that corresponds

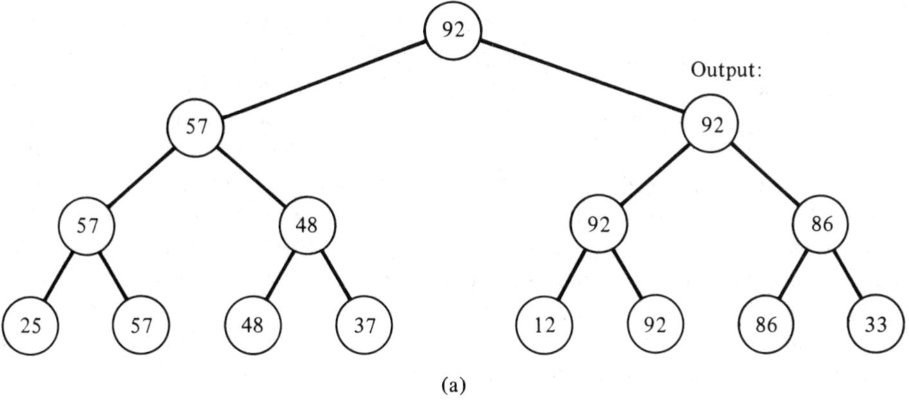

(a)

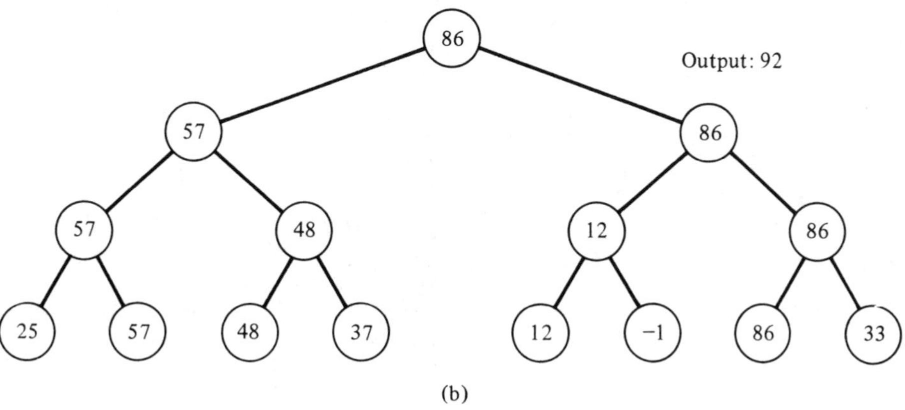

(b)

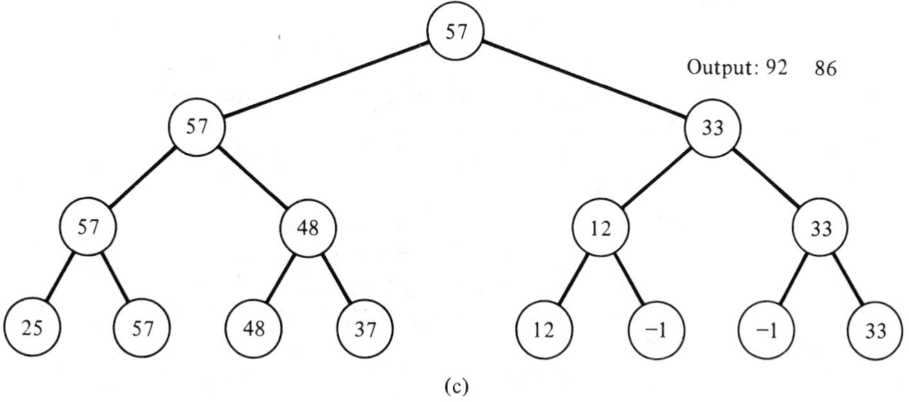

(c)

Figure 8.3.4.

to its contents. We therefore construct the complete binary tree in the following way: Each leaf contains an element of the original array. Each nonleaf node contains the index of the leaf node corresponding to the array element which the nonleaf node represents. If the content of a leaf node I, TREE(I), is moved up to a nonleaf node J, then TREE(J) is set to I (the index in the tree of the leaf node corresponding to the element) rather than TREE(I) (the actual element itself). The content of a nonleaf node (which is the index of the appropriate leaf node) is subsequently moved up the tree directly. Thus if I is a leaf node, then TREE(I) contains the actual element which node I represents; if I is a nonleaf node, then TREE(I) references the index of a leaf node and hence TREE(TREE(I)) references the actual element that node I represents.

For example, the array TREE representing the tree of Fig. 8.3.4(a) is initialized as follows (nodes 8 through 15 are leafs, nodes 1 through 7 are nonleafs).

I	TREE(I)
1	13
2	9
3	13
4	9
5	10
6	13
7	14
8	25
9	57
10	48
11	37
12	12
13	92
14	86
15	33

We may now code our program as follows:

```
TOURN:  PROC(X,N);
          DCL (X(*) ,N,SIZE,I,K)                    FIXED,
              SMALL                                 FIXED INIT(-99999);
          /*  determine the number of leafs in the tree   */
          SIZE=1;
          DO WHILE(SIZE<N);
             SIZE=SIZE*2;
          END;
          /*    SIZE is the number of leafs necessary       */
          /*  in the complete binary tree. The number       */
          /*              of nodes is 2*SIZE-1.             */
BLOCK:    BEGIN;
            DCL TREE(2*SIZE-1)                      FIXED;
            CALL INITIALIZE;  /*    creates initial tree      */
                              /*   as described in text       */
```

```
                /*    now that the tree is constructed, repeatedly     */
                /*    place the element represented by the root in     */
                /*     the next lower position in the array X and      */
                /*                  readjust the tree                  */
OUT:            DO K=N TO 2 BY -1;
                   I=TREE(1);        /*   I is the index of the leaf     */
                                     /*   node corresponding to the      */
                                     /*             root                 */
                   X(K) =TREE(I);    /*    place element referenced      */
                                     /*     by root in position K        */
                   TREE(I) =SMALL;
                   CALL READJUST(I);  /*   readjust tree based    */
                                      /*    on new contents of    */
                                      /*          TREE(I)         */
                END OUT;

                X(1) =TREE(TREE(1));
             END BLOCK;
             RETURN;
          END TOURN;
```

We now present the routines INITIALIZE and READJUST. Note that the level directly above the leafs must be treated differently than the other levels.

```
INITIALIZE:    PROC;
                  DCL (J,K)                       FIXED;
                        /*     initialize leafs of tree      */
                  DO J= 1 TO N;
                     TREE(SIZE+J-1) =X(J);
                  END;
                        /*    initialize remaining leafs    */
                  DO J=SIZE+J-1 TO 2*SIZE-1;
                     TREE(J) =SMALL;
                  END;

                        /*     compute upper levels of the tree      */
                        /*    the level directly above the leafs is  */
                        /*                treated separately          */
                  DO J=SIZE TO 2*SIZE-1 BY 2;
                     IF TREE(J)>=TREE(J+1) THEN TREE(J/2) =J;
                                            ELSE TREE(J/2)=J+1;
                  END;
```

```
                    /*   compute the remaining levels   */
                    K=SIZE/2;
NEXT_LEVEL:         DO WHILE(K>1);
                       DO J=K TO 2*K-1 by 2;
                          IF TREE(TREE(J))>=TREE(TREE(J+1))
                                      THEN TREE(J/2) =TREE(J);
                                      ELSE TREE(J/2) =TREE(J+1);
                       END;
                       K=K/2;
                    END NEXT_LEVEL;

                    RETURN;
                  END INITIALIZE;


READJUST:         PROC(I);
                    DCL(I,J)                    FIXED;
                      /*   now that TREE(I) has a new value (SMALL)   */
                      /*          we readjust all its ancestors       */

                      /*            adjust the father node            */
                    IF MOD(I,2) =0 THEN TREE(I/2) =I+1;
                                   ELSE TREE(I/2) =I-1;

                      /*            advance to the root               */
                    I=I/2;
BACKUP:             DO WHILE(I>1);
                      /*            J is the brother of I             */
                        IF MOD(I,2) =0 THEN J=I+1;
                                       ELSE J=I-1;
                        IF TREE(TREE(I))>TREE(TREE(J))
                                       THEN TREE(I/2) =TREE(I);
                                       ELSE TREE(I/2) =TREE(J);
                        I=I/2;
                    END BACKUP;

                    RETURN;
                  END READJUST;
```

Measuring the time and space requirements of this sort is straightforward. Observe that after the initial tree has been created and the root has been output, d comparisons are required to readjust the tree and move a new element to the root position, where d is the depth of the tree. Since d is approximately $\log_2 (N+1)$ and $N-1$ adjustments must be made to the tree, the number of comparisons is approximately $(N-1) \log_2 (N+1)$, which is $O(N \log N)$. Of course comparisons are made in creating the initial tree, but the number of such comparisons is $O(N)$ and is therefore dominated by the $O(N \log N)$ term.

The space requirements, in addition to temporary values, are the 2*SIZE memory units reserved for the array TREE, where SIZE is the smallest integral power of 2 which is greater than or equal to N. Since we insisted on a complete binary tree in this program, there may be some wasted space if, for example, the value of N is 33 or 129. Of course, if a linked implementation of trees is used, additional space is required for the links.

Heapsort

While the above program appears to be relatively efficient in all cases, it does have a serious shortcoming which is easy to remove. The upper levels of the tree contain pointers while the actual data is kept only at the lowest level. Because of this there is considerable work involved in bringing an element from the leaf to the root. Much of this work is unnecessary in the later stages of the sort when most of the leafs (and indirectly, many of the upper levels) contain the value SMALL, causing unnecessary comparisons to be made.

This drawback is remedied by the ***heapsort***. In this sort, only one node is reserved for each of the elements in the original file. This serves to eliminate the large amount of space allocated in the tournament sort and the redundant comparisons of the later stages of that sort. In fact, the original array is used as a workspace for the sort so that extra space is required only for temporary variables.

Define a ***heap of size n*** as an almost complete binary tree of n nodes such that the content of each node is less than or equal to the content of its father. (Recall that the definition of an almost complete binary tree in Section 7.3 requires such a tree to be strictly binary. If this requirement is dropped, an almost complete binary tree containing an even number of nodes exists. However, there would then be a nonleaf in the tree which has no right son; i.e., there is an i for which $2i+1$ is outside the array bounds. In the remainder of this section, the initial array x which is to be sorted may contain an even number of elements. Thus, an almost complete binary tree need not be strictly binary, and it is necessary to ensure that all array references are within bounds.)

If the array implementation of an almost complete binary tree is used as was done in the implementation of the tournament sort, then the requirement for a heap reduces to the inequality

$$info(j) \leqslant info(j/2) \text{ for } 1 \leqslant j/2 < j \leqslant n$$

(where the division is understood to be integer division). It is clear from this definition of a heap that the root of the tree (or the first element of the array) is the largest element in the heap. Assuming that the algorithm *create_heap*(i) creates a heap of size i consisting of the first i elements of the array x, a sorting method could be implemented as follows:

```
do i = n to 2 by -1;
   create_heap(i)
   interchange x(1) and x(i);
end;
```

As we shall see, however, it is not necessary to create the entire heap anew on each iteration; we can readjust the heap which was created on the previous iteration so that it remains a heap even after the interchange. Thus the heap sort consists of the following algorithm.

```
create_heap(n);
do i=n to 2 by -1;
   interchange x(1) and x(i);
   create a heap of order i-1 by readjusting the position of x(1);
end;
```

We must consider two problems: how to create the original heap and how to adjust the intermediate heaps. To create the original heap, start with a heap of size 1 consisting of $x(1)$ alone and try to create a heap of size 2 consisting of $x(1)$ and $x(2)$. This can be accomplished quite easily by interchanging $x(2)$ and $x(1)$ if $x(1)$ is less than or equal to $x(2)$. In general, in order to create a heap of size i by inserting node i into an existing heap of size $i-1$, compare node i with its father. If node i is greater, interchange the two and change i to point to the father. Repeat this process until the content of the father of node i is greater than or equal to the content of node i or until i is the root of the heap. Thus an algorithm to create a heap of order k may be written as follows:

```
do node=2 to k;  /*     insert x(node) into heap     */
   i=node;
   j=i/2;        /*        j is father of i          */
   do while (i is not the root & x(j) ≤ x(i));
      interchange x(i) and x(j);
      i=j;       /*     advance up the tree          */
      j=i/2;     /*        j is father of i          */
   end;
end;
```

To solve the second problem of finding the proper place for $x(1)$ in a tree which satisfies the requirements of a heap (except for the root), initialize i to 1 and repeatedly interchange the content of node i with the content of the larger of its two sons as long as its content is not larger than those of both its sons, resetting i to point to the larger son. The algorithm to readjust the heap of order k may be written as follows:

```
i=1;
/*   compute the larger of i's two sons and place in j   */
j=2;
if k≥3 & x(3) >x(2) then j=3;
do while (j≤k & x(j) >x(i));
   interchange x(i) and x(j);
   i=j;
   j=2*i;  /*  j=larger of i's sons   */
   if j+1≤k then if x(j+1) >x(j) then j=j+1;
end;
```

The last *if* statement reads

```
if j+1<=k then if x(j+1) > x(j) then j=j+1;
```

rather than

```
if j+1<=k & x(j+1) > x(j) then j=j+1;
```

because we must ensure that the references to $x(j+1)$ and $x(j)$ are within array bounds.

Figure 8.3.5 illustrates the creation of a heap of size 8 from the original file

25 57 48 37 12 92 86 33

The dotted lines in that figure indicate that two elements are interchanged.

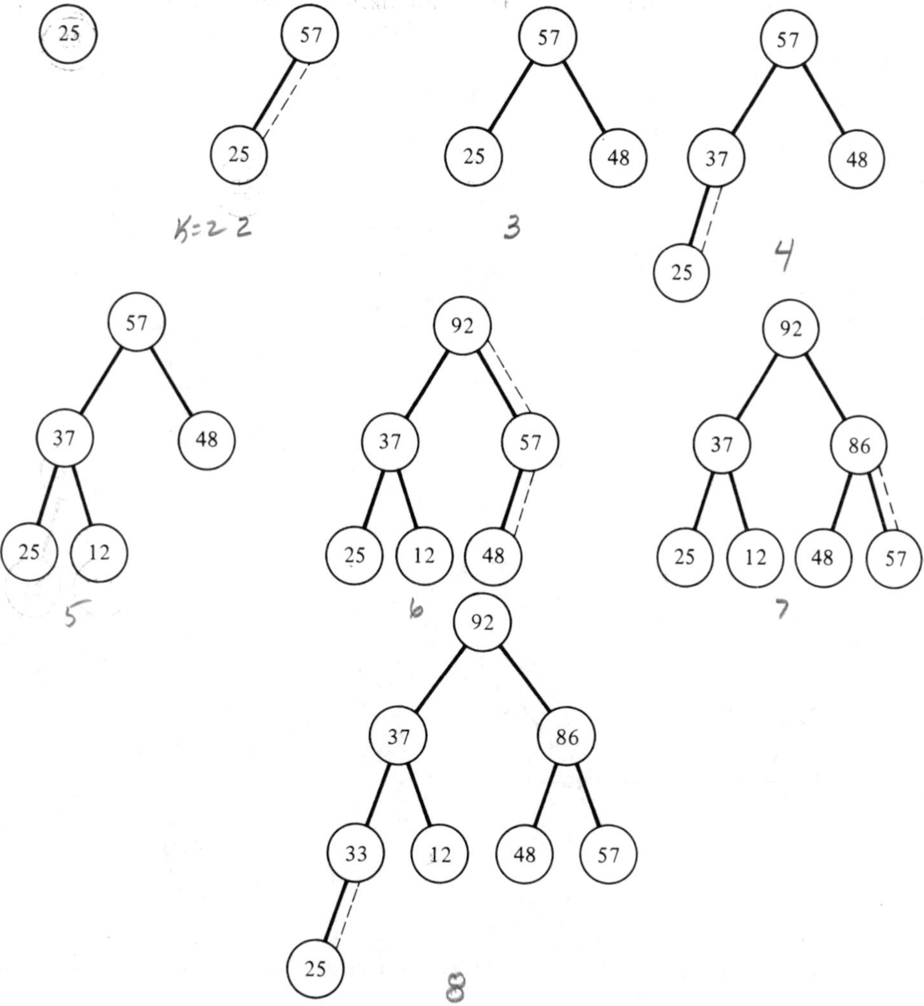

Figure 8.3.5. Creating a heap of size 8.

Figure 8.3.6 illustrates the adjustment of the heap as $X(1)$ is moved to its proper position in the original array, until all the elements of the heap are processed. Note that after an element has been "removed" from the heap it retains its position in the array; it is merely ignored in subsequent processing. Note also that the transformations in Fig. 8.3.6 illustrate a tournament in which after an element is inserted into a father node, the sons below it advance up the tree to take their proper position. This eliminates the redundant nodes and the redundant tests of the tournament sort.

In the program below we implement the heap sort. The statements of the program mirror the description above except that not all the interchanges called for are made immediately. The value whose correct position is being sought is kept in a temporary variable Y. Advances up or down the tree are made by adjusting pointers. N is assumed to be greater than or equal to 3.

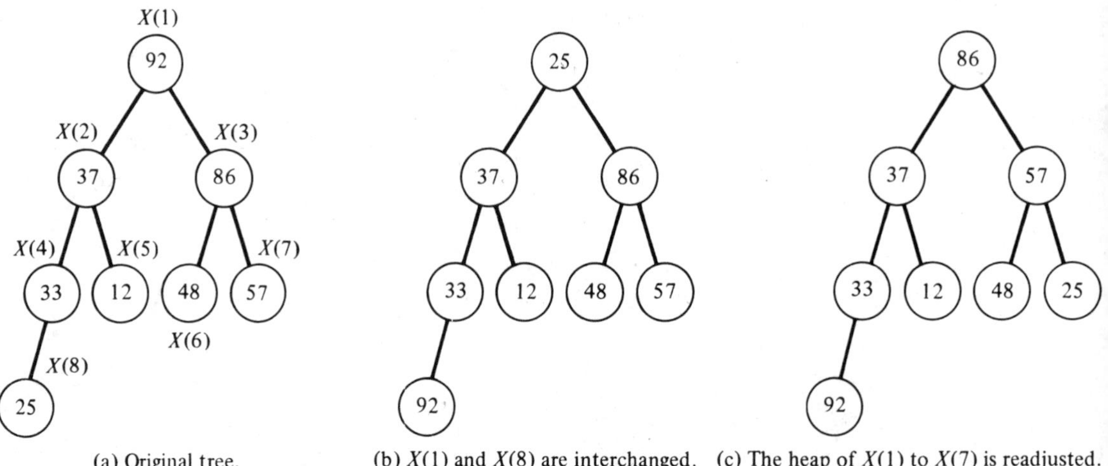

(a) Original tree.

(b) $X(1)$ and $X(8)$ are interchanged.

(c) The heap of $X(1)$ to $X(7)$ is readjusted.

(d) $X(1)$ and $X(7)$ are interchanged.

(e) The heap of $X(1)$ to $X(6)$ is readjusted.

(f) $X(1)$ and $X(6)$ are interchanged.

Figure 8.3.6. Adjusting a heap.

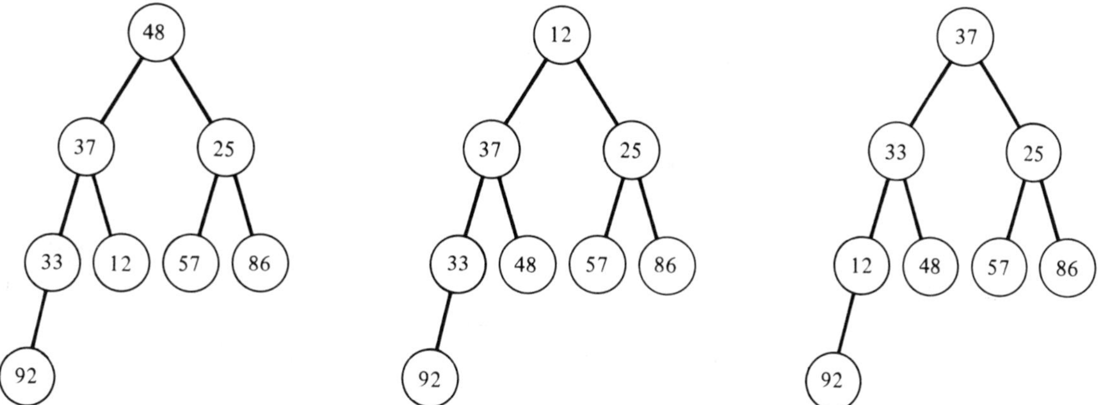

(g) The heap of $X(1)$ to $X(5)$ is readjusted. (h) $X(1)$ and $X(5)$ are interchanged. (i) The heap of $X(1)$ to $X(4)$ is readjusted.

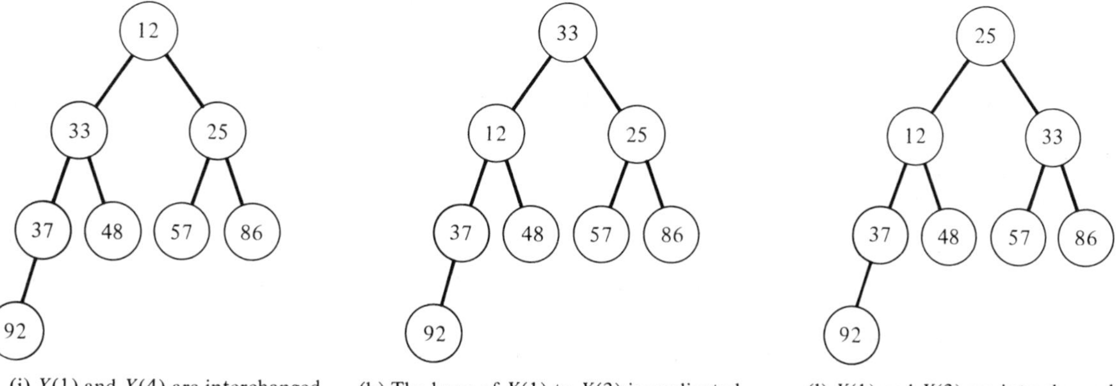

(j) $X(1)$ and $X(4)$ are interchanged. (k) The heap of $X(1)$ to $X(3)$ is readjusted. (l) $X(1)$ and $X(3)$ are interchanged.

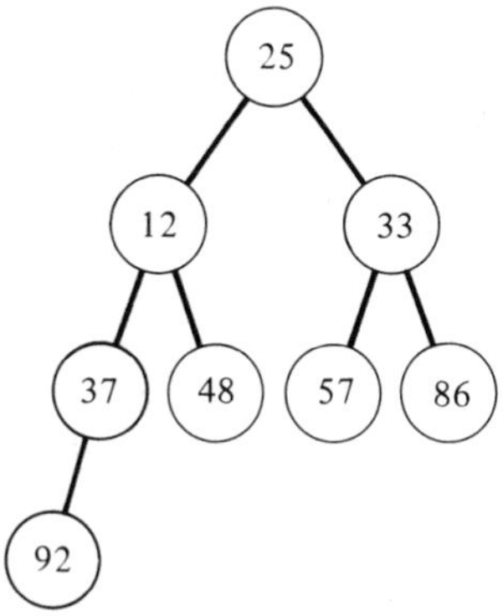

(m) The heap of $X(1)$ to $X(2)$ is readjusted. 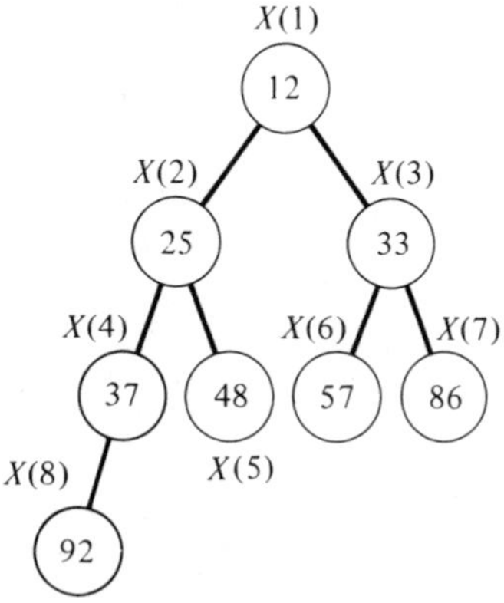 (n) $X(1)$ and $X(2)$ are interchanged. The array is sorted.

Figure 8.3.6 (*cont.*)

```
HEAP:  PROC(X,N);
         DCL (X(*) ,N,I,J,K,Y)                    FIXED;

            /*          create initial heap             */
CREATE_HEAP:
         DO K=2 TO N;
            /*   insert X(K) into existing heap of      */
            /*              size K-1                    */
           I=K;
           Y=X(K);
           J=I/2;   /*     J is the father of I         */
           DO WHILE(J>0);
              IF Y<=X(J) THEN GO TO DONE;
              X(I) =X(J);
              I=J;
              J=I/2;
           END;
DONE:      X(I) =Y;
         END CREATE_HEAP;

            /*   We remove X(1) and place it in its     */
            /*   proper position in the array. We       */
            /*         then adjust the heap.            */
ADJUST_HEAP:
        DO  K=N TO 2 BY -1;
           Y=X(K);
           X(K) =X(1);
            /*   readjust the heap of order K-1         */
            /*   move Y down the heap for proper        */
            /*              position                    */
           I=1;
           J=2;
           IF X(3)>X(2) & K-1>=3 THEN J=3;

            /*   J is the larger son of I in the        */
            /*         heap of size K-1                 */
           DO WHILE(J<=K-1  &  X(J)>Y);
              X(I) =X(J);
              I=J;
              J=2*I;
              IF J+1<=K-1 THEN IF X(J+1)>X(J) THEN J=J+1;
           END;

           X(I) =Y;
         END ADJUST_HEAP;

         RETURN;
      END HEAP;
```

To analyze the heapsort, note that a complete binary tree with n nodes (where n is one less than a power of 2) has $\log_2 (n+1)$ levels. Thus if each element in the array were a leaf, requiring it to be filtered through the entire tree both while creating and adjusting the heap, the sort would still be $O(n \log n)$. However, clearly not every element must pass through the entire tree. Thus while the sort is $O(n \log n)$, the multipliers are not as large as those for the tournament sort. The worst case for the heapsort is $O(n \log n)$; but it is not very efficient for small n (why?).

The space requirement for the heapsort is only one additional variable to hold the temporary for switching, provided the array implementation of an almost complete binary tree is used.

8.4. Insertion Sorts

Simple Insertion

An ***insertion sort*** is one which sorts a set of records by inserting records into an existing sorted file. An example of a simple insertion sort is the following program;

```
INSERT:     PROC(X,N);
              DCL  (X(*) ,N,I,K,Y)              FIXED;
               /*     Initially X(1) may be thought of as a       */
               /*     sorted file of one element. After each      */
               /*     repetition of the following loop, the       */
               /*  elements X(1) through X(K) are in order.       */
LOOP:          DO K=2 TO N;
               /*        insert X(K) into the sorted file         */
                  Y=X(K);

               /*     move down one position all numbers          */
               /*                greater than Y                   */
MOVEDOWN:         DO I=K-1 TO 1 BY -1 WHILE (Y<X(I));
                     X(I+1) =X(I);
                  END MOVEDOWN;

                  /*  insert Y at proper position   */
                  X(I+1) =Y ;
               END LOOP;

               RETURN;
            END INSERT;
```

If the initial file is sorted, only one comparison is made on each pass so that the sort is $O(N)$. If the file is initially sorted in the reverse order, the sort is $O(N^2)$ since the total number of comparisons is

$$(N-1) + (N-2) + \ldots + 3 + 2 + 1 = (N-1) * N/2$$

which is $O(N^2)$. However, the simple insertion sort is still usually better than the bubble sort. The closer the file is to sorted order, the more efficient the simple insertion sort becomes. The average number of comparisons in the simple insertion sort (by considering all possible permutations of the input array) is also $O(N^2)$. The space requirements for the sort consist of only one temporary variable Y.

The speed of the sort can be improved somewhat by using a binary search (see Sections 4.1, 4.2, and 9.1) to find the proper position for X(K) in the sorted file X(1), . . .,X(K–1). This reduces the number of comparisons from $O(N^2)$ to $O(N \log N)$. However, even if the correct position I for X(K) is found in $O(N \log N)$ steps, each of the elements X(I+1) , . . . ,X(K–1) must be moved one position. This latter operation performed N times requires $O(N^2)$ replacements. Unfortunately, therefore, the binary search technique does not significantly improve the overall time requirements of the sort.

Another improvement to the simple insertion sort can be made by using ***list insertion***. In this method there is an array LINK of pointers, one for each of the original array elements. Initially LINK(I) =I+1 for 1≤I<N, and LINK(N) =0. Thus the array may be thought of as a linear list pointed to by an external pointer FIRST initialized to one. To insert the Kth element, the linked list is traversed until the proper position for X(K) is found, or until the end of the list is reached. At that point X(K) can be inserted into the list by merely adjusting the list pointers without shifting any elements in the array. This reduces the time required for insertion but not the time required for searching for the proper position. The space requirements are also increased because of the extra LINK array. The number of comparisons is still $O(N^2)$, although the number of replacements in the LINK array is $O(N)$. You are asked to code both the binary insertion sort and the list insertion sort as exercises.

Shell Sort

More significant improvement can be achieved by using the ***shell sort*** (or ***diminishing increment sort***) named after its discoverer. This method sorts separate subfiles of the original file. These subfiles contain every kth element of the original file. The value of k is called an ***increment***. For example, if k is 5, the subfile consisting of $x(1)$, $x(6)$, $x(11)$, . . . is first sorted. Five subfiles, each containing one-fifth of the elements of the original file are sorted in this manner. These are (reading across):

subfile 1	⟶	$x(1)$	$x(6)$	$x(11)$	. . .
subfile 2	⟶	$x(2)$	$x(7)$	$x(12)$	. . .
subfile 3	⟶	$x(3)$	$x(8)$	$x(13)$	. . .
subfile 4	⟶	$x(4)$	$x(9)$	$x(14)$	. . .
subfile 5	⟶	$x(5)$	$x(10)$	$x(15)$	. . .

In general, the ith element of the jth subfile is $x(5(i-1)+j)$. If a different increment k is chosen, the k subfiles are divided so that the ith element of the jth subfile is $x(k(i-1)+j)$.

After the first k subfiles are sorted (usually by simple insertion), a new smaller value of k is chosen and the file is again partitioned into a new set of subfiles. Each of these larger subfiles is sorted, and the process is repeated yet again with an even smaller value of k. Eventually, the value of k is set to 1, so that the subfile consisting of the entire file is sorted. A decreasing sequence of increments is fixed at the start of the entire process. The last value in this sequence must be 1.

For example, if the original file is

25 57 48 37 12 92 86 33

and the sequence (5,3,1) is chosen, then the following subfiles are sorted on each iteration.

First iteration (increment = 5)
(x(1),x(6))
(x(2),x(7))
(x(3),x(8))
(x(4))
(x(5))

Second iteration (increment = 3)
(x(1),x(4),x(7))
(x(2),x(5),x(8))
(x(3),x(6))

Third iteration (increment = 1)
(x(1),x(2),x(3),x(4),x(5),x(6),x(7),x(8))

Figure 8.4.1 illustrates the shell sort on this sample file. The lines underneath each array join individual elements of the separate subfiles. Each of the subfiles is sorted using the simple insertion sort.

We present below a routine to implement the shell sort. In addition to the standard parameters X and N, it requires an array INCRMNTS containing the diminishing increments of the sort.

```
SHELL:          PROC(X,N,INCRMNTS);
                  DCL (X(*) ,N,INCRMNTS(*), J,K,SPAN,INCR,Y,NUMINC)
                                                              FIXED;
                  NUMINC=HBOUND(INCRMNTS,1);
NEXT_INCRMNT: DO INCR=1 TO NUMINC;
                     SPAN=INCRMNTS(INCR);  /*  SPAN is the size of    */
                                           /*     the increment       */

SUBFILESORT:         DO J=SPAN+1 TO N BY 1;
                        /*        insert element X(J) into its proper      */
                        /*            position within its subfile          */
                        Y=X(J);
```

```
MOVEDOWN:           DO K=J–SPAN TO 1 BY –SPAN WHILE(Y<X(K));
                         X(K+SPAN) =X(K);
                    END MOVEDOWN;
                    X(K+SPAN) =Y;
                END SUBFILESORT;

            END NEXT_INCRMNT;
            RETURN;
        END SHELL;
```

Be sure that you can trace the actions of this program on the sample file of Fig. 8.4.1. Notice that on the last iteration where SPAN equals 1 the sort reduces to a simple insertion.

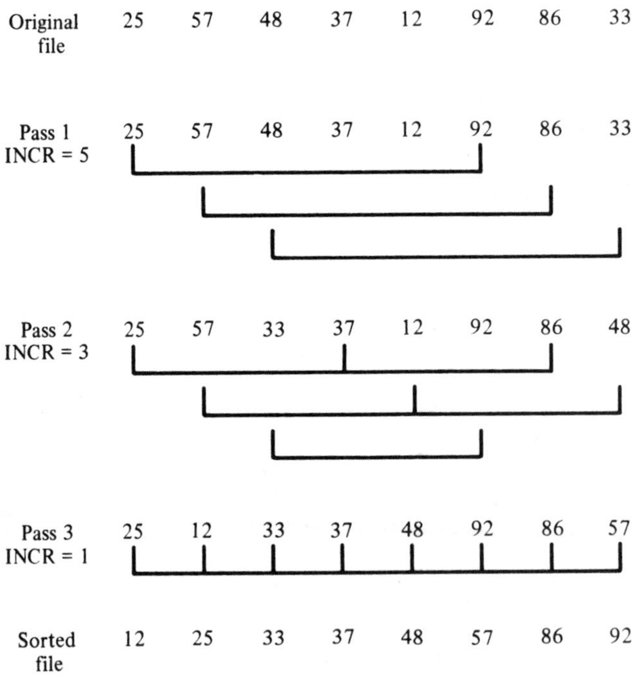

Figure 8.4.1.

The idea behind the shell sort is a simple one. We have already noted that the simple insertion sort is highly efficient on a file which is in almost sorted order. It is also important to realize that when the file size n is small, an $O(n^2)$ sort is often more efficient than an $O(n \log n)$ sort. The reason for this is that $O(n^2)$ sorts are generally quite simple to program and involve very few actions other than comparisons and replacements on each pass. Because of this low overhead, the constant of proportionality is rather small. An $O(n \log n)$ sort is generally quite complex and employs a large number of extra operations on each pass in order to reduce the work of subsequent passes. Thus its constant of proportionality is larger. When n is large, n^2 overwhelms $n \log n$ so that the constants of proportionality do not play a major role in determining the faster sort. However, when n is small, n^2 is not much larger than $n \log n$, so that a large difference in those constants often causes an $O(n^2)$ sort to be faster.

Since the first increment used by the shell sort is large, the individual subfiles are quite small, so that the simple insertion sorts on those subfiles are fairly fast. Each sort of a subfile causes the entire file to be more nearly sorted. Thus, although successive passes of the shell sort use smaller increments and therefore deal with larger subfiles, those subfiles are almost sorted due to the actions of previous passes. Thus, the insertion sorts on those subfiles are also quite efficient. In this connection, it is significant to note that if a file is partially sorted using an increment k and is subsequently partially sorted using an increment j, the file remains partially sorted on the increment k. That is, subsequent partial sorts do not disturb earlier ones.

The efficiency analysis of the shell sort is mathematically involved and beyond the scope of this book. The actual time requirements for a specific sort depend upon the number of elements in the array INCRMNTS and on their actual values. It has been shown that the order of the shell sort can be approximated by $O(n(\log n)^2)$ if an appropriate sequence of increments is used. One requirement that is intuitively clear is that the elements of INCRMNTS should be relatively prime (i.e., have no common divisors other than 1). You are asked to show why this is so as an exercise. This guarantees that successive iterations intermingle subfiles so that the entire file is indeed almost sorted when SPAN equals 1 on the last iteration.

Address Calculation Sort

As a final example of sorting by insertion, consider the following technique called sorting by ***address calculation*** (sometimes called sorting by ***hashing***). In this method a function f is applied to each key. The result of this function determines into which of several subfiles the record is to be placed. The function should have the property that if $x < y$, then $f(x) < f(y)$. Thus all of the records in one subfile will have keys which are less than the keys of the records in another subfile. An item is placed into a subfile in correct sequence by using any sorting method; simple insertion is usually used. After all of the items of the original file have been placed into subfiles, the subfiles may be concatenated to produce the sorted result.

For example, consider again the sample file

25 57 48 37 12 92 86 33

Let us create 10 subfiles, one for each of the 10 possible first digits. Initially, each of these subfiles is empty. An array of pointers F(0:9) is declared where F(I) points to the first element in the file whose first digit is I. After scanning the first element (25), it is placed into the file headed by F(2). Each of the subfiles is maintained as a sorted linked list of the original array elements. After processing each of the elements in the original file, the subfiles appear as in Fig. 8.4.2.

We present a routine to implement the address calculation sort. The routine assumes an array of two-digit numbers and uses the first digit of each number to assign that number to a subfile.

```
ADDR:       PROC(X,N);
              DCL (X(*) ,N,F(0:9) ,FIRST,I,Q,P,AVAIL,Y)        FIXED,
                    1 NODE(N),
                      (2 INFO,
                       2 NEXT)                                  FIXED;
                    /*   initialize available list   */
              AVAIL=1;
INITAV:       DO I=1 TO N-1;
                 NEXT(I) =I+1;
              END INITAV;
              NEXT(N) =0;
              F=0;              /*   initialize pointers   */


NEXT_NUMBER:
              DO I=1 TO N;
                 /*   we successively insert each element into its   */
                 /*      respective subfile using list insertion     */
                 Y=X(I);
                 FIRST=Y/10; /*   find the first digit of a two-     */
                             /*            digit number              */


                    /*   search the linked list   */
                 CALL PLACE(F(FIRST),Y);
                             /*   PLACE inserts Y into its   */
                             /*   proper position in the     */
                             /*   linked list pointed to     */
                             /*        by F(FIRST)           */
              END NEXT_NUMBER;


                 /*   copy numbers back into the array X   */
              I=0;

COPY_BACK:    DO J=0 to 9;
                 P=F(J);
                 DO WHILE(P¬=0);
                    I=I+1;
                    X(I) =INFO(P);
                    P=NEXT(P);
                 END;
              END COPY_BACK;


              RETURN;
            END ADDR;
```

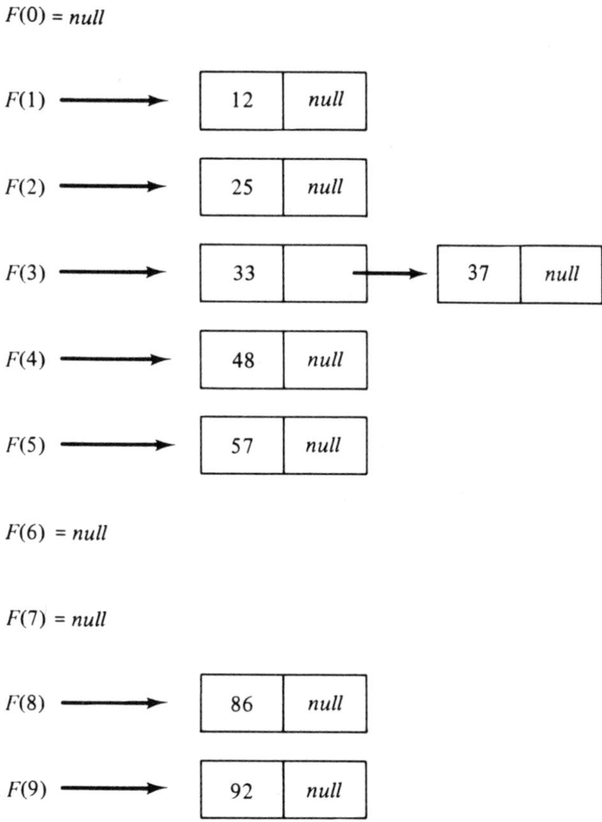

Figure 8.4.2. Address calculation sort.

The space requirements of the address calculation sort are approximately $2N$ (used by the array NODE) plus some header nodes and temporary variables. Note that if the original data is given in the form of a linked list rather than as a sequential array, it is not necessary to maintain both the array X and the linked structure NODE.

To evaluate the time requirements for the sort, note the following: If the n original elements are approximately uniformly distributed over the m subfiles and the value of n/m is approximately 1, the time of the sort is nearly $O(n)$ since the function assigns each element to its proper file and little extra work is required to place an element within its subfile. On the other hand, if n/m is much larger than 1, or if the original file is not uniformly distributed over the m subfiles, then significant work is required to insert an element into its proper subfile and the time is therefore closer to $O(n^2)$.

8.5. Merge and Radix Sorts

Merge Sorts

Merging is the process of combining two or more sorted files into a third sorted file. An example of a program that accepts two sorted arrays A and B and merges them into a third array C is the following:

```
MERGEARR:  PROC(A,B,C);
             /*   this program merges arrays A and B into array C    */
             DCL  (A(*) ,B(*) ,C(*))                     FIXED,
                  (APOINT,BPOINT,CPOINT)                 FIXED,
                  (ALIMIT,BLIMIT,CLIMIT)                 FIXED;
             ALIMIT=HBOUND(A,1);
             BLIMIT=HBOUND(B,1);
             CLIMIT=HBOUND(C,1);
             IF ALIMIT+BLIMIT¬=CLIMIT THEN DO;
                  PUT SKIP LIST('ARRAY BOUNDS INCOMPATIBLE');
                  STOP;
                                                  END;
             /*   APOINT and BPOINT are indicators of how far       */
             /*        we are in arrays A and B respectively        */
             APOINT,BPOINT=1;
MERGE:       DO CPOINT=1 BY 1 WHILE(APOINT<=ALIMIT & BPOINT<=
                                                            BLIMIT);
                IF A(APOINT)<B(BPOINT)  THEN DO;
                                       C(CPOINT)=A(APOINT);
                                       APOINT=APOINT+1;
                                             END;
                                         ELSE DO;
                                       C(CPOINT)=B(BPOINT);
                                       BPOINT=BPOINT+1;
                                             END;
             END MERGE;

               /*            add any remaining elements              */
FINISHA:     DO WHILE(APOINT<=ALIMIT);
                       /*   copy remaining elements from A    */
                C(CPOINT) =A(APOINT);
                CPOINT=CPOINT+1;
                APOINT=APOINT+1;
             END FINISHA;

FINISHB:     DO WHILE(BPOINT<=BLIMIT);
                       /*   copy remaining elements from B    */
                C(CPOINT) =B(BPOINT);
                CPOINT=CPOINT+1;
                BPOINT=BPOINT+1;
             END FINISHB;

             RETURN;
           END MERGEARR;
```

We can use this technique to sort a file in the following way. Divide the file into n subfiles of size 1 and merge adjacent (disjoint) pairs of files. We then have approximately $n/2$ files of size 2. Repeat this process until there is only one file remaining of size n. Figure 8.5.1 illustrates how this process operates on a sample file. Each individual file is contained in brackets.

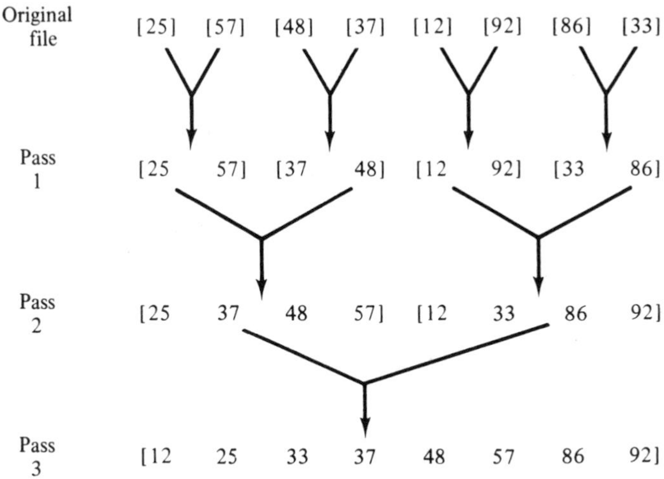

Figure 8.5.1. Successive passes of the merge sort.

We present a program to implement the above description of a ***straight merge sort***. An auxiliary array AUX of size N is required to hold the results of merging two subarrays of X. The variable SIZE is used to control the size of the subarrays being merged. Since at any time the two files being merged are both subarrays of X, lower and upper bounds are required to indicate the subfiles of X being merged. L1 and U1 represent the lower and upper bounds of the first file, and L2 and U2 represent the lower and upper bounds of the second file respectively. I and J are used to reference elements of the source files being merged, and K indexes the destination file. The program follows:

```
MSORT:      PROC(X,N);
              DCL  (X(*) ,N,AUX(N))                         FIXED,
                   (SIZE,L1,L2,U1,U2,I,J,K)                 FIXED;
             SIZE=1;      /*  merge files of size 1    */
NEXT_PASS:  DO WHILE(SIZE<N);
                 L1=1;   /*        initialize lower bound of first file        */
                 K=1;    /*          K is index for auxiliary array           */

NEXT_FILES:      DO WHILE(L1+SIZE<=N);  /*   check if there are two       */
                                        /*        files to merge          */
                     /*   compute remaining indices    */
                     L2=L1+SIZE;
                     U1=L2-1;
                     U2=MIN(L2+SIZE-1,N);
```

```
                        /*   proceed through the two subfiles    */
                        I=L1;
                        J=L2;
MERGE:                  DO K=K BY 1 WHILE(I<=U1 & J<=U2);

                           /*   enter smaller into the array AUX    */
                           IF X(I)<=X(J) THEN DO;
                                                 AUX(K) =X(I);
                                                 I=I+1;
                                              END;
                                         ELSE DO;
                                                 AUX(K) =X(J);
                                                 J=J+1;
                                              END;
                        END MERGE;
                        /*   At this point one of the subfiles has been    */
                        /*   exhausted. Insert any remaining portions      */
                        /*              of the other file.                 */
ENDFILE1:               DO K=K BY 1 WHILE(I<=U1);
                             AUX(K) =X(I);
                             I=I+1;
                        END ENDFILE1;

ENDFILE2:               DO K=K BY 1 WHILE(J<=U2);
                             AUX(K) =X(J);
                             J=J+1;
                        END ENDFILE2;

                        /*      advance L1 to start of next pair of files       */
                        L1=U2+1;
                      END NEXT_FILES;

                        /*   copy any remaining single file    */
SINGLEFILE:          DO I=L1 BY 1 WHILE(K<=N);
                        AUX(K) =X(I);
                        K=K+1;
                     END SINGLEFILE;

                        /*   adjust X and SIZE    */
                     X=AUX;
                     SIZE=SIZE*2;
                  END NEXT_PASS;

                  RETURN;
               END MSORT;
```

There is one deficiency in the above program which is easily remedied if the program is to be practical for sorting large arrays. Instead of merging each set of files into the auxiliary array AUX and then recopying the array AUX into X, alternate merges can be performed from X to AUX and from AUX to X. We leave this modification as an exercise for the reader.

The time required for the sort is $O(N \log N)$ since there are obviously no more than $\log N$ passes. The sort, however, does require an auxiliary array AUX into which the merged files can be stored.

There are two modifications of the above program which can result in more efficient sorting. The first of these is the ***natural merge***. In the straight merge, the files all had the same size (except perhaps for the last file). We can, however, exploit any order that may already exist among the elements and let the files be defined as the longest subarrays of increasing elements. You are asked to code such a program as an exercise.

The second modification uses linked allocation instead of sequential allocation. By adding a single pointer field to each record, the need for the array AUX can be eliminated. This can be done by explicitly linking together each input and output subfile. The modification can be applied to both the straight merge and the natural merge. You are asked to implement these as exercises.

Radix Sort

The next sorting method which we consider is called the ***radix sort***. This sort is based on the values of the actual digits in the positional representations of the numbers being sorted. For example, the number 235 in decimal notation is written with a 2 in the hundreds position, a 3 in the tens position, and a 5 in the units position. The larger of two such three-digit integers can be determined as follows: Start at the most significant digit and advance to the least significant digit as long as the corresponding digits in the two numbers match. The number with the larger digit in the first position in which the digits of the two numbers do not match is the larger of the two numbers. Of course, if all the digits of both numbers match, then the numbers are equal.

We can write a sorting routine based on the above method. Using the decimal base, for example, we can sort the numbers into 10 groups based on their most significant digit. (For simplicity, we assume that all the numbers have the same number of digits by padding with leading 0s, if necessary.) Thus, every element in the "0" group is less than every element in the "1" group, which is less than every element in the "2" group, etc. We can then sort within the individual groups based on the next significant digit. We repeat this process until each subgroup has been subdivided so that the least significant digits are sorted. At this point the original file is sorted. This method is sometimes called the ***radix-exchange sort***; its coding is left as an exercise for the reader.

Let us now consider an alternative to the method described above. It is apparent from the above discussion that considerable bookkeeping is involved in constantly subdividing files and distributing their contents into subfiles based on particular digits. It would certainly be easier if we could process the entire file as a whole rather than deal with many individual files.

Suppose we perform the following actions on the file for each digit, beginning with the least significant digit and ending with the most significant digit. Take each number in the order in which it appears in the file and place it into one of ten queues, depending on the value of the digit currently being processed. Then, starting with the queue of numbers with a 0 digit and ending with the queue of numbers with a 9 digit, return the numbers to the original file in the order in which they were placed onto the queue. When these actions have been performed for each digit, starting with the least significant and ending with the most significant, the file is sorted. This sorting method is called the ***radix sort***.

Notice that this scheme sorts on the least significant digit first. This allows processing of the entire file without subdividing the files and keeping track of where each subfile begins and ends. Figure 8.5.2 illustrates this sort on the sample file

25 57 48 37 12 92 86 33

Be sure that you can follow the actions depicted in the two passes of Fig. 8.5.2.

Original file

25 57 48 37 12 92 86 33

Queues based on least significant digit.

	Front	Rear
Q[0]		
Q[1]		
Q[2]	12	92
Q[3]	33	
Q[4]		
Q[5]	25	
Q[6]	86	
Q[7]	57	37
Q[8]	48	
Q[9]		

After first pass:

12 92 33 25 86 57 37 48

Queues based on most significant digit.

	Front	Rear
Q[0]		
Q[1]	12	
Q[2]	25	
Q[3]	33	37
Q[4]	48	
Q[5]	57	
Q[6]		
Q[7]		
Q[8]	86	
Q[9]	92	

Sorted file: 12 25 33 37 48 57 86 92

Figure 8.5.2. Illustration of the radix sort.

We can therefore outline an algorithm to sort in the above fashion as follows:

```
do k=least significant digit to most significant digit;
   do i=1 to n;
      y=x(i);
      j= kth digit of y;
      place y at rear of queue(j);
   end;
   do qu=0 to 9;
      place elements of queue(qu) in next sequential positions of x;
   end;
end;
```

We now present a program which implements the above sort on four-digit numbers. In order to save a considerable amount of work in processing the queues (especially in the step where we return the queue elements to the original file) we write the program using linked allocation. If the initial input to the subroutine is an array, then that input is first converted into a linear linked list; if the original input is already in linked format, then this step is not necessary and, in fact, space is saved. This is the same situation as in the program ADDR (address calculation sort) of Section 8.4. Again, as in previous programs, we do not make any internal calls to subroutines but rather perform their actions in place.

```
RADIX:    PROC(X,N);
            DCL (X(*),N,FRONT(0:9),REAR(0:9))              FIXED,
                 1 NODE(N),
                   (2 INFO,
                    2 NEXT)                                 FIXED,
                   (FIRST,P,Q,Y,I,J,K)                      FIXED;

            /*  initialize linked list  */
INITLIST:   DO I=1 TO N-1;
                 INFO(I) =X(I);
                 NEXT(I) =I+1;
            END INITLIST;
            INFO(N) =X(N);
            NEXT(N) =0;
            FIRST=1;  /*  FIRST is head of linked list  */


NXT_DIGIT: DO K=1 TO 4;
                 /*  assume we have four-digit numbers  */
                 REAR=0;
                 FRONT=0;  /*  initialize queues  */
```

```
                  /*     process each element on the list       */
NEXT_RECORD:   DO WHILE(FIRST¬=0);
                    P=FIRST;
                    FIRST=NEXT(FIRST);
                    Y=INFO(P);
                    J=MOD(Y/10**(K-1),10);  /*   extract Kth digit    */
               /*  insert Y into QUEUE(J)   */
                    Q=REAR(J);
                    IF Q=0  THEN FRONT(J) =P;
                                 ELSE NEXT(Q) =P;
                    REAR(J) =P;
               END NEXT_RECORD;
               /*   at this point each record is in its    */
               /*     proper queue based on digit K        */
               /*    we now form a single list from        */
               /*          all the queue elements          */
               /*            find first element            */
               DO J=0 TO 9 WHILE(FRONT(J) =0);
               END;
               FIRST=FRONT(J);

               /*   link up remaining queues    */
CONCATENATE:   DO WHILE (J<=9);  /*    check if finished     */
                    /*    find next element     */
                    DO I=J+1 TO 9 WHILE (FRONT(I) =0);
                    END;
                    IF I<=9 THEN LINK_UP:  DO;
                                              P=I;
                                              NEXT(REAR(J))=FRONT(I);
                                                        END LINK_UP;
                    J=I;
               END CONCATENATE;
               NEXT(REAR(P)) =0;

            END NXT_DIGIT;

               /*   copy back to original array    */
COPY_BACK:  DO I=1 TO N;
                 X(I) =INFO(FIRST);
                 FIRST=NEXT(FIRST);
            END COPY_BACK;

            RETURN;
         END RADIX;
```

The time requirements for the radix sorting method clearly depend on the number of digits (M) and the number of elements in the file (N). Since the outer loop NXT_DIGIT is traversed M times (once for each digit) and the inner loop N times (once for each element in the file), the sort is approximately $O(M*N)$. Thus the sort is reasonably efficient if the number of digits in the keys is not too large. The sort does, however, require space to store pointers to the fronts and rears of the queues in addition to an extra field in each record to be used as a pointer in the linked lists. If the number of digits is large, it is sometimes more efficient to sort the file by first applying the radix sort to the most significant digits and then using straight insertion on the rearranged file. In cases where most of the records in the file have differing most significant digits, this process eliminates wasteful passes on the least significant digits.

Bibliography and References

The most extensive material on sorting may be found in (Knuth, 1973B). Other references are (Flores, 1969) and (Lorin, 1975). Debugged PL/I programs for all the sorts in this chapter and more may be found in (Rich, 1972). A bibliography on sorting appears in (Rivest and Knuth, 1972). In addition to these comprehensive references, material on sorting may be found in most data structures and algorithms texts.

References for quicksort are (Hoare, 1962), (Knuth, 1974), (Sedgewick, 1975), and (Van Emden, 1970). References for heapsort are (Floyd, 1964) and (Williams, 1964). References for shell sort are (Boothroyd, 1963) and (Shell, 1959). Algorithms to find the Kth largest element of a file are discussed in (Aho, Hopcroft, and Ullman, 1974), (Knuth, 1973B) and (Reingold, Nievergelt, and Deo, 1977).

A discussion of the O notation and of the analysis of algorithm efficiency is contained in (Horowitz and Sahni, 1977).

chapter 9

searching

In this chapter, we consider various methods of searching through large amounts of data to find one particular piece of information. As we shall see, certain methods of organizing data make the search process more efficient. Since searching is such a common task in computing, a knowledge of these methods goes a long way towards making a good programmer.

9.1. Basic Search Techniques

Before we consider specific search techniques, let us define some terms. A ***table*** or a ***file*** is a group of elements, each of which is called a ***record***. Associated with each record is a ***key*** which is used to differentiate among different records. The association between a record and its key may be simple or complex. In the simplest form, the key is contained within the record at a specific offset from the start of the record. Such a key is called an ***internal key*** or an ***embedded key***. In other cases, there is a separate table of keys which includes pointers to the records. Such keys are called ***external***. For every file there is at least one set of keys (possibly more) that is unique (i.e., no two records have the same key value). Such a key is called a ***primary key***. For example, if the file is sorted as an array, then the index within the array of an element is a unique external key for that element. However, since any field of a record can serve as the key in a particular application, keys need not always be unique. For example, in a file of names and addresses, if the state is used as the key for a particular search, then it will probably not be unique, since there may be two records with the same state in the file. Such a key is called a ***secondary key***. Some of the algorithms we present assume unique keys; others allow for multiple keys. When adopting an algorithm for a particular application, the programmer should know whether the keys are unique and make sure that the algorithm selected is appropriate.

A ***search algorithm*** is an algorithm which accepts an argument a and tries to find a record whose key is a. The algorithm may return the entire record, or more commonly, it may return a pointer to that record. A successful search is often called a ***retrieval***. It is possible that the search for a particular argument in a table is unsuccessful; that is, there is no record in the table with that argument as its key. In such a case, the algorithm may return a special "null record" or a null pointer. Very often, if a search is unsuccessful, it may be desirable to add a new record with the argument as its key. An algorithm which does this is called a ***search and insertion algorithm***. In some cases it is desirable to insert a record with primary key *key* into a file without first searching for another record with the same key. Such a situation could arise if it has already been determined that no such record already exists in the file.

In subsequent discussions we investigate and comment upon the relative efficiency of various algorithms. In such cases, the reader should note whether the comments refer to a search, to an insertion, or to a search and insertion.

Note that we have said nothing about the manner in which the table or file is organized. It may be an array of records, a linked list, a tree, or even a graph. Because different search techniques may be suitable for different table organizations, a table is often designed with a specific search technique in mind. The table may be contained completely in memory, completely in auxiliary storage, or it may be divided between the two. Clearly different search techniques are necessary under these different assumptions. Searches in which the entire table is constantly in main memory are called ***internal searches***, while those in which most of the table is kept in auxiliary storage are called ***external searches***. As with sorting, we discuss only internal searching, and leave it to the reader to investigate the extremely important topic of external searching.

Sequential Searching

The simplest form of a search is the ***sequential search***. This search is applicable to a table which is organized either as an array or as a linked list. Let us assume that k is an array of n keys and r an array of records such that $k(i)$ is the key of $r(i)$. Let us also assume that *key* is a search argument. We wish to return the smallest integer i such that $k(i)$=*key* if such an i exists and 0 otherwise. The algorithm for doing this is as follows:

```
1       do i = 1 to n;
2          if key = k(i) then return (i);
3       end;
4       return(0);
```

The algorithm examines each key in turn; upon finding one that matches the search argument, its index (which acts a pointer to its record) is returned. If no match is found, 0 is returned.

This algorithm can easily be modified to add a record *rec* with key *key* to the table, if *key* is not already in the table. We begin the modification with line 4.

```
4       n=n+1;        /*    increase the size of the table      */
5       k(n)=key;     /*   insert the proper information in     */
6       r(n)=rec;     /*   the newly created array element      */
7       return(n);
```

Note that if insertions are made using the above revised algorithm only, then no two records can have the same key. When this algorithm is implemented in PL/I, we must ensure that increasing *n* by 1 does not make its value go beyond the upper bound of the array. To use a sequential insertion search on an array, sufficient storage must have been previously allocated for the array.

Storing a table as a linked list has the advantage that the size of the table can be increased dynamically as needed. Let us assume that the table is organized as a linear linked list pointed to by *table* and linked by a pointer field *next*. Then assuming, *k, r, key,* and *rec* as before, we may write the sequential insertion search for a linked list as follows:

```
q=null;
p=table;
do while (p¬=null);
   if k(p)=key then return(p);
   q=p;
   p=next(p);
end;
          /*   record must be inserted    */
s=getnode;
k(s)=key;
r(s)=rec;
next(s)=null;
if q=null then table=s;
          else next(q)=s;
return(s);
```

Another advantage of storing a table as a linked list rather than an array is that it is easier to delete a record from a linked list. Deleting an element from an array requires moving half the elements in the array on the average. (Why?)

One method of improving the efficiency of deleting a record from an array is to add a field *flag*(*i*) to each record. Initially, when there is no record in position *i*, *flag*(*i*) is off. When a record is inserted at position *i*, the flag is turned on. When the record at position *i* is deleted, its flag is turned off. New records are inserted at the end of the array. If there are a substantial number of insertions, all the space in the array is soon exhausted. If an attempt is made to insert a new record when there is no more room in the array, the array is condensed by overwriting all records whose flags are off. This yields an array which contains all valid records at the beginning, and room for new records at the end. The new record may then be inserted.

There is another method which avoids the necessity of periodically condensing the array but also entails lowered efficiency in individual insertions. In this method an insertion involves traversing the array sequentially, looking for a record which has been flagged as deleted. The new record is inserted over the first record whose flag is off. Yet another method is to link together all flagged records. This does not require any extra space since the information content of a deleted record is irrelevant and can therefore be overwritten by a pointer to the next deleted record. This available list of records can be maintained as a stack to make insertion more efficient. However, if an insertion is only performed after a search, then no efficiency gains result from these methods since the entire table must be searched for an existing record with the same key. We leave the development of these ideas into algorithms and the algorithms into programs as exercises for the reader.

Efficiency of Sequential Searching

How efficient is a sequential search? Let us examine the number of comparisons which must be made by a sequential search in searching for a given key. If we assume no insertions or deletions, so that we are searching through a table of constant size n, then the number of comparisons depends on where the record with the argument *key* appears in the table. If the record is the first one in the table, only one comparison is performed; if the record is the last one in the table, n comparisons are necessary. If it is equally likely for the argument to appear at any given table position, then a successful search will take (on the average) $n/2$ comparisons, and an unsuccessful search will take n comparisons. In any case, the number of comparisons is $O(n)$.

However, it is usually the case that some arguments are presented to the search algorithm more often than others. For example, in the files of a college registrar, the records of a senior who is applying for transcripts for graduate school, or of a freshman whose high school average is being updated are more likely to be called for than those of the average sophomore and junior. Similarly, the records of scofflaws and tax cheats are more likely to be retrieved from the files of a motor vehicles bureau or the Internal Revenue Service than those of a law-abiding citizen. (As we shall see later in this chapter, these examples are unrealistic because it is unlikely that a sequential search would be used for such large files; but for the moment, let us assume that a sequential search is being used.) Then, if frequently accessed records are placed at the beginning of the file, the average number of comparisons is sharply reduced since the most commonly accessed records take the least amount of time to retrieve.

Let us assume that $p(i)$ is the probability that record i is retrieved. ($p(i)$ is a number between 0 and 1 such that if m retrievals are made from the file, $m*p(i)$ of them will be from $r(i)$.) Let us also assume that $p(1) + p(2) + \ldots + p(n) = 1$ so that there is no possibility that an argument key is missing from the table. Then the average number of comparisons which are made in searching for a record is

$$p(1) + 2p(2) + 3p(3) + \ldots + np(n)$$

Clearly, this number is minimized if

$$p(1) \geqslant p(2) \geqslant p(3) \geqslant \ldots \geqslant p(n)$$

(Why?) Thus, given a large stable file, reordering the file in order of decreasing probability of retrieval achieves a greater degree of efficiency each time that the file is searched. Of course, this method implies that an extra field p is kept with each record which gives the probability of accessing that record, or that p can be computed based on some other information in each record.

Reordering a List for Maximum Search Efficiency

If many insertions and deletions are to be performed on a table, then a list structure is preferable to an array. However, even in a list it would be better to maintain the relationship

$$p(1) \geqslant p(2) \geqslant \ldots \geqslant p(n)$$

to provide for efficient sequential searching. This can be done most easily if a new item is inserted into the list at its proper place. This means that if *prob* is the probability that a record with a given key will be the search argument, then that record should be inserted between records $r(i)$ and $r(i+1)$, where i is such that

$$p(i) \geqslant prob \geqslant p(i+1)$$

Unfortunately, it is almost never the case that the probabilities $p(i)$ are known in advance. Although it is usual for certain records to be retrieved more often than others, it is almost impossible to identify those records. Also, the probability that a given record will be retrieved may change over time. To use the example of the college registrar given earlier, a student begins as a freshman (high probability of retrieval) and then becomes a sophomore and a junior (low probability) before becoming a senior (high probability). Thus it would be helpful to have an algorithm which would continually reorder the table so that more frequently accessed records would drift to the front while less frequently accessed records would drift to the back.

There are two search methods which accomplish this. One of these is known as the ***move-to-front*** method and is efficient only for a table which is organized as a list. In this method, whenever a search is successful (that is, when the argument is found to match the key of a given record), the retrieved record is removed from its current location in the list and is placed at the head of the list. The other method is the ***transposition*** method in which a successfully retrieved record is interchanged with the record which immediately precedes it. We present an algorithm to implement the transposition method on a table stored as a linked list. The algorithm returns a pointer to the retrieved record, or the null pointer if the record is not found. As before, *key* is the search argument, *k* and *r* are the tables of keys and records:

```
p = table;
q = null;        /*   q is one step behind p      */
s = null;        /*   s is two steps behind p     */
do while (p ¬= null);
   if k(p) = key  then do;
      /*   we have found the record, transpose the     */
      /*           records pointed to by p and q.      */
      if q = null then     /*   we have found the key   */
                           /*     at the first position */
                           /*     in the table so that  */
                           /*     no transposition is   */
                           /*          necessary        */
                     return (p);
```

```
            /*   remove node(p) from its position    */
            next(q) = next(p);
            next(p) = q;
            if s = null then table=p;
                        else next(s) =p;
            return(p);
                              end;
        s=q;
        q=p;
        p=next(p);
    end;
    return(null);
```

We leave the implementations of the transposition method for an array and the move-to-front method as exercises for the reader.

Both of these methods are based on the observed phenomenon that a record which has been retrieved is likely to be retrieved again. Since such records are advanced towards the front of the table, subsequent retrievals are more efficient. The rationale behind the move-to-front method is that since the record is likely to be retrieved again, it should be placed at the position within the table at which such retrieval will be most efficient. However, the counterargument for the transposition method is that a single retrieval does not yet imply that the record will be retrieved frequently; placing it at the front of the table reduces search efficiency for all the other records which formerly preceded it. By advancing a record only one position each time that it is retrieved, we ensure that it will advance to the front of the list only if it is retrieved frequently. Indeed it has been shown that, in general, the transposition method is more efficient than the move-to-front method.

Another advantage of the transposition method over the move-to-front method is that it can be applied efficiently to tables stored in array form as well as to list-structured tables. Transposing two elements in an array is a rather efficient operation, while moving an element from the middle of an array to its front involves (on the average) moving half the array. (However, in this case the average number of moves is not so large since the element to be moved most often comes from the upper portion of the array.)

Searching an Ordered Table

If the table is stored in ascending or descending order of the record keys, then there are several techniques which can be used to improve the efficiency of searching. This is especially true if the table is of fixed size. One immediately obvious advantage in searching a sorted file over searching an unsorted file is in the case that the argument key is absent from the file. In the case of an unsorted file, n comparisons are needed to detect this fact. In the case of a sorted file, assuming that the argument keys are uniformly distributed over the range of keys in the file, only $n/2$ comparisons (on the average) are needed. This is because we know that a given key is missing from a file which is sorted in ascending order of keys as soon as we encounter a key in the file which is greater than the given key.

Suppose that it is possible to collect a large number of retrieval requests before any of them are processed. For example, in many applications a response to a request for information may be deferred to the next day. In such a case, all requests in a specific day may be collected and the actual searching may be done overnight, when no new requests are coming in. If both the table and the list of requests are sorted on the same key, then the sequential search can proceed through both concurrently. Thus it is not necessary to search through the entire table for each retrieval request. In fact, if there are many such requests uniformly distributed over the entire table, then each request will require only a few lookups (if the number of requests is less than the number of table entries) or perhaps only a single comparison (if the number of requests is greater than the number of table entries). In such situations sequential searching is probably the best method to use.

Because of the simplicity and efficiency of sequential processing on sorted files, it may be worthwhile to sort a file before searching for keys in it. This is especially true in the situation described in the preceding paragraph, where we are dealing with a "master" file and a large "transaction" file of requests for searches.

The Indexed Sequential Search

There is another technique to improve search efficiency for a sorted file, but it involves an increase in the amount of space required. This method is called the ***indexed sequential*** search method. An auxiliary table, called an ***index***, is set aside in addition to the sorted file itself. Each element in the index consists of a key *kindex* and a pointer to the record in the file which corresponds to *kindex*. The elements in the index, as well as the elements in the file, must be sorted on the key. If the index is one-eighth the size of the file, then every eighth record of the file is represented in the index. This is illustrated by Fig. 9.1.1.

The algorithm used for searching an indexed sequential file is straightforward. Let *r*, *k*, and *key* be defined as before, let *kindex* be an array of the keys in the index and let *pindex* be the array of pointers within the index to the actual records in the file. We assume that the file is stored as an array, that *n* is the size of the file, and that *indxsze* is the size of the index.

```
do i=1 to indxsze while (kindex(i) <= key);
end;

if i=1 then lowlim = 1;
      else lowlim = pindex (i-1);
if i=indxsze+1 then hilim=n;
                  else hilim=pindex (i)-1;
do j=lowlim to hilim while (k(j) ¬= key);
end;
if j>hilim then return (0);
           else return (j);
```

Note that in the case of multiple records with the same key, the above algorithm does not necessarily return a pointer to the first such record in the table.

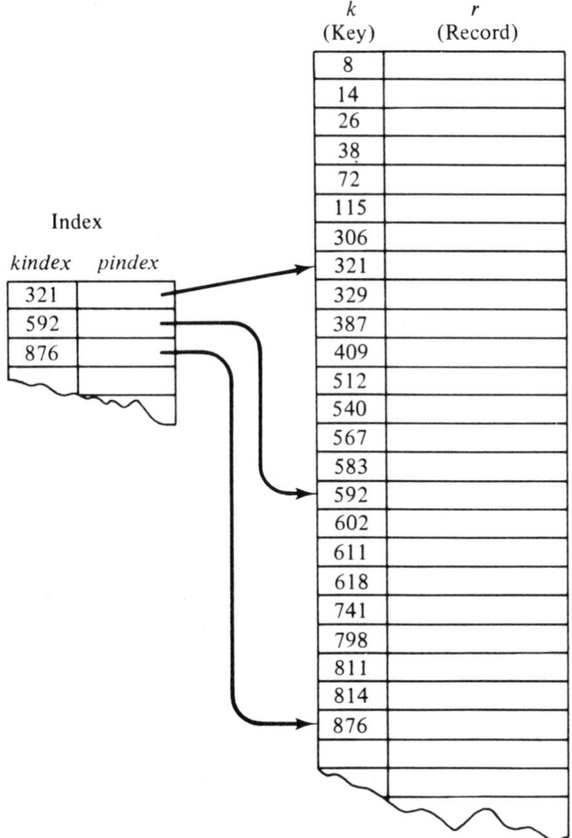

Figure 9.1.1. An indexed sequential file.

The real advantage of the indexed sequential method is that the items in the table can be examined sequentially if all the records in the file must be accessed, yet the search time for a particular item is sharply reduced. A sequential search is performed on the smaller index rather than on the larger table. Once the correct index has been found, a second sequential search is performed on a small portion of the record table itself.

The use of an index is applicable to a sorted table stored as a linked list, as well as to one stored as an array. Use of a linked list implies a larger space overhead for pointers, although insertions and deletions can be performed much more readily.

If the table is so large that even the use of an index does not achieve sufficient efficiency (either because the index is large in order to reduce sequential searching in the table, or because the index is small so that adjacent keys in the index are far from each other in the table), then a ***secondary index*** can be used. The secondary index acts as an index to the primary index which points to entries in the sequential table. This is illustrated in Fig. 9.1.2.

Deletions from an indexed sequential table can be made most easily by flagging deleted entries. In sequential searching through the table, deleted entries are ignored.

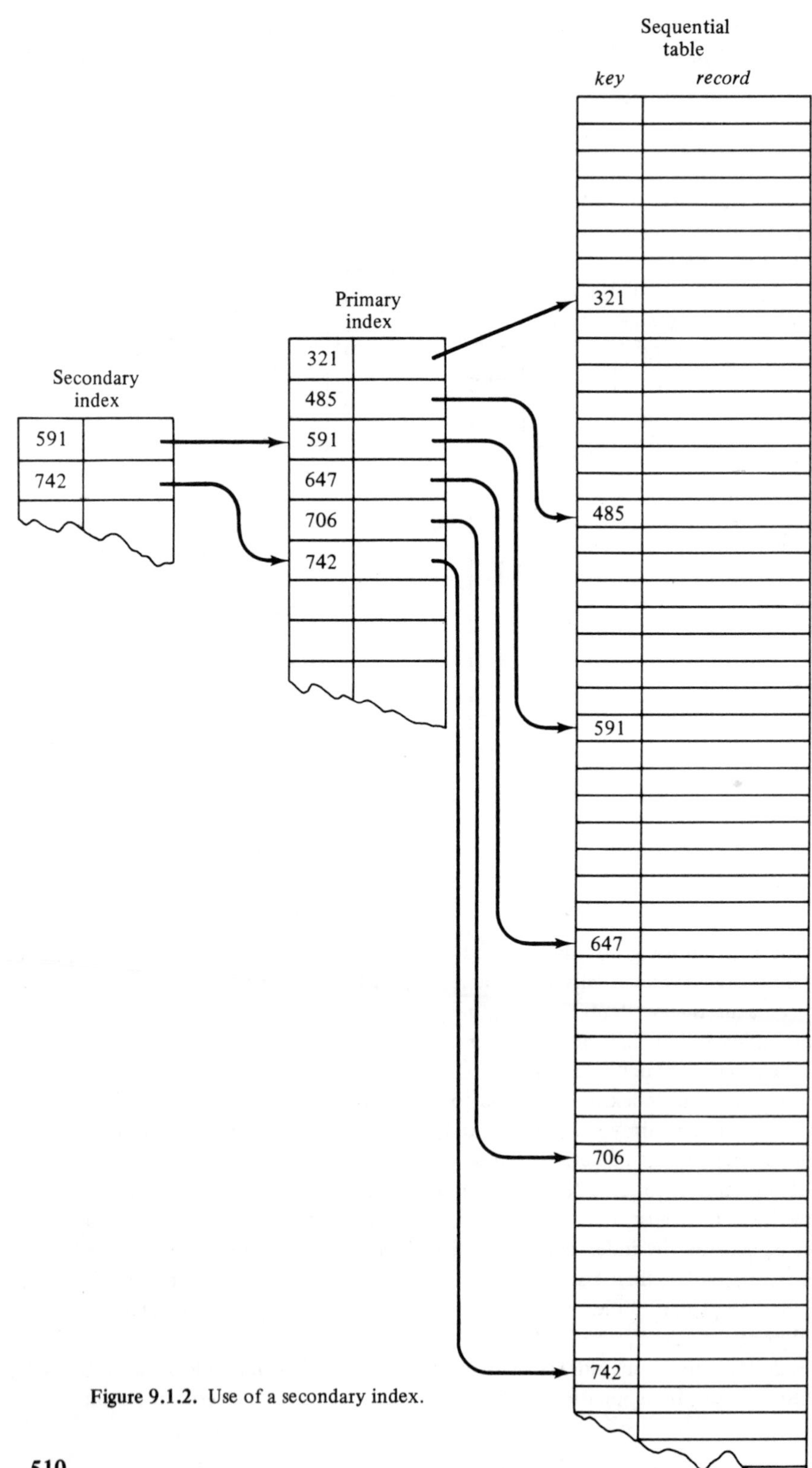

Figure 9.1.2. Use of a secondary index.

Note that if an element is deleted, then even if its key is in the index, nothing need be done to the index; only the original table entry is flagged.

Insertion into an indexed sequential table is more difficult since there may not be room between two already existing table entries, thus necessitating a shift in a large number of table elements. However, if a nearby item has been flagged as deleted in the table, then only a few items need be shifted and the deleted item can be overwritten. This may in turn necessitate alteration of the index if an item pointed to by an index element is shifted. An alternative method is to keep an overflow area at some other location and link together any inserted records. However, this would require an extra pointer field in each record of the original table. You are asked to explore these possibilities as an exercise.

The Binary Search

The most efficient method of searching a sequential table without the use of auxiliary indices or tables is the binary search. You should be familiar with this search technique from Sections 4.1 and 4.2. Basically, the argument is compared with the key of the middle element of the table. If they are equal, then the search ends successfully; otherwise, either the upper or lower half of the table must be searched in a similar manner.

In Chapter 4, it was noted that the binary search can best be defined recursively, and a recursive definition, a recursive algorithm, and a recursive PL/I program were presented for the binary search. However, the large overhead which is associated with recursion makes it inappropriate for use in practical situations in which efficiency is a prime consideration. We therefore present the following nonrecursive version of the binary search algorithm (in this algorithm we assume that division yields a truncated integer quotient):

```
low=1;
hi=n;
do while (low ≤ hi);
   mid = (low + hi)/2;
   if key=k(mid) then return (mid);
   if key < k(mid)  then hi=mid −1;
                         else low=mid +1;
end;
return(0);
```

Each comparison in the binary search reduces the number of possible candidates by a factor of 2. Thus the maximum number of key comparisons which will be made is approximately $\log_2 n$. (Actually, it is $2\log_2 n$ since in PL/I two key comparisons are made each time through the loop: *key=k(mid)* and *key<k(mid)*. However, in assembly language or in FORTRAN using an arithmetic IF statement, only one comparison is made. An optimizing PL/I compiler should be able to eliminate the extra comparison.) Thus, we may say that the binary search algorithm is $O(\log n)$.

Unfortunately, the binary search algorithm can be used only if the table is stored as an array. This is because it makes use of the fact that the indices of array elements are consecutive integers. For this reason the binary search is practically useless in situations where there are many insertions or deletions in which an array structure is inappropriate.

9.2. Tree Searching

In the last section we discussed search operations on a file that is organized either as an array or as a list. In this section we consider several ways of organizing files as trees and some associated searching algorithms.

In Sections 7.1 and 8.3 we presented a method of using a binary tree to store a file in order to make sorting the file more efficient. In that method, all the left descendants of a node with key *key* have keys that are less than *key* and all the right descendants have keys that are greater than or equal to *key*. The inorder traversal of such a binary tree yields the file in ascending key order.

Such a tree may also be used as a binary search tree. Using binary tree notation, the algorithm for searching for the key *key* in such a tree is as follows. (We assume that each node contains four fields: *k* which holds the record's key value, *r* which holds the record itself, and *left* and *right* which are pointers to the subtrees):

```
p=tree;
do while (p ¬= null);
   if key  =  k(p) then return (p);
   if key  <  k (p) then p=left (p);
                     else p=right(p);
end;
return(null);
```

Note that the binary search of Section 9.1 actually uses a sorted array as an implicit binary search tree. The middle element of the array can be thought of as the root of the tree, the lower half of the array (all of whose elements are less than the middle element) can be considered the left subtree and the upper half (all of whose elements are greater than the middle element) can be considered the right subtree.

A sorted array can be produced from a binary search tree by traversing the tree in inorder and inserting each element sequentially into the array as it is visited. On the other hand, many binary search trees correspond to a given sorted array. Viewing the middle element of the array as the root of a tree and viewing the remaining elements recursively as left and right subtrees produces a relatively balanced binary search tree (Fig. 9.2.1(a)). Viewing the first element of the array as the root of a tree and each successive element as the right subtree of its predecessor produces a very unbalanced binary tree (Fig. 9.2.1(b)).

The advantage of using a binary search tree over an array is that a tree enables search, insertion, and deletion operations to be performed efficiently. If an array is used, an insertion or deletion requires that approximately half of the elements of the array be moved (why?). Insertion or deletion in a search tree, on the other hand, requires that only a few pointers be adjusted.

Inserting into a Binary Search Tree

The following algorithm searches such a binary tree and inserts a new record into the tree if the search is unsuccessful. (We assume the existence of a function *maketree* which constructs a binary tree consisting of a single node whose information field is passed as a parameter and returns a pointer to the tree. This function is described in Section 7.1. However, in our particular version, we assume that *maketree* accepts two parameters: a record and a key.).

```
q=null;
p=tree;
do while (p¬=null);
   if key=k(p)  then return(p);
   q=p;
   if key<k(p)  then p=left(p);
                else p=right(p);
end;
v=maketree(rec, key);
if q=null  then tree=v;
           else if key<k(q)  then left(q)=v;
                             else right(q)=v;
return(v);
```

Note that after a new record is inserted, the tree retains the property of being sorted in an inorder traversal.

Deleting from a Binary Search Tree

We now present an algorithm which deletes a node with key *key* from a binary search tree and leaves the tree as a binary search tree. There are three cases to consider. If the node to be deleted has no sons, then it may be deleted without further adjustment to the tree. This is illustrated in Fig. 9.2.2(a). If the node to be deleted has only one subtree, then its only son can be moved up to take its place. This is illustrated in Fig. 9.2.2(b). If, however, the node p to be deleted has two subtrees, then its inorder successor s (or predecessor) must take its place. The inorder successor cannot have a left subtree (since a left descendant would be the inorder successor of p). Thus the right son of s can be moved up to take the place of s. This is illustrated in Fig. 9.2.2(c), where the node with key 12 replaces the node with key 11 and is replaced, in turn, by the node with key 13.

In the following algorithm, if no node with key *key* exists in the tree, the tree is left unchanged.

```
p=tree;
q=null;

/*       search for a node with key key, set p to point to     */
/*              the node and q to its father, if any.          */
do while (p¬=null & k(p)¬=key);
   q=p;
   if key<k(p)  then p=left(p);
                else p=right(p);
end;
```

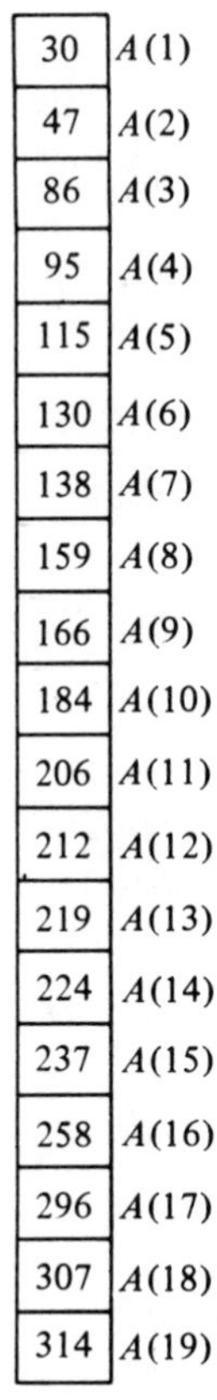

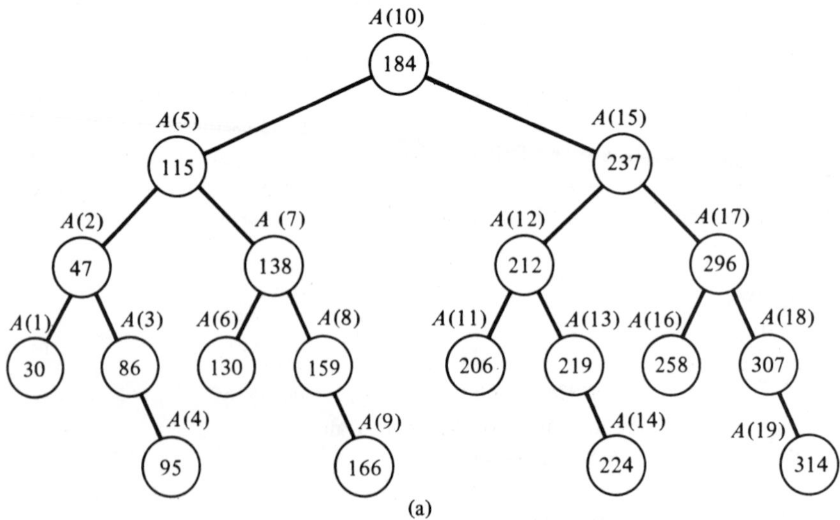

(a)

Figure 9.2.1. A sorted array and two of its binary tree representations.

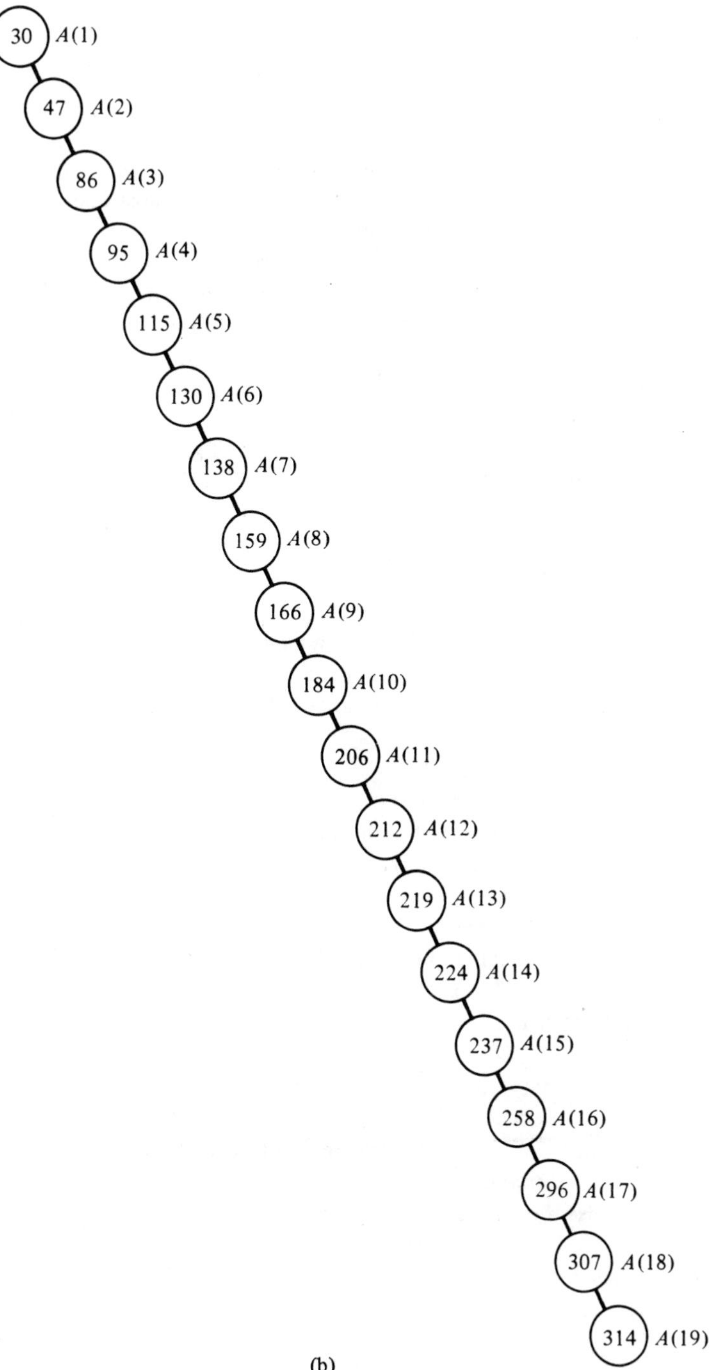

Figure 9.2.1. *(cont.)*

```
if p=null then   /*   the key does not exist in the tree   */
                 /*       leave the tree unchanged         */
                 return;

/*   set the variable v to the node which will replace node(p)    */
/*   first two cases: the node to be deleted has at most one son  */
if left(p)=null then v=right(p); else
   if right(p)=null then v=left(p);   else do;
      /*   third case: node(p) has two sons. Set v to   */
      /*     the inorder successor of p and t to the    */
      /*                father of v                     */
      t=p;
      v=right(p);
      s=left(v);   /*   s is always the left son of v   */
      do while (s ¬= null);
         t=v;
         v=s;
         s=left(v);
      end;
      /*   at this point, v is the inorder successor of p   */
      if t¬=p then   /*   p is not the father of v   */
                     /*        and v=left(t)         */
                     do;
         left(t)=right(v);
         /*    remove node(v) from its current position      */
         /*   and replace it with the right son of node(v)   */
         /*      node(v) takes the place of node(p)          */
         right(v)=right(p);
                     end;
      /*   set the left son of node(v) so that   */
      /*  node(v) takes the place of node(p)     */
      left(v)=left(p);
                                          end;
/*   insert node(v) into the position formerly   */
/*            occupied by node(p)                */
if q=null then   /*   node(p) was the root of the tree   */
              tree=v;
         else if p=left(q) then left(q)=v;
                           else right(q)=v;
freenode(p);
return;
```

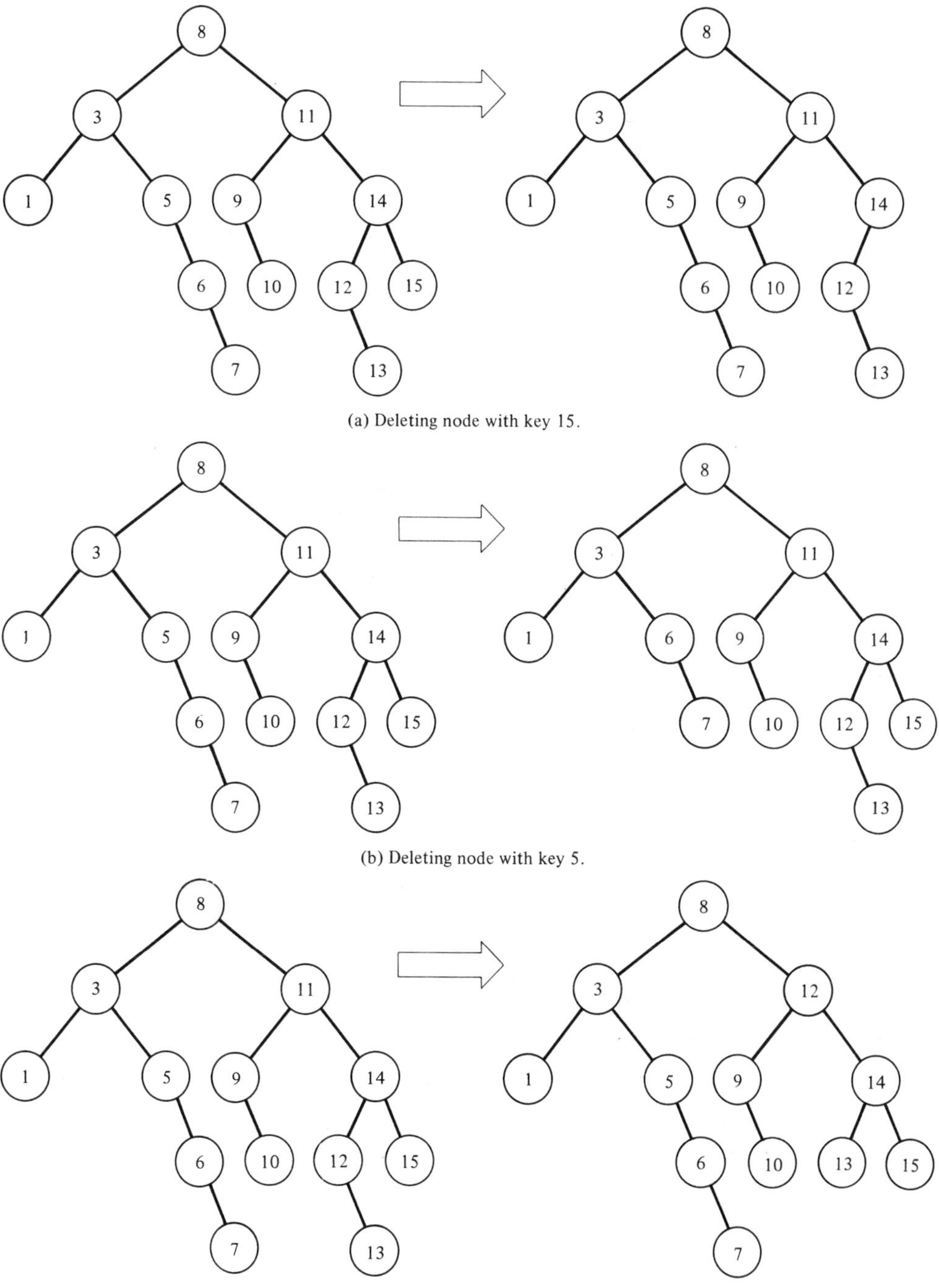

(a) Deleting node with key 15.

(b) Deleting node with key 5.

(c) Deleting node with key 11.

Figure 9.2.2. Deleting nodes from a binary search tree.

Note that the statement (in line 5):

```
do while (p¬=null & k(p)¬=key);
```

cannot be translated directly into PL/I since if p is *null*, the reference to $k(p)$ would result in an error. For alternate versions of this algorithm, see the Exercise Manual.

Efficiency of Binary Tree Search

As we have already seen in Section 8.3 (see Figs. 8.3.1 and 8.3.2), the time required to search a binary search tree varies between $O(n)$ and $O(\log n)$ depending on the structure of the tree. If elements are inserted into the tree by the insertion algorithm presented above, the structure of the tree depends on the order in which the records are inserted. If the records are inserted in sorted (or reverse) order, the resulting tree will contain all null left (or right) links, so that the tree search reduces to a sequential search. If, however, the records are inserted so that half the records inserted after a record with key k have keys smaller than k and half have keys greater than k, then a balanced tree is achieved in which approximately $\log_2 n$ key comparisons are sufficient to retrieve an element. (Again, it should be noted that examining a node in our insertion algorithm requires two comparisons: one for equality and the other for less than. However, in machine language and in some compilers, these can be combined into a single comparison.)

If the records are presented in random order (i.e., any permutation of the n elements is equally likely), balanced trees will result more often than not, so that on the average, search time will remain $O(\log n)$. However, the constant of proportionality will be greater on the average than in the specific case of an evenly balanced tree.

All of the preceding assumes that it is equally likely for the search argument to equal any key in the table. However, in actual practice it is usually the case that some records are retrieved very often, some moderately often, and some are almost never retrieved. Suppose that records are inserted into the tree so that a more commonly accessed record precedes one which is less frequently accessed. Then the most frequently retrieved records will be nearer the root of the tree, so that the average successful search time will be reduced. (Of course, this assumes that reordering the keys in order of reduced frequency of access does not seriously unbalance the binary tree, since if it did, then the reduced number of comparisons for the most frequently accessed records might be offset by the increased number of comparisons for the vast majority of records.)

If the elements to be retrieved form a constant set, with no insertions or deletions, then it may pay to set up a binary search tree which makes subsequent searches more efficient. For example, consider the binary search trees of Fig. 9.2.3. Both the trees of Fig. 9.2.3(a) and Fig. 9.2.3(b) contain three elements *K1*, *K2*, and *K3*, where $K1<K2<K3$, and are valid binary search trees for that set. However, a retrieval of *K3* requires two comparisons in Fig. 9.2.3(a), but requires only one comparison in Fig. 9.2.3(b). Of course, there are still other valid binary search trees for this set of keys.

The number of key comparisons necessary to retrieve a record is equal to the level of that record in the binary search tree plus 1. Thus a retrieval of *K2* requires one comparison in the tree of Fig. 9.2.3(a), but requires three comparisons in the tree of Fig. 9.2.3(b).

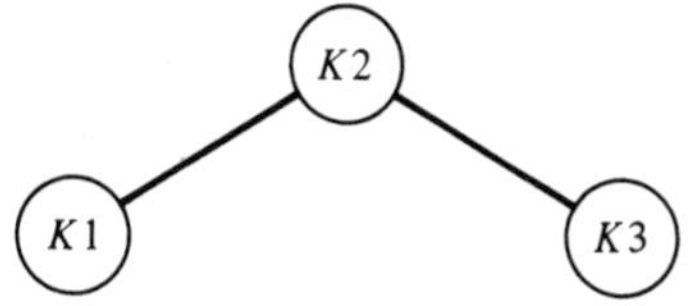

(a) Expected number of comparisons:
$2p1 + p2 + 2p3 + 2q0 + 2q1 + 2q2 + 2q3$

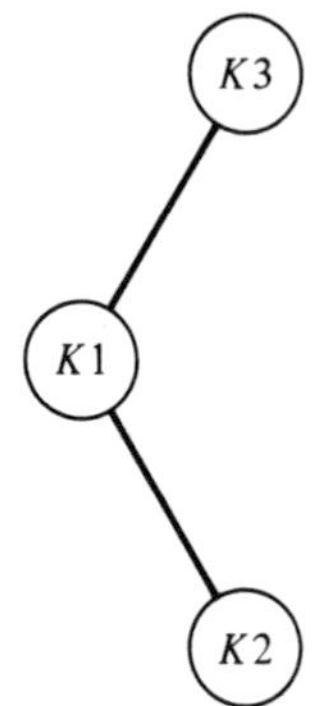

(b) Expected number of comparisons:
$2p1 + 3p2 + p3 + 2q0 + 3q1 + 3q2 + q3$

Figure 9.2.3. Two binary search trees.

An unsuccessful search for an argument lying immediately between two keys *a* and *b* requires as many key comparisons as the maximum number of comparisons required by successful searches for either *a* or *b* (why?). This is equal to 1 plus the maximum of the levels of *a* or *b*. For example, a search for a key lying between *K2* and *K3* requires two key comparisons in Fig. 9.2.3(a) and three comparisons in Fig. 9.2.3(b), while a search for a key greater than *K3* requires two comparisons in Fig. 9.2.3(a), but only one comparison in Fig. 9.2.3(b).

Suppose *p1*, *p2*, and *p3* are the probabilities that the search argument equals *K1*, *K2*, and *K3* respectively. Suppose also the *q0* is the probability that the search argument is less than *K1*, *q1* is the probability that it is between *K1* and *K2*, *q2* is the probability that it is between *K2* and *K3*, and *q3* is the probability that it is greater than *K3*. Then *p1+p2+p3+q0+q1+q2+q3*=1. The ***expected number*** of comparisons in a search is the sum of the probabilities that the argument has a given value times the number of comparisons required to retrieve that value, where the sum is taken over all possible search argument values. For example, the expected number of comparisons in searching the tree of Fig. 9.2.3(a) is

```
2p1+p2+2p3+2q0+2q1+2q2+2q3,
```

while the expected number of comparisons in searching the tree of Fig. 9.2.3(b) is

```
2p1+3p2+p3+2q0+3q1+3q2+q3.
```

This expected number of comparisons can be used as a measure of how "good" a particular binary search tree is for a given set of keys and a given set of probabilities. Thus, for the probabilities listed below on the left, the tree of Fig. 9.2.3(a) is more efficient; for the probabilities listed on the right, the tree of Fig. 9.2.3(b) is more efficient.

p1 = .1		p1 = .1	
p2 = .3		p2 = .1	
p3 = .1		p3 = .3	
q0 = .1		q1 = .1	
q1 = .2		q1 = .1	
q2 = .1		q2 = .1	
q3 = .1		q3 = .2	

Expected number for Fig. 9.2.3(a) = 1.7 Expected number for Fig. 9.2.3(a) = 1.9
Expected number for Fig. 9.2.3(b) = 2.4 Expected number for Fig. 9.2.3(b) = 1.8

A binary search tree which minimizes the expected number of comparisons for a given set of keys and probabilities is called ***optimum***. Although an algorithm to produce such a tree may be very expensive, the tree which it produces yields efficiencies in all subsequent searches. Unfortunately, however, it is rare that the probabilities of the search arguments are known in advance.

Balanced Trees

As noted above, if the probability of searching for a key in a table is the same for all keys, a balanced binary tree yields the most efficient search. Unfortunately, the search and insertion algorithm presented above does not ensure that the tree remains balanced—the degree of balance is dependent on the order in which keys are inserted into the tree. We would like to have an efficient search and insertion algorithm which maintains the search tree as a balanced binary tree.

Let us first define more precisely the notion of a "balanced" tree. The ***height*** of a binary tree is the maximum level of its leafs (this is also known sometimes as the ***depth*** of the tree). (For convenience, the height of a null tree is defined as –1.) A ***balanced binary tree*** (sometimes called an ***AVL tree***) is a binary tree in which the heights of the two subtrees of every node never differ by more than 1. The ***balance*** of a node in a binary tree is defined as the height of its left subtree minus the height of its right subtree. Figure 9.2.4(a) illustrates a balanced binary tree. Each node in a balanced binary tree has a balance of 1, –1, or 0 depending on whether the height of its left subtree is greater than, less than, or equal to the height of its right subtree. The balance of each node is indicated in Fig. 9.2.4(a).

Suppose that we are given a balanced binary tree and use the search and insertion algorithm above to insert a new node p into the tree. Then the resulting tree may or may not remain balanced. Figure 9.2.4(b) illustrates all possible insertions that may be made to the tree of Fig. 9.2.4(a). Each insertion that yields a balanced tree is indicated by a B. The unbalanced insertions are indicated by a U and are numbered from 1 to 12. It is easy to see that the tree will become unbalanced only if the newly inserted node is a

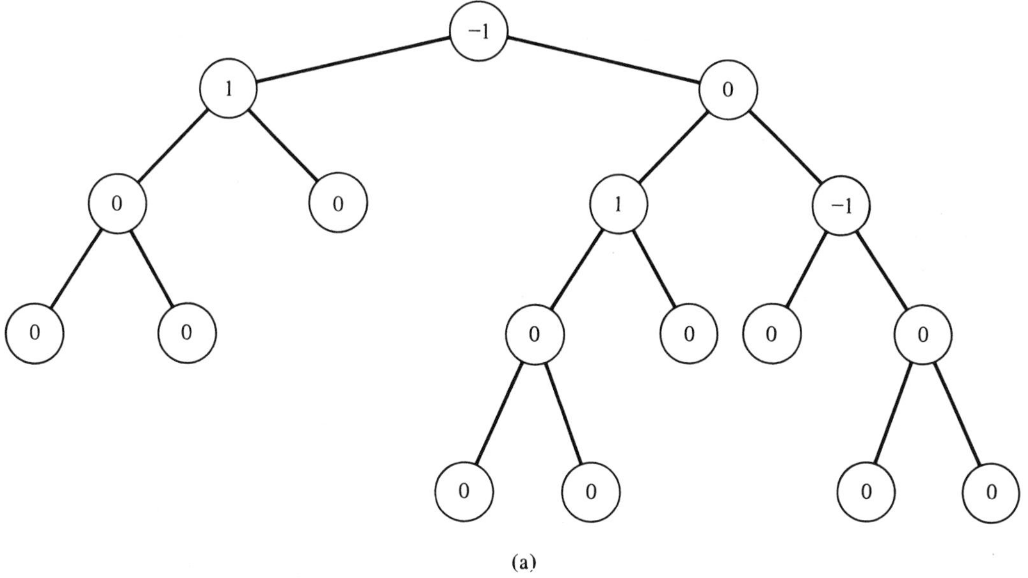

(a)

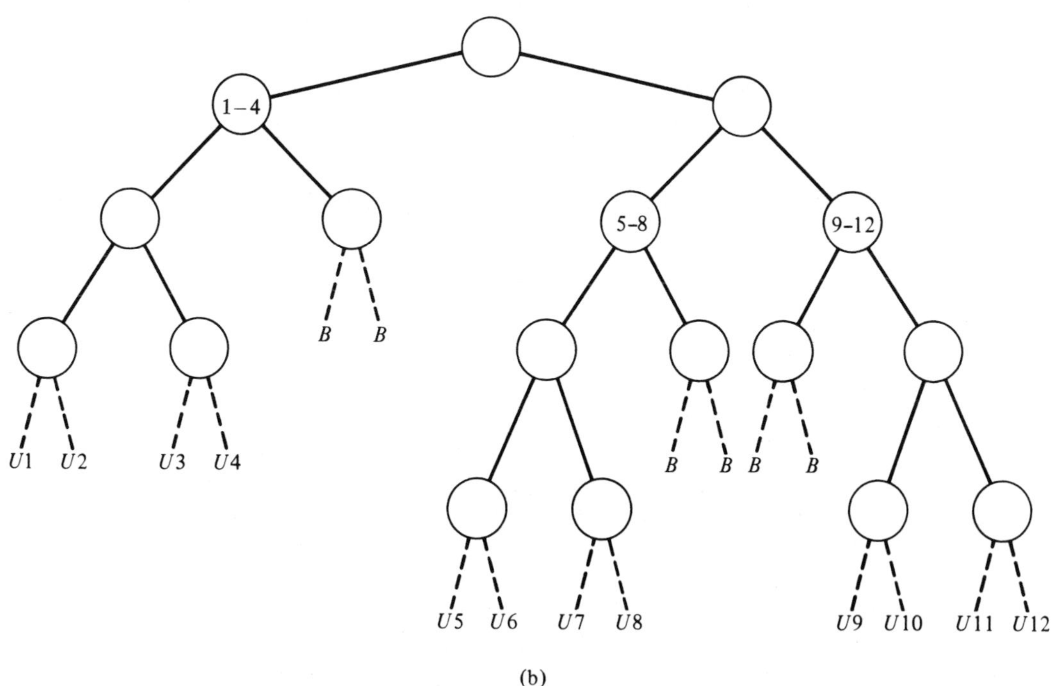

(b)

Figure 9.2.4. A balanced binary tree and possible additions.

left descendant of a node which previously had a balance of 1 (this occurs in cases *U1* through *U8* in Fig. 9.2.4(b)) or if it is a right descendant of a node which previously had a balance of −1 (cases *U9* through *U12*). In Fig. 9.2.4(b), the youngest ancestor which becomes unbalanced in each insertion is indicated by the numbers contained in three of the nodes.

Let us examine further the subtree rooted at the youngest ancestor to become unbalanced as a result of an insertion. We illustrate the case where the balance of this subtree was previously 1, leaving the other case to the reader. Fig. 9.2.5 illustrates this case. Let us call the unbalanced node *A*. Since *A* had a balance of 1, its left subtree was nonnull; we may therefore designate its left son as *B*. Since *A* is the youngest ancestor of the new node to become unbalanced, node *B* must have had a balance of 0. (You are asked to prove this fact as an exercise.) Thus, node *B* must have had (before the insertion) left and right subtrees of equal height *n* (where possibly $n=-1$). Since the balance of *A* was 1, the right subtree of *A* must also have been of height *n*.

There are now two cases to consider, illustrated by Figs. 9.2.5(a) and (b). In Fig. 9.2.5(a) the newly created node is inserted into the left subtree of *B*, changing the balance of *B* to 1 and the balance of *A* to 2. In Fig. 9.2.5(b) the newly created node is inserted into the right subtree of *B*, changing the balance of *B* to −1 and the balance of *A* to 2. In order to maintain a balanced tree, it is necessary to perform a transformation on the tree so that:

1. The inorder traversal for the transformed tree is the same as for the original tree (that is, the transformed tree remains a binary search tree).

2. The transformed tree is balanced.

Consider the trees of Figs. 9.2.6(a) and (b). The tree of Fig. 9.2.6(b) is said to be a ***right rotation*** of the tree rooted at *A* of Fig. 9.2.6(a). Similarly, the tree of Fig. 9.2.6(c) is said to be a ***left rotation*** of the tree rooted at *A* of Fig. 9.2.6(a).

An algorithm to implement a left rotation of a subtree rooted at *p* is as follows:

```
q=right(p);
hold=left(q);
left(q)=p;
right(p)=hold;
```

Let us call this operation *left_rotation(p)*. *right_rotation(p)* may be defined similarly. Of course, in any rotation the value of the pointer to the root of the subtree being rotated must be changed to point to the new root. (In the case of the above left rotation, this new root is *q*.) Note that the order of the nodes in an inorder traversal is preserved under both right and left rotations. It therefore follows that any number of rotations (left or right) can be performed on an unbalanced tree in order to obtain a balanced tree, without disturbing the order of the nodes in an inorder traversal.

Let us now return to the trees of Fig. 9.2.5. Suppose a right rotation is performed on the subtree rooted at *A* in Fig. 9.2.5(a). The resulting tree is shown in Fig. 9.2.7(a). Note that the tree of Fig. 9.2.7(a) yields the same inorder traversal as that of Fig. 9.2.5(a) and is also balanced. Also, since the height of the subtree of Fig. 9.2.5(a) was $n+2$ before

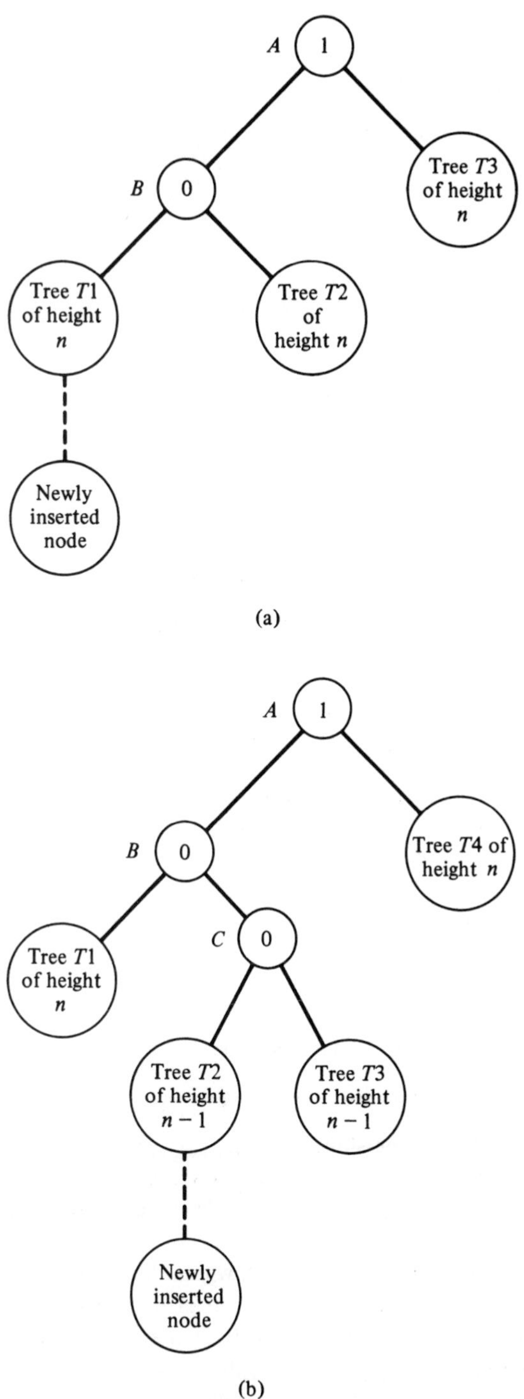

Figure 9.2.5. Initial insertion; all balances are prior to insertion.

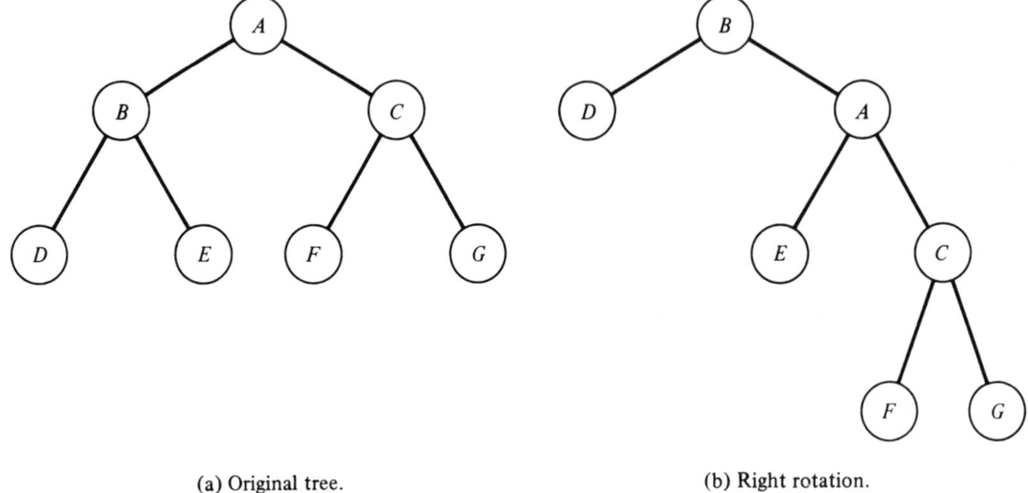

(a) Original tree.

(b) Right rotation.

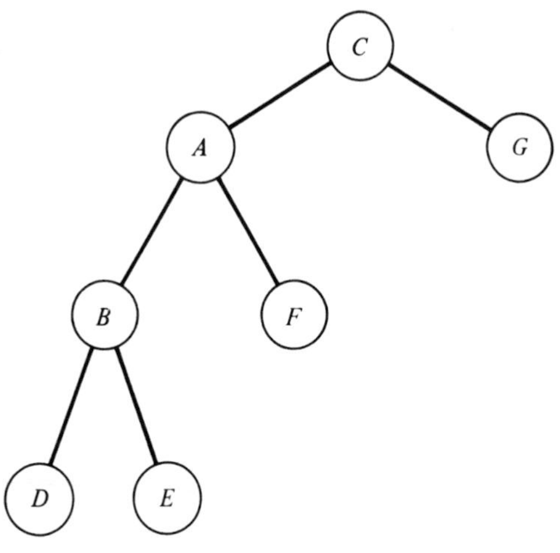

(c) Left rotation.

Figure 9.2.6. Simple rotation on a tree.

the insertion and the height of the subtree of Fig. 9.2.7(a) is n+2 with the inserted node, the balance of each ancestor of node A remains undisturbed. Thus, replacing the subtree of Fig. 9.2.5(a) with its right rotation of Fig. 9.2.7(a) guarantees that a balanced binary search tree is maintained.

Let us now turn to the tree of Fig. 9.2.5(b), where the newly created node is inserted into the right subtree of B. Let C be the right son of B. (There are three cases: C may be the newly inserted node, in which case n=–1, or the newly inserted node may be in the left or right subtree of C. Figure 9.2.5(b) illustrates the case where it is in the left subtree; the analysis of the other cases is analogous.) Suppose a left rotation on the subtree rooted at B is followed by a right rotation on the subtree rooted at A. Figure 9.2.7(b) illustrates the resulting tree. Verify that the inorder traversals of the two trees are the same and that the tree of Fig. 9.2.7(b) is balanced. The height of the tree in Fig. 9.2.7(b) is n+2, which is the same as the height of the tree in Fig. 9.2.5(b) before the insertion, so that the balance in all ancestors of A is unchanged. Therefore, by replacing the tree of Fig. 9.2.5(b) with that of Fig. 9.2.7(b) after insertion, a balanced search tree is maintained.

Let us now present an algorithm to search and insert into a nonempty balanced binary tree. Each node of the tree contains five fields: k and r, which hold the key and record respectively; *left* and *right*, which are pointers to the left and right subtrees respectively; and *bal*, whose value is 1, –1, or 0 depending on the node's balance. In the first

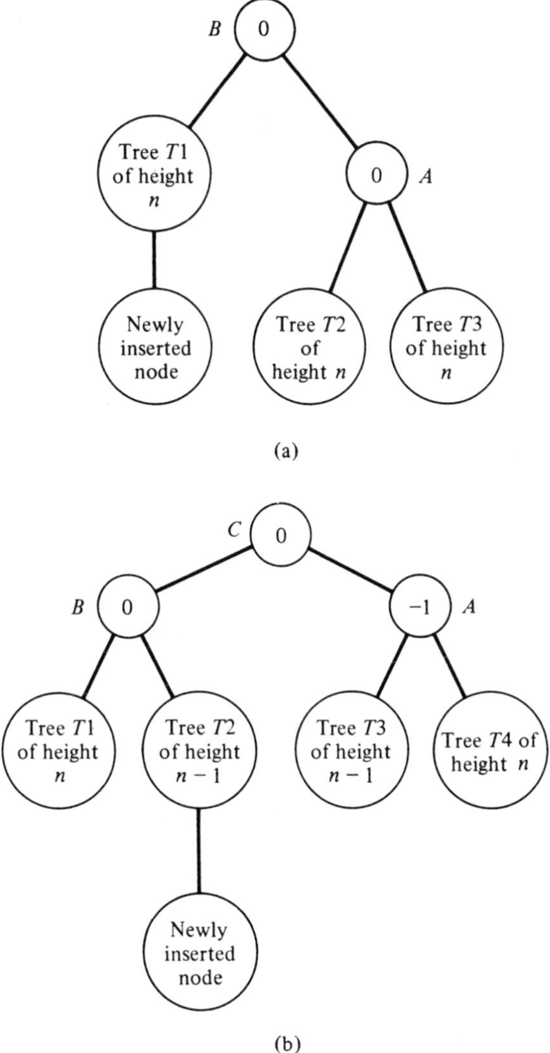

Figure 9.2.7. After rebalancing; all balances are after insertion.

part of the algorithm, if the desired key is not found in the tree already, a new node is inserted into the binary search tree without regard to balance. This first phase also keeps track of the youngest ancestor, *ya*, which may become unbalanced upon insertion. The algorithm makes use of the function *maketree* described above and routines *right_rotation* and *left_rotation* which accept a pointer to the root of a subtree and perform the desired rotation.

```
    /*   PART I: search and insert into the binary tree     */
s=null;
p=tree;
v=null;
ya=p;

      /*   ya points to the youngest ancestor which may become    */
      /*        unbalanced. v points to the father of ya, and s   */
      /*                  points to the father of p.              */
do while(p ¬= null);
   if key=k(p) then return(p);
   if key<k(p) then q=left(p);
                else q=right(p);
   if q ¬= null then
                 if bal(q) ¬=0 then do;
                                       v=p;
                                       ya=q;
                                    end;
   s=p;
   p=q;
end;

      /*                    insert new record                     */
q=maketree(rec,key);
bal(q)=0;
if key < k(s) then left(s)=q;
              else right(s)=q;
      /*   the balance on all nodes between node(ya) and node(q)  */
      /*                  must be changed from 0                  */

if key < k(ya) then p=left(ya);
                else p=right(ya);
s=p;
do while(p ¬= q);
   if key < k(p)  then do;
                          bal(p)=1;
                          p=left(p);
                       end;
```

```
                    else do;
                            bal(p)=-1;
                            p=right(p);
                         end;
end;


  /*   PART II: ascertain whether or not the tree is unbalanced     */
  /*     if it is, q is the newly inserted node, ya is its youngest  */
  /*      unbalanced ancestor, v is the father of ya and s is the    */
  /*           son of ya in the direction of the imbalance           */
if key < k(ya) then imbal=1;
               else imbal=-1;
if bal(ya)=0 then  /*  another level has been added to the tree  */
                   /*          the tree remains balanced          */
               do;
                  bal(ya)=imbal;
                  return(q);
               end;


if bal(ya) ¬= imbal then /*  the added node has been placed in the  */
                         /*    opposite direction of the imbalance   */
                         /*          the tree remains balanced       */
               do;
                  bal(ya)=0;
                  return(q);
               end;


  /*   PART III: the additional node has unbalanced the tree   */
  /*        rebalance it by performing the required rotations   */
  /*       and then adjust the balances of the nodes involved   */
if bal(s)=imbal then
  /*     ya and s have been unbalanced in the same direction    */
  /*             see Fig. 9.2.5(a) where ya=A and s=B           */
                  do;
                     p=s;
                     if imbal=1  then right_rotation(ya);
                                 else left_rotation(ya);
                     bal(ya)=0;
                     bal(s)=0;
                  end;
```

```
            else  /*     ya and s are unbalanced in opposite      */
                  /*          directions; see Fig. 9.2.5(b).      */
                  do;
                     if imbal=1  then do;
                                        p=right(s);
                                        left_rotation(s);
                                        left(ya)=p;
                                        right_rotation(ya);
                                     end;
                                 else do;
                                        p=left(s);
                                        right(ya)=p;
                                        right_rotation(s);
                                        left_rotation(ya);
                                     end;
/*    adjust bal field for involved nodes     */
             if bal(p)=0  then     /*    p was inserted node     */
                                 do;
                                    bal(ya)=0;
                                    bal(s)=0;
                                 end;
                          else if bal(p)=imbal  then

      /*    see Figs. 9.2.5(b) and 9.2.7(b)    */

                                 do;
                                    bal(ya)=-imbal;
                                    bal(s)=0;
                                 end;
                                            else
      /*      see Figs. 9.2.5(b) and 9.2.7(b)       */
      /*    but assume new node was inserted        */
      /*                  into T3                   */

                                 do;
                                    bal(ya)=0;
                                    bal(s)=imbal;
                                 end;
             bal(p)=0;
                end;

    /*    adjust the pointer to the rotated subtree      */
if v=null then tree=p;
        else if ya=right(v) then right(v)=p;
                         else left(v)=p;
return(q);
```

The algorithm to delete a node from a balanced binary search tree while maintaining its balance is even more complex and is left as an exercise. There are also other types of balance which may be used in designing tree structures for efficient search and insertion; see the Exercise Manual for further examples.

Digital Search Trees

Another method of using trees to expedite searching is to form a general tree based on the symbols of which the keys are comprised. For example, if the keys are integers, then each digit position determines one of 10 possible sons of a given node. A forest representing one such set of keys is illustrated in Fig. 9.2.8. If the keys consist of alphabetic characters, then each letter of the alphabet determines a branch in the tree. Note that every leaf node contains the special symbol *eok* which represents the end of a key. Such a leaf node must also contain a pointer to the record which is being stored.

If a forest is represented by a binary tree, as in Section 7.4.1, then each node of the binary tree contains three fields: *symbol,* which contains a symbol of the key; *son*, which is a pointer to the node's oldest son in the original tree; and *brother*, which is a pointer to the node's next younger brother in the original tree. The first tree in the forest is pointed to by an external pointer *tree*, and the roots of the other trees in the forest are linked together in a linear list by the *brother* field. The *son* field of a leaf in the original forest points to a record; the concatenation of all the *symbol*s in the original forest in the path of nodes from the root to the leaf is the key of the record. We make two further stipulations which will speed up the search and insertion process for such a tree. Each list of brothers is arranged in the binary tree in ascending order of the *symbol* field. The symbol *eok* is considered to be larger than any other.

Using this binary tree representation, we may present an algorithm to search and insert into such a nonempty ***digital tree***. As usual, *key* is the key for which we are searching and *rec* is the record which we wish to insert if *key* is not found. We also let *key*(i) be the ith symbol of the key. If the key has n symbols, we also assume that *key*(n+1) equals *eok*. The algorithm uses the *getnode* operation to allocate a new tree node, when necessary. It also uses the *addr* function to obtain the address of the record *rec* to be inserted. The algorithm returns a pointer to the record which is being sought.

```
p=tree;
father=null;   /*   father is the father of p   */
do i=1 by 1;
   q=null;   /*   q points to the older brother of p   */
   do while(p¬=null & symbol(p)<key(i));
      q=p;
      p=brother(p);
   end;
   if p=null | symbol(p)>key(i) then   /*   insert   */
```

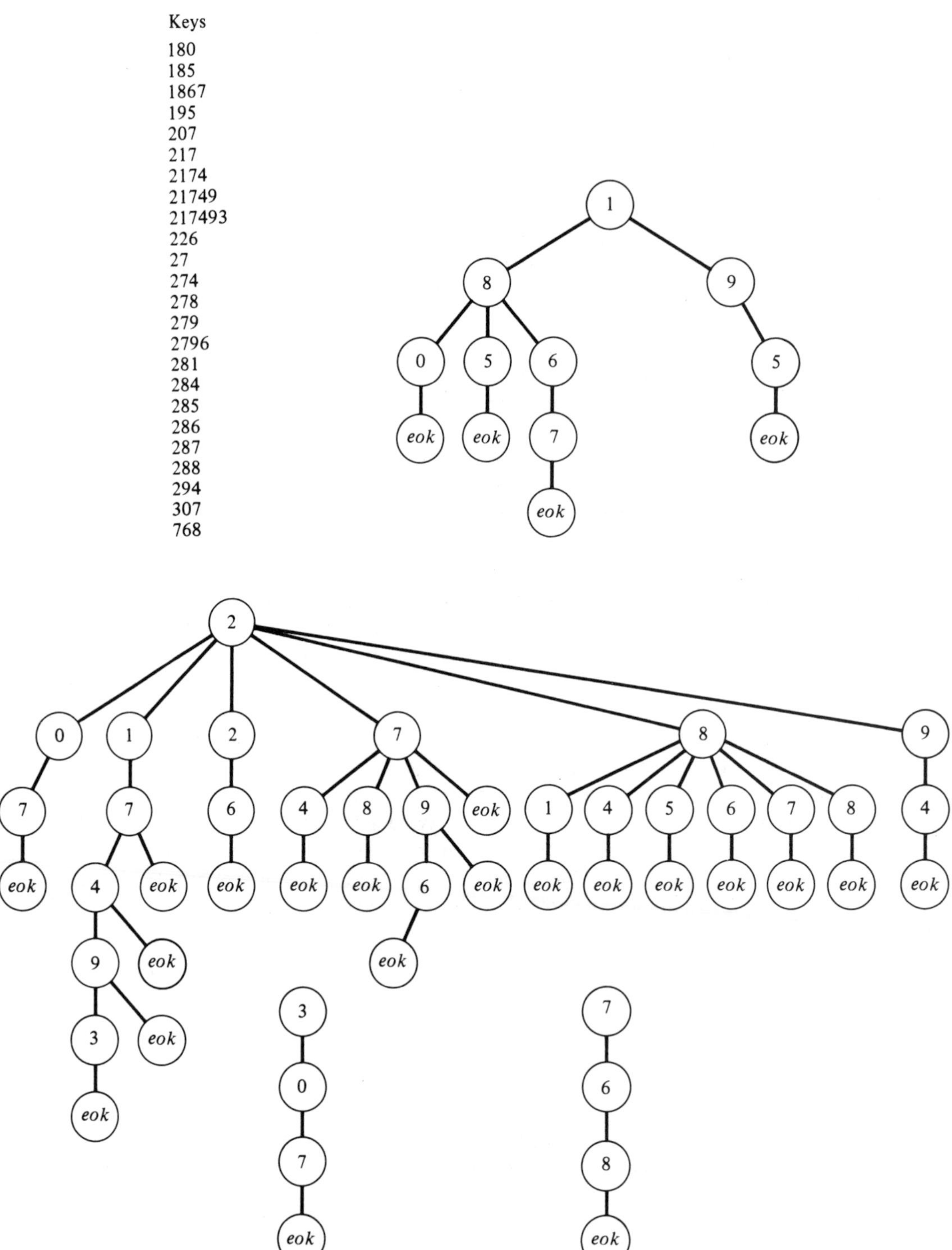

Figure 9.2.8. A forest representing a table of keys.

```
                    do;
            s=getnode;
            symbol(s)=key(i);
            brother(s)=p;
            if tree=null then tree=s;
                    else if q¬=null  then brother(q)=s;
                                     else if father=null
                                               then tree=s;
                                               else son(father)=s;
            do j=i by 1;
               if key(j)=eok then do;
                          son(s)=addr(rec);
                          return(son(s));
                                     end;
               father=s;
               s=getnode;
               symbol(s)=key(j+1);
               son(father)=s;
               brother(s)=null;
            end;
                    end;

    /*    at this point symbol(p) equals key(i)      */
    if key(i)=eok then return(son(p));
              else do;
                    father=p;
                    p=son(p);
                 end;
end;
```

Note that by keeping the table of keys as a general tree, we need search only a small list of sons to find whether a given symbol appears at a given position within the keys of the table. However, it is possible to make the tree even smaller by eliminating those nodes from which only a single leaf can be reached. For example, in the keys of Fig. 9.2.8, once the symbol '7' is recognized, the only key that can possibly match is 768. Similarly, upon recognizing the two symbols '1' and '9', the only matching key is 195. Thus the forest of Fig. 9.2.8 can be abbreviated to the one of Fig. 9.2.9. In that figure, a box indicates a key, while a circle indicates a tree node. A dashed line is used to indicate a pointer from a tree node to a key.

There are some significant differences between the trees of Figs. 9.2.8 and 9.2.9. In Fig. 9.2.8, a path from a root to a leaf represents an entire key; thus there is no need to repeat the key itself. In Fig. 9.2.9, however, a key may be recognized by its first few symbols. In those cases where the search is made for a key which is known to be in the table, then upon finding a leaf, the record corresponding to that key can be accessed. If, however, as is more likely, it is not known whether the key is present in the table, then it must be confirmed that the key is indeed correct. Thus, the entire key must be kept in the tree as well. Furthermore, a leaf node in the tree of Fig. 9.2.8 can be recognized because its contents are *eok.* Thus its *son* pointer can be used to point to the record which that leaf represents. However, a leaf node of Fig. 9.2.9 may contain any symbol. Thus in order to use the *son* pointer of a leaf to point to the record, an extra bit is required in each node to indicate whether or not the node is a leaf. We leave the representation of the forest of Fig. 9.2.9 and the implementation of a search and insertion algorithm for it as an exercise for the reader.

The tree representation of a table of keys is efficient when each node has relatively few sons. For example, in Fig. 9.2.9 only one node has as many as six (out of a possible ten) sons, while most nodes have only one, two, or three sons. Thus the process of searching through the list of sons to match the next symbol in the key is relatively efficient. However, if the set of keys is ***dense*** within the set of all possible keys (that is, if almost any possible combination of symbols actually appears as a key), then most nodes will have a large number of sons and the cost of the search process becomes prohibitive. For example, if the files of the Internal Revenue Service were keyed by social security number, the cost of a digital tree search would be prohibitive.

Tries

A modification of the digital tree proves to be quite efficient when the set of keys in the table is dense. Instead of storing the table as a tree, the table is stored as a two-dimensional array. Each row of the array represents one of the possible symbols which may appear in the key, and each column represents a node in a digital tree. Each entry in the array is a pointer to either another column in the array or to a key and its record. In searching for a key *key*, *key*(1) is used to index the first column of the array. The entry which is found at row *key*(1) and column 1 is either a pointer to a key and record, in which case there is only one key in the table which begins with the symbol *key*(1), or it is a pointer to another column of the array, say column *j*. Column *j* represents all keys in the table which begin with *key*(1). *key*(2) is used to index column *j* to determine either the only key in the table beginning with *key*(1) and *key*(2) or the column representing all keys in the table beginning with those two symbols. Similarly, each column in the array represents the set of all keys which begin with the same initial symbols. Such an array is called a ***trie*** (from the word re*trie*val).

Figure 9.2.10 illustrates a trie containing the keys of Figs. 9.2.8 and 9.2.9. A pointer to a key and its corresponding record is indicated by an unparenthesized number which is the actual key, while a pointer to a column is indicated by a parenthesized number. In an actual implementation, an extra bit would be required to differentiate between these two types of pointers.

For example, suppose a search is to be made for a record whose key is 274, in the trie of Fig. 9.2.10. In this case, *k*(1)=2, *k*(2)=7, and *k*(3)=4. *k*(1) is used to index column 1. Row 2 of column 1 points to column 4; thus column 4 represents all keys whose first character is 2. *k*(2) is then used to index column 4. Row 7 of column 4 points to column 9; thus column 9 represents all keys whose first two characters are 2 and 7 respectively. *k*(3) is then used to index column 9 in which row 4 contains the key 274. At this point the search is successful. Actually, since the array which forms the trie is dynamic (columns must be added as new records are inserted), a trie is best implemented as a gen-

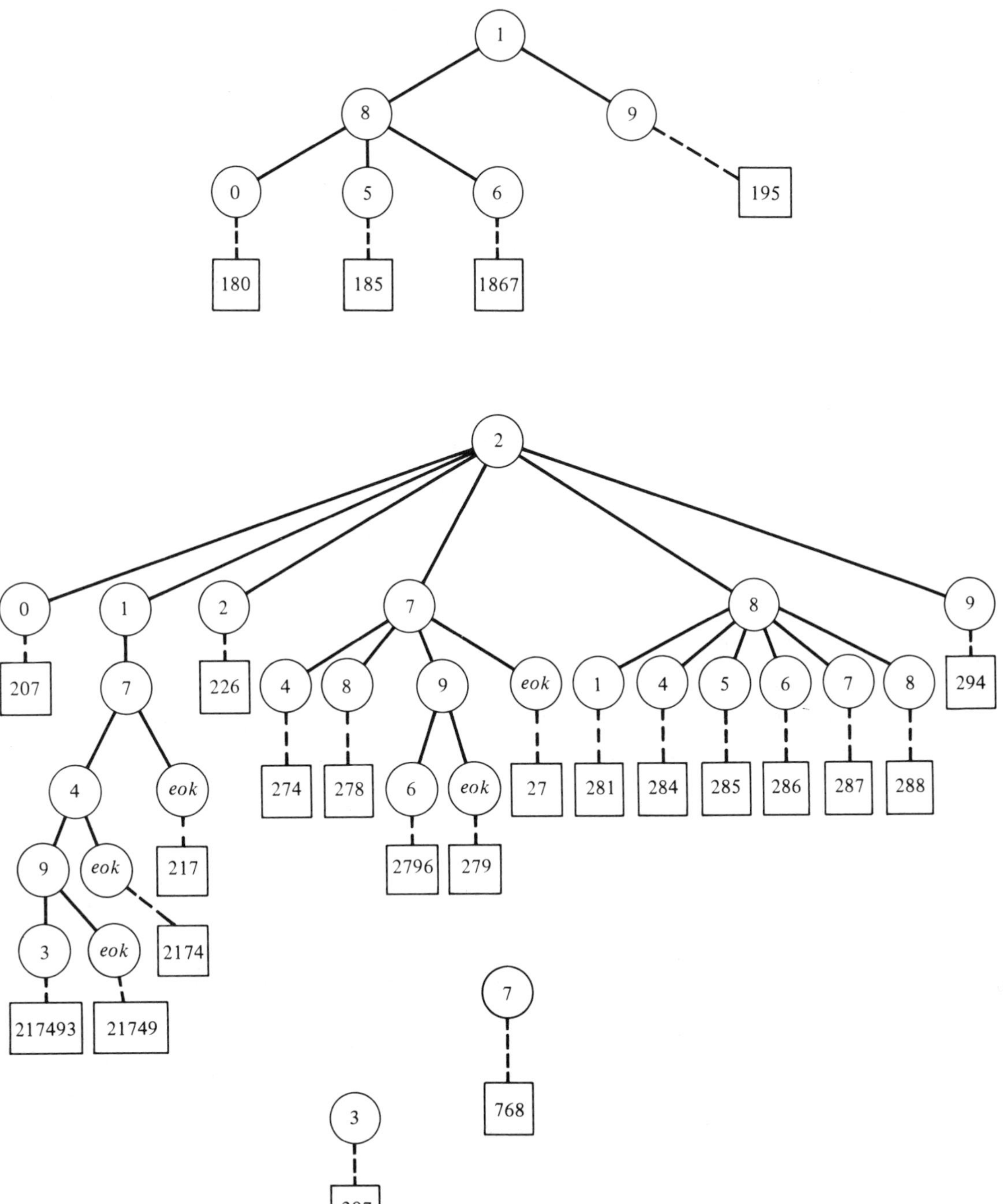

Figure 9.2.9. A condensed forest representing a table of keys.

	1	2	3	4	5	6	7	8	9	10	11	12	13	14
0			180	207										
1	(2)			(5)							281			
2	(4)			226										
3	307							217493						
4						(7)			274		284			
5			185								285			
6			1867							2796	286			
7	768			(9)	(6)						287			
8		(3)		(11)					278		288			
9		195		294			(8)		(10)					
eok						217	2174	21749	27	279				

Figure 9.2.10. A trie.

eral tree in which each node has a fixed number of sons. Each node of the general tree represents a column of the trie.

You will note that the trie of Fig. 9.2.10 contains a large amount of unused space. This is because the set of keys in this example is not dense, so that there are many digits at many positions which do not appear in a key. If the set of keys is dense, then most of the entries in the trie will be filled. The reason that a trie is so efficient is that for each symbol of the key only a single table lookup need be performed, rather than a list traversal.

9.3. Hashing

In the preceding two sections, we assumed that the record being sought was stored in a table and that it was necessary to pass through some number of keys before finding the desired one. The organization of the file (sequential, indexed sequential, binary tree, etc.) and the order in which the keys are inserted determine the number of keys that must be inspected before obtaining the desired one. Obviously, the efficient search techniques are those which minimize the number of these comparisons. Optimally, we would like to have a table organization in which there are no unnecessary comparisons. Let us see if such a table organization is feasible.

If a system is to be set up in which each key can be retrieved in a single access, then the location of the record within the table can depend only upon the key; it may not depend upon the locations of other keys as in a tree. The most efficient way to organize such a table is as an array; i.e., each record is stored at a specific offset from the base address of the table. If the record keys are integers, then the keys themselves can be used as indices to the array.

Let us consider an example of such a system. Suppose a manufacturing company has an inventory file consisting of 100 parts, each part having a unique two-digit part number. Then the obvious way to store this file is to declare an array:

```
DCL 1 PART(0:99),
      2 /*  record information associated with part  */
```

where PART(I) represents the record whose part number is I. In this situation, the part numbers are keys which are used as indices to the array. Even if the company stocks fewer than 100 parts, the same structure can be used to maintain the inventory file (providing the keys are two digits). While many locations in PART correspond to nonexistent keys, this waste is compensated by the advantage of direct access to each of the existent parts.

Unfortunately, however, such a system is not always practical. For example, suppose the company has an inventory file of more than 100 items and the key to each record is a seven-digit part number. To use direct indexing using the entire seven-digit key, an array of 100 million elements would be required. This clearly wastes an unacceptably large amount of space since it is extremely unlikely that a company stocks more than a few thousand parts.

What is necessary is some method of converting a key into an integer within a limited range. Ideally, no two keys should be converted into the same integer. Unfortunately, such an ideal method usually does not exist. Let us attempt to develop methods which come close to the ideal and determine what action to take when the ideal is not achieved.

Let us reconsider the example of a company with an inventory file in which each record is keyed by a seven-digit part number. Suppose the company has less than a thousand parts and that there is only a single record for each part. Then an array of 1000 elements is sufficient to contain the entire file. The array is indexed by an integer between 0 and 999 inclusive. The last three digits of the part number are used as the index for that part's record in the array. This is illustrated in Fig. 9.3.1. Note that two keys which are relatively close to each other numerically such as 4618396 and 4618996 may be further from each other in the table than two keys which are widely separated numerically such as 0000991 and 9846995. This is because only the last three digits of the key are used in determining the position of a record.

A function which transforms a key into a table index is called a ***hash function***. If h is a hash function and *key* is a key, then $h(key)$ is called the ***hash*** of *key* and is the index at which a record with key *key* should be placed. The hash function in the above example is $h(key) = mod(key,1000)$. The values which h produces should cover the entire set of indices in the table. For example, the function $mod(x,1000)$ can produce any integer between 0 and 999, depending upon the value of x. As we shall shortly see, it is a good idea for the table size to be somewhat larger than the number of records which are to be inserted. This is illustrated in Fig. 9.3.1, where several positions in the table are unused.

The above method has one flaw. Suppose two keys $k1$ and $k2$ are such that $h(k1)=h(k2)$. Then when a record with key $k1$ is entered into the table, it is inserted at position $h(k1)$. But when $k2$ is hashed, the position obtained is the same as where the record with key $k1$ is stored. Clearly, two records cannot occupy the same position.

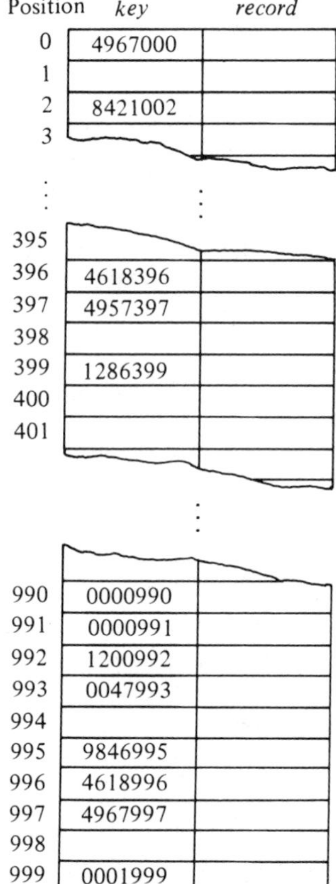

Figure 9.3.1. Part records stored in an array.

Such a situation is called a ***hash collision*** or a ***hash clash***. A hash clash occurs in the inventory example of Fig. 9.3.1 if a record with key 0596397 is added to the table. We will explore shortly how to resolve such a situation. However, it should be noted that a good hash function is one which minimizes collisions and spreads the records uniformly throughout the table. That is why it is desirable to have the array size larger than the number of actual records. The larger the range of the hash function, the less likely it is that two keys will yield the same hash value. Of course, this involves a space/time tradeoff. Leaving empty spaces in the array is inefficient in terms of space; but it reduces the necessity of resolving hash clashes and is therefore more efficient in terms of time.

Resolving Hash Clashes by Open Addressing

Let us consider what would happen if it was desired to enter a new part number 0596397 into the table of Fig. 9.3.1. Using the hash function *mod*(*key*,1000), we find that *h*(0596397)=397 and that the record for that part belongs in position 397 of the array. However, position 397 is already occupied since the record with key 4957397 is in that position. Therefore, the record with key 0596397 must be inserted elsewhere in the table.

The simplest method of resolving hash clashes is to place the record in the next available position in the array. In Fig. 9.3.1, for example, since position 397 is already occupied, the record with key 0596397 is placed in location 398, which is still open. Once that record has been inserted, another record which hashes to either 397 (such as 8764397) or 398 (such as 2194398) is inserted at the next available position, which is 400.

This technique is called ***linear probing*** and is an example of a general method for resolving hash clashes called ***rehashing*** or ***open addressing***. In general, a ***rehash function***, *rh*, accepts one array index and produces another. If array location *h*(*key*) is already occupied by a record with a different key, *rh* is applied to the value of *h*(*key*) to find another location where the record may be placed. If position *rh*(*h*(*key*)) is also occupied, then it too is rehashed to see if *rh*(*rh*(*h*(*key*))) is available. This process continues until an empty location is found. Thus, we may write a search and insertion algorithm using hashing as follows. We assume an array of size *m* indexed from 0 to $m-1$; a hash function *h* which accepts a key and returns an integer between 0 and $m-1$; and a rehash function *rh* which accepts an integer between 0 and $m-1$ and returns another integer in that range. The special value *nullkey* is used to indicate an empty record.

```
i=h(key);          /*   hash the key    */
do while(k(i)¬=key & k(i)¬=nullkey);
   /*   we must rehash    */
   i=rh(i);
end;
if k(i)=nullkey then      /*   insert record at empty position    */
                          do;
                               k(i)=key;
                               r(i)=rec;
                          end;
return(i);
```

In the example of Fig. 9.3.1, *h*(*key*) is the function *mod*(*key*,1000) and *rh*(*index*) is the function *mod*(*index*+1,1000) (i.e., the rehash of any index is the next sequential position in the array, except that the rehash of 999 is 0).

Let us examine the algorithm a bit more closely to see if we can determine the properties of a "good" rehash function. In particular, we focus our attention on the loop since the number of iterations determines the efficiency of the search. The loop can be exited in one of two ways: either *i* is set to a value such that *k*(*i*) equals *key* (in which case the record is found), or *i* is set to a value such that *k*(*i*) equals *nullkey* (in which case an empty position is found and the record may be inserted).

It may happen, however, that the loop may execute forever. There are two possible reasons for this. First, the table may be full so that it is impossible to insert any new records. This situation can be detected by keeping a count of the number of records in the table. When the count is equal to the table size, then no additional insertions are attempted.

However, it is possible for the algorithm to loop infinitely even if there are some (or even many) empty positions. Suppose, for example, that the function *rh*(*index*)=*mod*(*index*+2,1000) is used as a rehash function. Then any key which hashes into an odd integer rehashes into successive odd integers, and any key which hashes into an even integer rehashes into successive even integers. Consider the situation in which all odd positions of the table are occupied and all the even ones are empty. Despite the fact that half the positions of the array are empty, it is impossible to insert a new record whose key hashes into an odd integer. Of course, it is unlikely that all the odd positions are occupied while none of the even positions are. However, if the rehash function *rh*(*index*)=*mod*(*index*+200,1000) is used, each key can be placed in only one of five places (since *mod*(x,1000) = *mod*(x+1000,1000)) and it is quite possible for these five places to be full while much of the table is empty.

One property of a good rehash function is that for any index i, the successive rehashes *rh*(i), *rh*(*rh*(i)), . . . cover as many of the integers between 0 and $m-1$ as possible (ideally, all of them). The rehash function *rh*(i)=*mod*(i+1,1000) has this property. In fact, any function *rh*(i)=*mod*(i+c,m) where m is the size of the table and c is a constant value such that c and m are relatively prime (that is, they cannot both be divided evenly by a single integer other than 1) produce successive values which cover the entire table. You are invited to confirm this fact by choosing some examples; the proof is left as an exercise.

There is another measure of the suitability of a rehash function. Consider the case of the linear rehash. Assuming that the hash function produces indices which are uniformly distributed over the interval 0 through $m-1$ (that is, it is equally likely that *h*(*key*) is any particular integer in that range), then initially when the entire array is empty it is equally likely that a random record will be placed at any given empty position within the array. However, once entries have been inserted and several hash clashes have been resolved, this is no longer true. For example, in Fig. 9.3.1 it is five times as likely for a record to be inserted at position 994 than at position 401. This is because any record whose key hashes into 990, 991, 992, 993, or 994 will be placed in 994, while only a record whose key hashes into 401 can be placed in that location. This phenomenon, where two keys which hash into different values compete with each other in successive rehashes, is called ***clustering***.

The same phenomenon occurs in the case of the rehash function *rh*(i)=*mod*(i+c,m). For example, if m=1000, c=21 and positions 10, 31, 52, 73, and 94 are all occupied, any record whose key is any one of these five integers will be placed at location 115. In fact, any rehash function which depends solely upon the index causes clustering.

One way to eliminate clustering is to use ***double hashing***, which involves the use of two functions, *h1*(*key*) and *h2*(*key*). *h1*, which is known as the ***primary*** hash function, is first used to determine the position at which the record should be placed. If that position is occupied, the rehash function *rh*(*index*)=*mod*(*index*+*h2*(*key*),*m*) is used successively until an empty location is found. As long as *h2*(*key1*) does not equal *h2*(*key2*), records with keys *key1* and *key2* do not compete for the same set of locations. This is true despite the possibility that *h1*(*key1*) may indeed equal *h1*(*key2*). The rehash function depends not only on the index to be rehashed but also on the original key. Note that the value *h2*(*key*) does not have to be recomputed for each rehash–it need be computed only once for each key which must be rehashed. Optimally, therefore, one should choose functions *h1* and *h2* which distribute the hashes and rehashes uniformly over the interval 0 to $m-1$ and also minimize clustering. Such functions are not always easy to find.

Another approach is to allow the rehash function to depend on the number of times that the function is applied to a particular hash value. In this approach, the function *rh* is a function of two arguments. *rh(index,i)* yields the rehash of the integer *index* if the key is being rehashed for the *i*th time. One example is *rh(index,i)=mod(index+i,m)*. The first rehash yields *rh1=rh(h(key),1)=mod(h(key)+1,m)*, the second yields *rh2=mod(rh1+2,m)*, the third yields *rh3=mod(rh2+3,m)*, etc. Other rehash functions are presented in the Exercise Manual.

Resolving Hash Clashes by Chaining

There are several reasons why open addressing may not be an adequate method to deal with hash clashes. First, it assumes a fixed table size m. If the number of records grows beyond m, it is impossible to insert them without allocating a larger table and recomputing the hash values of the keys of all records already in the table using a new hash function. Furthermore, it is difficult to delete a record from such a table. For example, suppose record *r1* is at position *p*. To add a record *r2* whose key *k2* hashes into *p*, it must be inserted into the first free position from among *rh(p)*, *rh(rh(p))*, ... Suppose *r1* is then deleted, so position *p* becomes empty. A subsequent search for record *r2* begins at position *h(k2)*, which is *p*. But since that position is now empty, the search process erroneously concludes that record *r2* is absent from the table.

One possible solution to this latter problem is to mark a deleted record as "deleted" rather than "empty" and to continue searching whenever a "deleted" position is encountered in the course of a search. But this is viable only if there are a small number of deletions; otherwise an unsuccessful search would require a search through the entire table because most positions will be marked "deleted" rather than "empty."

Another method of resolving hash clashes is called ***chaining*** and involves keeping a linked list of all records whose keys hash into the same value. Suppose the hash function produces values between 0 and $m-1$. Then an array of header nodes of size m, called ***buckets***, is declared. *bucket(i)* points to the list of all records whose keys hash into i. In searching for a record, the list head which occupies position i in the *bucket* array is accessed and the list which it initiates is traversed. If the record is not found, then it is inserted at the end of the list. Figure 9.3.2 illustrates chaining. We assume a ten-element array and that the hash function is *mod(key,10)*. The keys in that figure are presented in the order:

75,66,42,192,91,40,49,87,67,16,417,130,372,227

We may write a search and insertion algorithm using chaining using a hash function h, a bucket array *bucket*, and nodes which contain three fields: k for the key, r for the record, and *next* as a pointer to the next node in the list.

```
i=hash(key);
q=null;
p=bucket(i);
do while(p ¬= null);
   if k(p)=key then return(p);
   q=p;
   p=next(p);
end;

   /*   the key has not been found, insert a new record   */
s=getnode;
k(s)=key;
r(s)=rec;
next(s)=null;
if q=null  then bucket(i)=s;
           else next(q)=s;
return(s);
```

Deleting a node from a table which is constructed by hashing and chaining involves simply removing a node from a linked list. A deleted node has no effect on the efficiency of the search algorithm; the algorithm continues as though the node had never been inserted. Note that the lists may be reordered dynamically for more efficient searching by the methods of Section 9.1.

The primary disadvantage of chaining is the extra space which is required for buckets and pointers. However, the initial array is usually smaller in schemes which use chaining than in those which use rehashing. This is because under chaining it is less catastrophic if the entire array becomes full–it is always possible to allocate more nodes and add them to the various lists. Of course, if the buckets are almost all full and the lists become very long, the whole purpose of hashing–direct addressing and resultant search efficiency–is defeated.

Choosing a Hash Function

Let us now turn to the question of how to choose a good hash function. Clearly, the function should produce as few hash clashes as possible; that is, it should spread the keys uniformly over the possible array indices. Of course, unless the keys are known in advance, it cannot be determined whether a particular hash function will disperse them properly. However, although it is rare to know the keys before selecting a hash function, it is fairly common to know some properties of the keys which will affect their dispersal.

For example, the most common hash function (which we have used in the examples of this section) uses the ***division method***, in which an integer key is divided by the table size and the remainder is taken as the hash value. This is the hash function *h(key)=mod(key,m)*. Suppose, however, that *m* equals 1000 and that all the keys end in the same three digits (for example, the last three digits of a part number might represent a plant number, and the program is being written for that plant). Then the remainder on dividing by 1000 will yield the same value for all the keys so that a hash clash will occur

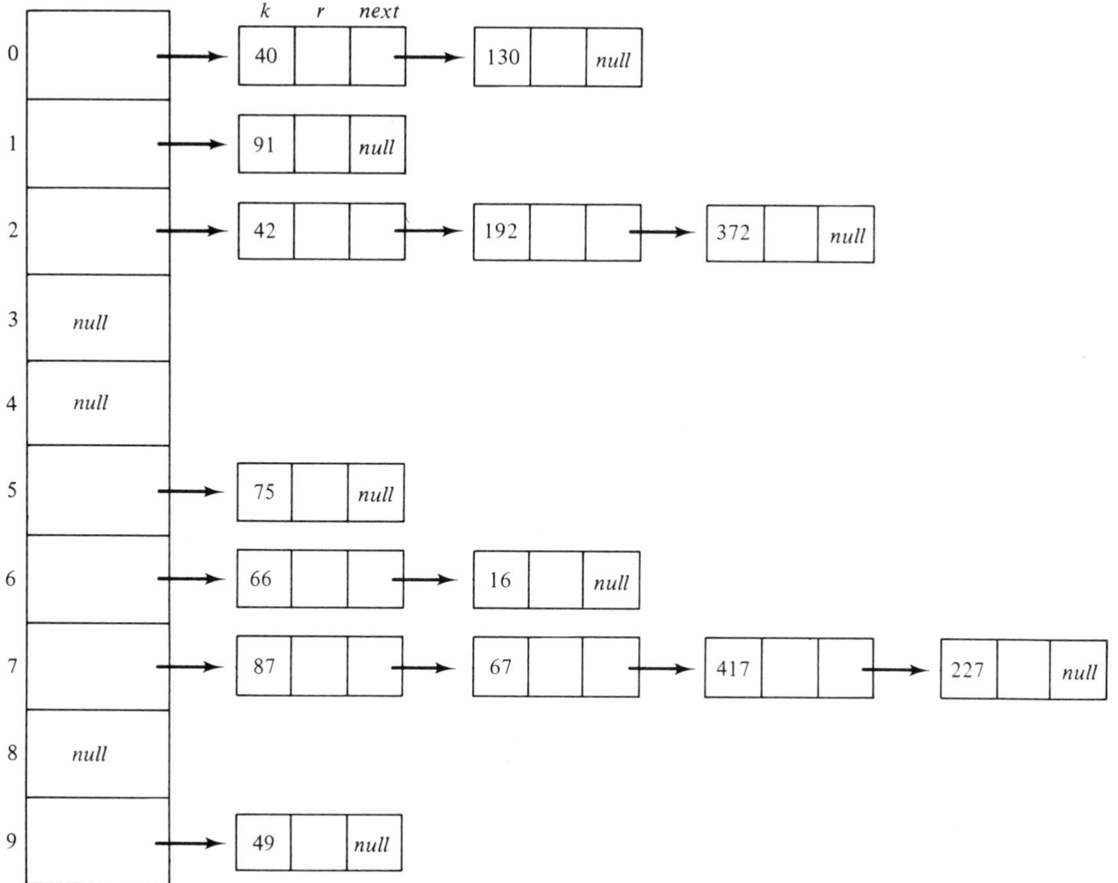

Figure 9.3.2. Resolving hash clashes by chaining.

for each record except the first. Clearly, given such a set of keys, a different hash function should be used.

It has been found that the best results with the division method are achieved when the table size m is prime (that is, m is not divisible by any positive integer other than 1 and m).

In another hash function, known as the ***mid-square method***, the key is multiplied by itself and the middle few digits (the exact number depends on the number of digits allowed in the index) of the square are used as the index. If the square is considered as a decimal number, then the table size must be a power of 10; if it is considered as a binary number, the table size must be a power of two. The ***folding method*** breaks up a key into several segments which are added or "exclusive or'ed" together to form a hash value. For example, suppose the bit string representation of a key is '010111001010110'B and five bits are allowed in the index. The three bit strings '01011'B, '10010'B, and '10110'B are exclusive or'ed to produce '01111'B, which is 15 as a binary integer. (The exclusive or of two bits is '1'B if the two bits are different, and '0'B if they are the same.)

There are many other hash functions, each with its own advantages and disadvantages, depending on the set of keys to be hashed. One consideration in choosing a hash function is efficiency of calculation; it does no good to be able to find an object on the first try if that try takes longer than several tries in an alternate method.

If the keys are not integers, they must be converted into integers before applying one of the above hash functions. There are several ways to do this. For example, for a character string the internal bit representation of each character can be interpreted as a binary number. One disadvantage of this is that the bit representations of all the letters or digits tend to be very similar on most computers. If the keys consist of letters alone, the index of each letter in the alphabet can be used to create an integer. Thus the first letter of the alphabet (A) is represented by the digits 01, while the fourteenth (N) is represented by the digits 14. The key 'HELLO' is represented by the integer 0805121215. Once an integer representation of a character string exists, the folding method can be used to reduce it to manageable size.

9.4. Examples and Applications

In this section, we reexamine several problems which were programmed in previous chapters to see how the search techniques of this chapter can be applied to make the solutions more efficient. We examine some tradeoffs in time and space among various solutions and show how searching plays an important role in problem solving.

Example 9.4.1: The Huffman Algorithm

Our first example is the Huffman algorithm of Section 7.3.1. The reader is asked to reread that section to refamiliarize himself with the problem and the solution presented therein.

We focus our attention on the program FINDCODE, especially on the loop labeled SEARCH. The nodes of a strictly binary tree with N leafs are represented by the integers between 1 and 2*N–1. The array FATHER of size 2*N–1 contains pointers to the fathers of the nodes in the tree, and the array FREQ of size 2*N–1 contains the information associated with each node.

We begin with FREQ(I) defined for I between 1 and N and with FATHER(I) equal to 0 for all I. That is, we are given frequencies for the original symbols each of which is a root of its own single-element binary tree. These nodes are to be combined into a single binary tree. The unoccupied nodes (from N+1 through 2*N–1) are thought of as an available list of nodes. The algorithm proceeds through this available list in sequence, setting each node as the father of two previously allocated nodes.

In choosing two previously allocated nodes to set as the sons of a newly allocated node, the algorithm searches for the two nodes without fathers with the smallest FREQ value. We now reproduce the section of code which accomplishes this. I is the index of the newly allocated node and MAXFREQ is a number bigger than the FREQ value of any allocated node. N1 and N2 point to the two nodes which are found by the search process.

```
N1,N2=0;
SMALL1,SMALL2=MAXFREQ;
```

```
SEARCH:  DO J=1 TO I-1;    /*   search through allocated nodes     */
              IF FATHER(J)=0 THEN    /*   node J has no father     */
                 IF FREQ(J) < SMALL1 THEN DO;
                                 SMALL2=SMALL1;
                                 SMALL1=FREQ(J);
                                 N2=N1;
                                 N1=J;
                                                  END;
                 ELSE IF FREQ(J)<SMALL2 THEN DO;
                                 SMALL2=FREQ(J);
                                 N2=J;
                                                        END;
         END SEARCH;
```

Once the two nodes N1 and N2 are identified, they are set as the sons of node I by the code

```
FATHER(N1)=-I;  /*   left son of I is N1    */
FATHER(N2)=I;   /*   right son of I is N2   */
FREQ(I)=FREQ(N1)+FREQ(N2);  /*   compute FREQ of the new node     */
```

This search process is inefficient because each time a new node is allocated, all the previous nodes must be examined in searching for the two root nodes with the smallest frequency.

The first improvement that can be made is to keep a separate list of root nodes (that is, nodes I such that FATHER(I)=0). If this is done, we need not search through all allocated nodes—only through those which have no father. Also, the test for whether FATHER(I) equals 0 can be eliminated from the loop. These benefits are not without disadvantages: extra space is required for the pointers which link together the list of root nodes, and extra time is required to add or delete an element from this list. These are the general disadvantages that must be faced in moving from an array to a list representation: in an array elements are ordered implicitly, while in a list they must be linked explicitly. In this case it is possible to use the FATHER field of all root nodes to link together the list. In the interest of clarity, we do not pursue this possibility here but leave it as an exercise for the reader.

Instead, we add an array NEXTROOT and a local variable FIRSTROOT declared by

```
DCL    FIRSTROOT          FIXED,
       NEXTROOT(2*N-1)    FIXED;
```

NEXTROOT(I) is undefined if I is not a root node. If I is a root node, then NEXTROOT(I) is the next root node after I on the list of root nodes. If I is the last root node on the list, then NEXTROOT(I) equals 0. FIRSTROOT is the index of the first root node on the list. These variables are initialized as follows:

```
FIRSTROOT=1;
DO I=1 TO N-1;
   NEXTROOT(I)=I+1;
END;
NEXTROOT(N)=0;
```

The search may then be rewritten as follows. K remains one step behind J in traversing the list of root nodes. K1 and K2 are set to the nodes immediately preceding N1 and N2 respectively on the list of root nodes.

```
         N1,N2,K1,K2,K=0;
         SMALL1,SMALL2=MAXFREQ;
         J=FIRSTROOT;
SEARCH:  DO WHILE(J¬=0);   /*  traverse the list of root nodes   */
            IF FREQ(J)<SMALL1 THEN DO;
                                  SMALL2=SMALL1;
                                  SMALL1=FREQ(J);
                                  N2=N1;
                                  N1=J;
                                  K2=K1;
                                  K1=K;
                                       END;
            ELSE IF FREQ(J)<SMALL2 THEN DO;
                                  SMALL2=FREQ(J);
                                  N2=J;
                                  K2=K;
                                            END;
            K=J;
            J=NEXTROOT(J);
         END SEARCH;
```

The code to remove nodes N1 and N2 from the list of root nodes, insert them into the binary tree, and insert the new root node I into the list of root nodes becomes more complex. The following code performs these tasks, inserting I in place of N2 and removing N1 from the list entirely.

```
/*  insert I into the binary tree   */
FATHER(N1)=-I;
FATHER(N2)=I;
FREQ(I)=FREQ(N1) + FREQ(N2);

/*  replace N2 in the list of root nodes by I   */
NEXTROOT(I)=NEXTROOT(N2);
IF K2=0  THEN FIRSTROOT=I;
         ELSE NEXTROOT(K2)=I;
IF NEXTROOT(I)=N1 THEN K1=I;
```

```
/*   remove N1 from the list of root nodes    */
IF K1=0  THEN FIRSTROOT=NEXTROOT(N1);
         ELSE NEXTROOT(K1)=NEXTROOT(N1);
```

This code can be simplified somewhat and made more efficient if the list of root nodes is maintained as a circular list. We leave this implementation as an exercise for the reader.

Further efficiency will be realized if the list of root nodes is kept sorted, ordered by increasing values of the FREQ field. Then the search for the two nodes of smallest frequency is eliminated—they are the first two nodes on the list. Thus the entire SEARCH loop can be replaced by the two statements

```
N1=FIRSTROOT;
N2=NEXTROOT(N1);
```

However, in order to keep the list sorted, the N original symbols must first be sorted using one of the sorting techniques of Chapter 8. Also each time a new node I is inserted into the list of root nodes, it must be inserted into its proper position. The code to insert I into the binary tree and the root node list therefore becomes:

```
          /*   insert I into the binary tree    */
          FATHER(N1)=–I;
          FATHER(N2)=I;
          FRQ,FREQ(I)=FREQ(N1)+FREQ(N2);

          /*   remove N1 and N2 from the root node list and     */
          /*                 insert I into that list            */
          FIRSTROOT=NEXTROOT(N2);
          K=0;
          J=FIRSTROOT;
SEARCH:   DO WHILE(J>0);
              IF FREQ(J)>=FRQ THEN GO TO OUT;
              K=J;
              J=NEXTROOT(J);
          END SEARCH;

OUT:      IF K=0  THEN FIRSTROOT=I;
                  ELSE NEXTROOT(K)=I;
          NEXTROOT(I)=J;
```

Thus the search process has been moved from the first step (finding the two nodes with lowest frequency) to the second (inserting a new node into its proper place). However, in the second step it is not necessary to search through the entire list of root nodes, but rather only until the proper position for the new node is found. Whether or not this is appreciably faster depends on the initial distribution of frequencies. For example, if the initial frequencies are successive integers starting at N, then the first root node allocated will have to be placed at the end of the list. In most cases, however, the search time is reduced by a factor of 2. (Why?)

This saving must be weighed against the cost of initially sorting the N original symbols which may be quite expensive. As N becomes larger and the saving in search time becomes more worthwhile, the cost of sorting increases. We leave to the reader to determine which method is more efficient for various values of N.

Example 9.4.2: A Scheduling Problem

Our next example of the application of search techniques is the scheduling problem of Section 7.6. Again, you should reread that section to refamiliarize yourself with the problem and the solutions which were presented therein.

The primary search problem of the scheduling algorithm is to search through the nodes of a graph represented by a linked data structure. This search takes place at two distinct points in the solution presented in Section 7.6: (We are now focusing our attention on the first solution presented in Section 7.6 in which a singly linked list is used for the graph nodes. This solution is presented in that section as the PL/I program named SCHEDULE.)

1. When a precedence relationship is read from a data card indicating that task INF1 must be performed before task INF2, an arc must be drawn from INF1 to INF2. All the nodes in the graph must be searched for nodes with contents INF1 and INF2 respectively. If no nodes with contents INF1 or INF2 exist, they must be allocated and added to the list of graph nodes. This search and insertion is performed by the function FIND which is called twice from within the loop labeled INPUT. (Actually an immediate saving in efficiency would result if the list of graph nodes were traversed only once for each input card to search for both INF1 and INF2 simultaneously.)

2. In the output phase of the program (the loop labeled TRAVGRAPH), the entire list of graph nodes must be searched during each time period to find those nodes whose COUNT field is 0. These nodes are removed from the graph and placed on another list from which they are subsequently printed. As noted in Section 7.6, the only reason that this search is necessary is because a node cannot be removed from a singly linked list without a pointer to its predecessor. This prevents us from placing a node on the output list at the time that its count is reduced to 0, because at that time we have only a pointer to the node itself and not to its predecessor. One way to eliminate this search, as noted in Section 7.6, is to keep the list of graph nodes as a doubly linked list so that a node contains a pointer to its predecessor as well as to its successor.

A careful analysis of the program SCHEDULE yields the interesting observation that there is no reason whatever to keep the graph nodes in a list except to perform the above two searches. The list of graph nodes is never traversed for any reason other than to search for particular nodes at one of the above two points. But since searching an unordered linear list is very inefficient, another way of organizing the graph nodes should improve the search efficiency significantly with no adverse effect to the remainder of the program.

What data structure shall we use to represent the graph nodes? In adding new nodes to the graph (point 1 above), it must be possible to access a graph node from the character string which names the task which it represents. Thus the INFO portion of the graph node acts as the key to the record which is the node itself. The most direct way to access a node from its key is by using a hash function. If a hashing method is to be used, we must determine how we shall handle hash clashes. This consideration leads directly into the issue of the number of graph nodes which are to be allowed. If hash clashes are resolved by rehashing, then the number of graph nodes is limited to the number of positions in the hash table. On the other hand, if collisions are resolved by chaining, then an unlimited number of graph nodes is permitted.

Since the array implementation was used in Section 7.6, we will adhere to that implementation and use rehashing to resolve collisions. Thus the set of graph nodes is declared by

```
DCL 1 GRAPHNODE(0:499),
      2 INFO CHAR(12) VAR INIT ((500)''),  /*      name of task       */
      2 COUNT          FIXED,              /* number of predecessors  */
      2 ARCPTR         FIXED,              /*  pointer to list of arcs */
      2 NEXTNODE       FIXED;              /*   used to link together */
                                           /*      the output list    */
```

Note that since the graph nodes are not linked together on a list, the pointer NEXTNODE in each graph node is not used until the node is placed in an output list.

We assume the existence of a hash function HASH which transforms a varying-length character string into an integer between 0 and 499 and a rehash function REHASH which accepts an integer in the same range. Then the function FIND can be written to search and insert a node into the graph as follows:

```
FIND:        PROC(INF)RETURNS(FIXED);
                DCL INF      CHAR(*) VAR,
                    (I,J)    FIXED;
                I=HASH(INF);
                IF INFO(I)='' THEN INFO(I)=INF;
                IF INFO(I)=INF THEN RETURN(I);
                J=REHASH(I);

TRYAGAIN:       DO WHILE(J¬=I);
                   IF INFO(J)='' THEN INFO(J)=INF;
                   IF INFO(J)=INF THEN RETURN(J);
                   J=REHASH(J);
                END TRYAGAIN;
                PUT SKIP(2) EDIT ('ERROR–',INF,
                  'CANNOT BE INSERTED INTO THE GRAPH') (A,X(1));
                STOP;
             END FIND;
```

By using the above FIND function, we can rewrite the loop labeled INPUT with very few changes from the way it appears in Section 7.6.

By representing a graph using a hash table, we have solved the first search problem. Let us see how we can solve the second. We first note that when a node is identified as a candidate for output (i.e., when its COUNT field becomes 0), it can be placed on the output list; however it is no longer necessary to remove it from the list of graph nodes since there is no list of graph nodes. Since the input phase and the output phase of the program are separate and no new nodes are added in the course of processing, it is unnecessary to delete any nodes from the hash table. (If it were necessary to delete nodes, chaining would be preferable to rehashing as the method for resolving hash clashes.) Thus our second problem, which was the necessity to traverse the entire set of graph nodes in order to remove a particular node, does not exist.

We may therefore write a revised version of the scheduling program as follows:

```
SCHEDULE:  PROC OPTIONS(MAIN);
             DCL 1  GRAPHNODE(0:499),
                      2 INFO          CHAR(20) VAR INIT((500)''),
                     (2 COUNT,
                      2 ARCPTR,
                      2 NEXTNODE)     FIXED,
                   1  ARC(500),
                     (2 NODEPTR,                  /*  to terminating node    */
                      2 NEXTARC)      FIXED,      /*  to next arc emanating  */
                                                  /*  from same graph node   */
                   AVAILARC           FIXED INIT(1),
                                  /*   available list of arcs   */
                   (INF1,INF2)        CHAR(20) VAR,
                   (P,Q,T,PERIOD,S,R,NEXTOUT,OUTPUT INIT(0)) FIXED;


INITAV:      DO I=1 TO 499;
                  NEXTARC(I)=I+1;
             END INITAV;
             NEXTARC(500)=0;
             COUNT=0;
             ON ENDFILE(SYSIN) GO TO STEP2;


             /*   construct the graph    */
INPUT:       DO WHILE ('1'B);
                  GET LIST(INF1,INF2);
                  P=FIND(INF1);
                  Q=FIND(INF2);
                  CALL JOIN(P,Q);
                  COUNT(Q)=COUNT(Q)+1;
             END INPUT;
```

```
STEP2:          /*    the graph has been constructed       */
                /*    traverse the hash table and place    */
                /*    all graph nodes with zero count      */
                /*           on the output list            */
INITOUT:        DO P=0 TO 499 BY 1;
                   IF INFO(P)¬='' THEN
                      IF COUNT(P)=0 THEN DO;
                                  NEXTNODE(P)=OUTPUT;
                                  OUTPUT=P;
                                       END;
                END INITOUT;

                /*   simulate the time periods   */
SIMTIME:        DO PERIOD=1 BY 1 WHILE (OUTPUT>0);
                   PUT SKIP(2)DATA (PERIOD);

                   /*   initialize output list for next period   */
                   NEXTOUT=0;
                   /*   traverse the output list   */
                   P=OUTPUT;
TRAVOUT:           DO WHILE(P>0);
                      PUT SKIP LIST (INFO(P));

                      /*   traverse arcs emanating from GRAPHNODE(P)   */
                      R=ARCPTR(P);
TRAVARC:              DO   WHILE(R>0);
                        S=NEXTARC(R);
                        /*   reduce count in terminating node   */
                        T=NODEPTR(R);
                        COUNT(T)=COUNT(T)-1;
                        IF COUNT(T)=0 THEN DO;
                          /*   place GRAPHNODE(T) on the   */
                          /*     next period's output list */
                          NEXTNODE(T)=NEXTOUT;
                          NEXTOUT=T;
                                          END;
                        CALL FREEARC(R);
                        R=S;
                      END TRAVARC;

                     /*   continue traversing the output list   */
                     P=NEXTNODE(P);
                   END TRAVOUT;

                   /*   reset output list for the next period   */
                   OUTPUT=NEXTOUT;
                END SIMTIME;
             END SCHEDULE;
```

Two points should be noted in passing. Because the list of graph nodes has been eliminated, it is no longer possible to test for cycles. Further, if chaining is used to resolve hash clashes, the list of all graph nodes whose contents hash into the same value must be linked together by their NEXTNODE pointer. Thus, we again have the problem of removing a graph node from a list before inserting it into the output list. This can be solved by using doubly linked lists as indicated in Section 7.6 or by adding another field to each node as in Exercise 3 of the Exercise Manual. An alternate method is to traverse the list of all nodes hashing to the same value from the initial hash bucket. This list should be relatively short and therefore would not involve the same overhead as a search through the entire list of graph nodes.

Example 9.4.3: An Airline Reservation System

Our next example is the application of search techniques to the airline reservation system of Section 6.3.1. Before we proceed with the example, a word of caution is necessary. Because a real-world reservation system must store huge quantities of information, the data is usually kept in an external file system. Thus such a system must be programmed using external search techniques which are not discussed in this text. Furthermore, a large portion of such a system consists of systems programs to handle remote terminals accessing the common data base. That type of programming is also beyond the scope of this text.

In this section we concern ourselves with the problem presented in Section 6.3.1. The reader is urged to review that section before proceeding. The program is to read two decks of cards: a control deck containing flight numbers and capacities and a deck of requests. A request may be one of three types: a reservation, a cancellation, or an inquiry. A reservation request specifies a passenger name and a flight number. The passenger is to be placed on the passenger list for that flight if there is room available; if not, he is placed at the rear of a waiting queue. A cancellation request also specifies a name and a flight number. The passenger is to be removed from the passenger list or the waiting list for the flight in question. An inquiry specifies a passenger name only. The program is to print out a list of all flights on which the passenger is either booked or waiting. Let us also assume that we wish to be able to print out the passenger list and the waiting list for a particular flight.

In the program of Section 6.3.1, each flight was represented as an array element containing pointers to two linked lists of passenger names, one representing the passenger list for that flight and the other representing the waiting list for that flight. Let us see what searches are required by this data organization to service our requests.

For a reservation request, a sequential search must be performed on the array of flights and then the name must be added to a passenger list or a waiting queue. The sequential array search (which is performed by the function FIND in Section 6.3.1) is inefficient, but not overly so if the number of flights is small. To improve the speed of the search, the flights could be stored in an array sorted by flight number, allowing the use of a binary search. The insertion into the appropriate list is a single operation which involves no searching. Thus the reservation operation can be said to be moderately efficient under the organization of Section 6.3.1.

For a cancellation request, a sequential search must be performed through the array of flights and then one or two sequential searches must be performed through the passenger list and the waiting list. These sequential searches are fairly inefficient.

An inquiry is the most inefficient operation under the organization of Section 6.3.1. A sequential search through every single passenger list and many waiting lists must be performed in searching for a particular name.

To print out the passenger list and waiting list for a particular flight, the array of flights must be searched sequentially and the two lists traversed. Thus any implementation of this operation is fairly efficient, since the list traversals are part of the problem specification.

We would like to develop data structures to improve the efficiency of a cancellation and an inquiry. To eliminate the sequential array search for a flight number, the table of flights may be kept as a binary search tree as described in Section 9.2. Whether or not the tree should be balanced depends upon the number of flights, the order in which they appear in the input, and the frequency with which searches are made for a particular flight. The question here is whether the efficiency of searching a balanced tree is worth the extra work involved in inserting elements into such a tree. If there are n flights, keeping them as a tree rather than as an array reduces the search time from $O(n)$ to $O(\log n)$. We leave the coding of the main program (which inserts the flights into the tree) and a function TREESEARCH(TREE, FLT) (which returns a pointer to the node which represents flight FLT in the tree pointed to by TREE) for the reader as exercises.

What information should each flight node contain? Surprisingly, the same information is needed as in Section 6.3.1, with the addition of left and right tree pointers. (If a balanced binary tree is used, a field containing the balance is also needed.) It is still necessary to have a passenger list emanating from each flight node so that the list may be traversed in constructing a passenger roster. However, since cancellations involve accessing a passenger node through the passenger name, the passenger list must be doubly linked to make it possible to delete a passenger node given only a pointer to that node. Similarly, it is necessary to have doubly linked waiting lists organized as queues so that the first passenger placed on a waiting list will be the first to get a seat in case of a cancellation. An indication of the capacity and current passenger count of each flight is also needed. In keeping with the program of Section 6.3.1, we use PL/I BASED storage in implementing our lists. Thus we may declare a flight node by

```
DCL 1 FLIGHT BASED(FLTPTR),
      2 FLTNO     CHAR(3),   /*       flight number          */
      2 CPCTY     FIXED,     /*          capacity            */
      2 COUNT     FIXED,     /*   number of passengers       */
      2 FLTHD     PTR,       /* pointer to passenger list    */
      2 WAITLIST,            /*        pointers to           */
        (3 FRONT,            /*       waiting queue          */
        3 REAR)   PTR,
     (2 RIGHT                /*       tree pointers          */
      2 LEFT)     PTR;
```

In order to make cancellations and inquiries more efficient, it must be possible to access a passenger node directly from the passenger name rather than by traversing a passenger list. In order to do this, the entire passenger list is kept as a hash table. Since it must be possible to remove passengers from a passenger list in case of a cancellation, and since it is not known how many passengers there will be, chaining is used to resolve hash clashes rather than rehashing.

Each passenger node contains the passenger name as well as three pointers: one to the next node on the same passenger list, one to the previous node on the same passenger list, and one to the next node which hashes into the same value. It is also necessary to keep an indication in the passenger node of which flight list a particular passenger is associated with and whether he is booked or waiting for that flight. This is necessary so that when making an inquiry of the flights that a particular passenger is on, the appropriate messages can be printed directly from the passenger node. Note that this information is unnecessary if a passenger node is accessed only through a flight node rather than directly through its hash. We may therefore declare a passenger node by

```
DCL 1 PASS_NODE     BASED(PASSPTR),
      2 NAME        CHAR(30), /*        passenger name            */
      2 FLTNUM      CHAR(3),  /*        flight number             */
      2 BOOKED      BIT(1),   /* '1'B if booked, '0'B if waiting  */
     (2 NEXTPASS,
      2 PREVPASS,             /*      for passenger lists         */
      2 NEXTHASH)   PTR,      /*      for hash clashes            */
```

Actually, there is much more information associated with each passenger, such as address, phone number, diet, etc., but we ignore these details here.

Our next decision is one which is crucial in many searching applications: choosing a key for our records. We use the passenger name as the key. Applying a hash function H to a passenger name yields an index of a bucket array. The entry at that index is a pointer to a list of passenger nodes (linked together by the NEXTHASH field), all of whose passenger names hashed into the same index. When a search is made for a specific passenger name on a specific flight (as in a cancellation), the passenger name is hashed and this list is traversed searching for the entry for that particular name. All reservations for a given passenger are on the same list. This means that there may be multiple records with the same key, which almost guarantees that hash clashes will occur. Thus the cancellation operation is somewhat inefficient since the chain must be searched sequentially. (The same inefficiency occurs when information is requested about a specific passenger on a specific flight.)

The solution to this inefficiency is to combine the passenger name field and the flight number as a single key. Then, when searching for a specific passenger on a specific flight, the combination can be hashed directly. However, in the present situation, such an extended key is impractical. In handling an inquiry for the list of all flights for a given passenger, it would be highly inefficient to combine the given passenger name with every possible flight number to produce a set of keys for hashing. Rather the passenger name alone is hashed to access a list of all the flights on which the name appears (this list might also contain extraneous nodes representing other passengers whose names happen to hash into the same value, but these nodes can be skipped). The number of flights on which an average passenger is booked is small enough so that in the case of a cancellation, it does not present an overhead significant enough to outweigh the alternative overhead in case of inquiry. This illustrates a general phenomenon in choosing a search key: placing more information in a key makes it easier to find a very specific item but more difficult to satisfy a general query.

Let us now examine the bucket table. The number of entries in this table should be slightly larger (about 10%) than the number of passenger names kept at any one time. This avoids long lists of names hashing into the same index and at the same time reduces storage requirements. The size of the table should also be a prime number since it has been found that taking a remainder upon division by a prime yields a good distribution of hash values. We arbitrarily assume approximately 900 passenger names (this is very small for a real system) and declare the bucket table by

```
DCL TABLE(0:1008)    PTR;
```

We now present two of the routines which satisfy service requests, leaving the main program and the other subroutines for the reader as exercises. The first routine, CANCEL, accepts a passenger name and a flight number and removes the passenger's reservation from that flight. We assume the global variables TREE, FLIGHT, PASS_NODE, and TABLE declared above, and the functions HASH and TREESEARCH described above. We also assume the existence of an auxiliary list manipulation routine DELETE(FPTR,P) which accepts two pointers, the first to a flight node and the second to a passenger node, and deletes the passenger node from either the passenger list or waiting queue (depending on the value of P->BOOKED) emanating from the flight node without freeing the node.

```
CANCEL:     PROC(NAM,FLT);
                DCL  (NAM,FLT)        CHAR(*),
                     (P,Q,R,FPTR)     PTR,
                     H                FIXED;

                FPTR=TREESEARCH(TREE,FLT);  /*  find the flight node   */
                IF FPTR=NULL THEN DO;        /*    no such flight      */
                          PUT SKIP LIST('ILLEGAL FLIGHT NUMBER');
                          RETURN;
                                    END;
                /*  hash the passenger name and search the hash list   */
                H=HASH(NAM);
                Q=NULL;
                P=TABLE(H)
TRAVHASH:       DO WHILE(P ¬= NULL);
                    IF (P->NAME=NAM) & (P->FLTNUM=FLT)
                                                    THEN GO TO FOUND;
                    Q=P;
                    P=P->NEXTHASH;
                END TRAVHASH;
                PUT SKIP LIST('NO SUCH PASSENGER FOR THAT FLIGHT');
                RETURN;
```

```
FOUND:      /*   at this point P points to the passenger node     */
            /*   remove P->PASS_NODE from the hash list            */
            IF Q=NULL THEN TABLE(H)=P-> NEXTHASH;
                     ELSE Q->NEXTHASH=P->NEXTHASH;
              /*   remove P->PASS_NODE from the passenger or waiting list    */
            CALL DELETE(FPTR,P);
            IF P->BOOKED THEN    /*   node was on the passenger list    */

PASSND:        DO;
                  PUT SKIP EDIT(NAM,'DELETED FROM FLIGHT', FLT)
                                                            (A,X(2));

                  Q=FPTR->FRONT;
                  IF Q¬=NULL THEN DO;

                     /*   remove first passenger from waiting queue     */

                     /*          and insert into passenger list         */
                     CALL DELETE(FPTR,Q);
                     Q->BOOKED='1'B;
                     R=FPTR->FLTHD;
                     FPTR->FLTHD=Q;
                     Q->PREVPASS=NULL;
                     Q->NEXTPASS=R;
                     IF R¬=NULL THEN R->PREVPASS=Q;
                     PUT SKIP EDIT(Q->NAME,
                                     'NOW BOOKED ON FLIGHT',FLT)
                                                            (A,X(2));
                                 END;

                          ELSE   /*   no one is waiting    */
                     FPTR->COUNT=FPTR->COUNT-1;
               END PASSND;

                     ELSE   /*   the node was on the waiting list    */
                  PUT SKIP EDIT(NAM,
                       'DELETED FROM WAITING LIST OF FLIGHT',FLT)
                       (A,X(2));
            FREE P->PASS_NODE;
            RETURN;
         END CANCEL;
```

The next routine we present is for an inquiry. We wish to list all flights on which a given passenger name appears. It is straightforward.

```
INQUIRE;     PROC(NAM);
                DCL NAM      CHAR(*),
                    P        PTR,
                    H        FIXED;
                PUT SKIP EDIT(NAM, 'FOUND ON FOLLOWING FLIGHTS:')
                                                          (A,X(2));
                H=HASH(NAM);
                P=TABLE(H);

TRAVERSE:       DO WHILE (P¬=NULL);
                   IF NAM=P->NAME THEN
                      IF P->BOOKED THEN
                         PUT SKIP EDIT('BOOKED ON',P->FLTNUM) (A,X(2));
                                  ELSE
                         PUT SKIP EDIT ('WAITING FOR', P->FLTNUM)
                                                          (A,X(2));
                   P=P->NEXTHASH;
                END TRAVERSE;
                PUT SKIP LIST('END OF LIST');
                RETURN;
             END INQUIRE;
```

Bibliography and References

The most extensive material on searching may be found in (Knuth, 1973B). A good discussion of much of the material in this chapter is contained in (Reingold, Nievergelt, and Deo, 1977) which has an excellent bibliography. Most texts on data structures or algorithms contain material on searching.

Dynamic reordering of sequential lists is discussed in (Bitner, 1976), (McCabe, 1965), and (Rivest, 1976). An algorithm for constructing optimum binary search trees is discussed in (Knuth, 1973B). Balanced binary trees were introduced in (Adelson-Velskii and Landis, 1962) and are discussed in (Knuth, 1973B) and (Reingold, Nievergelt, and Deo, 1977). The use of general trees for searching is described in (Knuth, 1973B).

Hashing is discussed in (Knuth, 1973B), (Reingold, Nievergelt, and Deo, 1977), and (Tremblay and Sorenson, 1976). A catalog of hash functions may be found in (Knott, 1975). The terms "rehash function" and "bucket" are used differently by different authors, and no standard terminology has yet evolved. The reader should be aware of this in examining other sources.

chapter **10**

storage management

A programming language which incorporates a large number of data structures must contain some mechanism for managing those structures, and in particular for controlling how storage is assigned to those structures. The previous chapters of this book illustrated some of those management techniques. As data structures become more complex and provide greater capabilities to the user, the management techniques grow in complexity as well. In this chapter, we look at several techniques for implementing dynamic allocation and freeing of storage. Most of these techniques are used by operating systems to grant or deny a program request. Others are used by a particular language processor directly. We begin by expanding the concept of a list.

10.1. General Lists

In Chapters 5 and 6, we examined linked lists. Each node of a simple linked list contains two fields: *info* and *next*. The *info* field represents the "contents" of that particular node, while the *next* field is used to connect that node to the remainder of the list. If all the elements of a list are of the same data type (e.g., FIXED), then the nodes of the list may be declared so that the *info* fields directly contain the list elements. For example, nodes on a list of integers may be declared by

```
DCL 1 NODE BASED(P),
      2 INFO          FIXED,
      2 NEXT          PTR;
```

However, it is sometimes necessary for a list to contain nonhomogeneous elements. This problem arose in connection with trees in Sections 7.2 and 7.4. For example, a list might contain both integers and character strings. In such a case, the same type of node cannot be used to hold every element on the list.

A solution to this problem is to allow the *info* field to be a pointer so that a list node contains two pointer fields: *infptr* and *nextptr*. A list node also includes a type indicator *type* which indicates whether the item to which *infptr* points is an integer (*type*='I') or a character string (*type*='C'). Such a type indicator is called a ***typecode***. It is also necessary to declare two other types of nodes: *cnode* and *inode*. These nodes contain character strings and integers respectively and are called ***atomic nodes***. The character strings and integers which they contain are called ***atoms***. (However, the terms "atom" and "atomic node" are often used interchangeably.) Atomic nodes are not directly contained in a list. Rather, they are pointed to by the *infptr* field of a list node, indicating that their contents are elements of a list.

Under this scheme, a list containing integers and character strings may be illustrated as in Fig. 10.1.1. The various nodes are declared in PL/I by

```
DCL INODE          FIXED BASED(IPTR),
    CNODE          CHAR(100) VAR BASED(CPTR),
    1 NODE         BASED(NDPTR),
      2 TYPE       CHAR(1),
     (2 INFPTR,
      2 NEXTPTR)   PTR;
```

(However, some PL/I compilers do not allow a varying-length character string variable to have the BASED attribute. If this is true for the compiler you are using, CNODE may be declared by

```
DCL CNODE          CHAR(100) BASED(CPTR);
```

Unfortunately, this may result in a large amount of wasted space and may yield different results in some character string manipulation operations. It is the programmer's responsibility to make sure that such results are correct.)

An atom is now referenced indirectly through a pointer. Thus a pointer to an atomic node containing an integer represents the integer, and a pointer to an atomic node containing a character string represents the string.

The *infptr* field of a list node may point to any type of data structure. In particular, it may point to a list node instead of an atom. In such a case, a list is itself a member of another list.

For example, consider the list *LIST2* of Fig. 10.1.2(a). This list contains four elements. Two of these are integers (the first element is the integer 5, the third element is the integer 2), and the other two are lists. The list which is the second element of *LIST2* contains five elements, four of which are integers (the first, second, fourth, and fifth elements) and one of which (the third element) is a list containing the integers 14, 9, and 3. The fourth element of *LIST2* is a list of the three integers 6, 3, and 10. The value of the *type* field for a list is 'L'.

The null list (the list with no elements) may also be a member of a list. This situation is represented by a null pointer in the *infptr* field of a list node. For example, in Fig. 10.1.2(b) the fourth element of *LIST3* as well as the second element of the list that is the second element of *LIST3*, are both null.

There is a convenient notation for specifying such general lists. A list may be denoted by a parenthesized listing of its elements separated by commas. For example, the list of Fig. 10.1.1 may be denoted by

LIST1=(5,12, 'STRING', 147, 'ANOTHER ONE').

The list of Fig. 10.1.2(a) may be denoted by

LIST2=(5,(3,2,(14,9,3),5,4),2,(6,3,10)).

The null list is denoted by an empty parenthesis pair (such as ( )). Thus *LIST3* of Fig. 10.1.2(b) is denoted by

LIST3=(16,(46,(),4),7,()).

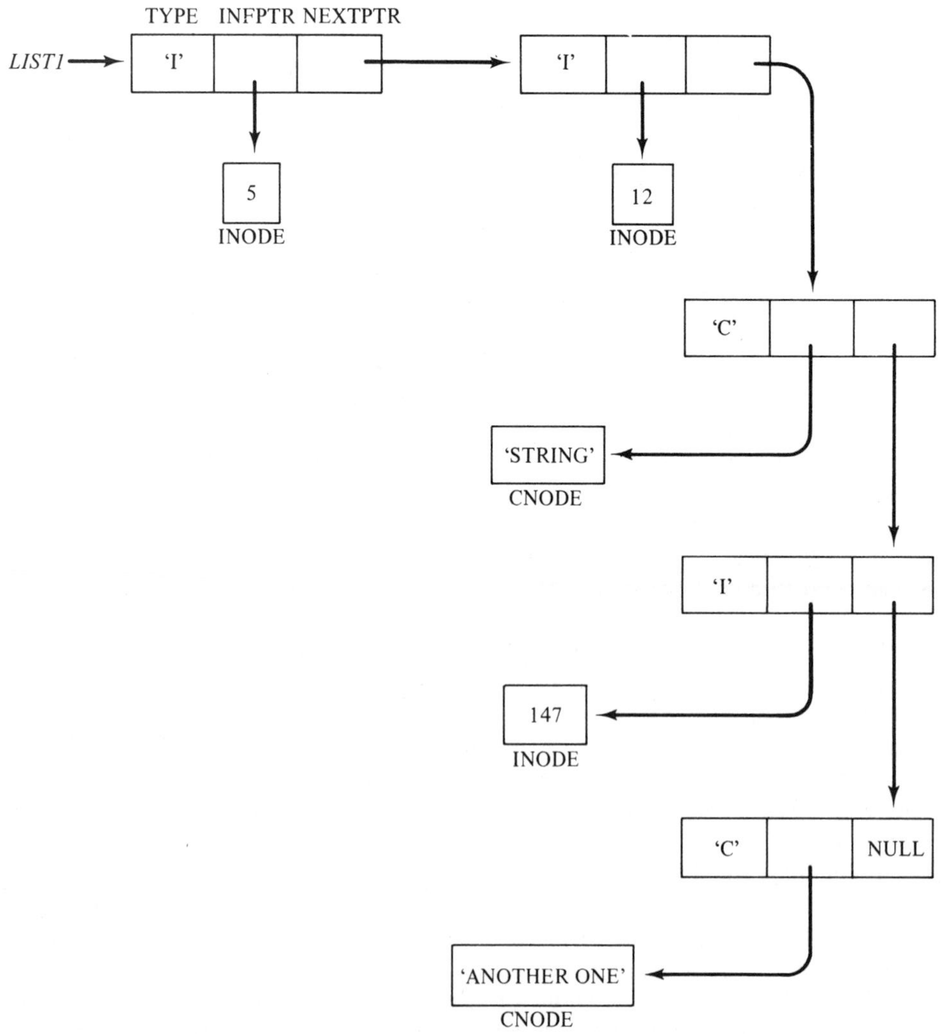

Figure 10.1.1. A list of integers and character strings.

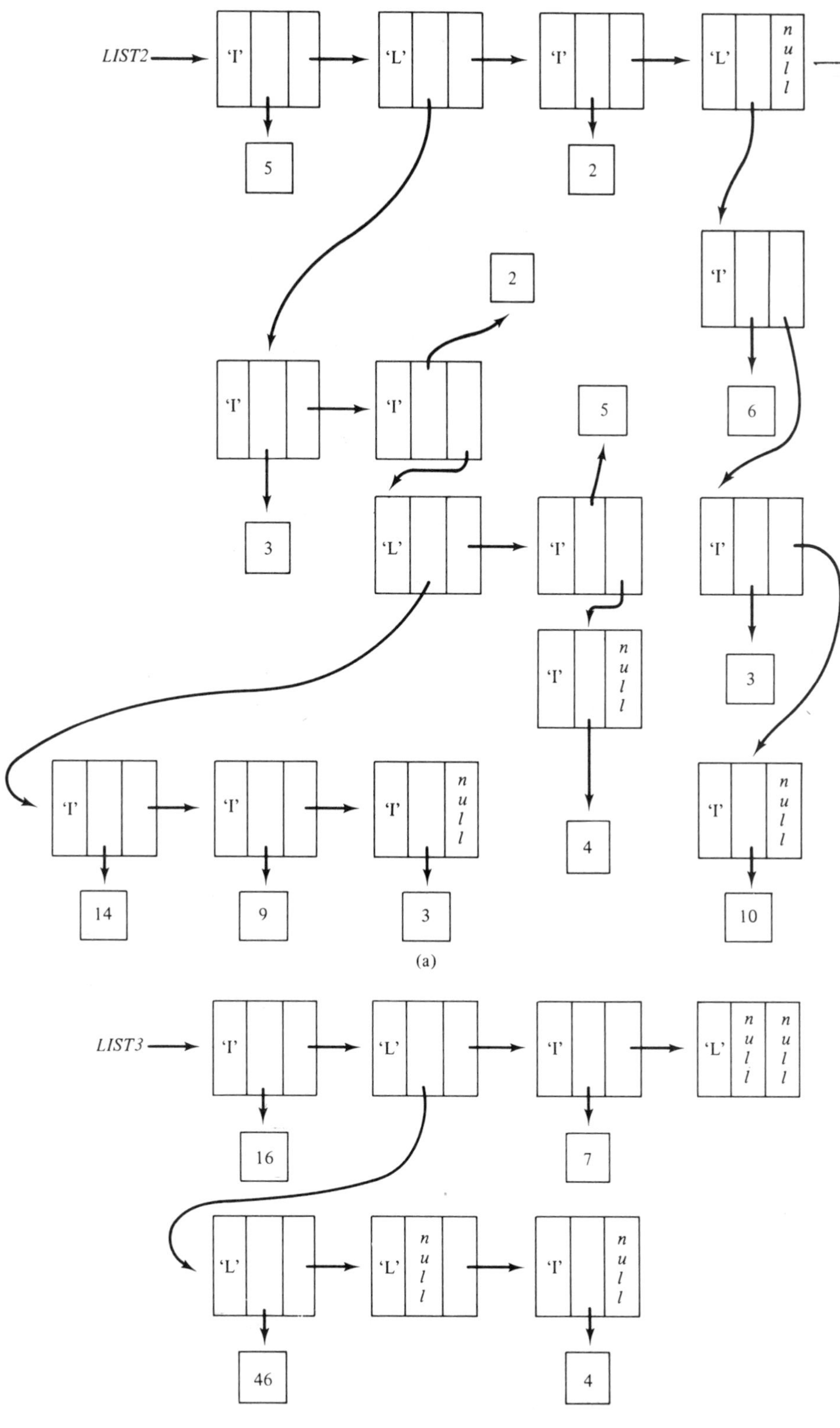
LIST2
'I'
'L'
'I'
'L'
null
5
2
'I'
2
'I'
'I'
5
6
3
'L'
'I'
'I'
'I'
null
3
'I'
'I'
'I'
null
'I'
null
4
14
9
3
10
(a)
LIST3
'I'
'L'
'I'
'L'
null
null
16
7
'L'
'L'
null
'I'
null
46
4
(b)

Figure 10.1.2.

Define an ***internal pointer*** as a pointer which is contained in a list node, and an ***external pointer*** as a pointer which is the value of a variable. For example, in Fig. 10.1.2, *LIST2* and *LIST3* are external pointers while all others are internal.

There are two operations which may be defined on lists. If *list* is a pointer to a list node, then *head*(*list*) is defined as the contents of *infptr*(*list*), and *tail*(*list*) is defined as the contents of *nextptr*(*list*). Note that if lists are constructed as we have described them in this section, then both *head*(*list*) and *tail*(*list*) are pointers. However, while *head*(*list*) may point to either a list node (if a list element is itself a list) or an atomic node (containing an integer, character string, or any other type of atom), *tail*(*list*) is either null or points to a list node. Since under this scheme an object is represented by a pointer to a node which contains it, the head of a list is the first element of the list while its tail is the list of remaining elements.

For example, if *LIST1*, *LIST2*, and *LIST3* are as in Figs. 10.1.1 and 10.1.2, then:

LIST1 = (5,12,'STRING',147,'ANOTHER ONE')
head(*LIST1*) = 5
tail(*LIST1*) = (12,'STRING',147,'ANOTHER ONE')
head(*tail*(*LIST1*)) = 12
tail(*tail*(*LIST1*)) = ('STRING',147,'ANOTHER ONE')
LIST2 = (5,(3,2,(14,9,3),5,4),2,(6,3,10))
head(*tail*(*LIST2*)) = (3,2,(14,9,3),5,4)
head(*head*(*tail*(*LIST2*))) = 3
LIST3 = (16,(46,( ),4),7,( ))
head(*tail*(*LIST3*)) = (46,(),4)
head(*tail*(*head*(*tail*(*LIST3*)))) = ()
tail(*tail*(*head*(*tail*(*LIST3*)))) = (4)
tail(*tail*(*tail*(*head*(*tail*(*LIST3*))))) = ()

Make sure that you understand these examples before proceeding.

Note that the *head* and *tail* operations are not defined if their argument is not a list (i.e., is not a pointer to a list node).

A ***sublist*** of a list *l* is a list which results from the application of zero or more *tail* operations to *l*.

PL/I Implementations of head *and* tail

We now implement the *head* and *tail* operations in PL/I. The TAIL function always produces a pointer to a list (possibly the NULL pointer), assuming that its argument points to a valid list. Thus this operation may be implemented as a simple PL/I function:

```
TAIL:  PROC(LIST)RETURNS(PTR);
          DCL   LIST                PTR;
          IF LIST=NULL THEN DO;
                                PUT SKIP LIST('ILLEGAL TAIL OPERATION');
                                STOP;
                            END;
          RETURN(LIST->NEXTPTR);
       END TAIL;
```

The TAIL function works properly if LIST does indeed point to a list node. It also detects an error if LIST is NULL. However, it cannot detect an error if LIST points to an entity other than a list node. Thus it is the programmer's responsibility to ensure that the argument passed to TAIL is a pointer to a list node.

We might be tempted to implement the *head* operation in a similar fashion, by simply returning the *infptr* field of the node to which the parameter points. However, there is a slight problem with this approach. If a list is correctly constructed, the TAIL function returns either the NULL pointer or a pointer to a list node, but the HEAD function can return a pointer to any of a variety of list or atomic nodes depending upon the elements of the list. Given only a pointer to such a node, there is no way for the programmer to determine the type of node which is being referenced. Without knowing the type of the node, the PL/I programmer cannot reference its contents.

For example, suppose we wanted to print the fourth element of the list *LIST1* of Fig. 10.1.1. Suppose P has been declared to be a pointer. After executing the PL/I statement

```
P = HEAD(TAIL(TAIL(TAIL(LIST1))));
```

P points to the atomic node containing the integer 147. However, the PL/I programmer does not know whether P points to an integer or a character string and therefore does not know whether to write

```
PUT LIST(P->INODE);
```

or

```
PUT LIST(P->CNODE);
```

To solve this problem we write HEAD as a subroutine with one input parameter (a pointer to a list node) and two output parameters. The first output parameter is a pointer to the first element of the input list, and the second is a code which specifies the type of that element. The subroutine is implemented as follows:

```
HEAD:  PROC(LIST,ELPTR,TCODE);
         DCL  (LIST,ELPTR)              PTR,
                TCODE                   CHAR(1);
         IF LIST=NULL THEN DO;
                                 PUT SKIP LIST('ILLEGAL HEAD OPERATION');
                                 STOP;
                               END;
         ELPTR=LIST->INFPTR;
         TCODE=LIST->TYPE;
         RETURN;
       END HEAD;
```

Using this subroutine, we can identify the first element of any list. If the first element is an integer, then ELPTR will point to an atomic node INODE containing that integer, and TCODE will be set to 'I' to indicate that fact. Similarly, if the first element is a character string, then ELPTR will point to an allocation of CNODE, and TCODE will be set to 'C'. If the first element is a list, then ELPTR will point to an allocation of NODE, and TCODE will be set to 'L'.

Note that neither HEAD nor TAIL changes the original list in any way. All fields retain the same values that they had before the routines were called (unless the first two parameters of HEAD are the same variable).

Examples

Let us look at some simple examples which use the HEAD and TAIL routines. Our first example is a routine to add 1 to every integer which is an element of a list. Character or list elements are left unchanged.

```
ADDONE:    PROC(LIST);
             DCL  (P,LIST,ELPTR)          PTR,
                    CODE                  CHAR(1);
             P=LIST;
TRAVERSE:    DO   WHILE(P¬=NULL);
                    CALL HEAD(P,ELPTR,CODE);
                    IF CODE='I' THEN ELPTR->INODE=ELPTR->INODE+1;
                    P=TAIL(P);
             END TRAVERSE;
             RETURN;
           END ADDONE;
```

Since P is used to traverse the list, the value of LIST is not changed by this subroutine. Also, since P always points to a list node (assuming the list is validly constructed), the HEAD and TAIL operations may be applied to P.

Our second example involves deletions. We wish to delete from a list all character string elements that begin with the letter 'W'. (Compare this example with the routine of Section 5.2.) A tentative solution follows (we will shortly see why the solution is tentative):

```
DELETEW:   PROC(LIST);
             DCL  (LIST,P,Q,R)            PTR,
                    CODE                  CHAR(1),
                    STRING                CHAR(100)VAR;
             Q=NULL;
             P=LIST;
```

```
TRAVERSE:   DO  WHILE(P¬=NULL);
                CALL HEAD(P,ELPTR,CODE);
                IF CODE='C' THEN DO;
                     STRING=ELPTR->CNODE;
                     IF SUBSTR(STRING,1,1)='W' THEN DO;
                                    R=P;


                       /*   remove P->NODE from the list   */
                                    IF Q=NULL THEN
                                         P,LIST=TAIL(LIST);
                                              ELSE DO;
                                         P=TAIL(P);
                                         Q->NEXTPTR=P;
                                                   END;
                                    FREE ELPTR->CNODE;
                                    FREE R->NODE;
                                    GO TO OVER;
                                                 END;
                             END;
                Q=P;
                P=TAIL(P);
OVER:       END TRAVERSE;
            RETURN;
          END DELETEW;
```

Note that when an element is removed from a list, both the list node which points to that element as well as the atomic node which contains the element must be freed. Otherwise, valuable space is wasted by allocated nodes which are not being used.

Before looking at a more complex example, let us define a new term. A node n is ***accessible*** from a pointer l if there is a sequence of *infptr*s and *nextptr*s from the node pointed to by l such that the last pointer in the sequence points to n. For example, in Fig. 10.1.2(a) the node containing 14 is accessible from *LIST2* since

14=*LIST2->nextptr->infptr->nextptr->nextptr->infptr->infptr->inode*

In fact, all the nodes shown in that figure are accessible from *LIST2*. When a node is removed from a list, it becomes inaccessible from the external pointer to that list.

Now let us consider the following problem. We wish to increase by 1 the value of every integer node accessible from a given list pointer LIST. We cannot simply traverse LIST since it is also necessary to traverse all lists which are elements of LIST as well as all lists which may be elements of elements of LIST, etc. One tentative solution involving recursion follows. It is a simple matter to remove the recursion and explicitly use a stack.

```
ADDONE2:   PROC(LIST) RECURSIVE;
             DCL (P,ELPTR,LIST)      PTR,
                   CODE              CHAR(1);
             P=LIST;
TRAVERSE:    DO WHILE(P¬=NULL);
                CALL HEAD(P,ELPTR,CODE);
                IF CODE='I' THEN ELPTR->INODE=EPTR->INODE+1;
                IF CODE='L' THEN CALL ADDONE2(ELPTR);
                P=TAIL(P);
             END TRAVERSE;
             RETURN;
           END ADDONE2;
```

Nodes on More Than One List

In the lists that we have encountered thus far, only a single pointer points to any single node (whether list or atomic). For example, in Fig. 10.1.2(a) there are two atomic nodes containing the integer 2, three containing the integer 3, and two containing the integer 5. We can conceive of a situation in which this duplication of atomic nodes is avoided by keeping only one copy of each integer and having several list nodes point to the same atomic node. This situation is depicted in Fig. 10.1.3(a). A similar situation occurs in Fig. 10.1.3(b) where the atomic node containing the string 'WHY' appears as the first and fourth elements of *LIST5*.

If this possibility is allowed, then the routines ADDONE, DELETEW, and ADDONE2 given above do not work correctly. For example, if DELETEW is applied to *LIST5* in Fig. 10.1.3(b), then when P equals *LIST5* at the start of the routine, the atomic node containing 'WHY' is freed. Thus the value of INFPTR in the fourth node of *LIST5* is a pointer to an unallocated node. A subsequent attempt to retrieve its value results in an error.

If ADDONE is applied to *LIST4* of Fig. 10.1.3(a), then the contents of the first atomic node on the list are changed to 6. The routine is supposed to add 1 only to integer atomic nodes on the list. However, by adding 1 to the atomic node, the contents of one of the sublists (the list pointed to by the fourth element of *LIST4*) are also changed. This violates the specification of the routine.

Similarly, if ADDONE2 is applied to *LIST4* in Fig. 10.1.3(a), when 1 is added to the integer 5 as the first element of *LIST4*, the contents of that atomic node are changed to 6. But the routine again adds 1 to that atomic node since it is pointed to by the INFPTR of another list element. Thus the final value of that atomic node is 7 rather than 6. Similarly, the values of the atomic nodes containing 2 and 3 will be changed to 4 and 6 respectively. This is clearly incorrect.

Let us look at these examples more closely. In the case of DELETEW, the program specification is to delete all character strings which start with 'W' from the list *LIST5*. In order to save space, when a list node is removed from the list, its storage, as well as that of the atomic node to which it points, is freed. In doing so, we incorrectly assume that the atomic node is being used in only one context. The freeing of the atomic node (or the list node, for that matter) is not part of the problem solution itself. The list node

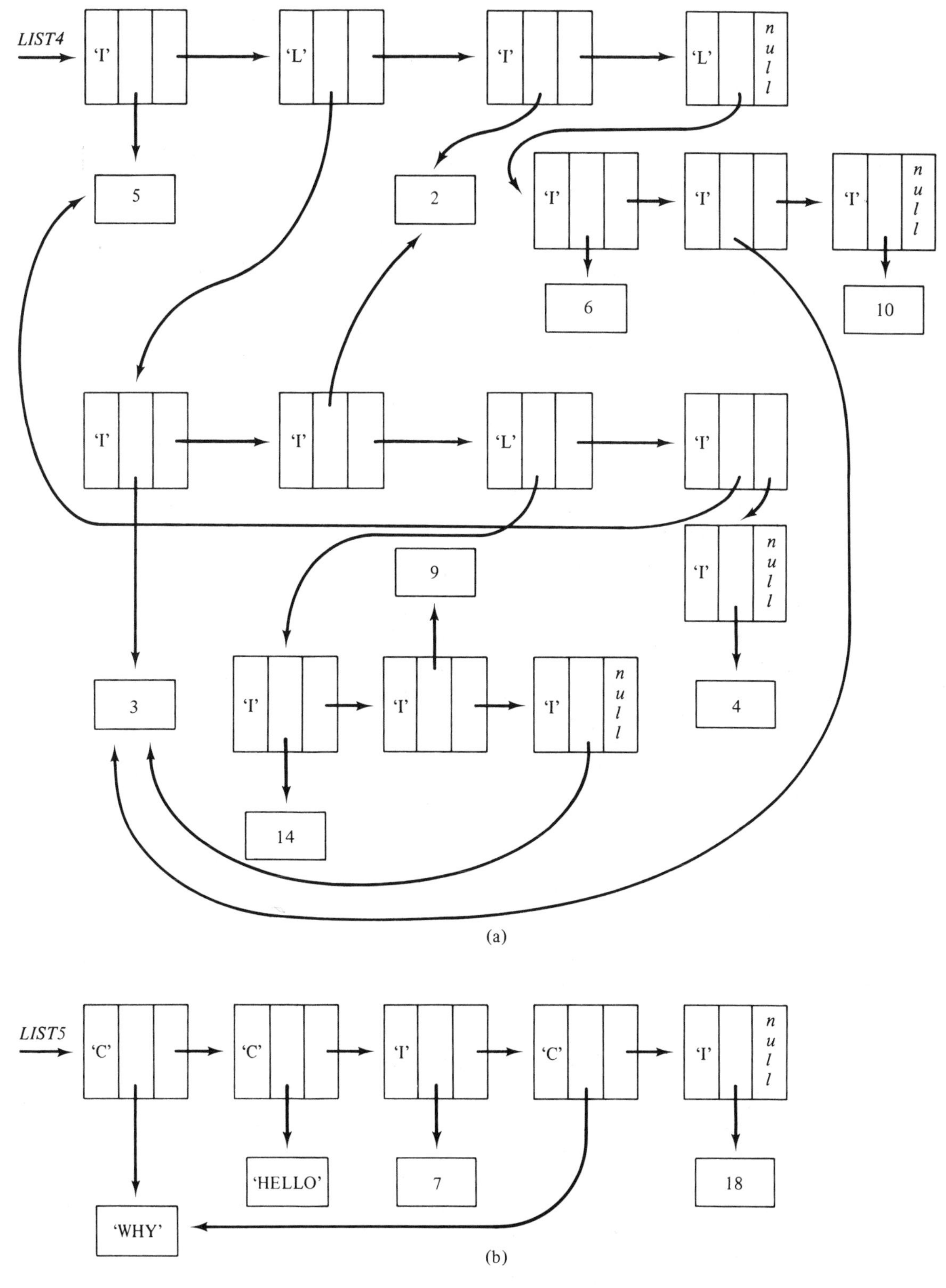
LIST4
'I'
'L'
'I'
'L'
null
5
2
'I'
'I'
'I'
null
6
10
'I'
'I'
'L'
'I'
'I'
null
9
'I'
'I'
'I'
null
3
4
14
(a)
LIST5
'C'
'C'
'I'
'C'
'I'
null
'HELLO'
7
18
'WHY'
(b)

Figure 10.1.3.

could just as well have been removed from the list without freeing it or the atomic node. The resultant list is the original list with all specified elements deleted, as required by the problem statement.

Why then did we bother to free the nodes? The answer is that we presumed that the subroutine is embedded in a large list processing application in which new nodes are constantly needed for insertions into lists. The available storage space is inadequate for all these nodes unless nodes are reused after they are no longer needed. In order to make a node available for reallocation in PL/I, it must be freed. Our error was that we mistakenly assumed that the atomic node containing 'WHY' was no longer needed once the first list node which points to it was removed from *LIST4*. Thus it was not the problem solution which we performed incorrectly, but rather the storage management which was embedded within that solution.

In the cases of ADDONE and ADDONE2, we have a slightly different but related problem. Changing the integer in an atomic node from 5 to 6 is equivalent to replacing the atomic node containing 5 by a new atomic node containing 6 and then freeing the node containing 5. But this again erroneously assumes that the node containing 5 is no longer needed. Indeed, each time that the contents of a node are changed or a node is deleted, we must first ensure that the old value is no longer needed.

One solution to this problem is to disallow use of the same atomic node in more than one context. That is, our lists should be constructed as in Fig. 10.1.2(a) rather than as in Fig. 10.1.3(a). It is rather easy to achieve this goal by insisting that each time that an atomic node is placed on a list, a new node must be allocated even if an atomic node containing the desired value already exists somewhere on the list. Therefore, once an atomic node is no longer needed in a particular context, it can be freed since no other list nodes point to it.

However, list nodes may also be on two lists at the same time. For example, consider Fig. 10.1.4 which illustrates two examples of list nodes being used in more than one list. In Fig. 10.1.4(a), the list (4,5,3,8) appears as both the second and the fourth elements of *LIST6*. However, instead of using two copies of the list (4,5,3,8), a single copy appears with two pointers to its first element. This method of using a list in two contexts is similar to the multiple use of atomic nodes in which a single atomic node appears as an element of several different lists or as several different elements of the same list.

In Fig. 10.1.4(b), the list (43,28) appears as a sublist of both *LIST7* which is (12,18,43,28) and *LIST8* which is (47,59,16,43,28). In this example the list nodes of the list (43,28) are not elements of another list but are subparts of two different lists. Imagine the chaos which would result if an attempt were made to remove the third element of *LIST7*.

Let us leave the resolution of this problem for Section 10.2. For now, let us examine why it is desirable to allow a list node to be used in more than one context.

The push, addon, sethead, *and* settail *Operations*

Thus far, we have been manipulating lists that are already in existence by extracting information from them or transforming them in some manner. Let us now turn to the question of how such lists are built in the first place.

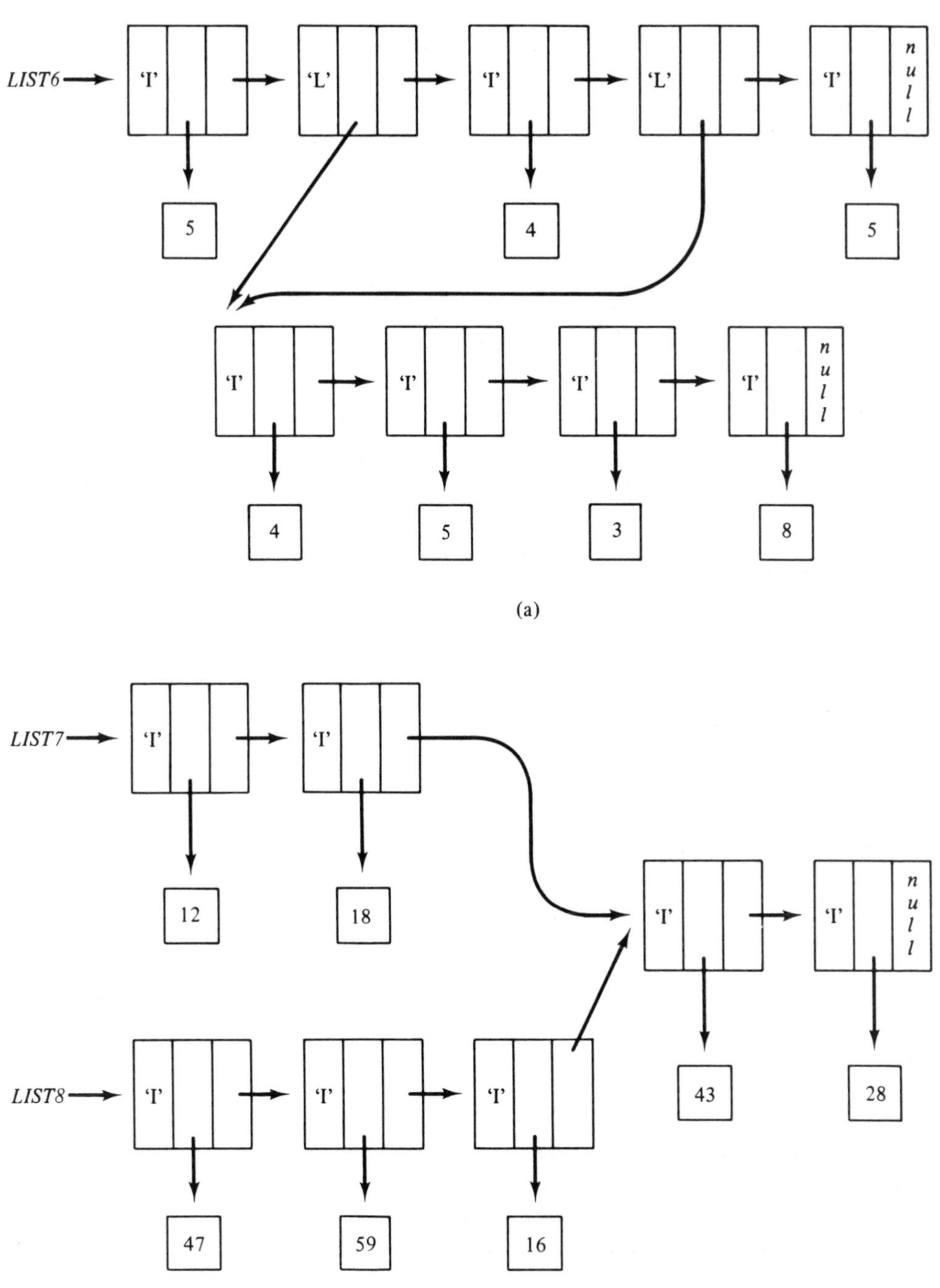

LIST6
'I'
'L'
'I'
'L'
'I'
null
5
4
5
'I'
'I'
'I'
'I'
null
4
5
3
8
(a)
LIST7
'I'
'I'
12
18
'I'
'I'
null
43
28
LIST8
'I'
'I'
'I'
47
59
16
(b)

Figure 10.1.4.

Recall the *push* operation of Chapter 3 and its list implementation in Section 5.2. If *list* points to a list and x is an atom, the operation *push*(*list*, x) adds x as an element to the front of the list.

We leave to the reader the PL/I implementation of this operation as it applies to general lists. We merely make some observations. Since the object to be pushed on the list can be of any type, the parameter X cannot be an atom in the PL/I implementation, but rather must be a pointer to an atomic node or list node. Alternatively, the PL/I subroutine PUSH requires a third parameter CODE to indicate the type of X being added as a list node. However, we ignore the PL/I implementation for the moment and write the *push* operation as though the atom itself were the second operand.

To illustrate the use of the *push* operation in constructing lists, consider the list

(5,10,8)

which can be constructed by the operations

```
list = null
push(list,8)
push(list,10)
push(list,5)
```

Note that the *push* operation changes the value of its first parameter so that it points to the newly created list. We introduce as a new operation the function

addon(*list*,*x*)

which returns a pointer to a new list which has x as its head and *list* as its tail. For example, if

L1 = (3,4,7)

then the operation

L2 = *addon*(*L1*,5)

creates a new list *L2* equal to (5,3,4,7). The crucial difference between *push* and *addon* is that *push* changes the value of its first parameter while *addon* does not. Thus, in the above example, *L1* retains the value (3,4,7). The operation *push*(*list*,*x*) is equivalent to *list* = *addon*(*list*,*x*). Since the *addon* operation is more flexible than *push*, and since *push* is usually used only in connection with stacks, we will henceforth use *addon* exclusively.

Two other operations which are used to modify lists are the *sethead* and *settail* operations. We have seen that the *head* operation is a function which returns the value of the first element of a list. (The fact that the PL/I HEAD procedure was a subroutine and that its output parameter was a pointer to an atomic node rather than the atom itself was due to the restrictions of the PL/I language. The *head* operation itself was defined as a function returning an atomic node or list pointer.) The *sethead* operation changes the contents of the first element of a list to a given value. Thus we may write

```
sethead(list,x)
```

to set the first element of the list *list* to *x*. This operation is only valid if *list* is a pointer to a list node. For example, if *list* = (5,10,8), then performing the operation

```
sethead(list,18)
```

changes *list* to (18,10,8) and performing the operation *sethead*(*list*,(5,7,3,4)) changes *list* to ((5,7,3,4),10,8).

The *sethead* operation is called the "inverse *head* operation" for an obvious reason. After performing the operation *sethead*(*list*,*x*), the value of *head*(*list*) is *x*. Note that *sethead*(*list*,*x*) is equivalent to

```
list = addon(tail(list),x)
```

Again, the comments which apply to a PL/I implementation of *push* apply as well to *addon* and *sethead* and most of the operations which we describe in this section.

The inverse *tail* operation, *settail*, is similar. After performing the operation *settail*(*list*,*x*), we desire that the value of *tail*(*list*) should be *x*. Since the value of the *tail* operation must be a list (assuming that *list* is well formed), the second parameter to *settail* must be a list. The *tail* operation is only defined on a nonnull list, so that the *settail* operation operates on two lists, the first of which is nonnull.

For example, if *list* = (5,9,3,7,8,6), then *settail*(*list*, (8)) changes the value of *list* to (5,8) and *settail* (*list*, (4,2,7)) changes its value to (5,4,2,7). Note that the operation *settail*(*list*, *l*) is equivalent to *list* = *addon*(*l*,*head*(*list*)).

Referencing Lists through Pointers

In all the foregoing discussions about lists, we have been purposely vague about a very important distinction which must now be made. We have often used the expression "the list *list*" to be synonymous with the expression "the list to which the pointer *list* points." That is, we have always identified a list with a pointer to its first element.

To see why this is ambiguous, let us look at an analogous situation using integers. Suppose that we declared two integer variables A and B and assigned the value 5 to both of them. Then it is correct to say that "the current values of A and B are the same." We often say this differently as "A and B are equal." However it would be incorrect to say that "A and B are the same," since they are clearly not the same. Rather, they are two different memory locations, each containing the same value.

Suppose we then executed the statement A = B+1; which changes the value of A to 6. If we later change the value of B to 10, the value of A does not change to 11; it remains at 6. This is because the statement A = B+1; does not mean "A now refers to 1 more than whatever value B refers to." If it did mean that, then whenever the value of B is changed, the value of A would be changed automatically, since the value of A could be determined only indirectly through the value of B. Rather, the statement A = B+1; means the following: "Add 1 to the current value of B and change the value of A to the sum." Thus it is not the storage location of A which is changed by the assignment statement, but only the contents of that location. A subsequent change in the value of B will not affect the value which had been originally placed into A.

Now let us examine the analogous situation with lists. Suppose, as before, that *L1* = (3,4,7) and the operation

L2 = addon(L1,5)

is performed. There are two possible ways to implement this operation as illustrated in Figs. 10.1.5(a) and (b). In the first method, which is called the ***pointer method***, the list (3,4,7) is represented by a pointer to it, *L1*. Thus, to create the list *L2*, an atomic node containing 5 is allocated and a list node is allocated as well. A pointer to the atomic node is placed in the *infptr* field of the list node, and the value of *L1* is placed in its *nextptr* field. Thus the list *L1* becomes a sublist of *L2*. In the second method, which is called the ***copy method***, the list (3,4,7) is copied before the new list element is added to it. Thus *L1* still points to the original version, while the new copy is made a sublist of *L2*.

The difference between these methods becomes apparent when we attempt to perform the operation

sethead(L1,7)

The resulting lists are shown in Figs. 10.1.6(a) and (b). If the copy method is used, then a change in list *L1* does not affect list *L2* (Figs. 10.1.5(b) and 10.1.6(b)); if the pointer method is used, any subsequent change in list *L1* also changes *L2* (Figs. 10.1.5(a) and 10.1.6(a)).

The *tail* operation can also be implemented by either the pointer method or the copy method. The implementation which we have presented in our PL/I function is the pointer method in which a pointer to the second list node in the input list is returned. Under a strict copy method, a new list would be created containing copies of all nodes from the second list node onwards. Here too, if the pointer method is used, then a subsequent change in either the input list or the output list (such as modifying its third element) causes a change in the other list.

The copy method is similar to the way that we define the statement A=B+1; so that a subsequent change in B does not change A. This is because the expression B+1 means "the new integer created by adding 1 to the integer found at location B." The variable B represents the integer stored at a given location and not the location itself. Similarly, in the copy method, although *L1* is a pointer, it really refers to the elements within the nodes of the list. In the pointer method, *L1* refers to the nodes themselves rather than their contents.

For reasons of efficiency, most list processing systems use the pointer method rather than the copy method. Imagine a 100-element list to which nodes are being constantly added (using *addon*) and from which nodes are being deleted (using *tail*). The overhead

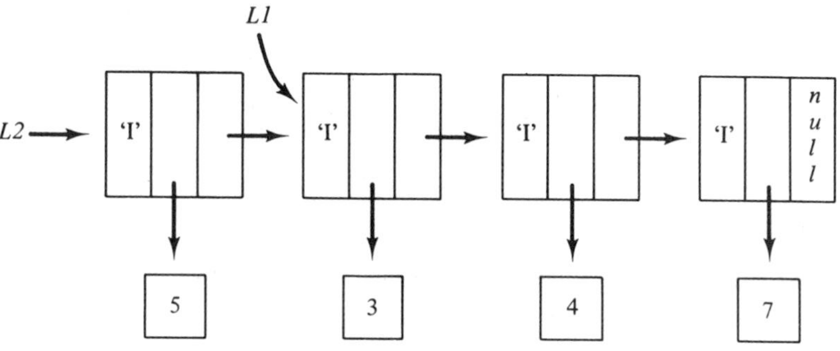

(a) The pointer method.

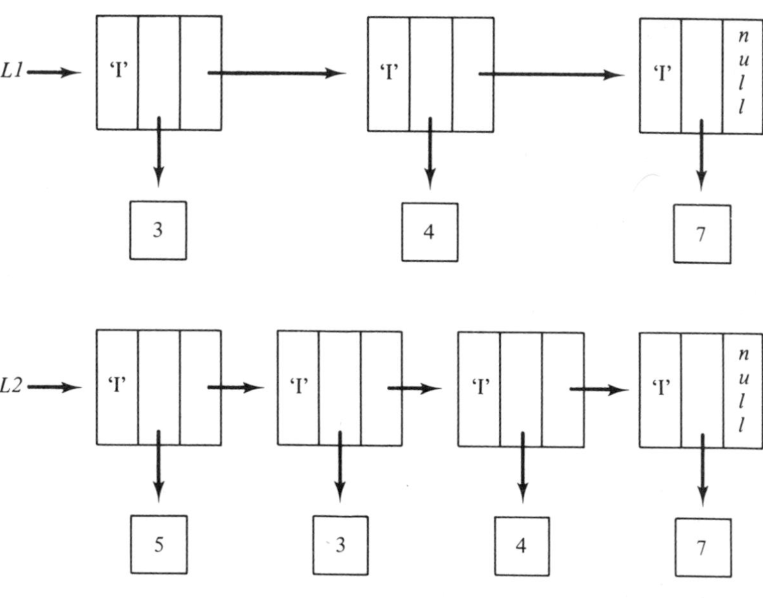

(b) The copy method.

Figure 10.1.5.

involved in both time and space in allocating and copying 100 list nodes (not to mention any atomic nodes or list nodes on any lists which appear as elements) each time that an operation is performed is prohibitive. Under the pointer method, the number of operations involved in adding or deleting an element is independent of the list size. However, in exchange for this efficiency, the user must be aware of possible changes to other lists.

In list processing systems which use the pointer method, an explicit copy operation is provided. The function

copy(*list*)

copies the list pointed to by *list* (including all list elements) and returns a pointer to the new copy. The user can use this operation whenever he wants to ensure that subsequent modifications to one list will not affect another.

As a result of the use of the pointer method, it is often the case that a list node is being used in more than one context.

The crlist *Operation*

Suppose that we wanted to create the list of Fig. 10.1.4(a). Then the following sequence of operations will accomplish this.

```
L = null
L = addon(L,8)
L = addon(L,3)
L = addon(L,5)
L = addon(L,4)
LIST6 = null
LIST6 = addon(LIST6,5)
LIST6 = addon(LIST6,L)
LIST6 = addon(LIST6,4)
LIST6 = addon(LIST6,L)
LIST6 = addon(LIST6,5)
```

Let us introduce the operation $L = crlist(a_1,a_2, \ldots ,a_n)$, where each a_i is an atom or a list pointer. This operation is defined as the sequence of statements

```
L = null
L = addon(L,an)
        ...
L = addon(L,a2)
L = addon(L,a1)
```

That is, $crlist(a_1,a_2, \ldots ,a_n)$ creates the list $(a_1,a_2 \ldots ,a_n)$. Then the above sequence of operations can be rewritten as

```
L = crlist(4,5,3,8)
LIST6 = crlist(5,L,4,L,5)
```

Notice that this is not the same as the single operation

```
LIST6 = (5,crlist(4,5,3,8),4,crlist(4,5,3,8),5)
```

Figures 10.1.7(a) and (b) illustrate the results of these two sequences.

We should note some problems which exist with our parenthesized list notation at this point. For example, the list of Fig. 10.1.7(b) can be denoted by

```
LIST6 = (5,(4,5,3,8),4,(4,5,3,8),5)
```

since there are two different lists (4,5,3,8) contained as members. However, in denoting the list of Fig. 10.1.7(a), it is important to express the fact that the same list (4,5,3,8) is a member of *LIST6* twice. Fortunately, there is an external pointer, *L*, to this list. Thus we may write

```
L = (4,5,3,8)
LIST6 = (5,L,4,L,5)
```

But how do we denote a list such as in Fig. 10.1.4(a) where there is no external pointer to the contained list? To solve this problem, we introduce local symbols within our list notation. The list of Fig. 10.1.4(a) can be denoted by

```
LIST6 = (5,L=(4,5,3,8),4,L,5)
```

That is, we define a temporary variable *L* so that we may refer to a list twice.

The list of Fig. 10.1.4(b) can be denoted as follows by using a colon to represent concatenation of lists and by using brackets to explicitly specify what operations are to be performed earlier.

```
LIST7 = (12,18):[L = (43,28)]
LIST8 = (47,59,16):L
```

These examples also illustrate several other points. The first is that the equal sign is used in two ways. Appearing as the second symbol in a line, it represents the declaration and definition of an external pointer. Anywhere else, it represents the declaration and definition of a local variable. Second, a local variable defined on one line can be used on another (*L* was defined and used within the definition of *LIST7* and is used in the definition of *LIST8*). Third, the colon has precedence over the equal sign, and brackets are necessary to reverse this order.

We leave as an exercise for the reader the job of finding a sequence of list operations which creates the lists *LIST7* and *LIST8* of Fig. 10.1.4(b). We also leave as exercises the PL/I implementations of *addon*, *sethead*, *settail*, and *crlist*. As we have already seen additional parameters for type codes are usually necessary in the PL/I implementations.

If the pointer method is used to implement list operations, we allow ***recursive lists***, which are lists which contain themselves as elements. For example, suppose the following operations are performed:

```
L = crlist(2,crlist(9,7),6,4)
L1 = tail(tail(L))
sethead(L1,L)
L2 = head(tail(L))
L2 = tail(L2)
sethead(L2,L)
```

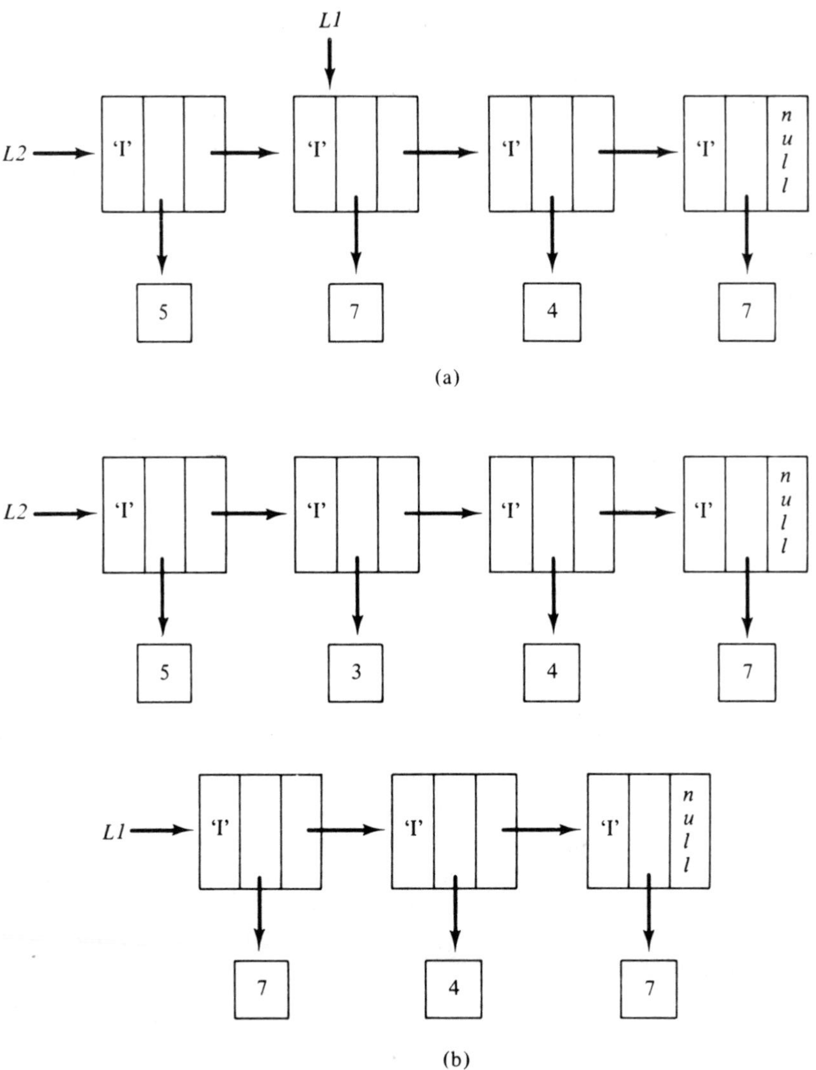

Figure 10.1.6.

Figure 10.1.8 illustrates the effects of each of these operations. At the end of the sequence (Fig. 10.1.8(f)) the list L contains itself as its third element. In addition, the second element of L is a list whose second element is L itself.

The Use of List Headers

In Chapter 5, list headers were introduced as a place to store global information about an entire list. In many general list processing systems, header nodes are used for other purposes as well. We have already seen two ways of implementing general lists: the pointer method and the copy method. There is a third alternative, called the ***header method***,

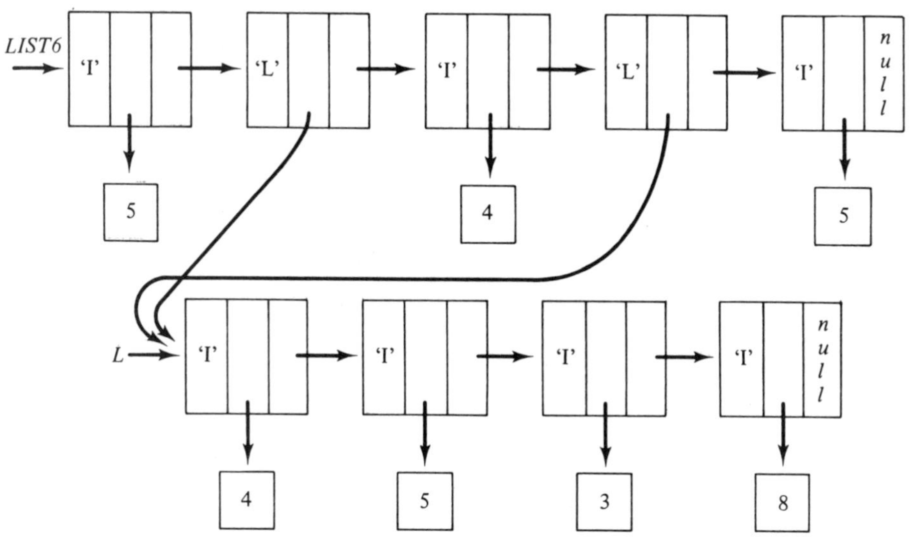

(a) Results of L = *crlist* (4, 5, 3, 8); *LIST6* = *crlist* (5, L, 4, L, 5);

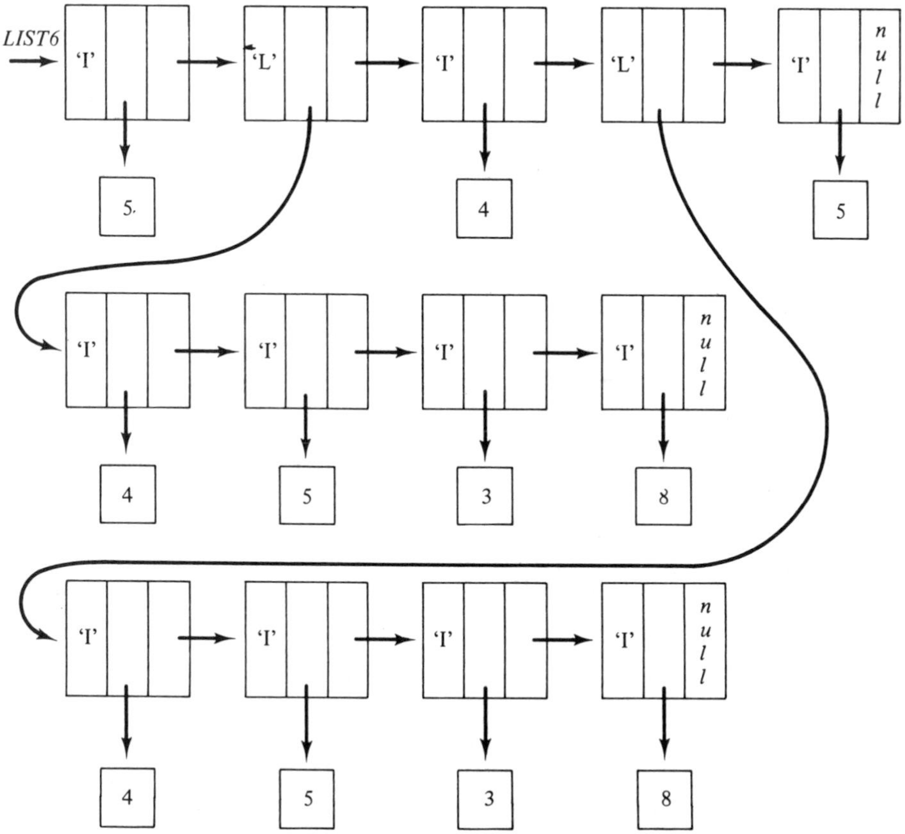

(b) The list *LIST6* = (5, *crlist* (4,5, 3, 8), 4, *crlist* (4, 5, 3, 8), 5);

Figure 10.1.7.

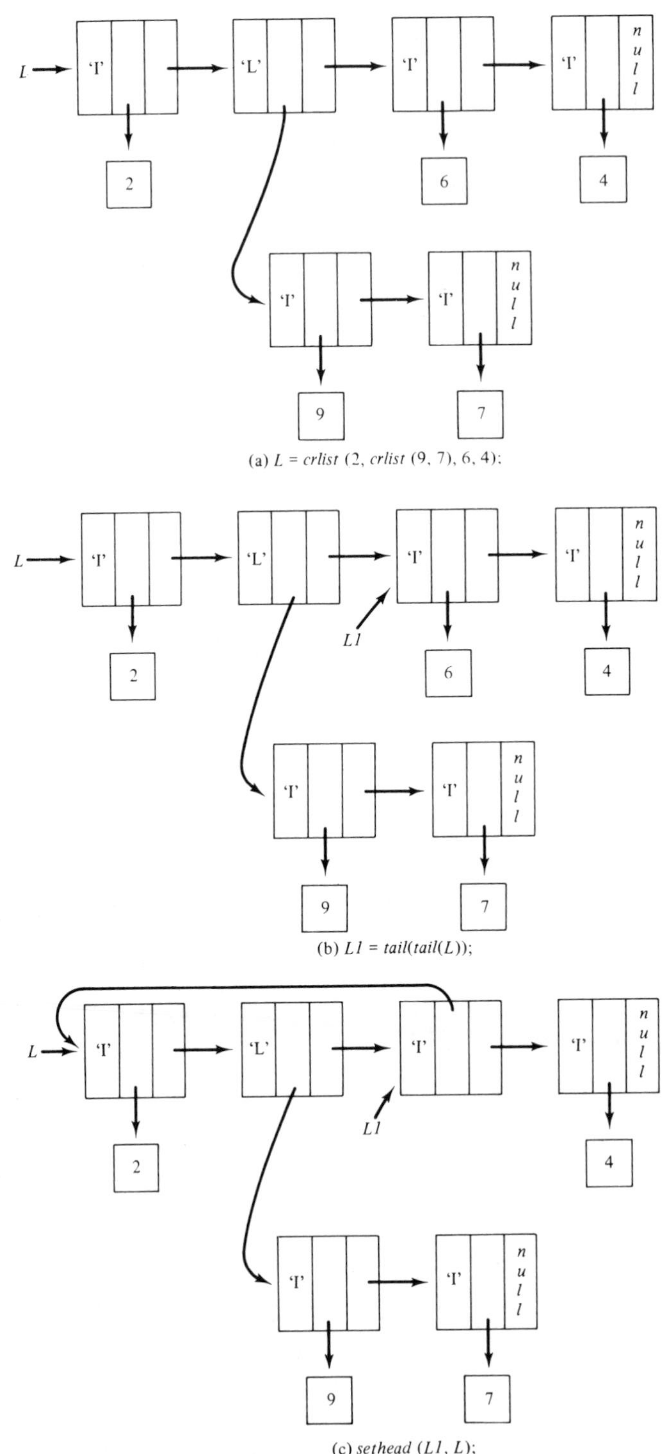

(a) L = *crlist* (2, *crlist* (9, 7), 6, 4);

(b) $L1$ = *tail*(*tail*(L));

(c) *sethead* ($L1$, L);

Figure 10.1.8.

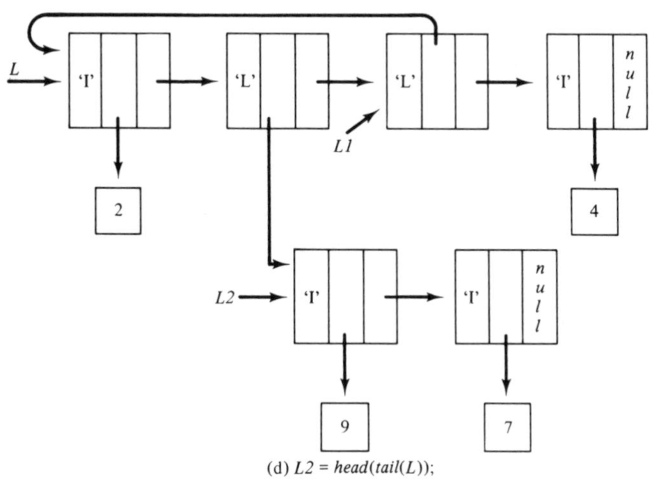

(d) $L2$ = *head*(*tail*(L));

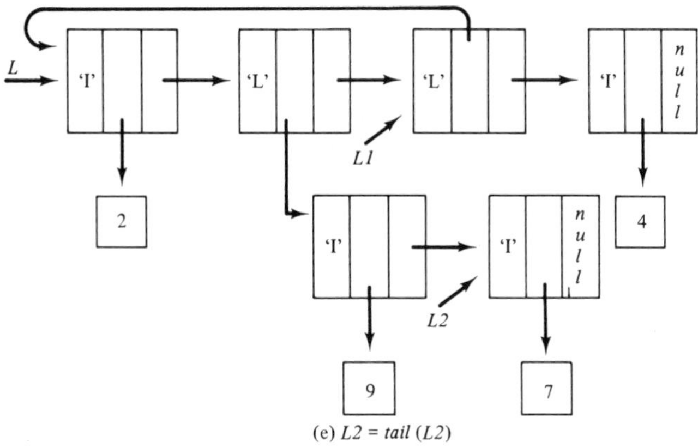

(e) $L2$ = *tail* ($L2$)

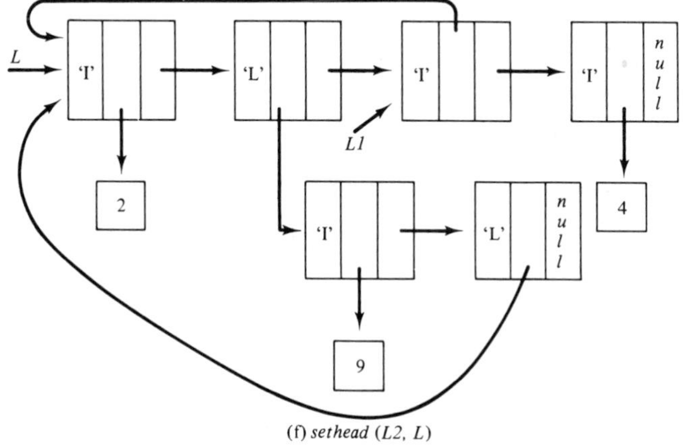

(f) *sethead* ($L2$, L)

Figure 10.1.8. (*cont.*)

which is widely used in list processing systems. Under this method, a header node is always placed at the beginning of any group of nodes which is to be considered a list. In particular, an external pointer always points to a header node. Similarly, if a list L is an element of another list, there is a header node at the front of L. Figure 10.1.9 illustrates the list of Fig. 10.1.2(b) using the header method. An 'H' in the type field indicates a header node. The *infptr* field in such a node can be used to hold global information about the list (such as the number of nodes in it, or a pointer to its last node). In the figure, this field is left blank. Note that a null list is now represented by a pointer to a header node containing a null pointer in its *nextptr* field, rather than by the null pointer itself.

The header method is similar to the pointer method in that a list is represented by a pointer to it. However, the presence of the header node causes significant differences. Let us examine some of these.

We made a distinction between the *push* and the *addon* operations. Thus if L is a list pointer, the operation

```
addon(L,x)
```

does not change the value of L, but rather adds a node containing x to the list and returns a pointer to that new node. *push*(L,x) changes the value of its parameter L to point to the new node. Under the header method, the *addon* operation becomes equivalent to *push*. Adding an element to a list involves inserting a node between the header and the first list node. Thus despite the fact that the value of L is not changed, the list which L represents has been altered. Figure 10.1.10 illustrates adding an element to the front of a list under the header method.

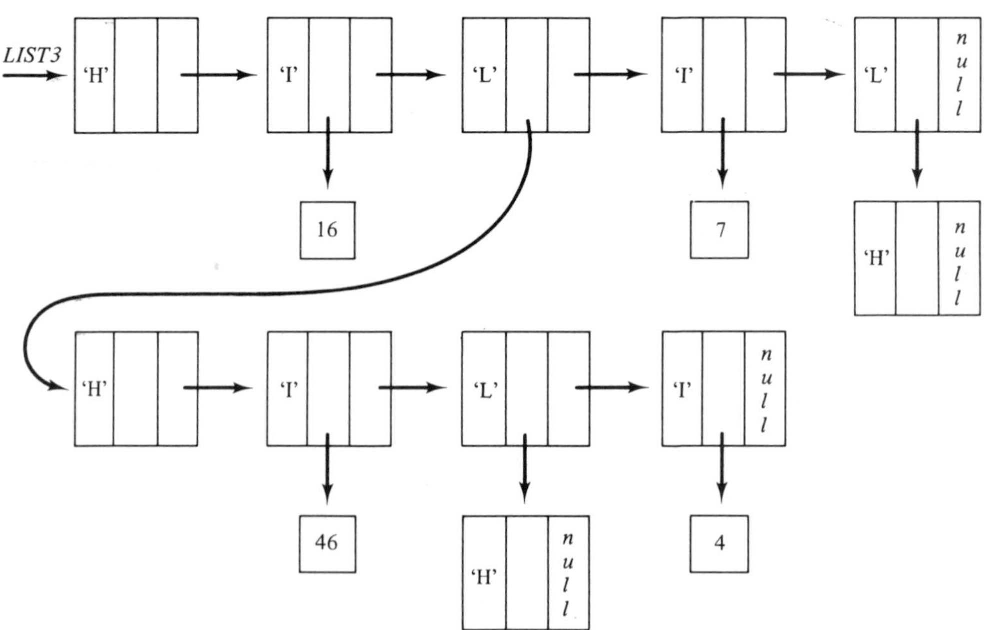

Figure 10.1.9.

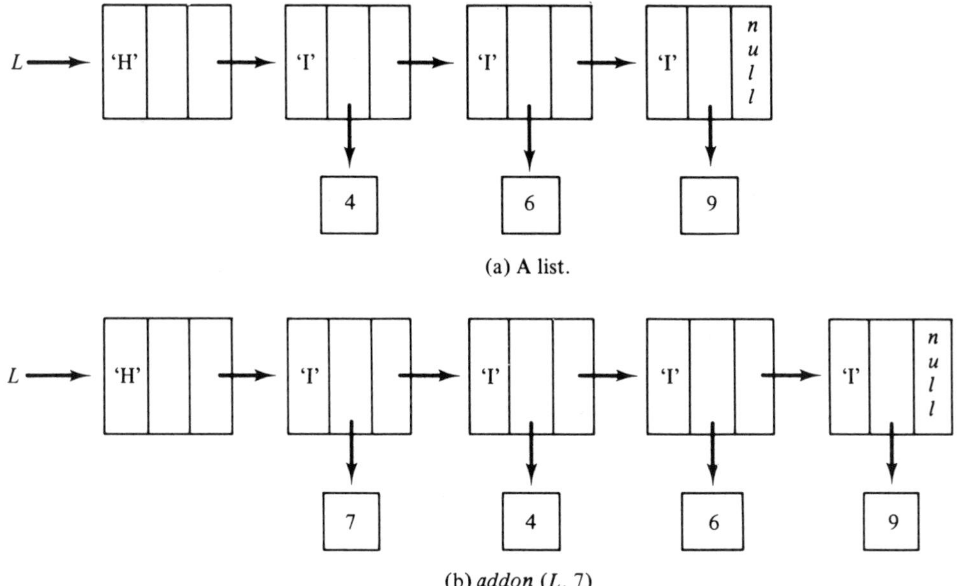

(a) A list.

(b) *addon* (*L*, 7)

Figure 10.1.10.

The *tail* operation involves allocating a new header node. Figure 10.1.11(a) illustrates executing the operation *L2* = *tail*(*L*) on the list of Fig. 10.1.10(b). Most systems would optimize execution of an operation such as *L* = *tail*(*L*) so that no additional nodes are allocated. Figure 10.1.11(b) illustrates the effects of this operation on the list of Fig. 10.1.10(b). We leave the implementation of the operations *head*, *sethead*, *settail*, and *crlist* under the header method as exercises. Note that any parameter which is a pointer to a list must now be a pointer to a header node for that list. Also any function which returns a pointer to a list must return a pointer to a header node.

As another illustration of the effects of a header node, consider Fig. 10.1.12(a), which represents the list of Fig. 10.1.7(a) with header nodes. Executing the operation *L* = *tail*(*L*) on the list of Fig. 10.1.7(a) under the pointer method leaves unchanged the second and fourth elements of *LIST6*. However, executing the same operation using header nodes (assuming that the system uses the optimized version of that operation's execution as described above) would also change these elements of *LIST6*. Figure 10.1.12(b) illustrates the result. This is because executing the operation does not involve changing the value of *L*, but rather the value of the pointer in the header node of *L*.

Freeing List Nodes

Earlier in this section, we saw that if an atomic node is to be used in more than one context (i.e., if the same atomic node is used as an element of more than one list, or as several elements of the same list), there is difficulty in determining when such a node can be modified or freed. One solution which is frequently used is to disallow such multiple use of atomic nodes. That is, operations on atomic nodes are performed by the copy method rather than the pointer method.

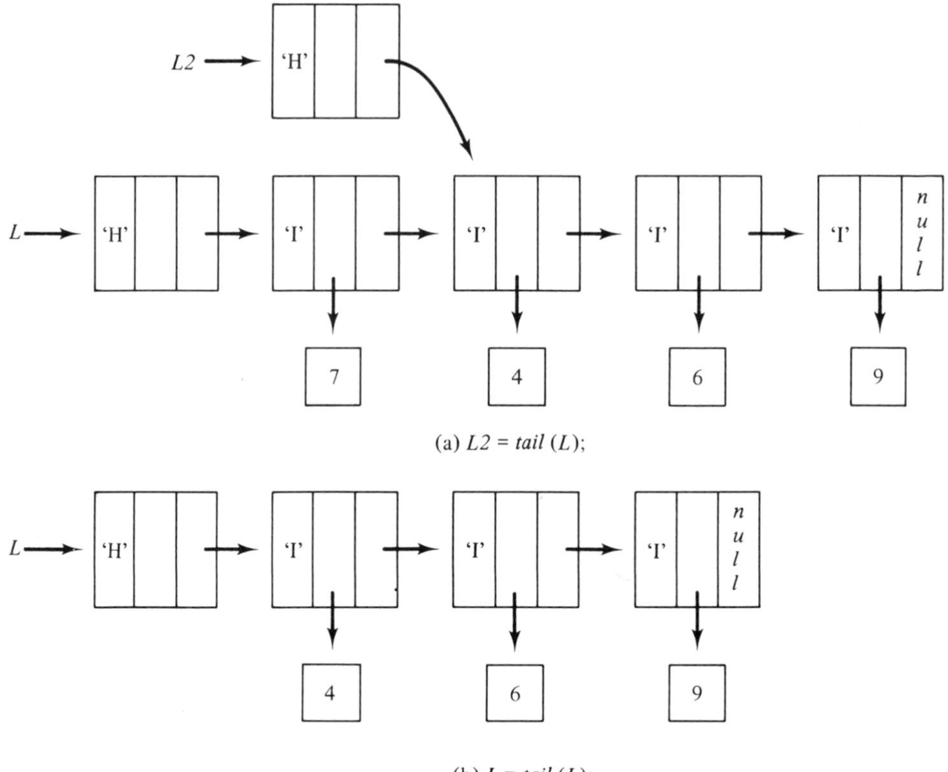

(a) *L2* = *tail* (*L*);

(b) *L* = *tail* (*L*);

Figure 10.1.11.

However, the copy method is highly inefficient when applied to list nodes, and the pointer method is the more commonly used technique. The same problems which arose in deciding whether or not to free an atomic node now occur in deciding whether or not to free all the nodes in a particular list. The situation is compounded by the fact that lists may contain other lists as elements. If a particular list is freed, it may also be necessary to free all the lists which are elements of it; however, if these lists are also elements of other lists, they cannot be freed. As an illustration of the complexity of the problem, consider *LIST9* of Fig. 10.1.13. The nodes in that figure are numbered arbitrarily so that we may refer to them easily in the text. This list can be written in parenthesized notation as

```
LIST9 = ((L1=(42):LIST11,L2=(5,7)),LIST10,12,L1)
LIST11 = (L2)
LIST10 = (14,28).
```

The local variables *L1* and *L2* are illustrated in the figure using dashed lines.

Suppose we wished to execute the operation

```
LIST9 = null
```

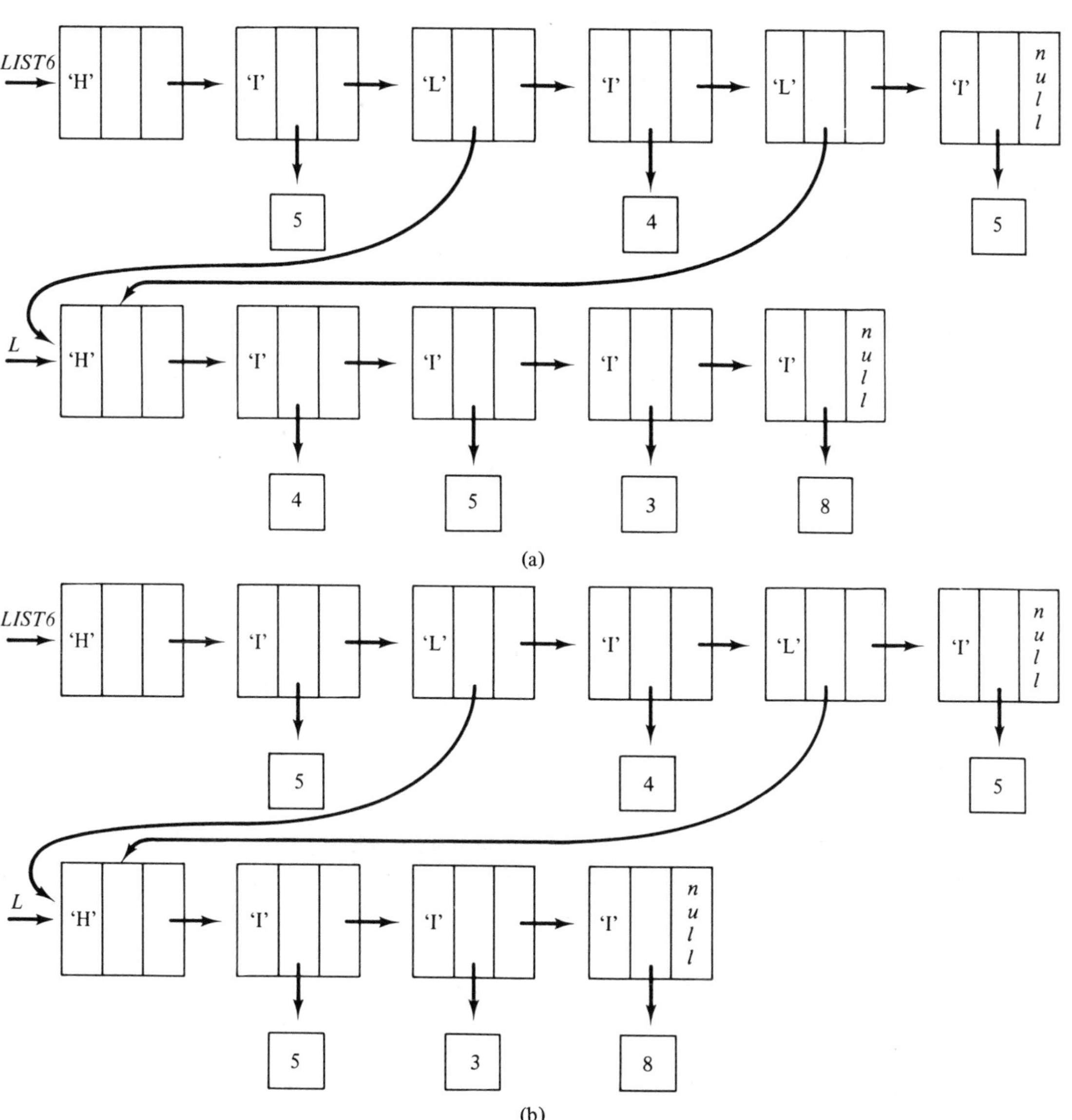

Figure 10.1.12.

Which nodes can be freed and which must be retained? Clearly, the list nodes of *LIST9* (nodes 1,2,3,4) and the atomic nodes to which they point (node 5) can be freed since no other pointers reference them. Freeing node 1 allows us to free nodes 17 and 18, since they too are accessed by no other pointers. Once node 17 is freed, can nodes 10, 11, and 12 also be freed? Node 10 can be freed because each of the nodes containing a pointer to it (nodes 17 and 4) can be freed. Thus atomic node 12 can also be freed. However, node 11 cannot be freed since *LIST11* points to it. *LIST11* is an external pointer, and therefore the node to which it points may still be needed elsewhere in the program. Since node 11 is kept, nodes 13, 14, 15, and 16 must also be kept (even though node 18 is being freed). Finally nodes 6,7,8, and 9 must be kept because of the external pointer *LIST10*.

The problem to be addressed in the next section is how to determine algorithmically which nodes are to be kept and which are to be freed. However, before considering possible solutions, let us make some comments about list processing languages and their design.

Programming Languages and Lists

In Section 1.1 we noted that a language implementation contains two classes of data types: those native to the machine and those implemented through software. Thus programs can be written using such entities as FIXED or FLOAT numbers and character strings. For more complex data structures, such as the stack, queue, tree, etc., it is necessary for the user to implement them in the language (i.e., defining how they will be represented and providing routines to perform elementary operations on them) before he can write programs using them.

Throughout this text, we have been treating a list as a compound data structure (a collection of nodes), rather than as a native data type (an elementary item such as FIXED numbers, character string, etc.). The reason for this is that we have been working closely with the PL/I language. In PL/I, one cannot make a declaration such as

```
DCL X LIST;
```

and apply such function as HEAD and TAIL to X directly. Rather, the programmer must implement lists himself and must write the necessary subroutines and functions for their manipulation. Other languages however, contain lists as elementary data structures with the operations *crlist*, *head*, *tail*, *addon*, *sethead*, and *settail* already built into the language. (A good example of such a language is LISP.)

One consequence of the fact that PL/I does not include list manipulation capabilities is that if a programmer programs a list manipulation application, he is responsible for allocating and freeing list and atomic nodes. As we have seen in this section, that problem is not at all trivial if lists are allowed in all their generality. However, any given application can usually be designed more easily using a specific type of list, tree, or graph, as we have seen in Chapters 5, 6, and 7. Indeed, general list manipulation techniques are more expensive in terms of both time and space than techniques which are designed specifically for a particular application. (This is a corollary to the axiom that a price is always paid for generality.)

However, in a system in which a general list is a native data type and into which list operations are built, the system must be able to deal with lists in all their generality. Since the fundamental objects with which the programmer deals are lists and atoms and not list nodes, the programmer cannot be responsible for allocating and freeing such nodes. Rather, when a program issues a statement such as

```
L1 = crlist(3,4,7);
```

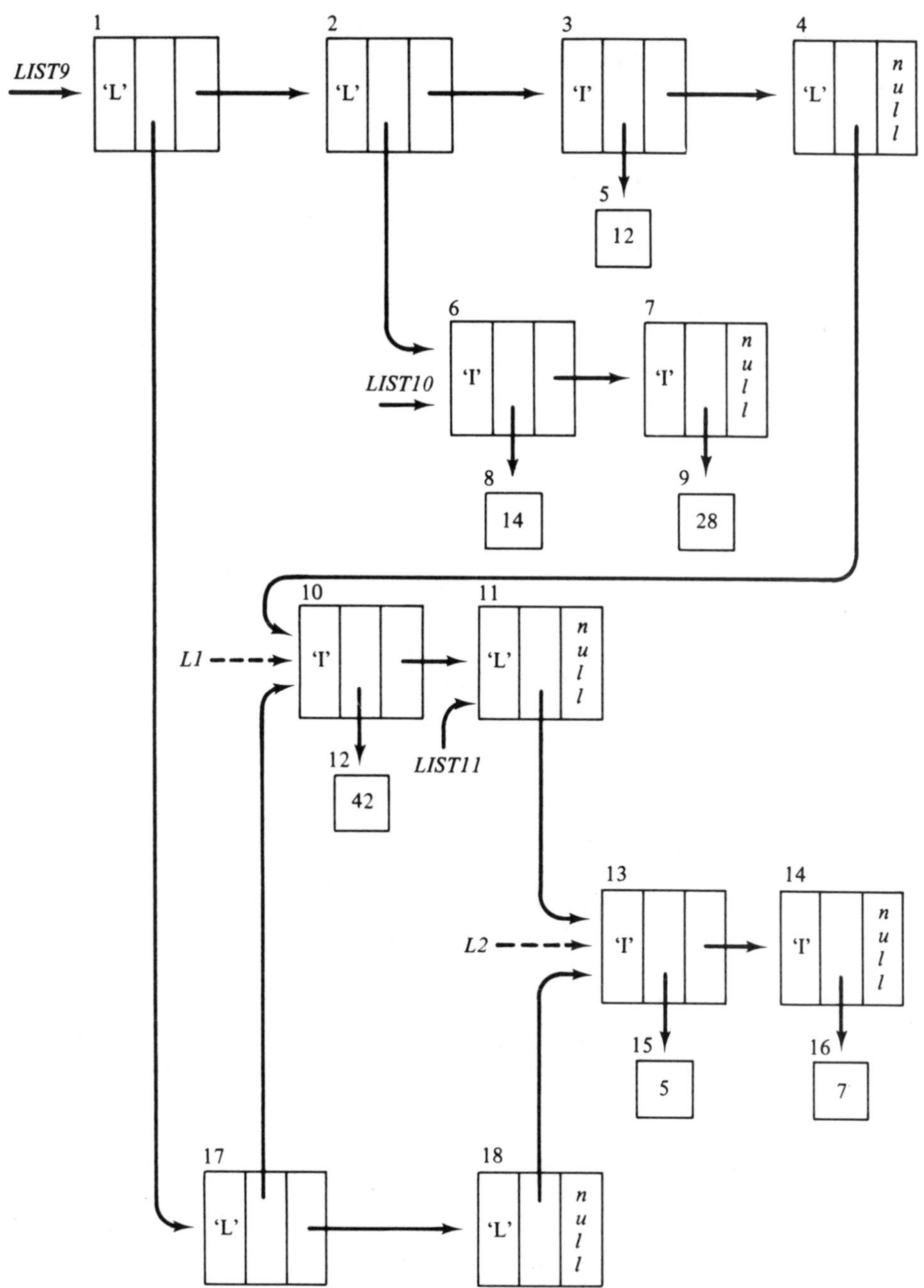

Figure 10.1.13.

the system is responsible for allocating sufficient list and atomic nodes and initializing the proper pointers. When the program later issues the command

```
L1 = null;
```

the system is responsible for identifying those nodes which were previously on list *L1* and which are now inaccessible and freeing them. If such nodes are not freed, available space would rapidly become exhausted.

In some sense languages which include lists as data types are of "higher level" than PL/I because the programmer is freed from so much of the bookkeeping activity which is associated with storage management. PL/I may be thought of as a higher-level language than FORTRAN in that PL/I includes data structures such as structures and varying-length character strings whereas FORTRAN does not. So too, a list processing system is of higher level than PL/I in that it includes lists whereas PL/I does not.

Another point which must be made concerns the implementation of lists. The implementation of lists as presented in this section is oriented towards PL/I. To see why this is so, let us reexamine Fig. 10.1.1. In that figure and the surrounding discussion, a distinction was introduced between list nodes and atomic nodes. All list nodes have the same format. Further, a typecode is included in each list node identifying the type of node to which its first pointer refers. The reason that this is necessary is because the PL/I language demands that the type of an object be known before it can be referenced. The only way that an object can be referenced in PL/I is through a constant or a variable. A constant can only be used to refer to an object whose value is known. Since a node's value is not known before referencing it, a constant cannot be used for this purpose. But in PL/I a variable must be declared as being of a specific type. Thus, the type of an object must be known before referencing it. Therefore, the list node must inform us of the type of the atomic node to which it points. For the same reason, each list node must have the same structure since the same variable must be used to refer to each list node.

To understand how clumsy this situation is, suppose there are 10 different types of atomic nodes (there is no reason that an atomic node may not be an array or a stack or a queue or a program label, etc.). Each of these must have a unique typecode. Further there must be a separate variable declared for each type of atomic node. Let us suppose that the typecodes used for 10 types are T1,T2, . . . ,T10 and that the atomic node variables are NODE1, NODE2, . . . , NODE10. Then each time that an atomic node is processed, we would need code such as:

```
IF TYPECODE = T1 THEN     /*  do something with NODE1    */;
IF TYPECODE = T2 THEN     /*  do something with NODE2    */;
                . . .
IF TYPECODE = T10 THEN    /*  do something with NODE10   */;
```

This is cumbersome.

However, some higher-level languages (many list processing languages included) do not require a variable to be declared as being of a particular type. Instead, a typecode appears in the initial portion of each data object informing the system as to how to interpret the remaining information. Thus a typecode is not needed in the list node but rather could be placed within the atomic node. Further, the programmer would no longer have the responsibility of recognizing the typecode and selecting an appropriate variable. The system would automatically recognize the code and interpret the object correctly. Any variable could be used to refer to any type of object.

Indeed, it may not be necessary to have atomic nodes at all. For example, the first portion of a list node can hold a pointer if the element happens to be a list, or it can hold an integer. Of course, then a typecode would be included with either the pointer or the integer. Thus "short" elements such as fixed- or floating-point numbers or single characters or labels or pointers can be contained within the list node itself, and an atomic node would not be required. In any case, any list processing system has its own convention for storing atoms and constructing lists.

In the next section of this chapter, we will examine techniques which are incorporated into the implementations of list processing systems in order to recover storage which is no longer needed. We retain the list structure conventions of this section, but it should be understood that they are not absolute. Because PL/I does not allow a single variable to refer to objects of different types, we present the techniques as algorithms rather than as PL/I programs.

10.2. Automatic List Management

In the last section we presented the need for algorithms to determine when a given list node is no longer accessible. In this section we shall investigate such algorithms. The philosophy behind incorporating such an algorithm into a programming system is that the programmer should not have to decide when a node should be allocated or freed. Instead, the programmer should code the solution to his problem with the assurance that the system will automatically allocate any list and atomic nodes which are necessary for the lists he wishes to create and that the system will make available for reuse any nodes which are no longer accessible.

There are two principal methods used in automatic list management: the reference count method and the garbage collection method. We now proceed to a discussion of each.

The Reference Count Method

Under this method, each node has an additional *count* field which keeps a count (called the ***reference count***) of the number of pointers to that node. Each time that the value of some pointer is set to the address of a node, the reference count in that node is increased by 1; each time that the value of some pointer which had been pointing to a node is changed, the reference count in that node is decreased by 1. When the reference count in any node becomes 0, that node can be returned to the available list of free nodes.

Reference counts may appear in both list and atomic nodes, thus allowing nodes of both types to appear in more than one context. However, the copy method is usually used for atomic nodes so that whenever a list node is freed, the atomic node to which it points (if any) may also be freed. Therefore, a reference count is unnecessary in atomic nodes.

Each list operation of a system using the reference count method must make provisions for updating that count and freeing any nodes whose count becomes 0. For example, to execute the statement

```
l = tail(l);
```

the following operations must be performed. If p is a pointer we denote the node to which p points, whether list or atomic, by *node*(p).

```
p=l;
l=nextptr(l);
nextptr(p) =null;
reduce(p);
```

where the operation *reduce*(p) is defined recursively as follows:

```
if p=null then return;
count(p) =count(p) −1;
if count(p) =0 then do;
                    r=nextptr(p);
                    reduce(r);
                    r=infptr(p);
                    if node(r) is atomic then free node(r);
                                         else reduce(r);
                    free node(p);
                  end;
```

reduce is coded as a recursive subprocedure which must be called each time that the value of a pointer to a list node is changed. Similarly, whenever a pointer variable is changed to a value which points to a list node, the *count* field of that node must be increased by 1. The *count* fields of free nodes are 0.

To illustrate the reference count method, let us reconsider the list of Fig. 10.1.13. The following set of statements creates that list:

```
LIST10=crlist(14,28);
LIST11=crlist(crlist(5,7));
L=addon(LIST11,42);
M=crlist(L,head(LIST11));
LIST9=crlist(M,LIST10,12,L);
M=null;
L=null;
```

Figure 10.2.1 illustrates the creation of the list using the reference count method. Each part of that figure shows the list after an additional group of the above statements has been executed. The reference count is shown as the leftmost field of each list node.

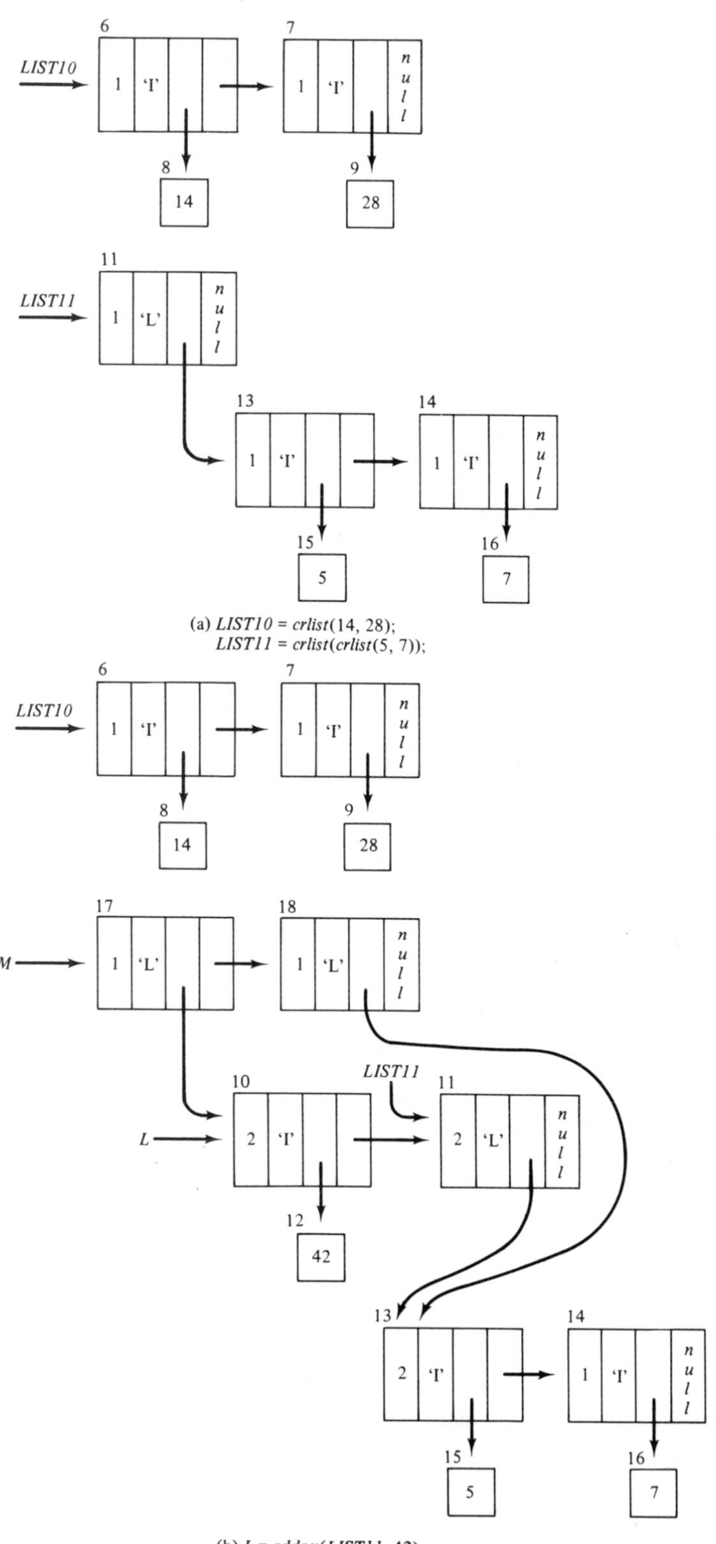

(a) *LIST10* = *crlist*(14, 28);
LIST11 = *crlist*(*crlist*(5, 7));

(b) *L* = *addon*(*LIST11*, 42);
M = *crlist*(*L*, *head*(*LIST11*))

Figure 10.2.1.

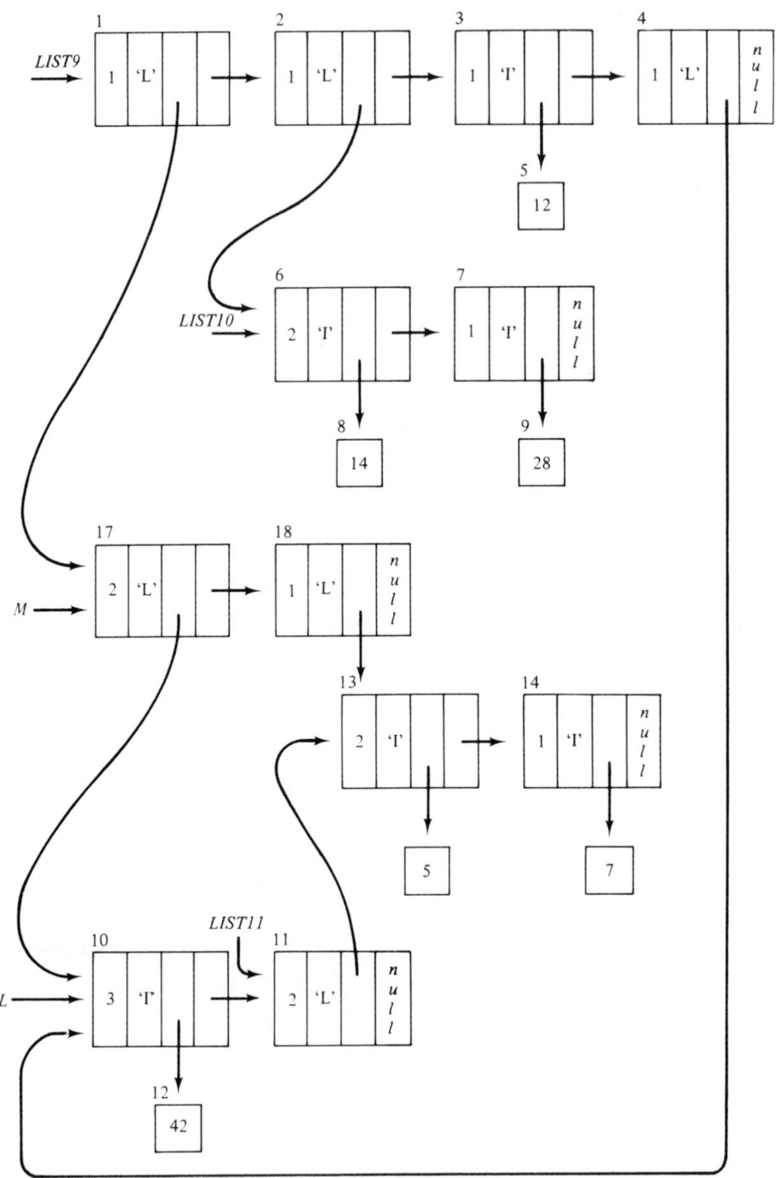

(c) *LIST9 = crlist(M, LIST10, 12, L)*

Figure 10.2.1. *(cont.)*

Each node in that figure is numbered according to the numbering of the nodes in Fig. 10.1.13. Make sure that you understand how each statement alters the reference count in each node.

Let us now see what happens when we execute the statement

```
LIST9=null;
```

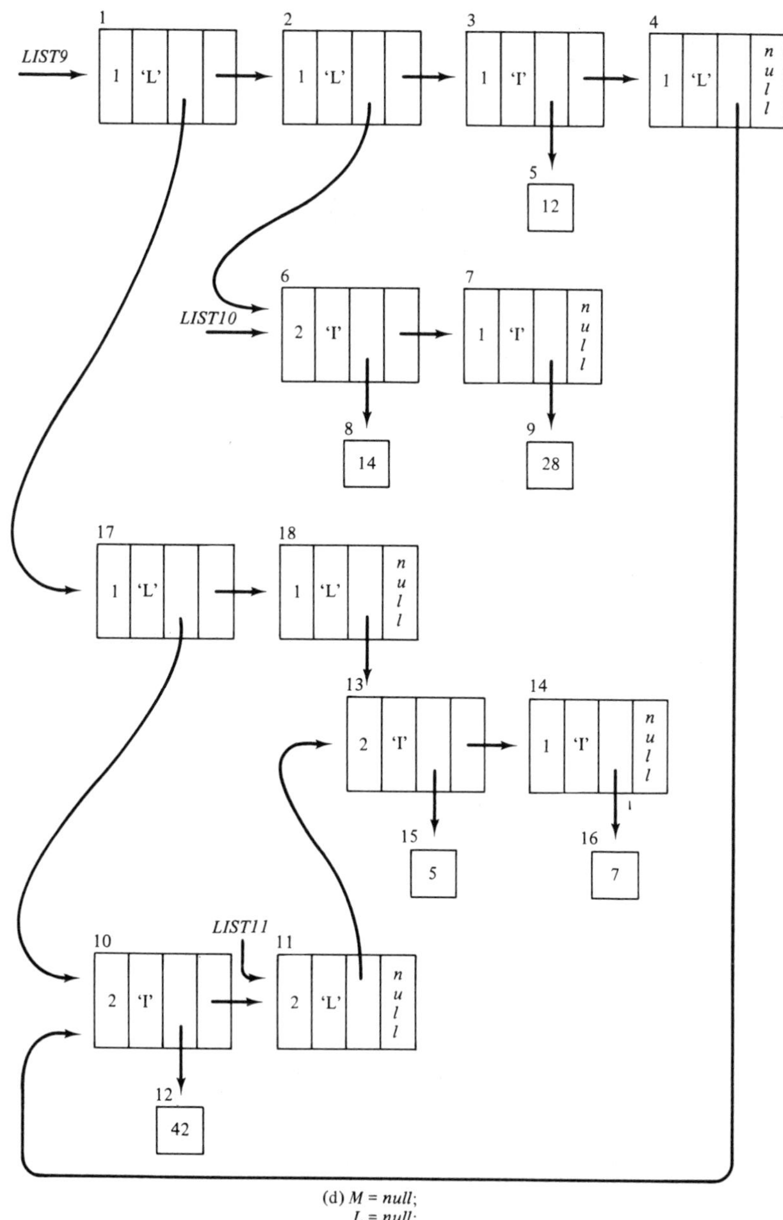

(d) M = *null*;
L = *null*;

Figure 10.2.1. (*cont.*)

The results are illustrated in Figs. 10.2.2 and 10.2.3, where freed nodes are shown by dashed lines. The following sequence of events may take place:

count of node 1 is set to 0

Node 1 is freed

counts of nodes 2 and 17 are set to 0

Nodes 2 and 17 are freed

counts of nodes 3 and 18 are set to 0

(Fig. 10.2.2) *counts* of nodes 6 and 10 are set to 1

Nodes 3, 5, and 18 are freed

count of node 4 is set to 0

count of node 13 is set to 1

Node 4 is freed

count of node 10 is set to 0

Nodes 10 and 12 are freed

(Fig. 10.2.3) *count* of node 11 is set to 1

Only those nodes which are accessible from the external pointers *LIST10* and *LIST11* remain allocated—all others are freed.

One drawback of the reference count method is illustrated by the above example. The amount of work which must be performed by the system each time that a list manipulation statement is executed can be considerable. Each time that the value of a pointer is changed, all nodes which were previously accessible from that pointer can potentially be freed. Often, the work involved in identifying the nodes to be freed is not worth the reclaimed space, since there may be ample space for the program to run to completion without reusing any nodes. After the program has terminated, a single pass through all of its lists reclaims all of its storage without having to worry about reference count values.

One solution to this problem can be illustrated by an alternate approach to the previous example. When the statement

```
LIST9=null;
```

is executed, the reference count in node 1 is reduced to 0 and node 1 is freed—that is, it is placed on the available list. However, the fields of this node retain their original values, so that it still points to nodes 2 and 17. (This means that an additional pointer field is necessary to link such nodes on the available list. An alternative is to reuse the reference count field for this purpose.) The reference count values in these two nodes remain unchanged. When additional space is needed and node 1 is reallocated for some other use, the reference counts in nodes 2 and 17 are reduced and they are placed on the available list. This removes much of the work from the deallocation process and adds it to the allocation process. If node 1 is never reused because enough space is available, then nodes 2, 17, 3, 4, 5, 10, and 18 are not freed during program execution. In order for this scheme to work best, however, the available list should be kept as a queue rather than as a stack, so that freed nodes are never allocated before nodes which have not been used for the first time.

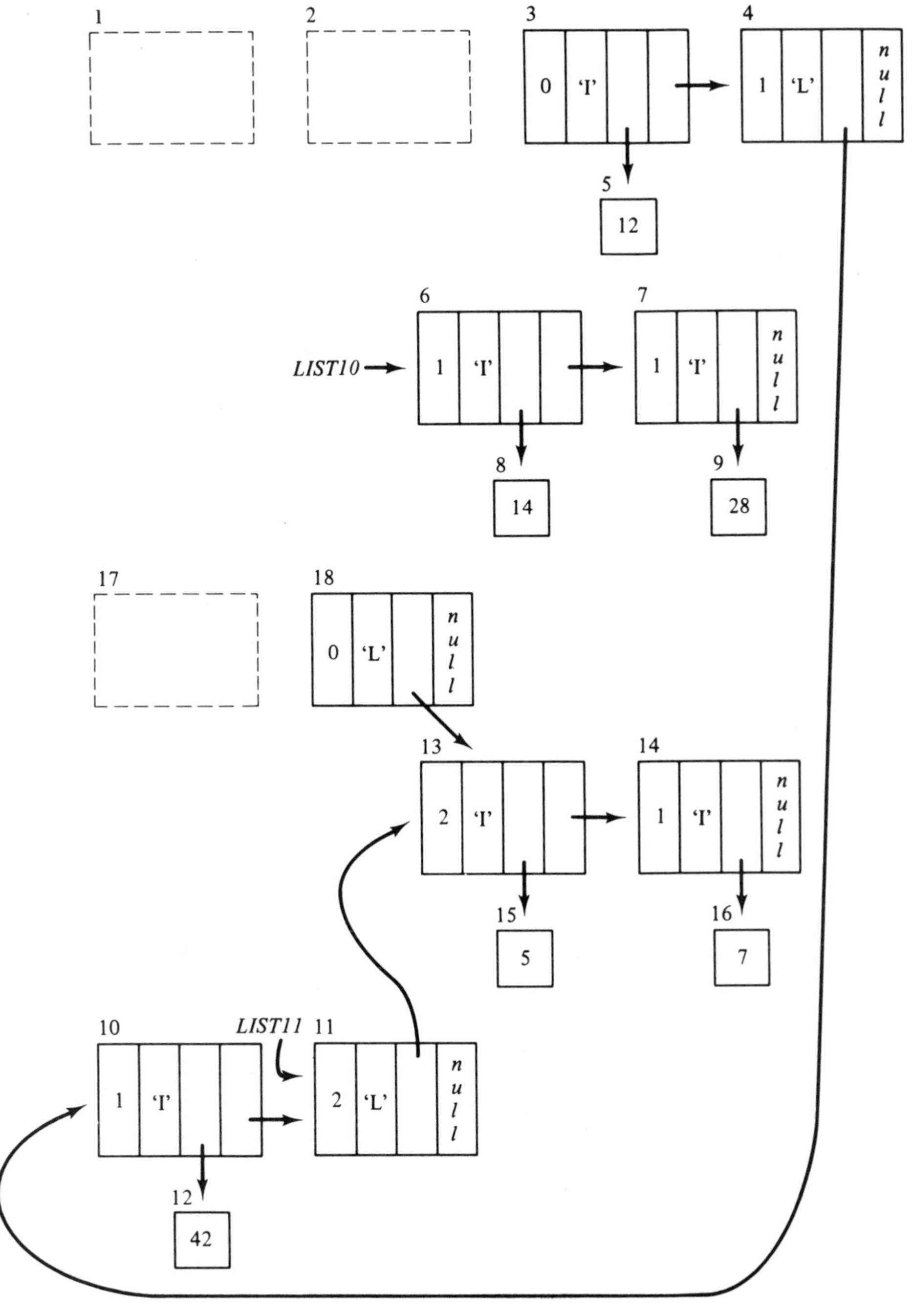
1
2
3
0
'I'
4
1
'L'
null
5
12
6
7
LIST10
1
'I'
1
'I'
null
8
14
9
28
17
18
0
'L'
null
13
14
2
'I'
1
'I'
null
15
5
16
7
10
LIST11
11
1
'I'
2
'L'
null
12
42

Figure 10.2.2.

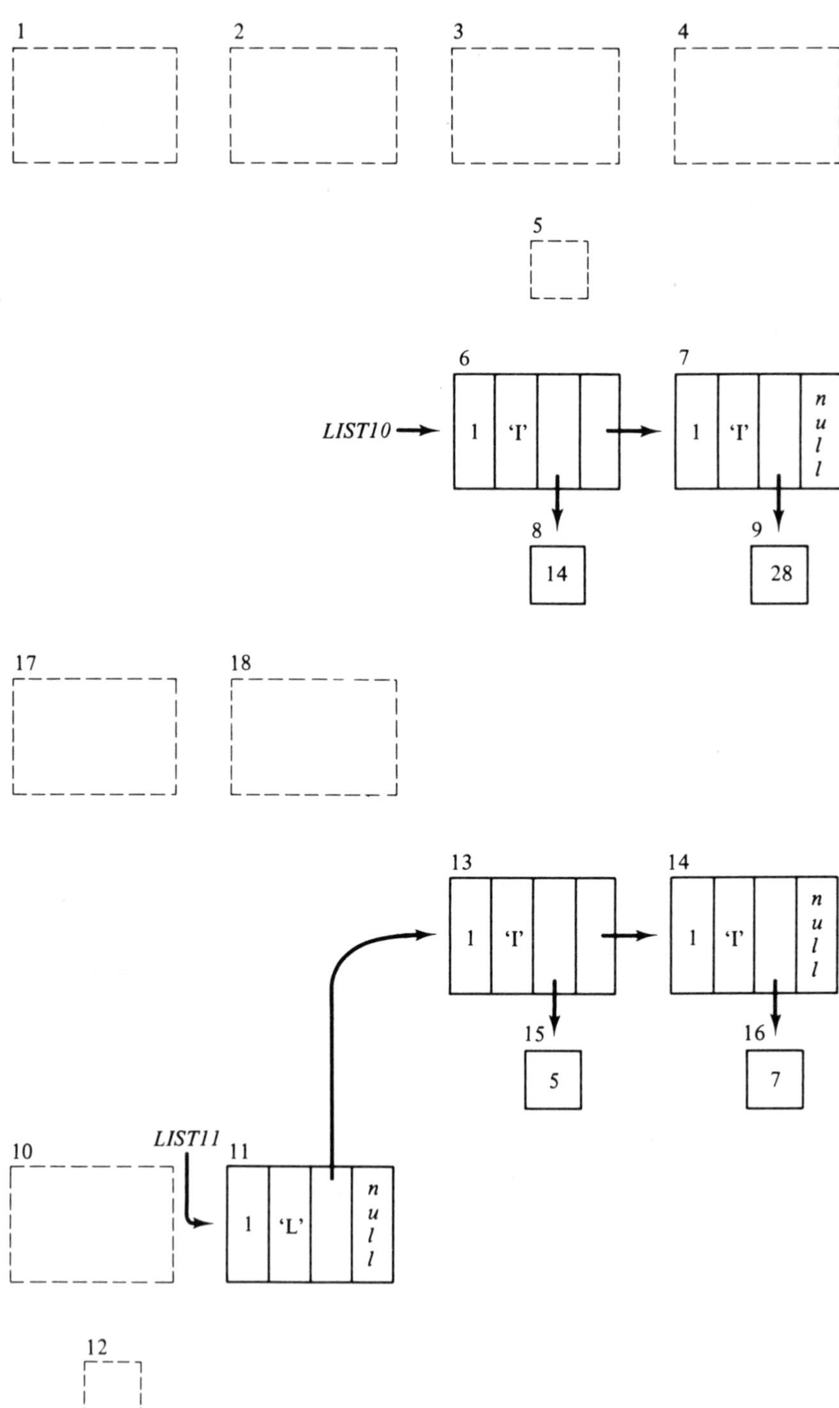
1
2
3
4
5
6
7
LIST10
1
'I'
1
'I'
null
8
9
14
28
17
18
13
14
1
'I'
1
'I'
null
15
16
5
7
10
LIST11
11
1
'L'
null
12

Figure 10.2.3.

There are two additional disadvantages to the reference count method. The first is the additional space that is necessary in each node for the count. This is not usually an overriding consideration, however. The problem can be somewhat alleviated if each list is required to contain a header node and a reference count is kept only in the header. However, this method requires that only a header node can be accessed by two pointers (i.e., a list such as in Fig. 10.2.4(b) would be prohibited). The counts are kept in the *infptr* field of the header node. The lists of Fig. 10.2.4 are analogous to those of Fig. 10.1.4 except that they include header nodes. When the count in a header node reaches 0, all the nodes on its list are freed and the counts in header nodes pointed to by *infptr* fields in the list nodes are reduced.

In particular, the *tail* operation must be modified so that the situation of Fig. 10.1.11(a) does not occur, and the *settail* operation must be modified so that the situation of Fig. 10.2.4(b) does not occur. One method of modification is to use the copy method in implementing these operations. Another method is to somehow differentiate between external pointers which represent lists (and therefore must point to a header node) and "temporary" external pointers which are used for traversal (and which can point directly to list nodes). When the count in a header node becomes 0, references to its list nodes through temporary pointers become illegal.

The other disadvantage of the reference count method is that the count in the first node of a recursive or circular list will never be reduced to 0. For example, Fig. 10.2.5(a) illustrates a circular list, and Fig. 10.2.5(b) a recursive list with reference counts. Executing the statement *L=null*; reduces the counts in the first nodes of both lists to 1, despite the fact that the nodes may be freed. Of course, whenever a pointer within a list is set to point to a node on that list, the reference count can be maintained rather than increased, but detecting when this is so is often a difficult task.

Garbage Collection

Under the reference count method, nodes are reclaimed when they become available for reuse (or under one version, when they are needed). The other principle method of detecting and reclaiming free nodes is called ***garbage collection***. Under this method, nodes which are no longer in use remain allocated and undetected until all available storage has been allocated. A further request for allocation cannot be satisfied until nodes which had been allocated but are no longer in use are recovered. When a request is made for additional nodes and there are none available, a system routine called the ***garbage collector*** is called. This routine searches through all of the nodes in the system, determines which are no longer accessible from an external pointer, and restores the inaccessible nodes to the available pool. The request for additional nodes is then fulfilled, and the system continues processing user requests for more space. When available space is exhausted again, the garbage collector is called once more.

Garbage collection is usually done in two phases. The first phase, called the ***marking phase***, involves marking all nodes which are accessible from an external pointer. The second phase, called the ***collection phase***, involves proceeding sequentially through memory and freeing all nodes that have not been marked. The collection phase is straightforward and need not be discussed further. We focus our attention on the marking phase.

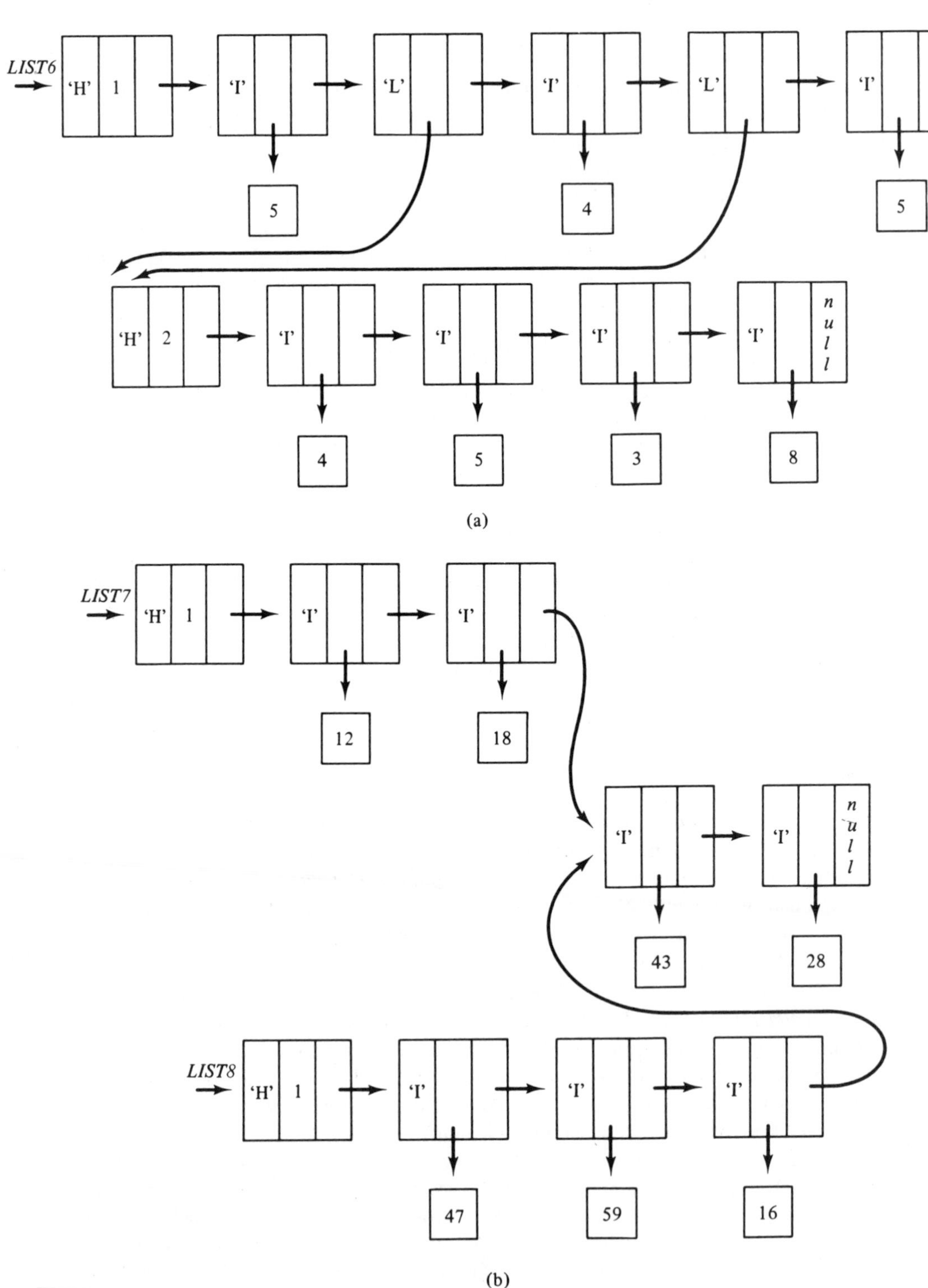
LIST6
'H'
1
'I'
'L'
'I'
'L'
'I'
null
5
4
5
'H'
2
'I'
'I'
'I'
'I'
null
4
5
3
8
(a)
LIST7
'H'
1
'I'
'I'
12
18
'I'
'I'
null
43
28
LIST8
'H'
1
'I'
'I'
'I'
47
59
16
(b)

Figure 10.2.4.

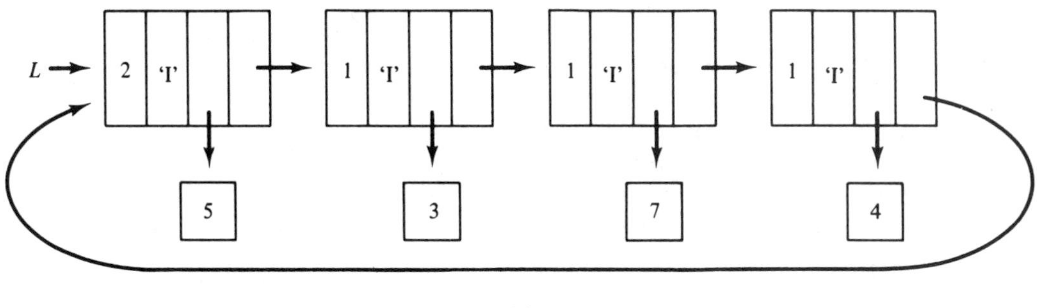

(a)

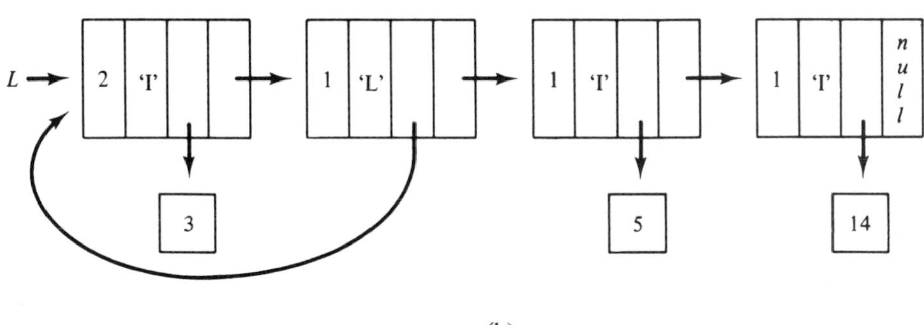

(b)

Figure 10.2.5.

One bit must be set aside in each node to indicate whether a node has or has not been marked. The marking phase sets the mark bit to 1 in each accessible node. As the collection phase proceeds, the mark bit in each accessible node is reset to 0. Thus, at the start and end of garbage collection, all mark bits are 0. User programs do not affect the mark bits.

It is sometimes inconvenient to reserve one bit in each node solely for the purpose of marking. In that case, a separate area in memory can be reserved to hold one long bit string of mark bits, one bit for each node which may be allocated.

One feature of garbage collection is that it must run when there is very little space available. This means that auxiliary tables and stacks must be kept to a minimum since there is not enough space available for them. An alternative is to reserve a specific percentage of memory for the exclusive use of the garbage collector. However, this effectively reduces the amount of memory available to the user and means that the garbage collector will be called more frequently.

Whenever the garbage collector is called, all user processing comes to a halt while the algorithm examines all allocated nodes in memory. For this reason, it is desirable that the garbage collector be called as infrequently as possible. For real-time applications, in which a computer must respond to a user request within a specific short time span, garbage collection has generally been considered an unsatisfactory method of storage management. We can picture a spaceship drifting off into the infinite as it waits for directions from a computer which is occupied with garbage collection. However, methods have recently been developed whereby garbage collection can be performed simultaneously with user processing. This means that the garbage collector must be called before all space has been exhausted so that user processing can continue in whatever space is left while the garbage collector recovers additional space.

Another important consideration is that users must be careful to ensure that all lists are well formed and that all pointers are correct. Usually, the operations which exist in a list processing system are carefully implemented so that if garbage collection does occur in the middle of one of them, the entire system will work correctly. However, some users try to outsmart the system and implement their own pointer manipulations. This requires great care so that the garbage collection will work properly. In a real-time garbage collection system, not only must we ensure that user operations do not upset list structures which the garbage collector must have, but also that the garbage collection algorithm itself does not disturb the list structures which are being used concurrently by the user. As we shall see, some marking algorithms do disturb (temporarily) list structures and are therefore unsuitable for real-time use.

It is possible that users are actually using almost all the nodes that are allocated at the time the garbage collector is called. Thus, almost all nodes are accessible, and the garbage collector recovers very little additional space. After the system runs for a short time, it will again be out of space; the garbage collector will again be called, only to recover very few additional nodes, and the vicious cycle starts again. This phenomenon in which the system storage management routines are executing almost all the time is called ***thrashing***. Clearly, thrashing is a situation to be avoided. One drastic solution is to impose the following conditions. If the garbage collector is run and does not recover a specific percentage of the total space, then the user who requested the extra space is terminated and removed from the system. All of that user's space is then recovered and made available to other users.

Now that we have mentioned some general concepts of garbage collection, let us proceed to present some marking algorithms.

The simplest method for marking all accessible nodes is to mark initially all nodes which are immediately accessible (i.e., those pointed to by external pointers) and then repeatedly pass through all of memory sequentially. On each sequential pass, whenever a node *n* which has already been marked is encountered, all nodes pointed to by a pointer within *n* are marked. These sequential passes continue until no new nodes have been marked in an entire pass. However, this method is as inefficient as it is simple. The number of sequential passes necessary is equal to the maximum path length to any accessible node (why?), and on each pass every list node in memory must be examined.

A somewhat more efficient variation is the following: Suppose that a node *n1* in the sequential pass has been previously marked and that *n1* includes a pointer to an unmarked node *n2*. Then node *n2* is marked, and the sequential pass would ordinarily continue with the node which follows *n1* sequentially. However, if the address of *n2* is less than the address of *n1*, the sequential pass resumes from *n2* rather than from *n1*. Thus, when the last node in memory is reached, all accessible nodes have been marked.

Let us present this method as an algorithm. Assume that all list nodes in memory are declared as an array:

```
DCL 1  NODE(0:NUM),
         2 TYPE          CHAR(1),
        (2 INFPTR,
         2 NEXTPTR)      FIXED,
         2 MARK          BIT(1);
```

This is the same format that was used in Section 10.1 except for three points. An array is used to convey the notion that we can step through all nodes sequentially. We also include a node called NODE(0). This is not a real node (since 0 represents the null pointer), but it is used as a dummy node so that a reference to INFPTR(0) (for example) does not generate an error. We assume that INFPTR(0) and NEXTPTR(0) are initialized to 0, TYPE(0) to 'L', and MARK(0) to '1'B and that these values are never changed throughout the system's execution. A MARK bit in each node is initially off and is turned on by the marking algorithm when a node is found to be accessible. The variable NUM is an integer whose value is the number of initially available list nodes. If INFPTR(I) points to another list node, then TYPE(I) is 'L'; if it points to an atomic node, then TYPE(I) is 'I', 'C', or whatever codes are legal for an atom. Of course, there are additional arrays of atomic nodes such as

```
DCL 1  INODE(NUMI),
         2 IINFO         FIXED,
         2 NEXTI         FIXED,
    1  CNODE(NUMC),
         2 CINFO         CHAR(100) VAR,
         2 NEXTC         FIXED,

    etc.
```

NUMI and NUMC indicate the total number of integer and character nodes available in the system, and NEXTI and NEXTC are used to link the unallocated atomic nodes of specific type in their own available list.

Note that the above conventions are very much PL/I oriented, so that the algorithms can be presented in PL/I style. Ordinarily the hardware of the computer imposes a sequential structure on all the nodes, both list and atomic, intermixed. Usually, a code indicating the type of a node is kept within the node itself rather than in the list node which points to it. The first byte of a node might be a typecode, another bit the mark flag (thus, atomic nodes as well as list nodes would have mark bits), and the next field possibly a length code specifying the length of the node. The actual contents of a node would come after all these bookkeeping fields. In such a scheme, a marking algorithm would mark all nodes, atomic and list, accessible from external pointers.

The algorithms which we present here mark only accessible list nodes. During the collection phase, when unmarked list nodes are restored to the available pool, the atomic nodes to which they point can be recovered as well. We also adopt the convention that the NEXTPTR field always points to a list node, or is null (equals 0, under our representation), while the INFPTR field may point to a list or an atomic node.

Now that we have disposed of questions of format and convention, we turn to the actual algorithm. Assume that ACC is an array containing external pointers to immediately accessible nodes. It is declared by

```
DCL ACC(NUMACC)    FIXED;
```

The algorithm is as follows (the variables refer to their capitalized versions declared in PL/I style above):

```
      /*   mark all immediately accessible nodes   */
do i=1 to numacc;
   mark(acc(i))='1'B;
end;

i=1;
      /*   begin a sequential pass through the list nodes    */
      /*   i points to the node currently being examined     */
do while(i<=num);
   j=i+1;
      /*   j points to the node to be examined next          */
   if mark(i) then    /*  mark nodes to which node(i) points  */
                do;
          if type(i)='L' & ¬mark(infptr(i))
                 /*  if infptr(i) points to an unmarked   */
                 /*              list node                */
                             then do;
                                   mark(infptr(i))='1'B;
                                   j=min(j,infptr(i));
                                end;
          if ¬mark(nextptr(i))
                 /*  if nextptr(i) points to an unmarked  */
                 /*                node                   */
                             then do;
                                   mark(nextptr(i))='1'B;
                                   j=min(j,nextptr(i));
                                end;
                end;
   i=j;
end;
```

As an exercise, you are asked to trace through the execution of this algorithm on a list distributed throughout memory such as in Fig. 10.1.13.

Although this method is better than successive sequential passes, it is still inefficient. Consider how many nodes must be examined if *node*(1) is immediately accessible and points to *node*(999), which points to *node*(2), etc. Thus it is usually too slow to use in an actual system.

A more desirable method is one which is not based on traversing memory sequentially, but rather traces down all accessible lists. Thus it examines only those nodes which are accessible, rather than all nodes.

The most obvious way to accomplish this is by use of an auxiliary stack. As each list is traversed through its *nextptr* fields, a pointer is stacked to any node whose *infptr* points to a list node. When the end of a list or a marked node is reached, the stack is popped and the list headed by the node at the top of the stack is traversed. In the algorithm which follows, we again assume that *mark*(0) equals '1'*B*.

```
do i=1 to numacc;
   /*    mark the next immediately accessible node and        */
   /*                    place it on the stack                */
   mark(acc(i))='1'B;
   push(stack,acc(i));

   do while(¬empty(stack));
      p=pop(stack);
      do while(p¬=0);
         if type(p)='L' & ¬mark(infptr(p)) then
               do;
                  mark(infptr(p))='1'B;
                  push(stack,infptr(p));
               end;
         if mark(nextptr(p)) then p=0;
                             else do;
                                        p=nextptr(p);
                                        mark(p)='1'B;
                                  end;
      end;
   end;
end;
```

This algorithm is as efficient as we can hope for in terms of time, since each node to be marked is visited only once. However, it has a very significant weakness because of its dependence on an auxiliary stack. A garbage collection algorithm is called when there is no extra space available. Where can sufficient space be obtained for the stack? In a list processing system, the stack itself might be implemented as a list using dynamic storage allocation, but a storage allocation request is what prompted garbage collection in the first place. A certain number of nodes can be set aside for the stack, and the size of the stack is never greater than the depth of list nesting. It is rare to find lists nested beyond some reasonable limit (such as 100), so that a specific number of nodes reserved for garbage collection would suffice in most cases. However, there is always the possibility that some user would want to nest nodes more deeply.

One solution is to use a stack limited to some maximum size. If the stack is about to overflow, we can revert to the sequential method given in the previous algorithm. We ask the reader to work out the details as an exercise.

Another solution is to use the allocated list nodes themselves as the stack. Clearly we do not want to add an additional field to each list node to hold a pointer to the next node on the stack, since the extra space would be better used for other purposes. Thus either the *infptr* or *nextptr* field of the list nodes must be used to link together the stack. But this means that the list structure is temporarily disturbed. Provision must be made for the lists to be restored properly.

In the above algorithm, each list is traversed using the *nextptr* fields of its nodes, and the value of each *infptr* to a list node is pushed onto a stack. When either the end of a list or a section of the list which had already been marked is reached, the stack is popped and a new list is traversed. Therefore, when a pointer to a node *nd* is popped, there is no need to restore any of the fields within *nd*.

However, suppose the stack is kept as a list, linked by the *nextptr* field. Then when a node is pushed onto the stack, its *nextptr* field must be changed to point to the next node in the stack. This implies that the field must be restored to its original value when the node is popped. But that original value has not been saved anywhere. (It cannot be saved on the stack, since there is no extra storage available for it.)

A solution to this problem can be described by the following scheme. Let us first assume a list with no elements which are themselves lists. As each node in the list is visited, it is pushed onto the stack and its *nextptr* field is used to link it onto the stack. Since each node preceding the current node on the list is present on the stack (the top of the stack is the last encountered element on the list), the list can be reconstructed easily by simply popping the stack and restoring the *nextptr* fields.

The situation is only slightly different in the case of one list as an element of another. Suppose *nd1* is a list node on *list1* and *nd2* is a list node on *list2* and that *infptr(nd1)* points to *nd2*. That is, *nd2* is the first node of *list2*, where *list2* is an element of *list1*. The algorithm has been traversing *list1* and is now about to begin traversing *list2*. In this case, *nextptr(nd1)* cannot be used as a stack pointer because it is needed to link *nd1* to the remainder of *list1*. However, the *infptr* field of *nd1* can be used to link *nd1* onto the stack since it is currently being used to link to *nd2*.

In general, when a node *nd* is pushed onto the stack, either its *infptr* field or its *nextptr* field is used to point to the previous top element. If the next node to be examined is pointed to by *infptr(nd)*, then the *infptr* field is used to link *nd* onto the stack; and if the node is pointed to by *nextptr(nd)*, then the *nextptr* field is used to link *nd* onto the stack. The remaining problem is how to determine for a given node on the stack whether the *infptr* or *nextptr* field is used to link the stack.

If the *infptr* of a list node points to an atomic node, then it is unnecessary to go down the *infptr* (because only list nodes are marked). If such a node appears on the stack, its *nextptr* must be in use as a stack pointer. Thus if the *type* field in a node popped from the stack is 'I' or 'C', or any of the codes used for atomic types, then its *nextptr* must be restored. However, a node with a typecode of 'L' is not so easily handled. Suppose that each time the *infptr* field is used to advance to the next node, the *type* code in the list node is changed from 'L' to some new code (say 'S' for stack) which is neither 'L' nor any of the codes which denote atomic elements. Then when a node is popped from the stack, if its type code is 'L', its *nextptr* must be restored and if its *type* code is 'S', its *infptr* must be restored and the *type* code changed back to 'L'.

Figure 10.2.6 illustrates how this stacking mechanism works. Figure 10.2.6(a) shows a list before the marking algorithm begins. The pointer *p* points to the node currently being processed; *top* points to the stack top, and *q* is an auxiliary pointer. The mark bit is shown in each node immediately following the type code. Figure 10.2.6(b) shows the same list immediately after node 4 has been marked. The path taken to node 4 is through the *nextptr* fields of nodes 1, 2, and 3. This path can be retraced in reverse order, beginning at *top* and following along the *nextptr* fields. Figure 10.2.6(c) shows the list after node 7 has been marked. The path to node 7 from the beginning of the list was from node 1, through *nextptr*(1) to node 2, through *infptr*(2) to node 5, through *nextptr*(5) to node 6, and then from *nextptr*(6) to node 7. The same fields which link together the stack are used to restore the list to its original form. Note that the *type* code in node 2 is 'S' rather than 'L' to indicate that its *infptr* field, not its *nextptr* field, is being used as a stack pointer. The algorithm which incorporates these ideas is known as the Schorr and Waite algorithm, after its discoverers.

Now that we have described the temporary distortions which are made in the list structure by the Schorr and Waite algorithm, we present the algorithm itself. We invite the reader to trace through the effects of the algorithm on the lists of Figs. 10.2.6(a) and 10.1.13.

```
accloop:  do i=1 to numacc;
              /*     for each immediately accessible node,    */
              /*            trace through its list            */
              p=acc(i);
              /*         initialize the stack to empty        */
              top=0;

traverse:     /*          traverse the list through its        */
              /*       nextptrs, marking each node and         */
              /*          placing it on the stack until a      */
              /*     marked node or the end of the list is     */
              /*     reached; recall that, by conventions,     */
              /*               mark(0) = '1'B.                 */
              do while (¬mark(p));
                 mark(p)='1'B;
                    /*   place node(p) on the stack, saving    */
                    /*          a pointer to the next node     */
                 q=nextptr(p);
                 nextptr(p)=top;
                 top=p;
                    /*          continue to the next node      */
                 p=q;
              end traverse;
```

```
                /*    at this point, trace the way back       */
                /*   through the list, popping the stack      */
                /*  until a node is reached whose infptr      */
                /*  is to an unmarked list node, or until     */
                /*             the list is empty              */
unravel:        do while(top¬=0);
                   /*    restore infptr(p) or nextptr(p) to p      */
                   /*               and pop the stack              */
                   p=top;

                   /*    restore the proper field of node(p)      */
                   if type(p)='S' then do;
                               /*       infptr was used as the stack link        */
                               /*              restore the type field            */
                               type(p)='L';
                               /*                 pop the stack                  */
                               top=infptr(top);
                               /*             restore the infptr field         */
                               infptr(p)=q;
                               q=p;
                                         end;
                                   else do;
                               /*       nextptr was used as the stack link       */
                               /*                 pop the stack                  */
                               top=nextptr(top);
                               /*             restore the nextptr field          */
                               nextptr(p)=q;
                               q=p;

                               /*     check whether we must travel down          */
                               /*                    infptr(p)                   */
                               if type(p)='L' then do;
                                     /*      indicate that infptr(p) is      */
                                     /*         used as the stack link       */
                                     type(p)='S';
                                     q=infptr(p);
                                     /*    push node(p) onto the stack       */
                                     infptr(p)=top;
                                     top=p;
                                     /*      advance to the next node        */
                                     p=q;
                                     /*           begin traversing the new list           */
                                     go to traverse;
                                                   end;
                                         end;
                end unravel;
              end accloop;
```

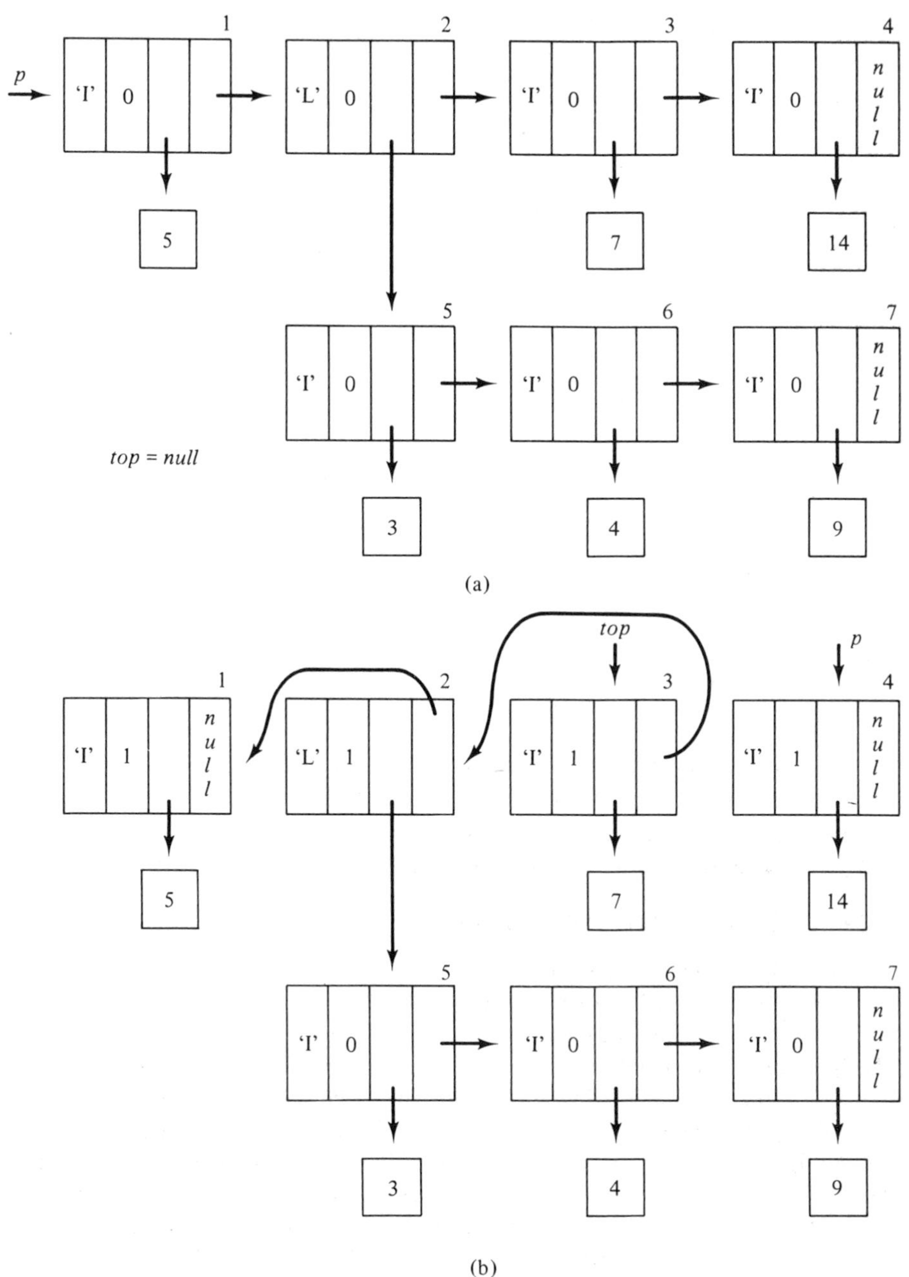

Figure 10.2.6.

Although this algorithm is advantageous in terms of space, since no auxiliary stack is necessary, it is disadvantageous in terms of time because each list must be traversed twice: once in pushing each node in the list on the stack and once in popping the stack

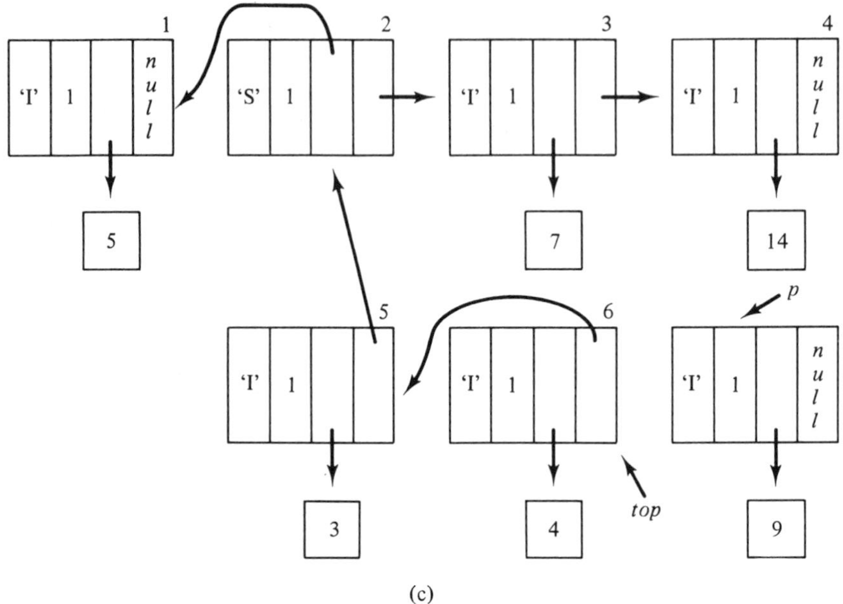

(c)

Figure 10.2.6. (*cont.*)

This can be contrasted with the relatively few nodes which must be stacked when an auxiliary stack is available.

Of course, several methods of garbage collection can be combined into a single algorithm. For example, an auxiliary stack of fixed size can be set aside for garbage collection, and when the stack is about to overflow, the algorithm can switch to the Schorr-Waite method. We leave the details as an exercise.

10.3. Dynamic Memory Management

Previously we assumed that storage is allocated and freed one node at a time. There are two characteristics of nodes which make the previous methods suitable. The first is that each node of a given type is of fixed size, and the second is that the size of each node is fairly small. In some applications, however, these characteristics do not apply. For example, a particular program might require a large amount of contiguous storage (e.g., a large array). It would be impractical to attempt to obtain such a block one node at a time. Similarly, a program may require storage blocks in a large variety of sizes. In such cases, it is necessary to have a memory management system that processes requests for variable-length blocks. In this section we discuss some systems of this type.

As an example of this situation, consider a small memory of 1024 words. Suppose a request is made for three blocks of storage of 348, 110, and 212 words respectively. Let us further suppose that these blocks are allocated sequentially, as shown in Fig. 10.3.1(a). Now suppose that the second block of size 110 is freed, resulting in the situation of Fig. 10.3.1(b). There are now 464 words of free space; yet a request for a block of 400 words could not be satisfied because the free space is divided into noncontiguous blocks.

Suppose block 3 were now freed. Clearly, it is not desirable to retain three free blocks of 110, 212, and 354 words. Rather the blocks should be combined into a single large block of 676 words so that further large requests can be satisfied. After combinations, memory will appear as in Fig. 10.3.1(c).

This example illustrates that it is necessary to keep track of the space that is available, to allocate portions of that space when allocation requests are presented, and to combine contiguous free spaces when a block is freed.

Compaction

One scheme sometimes used involves compaction of storage as follows: Initially memory is one large block of available storage. As requests for storage arrive, blocks of memory are allocated sequentially starting from the first location in memory. This is illustrated in Fig. 10.3.2(a). A variable *freepoint* contains the address of the first location after the last block allocated. In Fig. 10.3.2(a), *freepoint* equals 950. Note that all memory locations between *freepoint* and the highest address in memory are free. When a block is freed, *freepoint* remains unchanged and no combinations of free spaces take place. When a block of size n is allocated, *freepoint* is increased by n. This continues until a block of size n is requested and $freepoint+n-1$ is larger than the highest address in memory. The request cannot be satisfied without further action being taken.

At that point, user routines come to a halt and a system compaction routine is called.

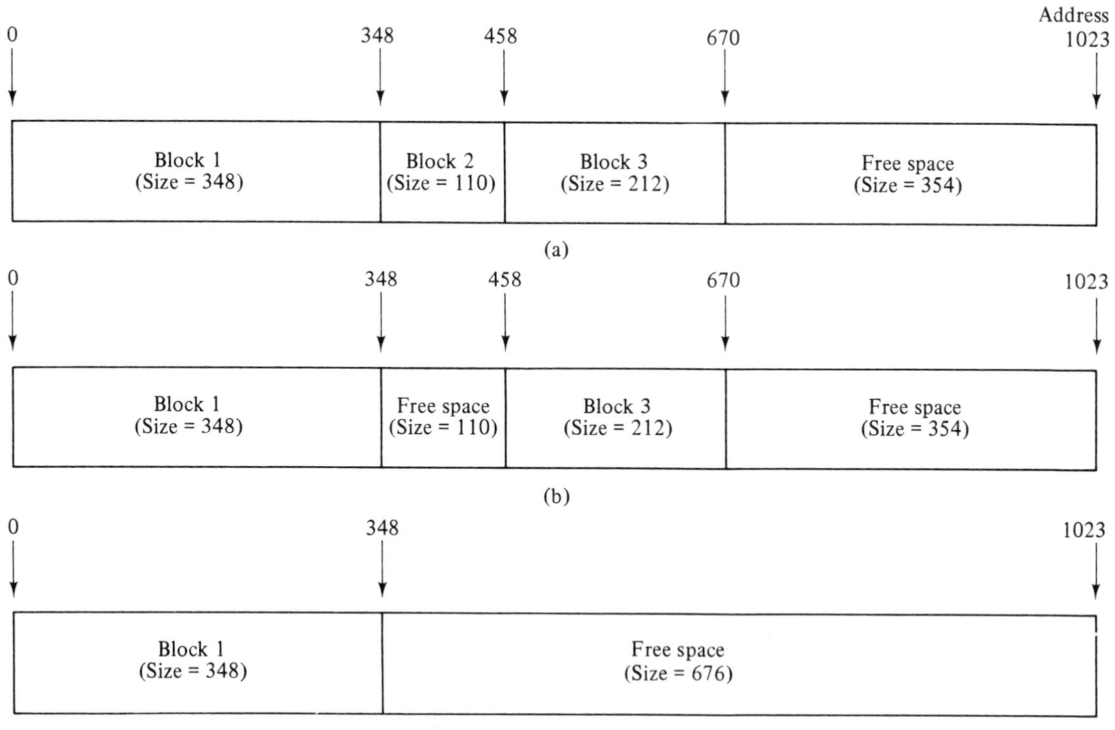

Figure 10.3.1.

This routine copies all allocated blocks into sequential memory locations starting from the lowest address in memory. Thus all free blocks which were interspersed with allocated blocks are eliminated, and *freepoint* is reset to the sum of the sizes of all the allocated blocks. One large free block is created at the upper end of memory, and the user request may be filled if there is sufficient storage available. This process is illustrated in Fig. 10.3.2 on a memory of 1024 words.

When allocated blocks are copied into lower portions of memory, special care must be taken so that pointer values remain correct. For example, the contents of memory location 420 in allocated block 2 of Fig. 10.3.2(a) might contain the address 340. After block 2 is moved to locations 125 through 299, location 140 contains the previous contents of location 340. In moving the contents of 420 to 220, those contents must be changed to 140. Thus in order for compaction to be successful, there must be a method to determine if the contents of a given location are an address.

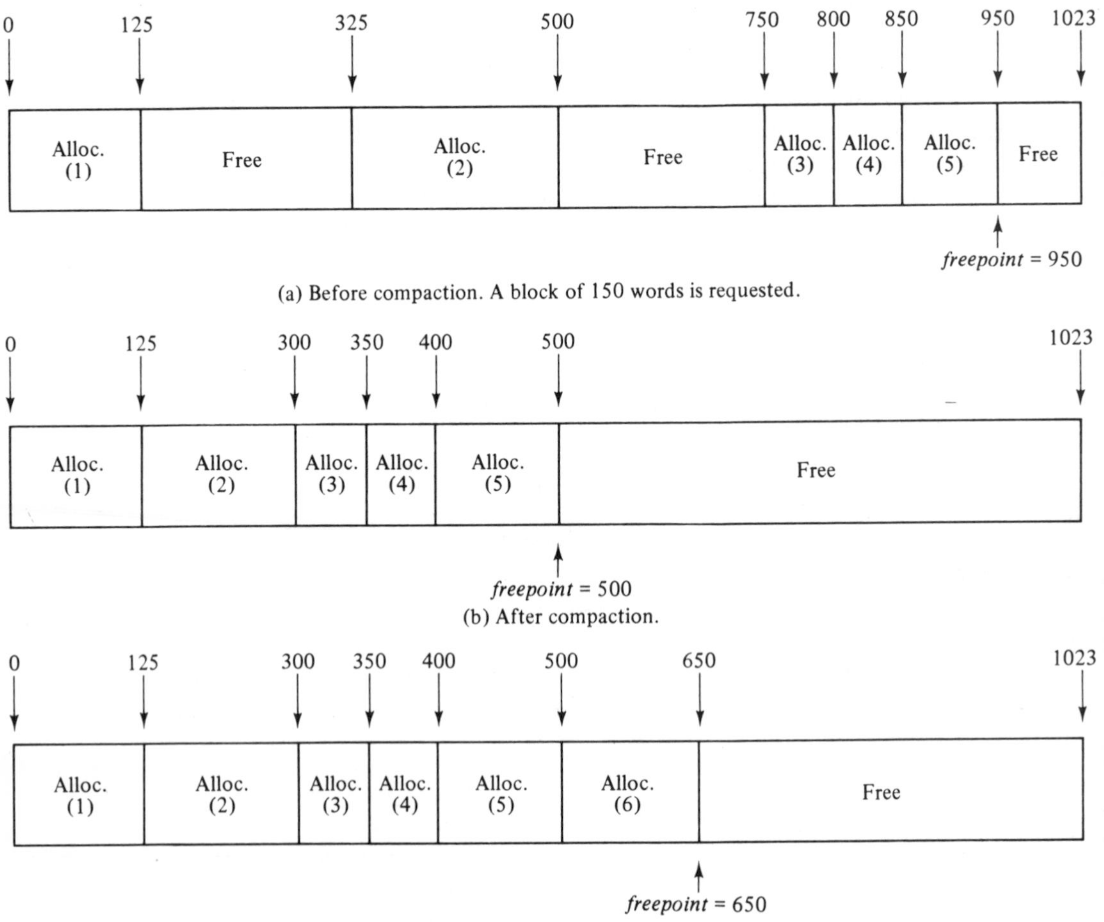

Figure 10.3.2. Compaction.

Exercise 10.2.18 of the Exercise Manual asks you to develop a compaction algorithm for list structures which contain many addresses. An alternative is a system which computes addresses as offsets from some base register. In that case, only the contents of the base register must be changed, while the offset in memory need not be altered. For example, in the previous instance, location 420 would contain the offset 15 before compaction, rather than the address 340. Since the base address of the block is 325, the address 340 would be computed as the base address 325 plus the offset 15. When the block is moved, its base address is changed to 125, while the offset 15 is moved from location 420 to location 220. Adding the new base address 125 to the offset 15 yields 140, which is the address to which the contents of 340 have been moved. Note that the offset 15 contained in memory has not been changed at all. A compaction routine requires a method by which the size of a block and its status (allocated or free) could be determined.

Note that compaction is similar to garbage collection in that all user processing must stop as the system takes time to clean up its storage. For this reason, and because of the pointer problem discussed above, compaction is not used as frequently as the more complicated schemes which are presented below.

First Fit and Best Fit

If it is not desirable to move blocks of allocated storage from one area of memory to another, then it must be possible to reallocate memory blocks which have been freed dynamically as user processing continues. For example, if memory is fragmented as shown in Fig. 10.3.1(b) and a request is made for a block of 250 words of storage, locations 670 through 919 would be used. The result is shown in Fig. 10.3.3(a). If memory is as shown in Fig. 10.3.1(b), then a request for a block of 50 words could be satisfied by either words 348 through 397 or words 670 through 719 (see Figs. 10.3.3(b) and (c)). In each case, part of a free block becomes allocated, leaving the remaining portion free.

Each time that a request is made for storage, a free area large enough to accommodate the size requested must be located. The most obvious method for keeping track of the free blocks is to use a linear linked list. Each free block contains a field containing the size of the block and a field containing a pointer to the next free block. These fields are in some uniform location (say, the first two words) in the block. If *p* is the address of a free block, the expressions *size*(*p*) and *next*(*p*) are used to refer to these two quantities. A global pointer *freeblock* points to the first free block on this list. Let us see how blocks are removed from the free list when storage is requested. We will then examine how blocks are added onto this list when they are freed.

Reconsider the situation of Fig. 10.3.1(b), reproduced in Fig. 10.3.4(a) to show the free list. There are two principal methods of selecting the free block to use when requesting storage. In the ***first-fit*** method, the free list is traversed sequentially to find the first free block whose size is larger than or equal to the amount requested. Once the block is found, it is removed from the list (if equal in size to the amount requested) or is split into two portions (if greater than the amount requested). The first of these portions remains on the list, and the second is allocated. The reason for allocating the second portion rather than the first is that the free list *next* pointer is at the beginning of each free block. By leaving the first portion of the block on the free list, this pointer need not be

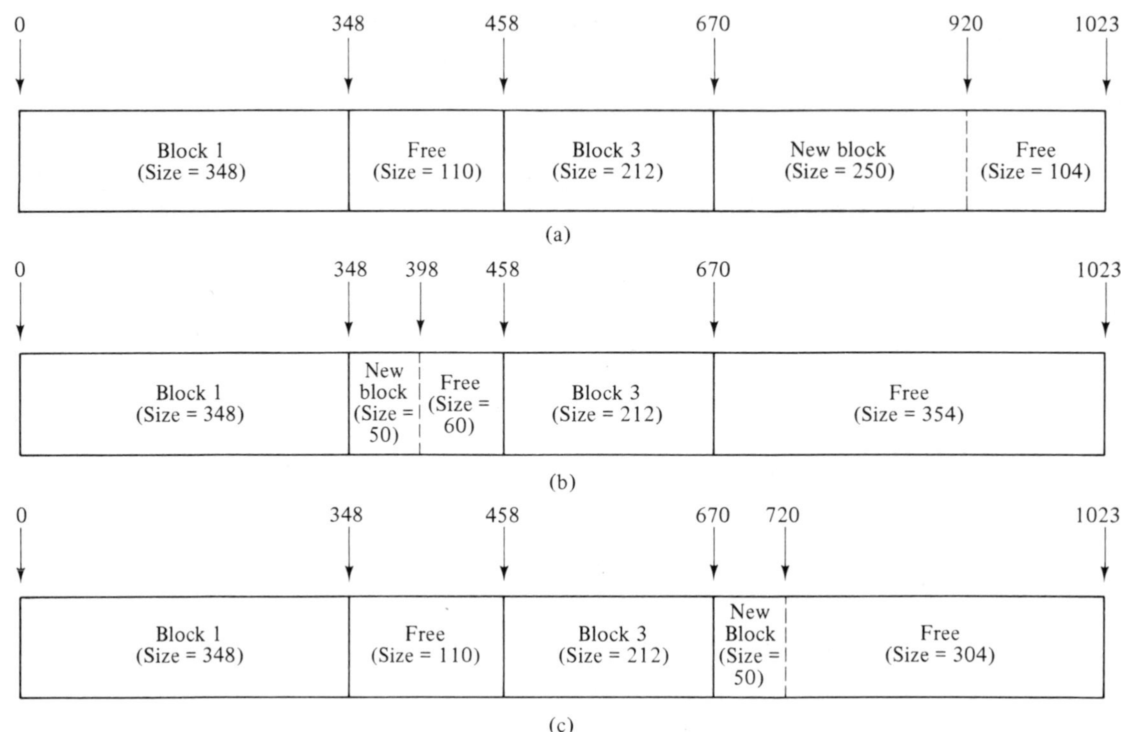

Figure 10.3.3.

copied into some other location and the *next* field of the previous block in the list need not be changed.

Before presenting an allocation algorithm using the first-fit method, let us examine some general issues which are raised in implementing dynamic allocation algorithms. As noted above, the blocks of storage being manipulated are of variable length. There is often a need to locate a word which is a specific number of words past the location designated by a pointer p. For example, when a free block of size s beginning at location p is split into two to provide a block B of size n, the location of B is at $p+s-n$. Thus, we must have the ability to perform arithmetic operations on addresses. For these reasons, it is cumbersome to implement these algorithms in PL/I. Also it is often necessary to interpret information within the computer's memory in different data formats. For example, if the size of a free block is contained in the first word of that block and the *next* pointer is contained in its second word, and if p is the location of a free block, then $size(p)$ refers to the information stored at location p interpreted as an integer, while $next(p)$ refers to the information stored at location $p+1$ interpreted as an address. In the exercises, there is a scheme by which the algorithms of this section can be implemented in PL/I. However, for the sake of clarity and ease of expression, storage management methods will be presented as algorithms rather than as PL/I programs.

The first-fit allocation algorithm returns the address of a free block of storage of size n if one is available and the null address if it is not.

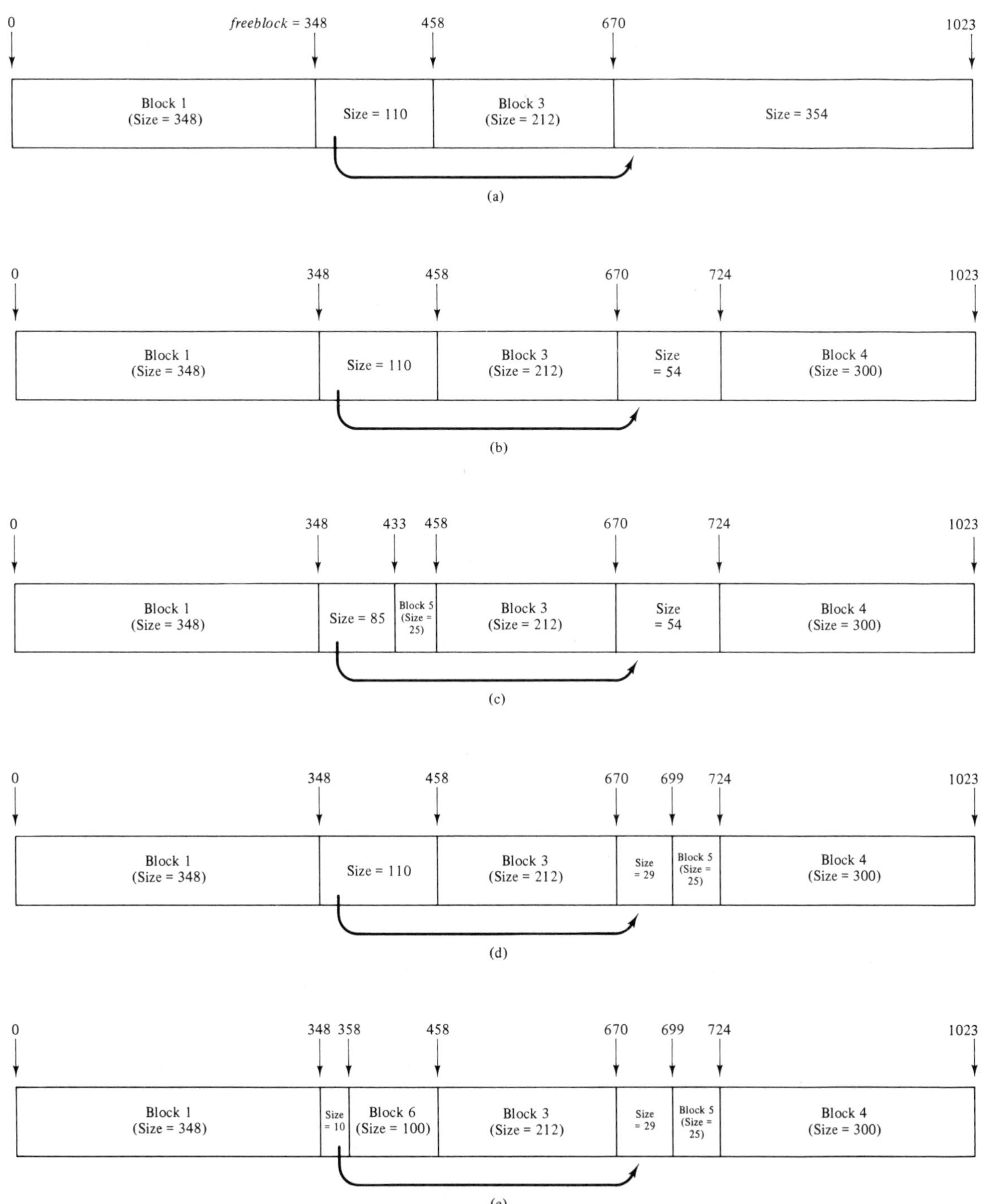

0
freeblock = 348
458
670
1023
Block 1
(Size = 348)
Size = 110
Block 3
(Size = 212)
Size = 354
(a)
0
348
458
670
724
1023
Block 1
(Size = 348)
Size = 110
Block 3
(Size = 212)
Size
= 54
Block 4
(Size = 300)
(b)
0
348
433
458
670
724
1023
Block 1
(Size = 348)
Size = 85
Block 5
(Size =
25)
Block 3
(Size = 212)
Size
= 54
Block 4
(Size = 300)
(c)
0
348
458
670
699
724
1023
Block 1
(Size = 348)
Size = 110
Block 3
(Size = 212)
Size
= 29
Block 5
(Size =
25)
Block 4
(Size = 300)
(d)
0
348
358
458
670
699
724
1023
Block 1
(Size = 348)
Size
= 10
Block 6
(Size = 100)
Block 3
(Size = 212)
Size
= 29
Block 5
(Size =
25)
Block 4
(Size = 300)
(e)

Figure 10.3.4.

```
p=freeblock;
alloc=null;
q=null;
do while(p¬=null & size(p)<n);
      /*    traverse the free list    */
   q=p;
   p=next(p);
end;

if p=null then /*      there is no block which is large enough        */
               return(p);
s=size(p);
alloc=p+s−n;
if s=n then
               /*         remove the block from the free list          */
         if q=null then freeblock=next(p);
                  else next(q)=next(p);
      else
               /*            adjust the size of the remaining free block             */
           size(p)=s−n;
return(alloc);
```

The ***best-fit*** method traverses the entire free list and obtains the free block closest in size to the desired size *n* which is larger than or equal to *n*. An algorithm using this method follows. We assume that *memsize* is the number of total words in memory.

```
p=freeblock;         /*   p is used to traverse the free list      */
q=null;              /*        q is one block behind p             */
r=null;              /*   r points to the desired free block       */
rq=null;             /*        rq is one block behind r            */
rsize=memsize+1;     /*   rsize is the size of the block at r      */
alloc=null;          /*   alloc will point to the block to be      */
                     /*                allocated                   */

do while(p¬=null);
   if size(p)>=n & size(p)<rsize then do;
       /*    we have found a free block closer in size    */
       r=p;
       rq=q;
       rsize=size(p);
                                             end;
   /*           continue traversing the free list           */
   q=p;
   p=next(p);
end;
```

```
if r=null then          /*   there is not block of sufficient size     */
               return(null);
alloc=r+rsize-n;
if rsize=n  then
                        /*   remove the block from the free list       */
                 if rq=null then freeblock=next(r);
                            else next(rq)=next(r);
          else
                        /*   adjust the size of the free block         */
                 size(r)=rsize-n;
return(alloc);
```

To see the difference between the first-fit and best-fit methods, consider the following examples. We begin with memory fragmented as in Fig. 10.3.4(a). There are two blocks of free storage, of sizes 110 and 354. If a request is made for a block of 300 words, the block of 354 is split as shown in Fig. 10.3.4(b), under both the first-fit and best-fit methods. Suppose a block of size 25 is then requested. Under first-fit, the block of size 110 is split (Fig. 10.3.4(c)), while under best-fit, the block of size 54 is split (Fig. 10.3.4(d)). If a block of size 100 is then requested, the request can be fulfilled under best-fit since the block of size 110 is available (Fig. 10.3.4(e)), but it cannot be fulfilled under first-fit. This illustrates an advantage of the best-fit method in that very large free blocks remain unsplit so that requests for large blocks can be satisfied. In the first-fit method, a very large block of free storage at the beginning of the free list is nibbled away by small requests so that it is severely shrunken by the time a large request arrives.

However, it is also possible for the first-fit method to succeed where the best-fit method fails. As an example, consider the case in which the system begins with free blocks of size 110 and 54 and then makes successive requests for 25, 70, and 50 words. Figure 10.3.5 illustrates that the first-fit method succeeds in fulfilling these requests, while the best-fit method does not. The reason is that remaining unallocated portions of blocks are smaller under best-fit than under first-fit.

The major reason for choosing one method over the other is efficiency. The best-fit method must traverse the entire free list in its search for the best fit each time that a block is allocated. The first-fit method traverses the list only until it finds a block large enough. (However, if the free list is maintained in sorted order based on size, then the search process for allocation using best-fit is as efficient as the search in the first-fit method.) Additionally, in the best-fit method, small slivers of free space remain which are for all intents and purposes useless. For these reasons, first-fit is the preferred method.

Improvements in the First-Fit Method

There are several improvements which can be made in the first-fit method. If the size of a free block is only slightly larger than the size of the block to be allocated, the portion of the free block which remains free is very small. Very often, this remaining portion is so small that there is very little likelihood of its being used before the allocated portion is freed and the two portions are recombined. Thus there is little benefit to be achieved by leaving that small portion on the free list. Also recall that any free block must be of some minimum size (in our case, two words) so that it may contain *size* and *next* fields. What if the smaller portion of a free block is below this minimum size after the larger portion has been allocated?

	Blocks remaining using	
Request	First-fit	Best-fit
Initially	110, 54	110, 54
25	85, 54	110, 29
70	15, 54	40, 29
50	15, 4	cannot be fulfilled

Figure 10.3.5.

The solution to these problems is to insist that no block may remain free if its size is below some reasonable minimum. If a free block is about to be split and the smaller portion is below this minimum size, the block is not split. Instead, the entire free block is allocated as though it were exactly the right size. This allows the system to remove the entire block from the free list and does not clutter up the list with very small blocks. The phenomenon in which there are many small, noncontiguous free blocks is called ***external fragmentation*** because free space is wasted outside allocated blocks. This contrasts with ***internal fragmentation*** in which free space is wasted within allocated blocks. The above solution transforms external fragmentation into internal fragmentation. The choice of what minimum size to use depends on the pattern of allocation requests in the particular system. It is reasonable to use a minimum size such that only a small percentage (say 5%) of the allocation requests are less than or equal to that size. Note that the possibility of small slivers remaining is even greater under the best-fit method than under first-fit, so that the establishment of such a minimum size is of correspondingly greater importance under that method.

Another significant improvement in the first-fit method can be made. As time goes on, smaller free blocks will tend to accumulate near the front of the free list. This is because a large block near the front of the list is reduced in size before a large block near the back of the list. Thus, in searching for a large or even a moderate size block, the small blocks near the front are skipped. The algorithm would be more efficient if the free list were organized as a circular list whose front could vary dynamically as blocks are allocated. Two ways of implementing this dynamic variance suggest themselves. In the first, *freeblock* (which is the pointer to the first free block on the list) is set to *next*(*freeblock*), so that the front of the list advances one block each time that a block is allocated. In the second, *freeblock* is set to *next*(*alloc*), where *alloc* points to the block which was just chosen for allocation. Thus all blocks which were too small for this allocation request are in effect moved to the back of the list. The reader is invited to investigate the advantages and disadvantages of both techniques.

Freeing Storage Blocks

Thus far, nothing has been said about how allocated blocks of storage are freed and how they are combined with contiguous free blocks to form larger blocks of free storage. Specifically, three questions arise:

1. When a block of storage is freed, where is it placed on the free list? The answer to this question helps determine how the free list is ordered.
2. When a block of storage is freed, how can it be determined whether the blocks of storage on either side of it are free (in which case the newly freed block must be combined with an already existing free block)?
3. What is the mechanism for combining a newly freed block with a previously free contiguous block?

The reader is asked to consider these questions (especially the first two) before proceeding.

The term ***liberation*** is used for the process of freeing an allocated block of storage; an algorithm to implement this process is called a ***liberation algorithm***. The free list should be organized to facilitate efficient allocation and liberation.

Suppose that the free list is organized arbitrarily, so that when a block is freed, it is placed at the front of the list. It may be that the block just freed is adjacent to a previously free block. In order to make a single large free block, the newly freed block should be combined with the adjacent free block. There is no way, short of traversing the free list, to determine if such an adjacent free block exists. Thus each liberation would involve a traversal of the free list. For this reason it is inefficient to maintain the free list this way.

An alternative is to keep the free list sorted in order of increasing memory location. Then, when the free list is traversed and a free block whose starting address is greater than the starting address of the block being freed is encountered, the list need not be traversed further. If a contiguous free block has not been found, such a block does not exist and the newly freed block can be inserted into the previous position of the free list. This means that the entire free list need not be traversed. Instead, only half the list must be traversed on the average.

The following liberation algorithm implements this scheme, assuming that the free list is linear (not circular) and that *freeblock* points to the free block with the smallest address. The algorithm frees a block of size *n* beginning at address *alloc*.

```
q = null;
p = freeblock;
/*      p traverses the free list. q remains one step behind p.      */
do while(p¬=null & p<alloc);
   q=p;
   p=next(p);
end;
```

```
/*    At this point, either q=null or q<alloc, and either p=null     */
/*    or alloc<p. Thus if p and q are nonnull, the block must be     */
/*    combined with the blocks beginning at p or q or both, or       */
/*    must be inserted in the list between the two blocks.           */

if q=null   then freeblock=alloc;
            else if q+size(q)=alloc then
                       /*    combine with previous block    */
                                 do;
                                    alloc=q;
                                    n=size(q)+n;
                                 end;
                           else  next(q)=alloc;

if p¬=null & alloc+n=p then do;
                       /*    combine with subsequent block     */
                             size(alloc)=n+size(p);
                             next(alloc)=next(p);
                           end;
                       else do;
                             size(alloc)=n;
                             next(alloc)=p;
                           end;
return;
```

Note that if the free list is implemented as a circular list, the first-fit allocation algorithm begins traversing the list from varying locations. However, in order to traverse from the lowest location during liberation, an additional external pointer, *lowblock*, to the free block with the lowest location is required. Ordinarily, traversal starts at *lowblock*. However, if it is found that *freeblock*<*alloc* when the block which starts at *alloc* is about to be freed, traversal starts at *freeblock*, so that even less search time is used during liberation. The reader is urged to implement this variation as an exercise.

The Boundary Tag Method

It is desirable to eliminate all searching during liberation to make the process more efficient. One method of doing this comes at the expense of keeping extra information in all blocks (both free and allocated).

The reason that a search is necessary during liberation is to determine if the newly freed block may be combined with some existing free block. There is no way of detecting whether such a block exists or which block it is without a search. However, if such a block exists, it must immediately precede or succeed the block being freed. The first address of the block which succeeds a block of size n at *alloc* is *alloc+n*. Suppose every block contains a single bit field *flag* which is on if the block is allocated and off if the block is free. Then by examining *flag(alloc+n)*, we can determine whether or not the block immediately succeeding the block at *alloc* is free.

It is more difficult to determine the status of the block immediately preceding the block at *alloc*. The address of the last location of that preceding block is, of course, *alloc*−1. But there is no way of finding the address of its first location without knowing its size. Suppose, however, that each block contains two flags, *fflag* and *bflag*, both of which are on if the block is allocated and off otherwise. *fflag* is at a specific offset from the front of the block, and *bflag* is at a specific negative offset from the back of the block. Thus, to access *fflag*, the first location of the block must be known; to access *bflag*, the last location of the block must be known. The status of the block following the block at *alloc* can be determined from the value of *fflag(alloc+n)*, and the status of the block preceding the block at *alloc* can be determined from the value of *bflag(alloc*−1). Thus when a block is to be freed, it can immediately be determined whether it must be combined with either of the two blocks on its sides.

A list of the free blocks is still needed for the allocation process. When a block is freed, its neighbors are examined. If both are allocated, the block can simply be appended to the front of the free list. If one (or both) of its neighbors is free, the neighbor can be removed from the free list and combined with the newly freed block, and the newly created large block can be placed at the head of the free list. Note that this would tend to reduce search times under first-fit allocation as well, since a previously allocated block (especially if it has been combined with other blocks) is likely to be large enough to satisfy the next allocation request. Since it is placed at the head of the free list, the search time is reduced sharply.

In order to remove an arbitrary block from the free list (to combine it with a newly freed block) without traversing the entire list, it is necessary that the free list be doubly linked. Thus each free block must contain two pointers *next* and *prev* to the next and previous free blocks on the free list. It is also necessary to be able to access these two pointers from the last allocation of a free block. (This is needed when combining a newly freed block with a freed block which immediately precedes it in memory.) Thus it is necessary to be able to access the front of a free block from its rear. One way to do this is to introduce a *bsize* field at a given negative offset from the last location of each free block. This field contains the same value as the *size* field at the front of the block. Figure 10.3.6 illustrates the structure of free and allocated blocks under this method, which is called the ***boundary tag method***. Each of the control fields, *fflag*, *size*, *next*, *prev*, *bsize*, and *bflag*, is shown as occupying a complete word, although in practice they may be packed together, several to a word. In particular *fflag* and *bflag* need only a single bit each.

We now present the liberation algorithm using the boundary tag method. For clarity, we assume that *fflag* and *bflag* are single characters and that 'A' indicates an allocated block and 'F' indicates a free block. The algorithm frees a block of size n at location *alloc*. (We assume that *bflag*(0) and *fflag*(m+1), where m is the size of memory, are both 'A'.) It makes use of an auxiliary routine *remove* which removes a block from the doubly linked list. The details of that routine are left as an exercise for the reader.

```
/*   check the preceding block   */
if bflag(alloc-1) = 'F' then do;
   /*   the block must be combined with the preceding block   */
   /*          find the initial address of the block           */
   start = alloc-bsize(alloc-1);
   /*          remove the block from the free list             */
   remove(start);
   /*        increase the size and combine the blocks          */
   n = n + size(start);
   alloc = start;
                          end;

/*   check the following block   */
if fflag(alloc+n) = 'F' then do;
   /*   combine the block with the following block   */
   start = alloc+n;
   n = n+size(start);
   remove(start);
                          end;
```

fflag
size
next
prev
{ Unused
bsize
bflag

Free block

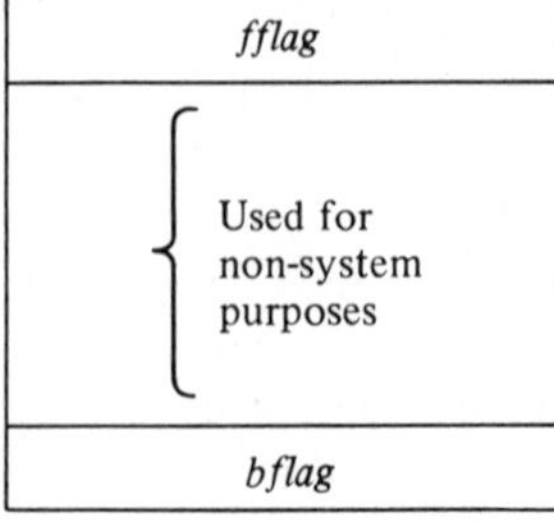

Allocated block

Figure 10.3.6. Structure of blocks under the boundary tag method.

```
/*   add the newly free, possibly combined block to the free list    */
next(alloc) = freeblock;
prev(freeblock) = alloc;
prev(alloc) = null;
freeblock = alloc;

/*                 adjust all fields in the new block                */
fflag(alloc) = 'F';
bflag(alloc+n-1) = 'F';
size(alloc) = n;
bsize(alloc+n-1) = n;
return;
```

The Buddy System

An alternate method of handling the storage management problem without frequent list traversals is to keep separate free lists for blocks of different sizes. Each list contains free blocks of only one specific size. For example, if memory contains 1024 words, it might be divided into fifteen blocks: one block of 256 words, two blocks of 128 words, four blocks of 64 words, and eight blocks of 32 words. Whenever storage is requested, a block whose size is closest to the size needed is reserved. For example, a request for a block of 97 words is filled by a block of 128. There are several drawbacks to this scheme. First, space is wasted due to internal fragmentation. (In the example, 31 words of the block are totally unusable.) Second, and more serious, is that a request for a block of size 300 cannot be fulfilled since the largest size maintained is 256. Also, if two blocks of size 150 are needed, the requests cannot be filled even if sufficient contiguous space is available. Thus the solution is impractical. The source of the impracticality is that free spaces are never combined. However, there is a variation of this scheme which is quite useful. This variation is called the ***buddy system***.

Several free lists consisting of various-sized blocks are maintained. Adjacent free blocks of smaller size may be removed from their lists, combined into free blocks of larger size, and placed on the larger size free list. These larger blocks can then be used intact to satisfy a request for a large amount of memory, or they can be split once more into their smaller constituent blocks to satisfy several smaller requests.

The method outlined below works best on binary computers in which the memory size is an integral power of 2 and in which multiplication and division by 2 can be performed very efficiently by shifting. Originally, the entire memory of size 2^m is viewed as a single free block. For each power of 2 between one (which equals 2^0) and 2^m, a free list containing blocks of that size is maintained. A block of size 2^i is called an ***i-block***, and the free list containing i-blocks is called the ***i-list***. (In practice, it may be unreasonable to keep free blocks of sizes 1, 2, and 4 so that 8 is the smallest free block size allowed; we will ignore the possibility.) However, it may be (and usually is) the case that some of these free lists are empty. Indeed, initially all the lists except the m-list are empty.

Blocks may be allocated only in sizes 2^k for some integer k between 0 and m. If a request for a block of size n is made, an i-block is reserved where i is the smallest integer such that $n \leqslant 2^i$. If no i-block is available (the i-list is empty), an $(i+1)$-block is removed from the (i+1)-list and is split into two equal-size buddies. Each of these buddies is an i-block. One of the buddies is allocated, and the other remains free and is placed on the i-list. If an $(i+1)$-block is also unavailable, an $(i+2)$-block is split into two $(i+1)$-block buddies, one of which is placed on the $(i+1)$-list and the other is split into two i-blocks. One of these i-blocks is allocated, and the other is placed onto the i-list. If no $(i+2)$-block is free, this process continues until either an i-block has been allocated or an m-block is found to be unavailable. In the former case, the allocation attempt is successful; in the latter case, a block of proper size is not available.

The buddy system allocation process can best be described as a recursive function *getblock*(n) which returns the address of the block to be allocated or the null pointer if no block of size n is available. An outline of this function follows:

```
find the smallest integer i such that 2^i>=n;
if the i-list is not empty then do;
        p = the address of the first block on the i-list;
        remove the first block from the i-list;
        return(p);
                                    end;
/*   at this point, the i-list is empty    */
if i = m then return (null);
p = getblock(2^(i+1));
if p=null then return (null);
put the i-block starting at location p on the i-list;
return(p+2^i);
```

In the above outline, if an $(i+1)$-block starts at location p, then the two i-blocks into which it is split start at locations p and $p+2^i$. The first of these remains on the free list, and the second is allocated.

Initially, only a single free m-block exists. Thus each block is created by splitting a block of one size higher. If an $(i+1)$-block is split into two i-blocks *B1* and *B2*, then *B1* and *B2* are ***buddies*** of each other. The buddy of an i-block at location p is called the ***i-buddy*** of p. Note that a block at location p can have several buddies but only one i-buddy.

If an i-block is freed and its i-buddy is already free, the two buddies are combined into the $(i+1)$-block from which they were initially created. In this way, a larger free block of storage is created to satisfy large requests. If the i-buddy of a newly freed i-block is not free, then the newly freed block is placed directly on the i-list.

Suppose a newly freed i-block has been combined with its previously free i-buddy into an $(i+1)$-block. It is possible that the $(i+1)$-buddy of this recombined $(i+1)$-block is also free. In that case, the two $(i+1)$-blocks can be recombined further into an $(i+2)$-block. This process continues until a recombined block is created whose buddy is not free or until the entire memory is combined into a single m-block.

The liberation algorithm can be outlined as a recursive procedure *liberate*(*alloc*,*i*) which frees an i-block at location *alloc*.

```
if (i=m) or (the i-buddy of alloc is not free)
   then do;
      add the i-block at alloc to the i-list;
      return;
         end;
remove the i-buddy of alloc from the i-list;
combine the i-block at alloc with its i-buddy;
p = the address of the newly formed (i+1)-block;
liberate(p, i+1);
return;
```

Let us refine the outline of *liberate*; we leave the refinement of *getblock* as an exercise for the reader.

There is one obvious question which must be answered. How can the free status of the *i*-buddy of *alloc* be established? Indeed, how can it be determined whether an *i*-buddy of *alloc* exists at all. It is quite possible that the *i*-buddy of *alloc* has been split and part (or all) of it is allocated. Additionally, how can the starting address of the *i*-buddy of *alloc* be determined? If the *i*-block at *alloc* is the first half of its containing (*i*+1)-block, then its *i*-buddy is at $alloc+2^i$; if the *i*-block is the second half of its containing block, then its *i*-buddy is at $alloc-2^i$. How can it be determined which is the case?

At this point, it would be instructive to look at some examples. For illustrative purposes, consider an absurdly small memory of 1024 ($=2^{10}$) words. Figure 10.3.7(a) illustrates this memory after a request for a block of 100 words has been filled. The smallest power of two which contains 100 words is 128 ($=2^7$). Thus, the entire memory is split into two blocks of size 512; the first is placed on the 9-list and the second is split into two blocks of size 256. The first of these is placed on the 8-list, and the second is split into blocks of size 128, one of which is placed on the 7-list and the second of which is allocated (block *B1*). At the bottom of the figure, the starting addresses of the blocks on each nonempty *i*-list are indicated. Make sure that you follow the execution of the functions *getblock* and *liberate* on this and succeeding examples.

Figure 10.3.7(b) illustrates the sample memory after filling an additional request for 50 words. There is no free 6-block, so that the free 7-block at location 768 is split into two 6-blocks. The first 6-block remains free, and the second is allocated as block *B2*. In Fig. 10.3.7(c) three additional 6-blocks have been allocated in the order *B3*, *B4*, and *B5*. When the first request is made, a 6-block at location 768 is free, so that no splitting is necessary. The second request forces the 8-block at 512 to be split into two 7-blocks and the second 7-block at 640 to be split into two 6-blocks. The second of these is allocated as *B4*, and when the next request for a 6-block is made, the first is also allocated as *B5*.

Note that in Fig. 10.3.7(a) the block beginning at 768 is a 7-block, while in Fig. 10.3.7(b) it is a 6-block. Similarly, the block at 512 is an 8-block in Figs. 10.3.7(a) and (b), but a 7-block in Fig. 10.3.7(c). This illustrates that the size of a block cannot be determined from its starting address. However, as we shall soon see, a block of a given size can start only at certain addresses.

Figure 10.3.7(d) illustrates the situation after blocks B4 and B3 have been freed. When block *B4* at location 704 is freed, its buddy is examined. Since *B4* is a 6-block

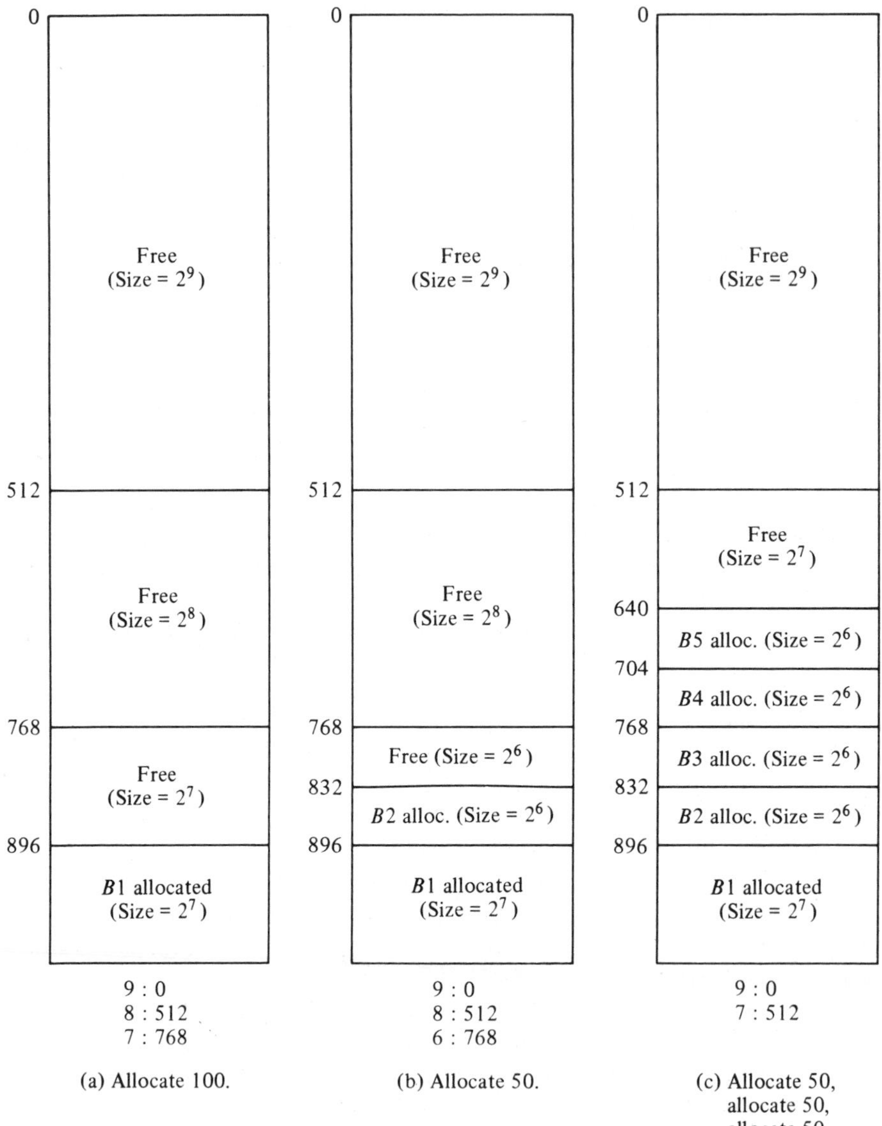

(a) Allocate 100.

(b) Allocate 50.

(c) Allocate 50, allocate 50, allocate 50.

Figure 10.3.7. Memory management under the buddy system.

which is the second half of the 7-block from which it was split, its buddy is at location $704-2^6=640$. However, the 6-block at location 640 (which is B5) is not free, so no combination can take place. When *B3* is freed, since it is a 6-block and was the first half of its containing 7-block, its 6-buddy at $768+2^6=832$ must be examined. However, that 6-buddy is allocated, so again no combination can take place. Notice that two adjacent blocks of the same size (6-blocks *B4* and *B3* at 704 and 768) are free but are not combined into a single 7-block. This is because they are not buddies; i.e., they were not ori-

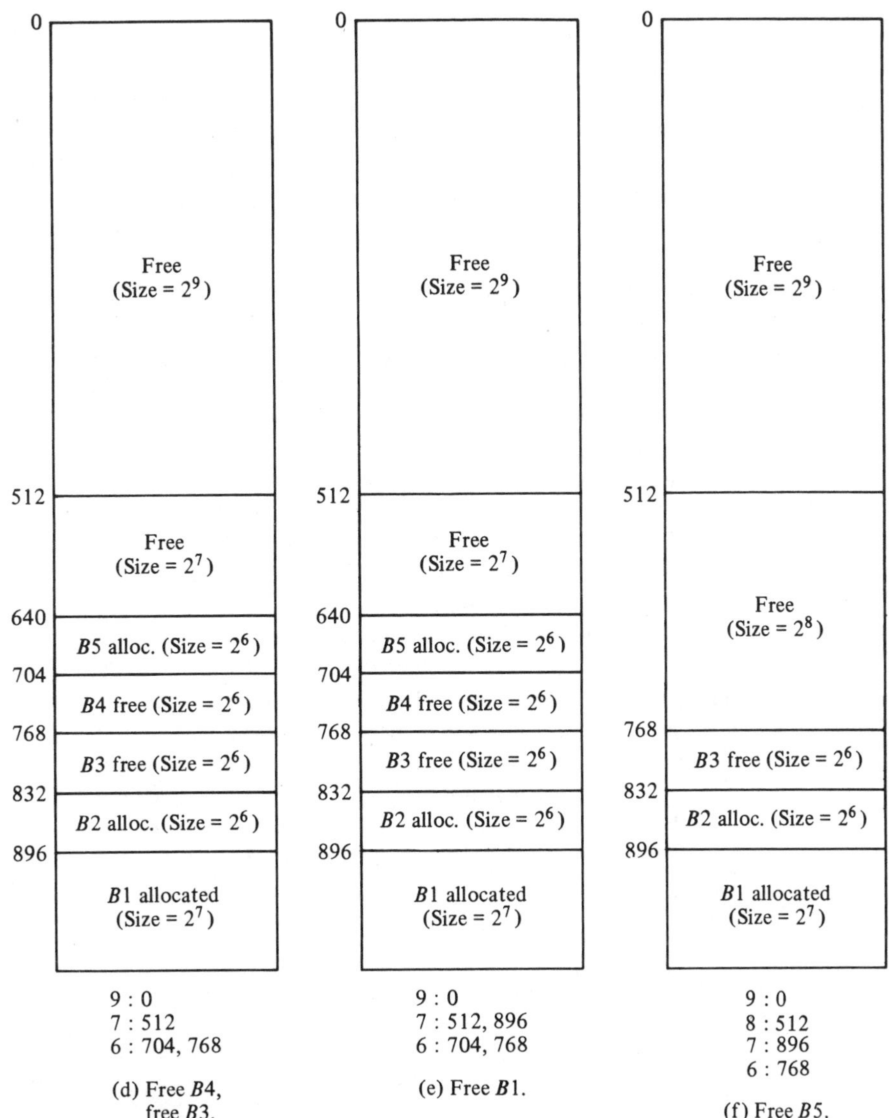

(d) Free *B*4, free *B*3.

(e) Free *B*1.

(f) Free *B*5.

Figure 10.3.7. *(cont.)*

ginally split from the same 7-block. *B4* can be combined only with its buddy *B5*, and *B3* can be combined only with its buddy *B2*.

In Fig. 10.3.7(e), the 7-block *B1* has been freed. *B1* is the second half of its 8-block, so its 7-buddy is at $896-2^7=768$. Although block *B3* which starts at that location is free, no combination can take place. This is because block *B3* is not a 7-block, but only a 6-block. This means that the 7-block starting at 768 is split and, therefore, partially allocated. We see that it is not yet ready for combination. Both the address and the size of a given free block must be considered when making a decision as to whether or not to combine buddies.

In Fig. 10.3.7(f), the 6-block *B5* at location 640 is freed. *B5* is the first half of its containing 7-block, so its 6-buddy is at $640+2^6=704$. That 6-buddy (block *B4*) is already free, so the two can be combined into a single 7-block at 640. That 7-block is the second half of its containing 8-block, so its 7-buddy is at $640-2^7=512$. The 7-block at that location is free, so that the two 7-blocks can be combined into an 8-block at 512. That 8-block is the first half of its containing 9-block, so its 8-buddy is at $512+2^8=768$. But the block at location 768 is a 6-block rather than an 8-block, so no further combination can take place.

The above examples illustrate that it is necessary to be able to determine whether a given i-block is the first or second half of its containing $(i+1)$-block in order to compute the location of its i-buddy.

Clearly, there is only one m-block in memory, and its starting location is 0. When this block is split, it produces two $(m-1)$-blocks starting at locations 0 and 2^{m-1}. These split into four $(m-2)$-blocks at locations 0, 2^{m-2}, 2^{m-1}, and $3*2^{m-2}$. In general, there are 2^{m-i} i-blocks starting at locations which are integer multiples of 2^i. For example, if $m=10$ (memory size is 1024), there are $2^{10-6}=16$ 6-blocks starting at locations 0, 64, 128, 192, 256, 320, 384, 448, 512, 576, 640, 704, 768, 832, 896, and 960. Each of these addresses is an integral multiple of 64 (which is 2^6), from $0*64$ to $15*64$.

Notice that any address which is the starting location of an i-block is also the starting location of a k-block for all $0 \leqslant k < i$. This is because the i-block can be split into two $(i-1)$-blocks, the first of which begins at the same location as the i-block. This is consistent with the observation that an integral multiple of 2^i is also an integral multiple of 2^{i-1}. However, the reverse is not necessarily true. A location which is the starting address of an i-block is the starting address of an $(i+1)$-block only if the i-block is the first half of the $(i+1)$-block, but not if it is the second half. For example, in Fig. 10.3.7, addresses 640 and 768 begin 7-blocks as well as 6-blocks and 768 begins an 8-block as well. However, addresses 704 and 832 begin 6-blocks but not 7-blocks.

After making these observations, it is easy to determine whether a given i-block is the first or second half of the $(i+1)$-block from which it was split. If the starting address p of the i-block is evenly divisible by 2^{i+1}, then the block is the first half of an $(i+1)$-block and its buddy is at $p+2^i$; otherwise, it is the second half of an $(i+1)$-block and its buddy is at $p-2^i$.

We can therefore introduce a function *buddy*(p,i) which returns the address of the i-buddy of p:

```
if mod(p,2^(i+1))=0 then return(p+2^i);
                    else return(p-2^i);
```

Now that the address of a newly freed block's i-buddy can be found, how can we determine whether or not that buddy is free? One way of making that determination is to traverse the i-list to see if a block at the desired address is present. If it is, then it can be removed and combined with its buddy. If it is not, then the newly freed i-block can be added to the i-list. Since each i-list is generally quite small (because as soon as two i-buddies are free, they are combined into an $(i+1)$-buddy and removed from the i-list), this traversal is not very inefficient. Furthermore, to implement this scheme, each i-list need not be doubly linked since a block is removed from the *i*-list only after the list is traversed, so that its list predecessor is known.

An alternate method which avoids list traversal is to have each block contain a one-bit flag to indicate whether or not it is allocated. Then when an *i*-block is freed, it is possible to determine directly whether or not the block beginning at the address of its buddy is already free. However, this flag alone is insufficient. For example, in Fig. 10.3.7(e), when 7-block *B1* at location 896 is freed, its buddy's starting address is calculated as 768. The block at 768 is free, and its flag would indicate that fact. Yet the two blocks at 768 and 896 cannot be combined because the block at 768 is not a 7-block, but a 6-block whose 6-buddy is allocated. Thus an additional *power* field is necessary in each block. The value of this integer field is the base-2 logarithm of its size (e.g., if the block is of size 2^i, the value of *power* is *i*). When an *i*-block is freed, its buddy's address is calculated. If the *power* field at that address is *i* and if the flag indicates that the buddy is free, the two blocks are combined.

Under this method, the *i*-lists are required only for the allocation algorithm so that a block of proper size can be found efficiently. However, because blocks are removed from the *i*-lists without traversing them, the lists must be doubly linked. Thus each free block must contain four fields: *flag*, *power*, *prev*, and *next*. The last two are pointers to the previous and next blocks on the *i*-list. An allocated block need contain only the *flag* field.

We present the second method of liberation, leaving the first to the reader as an exercise. We assume an array of pointers *list*(*o*:*m*), where *list*(*i*) points to the first block on the *i*-list. We also replace the recursive call to *liberate* by a loop in which successively larger blocks are combined with their buddies until a block is formed whose buddy is not free. The procedure *liberate*(*alloc*,*i*) frees an *i*-block at location *alloc*. For completeness, let us establish that *buddy*(*p*,*m*) equals 0. For clarity, we also expand the *flag* field to a character so that it can hold the value 'A' for an allocated block and 'F' for a free block.

```
p=alloc;
j=i;
bud=buddy(p,j);
do while ((j<m) & (flag(bud)='F') & (power(bud)=j));
     /*    remove the j-buddy of p from the j-list    */
   q=prev(bud);
   if q=null then list(j)=next(bud);
             else next(q)=next(bud);
   if next(bud)¬=null then prev(next(bud))=q;

     /*    combine the j-block at p with its buddy    */
   if mod(p,2**(j+1))¬=0 then
     /*       the combined block begins at bud        */
                               p=bud;
   j=j+1;
   bud=buddy(p,j);
```

```
        /*  attempt to combine the larger block with its  */
        /*                  buddy                          */
end;

        /*        add the j-block at p to the j-list       */
q=list(j);
prev(p)=null;
next(p)=q;
list(j)=p;
if q¬=null then prev(q)=p;
        /*          adjust fields in the j-block           */
power(p)=j;
flag(p)='F';
return;
```

There are two primary disadvantages to the buddy system. The first is internal fragmentation. Only blocks whose sizes are integral powers of 2 can be allocated without waste. This means that a little less than half the storage in each could be wasted (for example, to satisfy a request for 65 words, a block of 128 words must be allocated). The other disadvantage is that adjacent free blocks are not combined if they are not buddies. However, simulations have shown that the buddy system works well and that splitting and combinations take place infrequently once the pattern of memory allocations and liberations stabilizes.

Bibliography and References

Two excellent sources for material related to this chapter are (Knuth, 1973A) and (Pfaltz,1977).

The Schorr-Waite algorithm for garbage collection was introduced in (Schorr and Waite, 1967). The buddy system was introduced in (Knowlton, 1965). Variations of the buddy system may be found in (Cranston and Thomas, 1975), (Hinds, 1975), (Hirschberg, 1972), (Peterson and Norman, 1977), and (Shen and Peterson, 1974). A mathematical analysis of the buddy system is found in (Purdom and Stigler, 1970).

Simulations of dynamic memory allocation methods are described in (Knuth, 1973A), (Peterson and Norman, 1977), (Pfaltz, 1977), (Nielson, 1977), (Shore, 1975) and (Shore, 1977).

bibliography and references

The following bibliography is in no way complete. However, it is an attempt to list a large number of sources and references for further reading. After each entry is a list of the sections of this book to which the entry applies. If the letter A appears in this list, then the entry is a general reference to the topic of algorithms and their development and efficiency; if the letter D appears, then the entry is a general reference to the topic of data structures, their implementations and applications. Such entries are relevant to most of the topics discussed in this book and are therefore not categorized further. If the letter P appears after an entry, then the entry is a general reference to the PL/I language. Other entries contain either an integer, in which case they are relevant to an entire chapter, or a section number (of the form X.X), in which case they are relevant to a particular section.

Adelson-Velskii, G. M. and E. M. Landis: "An Algorithm for the Organization of Information," *Dokl. Akad. Nauk SSSR*, Mat., **146**(2):263-66, 1962. **(9.2)**

Aho, A., J. Hopcroft, and J. Ullman: *The Design and Analysis of Computer Algorithms*, Addison-Wesley, Reading, Mass., 1974. **(A)**

Allen, F. E. and J. Cocke: "A Catalogue of Optimizing Transformations," in *Design and Optimization of Compilers*, Prentice-Hall, Englewood Cliffs, N.J., 1972. **(2.3)**

Amble, O. and D. E. Knuth: "Ordered Hash Tables," *Comp. J.*, **18**:135-142, 1975. **(9.3)**

Augenstein, M. and A. Tenenbaum: "A Lesson in Recursion and Structured Programming," *SIGCSE Bulletin*, **8**(1):17-23, February, 1976. **(4.4)**

Augenstein, M. and A. Tenenbaum: "Approaches to Based Storage in PL/I," *SIGCSE Bulletin*, **9**(1):145-150, February, 1977. **(6)**

Augenstein, M. and A. Tenenbaum: "Program Efficiency and Data Structures," *SIGCSE Bulletin*, **9**(3):21-37, August, 1977. **(5.4, 7.3)**

Auslander, M. A. and H. R. Strong: "Systematic Recursion Removal," *Commun. ACM*, **21**(2), February 1978. **(4.4)**

Barron, D. W.: *Recursive Techniques in Programming,* American Elsevier, 1968. **(4)**

Bates, F. and M. L. Douglas: *Programming Language/One*, 3d ed., Prentice-Hall, Englewood Cliffs, N.J., 1975 **(P)**

Bays, C.: "A Note on When to Chain Overflow Items Within a Direct-Access Table," *Commun. ACM*, **16**(1), January 1973. **(9.2)**

Bellman, R.: *Dynamic Programming*, Princeton, Princeton, N.J., 1957. **(A)**

Berge, C.: *Theory of Graphs and Its Applications*, Methuen, 1962. **(7.5, 7.6)**

Berge, C.: *Graphs and Hypergraphs*, North-Holland, Amsterdam, 1973. **(7.5, 7.6)**

Berztiss, A. T.: *Data Structures, Theory and Practice*, 2d ed., Academic, New York, 1977. **(D)**

Bird, R. S.: "Notes on Recursion Elimination," *Commun. ACM*, **20**(6):434, June 1977. **(4.4)**

Bird, R. S.: "Improving Programs by the Introduction of Recursion," *Commun. ACM*, **20**(11), November 1977. **(4.4)**

Bitner, J. R. and E. M. Reingold: Backtrack Programming Techniques, *Commun. ACM*, **18**:651-656, 1975. **(4.3)**

Bitner, J. R.,: "Heuristics that Dynamically Alter Data Structures to Decrease Their Access Time," Ph. D. thesis, University of Illinois, Urbana, Ill., 1976. **(9.1, 9.2)**

Blum, M., R. W. Floyd, V. Pratt, R. L. Rivest, and R. E. Tarjan: "Time Bounds for Selection," *J. Comput. Syst. Sci.*, **7**:448-461, 1973. **(8.3)**

Bohl, M.: *A Guide for Programmers*, Prentice-Hall, Englewood Cliffs, N.J., 1978. **(2)**

Boothroyd, J.: "Algorithm 201 (Shellsort)," *Commun. ACM*, **6**:445, 1963. **(8.4)**

Brillinger, P. C. and D. J. Cohen: *Introduction to Data Structures and Non-numeric Computation*, Prentice-Hall, Englewood Cliffs, N.J., 1972. **(D)**

Brown, P. J.: "Programming and Documenting Software Projects," *ACM Comput. Surv.*, **6**(4), December 1974. **(2)**

Bruno, J. and E. G. Coffman: "Nearly Optimal Binary Search Trees," *Proc. IFIP Congr. 71*, North-Holland, Amsterdam, 1972, pp. 99-103. **(9.2)**

Burge, W. H.: "A Correspondence Between Two Sorting Methods," *IBM Research Report RC 6395*, IBM Thomas J. Watson Research Center, Yorktown Heights, N.Y., 1977. **(8.3)**

Carter, J. L. and M. N. Wegman: "Universal Classes of Hash Functions," *IBM Research Report RC 6495*, IBM Thomas J. Watson Research Center, Yorktown Heights, N.Y., 1977. **(9.3)**

Chartres, B. A.: "Algorithms 310-311: Prime Number Generators 1 and 2," *Commun. ACM*, **10**(9), September 1967. **(2.2)**

Conway, R. and D. Gries: *An Introduction to Programming*, 2d ed., Winthrop, Cambridge, Mass., 1975. **(P)**

Cranston, B. and R. Thomas: "A Simplified Recombination Scheme for the Fibonacci Buddy System," *Commun. ACM*, **18**(6), June 1975. **(10.3)**

Deo, N.: *Graph Theory with Applications to Engineering and Computer Science*, Prentice-Hall, Englewood Cliffs, N.J., 1974. **(7.5, 7.6)**

Dijkstra, E.: "Notes on Structured Programming," in *Structured Programming*, Academic, New York, 1972. **(2)**

D'Imperio, M. E.: "Data Structures and their Representation in Storage," Vol. 5, *Annual Review in Automatic Programming*, Pergamon, 1969, pp. 1-75. **(D)**

Earlson, I. M.: "Sherlock Holmes and Charles Babbage," *Creative Comput.*, 3(4):106-113, July-August 1977. **(4.3)**

Elson, M.: *Data Structures*, Science Research, Palo Alto, Calif., 1975. **(D)**

Even, S.: *Graph Algorithms*, Computer Science, Potomac, Md., 1978. **(7.5, 7.6)**

Fishman, G. S.: *Concepts and Methods in Discrete Event Digital Simulation*, Wiley, 1973. **(5.3)**

Flores, I.: *Computer Sorting*, Prentice-Hall, Englewood Cliffs, N.J., 1969. **(8)**

Flores, I.: *Data Structure and Management*, Prentice-Hall, Englewood Cliffs, N.J., 1970. **(D)**

Flores, I. and G. Madpis: "Average Binary Search Lengths for Dense Ordered Lists," *Commun. ACM*, **14**(9), September 1971. **(9.1)**

Floyd, R. W.: "Algorithm 245 (Treesort3)," *Commun. ACM*, **7**:701, 1964. **(8.3)**

Floyd, R. W. and R. L. Rivest: "Algorithm 489 (Select)," *Commun. ACM*, **18**(3):173, March 1975. **(8.3)**

Floyd, R. W. and R. L. Rivest: "Expected Time Bounds for Selection," *Commun. ACM*, **18**(3), March 1975. **(8.3)**

Ford, L. R. and D. R. Fulkerson: *Flows in Networks*, Princeton University Press, Princeton, N. J., 1972. **(7.5)**

Foster, C. C.: "A Generalization of AVL Trees," *Commun. ACM*, **16**(8), August 1973. **(9.2)**

Fulkerson, D. R.: "Flow Networks and Combinatorial Operations Research," *Am. Math. Mon.*, **73**:115, 1966. **(7.5)**

Golomb, S. W. and L. D. Baumert: "Backtrack Programming," *J. ACM*, **12**:516, 1965. **(4)**

Goodman, S. E. and S. T. Hedetniemi: *Introduction to the Design and Analysis of Algorithms*, McGraw-Hill, New York, 1977. **(A, 4)**

Gordon, G.: *System Simulation*, Prentice-Hall, Englewood Cliffs, N.J., 1969. **(5.3)**

Gries, D.: *Compiler Construction for Digital Computers*, Wiley, New York, 1971. **(2.2, 4.2, 4.4, 9.3)**

Hantler, S. L. and J. C. King: "An Introduction to Proving the Correctness of Programs," *ACM Comput. Surv.*, 8(3):331-353, September, 1976. **(2.3)**

Harary, F.: *Graph Theory*, Addison-Wesley, Boston, 1969. **(7.5, 7.6)**

Harrison, M. C.: *Data Structures and Programming*, Scott Foresman, Glenview, Ill., 1973. **(D)**

Hetzel, W. C.: *Program Test Methods*, Prentice-Hall, Englewood Cliffs, N.J., 1972. **(2.3)**

Hinds, J.: "An Algorithm for Locating Adjacent Storage Blocks in the Buddy System," *Commun. ACM*, **18**(4), April, 1975. **(10.3)**

Hirschberg, D. S.: "A Class of Dynamic Memory Allocation Algorithms," *Commun. ACM*, **16**(10):615-618, October 1973. **(10.3)**

Hirschberg, D. S.: "An Insertion Technique for One-sided Height-Balanced Trees," *Commun. ACM*, **19**(8), August 1976. **(9.2)**

Hoare, C. A. R.: "Quicksort," *Comput. J.*, **5**:10-15, 1962. **(8.2)**

Horowitz, E. and S. Sahni: *Fundamentals of Data Structures*, Computer Science, Woodland Hills, Calif., 1975. **(D)**

Horowitz, E. and S. Sahni: *Algorithms: Design and Analysis*, Computer Science, Potomac, Md., 1977. **(A)**

Huang, J. C.: "An Approach to Program Testing," *ACM Comput. Surv.*, **7**(3), September 1975. **(2.3)**

Huffman, D.: "A Method for the Construction of Minimum Redundancy Codes," *Proc. IRE*, **40**, 1952. **(7.3)**

Hughes, J. K.: *PL/I Programming*, Wiley, New York, 1973. **(P)**

Hughes, J. K. and J. I. Michton: *A Structured Approach to Programming*, Prentice-Hall, Englewood Cliffs, N.J., 1977. **(2)**

IBM: *Techniques for Processing Data Lists in PL/I*, IBM Corporation, White Plains, N.Y., 1971 (order no. GF 20-00018). **(6)**

IBM: *Introduction to the List Processing Facilities of PL/I*, IBM Corporation, White Plains, N.Y., 1972A (order no. GF 20-0015). **(6)**

IBM: *Techniques for Processing Pointer Lists and Lists of Lists in PL/I*, IBM Corporation, White Plains, N.Y., 1972B (order no. GF 20-0019). **(6, 10.1)**

IBM: *System/360 Operating System PL/I(F) Language Reference Manual*, IBM Corporation, New York, 1972C (file no. S360-29, order no. GC28-8201). **(P)**

IBM: *PL/I Checkout and Optimizing Compilers: Language Reference Manual*, IBM Corporation, San Jose, Calif., 1976 (order no. GC 33-0009). **(P)**

Isoda, S., E. Goto, and I. Kimura: "An Efficient Bit Table Technique for Dynamic Storage Allocation of 2^n Word Blocks," *Commun. ACM*, **14**(9), September 1971. **(10.3)**

Kernighan, B. W. and P. J. Plauger: *The Elements of Programming Style*, McGraw-Hill, New York, 1970. **(2)**

Kernighan, B. W. and P. J. Plauger: "Programming Style: Examples and Counter Examples," *ACM Comput. Surv.*, **6**(4), December 1974. **(2)**

Kernighan, B. and P. J. Plauger: *Software Tools*, Addison-Wesley, Reading, Mass., 1976. **(8)**

Kleinrock, L.: *Queuing Systems*, Wiley, 1975. **(5.3)**

Knott, G. O.: *Hashing Functions, Comp. J.*, **18**, August 1975. **(9.3)**

Knowlton, K.: "A Fast Storage Allocator," *Commun. ACM*, 8(10), October 1965. **(10.3)**

Knuth, D. E.: "Optimum Binary Search Trees," *ACTA Inf.*, **1**:14-25, 1971. **(9.2)**

Knuth, D. E.: "Structured Programming with Goto Statements," *ACM Comput. Surv.*, **6**(4):261, December 1974. **(2.1, 4.4, 8.2)**

Knuth, D.: *Fundamental Algorithms*, 2d ed., Addison-Wesley, Reading, Mass., 1973A. **(D, A)**

Knuth, D.: *Sorting and Searching*, Addison-Wesley, Reading, Mass., 1973B. **(8, 9)**

Korfhage, R. R.: *Discrete Computational Structures*, Academic, New York, 1974. **(7.5)**

Kosaraju, S. R.: "Insertions and Deletions in One-Sided Height Balanced Trees," *Commun. ACM,* **21**(3), March, 1978. **(9.2)**

Ledgard, H.: *Programming Proverbs*, Hayden, Rochelle Park, N.J., 1975. **(2)**

Lewis, T. G. and M. Z. Smith: *Applying Data Structures*, Houghton Mifflin, Boston, 1976. **(D)**

Lockyer, K. G.: *An Introduction to Critical Data Analysis*, Pitman, London, 1964. **(7.6)**

Lockyer, K. G: *Critical Path Analysis: Problem and Solutions*, Pitman, London, 1966. **(7.6)**

Lum, U. Y.: "General Performance Analysis of Key-to-Address Transformation Methods using an Abstract File Concept," *Commun. ACM*, **16**(10):603, October 1973. **(9.3)**

Lum, U. Y. and P. S. T. Yuen: "Additional Results on Key-to-Address Transform Techniques: A Fundamental Performance Study on Large Existing Formatted Files," *Commun. ACM*, **15**(11):996, November 1972. **(9.3)**

Lum, U. Y., P. S. T. Yuen, and M. Dodd: "Key-to-Address Transform Techniques: A Fundamental Performance Study on Large Existing Formatted Files," *Commun. ACM*, **14**:228, 1971. **(9.3)**

Mairson, H. G.: "Some New Upper Bounds on the Generation of Prime Numbers," *Commun. ACM*, **20**(9), September 1977. **(2.2)**

Manna, Z. and A. Shamir: "The Optimal Approach to Recursive Programs," *Commun. ACM*, **20**(11), November 1977. **(4.4)**

Martin, W.: "Sorting," *Comput. Surv.*, **3**(4):147, 1971. **(8)**

Maurer, H. A. and M. R. Williams: *A Collection of Programming Problems and Techniques*, Prentice-Hall, Englewood Cliffs, N.J., 1972. **(A)**

Maurer, H. A.: *Data Structures and Programming Techniques*, Prentice-Hall, Englewood Cliffs, N.J., 1977. **(D)**

Maurer, W. and T. Lewis: "Hash Table Methods," *Comput. Surv.*, **7**(1):5-19, March 1975. **(9.3)**

McCabe, J.: "On Serial Files with Relocatable Records," *Oper. Res.*, **12**:609-618, 1965. **(9.1)**

Mills, H. D.: "Top Down Programming in Large Systems," in R. Rustin (ed.), *Debugging Techniques in Large Systems*, Prentice-Hall, Englewood Cliffs, N.J., 1971. **(2.2)**

Morris, R.: "Scatter Storage Techniques," *Commun. ACM*, **11**(1):38-44, January 1968. **(9.3)**

Munro, I.: "Efficient Determination of the Transitive Closure of a Directed Graph," *Inf. Process. Lett.*, **1**:56, 1971-1972. **(7.5)**

Nielson, N. R.: "Dynamic Memory Allocation in Computer Simulation," *Commun. ACM*, **20**(11), November 1977. **(10.3)**

Nievergelt, J., J. C. Furrar, and E. M. Reingold: *Computer Approaches to Mathematical Problems*, Prentice-Hall, Englewood Cliffs, N.J., 1974. **(A)**

Nievergelt, J. and E. M. Reingold: "Binary Search Trees of Bounded Balance," *SIAM J. Comput.*, 2:33, 1973. **(9.2)**

Nievergelt, J. and C. K. Wong: "On Binary Search Trees," *Proc. IFIP Congr. 71*, North-Holland, Amsterdam, 1972, pp. 91-98. **(9.2)**

Nijenhuis, A. and H. S. Wilf: *Combinatorial Algorithms*, Academic, New York, 1975. **(A)**

Nilsson, N.: *Problem-solving Methods in Artificial Intelligence,* McGraw-Hill, New York, 1971. **(7.4)**

O'Neil, P. E. and E. J. O'Neil: "A Fast Expected Time Algorithm for Boolean Matrix Multiplication and Transitive Closure," *Inf. Control*, **22**:132-138, 1973. **(7.5)**

Ore, O.: *Theory of Graphs*, vol. 38, American Mathematical Society, Providence, R.I., 1962. **(7.5, 7.6)**

Ore, O.: *Graphs and their Uses*, Random House, New York, and Singer, Syracuse, N.Y., 1963. **(7.5, 7.6)**

Page, E. S. and L. B. Wilson: *Information Representation and Manipulation in a Computer*, Cambridge, London, 1973. **(D)**

Peterson, J. L. and T. A. Norman: "Buddy Systems," *Commun. ACM*, **20**(6), June 1977. **(10.3)**

Pfaltz, J. L.: *Computer Data Structures*, McGraw-Hill, New York, 1977. **(D)**

Pohl, I.: "A Sorting Problem and its Complexity," *Commun. ACM*, **15**(6), June 1972. **(8.1)**

Pollack, S. V. and T. D. Sterling: *A Guide to PL/I*, 2d ed., Holt, New York, 1976. **(P)**

Polya, G.: *How to Solve It*, Doubleday, Garden City, N.Y., 1957. **(A)**

Pooch, U. W. and A. Nieder: "A Survey of Indexing Techniques for Sparse Matrices," *Comput. Surv.*, **15**:1Q9, 1973. **(6.3)**

Pratt, T. W.: *Programming Languages: Design and Implementation*, Prentice-Hall, Englewood Cliffs, N.J., 1975. **(1.2, 1.3, 2.2, 3.4, 4.2, 4.4)**

Price, C.: "Table Lookup Techniques," *Comput. Surv.*, **3**(2):49-65, 1971. **(9)**

Purdom, P. W. and S. M. Stigler: "Statistical Properties of the Buddy System," *Commun. ACM*, **17**(4), October 1970. **(10.3)**

Reingold, E. M., J. Nievergelt, and N. Deo: *Combinatorial Algorithms: Theory and Practice*, Prentice-Hall, Englewood Cliffs, N.J., 1977. **(A)**

Rich, R. P.: *Internal Sorting Methods Illustrated with PL/I Programs*, Prentice-Hall, Englewood Cliffs, N.J., 1972. **(8)**

Rivest, R.: "On Self-Organizing Sequential Search Heuristics," *Commun. ACM*, **19**(2), February 1976. **(9.1)**

Rivest, R. L. and D. E. Knuth: "Bibliography 26: Computer Sorting," *Comput. Rev.*, **13**:283, 1972. **(8)**

Rustin, R., ed.: *Debugging Techniques in Large Systems*, Prentice-Hall, Englewood Cliffs, N.J., 1971. **(2.3)**

Schorr, H. and W. M. Waite: "An Efficient Machine-Independent Procedure for Garbage Collection in Various List Structures," *Commun. ACM*, **10**(8):501-506, August 1967. **(10.2)**

Sedgewick, R.: "Quicksort," *Report no. STAN-CS-75-492*, Department of Computer Science, Stanford, Stanford, Calif., May 1975. **(8.2)**

Sedgewick, R.: "Permutation Generation Methods," *ACM Comput. Surv.*, **9**(2):137, June 1977. **(4.3)**

Severance, D. G.: "Identifier Search Mechanisms: A Survey and Generalized Model," *Comput. Surv.*, **6**(3), September 1974. **(9)**

Shell, D. L.: "A High Speed Sorting Procedure," *Commun. ACM*, **2**(7), July 1959. **(8.4)**

Shen, K. K. and J. L. Peterson: "A Weighted Buddy Method for Dynamic Storage Allocation," *Commun. ACM*, **17**(10):558-562, October 1974. **(10.3)**

Shore, J.: "On the External Storage Fragmentation Produced by First-fit and Best-fit Allocation Strategies," *Commun. ACM*, **18**(8):433, August 1975. **(10.3)**

Shore, J.: Anomalous Behavior of the Fifty-percent Rule in Dynamic Memory Allocation," *Commun. ACM*, **20**(11), November 1977. **(10.3)**

Shortt, J. and T. C. Wilson: *Problem Solving and the Computer: A Structured Concept with PL/I (PL/C)*, Addison-Wesley, Reading, Mass., 1976. **(P)**

Sprugnoli, R: "Perfect Hashing Functions: A Single Probe Retrieving Method for Static Sets," *Commun. ACM*, **20**(11), November 1977. **(9.3)**

Stanat, D. F. and D. F. McAllister: *Discrete Mathematics in Computer Science*, Prentice-Hall, Englewood Cliffs, N.J., 1977. **(7.5)**

Stephenson, C.J.: "A Method for Constructing Binary Search Trees by Making Insertions at the Root," *IBM Research Report RC 6298*, IBM Thomas J. Watson Research Center, Yorktown Heights, N.Y., 1976. **(9.2)**

Stone, H.: *Introduction to Computer Organization and Data Structures*, McGraw-Hill, New York, 1972. **(1.1)**

Tenenbaum, A.: "Simulations of Dynamic Sequential Search Algorithms," *Commun. ACM*, **21**(9), September, 1978. **(9.1)**

Tenenbaum, A. and E. Widder: "A Comparison of First-fit Allocation Strategies," *Proc. ACM78*, December, 1978. **(10.3)**

Tremblay, J. P. and R. P. Manohar: *Discrete Mathematical Structures with Applications to Computer Science*, McGraw-Hill, New York, 1975. **(7.5)**

Tremblay, J. P. and P. G. Sorenson: *An Introduction to Data Structures with Applications*, McGraw-Hill, New York, 1976. **(D)**

Van Emden, M. H.: "Increasing Efficiency of Quicksort," *Commun. ACM*, **13**:563-567, 1970. **(8.2)**

Van Tassel, D.: *Program Style, Design, Efficiency, Debugging and Testing*, Prentice-Hall, Englewood Cliffs, N.J., 1974. **(2)**

Wadler, P. L.: "Analysis of an Algorithm for Real Time Garbage Collection," *Commun. ACM*, **19**(9), September 1976. **(10.2)**

Waite, W. M.: *Implementing Software for Non-numeric Applications*, Prentice-Hall, Englewood Cliffs, N.J., 1973. **(D)**

Walker, W. A. and C. C. Gotlieb: "A Top Down Algorithm for Constructing Nearly Optimal Lexicographic Trees," in R. Read (ed.), *Graph Theory and Computing*, Academic, New York, 1972. **(9.2)**

Warnier, J. D.: *Logical Construction of Programs*, Van Nostrand Reinhold, New York, 1974. **(2.1)**

Warren, Henry S.: "A Modification of Warshall's Algorithm for the Transitive Closure of Binary Relations," *Commun. ACM*, **18**(4), April 1975. **(7.5)**

Warshall, S.: "A Theorem on Boolean Matrices," *J. ACM*, **9**(1):11, 1962. **(7.5)**

Weinberg, G.: *PL/I Programming: A Manual of Style*, McGraw-Hill, New York, 1970. **(P)**

Weinberg, G., N. Yasukawa, and R. Marcus: *Structured Programming in PL/C: An Abecedarian*, Wiley, New York, 1973. **(P)**

Wickelgren, W. A.: *How to Solve Problems: Elements of a Theory Problems and Problem Solving*, Freeman, San Francisco, 1974. **(A)**

Williams, J. W. J.: "Algorithm 232 (Heapsort)," *Commun. ACM*, **7**:347-348, 1964. **(8.3)**

Wirth, N.: *Systematic Programming: An Introduction*, Prentice-Hall, Englewood Cliffs, N.J., 1973. **(2.2)**

Wirth, N.: "On the Composition of Well-structured Programs," *ACM Comput. Surv.*, **6**(4), December 1974. **(2.1, 2.2)**

Wirth, N.: *Algorithms + Data Structures = Programs*, Prentice-Hall, Englewood Cliffs, N.J., 1976. **(D)**

Yohe, J. M.: "An Overview of Programming Practices," *Comput. Surv.*, 6(4), December 1974. (2)

Yourdon, E.: *Techniques of Program Structure and Design*, Prentice-Hall, Englewood Cliffs, N.J., 1975. (2)

index

This index references both the text and the Exercise Manual. References to the exercises are by section number and exercise number and appear following the text references; they are indicated by an E and are enclosed in parentheses. In those cases where the exercises of an entire chapter or section are relevant to a particular topic, a chapter or section reference appears. For example, E(6, 7.2, 9.3.11) means that the term appears in all the exercises of Chapter 6 and Section 7.2, as well as in Exercise 9.3.11.

A

T

U

V

W

Z